Philosophy and Revolution

Philosophy and Revolution

From Kant to Marx

◆

STATHIS KOUVELAKIS

Translated by G.M. Goshgarian

Preface by Fredric Jameson

New Afterword by Stathis Kouvelakis
and Sebastian Budgen

VERSO

London • New York

In memory of Nicos Poulantzas

This book is supported by the French Ministry of Foreign Affairs
as part of the Burgess Programme, headed for the French Embassy
in London by the Institut Français du Royaume-Uni

Liberté • Égalité • Fraternité
RÉPUBLIQUE FRANÇAISE

This edition published by Verso 2018
First published by Verso 2003
© Stathis Kouvelakis 2003, 2018
Translation © G.M. Goshgarian 2003, 2018
Preface © Fredric Jameson 2003, 2018
Afterword © Stathis Kouvelakis and Sebastian Budgen 2018

1 3 5 7 9 10 8 6 4 2

Verso
UK: 6 Meard Street, London W1F 0EG
US: 20 Jay Street, Suite 1010, Brooklyn, NY 11201
versobooks.com

Verso is the imprint of New Left Books

ISBN-13: 978-1-78663-578-5
ISBN-13: 978-1-78663-579-2 (UK EBK)
ISBN-13: 978-1-78663-580-8 (US EBK)

British Library Cataloguing in Publication Data
A catalogue record for this book is available from the British Library

Library of Congress Cataloging-in-Publication Data
A catalog record for this book is available from the Library of Congress

Typeset in Baskerville
Printed and bound by CPI Group (UK) Ltd, Croydon, CR0 4YY

Contents

Acknowledgements

To my mother, Mitzi Koudounis, who was always at my side at the most important moments, notably during the composition of this work, but who left us unexpectedly.

To Georges Labica and Jean-Marie Vincent, without whom this research would have proved impossible.

To Fredric Jameson, Jacques Bidet and Kostas Vergopoulos, whose support never faltered.

To Étienne Balibar, Sebastian Budgen, Gregory Elliott, Jacques Guilhaumou, Annie Mordrel, Emmanuel Renault and André Tosel, who, in different ways, examined all or a part of this bulky manuscript.

To my former colleagues at the Department of European Studies of the University of Wolverhampton and particularly to Mike Haynes.

To Marie-José Gransard, for her indispensable generosity.

To G.M. Goshgarian, whose lessons in rigour and method I am not going to forget.

To the whole Verso team, for their goodwill and their hard work.

The revolution is one and indivisible.

Heinrich Heine

Preface

FREDRIC JAMESON

If it is a truism that every generation rewrites Marx in a new way, what has to be added is that every age also brings its own historically specific mode of rewriting to the process. This one, for example, is characterized by a paradoxical combination of a distrust of teleology, and even historical narrative as such, with an extraordinary renaissance of biographical writing. The apparent paradox can be reduced if we begin to grasp the way in which nowadays narratives of emergence, influence, causality, and formation in reality have begun to function as devices for highlighting and foregrounding the component parts of structure as such: a narrative trajectory serving as a visible pathway on a multidimensional construct formed out of tubes of distinctly coloured beams of light.

This is the sense in which Stathis Kouvelakis's remarkable new history of the formation of Marx's thought – perhaps the first truly original new version of that formation since Auguste Cornu's monumental postwar history – is not to be taken only as an account of the contingencies and encounters, the accidents of intellectual discovery and the unpredictable exposure to the winds of the *Zeitgeist*; but also as a new theory of what is structurally most central and distinctive in Marx's achievement: namely, the unique political nature and powers of the proletariat.

As for Marx's formation and development, the classical narrative was already constructed by Engels: the confluence of German philosophy, British political economy, and French revolutionary politics. It was an enormously satisfying dialectical synthesis, which positioned 'Marxism' (about which it is today generally agreed that it was Engels who invented it) centrally as the inheritor of European thought as such. Today, perhaps, in the light of globalization and the new thought modes it is in the process of teaching us, and also in the hindsight of Moses Hess's notion (rediscovered here) of a *triarchy* of relations between Paris, Germany and Manchester (rather than London), we may grasp this as something like a

spatial or geographical force-field, the after-image in thought of an
international and cross-cultural pattern of the type most universally
revealed today in the current world system. This is, so to speak, the
geopolitical substratum of philosophy; and Kouvelakis's book reminds us
insistently of the perceptual and intellectual advantages of figures we
might once have considered as exiles, but who come before us today as
the bearers and vehicles of transnationality.

The first dramatic crystallization of this process is to be identified in
the French Revolution itself, which resonated beyond all the old national
boundaries with the shattering and terrifying force of an event – and,
indeed, an event of wholly new historical structure, which now redefines
our conception of *événementialité* or 'eventfulness', even of history itself.
Revolution now becomes a new kind of collective event, and the historical
chronicle is suddenly and dramatically reorientated around it in a radically new kind of historicity, which in the process changes all the conditions of philosophizing as such.

Kouvelakis demonstrates this process centrally at work in the renewal
of philosophy by Kant and Hegel. Characteristically, the Anglo-American
perspective on these thinkers has never been passionately committed to
any curiosity about their political positions, beyond some vague sense that
Kant was an Enlightenment figure and Hegel a seemingly more conservative or even reactionary one. We therefore have everything to learn from
the newer French and Italian intellectual scholarship, and Kouvelakis's
discussion may well serve, not only as an introduction to this new material,
but as a way of producing new kinds of philosophical problems. Thus
André Tosel has demonstrated the centrality of the French Revolution for
Kant, and Domenico Losurdo has definitively dispelled the myth of a
reactionary Hegel: these are positions more in consonance with Lukács's
views than with those of Althusser, which are systematically and punctually
questioned throughout the present work. Yet all this scarcely betokens a
return to Lukács either (unless we posit a considerable rewriting of his
work as well), and in fact suggests the possibility of an opening up of
philosophy beyond its current disciplinary boundaries and, very specifically, a new sense of the necessary and constitutive political dimension of
thought as such.

Of thought; but also of other forms of culture. Indeed, nothing is more
dramatic, in the present book, than the reconsideration of the role and
status of Heinrich Heine in the history of post-Hegelian German philosophy and the emergence of Marxism. This poet – a kind of German
Baudelaire, the first 'ironic German' and the inventor of a unique
combination of satire and lyric, who was also the purveyor of an advanced

French culture to a provincial Germany, and the author of the first great popular account of the development and potentialities of post-Hegelian German thought; the target, as well, of the first, shall we say experimental, cultural anti-Semitism – remains to this day a profoundly ambivalent figure: his historical assessment still in doubt, his literary status still contested as though he had written only yesterday (Adorno's essay 'Heine as Wound' gives a vivid and exemplary picture of these contradictions and uncertainties).

It is Kouvelakis's supreme insight to have displaced the old story of Marx and the Young Hegelians (Bruno Bauer *et al.*), and to have positioned Heine centrally as the most representative radical Hegelian German, and the very source of the seminal new concept of the proletariat. As if this were not enough, his extended analysis shows that the thematics of the crowd, the great city and the *flâneur* were not original with Benjamin's Baudelaire, but of a piece with a thought that opens a new path – that of the social – between the seemingly exhaustive alternatives of the political and the philosophical. Thereby an unexpected and neglected seam is opened up which runs far more directly than hitherto from Hegel to communism.

After this, it is clear that the old story will no longer do. Yet it is not necessarily a disservice to Engels to deprive him of the honorific status of godfather to Marx's brainchild, 'the proletariat'. On the contrary, his own originality as a spatial and geographical analyst is sharpened by this attention to his limits, just as the work of Moses Hess (an eternal candidate, in every generation, for the intellectual rediscovery he so richly deserves) is not at all discredited by the abandonment of a second traditional narrative of synthesis (Hess's notion of communism connecting up with Engels's notion of the proletariat).

The true beneficiary of this redistribution of merits and discoveries is Marx's early journalism, which gives density and concrete content to the intellectual and speculative ferment all around him. The new approach to this material, however, does away with the hierarchy of the disciplines, with the inequality between facts and principles, for example, or between philosophy and its examples, or historical *faits divers* and political or social 'laws': all these 'levels' now feed into a conjuncture of acts and events; all are grist for the drama of emergence.

At the same time, however, the work of the 'early' Marx will be reviewed with the intention of forming some new and more accurate picture of his relations with Hegel – indeed, the mediations linking Marx back to Hegel himself are the narrative frame of the book. Two now traditional options can thereby be avoided: the Althusser/Colletti denunciation of Hegel's

idealism, a critique to be attributed, not only to the early Marx, but to
Marxism itself as a materialism; and the antithetical notion that while the
young Marx focused with satirical attention on Hegel's faults and flaws,
the more mature one returned in the 1850s to the *Logic*, whose architec-
tonic can henceforth be found in what was achieved of *Capital* itself.

But in fact, the influence of Hegel today lies neither in his idealism
('the System or Substance as Subject') nor in his dialectic of the logical
categories: it lies in the appropriation of the notion and problematics of
civil society [*bürgerliche Gesellschaft*] by liberal and 'post-socialist' thinkers.
Hegel is himself in part responsible for the contemporary Western misap-
propriation of his thought on the subject, owing to its profoundly contradictory formulations in his own work. A new interpretation thereby
becomes possible in which Hegel is not simply stigmatized as a conservative thinker (or a forerunner of liberalism either) but, rather, recognized
as having touched, at this point, at the limit of what could be thought in
his historical situation. The originality of Kouvelakis's reading here lies in
his assertion that, particularly in connection with the conceptualization of
'civil society', the young Marx criticizes Hegel, in effect, for not being
Hegelian enough.

It is at this point, then, that a new and distinctively political Marx
becomes available – quite different from the Marx who stereotypically
turns from politics to the philosophy of alienation, or later on to economics as such. At a time when new political thoughts seem particularly scarce
on the left (if not, indeed, everywhere), such a Marx could be of the
greatest interest and value for us.

Introduction:
From Philosophy to Revolution

Philosophy and Revolution: From Kant to Marx is a rather imposing title that calls for a good deal of preliminary comment. At the risk of disappointing certain expectations, I shall begin with a remark that may seem insignificant, because it bears 'only' on the little preposition sandwiched between the names 'Kant' and 'Marx'. It should be made clear at the outset that this 'to' is not to be understood as the expression of a progressive movement, the culmination of a development that brings to full maturity something that was already present 'in embryo' from the start. On the contrary, it expresses, as the index of an order of investigation, a backward movement. For I have begun at the end, that is, from what the name 'Marx' signified at a moment when there was no denying that that which constituted this signifier's relationship to the world and especially to political practice during the short twentieth century had come face to face with the moment of its defeat.

I have, however, wagered that such a conjuncture is also one of those which require that we reconstruct a genealogy, in a very precise sense: an attempt to go back to a constitutive moment with a view to grasping, setting out from a nodal point, turning point, or event, the stakes of a long historical period from which our present is descended. Here I am thinking, in particular, of both the frequently misunderstood later project of Georg Lukács,[1] who sought to situate the decisive bifurcation of modern thought, and that of the Gramsci of the *Prison Notebooks*, who retraces the formation of the European nation-states and reassesses the importance of the Jacobin moment in modern politics. Whatever the merits and limitations of the contributions of these two thinkers, whose virtues and faults could provide matter for lengthy debates, their profoundly self-critical, innovative reaction to the catastrophic rise of European fascism unquestionably opened up a seam whose fecundity, in my view, has yet to be exhausted. The chapters below, at any rate, strike out on this path, by tracing diverse trajectories that all lead from Marx towards Kant – which means, as we shall see, towards the French Revolution, as the founding moment in which the cluster of questions, conflicts and historical tendencies called 'modernity' first emerged.

Kant, as Michel Foucault points out in a now classic commentary, is no doubt the first to have redeployed the reflexivity of the subject as a 'sagittal' relationship to his own present [*actualité*] rather than as a trajectory internal to a consciousness that has withdrawn into its own depths. He thus poses the question of the present in its subjectivity, the question of the present as event. This event can, in its turn, be understood only as the effect of another, of the event *tout court* – that is, the revolution, or, more precisely, the French Revolution. Grasping the revolution as event thus means – according to Kant, whom Foucault follows on this point – grasping it as a subjective disposition to the enthusiasm that it inspires, an enthusiasm attesting to a possibility immanent in the human species: autonomy, or the subject's capacity for self-development.

It is, however, Foucault, not Kant, who gives the name 'modernity' to this attitude or this mode of subjectivation. He thus draws our attention to the indissoluble bond between it and the revolution, which shows that such enthusiasm plays a constitutive role in the formation of modern consciousness; Baudelaire's 'spleen' later appears as its mirror-opposite. But – and this is the crucial point – if it is precisely at this moment that Foucault returns to Kant, and, by way of Kant, to modernity's inaugural moment, he does so not out of an academic desire to document the sources of the modern, but because he recognizes something of himself in the position Kant takes *vis-à-vis* the present, or – if you prefer – something of his own relevance to the present [*actualité*]. It is something that allows him to assume the revolution's founding (and still active) role in modern reflexivity, and, simultaneously, that reflexivity's radical distance from the event marking its emergence: what matters is not the revolution's content or its development as seen by those who make it, but merely its status as a *sign* or *spectacle* revealing the potential for autonomy characteristic of the human species ('progress' in the Kantian sense).

Foucault thus reaches a point of equilibrium on a question that had tormented him for years: 'what are we to make of the Revolution?' (a question soon reformulated to read: 'what are we to make of the will to revolution?') and, therefore, of the Enlightenment, since 'the revolution plainly continues and completes the basic process of the Enlightenment'.[2] This question haunts the shift in his work towards the mechanisms of power over life and populations – towards, that is, the 'bio-power' that culminates in contemporary racism[3] – as well as his commitment to the

Iranian revolution. A revolution against the Enlightenment – in the sense
in which Gramsci called October 1917 a 'revolution against *Capital*' – and,
above all, against the version of the Enlightenment associated with Marxism, the Iranian revolution is posed as a possible alternative, for the space
of an instant or an illusion, to the trajectory of the revolutions that turned
into states, a trajectory that also led Foucault to approve those who
regarded the latter enterprise as the realization of a promise and a desire
leading straight to the Gulag.[4]

Foucault's adoption of the Kantian attitude, closely bound up with the
turn taken by events in Iran,[5] is, in this sense, the sign of a reformulation
that implicitly rectifies his positions of 1977–79. Continuing to pose the
question of the revolution no longer appears as a symptom of the desire
fuelling totalitarianism, and the connection of this question to the
Enlightenment is reaffirmed. And yet 'we would not make [this revolu-
tion] again if given the choice'.[6] Being modern means facing up to the
question posed by the Enlightenment and the Revolution; but it means
doing so at an irreducible distance from the action, as a spectator who,
albeit sympathetic, is also forever separated from the event.

This position is symptomatic of the oscillations of Foucault, and,
through him, of an entire period which lived out the 'passion for the real'
that is – if we are to accept Alain Badiou's thesis – the defining feature of
the twentieth century.[7] Hence it does not seem inappropriate to compare
Foucault's thought, in this respect, with that of a writer who is generally
taken to be a 'paradigmatic representative'[8] of an intelligentsia swept up
by the passion of the century: Lukács – more precisely, the Lukács we find
reacting to the founding event of the past century, October 1917, and the
name that designates it, Lenin. It is, to be sure, unusual to compare these
two thinkers; but the comparison appears less surprising once it becomes
clear that both approach the question of the age in terms of the same
category, that of actuality [*actualité*].

Lenin grasps the actuality of the revolution: indeed, it is precisely in so
far as he does, says Lukács, that he embodies October 1917 and that this
event, far from being a Russian particularity, breaks the flow of world
history. By the radically self-referential phrase 'actuality of the revolution',
Lukács means precisely what Foucault defines as a 'sagittal' relation to the
present: the capacity to 'recognize the fundamental problem of our time
. . . at the time and place of its first appearance'.[9] The actuality of the
revolution is not – or, at any rate, not necessarily – its imminence, and
even less its pure contingency; it is 'merely' the fact that 'every question
of the day – precisely as a question of the day – at the same time became
a fundamental problem of the revolution'.[10]

This, Lukács goes on, is what some people, especially 'vulgar Marxists',[11] fail to see whenever bourgeois society is functioning 'normally'; but it comes into view as soon as one adopts the 'perspective' of the event,[12] of decisiveness in all everyday actions – something that requires the actuality of the revolution as its 'sure', because wholly internal, 'touchstone'.[13] To think the actuality of the revolution – or, if you prefer, the actuality of actuality[14] – is to acknowledge that one is, in some way, always-already caught up in this process of everyday decision, in which *every* question, subjectively grasped as a 'question of the day', becomes 'a fundamental problem of the revolution'. This is what Lukács calls 'the standpoint of the totality', or, alternatively, the standpoint of the transcending of the subject–object split, which, as is well known, is in his view the 'heart of Marx's method'[15] understood as revolutionary dialectics.

But it is here that the difference between Foucault's and Lukács's positions is most obvious; for Lukács's argument, even before it diverges from Foucault's over the question of the totality or the dialectic, plainly excludes the Kantian possibility of the spectatorial position taken up by Foucault (albeit without the transcendental subject). We must also ask what bearing this position has on the 'experience of the outside' in Foucault's work of the 1960s, on the 'systematic description of a discourse-object' of his archaeological project, or on the 'clear, pure, unruffled' transcription of the Greeks' techniques of the self, the subject of his late work.[16]

A position '*à la* Kant' is illusory not because it presents itself as subjective, but, in a certain sense, because it is not subjective enough: because it holds that an 'objective' upheaval can take place in the world on a level that is indifferent and, as it were, external to the deliberations of a subject confined to his enthusiasms for the 'spectacle' of a remote battle. This observing consciousness does not take into account the 'always-already' of the network of day-to-day decisions in which subjective activity is entangled. By dissociating the form of the event from its content, this consciousness condemns itself to oscillating between enthusiasm at a distance and aestheticized indifference to worldly affairs.

In this sense, the difference that opposes Lukács to the Kantian Foucault over the questions of the event and the totality (or, again, the dialectic) originates, first and foremost, in their diverging views on the intelligibility of revolutionary practice. The standard interpretations notwithstanding, this is not because Lukács suppresses (in the name of the Grand Proletarian Subject or the Laws of History) the singularity of the event, or the dimension of subjective action. Quite the contrary: what the author of *History and Class Consciousness* emphasizes about Lenin is, rather, his sense of initiative and his grasp of the concrete situation, which allows him to break with both the economistic determinism of 'orthodox' Marxism (Kautsky's is the standard example) and the linear vision of the development of class struggles (and class consciousness) characteristic of spontaneism. To put it simply: for Lukács, even the disposition to enthusiasm called forth at a distance by the revolutionary event can only be understood only as immanent in the kind of intervention specific to revolutionary practice as defined by the third Thesis on Feuerbach: 'self-change [*Selbstveränderung*]' or the 'coincidence of the changing of circumstances and of human activity'.[17]

But the fact remains – to adopt Foucault's standpoint now – that it is hard to believe that the power of these famous lines could remain unaffected by the experience of the last years of the previous century, which saw – in André Tosel's uncompromising words – 'the movement of the masses go down to the most terrible defeat in its history, to the point that it disappeared from view, its very substance dissolved in the void created by the restoration of an unrestrained, globalized capitalism'.[18] In other words, even if we refuse to dismiss Lukács's argument as a now useless accessory, it is undeniable that the picture that began to emerge in the 1980s contrasts radically with the perspectives opened up by October 1917. Clearly, it is this difference which Foucault's doubt invites us to think about.

Marked as it is by the defeat of what styled itself 'communism', our present once again brings us face to face with the nodal point constitutive of modernity and revolution. Here I have interrogated the past from the standpoint of this present, but also with a view to breaking its grip, directing my attention to a period very different from our own, during which the explosion of the revolutionary event continued to exercise powerful effects. It is, without doubt, a privileged period for anyone who wishes to home in on the indefinitely deferred promises of emancipation held out by modernity, a period diametrically opposed to the one we are living through, even if everyone knows that the opening it created was short-lived and that it foundered on the outcome of the revolutions of 1848 – 'our first defeat since 1794', as Alexander Herzen put it.

Following Foucault, I begin my inquiry with the German Enlightenment (in particular, Kant). I do not, however, confine myself to this period, since my aim is to traverse the entire sequence that stretches between the two 'crests' of the European revolution that occurred in 1789 and 1848. Yet the chapters that follow do focus mainly on Germany, especially on the German theory of the period known as the *Vormärz* (beginning with the 1830 July Days in Paris and ending with the revolution of March 1848): their purpose is to re-examine the familiar paradox (of which both the first German Jacobins and their detractors were equally aware) according to which French revolutionary practice found its expression and its fullest reflection in this *German* theory. Accordingly, we have to deal with a double paradox, inasmuch as geographical distance serves here as a trope for that other distance which separates the revolution – revolutionary politics – from philosophy, or, if you like, theory from practice. If we add to these two doublets a third term, the economy, 'represented' by England, 'the world's workshop', we arrive at the three-fold division, at once both symbolic and geopolitical, that finds condensed expression in Moses Hess's phrase 'the European triarchy'. It is not hard to make out, in this tripartite division, the 'three sources' of Marx's theory, as systematized in Engels's account and canonized by tradition, especially by Kautsky. For, as I have already pointed out, the theoretical sequence examined below culminates, in the order of exposition I adopt, in the trajectory of the early Marx.

Our road runs, then, from Kant to Marx, but it now appears in a slightly different perspective: it is not a 'natural' progression towards a triumphant conclusion, but the product of a decision that takes full responsibility for its retroactive character: I have chosen to approach the early Marx's trajectory as a theoretical event that is utterly incomprehensible when it is considered apart from the sequence that precedes it (chronologically, to begin with, but also in the order of my exposition), yet is radically irreducible to it. Marx becomes Marx only under certain conditions that are, inseparably, both historical and theoretical; but this process can be understood only as a distantiation, a forceful separation from its conjuncture. Unpredictable, even highly improbable, this rupture radically reorders, by virtue of the opening or innovation it makes possible, the whole of the preceding sequence. Such, at any rate, is the hypothesis underlying my own interpretative decision.

The fact remains that it is entirely possible to imagine ways of telling this story that would not assign Marx a privileged position. This is one of the things I wish to suggest by opting for a mode of exposition and composition that proceeds by arranging, in a montage, chapters that are largely autonomous, like so many separate building blocks: the length and cast of each make them into virtual monographs. At the limit, these parts can be read out of order, in somewhat kaleidoscopic fashion, in order to multiply angles of approach and culminating points (Hess or Heine instead of Marx, or instead of Engels, and vice versa). Still, it would be foolish to deny that, among these various possibilities, the order of exposition privileges one in particular, whose whys and wherefores I now need to say something about.

The chapters below are organized around five itineraries, the aim of which is to re-create five decisive scansions of a process that saw the trajectory of classical German philosophy intersect that of the revolution-ary event in ways that are themselves theoretical, and defined by the irreducible distance separating each from all the others. The inaugural moment (Chapter 1) is that of Kant and Hegel, a contradictory pair who put the relation between philosophy and revolution under the constitutive sign of ambiguity; the play internal to this relation provides, to some extent, the matrix for later developments (of which the Lukács/Foucault comparison constitutes an outline).

The other four chapters take us into the period of the *Vormärz* itself: they correspond to four different moments in the radicalization of Hegel's posterity – or, at least, of a part of it. With Heine (Chapter 2), who represents the veritable pivotal point between the divergent post-Hegelian movements, the relation between philosophy and revolution confronts its own impossibility; its spectral dimension comes into view, opening up a new perspective, that of the actuality [*actualité*] of a German revolution. With Moses Hess (Chapter 3), and then with his most brilliant recruit, Friedrich Engels (Chapter 4), the grafting of philosophy on to the revolution engenders a third term, the 'social', which holds out a vision of harmony that purports to close the gap that is internal to the revolution while realizing its promises of liberation.

This is the illusion that will be categorically rejected with the advent of the Marxian moment (Chapter 5): Marx – recapitulating, *ex post facto*, all the terms of the German matrix – is led to consummate a political rupture that allows him to take up the thread of Heine's work while endowing it, this time, with the corresponding theoretical status. In encountering its concept – namely, the German revolution – philosophy exceeds its own limits. To preserve its truth content, it is duty-bound to consent to its own displacement; philosophy as a discourse divorced from politics and social practice is dissolved. This is the other way of conceiving the belatedness of the owl of Minerva: it consists in looking at the dusk from the perspective of the dawn that will follow.

'From Kant to Marx' now appears from a third and last angle, the one that profiles a 'transition' from philosophy to revolution in which philosophy loses its pre-eminence and autonomy only in the course of transforming revolution, in the very process of their mutual self-criticism. Philosophy now becomes the theoretical moment of a transformative political practice, the fold internal to it; it opens on to a new revolution or, rather, revolutionizes the revolution itself – a revolution within the revolution.

As I have already said, these chapters were written from the perspective of the present. A present defined against a backdrop of defeat and denial of the idea of revolution could – perhaps paradoxically – offer a new, because distanced, angle of approach to the bifurcation that founded modernity. But, in the opposite sense, this turn back to the past could help us to free ourselves to some extent from the trammels of our present, with its falsely familiar, self-evident truths that are in reality so many points of closure. For whenever the prospect of a transformation of the world is obscured, under the impact of a traumatic defeat, it is politics itself that is repressed and the antagonism inherent in the historical real that is quelled, only to return to haunt the present in spectral form. To some extent, the defeat of the revolution is fully registered in its actuality, which it confirms without, for all that, offering any guarantee whatsoever for the future.

It seems to me that this offers rich food for thought about history, which is, as we all know, a force that we encounter not in person, by virtue of a mystical illumination or founding anthropological experience, but only indirectly, through its effects. And if it is true that those effects are always apprehended as limits that individual and collective action comes up against in traumatic moments, the fact remains that these limits do not originate in a transcendent absolute; they can therefore be displaced, though not ignored or abolished. This, perhaps, is the only acceptable definition of an absolutely historicist approach, such as the one I have tried to adopt, and, simultaneously, the corresponding political practice, which deserves to be put to the test of experience or, at the very least, of thought.

1

Kant and Hegel, or the Ambiguity of Origins

Like other truths that have been too often repeated, the picture of a Germany, even a 'thinking man's' Germany, hailing the Paris events of July 1789 with a single voice has to be more finely shaded.[1] Yet the broad wave of goodwill that swept over 'enlightened' German public opinion with the storming of the Bastille, and the euphoric period that followed, are not just the stuff of myth. This reaction was not confined to the princely courts that were most receptive to the ideas of the *Aufklärung*. From Bavaria to Weimar, even to Prussia, many a German momentarily succumbed – although the moment was strictly delimited by the prospect of establishing a liberal monarchy (this was, then, the moment before Varennes and, especially, the August 1792 insurrection) – to a taste for the unprecedented freedom then spreading from Paris to the whole of Europe. This provides some indication of the depth of the enthusiasm that the revolutionary event called up in the most militant wing of the German Enlightenment, particularly in Kant and Fichte, to mention no one else. Yet the concern of the thinkers who were then at the centre of the philosophical stage was not merely to defend this event, but, even more, to *theorize* it – so much so that it hardly seems an exaggeration to say that German philosophy as such became the philosophy of the Revolution *par excellence*. Hannah Arendt's observation is therefore right on the mark:

> the model for this new revelation [of the philosophers' old absolute] by means of historical process was clearly the French Revolution, and the reason why post-Kantian German philosophy came to exert its enormous influence on European thought in the twentieth century, especially in countries exposed to revolutionary unrest – Russia, Germany, France – is not its so-called idealism but, on the contrary, the fact that it had left the sphere of mere speculation and attempted to formulate a philosophy which would correspond to and comprehend conceptually the newest and most real experience of the time.[2]

Contrary to what Arendt goes on to suggest, however, Kant and Fichte not only initiated this movement, but also remained faithful to it, even in the Jacobin period; they defended the Revolution's universal significance at a time when others were turning away from it and abandoning previously held positions to seek refuge in the exalted spheres of art – or, conversely, to lose themselves in the depths of their own tormented souls. Yet it would be hard to overemphasize the fact that this enthusiasm and this fidelity were inseparable from their other face, German theory's fundamental *ambivalence* towards the revolutionary phenomenon, an ambivalence that the next generation, the *Vormärz* generation, repeatedly came up against: it may be regarded as constitutive of the whole problematic of the 'German road' towards political and social modernity. Accepted as a fundamental point of reference, even admired, the Revolution was nevertheless also the object of an ongoing denial, doubtless for reasons having to do with the traumatic charge carried by the event and the many representations of it. Viewed from across the Rhine, the upheaval at the origins of the reflexivity crystallized in the modern sense of the word 'timeliness' [*actualité*] seemed simultaneously to bear the marks of a no less radical 'untimeliness' [*inactualité*] that had to do with the *hic et nunc*, with Germany itself and the fate of its *ancien régime*.

Kant is a good case in point. Even as he hails the event, the Jacobin moment not excepted, and unsparingly denounces the French and the foreign counter-revolution, he declares categorically that a revolutionary perspective is untimely and undesirable for Germany. Kant manages to theorize the revolution as the revelation of the secular millenarianism of history, a manifestation of the moral disposition of the human race and a sure sign of its immanent tendency towards progress, while *simultaneously* theorizing the insurmountable *distance* between this revolution and anyone who merely contemplates it from a spectator's position. *Committed* spectator though he is, Kant takes pains to remain above the fray: 'this revolution', he says, 'has aroused in the hearts and desires of all spectators who are not themselves caught up in it a *sympathy* which borders almost on enthusiasm, although the very utterance of this sympathy was fraught with danger. It cannot therefore have been caused by anything other than a moral disposition within the human race.'[3] The revolution is thus a 'historical sign'[4] – contingent in itself, and therefore an 'event' external to the causal order – which nevertheless offers a concrete manifestation of the teleological unity of nature and human freedom. The meaning of this sign can be deciphered only by a spectatorial consciousness; the gap between such a consciousness and the event, between the order of causes and ends, remains irreducible. It is not at all difficult to grasp the political significance of this operation by which the event is reduced to its hermeneutical reception: it means that one can express one's approval of the revolution as sign even while publicly exhibiting, especially for the benefit of the existing (absolutist) state, either a conspicuous lack of interest in the outcome of the actual revolution, or even – since all that matters is the impact the revolution has on the spectatorial consciousness – unfeigned hostility to seeing it spread.

Fichte's language seems more radical. But, in its fashion, it reflects the same ambiguity. On the one hand, it is a defence of the 'legitimacy of revolutions', a paean to 'action', a wink to the reader about 'the dawn [that] will soon break and the glorious day [that] will follow it'. On the other, it proclaims its desire for an emancipation achieved 'without disorder' and 'from the top down',[5] and ultimately defines the 'action' it celebrates as conformity to the moral law, assigning it to the sphere of the inner self and the individual consciousness. Such action is resolutely non-violent and generates its effects only very gradually; it is radically distinct from political action and, *a fortiori*, from any form of concrete revolutionary activity.[6] At the limit, the very meaning of the word 'revolution' changes. It falls to 'another' revolution, one that is 'incomparably more important' than the French Revolution, yet complementary to it for as long as the French Revolution is just an enlightening 'canvas'[7] to be contemplated at a distance from the spectatorial position defined by Kant – it falls to the revolution that Kant himself has wrought in the philosophical realm to carry out the work of liberation by contributing to the progress of civic and spiritual education, thereby making further revolutions superfluous.

There, in a nutshell, are the founding themes of the 'German road'. For, if civic and spiritual education – *Bildung* in Fichte's terms – or the slow spread of 'publicity' or 'aesthetic education' in Kant's or Schiller's, or even the 'reform in inwardness' (that is, in the sphere of culture) celebrated by Hegel do not simply signal so many inevitable detours (or, rather, so many constitutive moments of the revolution considered as a process), but clearly mark out a distinct German path (whose results may well partially converge with its French equivalent, if only in a future as distant as it is indeterminate), when they do not name a historical possibility *superior* to the 'French original', then the whole meaning of the France–Germany relationship changes. Germany ceases to be a laggard, a mere spectator of events unfolding on a remote stage which is like no other; it becomes the protagonist of a distinct process, inasmuch as it strikes out on a path which – even if it remains, in a sense, derivative of, and dependent on, the revolutionary prototype – nevertheless *displaces* that prototype beyond the bounds of the political domain, and thereby *supersedes it* even while managing to do without it.

A FOUNDATION FOR POLITICS?

The impossible compromise

German Idealism, once posited as the philosophy of the revolution, takes its place under the sign of a paradoxical dialectic of compromise: to keep faith with the revolution, one must finally demonstrate that one can do without it, even if this requires transposing it to a very different realm. The most rigorous formulation of the idea is doubtless the one furnished by the old sage of Königsberg: the goal is plainly a republican form of government (as distinguished from democracy), 'this one and only perfectly lawful kind of constitution';[8] but the 'German road' is the road of reform, not revolution, which is (and should continue to be) restricted to the French case. More precisely, the German road is that of a 'reform from the top downwards', charged with undermining the feudal order and ushering in the reign of freedom while avoiding a break with the legal order:

> it can still be required of the individual in power that he should be intimately aware of the maxim that changes for the better are necessary, in order that the constitution may constantly approach the optimum end prescribed by laws of right. A state may well *govern* itself in a republican way, even if its existing constitution provides for a despotic *ruling power*, and it will gradually come to the state where the people can be influenced by the mere idea of the law's authority, just as if it were backed up by physical force, so that they will be able to create for themselves a legislation ultimately founded on right.[9]

The philosopher, unlike 'official' professors of law and 'jurists' working in the service of absolutism, is undoubtedly duty-bound to elaborate a theory of freedom and put it to public use. However, he addresses himself, first and foremost, to a cultivated public and the king, whom he seeks to enlighten; he does not turn to the people with a view to inciting it to rebellion.[10] He has no ambition to govern, but, rather, seeks to promote all necessary reforms by means of the counsel he offers the enlightened elites. Indeed, the place Kant assigns intellectuals is a crucial component of the compromise that he proposes. The Kantian intellectual is not the Platonic 'philosopher-king', given that the tension between power and truth is irreducible in Kant. He is a moderate version of the French

Enlightenment thinker, an intellectual whose mission is that of a counsellor to the powerful; he enjoys freedom of expression, but has no direct political stake in the exercise of power. He is an educator and researcher devoted to the service, not of the monarch, but of what is ultimately the sole legitimate form of sovereignty, that of a 'sovereign people', an autonomous humanity capable of self-government.

Here are the exact terms of the pact Kant proposes:

> It is not to be expected that kings will philosophise or that philosophers will become kings; nor is it to be desired, however, since the possession of power inevitably corrupts the free judgment of reason. Kings or sovereign peoples (i.e. those governing themselves by egalitarian laws) should not, however, force the class of philosophers to disappear or to remain silent, but should allow them to speak publicly. This is essential to both in order that light may be thrown on their affairs. And since the class of philosophers is by nature incapable of forming seditious factions or clubs, they cannot incur suspicion of disseminating propaganda.[11]

Yet the fact remains that, even in this moderate version, the proposed pact looks less like an immediately applicable compromise than an ideal addressed to a future 'sovereign people' – to, that is, a republican government based on popular sovereignty.

What the existing state is invited to do here and now is to tolerate philosophers' criticisms, respect their autonomy, and even seek to benefit from their advice, which can only sustain it on its reform course. In exchange, philosophers are to keep strictly to the reformist road without attempting to elude the censors so as to forge direct contacts with the people – by, for example, distributing clandestine literature the way their French counterparts do, to say nothing of direct involvement in 'subversive' political action (again, in the clandestine forms exemplified by the proliferating secret societies and clubs patterned after the French model).[12] Kant's discussion, in fact, focuses on these points. What he advocates is a kind of self-imposed limitation – not so much on the Enlightenment project as such, but on the way it is concretely publicized. His aim is to relieve this project of the burden represented by what Reinhart Koselleck calls its 'twin brother'[13] – that is to say, its non-public face, guaranteed by the secret organization of the Freemasons and, to a lesser extent, by the obscurity of the intellectuals' idiom.

Kant makes it abundantly clear that he has a top–down reform in mind, rather than anything resembling an initiative from below – that is, a popular initiative, even one of a gradualist kind:

It is certainly *agreeable* to think up political constitutions which meet the requirements of reason (particularly in matters of right). But it is foolhardy to put them forward seriously, and *punishable* to incite the people to do away with the existing constitution.... But it is not merely *conceivable* that we can continually approach such a state; so long as it can be reconciled with the moral law, it is also the *duty* of the head of state (not of the citizens) to do so.[14]

Here too, however, what Kant says is immediately qualified by a restriction that reduces its import. A few lines earlier, he had observed that 'it is our duty to enter into a constitution of this kind; and in the meantime, since it will be a considerable time before this takes place, it is the duty of monarchs to govern in a *republican* . . . manner'.[15] In other words, the fact that Kant leaves the initiative to the rulers alone is dictated by pragmatic considerations, not derived from a postulate of practical reason. A different reading of the passage is thus authorized in advance. That is why it is a mistake to accuse Kant, as a certain philosophical 'common sense' does, of neglecting practice for the sake of the pure formalism of theory and the 'ought'.[16] The question nevertheless arises as to whether the mediations designed to bridge the gulf that separates, *ex ante*, the 'is' and the 'ought' can be effective, or whether they merely reinforce the circle of political impotence.

One need not go so far as to accept Koselleck's argument that the denial of politics in the name of morality paradoxically establishes the political and, indeed, revolutionary character of the *Aufklärung*, in order to recognize that impotence is also a political position – or, at any rate, a position that has determinate political effects. In the suffocating conditions of Prussian absolutism, Kant, who was more representative of the radical wing of the German intelligentsia in this respect than is commonly supposed, strikes out, both theoretically and practically, on the path of a laboured, ambiguous compromise, which aims to have done with the *ancien régime* without provoking a revolutionary rupture and, above all, without sparking off a mass mobilization, which Kant both fears and, in the German case, deems utopian. Self-censorship and a willingness to respect the divide between intellectuals and 'the lower orders', taken to the point of cultivating a deliberately obscure style, set the boundaries that can never be crossed in this endless negotiation over the limits of the public sphere.[17] Fichte's sole, short-lived act of daring consisted in trying to shift, however slightly, the border that ran between 'esoteric truths' and 'exoteric truths';[18] he ventured so far as to launch an 'Appeal to the Public' that brought him into disgrace in Jena.

The career of Georg Forster,[19] generally regarded as one of the very small handful of German Jacobins, shows us the aporias of the German road as if under a magnifying glass. As the leader of the ephemeral Republic of Mainz, and one of the first exiles on French soil, Forster had nothing of the unworldly intellectual about him. Inverting, as it were, the terms of Kantian 'moderantism', Forster heaped praise, *in public*, on the role that the people of Paris had played in establishing the Jacobin Republic. Even as he did so, however, he was coming to the conclusion, *in private*, that a reawakening of the German people was both impossible and undesirable: 'the French volcano might well serve to protect France from an earthquake'.[20] To be sure, Forster himself did indeed risk getting involved in the world of practice, conducting one of the rare republican experiments on German soil. But the fragile Republic of Mainz, which had little popular support, owed its survival to the presence of French troops; as Forster was aware, this distinguished it from an indigenous revolutionary process. For *Germany*, this German republican advocated developing 'intellectual and moral culture', going so far as to argue that this path of development would '*necessarily* lead, *as if by itself*, to freedom'.[21] Thus the tragic dimension of Forster's trajectory – that of a revolutionary inwardly opposed to the revolution, a German patriot whose republicanism grew out of fidelity to a foreign revolutionary cause – is graphically illustrative of the constitutive impossibility of German political practice.

Between the republic without revolution (the reformist option) and dissimulation – or even accommodation to the existing order, in exchange for a certain tolerance of intellectuals – the way proved particularly strait, when it was not simply impracticable. Domenico Losurdo observes that 'defence of the French Revolution cannot and must not be understood as an appeal to overturn the established order in Germany – not only because censorship and the balance of forces ruled that out, but also because the balance of forces had in some sense been internalized to the point of affecting, at a fundamental level, the structure of thought itself, thus preventing formulation of a coherent theory of the bourgeois revolution'.[22] Arguing along the same lines, others have stressed the abiding lag between the audacity of Spirit and the political absurdity of an essentially heteronomous German Jacobinism[23] whose divorce from political practice took the peculiar form of dependence on the French model. This dependence manifested itself both on the intellectual plane (a real revolution theorized at a distance) and in the abortive attempts at practical action adapted to the military balance of power and the presence of foreigners whose conduct had soon disappointed even those in the thin ranks of their fervent partisans.

Politics between a foundation and the *salto mortale*

There can be little doubt as to where the ticklish point in Kant's project lies. Contrary to a widespread misconception, Kant does not by any means believe that it is enough to cultivate inner virtue, perfect individual consciousness, or preach reform in order to promote progress in morality and right. On the contrary, he stresses the decisive role of institutions, and conceives right, which operates in the public sphere, as a means of squaring morality with politics. Furthermore, he rejects the road defended by his disciple Schiller,[24] who, alarmed by the turn contemporary events had taken (the first nine letters in *On the Aesthetic Education of Man*, written in September–October 1794, are an immediate reaction to the fall of Robespierre), abjured politics, although he renounced neither the project nor the achievements of the Revolution: the establishment of a universal foundation for moral values and political liberties within the framework of a rational state. Thereafter, Schiller devoted himself to establishing a different kind of mediation, which was to proceed by way of aesthetic education and the spiritual elevation of humanity; this was, as he saw it, the precondition for winning freedom and avoiding the dreaded state of 'barbarity', the unleashing of the 'crude, lawless impulses' of the 'lower classes', 'hastening with ungovernable fury to their brutal satisfaction'.[25] This project of aesthetic mediation is based on a clear-cut separation between the ideal objective of the revolution and actual political practice. The 'aesthetic state' that Schiller interposes between the physical and moral state – halfway between the passivity of nature and juridical-political autonomy – is conceived as education through Beauty; the sole active state is thought, the activity of the subject as lawgiver in his encounter with the object.[26] Hence Schiller's praise for the ear and the eye (to the detriment of the sense of touch) and his insistence on maintaining a sharp distinction between the ideal and its realization, which, he says, is external to the aesthetic state.[27] In fact, Schiller's defence of a radical break between *Kultur* and political practice plainly risks relapsing into a position short even of Kantian reformism.

In a certain sense, Kant presents himself as a thinker of 'objective morality', not an advocate of improving Humanity with the help of the Beautiful, or a believer in the superiority of private virtue. Yet his conception of ethical life poses the relationship between morality and politics as the external action of morality *on* politics (through the mediation of right), and, ultimately, as the subordination of the one to the other. As a mechanics of forces, as technico-pragmatic action, politics is subject to the rationalization of juridical norms, and its legality is defined from the standpoint of its external conditions as simple conformity or nonconformity with the law, without regard for motives. The legal norm, in its turn, is summoned before the bar of morality, which examines it in its internality, taking as its criterion the harmony between the motives for an act and the idea of duty according to the law.

However, the tension constitutive of politics proves undecidable if we do not move to the higher level represented by morality, which plainly has the last word:

> A true system of politics cannot therefore take a single step without first paying tribute to morality. And although politics in itself is a difficult art, no art is required to combine it with morality. For as soon as the two come into conflict, morality can cut through the knot which politics cannot untie. The rights of man must be held sacred, however great a sacrifice the ruling power may have to make. There can be no half measures here; it is no use devising hybrid solutions such as a pragmatically conditioned right halfway between right and utility. For all politics must bend the knee before right.[28]

Applying this criterion, Kant distinguishes 'the moral politician'[29] – that is, the leader who accepts the subordination of politics to moral imperatives and takes the path of reforms, sacrificing his own interests in the process, if need be – from the 'moralising politician', who utilizes morality as mere window-dressing for his defence of the interests of authority, or as cover for the violation of right by the powerful. Concretely, this distinction serves to draw a line of demarcation between a policy of 'reform from the top down', implemented by statesmen guided by reason and enlightened by the counsel of philosophers, and those leaders and courtiers who stubbornly defend absolutism and cling to their privileges, opposing reform and blocking gradual progress towards the rule of law.[30] In accordance with the classical tradition of political philosophy, 'true politics', which here means moral politics, is understood as the subordination of politics to a truth located beyond it in an ontological position from which it can survey politics from on high. As usual, this truth provides both a foundation for politics and its ultimate meaning. It is rooted in subjective freedom – a specifically Kantian feature that attests its inscription in a secularized world-view – not in its conformity with a natural/cosmic order, as in ancient philosophy. The metapolitical principle serves, in turn, to define and ground a line of conduct in politics; it presents itself as the rational ideal with which empirical individuals are invited to bring their actions into conformity *ex post facto*. The act that founds politics appeals to an element that abolishes politics while simultaneously assigning it a totalizing meaning.

But it is precisely here that the real indeterminateness of Kant's proposed criterion stands out most sharply. The category that makes it possible to provide a rational foundation for the pursuit of reforms from on high, the road of 'moral politics', also serves to justify both the dictatorship of Robespierrean virtue and . . . its Thermidorean 'rectification'.[31] The moral criterion, for its part, turns out to be unmanageable, in the literal sense of the word: the Enlightenment thinkers' reactionary adversaries are certainly not the only 'moralizing politicians', since moral precepts can typically be invoked to justify any brand of politics whatsoever, at least if the politics in question is not legitimized in absolutist terms.[32] As soon as morality consents to confront real situations, it splits in two, reflecting the contradictions of those situations within itself and revealing, in the process, its political overdetermination. It should now be clearer how the revolutionary event dangerously undermines Kant's construction at its nodal point – the point at which it tries to articulate the two previously distinct legal orders, positing that a gradual historical process can bring about their reunification. For the revolution suspends the existing legal order and plunges society into a legal vacuum, even if it eventually produces a new system of right in closer conformity with freedom. Right, as the form of the external (intersubjective) conditions of freedom, does not arrive together with the means of establishing it; politics, at its culminating point – the revolutionary event – asserts itself independently of any moral foundation; the revolution, precisely as an event, overturns the conception of a historically homogeneous time orientated, in linear fashion, towards progress. Such is the triple antinomy that Kant allows us to think; but, once reflection has grasped it, his whole system threatens to disintegrate as a result.

Kantian reformism, which tries to plug the resulting gaps and maintain the coherence of the doctrine, is premised on the gradual extension of the sphere of publicity [Publizität], conceived as the domain in which progress is made towards the juridical-moral subsumption of politics. Here, every action is subject to the test of the transcendental principle of public right: 'All actions affecting the rights of other human beings are wrong if their maxim is not compatible with their being made public.'[33] Publicity thus makes it possible to bring the two faces of the Kantian empirico-transcendental doublet together on the same experiential grounds, while preserving the distinction between them. Once any action has passed the test that consists in its being made public, it may be considered both free and necessary.

The subject of civil law then becomes coextensive with the intelligible subject, and the *res publica* effectively offers, at the phenomenal level, a concrete manifestation of the noumenal order (the Idea of freedom). But this is so only under certain empirical conditions: only property-holders have access to the public sphere and enjoy full-fledged citizenship, once obstacles of a feudal kind (the division into estates and hereditary privileges) have been swept away and 'equality of opportunity' ensured.[34] This assumption testifies to a typically liberal confidence in a certain natural order (the market) capable of uniting, in a single empirico-transcendental political community, the proprietor-citizen, who acts in the sphere of right (of freedom in its external aspects), and the inwardly free man, who is subject to the moral law.[35] So defined, the maxim of publicity reinforces the terms of the compromise between the intelligent-sia and the established order by preventively eliminating the temptation to engage in illegal activity;[36] it also forestalls the emergence of an organic bond between intellectuals and the subaltern classes. Even if this presents certain disadvantages for the rulers, it remains preferable, from their own standpoint, to accept a public sphere carefully confined to the bourgeois strata rather than to eliminate the legal margin for free expression at the risk of seeing it informally or secretly extended to the lower orders, a development that would have the additional consequence of transforming the philosophers who would bear the brunt of repression into subversive propagandists and agitators. It is at this price that the establishment of Publicity may be proffered as a 'substitute for any imaginable revolution'.[37] But it is precisely this price that would seem exorbitant to the *Vormärz* generation, from Ruge to Marx: a generation that had had its fill of the reformist rationalism of the German intelligentsia – synonymous, in its eyes, with impotence and inefficacy.

The force of events

Kant's solution appears fraught with uncertainties even to Kant himself. Inasmuch as idealism's affirmation of the primacy of morality over politics proves inseparable from a philosophy of the teleological nature of the historical process,[38] the irruption of a revolutionary temporality can only throw it into permanent crisis. The fierce confrontation between revolu-tion and counter-revolution, the brutal reaction of the classes threatened by this unprecedented event, and the war unleashed by the European monarchies were all hard to reconcile with the schema of the slow but sure spread of culture and the Spirit of reform. In the last text he published, Kant allows himself to air a doubt as to the ability of the princely courts to undertake reforms and tolerate public criticism, even if it comes only from philosophers and respectable citizens. To the question posed in the title of Section 10 of 'The Contest of Faculties', 'What Sequence Can Progress Be Expected to Follow?', the answer Kant gives in the rest of the text seems, at the very least, sceptical.

Kant now deems the path based on cultural reform and education of the younger generation unrealistic if it does not issue in a general reform of the state; but such reform, for its part, will run up against the obstacle represented by the need to educate the educators. Barring appeals to Providence, the only other possibility that Kant can see is that a regulatory use of warfare might give rise to a certain 'negative wisdom' which would eventually make aggression a thing of the past. Yet, as Kant himself has already abundantly demonstrated in 'Perpetual Peace', this state of affairs can come about only on the basis of a prior political transformation, a republican transformation that would, by preventing rulers from making war without first consulting the people, put an end to *guerres de cabinet*, colonialist pillage, and the rapine associated with the slave trade. Furthermore, at the very moment when Kant makes his plea for publicity as a means of avoiding revolution, he also observes that the state, 'whose only wish is to rule', will do everything in its power to stigmatize philosophers and thwart the creation of a public sphere, thus depriving the people of all means of expressing (*peacefully*, is the unspoken implication) its needs and discontents.[39]

Moreover, Section 8 of 'The Contest of Faculties' bears the significant title, 'The *Difficulty* of Maxims Directed Towards The World's Progressive Improvement As Regards their Publicity'.[40] In the final analysis, we see here, it may be the task of *revolutions* to bring about the acceleration needed to ensure the historical progress of freedom, and thus resolve the decidedly too antinomical 'paradoxes' of enlightened absolutism. Kant now goes so far as to legitimize popular rebellions and the use of force, at least in certain extreme cases – but is every revolutionary situation not, precisely, a state of exception? In this sense, there does indeed exist a Kantian theory of revolution – what Jürgen Habermas calls the 'semi-official reading' of Kant. That is clearly how Kantian theory appeared to Kant's contemporaries, who either damned it, if they were supporters of absolutism, or, like the Rhenish leader Joseph von Görres, hailed it as the 'German theory of the French Revolution'.[41]

In this perspective, the revolution appears as a 'call of nature' and a '*salto mortale*' which makes possible a transition from one legal order to the next: 'But this counsel of desperation (*salto mortale*) means that, since there is no appeal to right but only to force, the people may themselves resort to force and thus make every legal constitution insecure. If there is nothing which commands immediate respect through reason, such as the basic rights of man, no influence can prevail upon man's arbitrary will and restrain his freedom.'[42] The revolutionary enterprise is, to be sure, absolutely unjustifiable from a *legal* point of view, since the creation of a new legal order presupposes the abrogation of the one that preceded it, and therefore represents a moment of legal vacuum and a radical discontinuity in the sphere of right: 'But revolution under an already existing constitution means the destruction of all relationships governed by civil right, and thus of right altogether. And this is not a change but a dissolution of the civil constitution; and the transition to a better one would not then be a metamorphosis but a palingenesis, for it would require a new social contract on which the previous one (which is now dissolved) could have no influence.'[43]

What Kant finds alarming is precisely the moment of vacuum thus created, in so far as it implies the threat of regression to a state of nature: 'for such procedures, if made into a maxim, make all lawful constitutions insecure and produce a state of complete lawlessness (*status naturalis*) where all rights cease at least to be effectual'.[44] This explains why he disallows the 'right to resistance' – a position that is often interpreted, wrongly, as condemnation of the French revolutionary experience. Restored to its context, that of a war waged by a European coalition against a French Republic that was simultaneously faced with a domestic rebellion in the Vendée, Kant's position is in fact as much a defence of the legitimacy of the new republican state against the domestic and European counter-revolutionary 'resistance' as it is an attempt to delegitimize any new revolution. Moreover, what Kant contests is not the historically progressive character of 'resistance', but the claim that such resistance has the character of *right*. Kant's rigour allows him to state clearly that the revolution is irreducible to any *legal* foundation.

Out of joint from the legal point of view, the revolution is, by the same token, objectionable from the standpoint of individual morality, which dictates obedience to existing laws in order to preserve the foundations of the community.[45] Yet, once he has established this, Kant at no point rejects the revolutionary regime on moral grounds; on the contrary, he defends both its legality and its internal link to the imperatives of 'moral politics', even in the case of the Jacobin Terror. Indeed, he would appear to criticize the Jacobins less for resorting to force than for the plebeian social dimension of their policy – in other words, for raising broad egalitarian demands. In this sense, he is a Thermidorean *avant la lettre* who anticipated the closure of the debate on equality opened by the revolution of 10 August 1792. For Kant – as I have already pointed out in discussing the conditions of access to the public sphere – 'this uniform equality of human beings as subjects of a state is . . . perfectly consistent with the utmost inequality of the mass in the degree of its possessions, whether these take the form of physical or mental superiority over others, or of fortuitous external property and of particular rights (of which there may be many) with respect to others'.[46] The implication is that

> the only qualification required of a citizen (apart, of course, from being an adult male) is that he must be his *own master* (*sui juris*), and must have some *property* (which can include any skill, trade, fine art or science) to support himself. . . . The domestic servant, the shop assistant, the labourer, or even the barber, are merely labourers (*operarii*), not *artists* (*artifices*, in the wider sense) or members of the state, and are thus unqualified to be citizens.[47]

But let us turn back to Kant's conception of the revolution-event. Defying all legal-moral norms, the revolution appears as a 'natural'-objective fact whenever the use of force by the dominant provokes a riposte from the dominated; but it is also an opportunity to be seized, for it makes the emergence of right and freedom possible:

> Thus political prudence, with things as they are at present, will make it a duty to carry out reforms appropriate to the ideal of public right. But where revolutions are brought about by nature alone, it will not use them as a good excuse for even greater oppression, but will treat them as a call of nature [*Ruf der Natur*] to create a lawful constitution based on the principles of freedom, for a thorough reform of this kind is the only one which will last.[48]

Plainly, Kant ultimately hails the revolution, assigning it its place in his vision of universal history as a phenomenon that will inevitably recur: 'For the occurrence in question is too momentous, too intimately interwoven with the interests of humanity and too widespread in its influence upon all parts of the world for nations not to be reminded of it *when favourable circumstances present themselves*, and to rise up and make *renewed attempts of the same kind as before.*'[49]

'*Salto mortale*' or 'call of nature', the revolutionary *event* breaks with the representation of time as homogeneous and linear. It entails a risk (which is what makes this leap 'perilous', *mortale*); its results are not guaranteed in advance; it arrives without warning; in short, it is *always* untimely. More than a mere acceleration of history, what begins to emerge beneath the surface here is an *opening up* of history – to the contingency of events (a revolution is not predictable, it develops as a function of 'circumstances'), a range of different possibilities (reform, revolution, restoration), different partisan positions (not everyone shares the 'enthusiasm' of the Francophiles), and either/or alternatives: who will carry the day, the republic or the Vendée? France, or the coalition of monarchies?

Deprived of a legal-moral foundation, but not of historical legitimacy or political-institutional productivity, the revolution is stubbornly resistant to something that is at the heart of Kant's enterprise: the subsumption of politics under the moral law. For the revolution defies all notions of foundation. It leaves in its wake the total absence of a divine signifier, a void that Kant lucidly faces up to even as he strives – unsuccessfully – to fill it. The Kantian conception of politics and the philosophy of history underlying it are thus taken to their limit, which is, at one and the same time, the point of theory's greatest advance and the boundary beyond which the whole edifice collapses. With Kant, philosophy settles in for a very long crisis.

SUPERSEDING THE REVOLUTION?

Is the revolution Kantian?

Hegel means his move to be radical: eliminating Kant's empirical-transcendental dualism and positing the rationality internal to the real as the only process through which the absolute freedom of spirit unfolds, he does away, by the same token, with the problem of the moral foundation of right. His position is rooted in a radical critique of the claim that such a foundation can be provided by subjective morality and the individual consciousness. Yet neither subjective morality nor the individual consciousness is negated; both are rather positioned within a process which, endlessly decentring them, endlessly realizes higher forms of political rationality. Subjective morality, the morality of Kant's empirical-intelligible subject, is preserved/sublated in the mutual implication of the spheres that go to make up *Sittlichkeit* ('ethical life' or 'objective morality', depending on the translation), that is, the family, civil society, and the state; *Sittlichkeit* is defined as the concrete identity of freedom and the *subjective will*.[50] It follows that pitting morality against politics at the level, precisely, of concrete intersubjective action, only to unite them *ex post facto* under the auspices of the transcendental principle, simply indicates the persistence of a false question, a regression towards the horizon of abstract right and subjective morality.[51]

Hegel credits Kant with establishing the right of the subjective will, and positing duty as an expression of its pure self-determination. He contends, however, that leaving matters there comes down to conceptualizing right and freedom as the mere coexistence of mutually restrictive subjective freedoms that are incapable of becoming anything more than formal moral imperatives.[52] The divorce between the 'is' and the 'ought' inevitably points back to an objective indeterminateness that reduces morality to hollow formalism while exposing the undecidability of moral imperatives at the practical level; these can be invoked to justify, *ex post facto*, any concrete action whatever.[53] Clinging to the illusory force of moral certainty in the hope of closing the gap between itself and the world, subjectivity constantly runs up against, and perpetuates, its own real impotence. For Hegel, withdrawal to the closed world of such moral certainty exemplifies, as a one-sided valorization of the conformity of action to duty, the bad infinity of a subjectivity that reflects only itself, posits itself as the supreme absolute, and experiences its own one-sidedness amid the pangs of its bad conscience.[54] Stubbornly refusing to go down the path of objective morality, the subjective consciousness loses itself in the labyrinth of hypocrisy, carried away by the extravagant pretension that it can justify its actions simply by invoking its good intentions. From the heights of this 'solitary divine worship', it topples into the complacency of those who share 'the rejoicing over this mutual purity, and the refreshing of themselves in the glory of knowing and uttering, of cherishing and fostering such an excellent state of affairs': the community of beautiful souls.

Yet Hegel, contrary to the common conception of him as an 'organicist', state-centred thinker hostile to individual rights, accords great importance to subjectivity, both as possessed of specific rights – which the sphere of *Sittlichkeit* does not abolish but, rather, puts in a broader framework – and as an active principle, the subject of endless, active self-development, thanks to which the objectivity of the ethical totality is mediated and can become concrete universality: 'that which implements and externalises this universal principle and gives it reality is the activity of individuality, which translates the inner essence into reality. It thereby brings what is wrongly described as reality, i.e. the world of mere externals, into conformity with the Idea.'[55] The real cannot maintain itself as such unless subjective activity takes place within it – through, not least, the elaboration of objectivity in the moment of particularity: 'the individual does not invent his content, but merely activates the substantial content which is already present within him. But this universal substance which every individual must translate into activity [is] an activity by which the whole of ethical life is sustained.'[56]

However, Hegelian phenomenology conceives this subjective position as inseparable from a structure of misrecognition, typical of self-consciousness, which tends towards truth only at the price of an infinitely repeatable 'missed encounter' with its object. Thus Hegel cannot but object to Kant's attempt to articulate theory with practice, even if, like his predecessor, he puts revolution at the centre of the relationship between them. His 'enthusiasm' (Hegel uses Kant's word) for the French Revolution, palpable even in a late text like *The Philosophy of History*, is no less intense than Kant's; *The Philosophy of History* celebrates the Revolution as the destruction of the accumulated 'injustices' of the *ancien régime*, the sudden emergence of the principle of right, a 'sublime' attempt to reconstitute the real on a rational basis. The Revolution is, says Hegel, a radical (new) beginning, an upheaval of truly cosmic dimensions, a 'glorious mental dawn', the event of universal significance *par excellence*.[57] Thus we find in Hegel, as in all the other German Idealists, the core of the Jacobin conception of the Revolution, especially in the central importance he ascribes to the moment of the Terror as a key to understanding the revolutionary process. No wonder, then, that Hegelian thought has been deemed 'the most far reaching consequence of the French Revolution' (Arendt), or that it has called forth judgements such as Ritter's: 'no other philosophy . . . is a philosophy of revolution to such a degree and so profoundly'.[58]

But Hegel does not leave matters at that. Like the standpoint of subjective morality, the freedom created by the French Revolution must also be grasped in its internal limits, in the movement of self-transcendence triggered again and again by the very spectacle of its defeat. The Revolution is by no means finished; it is not a shore that has been left behind and can now be safely contemplated from afar. It dominates the whole of the historical period that followed it, as is shown in the astounding section of the *Phenomenology* devoted to 'absolute freedom and the Terror'.[59] At the moment when consciousness turns back upon itself, it retrospectively grasps its own progression by confronting the void, the constitutive lack formed by the absolute negativity at its core. It recognizes its own becoming in the Revolution. It is in this sense that even the moment of the Terror – the moment, precisely, in which absolute freedom changes into its opposite and is identified with death and nothingness – enters into the process by which freedom becomes necessity; that is to say, it is in this sense that the Terror is always-already there, behind us and within us. In other words, it is at the moment when, under the impact of this retroactive performativity, consciousness recognizes that its own freedom is realized in the state's that it posits the necessity of the Terror, and assigns it its significance: that of an internal precondition for the emancipatory process.

Hegel's critique thus challenges what might be termed the Kantian political illusion as an illusion of the spectatorial consciousness, which putatively stands outside a process that affects only its inner disposition – an illusion that is coextensive with the radical disjunction that this consciousness establishes between freedom and causality (the revolution is a 'sign' but not a 'cause' of progress). The relationship between theory and practice must consequently be rethought; it must be displaced under the effect of a new question. 'The same principle [that of formal will] obtained speculative recognition in Germany in the *Kantian* philosophy. According to it,' Hegel goes on, in a famous passage in *The Philosophy of History* just before the celebration of the French Revolution quoted above,

> the simple unity of Self-consciousness, the Ego, constitutes the absolutely independent Freedom, and is the fountain of all general conceptions – i.e., all conceptions elaborated by Thought–Theoretical Reason; and likewise of the highest of all practical determinations [or conceptions] – Practical Reason, as free and pure Will; and Rationality of Will is none other than the maintaining one's self in pure Freedom – willing this and this alone – Right purely for the sake of Right, Duty purely for the sake of Duty. Among the Germans this view assumed no other form than that of tranquil theory; but the French wished to give it practical effect. Two questions, therefore, suggest themselves: Why did this principle of Freedom remain merely formal? and why did the French alone, and not the Germans, set about realizing it?

These formulations should give us pause. They sketch a displacement of the terms of the problem, the consequences of which were to continue to make themselves felt throughout the whole of a historical period running down to the 1848 revolution and even beyond, in so far as Germany – which in this respect was quite Hegelian – repeatedly 'missed' the moment of its democratic revolution.

The displacement in question, then, is double. On the one hand, from a theoretical point of view, Kant is plainly contemporaneous with the French Revolution. But a typically Hegelian reversal allows us to state the same thing the other way round: the French Revolution is Kantian. A critique of the one thus applies to the other as well. None the less, from the standpoint of the concrete historical totality, the German situation has not progressed beyond 'tranquil theory'. It is therefore *not* contemporaneous – except in the one-sidedness of theory – with the revolutionary event; from this point of view, Kant falls behind his historical moment. This throws up two sets of questions. What part is theory – that is, philosophy – to play in this historical period? How can Germany not only catch up with the French Revolution, but even overtake it, in order to become contemporaneous with its own times? – and what, ultimately, would it mean to 'overtake' the French Revolution?

Revolution as process, revolution as event

Hegel objects to the radical lag [*décalage*] that Kant puts between the spectatorial consciousness and the real event – not, as has often been said, by calling the existence of freedom and contingency into question, but by showing how necessity is engendered, as a retroactive effect,[60] by this contingency and the activity of subjects. Such is the truth of the retroaction [*après-coup*] constitutive of philosophy. The event, in its emergence, poses its own premises, determining that they were the conditions for its realization. This transition is always the result of a *salto mortale*, which is a creative act in the sense that it gives the preceding links in the chain of events their meaning. Thus the moment of the Terror 'yields up' its inner meaning only as an effect of the shift in perspective imposed by the emergence of the modern post-Revolutionary state. A possibility, by becoming 'historical', can appear as the bearer of a different kind of universality, a form of the real that abolishes the existing order of things. Thought recognizes the event as a sign by refusing to succumb to the retrospective illusion according to which everything was decreed in advance, whether in an abstract Absolute standing outside history or in the subjective intentions of its agents. In reality, the lag is located not between the subject and the event, but *within the event itself*, in the retroactive, self-referential structure of its necessity. That is why the only viable conception of practice involves treating it as a movement of ongoing adjustment immanent in the real, and why revolution must be conceived as a process – or, more precisely, as an irreducible duality oscillating between process and event.

Philosophy – whose task, for Hegel, consists in attaining knowledge of the becoming-history of truth – cannot remain indifferent to such a process; for that which, in the real, attains to the level of the concept is reflected, precisely, in philosophy, as is that which, conversely, lapses into inactuality and absurdity:[61] 'It has been said that the French Revolution resulted from Philosophy, and it is not without reason that Philosophy has been called "Weltweisheit" [World Wisdom]; for it is not only Truth in and for itself, as the pure essence of things, but also Truth in its living form as exhibited in the affairs of the world. *We should not, therefore, contradict the assertion that the Revolution received its first impulse from Philosophy.*'[62] The Hegelian present clearly opens on to the future,[63] because it makes it possible to recognize the real tendencies that shape the present from within, and are the driving force behind the progress of Spirit. Should we, then, say that Hegel was the theoretician of the revolution – that is, of a conception of revolutionary activity as the correct [*juste*] articulation of theory with practice? To do so would no doubt be to proceed, once again, somewhat too hastily.

Hegelian thought, too, was never to overcome a fundamental ambiguity, a mixture of fascination and repulsion in the face of the revolutionary phenomenon: admiration for its universal significance and sympathy for the demands of a suffering humanity to which it gave voice; but also apprehension about uncontrollable mass movements and the chronic instability they breed. At the very moment when Hegel justifies philosophy's role as midwife to the revolution – its greatest sin, according to the overwhelming European reaction of his day[64] – he downplays the importance of the French experience from a practical point of view, and, no less, at the theoretical level. The philosophy from which freedom receives its basic impulse 'is in the first instance', Hegel is quick to say, 'only abstract Thought, not the concrete comprehension of absolute Truth – intellectual positions between which there is an immeasurable chasm'.[65] This philosophy is abstract because, in Catholic France, the target of the thinkers of the Enlightenment was from the outset the Church, whereas Protestant Germany reaped the fruits of a secularization whose driving spirit was the Reformation.[66] In attacking religion, which we should understand, in this context, as a form of collective life rooted in subjective inwardness – that is, 'religion' in the etymological sense of 'bond' [*relicare*] – the French Enlightenment absolutized particularity, the individual will, and the formal moment. Hegel takes issue with the contractualist model that is the inevitable consequence of such an approach:

> that formal, individual Will is in virtue of the abstract position just mentioned made the basis of political theories; Right in Society is that which the Law wills, and the Will in question appears as an isolated *individual* [*einzeln*] will; thus the State, as an aggregate of many individuals, is not an independently substantial Unity, and the truth and essence of Right in and for itself – to which the will of its individual members ought to be conformed in order to be true, free Will; but the volitional atoms are made the starting point, and each will is represented as absolute.[67]

Thus French freedom is inherently incapable of going beyond the moment of the subjective will and the atomistic conception of the state that flows from it. The sunrise of 1789 can therefore only be followed by the twilight of the gods. . . . Incapable of transforming consciousness from within, the subjective will, promoted to the rank of sole possible foundation for the state and public virtue, necessarily becomes sheer coercion, brought to bear on the individual consciousness from without. It is identified with the policing of individual feeling and the destruction of singularities by a 'simple, inflexible, cold' universality;[68] it is changed into its opposite, becoming a form of tyranny – the Robespierrean Terror[69] – only to culminate, after the Napoleonic interlude, in the Restoration. (Let us remark in passing that Hegel, often described as an apologist for this Restoration, calls it a 'farce' in discussing the Bourbon monarchy, and a 'rotten despotism'[70] when he writes about the Italian principalities.) French freedom, formal and abstract, is still only the freedom of liberalism. But, in Hegel's estimation, liberalism remains external to the spirit of the peoples; it is incapable of creating a self-sustaining form of collective life, of constituting an actual community. Revolutions give way to counter-revolutions and securely entrenched regimes, but 'agitation and unrest' do not therefore come to an end.[71]

Short of liberalism, and beyond it

Hegel's critique of liberalism, the heart of his critique of the French Revolution, fans out in a number of different directions; it is by no means clear that it constitutes a coherent whole, despite the multiple connections between the themes Hegel develops. This amounts to saying that the Hegelian critique is fundamentally ambiguous and thus capable of sustaining the diverse readings which were later to find systematic expression in so many competing 'Hegelianisms'. Hegel's basic argument is that liberalism absolutizes the viewpoint of civil society, which it tends systematically to confound with the state. Liberalism thus remains trapped in the atomism of individual interests, and is incapable of rising to the level of *Vereinigung* (union or association), of collective existence in its objectivity and universalizing significance:

If the state is confused with civil society and its determination is equated with the security and protection of property and personal freedom, the interest of individuals [*der Einzelnen*] as such becomes the ultimate end for which they are united; it also follows from this that membership of the state is an optional matter. But the relationship of the state to the individual [*Individuum*] is of quite a different kind. Since the state is objective spirit, it is only through being a member of the state that the individual [*Individuum*] himself has objectivity, truth, and ethical life. Union [*Vereinigung*] as such is itself the true content and end, and the destiny of individuals is to lead a universal life.[72]

With this as his point of departure, Hegel goes on to criticize liberalism from a threefold point of view, which I shall describe here, in order to simplify the discussion, as legal-political, cultural, and social.

All Rousseau's fault?

From a *legal-political* standpoint, Hegel's critique of liberalism is closely bound up with his critique of contractualism, although it should be made clear from the start of our discussion that there is no necessary connection between these two, which are very far from being simply identical. The same holds for their respective antitheses, anti-liberalism and anti-contractualism. Bentham, for instance, is a liberal hostile to contract theory; Rousseau, whom Hegel explicitly criticizes, stands as an example of a contract theorist who fiercely attacks the economic and moral foundations of liberalism ('luxury', private property, cities, trade, the progress due to the 'arts and sciences', and so on).[73] Hegel, however, pursues his two critiques conjointly, constantly citing the French Revolution as a splendid illustration of the dire consequences of contractualism. Arguing against Rousseau, whom he considers a representative figure of political Jacobinism, Hegel nevertheless credits him with having established the principle of the will in its universality 'as the principle of the State'; Rousseau's merit, in other words, is to have established the essentially spiritual content of the concept of the state. But, Hegel objects, Rousseau is unable to assign the will a substantial content, so that it remains abstract; moreover, he conceives it on the model of personal volition, the arbitrary will of the individual.[74] Hence he treats the general will as an aggregate of such particular wills, or as a reduction of them to their common denominator: in other words, as a contract. Rousseau's general will is thus too dependent on the particular will, and his conception of it ultimately remains in its shadow. In the final analysis, it misses the specificity of the state, a totality immanent in the spheres of social life and greater than the sum of its parts; it dissolves the state into the sphere of exchanges between contracting property-holders, which, for Rousseau, basically makes the state what it is. Hegel's criticism of the revolutionary contract theory of Rousseauesque inspiration coincides, on this point, with his criticism of the bourgeois liberalism which, in the spirit of the July monarchy, obliterates the distinction between the 'general will' and the 'will of the many', reducing the former to the '*empirically* general will',[75] and thus subordinating the state to the arbitrary power of individuals and groups.

But Hegel's anti-contractualist polemic does not stop here. It becomes more radical, peaking in a global rejection of the idea of democracy as self-government by the people. If *The Philosophy of History* explicitly challenges only the principle of majority rule,[76] *Elements of the Philosophy of Right*, as everyone knows, denies the representative principle, elections, and the franchise all validity, except in the form of organic representation by estates [*Stände*] and corporations, or the designation of deputies for their competence and the popular confidence they enjoy.[77] Hegel rejects representation both as an abstract reproduction of the general will which is incompatible with the universalization of different interests (by way of the 'organic' mediation of the corporations) that it is the state's task to ensure, and also as a constant source of political disorder. In evidence here, once again, is his fear of the masses, an 'irrational, barbarous, and terrifying'[78] element that is condemned to oscillate between the status of a subject of revolutionary exaltation and an object of counter-revolutionary manipulation.[79] This throws into sharp relief the limits of a political philosophy that culminates in an amalgam of anti-liberal themes, the refutation of contract theory, and the rejection of democracy.

So, for Hegel, runs one of the lessons of 1789: the attempt to translate contractualist abstractions into reality inevitably drew the 'dawn' of French freedom towards disaster:

> when those abstractions were invested with power, they afforded the tremendous spectacle, for the first time we know of in human history, of the overthrow of all existing and given conditions within an actual major state and the revision of its constitution from first principles and purely in terms of *thought*; the intention behind this was to give it what was *supposed* to be a purely *rational* basis. On the other hand, since these were only abstractions divorced from the Idea, they turned the attempt into the most terrible and drastic event.[80]

Hegel's verdict would seem to brook no appeal. Yet we would do well to notice that this critique is incomparably more profound than the straightforward expression of a defensive conservative reaction to a popular uprising. What Hegel dismantles here is the mechanism of a certain political illusion that found extreme, but not exclusive,[81] expression in the revolutionary consciousness: contractualism, incapable of fully grasping the real processes by which the state is formed, counterposes to them, in arbitrary fashion, an a priori construction, a ready-made programme whose implementation takes on the appearance of a radical new beginning. The formalism of freedom must thus oscillate between, on the one hand, the illusion of a certain political rationalism which claims that it can construct a new state by making a clean sweep of all mediations, and is therefore doomed to fail; and, on the other, the gradualist road taken by the July monarchy, which reintroduces chronic instability and opens the way to fresh revolutions. Abandoned by the sphere of subjectivity, isolated, blinded by its delirious joy at founding something new, abstract freedom ends up destroying itself, while constantly threatening to turn into its opposite: unfreedom and coercion.

The harbinger of a new freedom

Let us now turn to the second aspect of Hegel's critique of liberalism. *Culturally*, as I have already pointed out, liberalism cannot engender any form of collective life for as long as it remains cut off from 'inwardness', disconnected from the movement of cultural and intellectual reform inaugurated by Protestantism. This puts German backwardness in a different light. Because the Germans have not tried to realize the principle of freedom that they themselves have produced at the theoretical level, says Hegel, they lag behind the moment of the French Revolution; but they are also, in a certain sense, in advance of it, thanks to the intellectual movement rooted in that 'other' revolution known as the Reformation. In effect, the Germans have carried out a revolution in 'inwardness';[82] it combines a break with a corrupt institution, the Church, and a radical experience in winning freedom of conscience and freedom of thought. Hence the Germans are beyond the division between subjective consciousness and the temporal order characteristic of the Latin, Catholic world.

Despite Hegel's patent aversion for Catholicism, we would be ill advised to dismiss him as a narrow-minded champion of the superiority of the German-Lutheran mind. To begin with, it should be recalled that, in Hegel's day, conversions to Roman Catholicism were mushrooming in the Romantic and nationalistic circles that were radically hostile to the Enlightenment and the spirit of 1789 and critical of precisely that which, as far as Hegel was concerned, constituted the Reformation's chief merit: the fact that it had laid the groundwork for the Revolution.[83] Secondly, if, in Hegel's view, Catholicism had degenerated to the point of becoming a purely external means of bringing the subject into conformity with the world (through the formal observance of rituals, or repression-inquisition) – if, in a word, it had a purely decorative function in a waning feudal order – Protestantism, for its part, had degenerated into 'minute and painful introspection' focused on the state of one's soul, and had 'for a long time [been] characterized by a self-tormenting disposition and an aspect of spiritual wretchedness'.[84] In short, in Hegel's day, philosophy was to assume the role formerly played by both Catholicism and Protestantism; but philosophy owed as much to the Revolution as to the Reformation, to French revolutionary practice as to the German experience of inner, intellectual freedom.

By standing the significance of German backwardness on its head, Hegel adumbrates a possibility that is undoubtedly in contradiction with arguments he makes elsewhere, but nevertheless held a deep, lasting fascination for the *Vormärz* generation. He gives his reader to understand that a 'transformation of [the world's] political condition' – by which he unmistakably means, since he cites the German peasant uprisings, a transformation of a *revolutionary* kind – was 'a consequence of ecclesiastical reformation', that is, a transition from the reform of the inner man to 'a change affecting the state of things outside'.[85] But this political transformation, for which 'the world was not yet ripe' in Münzer's day, was then indefinitely suspended in the Protestant world, especially in Germany. Hence the possibility, which Hegel briefly evokes *a contrario*, of a movement capable of overcoming the division between the temporal order and the subjective consciousness in its inwardness; a movement which, superseding liberal individualism, would combine Reformation and Revolution: 'for it is a false principle that the fetters which bind Right and Freedom can be broken without the emancipation of conscience – that there can be a Revolution without a Reformation'.[86]

If, down to Hegel's time, two aspects of a single process, the 'internal' and the 'external' revolution, have developed separately, nothing prevents us from imagining their combination. Indeed, Hegelian logic strongly predisposes us to do just that. Here we find the idea that Germany is, as it were, holding its history in reserve, that the country's lag can become a lead, that its non-contemporaneousness with the present – or, rather, its one-sidedly *theoretical* contemporaneousness with the present – can issue in a higher totality, the principle of a new freedom of a kind as yet unknown. The reversal that Hegel announces here is of decisive importance. It is a matter not so much of 'catching up' to the level already reached by others, but of making – as Kant would say – a 'perilous leap' in order to open the present to the future it bears within it.

The aporias of bourgeois society

Finally, liberalism suffers from a third limitation that can only be described as *social*. Hegel does not by any means subscribe to Kant's definition of property, or to his assumptions about the harmony of civil society. He refuses to identify the highest forms of collective life with the 'social' sphere delimited by property law and the system of needs and labour. Thus he rejects the kind of liberal vision, especially Kant's, which subordinates constitutional law to civil law – itself intrinsically defined in terms of proprietary individualism – and treats the latter as the ultimate objective of the former. Within the sphere of ethical life [*Sittlichkeit*], civil society [*bürgerliche Gesellschaft*, which might also be translated as 'bour-geois-civil society'] represents, precisely, the moment of division or conflict; indeed, it is a limit-situation of social life that calls for its own supersession. Civil society, in an intermediate position between the immediate unity of the family and the articulated unity of the state, has a mediating function that creates a certain bond among its members, even if this remains a purely external tie that is incapable of leading them beyond their separate existences as independent individuals.[87] As the merely 'external State', civil society reveals that its true foundation is the political state, which is both a power transcending it that fully corresponds to true ethical life, and the immanent objective of the relations governing it.[88]

Within civil society, individuals do indeed appear as creatures of need; their needs are an index of their finite subjectivity, and also form a network or system of needs. This system is an indication of the social existence inherent in need, which is always more than simple biological demand, since need cannot assert itself unless it is *recognized*, and represented as such, in the context of a socialized existence.[89] But individuals are also the subjects of a specific activity, labour; it, too, takes the form of a system, that of social labour culminating in industrial society, for it is through the mediation of labour that individuals can reciprocally satisfy their needs.[90] In both cases – the system of needs, social labour – the unity that appears among individuals (to put it in other terms: the type of social bond) and defines a particular kind of civil society remains an external unity operating behind the back of its agents. Their integration into a vast overarching whole, which confers a general social meaning on their activities, is brought about in an extrinsic manner, and thus goes unnoticed by the individual consciousness, convinced that it is merely pursuing its own private ends and inclinations.

In this perspective, *bürgerliche Gesellschaft* is identical to *bourgeois* society; for all the members of this society, trapped within the horizon defined by their pursuit of their atomistic interests, exist as *bourgeois* (in this particular instance, Hegel uses the French word).[91] Yet this is plainly how a first form of ethical life springs up; it finds a means of concretization in the division of society into corporations, and the recognition of the different trades and occupations which that division engenders. Smith's famous 'invisible hand', which Hegel had profoundly understood, clearly operates like a 'ruse of reason',[92] with the crucial difference that in the case of civil society, we are dealing with a subaltern moment of rationality, the analytical activity of the understanding, which puts back together what it had earlier broken down into its various parts. Hence civil society is not the rational in itself and for itself, the concrete Idea of ethical life embodied by the political community.

Its finitude makes itself felt in its inability to respect its own principle – that of guaranteeing everyone, even if only in unequal fashion, access to work and property – without encountering insuperable internal limits. To be sure, the activity of industrious acquisition introduces, as I have emphasized, a division of labour involving not only the differentiation of productive tasks, but also the production of the representations and forms of consciousness, 'practical education' and 'language',[93] which ensure its cohesion. This complex system is internally divided into 'estates' (*Stände*, in the sense in which there were three *Stände* or estates under the *ancien régime*), the highest form of mediation in civil society. It is as a member of an estate, within the framework of a corporation, that an individual first becomes aware of the bonds that unite him with others and the purposes of society as a whole. But the fragility of this cohesion quickly becomes apparent. The internal development of civil society tends to (re)produce, through the play of its own contradictions, a *polarization* of social conditions that calls the very unity of society into question, threatening to destroy the 'estates' [*Stände*] by transforming them into 'classes' [*Klassen*].[94]

Antagonism, temporarily displaced by foreign expansion, colonization and wars of conquest, seems to Hegel to be an ineradicable feature of civil society.[95] Only the state makes it possible to restore unity by fully internalizing the characteristic mediations of the family and civil society, appearing, in its turn, as their true foundation. Confronted with the reality of extreme poverty, Hegel speaks of the need for public institutions, especially corporations – centres of mutual assistance for their members which have a public character in so far as they are integral parts of the state.[96] He does not think that private aid and voluntary charity are sufficient, although they are the sole legitimate forms of support in the view of the liberals, who scream social subversion at the merest suggestion that the rights of the poor or their claims to assistance should be made into legal entitlements.[97] Hegel does not deny that private charity serves a useful purpose; as he sees it, however, the struggle against poverty cannot be made to depend on the contingency and caprice of individual virtue: laws and institutions are indispensable here.[98] The reason, as we have just seen, is that, in his view, poverty has objective causes which have their roots in the contradictions inherent in the functioning of bourgeois society. Contrary to the liberals' basic assumption, the poor are not responsible for their lot; even the destructive, antisocial and anti-state spirit of the rabble, its faltering sense of honour and its aversion to work, arise from objective circumstances and contradictions that cannot be resolved within the limits of the existing order of things.

Hegel goes so far as to defend the 'right of necessity' [*Notrecht*], the right of the dispossessed whose very existence is endangered.[99] He makes it quite clear that this is a matter of right, not charity or equity law, and that the right in question limits property rights in the name of the higher right to life. What Hegel demolishes here is the very matrix of the liberal thought of his day: a new type of rationality based on the diagram[100] of a well-ordered society regulated by the principle of individual responsibility and the unconditional right to hold and enjoy property. For Hegel, property is merely the form of a 'limited existence of freedom', and violations of property rights are justified in the face of the 'infinite injury to existence' and 'total loss of rights' represented by penury and hunger. In addition to defending this right of necessity, Hegel affirms that 'the livelihood and welfare of individuals should be secured ... as a *right*'; to this end, he does not hesitate to propose 'regulations' which would fix 'the values of the commonest necessities of life'.[101] Refusing to isolate economics from politics, he affirms the primacy of the latter over the former. For Hegel, it is impossible 'to create a space of real freedom if one ignores the economy'.[102] On this point, at any rate, he is receptive to the anti-liberal project pursued by the social movements in city and countryside during the French Revolution.[103] Conceived, notably by Robespierre, as the 'right to existence', 'the only property left to the propertyless', it was translated into reality, albeit only partially, in the maximum programme.

On the Terror, Hegel takes a position that is the exact opposite of Kant's. In the dictatorship of virtue, Kant sees only the extreme form of a moral politics that he basically approves; its excesses, he thinks, can easily be rectified later (hence the necessity, for Kant, of the Thermidorean moment). On the other hand, he is ill at ease whenever the populace gets out of hand, or property is in any way jeopardized. Conversely, for Hegel, the imposition of virtue constitutes an external constraint on consciousness; it testifies to the nothingness inherent in the moment of 'absolute' freedom precipitated by the revolutionary process, illustrating its abstraction and one-sidedness. The least one can say, however, is that Hegel shows that he understands the social dimension of the revolution, and that he grasps its inherent importance as well as its class dynamics. Indeed, the same holds for his position on all the popular uprisings that punctuate history, pitting plebeians against patricians in ancient Rome, German or Swiss peasants against foreign aristocrats or kings, or Dutch artisans against the Spanish monarchy.

In the framework of Hegel's categories, it is literally unthinkable that anything whatsoever should be traced to a 'class viewpoint'; the eruption of the 'rabble', a veritable anti-people,[104] is for Hegel symptomatic of the dissolution of the social bond, and does not open on to any form of universality. Nevertheless, at the level of the philosophy of history, world spirit displays a marked inclination to take sides – so much so, indeed, that it is no exaggeration to say that 'freedom's tortuous advance appears to follow the varying fortunes of plebeian class struggle'.[105] As a limit case, the right of necessity reveals the finitude of right,[106] its inability to create the concrete conditions under which everyone can freely develop his personality and acquire property within the existing social order. This represents the irresolvable aporia of right; it amounts to a confession that antagonisms are irreconcilable in civil society as a whole.

It is essential, if not very original, to stress the significance of Hegel's analysis of civil society, given the prevailing misconceptions. Thanks to Hegel, the sphere of civil society acquires real consistency. It ceases to be conceptualized in legal terms and appears as a distinct order characterized by its own peculiar laws and contradictions; they account for the division that traverses the modern world. The social is conceived in its own right; it emerges at the theoretical level in the same movement that founds political philosophy – as is too often forgotten in the age of the 'rehabilitation of political philosophy' – amid a confrontation between politics and the contradictions that both condition it and tend constantly to 'go beyond' it. With Hegel, the encounter with the experience of revolutionary politics integrates the achievements of political economy, understood literally – that is, in terms of the relationship that political economy establishes between politics and economics; in his estimation, it is one of the 'sciences' 'which have originated in the modern ages as their element', and take as their object nothing less than the 'mass relationships and mass movements in their qualitative and quantitative determinacy and complexity'.[107] This approach allows him to grasp the necessary, internal link between revolution and bourgeois society;[108] thus he radically displaces the problematic of the revolution, shifting it away from the terrain staked out by the debate about its legal-moral legitimacy.

A state beyond politics?

There can be no question of giving a full account of the Hegelian doctrine of the state here. It has already been convincingly shown, in my view, that Hegel neither defends absolutism nor yearns for the restoration of the theological-political order, but is, rather, the pioneering theorist of the modern state; there is no need to rehearse the argument.[109] For the purposes of our discussion, however, three points are worth emphasizing: the reformist, reforming spirit that animates Hegel's argument about the state; the internal instability and uncertainty of this argument, a consequence of its ambition to establish a philosophical foundation for the political; and, finally, the status it accords philosophy. While Hegel never denied the accomplishments of the French Revolution, but continued to defend them against apologists for absolutism and feudal reaction – the Savignys, Baaders, Hallers, and so on – it is clear that he did not look to revolution to bring about political progress. He was frightened by initiatives 'from below' and the attendant 'irrational', 'barbarous' mass movements, and expected nothing good to come of them at the political level. Although he was not in the least nostalgic for the 'farce' of the Restoration, he had difficulty hiding his apathy after the July Revolution. He wanted to see peace re-established in Europe, but harboured few illusions that things would develop peacefully in the years to come. He could see that the 'knot' which history (decidedly refractory to closure of any sort) would have to untie in the future was forming around the question of representative government and universal suffrage; but he was far from thrilled at the prospect.[110]

To grasp the significance of Hegel's position, it is perhaps worth recalling, if only in passing, that in almost all the countries of Europe, and especially in Germany, the aristocracy still wielded considerable political and cultural power in the early decades of the nineteenth century. Contemporary historians even talk about a pre-bourgeois Europe led by aristocratic elites – in a word, of the 'persistence of the old regime' down to the First World War period, which saw the beginnings of its real dissolution.[111] Needless to say, the Germany of the Junkers, imperial absolutism, and militarism provides an excellent illustration of the fact that the revolution-as-process was a (very) long-drawn-out process indeed. This complicates any attempt to map the contending forces, and makes it particularly difficult to gauge the significance of the opposition between the throne and parliaments often heavily dominated by feudal elements fiercely opposed to any kind of reform.

To do away with the *ancien régime*, break the power of the aristocracy, and finish with absolutism – a task he considered decisive, whereas the liberal critique tended to ignore it – Hegel favoured gradual change.[112] The moving force behind it was to come from the very highest levels of society, aided and abetted by philosophy. Hegel's wager, as we have seen, did not fundamentally differ from Kant's. That is, Hegel too counted on a 'reform from on high'; undeniably, he would emerge as its greatest theoretician. He advocated a rationalization of state institutions, carried out within the framework of a constitutional monarchy that would modernize and pursue the anti-feudal initiative taken by enlightened absolutism. For Hegel, 'the transition from feudalism to monarchy' (to cite the title of Part I, Chapter 3 of *The Philosophy of History*), the end of aristocratic polyarchy, and the unification and centralization of the state were identified with the 'abrogation of servitude', the primacy of law and right, and the birth of 'real freedom'.[113] His account of the emergence and consolidation of the absolutist state focuses, above all, on absolutism's challenge to the power of the feudal nobility, and the creation of a modern administration that would abolish aristocratic privilege.

As is well known, Hegel was a proponent of constitutional monarchy. Yet this category – far from legitimizing absolutism, as the *doxa* that makes Hegel an apologist for the Prussian king would have it – was regarded as highly suspect in the Europe of the Holy Alliance. Let me first point out that Hegel conceives of the king's role as a *function* to be exercised within very narrow limits: the king is a personal incarnation of the ideal will, one and indivisible, of the state.[114] The word 'incarnation' must be taken literally: the state is, for Hegel, the emanation of reason in itself and for itself – an earthly divinity, in a revealing Hegelian phrase[115] – inasmuch as its *absolute* freedom (its non-dependence *vis-à-vis* all external constraints or determinations) makes it something akin to an absolute. The absolute Hegel has in mind is not transcendent, but immanent in the totality of social life, of which it is simultaneously the ground and the result; hence its sovereignty designates the absolute power of a collectivity posed as a fully developed totality and symbolized in the person of the king. If the state is 'a hieroglyphic of reason which becomes manifest in actuality', the power of the king is, precisely, hieroglyphic, that is, symbolic;[116] it is the power of a 'name', a signature, the power of one who restricts himself to 'say[ing] yes and dot[ting] the "i"', to cite the terms Hegel chose to use when he was less inhibited by self-censorship than he was in his lecture courses.[117] The king thus clearly exercises a personalizing function that is inherent in the state as such (at the limit, any state that fully corresponds to its concept is endowed with this monarchical dimension); it is by no means insignificant,[118] but it remains symbolic.

Contrary to a widely held view, Hegel's conception of the state is no more 'totalitarian' than it is absolutist. Far from deprecating civil society, it mobilizes the mediations produced by civil society in order to invest them with a new legitimacy and permit them to participate in the creation of unity while maintaining/sublating their particularity. The corporations, higher institutions engendered by civil society, constitute the privileged mediation and point of contact between the particular and the universal;[119] this mediation endows individuals with the consciousness of their social being, operating as if it were a machine for producing social cohesion and defusing the antagonisms of civil society. As we have already noted, however, the corporations cannot resolve the conflicts of civil society by themselves; all that they can convert into the universal is a 'limited and finite end'.[120] It falls to the organs of the state – assemblies, the government, the various administrations – to subsume the particular under the universal; that is, to develop the content of decisions validated by the sovereign in order to maintain the connection between the rational principle of state unity and the complex hierarchy of mediations. At stake here is not the traditional separation of powers, which makes no sense whatever from the standpoint of the totality formed by the Hegelian state, but a differentiation that is internal to power,[121] and immanent in its principle, which distinguishes the sovereign from those organs that give material expression to a competence or a body of theoretical knowledge. The organs possess no power of their own, inasmuch as their power is theirs by delegation; they are composed of civil servants, who must here be considered intellectuals, and whose knowledge is wholly devoted to the public interest and the service of the sovereign.

For Hegel, as for Kant, intellectuals are privileged mediators of the universal. This proposition must be understood in two senses: the universal constitutes 'the end of [intellectuals'] essential activity',[122] and, by way of this activity, it is the universal which expresses itself in person. But – unlike Kant's philosophers, who are relatively autonomous *vis-à-vis* the state – the people meant here are civil servants, 'exempted from work for the direct satisfaction of [their] needs' thanks to the indemnity paid them by the state. They are veritable specialists of the universal, possessing real and varied areas of competence. They comprise the 'universal estate' [*allgemeiner Stand*]¹²³ that crowns the whole social edifice. Hegel does not defend a theory of the 'philosopher-king' – these civil servants are not supposed to have any power in their own right; rather, using quite modern terminology, he theorizes the role a technocracy can play as a result of its real competence. The technocracy, as he envisages it, fulfils the old Enlightenment ambition for universality; denying its potentially subversive character, however, he affirms that it functions 'especially – or solely – in the service of the state'.¹²⁴ Public affairs, for Hegel, are above all the business of those 'who know', not of the ignorant populace, which can, at any moment, change into an uncontrolled, threatening mass.¹²⁵ He rejects the Platonic Idea; however, the philosophical utopia of a knowledge as transparent as it is omnipotent reappears here in all its purity, because the cohesion of the whole depends, in the last instance, on the 'universal class' that possesses this knowledge, though it does not, precisely, derive any power of its own from exercising its function. The resulting problem remains unthought in Hegel, and doubtless testifies to the limits of Hegelian immanence: the 'earthly divinity', the state that fully corresponds to objective Spirit, preserves something of the divine *tout court*.

Hegel thinks that he has solved the problem of the unity of the state and the sphere of *Sittlichkeit* as a whole once and for all, by way of the vertical equilibrium or hierarchical imbrication of levels whose substance is drawn from a unique, indivisible power. The state is accordingly posed as the ultimate, fully accomplished form of social life. In coming back towards itself, the state shows that it is the true foundation of the spheres of *Sittlichkeit*; yet it has emerged, in the course of Hegel's discussion, as its result, not in the chronological but in the logical sense.¹²⁶ Without denying the specificity of *Sittlichkeit*, Hegel rejects the liberal conception of the relationship between civil society and the state as a relationship between two distinct, mutually limiting orders that fall under the jurisdiction of different systems of right. Civil society – which cannot simply be identified with a natural market-based order, and which, moreover, includes public apparatuses such as the corporation – is merely an 'external state', one particular aspect of the idea of the state in its moment of division. 'An absolute and unmoved end in itself'¹²⁷ that is already contained in its origins, the state now appears to have it in its power to banish the antagonisms of civil society and the impotence of a philosophy limited to affirming an abstract 'ought'; consequently, it seems to have it in its power to banish politics. Thanks to Hegel, political philosophy is revealed for what it is: it attains to the fullness of its concept in becoming the 'philosophy of the state', 'a philosophical science of the state',¹²⁸ the theoretical instance which, motivated by the 'universal estate's' propensity for reform, rationalizes the state's conduct. He can therefore present the state as the solution to the riddle of history: it makes the achievements of the revolution its own even while managing to avoid the revolution itself and make it impossible in the future.[129]

But has the problem been solved, or merely displaced? As was to be feared, antagonism, the object of a brilliantly orchestrated denial, re-emerges precisely where one would expect it to. For what is to prevent this 'universal estate' from being transformed into a corporation which, like all the others, seeks to defend its special interests?[130] Is it its twofold subjection to the control of the sovereign and the other corporations – that is to say, the fact that it takes its allotted place within the hierarchical system of *Sittlichkeit*? But that is merely a formal solution which, by distinguishing the authorities and civil servants from the people, only reproduces the conditions that make it possible to fall back into the disorder of civil society. Thus we are brought face to face with 'the extreme contradiction', 'this collision, this nodus, this problem' 'with which history is now occupied, and whose solution it has to work out in future'.[131]

Hegel's political testament, his controversial text on the English Reform Bill, offers an exemplary condensation of the aporia that plagues its author. To begin with, the essay places the question of electoral reform in the broader English social context. Its uncompromising analysis of the explosive antagonisms of British society strikingly decentres the political. Hegel depicts the ongoing suppression of the peasantry by arrogant, intransigent feudal lords supported by a corrupt clergy; the oppression of the starving Irish people, victimized by a policy of conquest that might well be termed quasi-genocidal;[132] the widespread corruption and clientel-ism at the heart of the representative system; a system of justice taken over by the aristocracy and operating for its benefit alone – in short, the 'enormous' 'contrast ... between prodigious wealth and utterly embar-rassed penury';[133] between the prevailing feudal relations of domination on the one hand, and commercial and industrial prosperity on the other. The picture he draws demolishes the reigning myth of the golden age of Manchesterian capitalism. In the face of this barbaric disorder, Hegel defends the principles of the 'civilized states of the Continent' and the 'principles of real freedom'. We have only to look carefully at this text – which, it should be remembered, was subject to the pressure of a censor-ship reinforced by autocensorship – in order to understand that what Hegel envisages here is the principles of the French Revolution adapted to the reformist spirit of the constitutional monarchy. The text is a warning that any application of these principles that strays from the reformist road is likely to spark off a revolutionary upheaval. But even an electoral reform that leaves the interests of the aristocracy intact will inevitably open the doors of Parliament to men who defend such principles and must therefore, given the framework of English institutions (a weak monarch, a representative assembly), turn towards the opposition and engage in agitation aimed at the 'the lower [class], although the latter is extremely numerous in England, and most receptive to such formalism'. The result, in other words, will inevitably be to open the door to the French version of the principles of freedom. Thus we are led towards the 'the extreme contradiction within whose circle a nation revolves as soon as the formal categories have come to dominate it'. Through the play of its contradictory, counter-intentional effects, Hegel concludes in his last text, electoral reform may well serve as a prelude to the English revolution.[134]

History, then, is not over. A tenacious myth notwithstanding, Hegel affirms the very opposite, in black and white: 'the process of the world's history ... [is] still incomplete'.[135] This is by no means an isolated statement for Hegel, given his profound conviction that 'dichotomy ... is the fundamental condition of the modern age'.[136] Both the question of the representative regime, as we have seen, as well as the social question, remain in suspense; they testify to the finitude that distinguishes this moment of Spirit's trajectory. The forward march of the Idea does not come to a halt at the frontiers of the field of right and the state, which is the realization of a particular *Volksgeist* corresponding to the position of Objective Spirit. Spirit passes beyond this sphere once it has become aware of its ineluctable limits, attaining the position of absolute Spirit – of art, religion, and, at a still higher level, philosophy.[137] In these spheres, the movement of Spirit unfolds in a new element that transcends those of right and the state, and therefore also of politics, even while it remains internal to history. Philosophy cannot be reduced to the science of the state, or, if you prefer, to political philosophy. In superseding the sphere of right and the state, it lays the groundwork for a new rationality; but, as a result of this very movement, it also abandons – after fully integrating – the rationality of politics.

2

Spectres of Revolution:
On a Few Themes in Heine

> Was it possible that a revolution could hide behind these professors, behind their obscure, pedantic phrases, their ponderous, wearisome periods? Were not precisely those people who were then regarded as the representatives of the revolution, the liberals, the bitterest opponents of this befuddling philosophy? But what neither governments nor liberals saw was seen at least by one man as early as 1833, and this man was none other than Heinrich Heine.
>
> (Friedrich Engels[1])

Hegel died of cholera in 1831, haunted by the shadow of a new wave of revolutions, English electoral reform, and the immediate repercussions of the July Days in Paris. The owl of Minerva seemed to be suspended in midair, caught in the snares of a twilight fraught with danger. Or did this turbulence announce the dawn of a new day? For Hegel's disciple Heine,[2] the same year, 1830, was one of those dates that mark the beginning of a new period; the first reports of the July events woke him – this time for good – from the German reveries and meditations of which he was all too fond. A herald of the new spirit of the day, Heine could no longer live (or die) anywhere but in its epicentre, Paris – the 'chief city', as he put it, not 'just of France, but of the whole civilized world';[3] 'the capital of the nineteenth century', as Walter Benjamin would say, in a time closer to our own.

Like his teacher before him, Heine saw an English revolution brewing in the working-class agitation for universal suffrage. But he was not in the least alarmed by it. Even before the passage of the Reform Bill, he had arranged to 'smuggle' long extracts from the English 'radicals'' pamphlets past the authorities by weaving them into his *Reisebilder*, a method he liked to use whenever he wanted to dance his way around the censors' scissors. He made no secret of his sympathy for the English movement, whose vision of history he had by and large adopted.[4] As for the 1831–32 cholera epidemic, not only did Heine emerge from it unscathed, although he had deliberately taken the risk of remaining in Paris when it was at its height, but he even made it the theme of a narrative.[5] Simultaneously epic and allegory, his account of the epidemic paints the sombre, intimidating features of the big city (mob violence, the omnipresence of anonymous mass death, the resurfacing of the 'dregs' of society, and so on) as a backdrop against which, through the play of contrasts, the power of the 'life' of the community is affirmed.

Heine belonged to a generation that had from the first been confronted with the consequences of the crisis sparked by the revolutionary rupture. For this generation, which had to come to terms with a wholly unprecedented situation, historical time had always been out of joint: the present seemed to escape its control, because it appeared to be determined by the successes and failures of the past revolution and its secondary effects – the shifting sands of the counter-revolution and the impossible Restoration. Heine was the more sensitive to the aftershocks of this crisis in that, with the greater authoritarianism of the Prussian regime after the Carlsbad Decrees (1819), Germany's political backwardness had simply been confirmed, while all hopes of seeing Prussia adopt a reform course had been shattered. But Heine, unlike many others, was not labouring under the delusion that things would return to 'normal'. He chose to swim against the current of an age which, haunted by its revolutionary past, desperately craved harmony, social peace, and political moderation.

Born in a Rhineland that had been indelibly marked by the French presence, Heine grew up to the sounds of the drum that symbolized it; the victories and defeats of the cause of freedom in Europe had been accompanied by the beating of that drum.[6] Heir to the 1789 Revolution, he wanted to incarnate that of July 1830, which, 'so to speak, split our era in half'.[7] He was an eyewitness to the recurrent rebellions that punctuated the reign of Louis-Philippe (1832, 1834, 1839); his physical collapse during a May 1848 visit to the Louvre, a collapse from which he would never recover, seemed to portend the violent repression of the June Days. Buried alive in his mattress-grave, the poet deliberately turned his suffering and physical decline into an allegory of the defeat of the people's attempt to win freedom – the ultimate form of identification with what had always been his 'great task in life'.[8]

Of the many personae that went to make up this complex individual, the one on which we will be focusing in the following pages belongs to a happier time than that just evoked. It is the period in which Heine settled in Paris – not as a defeated *émigré*, but amid the euphoria called up by the July Revolution, at the beginning of an exile that served notice of his resolutely combative posture. Heine meant to work towards forging a Franco–German political and cultural alliance, the condition for the success of a new revolutionary wave in Europe which, he hoped, would be broader and more radical than its predecessor. It could not, he felt, be long in coming. Moreover, the experience of these auspicious years, the years of the *Vormärz*, no doubt goes a long way towards explaining the aggressive vigour that was his right up to the very end of his life, when he had to cope with political catastrophe and his own physical decay.[9]

The Heine whom we will be discussing in what follows was above all an event that was, inseparably, both poetic and theoretical; for Heine's poetry was quite as philosophical as his essays, even if it was so in a *different way* – in a specifically poetic mode that sharply distinguished it from the tendentious versifying already fashionable at the time, especially in the movement known as 'Young Germany'. Our attention, then, will be directed towards the Heine who forged a new kind of poetry – or, rather, a poetics that informs both his prose and his verse, dialectical and critical down to its very form. It is a poetics that opens the German language and the German lyric to the world of the big city and its ephemeral brilliance, that of the faceless crowd and venal love; a poetics of everyday language and subversive irony; a poetics which, two decades before Baudelaire, captured the spirit of modernity and founded it aesthetically, even as it invoked the founding themes of Romanticism in the specifically Heinean mode of the 'last time', with the firm intention of dismissing them for good and all as historicist clichés – and yet not without a certain fondness, and not without realizing the promise they contained.

But we cannot truly understand this Heine, a pioneer of modernity, unless we make our acquaintance with the Heine who was a disciple of Hegel and the initiator of an interpretation of Hegelian philosophy that was not merely 'progressive'[10] but – as both Engels and Lukács[11] have pointed out – explicitly *revolutionary*. Despite the fact that Heine's was a popular-philosophical exposition of Hegel's thought, the poet's revolutionary Hegelianism, often mentioned but rarely examined, represented the Hegelian left's real point of departure. It is coextensive with his poetics. Heine mobilizes the Hegelian categories, particularly those which ground Hegel's philosophy of history – not, as received wisdom would have it, to bend them to the imperatives of a new system, or even to distinguish what belongs to the (obsolete and conservative) 'system' from what belongs to the (modern and revolutionary) 'method',[12] but, much more radically, in the Heinean mode of 'the last time': taking his leave of them, he nevertheless preserves their truth content; acknowledging that their crisis is irreversible, he nevertheless makes them the heralds of a new cycle of German history and thought.

Heine's text-manifesto on German philosophy and religion was published before David Friedrich Strauß's *The Life of Jesus Critically Examined*,[13] although Strauß's book is all but unanimously held to mark the inception of the Young Hegelian movement. (*The Life of Jesus* recapitulates a controversy that had swirled for more than a decade around the exploitation of religious questions as legitimizing principles for the German-Christian Restorationist state, a subject that anyone attempting to challenge that state had to take into account.) Above all, Heine 'goes beyond' Strauß by setting over against the properly German, theological-critical current that he represented a trajectory which, to be sure, preserves the achievements of classical idealism's critique of religion, but also imbues that critique with the French spirit, that is, the heritage of 1789–93. Rather than glossing the Holy Scriptures, Heine, in exile, finally casts the rules of compromise and self-censorship to the winds. He frankly names the directly political stakes of German philosophy, thereby making 'detours through religion' appear futile, even retrograde; and he redefines the project for a political-intellectual alliance spanning the Rhine under the new political and theoretical conditions posed by both the July Revolution and the development of Hegelian doctrine after the philosopher's death.

A Romantic at odds with the Romantic movement, a student of Hegel who knew both Goethe and Marx, a Parisian *flâneur* who beat the drum for revolutionary German democracy, a dandy who wielded the weapon of irony with consummate skill, and was nevertheless a popular poet by virtue of both his audience and, especially, the subject matter of his poetry: Heine was all this at once. He was an event situated at the point where the universalistic revolutionary movement intersected a national cultural tradition – a decisive, constitutively Franco–German turning point in the revolution's critical reflection upon itself.

Flânerie as dialectical exercise

'I am the son of the Revolution,' Heine exclaimed on learning the news of the July events, 'and I take up the charmed weapons upon which my mother has breathed her magic blessing.'[14] He had a fair claim to that heritage, for, to Heine – if we restrict ourselves to the family romance that the poet was particularly fond of reciting – the revolution does not simply appear as his foster mother, amid the images of fusion and undying loyalty that such a relationship implies; it also points to the primal scene that turns on the murder of the father, the paternal authority figure evoked by both the theme of the real/symbolic decapitation of the king and the dialectic of the executioner and the despot. This scene was concealed, yet bourgeois society never ceased to come up against it; it was destined to play it again and again precisely because it sought to conceal it, to turn a blind eye to the symptoms that betrayed its conflictual content. In Heine's view, post-Revolutionary bourgeois society functioned by denial; amnesia was one of its characteristic features. This forgetfulness enabled it to live in a perpetual present devoid of all historical depth: 'the society of those in power really believes in its eternal duration, when the annals of universal history, the fiery *Mene tekel* of the daily journals, and even the loud voice of the people in the streets, cry aloud their warnings'.[15]

Even after the warnings could no longer be ignored, and the old fears had resurfaced, the denial went on. Now it took the form of a false wisdom that misled the powerful into projecting their beliefs on to their enemies. The dominant had convinced themselves, Heine says, that they could easily pull the wool over the eyes of those they dominated, whereas in fact they only redoubled their own blindness, thereby hastening the very outcome they wished to avoid. Louis-Philippe pretended, for example, that he was fortifying Paris to protect it against the possibility of attack by the Holy Alliance, although everyone knew that the king was lying, and that his real concern was to defend himself against the domestic threat of a new insurrection by hostile citizens. For Heine, there was nothing fortuitous about Louis-Philippe's mistake. The fact that he lied to the people and stubbornly clung to his lie was simply the effect of a deeper mechanism – the 'forgetting', that is, denial – of the fact that the king's own authority stemmed from the barricades: that, in other words, it was simply the result of his confiscation of the popular victory of July.[16] Between the hypocrisy of the authorities and a populace aware that it was being deceived, the spiral that began to emerge in this period lent an air of 'fatality' to the revolutionary dénouement: 'It is always this ancient curse that hurls clever men headlong to destruction; they believe themselves to be shrewder than whole races, and yet experience has shown that the masses always judge rightly, and always see through the intentions, if not the plans, of their rulers.'[17]

Did Heine, in prophesying the end of the Orléanist regime, fall into the trap set for him by the prophetic posture of his own writing? Did he, in a certain sense, take the alarmist discourse of the authorities at its word?[18] Let us say, rather, that he borrowed certain elements from the event in question and the discourse that accompanied it, using them to develop a deeply anchored set of themes: that is, to decipher, in the enchanted image that bourgeois society projected of itself, the signs that betokened its approaching end. The appearance of a new *name*, communism, was, precisely, one such sign, decisive and, in a certain way, irreversible. I shall discuss this at greater length below,[19] but let me note straight away that the new name is inserted into the narrative sequence that is the object of Heine's chronicle for 11 December 1841, a *flânerie* cast in the form of a three-step syllogism. Heine makes use of a dialectical framework here, but this framework is heavily marked by ironical distantiation; the ironical perspective reveals the ultimate significance of this reflection on history. Jean-Pierre Lefebvre has shown that Heine's late poetic work *Romancero* is structured by a deliberately twisted dialectical syllogism.[20] This quite rightly leads him to the conclusion that Heine, by thus decomposing an optimistic (and therefore, as he saw it, Hegelian) vision of the course of history in a sceptical, satirical mode, shows that he is 'the poet of times of crisis'; *Romancero*, Lefebvre adds, provides 'a précis of this crisis of modern lyricism'.[21] In what follows, I would like to demonstrate that the same type of syllogism structures other Heinean texts – prose works and, above all, works that antedate his experience of the defeat of the 1848 revolutions. This is to say that Heine calls Hegel into question even before the turning point of 1848: the insurmountable crisis of the philosophy of history traverses his writing from one end to the other.

Let us observe the way this deconstruction of the canonical dialectical narrative works in actual practice. Its first moment brings the 'ordinary *flâneur*' face to face with an abstract universality that is as yet external to his consciousness:

> if a man is not a great politician, but only an ordinary *flâneur* who troubles himself little as to the shade or tint of Dufaure and Passy, yet pays attention to the people in the streets . . . he will attain the firm conviction that sooner or later the whole *bourgeois* comedy of France, with its parliamentary dramatic heroes and supernumeraries, will have an awful end amid hideous hisses, and that there will be an after-piece called the Rule of the Communists.[22]

Encountering the theatre of history, itself fallen to the level of a comic spectacle, the ordinary consciousness has a sombre presentiment of finitude, which it immediately tries to dismiss: 'The late political trials might have opened the eyes of many, but blindness is too agreeable. No one would be willingly reminded of tomorrow's dangers while he enjoys today.'[23] Momentarily abandoned for the pitiful, alarming spectacle offered by politics, merchandise once again demands its due – and it is certain to get it.

Whence the second moment of this dialectic, the particularity of the *flâneur* who, from the depths of his melancholy, suddenly jumps at the promise of happiness, the eternal present of the phantasmagoria of merchandise: 'But let us quit this sad theme and return to the more pleasing objects behind the vast plate-glass panes of the rue Vivienne and the Boulevards. How they gleam and glitter, laugh and allure! Vigorous life, expressed in gold, silver, bronze, gems, in all possible forms, especially in the forms of the Renaissance, the imitation of which is at present all the fashion.'[24] Alas, this phantasmagoric pleasure lasts but a dazzling, fleeting instant. The *flâneur* who thought he could escape history soon finds himself drawn back into it; the tragicomedy of politics now gives way to an evocation of the past cast in the mode peculiar to fashion, the power of the mimetic situated at the very heart of the world of merchandise.

The *flâneur* (the first-person narrator) is left facing a new problem: how can he account for this leap into a past that is itself turned towards another and still more remote past? 'What is the cause of this predilection for the Renaissance, that new birth, or rather resurrection, when the antique world rose from the tomb to make the Middle Ages more beautiful in their dying hours? Does our time feel an affinity with that age, which sought in the past, even as we are doing, a rejuvenating fountain, thirsting for the cool and refreshing draught of life?'.[25] In reality, this resuscitation of archaic images from a distant age very quickly turns out to be, in its turn, profoundly ambiguous and unstable. It summons up the images the beholder longs to see, and, simultaneously, signs of approaching death. Between the two, from the standpoint of the present, there can be no reconciliation: 'that age of Francis I and his contemporaries exerts on us an almost terrible charm, like the memory of things seen and a life lived in dreams'.[26]

This fascination, we learn, is bound up with a sense of loss that throws the disparity between the past and the present into sharp relief. The present is modern, emptied of 'magic', 'boldness' and 'originality'. It can call up features of the past only by imitating them, whether in the manner (already touched on) of the commercial pastiche or in that of the dry, academic reproduction typical of the neoclassical art of a David:

> there is something magic and mysteriously original in the way and manner in which that age worked rediscovered antiquity into itself. Here we do not see, as in the school of David, a dry academic imitation of Greek plastic art, but a fluent blending of it with Christian spiritualism. In the forms of art and of life

which owe their daringly original existence to that fusion of most unlike elements, there lurks such a sweetly melancholy humour, such an ironic kiss of reconciliation, such flourishing disdain, such a superbly elegant horror, that we are subdued by an unearthly spell, we know not how.[27]

The price to be paid for such particularistic withdrawal into the magic world of merchandise is the equivalent of an experience of loss – the loss of the beautiful totality of the work of art and its aura – and a new division of consciousness that throws the *flâneur* into disarray. His attempt to escape history has been transformed into an obsessive relation to the past, one that is dominated by repetition and decline.

After this new failure, the *flâneur* can only continue to wander over the cobblestones of the *grands boulevards*, leading us towards the third moment of the syllogism, singularity. Consciousness sloughs off its old skin, abandoning it to others, and endeavours to return to itself. Moreover, although its wanderings began in an unnamed place (the moment of abstract universality), and were pursued the length of the rue Vivienne, with its shop windows (the moment of particularity), they now bring it to the boulevard Montmartre, very close to where Heine lived. The '*vrai flâneur*', the last of the roles assumed by the narrator – who here shifts from the 'I' to the narrative 'we' – can now make his entry. It is, as usual,[28] a peculiar kind of merchandise that catches his eye: 'just as we leave politics, for today, to the petty professionals, so we will also abandon to the duly patented historians the exact determination of the degree to which our time is allied with that of the Renaissance, and, *en vrais flâneurs*, stop on the Boulevard Montmartre before an engraving which Messieurs Goupil & Rittner have there exhibited, and which attracts all glances'.[29] This engraving is a reproduction of *The Fishermen*, a painting by Léopold Robert.

Even before considering the subject of this painting, we need to note the extreme importance that it has for Heine. In 'The Salon of 1831', he had already devoted a long review essay to Robert, focusing on the painting with which *The Fishermen* forms a contradictory pair, *The Reapers* (which had also been reproduced as an engraving).[30] These two pictures were among the very first that Heine hurried to see upon his arrival in Paris, and they would forever embody, in his eyes, the spirit of the July Days. He no doubt detected something of this spirit in the engraved reproductions of them. He dwells at considerable length on the differences between the originals and the copies; in a way, they compensate, by inversion,[31] for the fact that one of the paintings is much better than the other, since the more successful engraving corresponds to the less success-

ful painting, and vice versa. Although these engravings, published by a
pioneer in the capitalist transformation of this sector, can be categorized
as 'mass reproductions',[32] they have a special aura about them; for, like
icons, they decorated the walls of Heine's various dwellings until the day
he died[33] – a circumstance that dispels all doubts as to whether his
phenomenology of the *flâneur* has autobiographical implications.

A comparison of the two texts about Robert, the second of which was
written ten years after the first, reveals the reasons for Heine's lifelong
fascination with the painter. In both texts, Heine's commentary begins
with the same question: where does Robert stand with respect to the
traditional opposition between historical painting and genre painting?
But the answer Heine gives in the first piece is the exact opposite of
the one he proposes in the second. In 'The Salon of 1831', he sets out
from the observation that the opposition historical painting/genre painting is itself historically obsolete, since what is common to the two categories, which have both become mere caricatures of what they once
were, is their escapism. Historical painting has turned to a medieval-
Catholic past; genre painting has set out in pursuit of a cheap, folksy-
bucolic picturesque. But, says Heine, Robert concretely trandscends this
obsolete opposition by forging a higher totality in which elements from
both traditions are reconciled. His paintings owe their success, typified by
that of *The Reapers*, to the fact that they offer both 'depictions drawn
from world history' and representations 'of ordinary life'.[34] They hold
out the image of a reconciled humanity, abolishing the opposition of
matter and spirit, body and soul; Robert paints a Saint-Simonian
humanity that has recovered its original purity, and risen to take the
place of the divinity.

The picture that catches the eye of the experienced *flâneur* of 1841 is
very different. If Heine again mentions *The Reapers*, he does so only in
order to bring out, by contrast, the signification of *The Fishermen*: 'as much
as the first picture calms and enraptures us, so the other fills us with
revolutionary wrath'.[35] *Exit* Saint-Simon; enter Buonarroti, 'the stormy
Titan, the wild thunder-god of the "Last Judgement", whom [Robert]
adored and idolized'.[36] To invoke Buonarroti in 1841 was anything but
innocent: the 1828 publication of his book on Babeuf's conspiracy may
be said to have rung in a new era,[37] making it possible to forge a link with
the past that restored the historical continuity of the revolutionary movement. Buonarroti's major contribution to propagating Babeuf's heritage
made him one of the central figures behind *communism*'s reappearance
on the public scene in the 1840s. The fact that Heine now substitutes
Buonarroti's name for Saint-Simon's in a list of those who inspired Robert

thus signals the transition from a vision of harmony and reconciliation to a logic of antagonism that is more appropriate to the new situation.

No sooner has it been evoked than the reconciliation which this third stage seemed to promise vanishes before the *flâneur*'s eyes, fading away like a mirage that had briefly shimmered on the sands. But the reaffirmation of the primacy of antagonism comes at the price of a tragic division. What is exemplary now is not Robert's success but his failure, for his revolutionary *élan* is inseparably linked to his death. The magnificent totality characteristic of the period following the 1830 revolution has disintegrated; it is obvious that 'it is only by the colours that what is incongruous in the original picture is balanced, so that the whole receives an air of unity'.[38] But it is merely an *air* of unity: for, in Robert's paintings, we can detect the traces of 'wearisome painful strife with the subject which he could only overcome by the most desperate effort'. This struggle issued in a defeat that the painter's suicide simply confirmed:[39] 'the true cause of his death was the bitter irritation of the genre painter who yearns to be a supremely great historical artist; he died of a missing link in his power of execution'.[40]

Heine offers his own interpretation of the painter's suicide as a way of suggesting that Robert's is not merely artistic or individual impotence, but the impotence of an age that lives in the prosaic present of bourgeois society while dreaming of a History inspired by the glorious figures of the past. Yet this dream hovers constantly on the verge of nightmare. At the end of his promenade, the *flâneur* observes that he has gone from one failure to another, one unrealized promise to the next. His walk has turned into a *via dolorosa* with no possibility of redemption, an attempt to break free of the history of successive failures only a breath away from death.

The philosophy of history:
A clinical description of decomposition

The phenomenology of the *flâneur* and his abortive dialectic provides a model for the ironical, distantiated reappropriation of the Hegelian syllogism that is a hallmark of Heine's writing. It is characteristic not only of the way it handles its themes, but also of its formal structures: the elaborate, rigorous arrangement of its component elements – both the poetic 'cycles' and the collections of chronicles, essays, fragments, and so on. If it is true that the special beauty of many of Baudelaire's poems comes from one's impression that their first lines 'emerge from the abyss',[41] the beauty of Heine's has to do with the fact that their closing lines seem to lose themselves in it. This is how the famous 'Heine effect'[42] works: Heine's texts first enchant us with their lyricism, the half-glimpsed promises of satisfaction and the enticing images that gleam before our mind's eye; and then, suddenly, as the result of an intrusive interpolation or, indeed, a 'collage' – a play on words, a vulgar expression, a cliché – the pseudo-harmony of the lyricism suddenly grates on our ears, and we experience a sudden falling off, or disappointment, or anguish. But we are not on a treadmill. By dint of this very failure, we advance: towards a new vision, disenchanted and at the same time more dynamic; towards an attitude that breaks with everything that would lull the senses and the understanding. In the final analysis, the 'Heine effect', a transcription into the very letter of the text of the experience of the shock of modern life, is nothing more nor less than a sloughing off of obsolete poetic and narrative forms (and, consequently, of social forms *tout court*): they are called up one last time only so that they may be dismissed for good and all by the author, but also by a reader who is directly addressed, thrown off balance, compelled to take an active stance.

History is the very stuff of Heine's poetry. This is so even where history does not appear as such. In the ambivalence of love, which marks the end of sickly, mawkish sentimentality *à la* Werther, or in the way the 'city-dweller' regards a nature that has become a mere canvas on which the poet projects his inner world, there emerges the same experience of being and time introduced by the figures of the *flâneur* and the allegorist. This comes down to saying that Heine's poetry communicates directly with his reflections on history and politics: if the poetry offers an account of the crisis of modern lyricism, we also need to look for its complement, an account of the crisis of the 'narrative of narratives', that is, of the philosophy of history. Not surprisingly, this account exists only in a fragmentary state; it is at once impossible to find and omnipresent, disseminated throughout the poetic work, leaving its mark in the very arrangement of its themes or surging up in the midst of reflections on art, current events, or philosophy. Heine does not offer to re-establish a connection between the 'facts' and a narrative that would deliver up their Meaning; his is not one more attempt to shuttle back and forth between the banks of the empirico-transcendental doublet;[43] he does not seek, in other words, to construct, even in the practical state, a 'different' philosophy of history. Rather, he offers us a clinical description of history, as if he were analysing an organism already haunted by death: a précis of decomposition that nevertheless announces the emergence of new forms of life.

Political revolution, social revolution

We have already begun to grasp the paradoxical logic of the revolutionary event. It is a logic of the counter-intentional and the unpredictable that is nevertheless not that of sheer contingency, since it intersects a certain objectivity of the historical process. At first sight, it might appear that the categories capable of accounting for this logic are Hegel's; the definition of the revolution, or, rather, of the 'main idea' behind it – the definition, then, of the revolution according to its concept – reproduces the main lines of the philosophical-historical narrative, while introducing an organicist metaphor:

> When the intellectual developments or culture of a race are no longer in accord with its old established institutions, there results necessarily a combat in which the latter are overthrown; this is called a revolution. Until the revolution is complete, until that reformation of institutions does not perfectly agree with the intellectual development and the habits and wants of the people, just so long the national malady is not perfectly cured, and the sickly and excited people will often relapse into the weakness of exhaustion, yet ever and anon be subject to attacks of burning fever, when they tear away the tightest bandages and the most soothing lint from the old wounds, throw the most benevolent, noblest nurses out of the window, and roll about in agony until they finally find themselves in circumstances, that is, adapt themselves to institutions which suit them better.[44]

Thus there are objective causes for revolution: the lag between, on the one hand, the state of *Sittlichkeit* (intellectual culture, customs and needs), which Heine also designates as 'social' conditions, or, again, 'the inner life of the people',[45] and, on the other hand, obsolete, ossified political institutions. When a revolution breaks out, it is obeying an imperative that is also objective – the need to overcome this lag. The revolution is ineluctable, like the crisis that occurs in the course of an illness, and it is equally essential that it be prolonged until 'recovery' (or death?) – until, that is, harmonious relations have been established between political institutions and *Sittlichkeit* (or social conditions). Heine insists on this point: nothing can stop the revolutionary process, except perhaps temporarily, until this stage is reached – certainly not the obstacles which are thrown up in the way of popular action, even when they are the products of a benevolent paternalism. A revolution attains its end, in both senses of the word, only when the people has forged suitable institutions (that is, institutions which suit it) 'by itself': freedom is won, not granted. The progress of freedom is inscribed in an evolving history, revealing that history's truth and immanent rationality. Such, in broad outline, was Heine's conception of revolution when he sat down to write a book on the French Revolution – a project which, as we have seen, came to an abrupt end, owing, in particular, to the impact of contemporary events: a cholera epidemic broke into the sixth French chronicle, turning it in a new and unforeseen direction.

The first major implication of Heine's definition of revolution is that a revolution – or, more precisely, a revolution that corresponds to its concept – is, by virtue of the lag between the social and the political in which it originates, a *Sittenrevolution*, a revolution in the sphere of objective morality, a social revolution. In this sense, the French Revolution, contrary to what Hegel affirmed,[46] did indeed rise to the level of its concept; it was not a revolution without a Reformation, confined to the abstractions of liberalism: 'here [in France] we stand on a ground where that great female despot, the Revolution, has exercised for fifty years her arbitrary power, tearing down here, sparing there, but shaking violently everywhere at the foundations of social life'.[47]

Thus France differs sharply from England, which has also undergone a revolution, but one that remains unfinished, politically and socially:

> no social overthrow took place in Great Britain; the framework of civil and political institutions remained undisturbed, the tyranny of castes and of guilds has remained there down to the present day, and though penetrated by the light and warmth of modern civilization, England is still congealed in a medieval condition, or rather in the condition of a fashionable Middle Age.... The religious reformation in England is consequently but half perfected.... Nor has it succeeded much better with the political reformation.[48]

In France, in contrast, thanks to 'those latter-day preachers of the mountain, who from the summit of the Convention in Paris preached a tri-colored gospel ... not only the form of the State but all social life was to be, not patched, but formed anew, and to be not only newly founded, but newly born'.[49] The problem to be resolved is thus not (we shall come back to this) whether the French Revolution did or did not have a 'social' character, but, rather, the question of its *unfinished* nature, which, pre-cisely, made it possible to separate the socioeconomic from the political. Büchner, a contemporary (and powerful reader) of Heine, makes much the same point when he puts Saint-Just's words in Robespierre's mouth: 'the social revolution is not yet ended; to carry out a revolution by halves is to dig your own grave'.[50]

This difference between Heine's and Hegel's assessment of the Revolution is reflected in Heine's analysis of both the pre-Revolutionary and post-Revolutionary periods. If – emphatically and on several different occasions – Heine repeats Hegel's idea that the Reformation, Peasant Wars, Enlightenment, and French Revolution form a single sequence, the properly religious content of the first moment of this sequence holds little interest for him. His vision of the Reformation is, as we shall see, completely secularized and indifferent to the destiny of 'inwardness', which is subordinated to the political stakes of the emergence of the Protestant movement. Similarly, whereas Hegel, while endorsing the emancipatory mission of the French Enlightenment, focuses on its abstraction and one-sidedness, which he attributes to its detachment from religious/national feeling, Heine considers the Enlightenment to be a model for an authentic intellectual and moral reform profoundly rooted in the national life of the people; its impact on the very nature of the revolutionary event was, in his view, as decisive as it was beneficial. He thus rejects not only, as goes without saying, the classic reactionary leitmotiv (particularly in its German variant: 'it's all Voltaire's fault, it's all Luther's fault'), but also (and here his target is Hegel) everything which tends to suggest that the German road – the only one to have withstood the test of practice – is preferable to the French.

The same unwillingness to minimize Germany's backwardness was to lead Heine to take a more finely shaded view of England after the passage of the Reform Bill, despite the aversion he continued to feel for the country and, especially, his unrelenting hatred for its attachment to archaic aristocratic traditions. To be sure, his basic approach hardly changed. He still regarded English freedom as an exaltation of particularism and traditionalism with far too pronounced an aristocratic and feudal flavour; it fell far short of the universal aims associated once and for all with the French Revolution.[51] But the poet admitted that the English nobility – whose power, he insisted, had remained intact since feudal times – had succeeded in concluding a successful alliance with the people in order to win the 'civil freedom' (carefully distinguished from 'social equality') that was now a solidly established feature of British life.

This freedom, distinguished from equality (again at the 'civic' level), lacks, says Heine, the universal ambition that characterizes the French. It nevertheless has important effects, in that it fosters public political *action* and endows the English with the *practical* character that contrasts sharply with the passivity and inhibition – the famous 'prudence', a combination of censorship and self-censorship – of the Germans, intellectuals included. 'Many German thinkers have gone to their graves without ever having expressed an opinion on any great question,' Heine notes bitterly. And, when they have dared to, their ideas, 'weak as the brain from which they come',[52] have proved inapplicable and, in fact, superfluous, even when their authors were imprisoned for them:[53] in Germany, even the incarceration of intellectuals for political reasons has something farcical about it! In other words, a critique of the English brand of liberalism and an understanding of its limits, which coincided with class inequalities,[54] cannot in any sense be transformed into a justification – even an indirect one – of Germany's political *misère* and superannuated absolutism.

It is true that in Heine's later writings the theme of social revolution seems to be more clearly distinguished from – even opposed to – that of political revolution. These texts foreground the antagonisms internal to the sphere of *Sittlichkeit*, that is to say, class struggles, thereby diminishing the importance of the question of the political regime. But the word 'social' has a special ring to it in Heine's work, as in the political vocabulary of the 1840s generally, owing, on the one hand, to the influence of socialist theories and the workers' movement, with their strong anti-political bent; and, on the other, to the consolidation of a moderate republican tendency (in France, for example, around the newspaper *Le National*), which was concerned not to upset the social order unduly. Thus the trend was towards an ever wider divergence between the 'social' and the 'political', even as each of the terms within this opposition was being redefined.

Major events punctuated the years in which this shift was coming about. One was the abortive Chartist uprising of summer 1842. Heine reacted to it with an outpouring of pro-English feeling, exceptional in his case; he went so far as to predict that England would be the site of a future social revolution – an idea that Moses Hess had developed in Germany, a year earlier, in *The European Triarchy*.[55] What is more, Heine declared that the eventuality of an 'alliance [between the Chartists] and the discontented workers is perhaps the most important phenomenon of the present time'.[56] He went so far as to call for an *allegorical* reading of the Chartist programme that could discern the social content behind the *shibboleth* of its purely political demands;[57] this social content was latent, of course, but, with 'one step more', it 'must lead, if not to a community of goods, certainly to the undermining of the ancient principle of property – the pillar of modern society'. On the English horizon, then, one could make out the possibility of 'a social revolution compared with which the French Revolution will seem tame and modest'.[58] This is perhaps the sole occasion on which Heine suggests that, as far as its level of historical development was concerned, England might well have outstripped France – or, at least, have progressed beyond the moment represented by 1789.[59] A few months later, other letters – written this time by a young German publicist living

in England, one Friedrich Engels[60] – considerably extend these arguments, while accentuating their anti-political features.

Of course, a certain form of the anti-political is to be found in Heine
as well; indeed, it is a constant in his thinking. An 1832 text, 'An Appeal
to Democrats',[61] is particularly eloquent in this regard. It shows that Heine
plainly shared one of Hegel's fundamental positions: he, too, put a higher
premium on the sociopolitical principle, whose definition always involves
a twofold reference to *democracy* and the *revolution*, than on the question
as to what form of government to adopt. Hence his critique of a certain
republicanism, even in the strictly political, anti-feudal realm. Like Hegel
– and often using the same examples – Heine maintained that the
republican form of government could turn out to be a lure (as it had, for
instance, in the oligarchic cities of Italy); that advance towards a representative regime was not necessarily synonymous with progress (if such a
regime were imposed by assemblies dominated by the aristocracy); and
that a constitutional monarchy could help to accomplish the fundamental
task of the day: smashing the power of the aristocracy, and its political
and ideological sources of support. 'All constitutions,' Heine repeated,
'even the best, cannot help us until the whole nobility is torn up to the
last root.'[62] Nothing was more natural than that Saint-Simonianism should
be grafted on to this Hegelian matrix, of which it seemed to be the logical
extension, both in its attempt to analyse civil society and in its ambition
to found a secularized, pantheistic religion.[63] Even before settling in
France, Heine had shown sympathy for Hegel's position on this matter –
as had other progressive disciples of the philosopher, especially Édouard
Gans, with whom he had rubbed shoulders in the *Verein für Cultur und
Wissenschaft der Juden.*[64] Let us add that Heine's depreciation of the
question of the political regime would later spark polemics with other
representatives of the democratic German intelligentsia; it goes a long
way towards explaining why he fell out with Ludwig Börne.

Heine, however, kept coming back to the question without ever definitively settling it for himself; thus the declarations of faith in the monarchy
to be found in some of the essays he wrote in the 1830s,[65] which were
subject to harsh censorship and self-censorship, are not to be taken at
face value. There is a properly theoretical reason for thinking so: more
than anyone else, perhaps, Heine insisted on the importance of the
symbolic 'decapitation' of the absolutist regime, regarding it as the
indispensable condition, however traumatic, for the desacralization and
democratic transformation of political power in general.[66] Moreover, the
Heine of the 1840s was well aware that a social transformation which
challenged not only the power of the aristocracy, but also bourgeois

property rights, would be inconceivable for as long as there was no change in the political regime itself: 'the bourgeoisie will before all things have order and protection of the laws of property – needs which a republic can satisfy as well as a kingdom. But these shopkeepers know . . . by instinct that the Republic of today would not represent the principles of 1789, but only the form under which a new and unheard-of reign of proletarians would realise all the dogmas of the community of property.'[67]

The republic, then, represented the (political) *form* of a future proletarian regime. Hence its kinship with what others were to describe, some three decades later, as the 'true secret' of the proletariat's first real experiment in exercising power, the Paris Commune, that short-lived, posthumous revenge of the insurgents of June 1848: this 'true secret' resided in the fact that the Commune represented the expansive political form required by the emancipation of labour.[68] For not all republics are the same. After evoking the likelihood that a revolutionary upheaval would bring a European war in its wake, Heine concludes that

> the bourgeoisie, which has to defend its painfully achieved work, the new constitution of the state, against the pressure of the people, which cries for a radical overthrow of society, is certainly too weak to resist if foreigners should attack it four to one. Before it came to an invasion, the bourgeoisie would abdicate; the lower classes would assume their place as in the terrible time of 1790, but better organised, with clearer consciousness of what they need, with new doctrines, new divinities, and new earthly and heavenly powers; so that the foreigners would have to contend with a social instead of with a political revolution.[69]

A new 1789 would thus be followed by a new 1793, which the communists' programme simultaneously prolonged and transcended. The novelty was real, and made it possible to imagine an outcome different from Thermidor; it was not, however, radical. Considered as the whole set of sequences that made it up, the French Revolution was simultaneously a political and a social revolution; more precisely, the democratic revolution was a single expansive process, which, as it unfolded, constantly called the separation of the social and the political into question. Thus it is no accident that Heine, like Büchner, should mention the Year II as a means of introducing the radical (or 'social') reference as one 'moment' of a development internal to the revolutionary process. When he wants to hold the threat of a new revolution over the heads of the dominant classes, Heine quotes *Le Moniteur*, the official organ of the first French Republic; but the only texts he cites date from 1793, for they alone are capable of 'calling the dead from their graves'.[70] It seems plain to Heine

– who, shortly after his arrival in Paris, took issue with both the Orléanist partisans of the *juste-milieu* (the Orléanists wanted to restrict the significance of the *Trois Glorieuses* to the application of the principles of the *Charte*) and the German conservatives (for whom the question of the revolution had already been laid to rest) – that one and the same process has been, and still is, under way in France. It runs like a red thread from 1789 through 1793 and on to the July Days: 'Today is the result of yesterday. We must find out what the former would, before we can find what it is the latter will have. The Revolution is always one and the same. It is not as the doctrinaires would have us think; it was not for the *Charte* that they fought in the great week, but for those same Revolutionary interests for which the best blood in France has been spilt for forty years'.[71]

Thus Heine identifies the democratic revolution with an *uninterrupted* process that constantly pushes back its own limits and has certainly not yet said all it has to say; for, if something new is to be brought into existence, something new will nevertheless always remain to be said: 'the revolution may in no case be declared finished, if it is not to betray itself'.[72] Ten years later, when Heine had a clearer perception of class antagonism, he defended the same position: 'There may yet pass in Paris scenes compared to which all those of the former Revolution will seem to be a Midsummer Night's Dream! The former Revolution? No; the Revolution is ever one and the same; we have as yet only seen the beginning, and many of us will not survive the middle of it.'[73]

It should be emphasized that Heine's line of argument harks back to the basic themes common to Robespierre and Babeuf, the experience of the Year II, and the revolutionary movement of the 1830s, particularly its neo-Babouvist wing: that is, the themes of the continuity and permanence of the revolution. This question began to crystallize in the immediate aftermath of the Montagnarde victory of 1792. Against the moderate bloc – eager to have done with the revolution, even at the risk of capsizing it – Robespierre, who considered the moderates' haste suspect, to say the least, defended the new revolution of 10 August 1792, and asked the essential question: 'Citizens, do you want a revolution without a revolution . . .? Who can determine, after the fact, the precise point at which the waves of popular insurrection should break?'.[74] The movement characteristic of popular revolutions, Robespierre was to add later, was radically different from that of astronomical revolutions;[75] it comprised neither pre-established trajectories nor pre-established cycles. As for Saint-Just, he concluded that 'those who make revolutions in this world, those who want to do good, should sleep nowhere but in the grave'.[76]

But it was above all Babeuf and his political heirs who were to give systematic expression to the idea of an uninterrupted revolution that had always to be begun anew, until the happiness of all had been secured:

> [the revolution] is not finished, since nothing has been done to secure the people's happiness, while everything is done to exhaust the people, so that its blood and sweat will flow eternally into the golden vases of a handful of despicable rich men. Therefore this revolution must be pursued until it has become the revolution of the people. Therefore those who complain about 'people who want to make revolution without end' can only be considered enemies of the people.[77]

It was, of course, no accident that, hard on the heels of the various hypotheses about the permanent revolution, the term 'communism' should appear in the circles close to both Babeuf and the Robespierreans.[78] Communism emerged at a very precise moment in the course of the French Revolution: at the turning point of 1795–96, when, although the bourgeoisie seemed to have carried the day, the most advanced fractions of the popular movement in Paris were re-examining the reasons for the defeat of Thermidor. It emerged, then, at the moment when, in the wake of these convergent self-criticisms, Babeuf and the Robespierreans on the one hand, and the Jacobins and radical *sans-culottes* on the other, were closing ranks. In other words, its birth can be traced to the moment when these two fractions, whose clashes during the Year II had proved fatal to the short-lived experience of popular rule, began to overcome their divisions with a view to pursuing the revolution until genuine equality had been attained. Heine's rhetoric takes its place in the ongoing tradition of this internal self-criticism of the democratic revolution.

The revolution as the right of (and to) life

Let us now turn back to Heine's 1832 definition. A revolution is the result of an unbearable contradiction between social conditions and political institutions; Heine compares it to the organic process or cathartic crisis as a result of which a diseased body regains its health. There is, of course, nothing original about this comparison: in Enlightenment discourse as well, references to natural or biological phenomena served to bring out the objective character of the revolutionary process, and thus to counter the reactionary themes of conspiracy or divine punishment. But they also raised the price that the notion of revolution had to pay in order to achieve – via the philosophy of history – theoretical respectability. Revolution, a means of access to a superior sociopolitical totality, embodies a critically important moment in historical 'development', conceived as a process that allows its own immanent rationality to unfold. Revolution thus establishes its theoretical pedigree, but it takes on a sharply teleological colouring in the process: it is now 'necessary' not simply in the sense that it represents the one possible way of resolving an otherwise irresolvable contradiction, but also in the sense that it is inevitable, does not require any specific practical intervention, and is thus assigned its place, in advance, in the course of a history orientated towards progress. It is precisely these implications of the historical-philosophical conception that Heine strongly resists.

He has an acute grasp of the central problem they throw up: 'Will things come by themselves, without the help of individuals?', he wonders in a 1 April 1831 letter to Varnhagen von Ense. 'That is the great question to which I answer yes today and no tomorrow – responses by which my particular activities are then always influenced and even determined.'[79] One could hardly provide a better description of either the importance of what was in question for Heine, or his chronic inability to make up his mind about it. He was not the only one tormented by this question: a famous letter that Büchner wrote in January 1834 shows that the playwright was at least as deeply torn between his understanding of the tragedy of the French Revolution and his overwhelming sense of the ineffectiveness of human action. The ambivalence of Büchner's attitude, the fact that he could oscillate between two extreme positions, stands out the more sharply in that this letter, with its radically pessimistic, fatalistic tone (it treats the individual's efforts as nothing more than 'a ludicrous struggle against an iron law', which it is our 'supreme duty to recognize', but which is 'impossible to master'),[80] was written shortly before Büchner turned to direct action, calling on the Hessian peasants to rise up in revolt,[81] and participating in clandestine organizational work – activities that nearly cost him, like his comrades, a long prison term, or even his life.

The hesitation that marked Heine's thinking on this question was less radical, but no less interesting for all that. A text which went unpublished in his lifetime, written at almost exactly the same moment as Büchner's letter and given the title 'Differing Conceptions of History'[82] by its first publisher, makes it easier to understand his reluctance to embrace the rationalism of the philosophy of history, as well as his attempts to find a new way out of his dilemma. In this text, Heine contrasts two different conceptions of historical time. The first is that of the traditional cyclical vision of history; it mobilizes, for the greater benefit of the reactionary regimes, a pedagogy of renunciation and disabused passivity. It is defended by the partisans of conservatism and political indifferentism, 'the sages of the Historical School and the poets of Wolfgang Goethe's artistic period [*Kunstperiode*]'.[83] The second, more sanguine conception is that of historical rationalism, defended by the 'philosophers of humanity and the philosophical school', with which we may associate the names of Schiller and Hegel. It is informed by an idea of human progress, of gradual human improvement, which will lead mankind towards a reconciled state form and social life. Remarkably, even if Heine judges the second conception obviously preferable to the first, he takes his distance from both, and sets out to explore a *third* possibility. He justifies his rejection of both conceptions with two arguments. The first turns on the priority he accords the present, that is, his refusal to subordinate it to an extrinsic end located in a beyond with respect to which it is only a 'means'. The second challenges the very idea that notions of means and ends apply to nature and history, given that such notions are merely human projections which contradict the conception of the universe as *causa sui*.

So far, there is nothing here that is radically incompatible with Hegel's positions.[84] An affirmation of the primacy of the present is basic to the Hegelian conception of historical time: in so far as it is 'the existent Notion itself',[85] time can be understood only in the present, as the self-presence of the concept at a given moment of its immanent development. In a certain sense, the present simultaneously contains both the past, whose different moments it recapitulates, and the future towards which it tends, driven by the inexorable progress of the Concept that progressively internalizes all external determinations. The present that fascinates both Hegel and Heine is a present that is always in excess of itself and endowed with an exceptional historical depth, of which it represents the necessary culmination. But this is true only on condition that it also anticipates the future, that it is a new point of departure, that it is always-already in *transition* – a fundamental Hegelian category – towards the next stage in the endless internal development of the Idea in the world: 'it is not difficult to see that ours is a birth-time and a period of transition to a new era. Spirit has broken with the world it has hitherto inhabited and imagined, and is of a mind to submerge it in the past, and in the labour of its own transformation. Spirit is indeed never at rest but always engaged in moving forward'.[86]

Hegel was perfectly aware that the course of history is a far cry from that of a long, peacefully flowing river; at the heart of his exposition of world history we find the labour of the negative, the moments of tragedy, both individual and collective, as well as sorrow and mourning over the field of ruins that the activity of spirit leaves in its wake.[87] Indeed, these features occupy the *whole* historical field, Hegel points out in a famous passage in *The Philosophy of History*: 'The History of the World is not the theatre of happiness. Periods of happiness are blank pages in it, for they are periods of harmony – periods when the antithesis is in abeyance.'[88] Philosophers, in other words, should study the pages that have been thoroughly blackened by the conflict and grime of history. By the same token, Spirit in Hegel is radically incompatible with the naive theological figure of a creator God, or a providential plan that history is charged with realizing one step at a time. Historical rationality is posed in its radical immanence as substance and infinite power;[89] it contains the form and material of its activity within itself, and has no existence prior to that activity.

Thus, if Heine parts company with the man who was his teacher in Berlin, it is not because of the emphasis Hegel puts on the present, the contradiction between means and ends, or the irreducibility of individual tragedy. The generally more sombre tone of the poet's work aside, the divergence stems, rather, from his invocation of a principle capable of opening up a third way distinct from both the cyclical conception of history *and* a progressive evolutionism. This principle is 'life', the only principle to take into account the twofold constraint imposed by the finitude of all human effort and, simultaneously, the irreducible value of the present; for it is the only principle commensurate with the idea of an absolutely free totality: 'everything [that], like the world itself, exists and occurs for its own sake'.[90]

Here again, what is in question seems at first sight to be nothing more than a restatement of the theme of the life of the spirit, the infinite activity that consists in elaborating the raw material internal to life itself. Hegel, too, had occasion to defend 'the life and freedom of the Present' against the 'pallid shades' of a priori generalizations.[91] What is more, Heine's formulations are virtually identical with his former teacher's: 'Reason ... is exclusively its own basis of existence', says Hegel;[92] 'my motto', Heine seems to echo back, 'is ... Life for Life's sake'.[93] Let us note that – certain overhasty interpretations notwithstanding[94] – we are poles apart here from anything resembling a 'vital principle' that would function as a joint ontological, political and ethical foundation, and thus serve to legitimize a hierarchical, racialist, aristocratic vision of life. Only someone who is literally blind to these texts could take the Hegelian–Heinean conception of life for anything other than the most complete

refutation of the following definition: 'life itself is essentially appropriation, injury, overpowering of the stranger and weaker, suppression, severity, imposition of one's own forms, incorporation and, at the least and
mildest, exploitation'.[95]

More generally, the parallels often drawn between Heine and Nietzsche – on the basis, invariably, of their ostensibly convergent critiques
of religion and moral asceticism – seem extremely superficial. Even
when he was assailing, notably, Börne's 'Jewish' or 'Nazarene' temperament in his 'sensualist' period, Heine, faithful to the spirit of an age
that was always ready to invoke a 'Christ of the barricades',[96] carefully
distinguished, within Christianity, the spiritualistic constraints imposed
on the body, which he rejected, from Christianity's social, egalitarian and
messianic dimension, which he wholeheartedly endorsed and never
ceased to invoke: that of a religion of the 'weak' and the oppressed
which had inspired popular revolts for nearly two thousand years.[97] In
what is by common consensus his most militant collection of poetry
(written before his post-1848 'religious turn'), he portrays Christ as the
Messiah of the disinherited, a prophet of subversion and the enemy of
the commercial order.[98] In this he is, of course, at the opposite pole
from Nietzsche, who treats the message of Jesus as a religion of the weak,
a slave morality responsible for the malaise of modern times: the unjus-
tified preservation of what was doomed to disappear, the stunting of the
human figure, and – abomination of abominations – the *corruption of the
European race*.[99]

What is more, Heine does not make his critique of a Judaeo-Christian
morality based on asceticism and renunciation of the world in the name
of a mythical leap back into the early history of mankind, towards the
primitive exhilaration of a Dionysiac religion reserved for the 'strong'. His
aim is, rather, to transcend, dialectically, the 'Jewish' and 'Greek' components of Western culture in a higher totality uniting spirit and body,
freedom and equality. It was in Shakespeare, 'at once Jew and Greek', that
Heine found his model for this ideal, inspired by a Spinoza refracted
through the prism of the *Pantheismusstreit*. 'Is such a harmonious fusion of
both these elements perhaps the task of all of European civilization?', the
poet asks, only to conclude that 'we are still very far removed from such a
goal'[100] – a conclusion that banishes the temptation to sink into an
irrationalist vitalism animated by obsessive hatred of the French Revolution, buttressed by contempt for – and fear of – democratization and
popular participation in the political process.[101]

To make matters still clearer, Heine promptly spells out his conception
of 'life':

Life is neither end nor means; life is a right. Life wants to enforce its right against the cold hand of death, against the past, and this enforcement is revolution. The elegiac indifference of historians and poets shall not paralyse our energies as we go about this business; and the rhapsodies of starry-eyed prophets shall not seduce us into jeopardizing the interests of the present and of the first human right that needs to be defended – the right to live. 'Bread is the people's first right', said Saint-Just, and that is the greatest declaration made in the entire French Revolution.[102]

To declare life to be a 'right' is to identify it with the irreducible necessity of taking sides in a struggle. It is also to defend an unconditional right that corresponds, not to a rationally grounded categorical imperative, but to the fact – a reflection of the antagonism internal to social relations – that certain realities are subjectively intolerable: it is to defend life as a right, the right to live, against everything that consistently tends to deny this right, everything that carries death into the life of the people, robbing it even of the right to bread. This commitment appears under its true name: revolution.

To carve out a third path, then, Heine makes a conceptual 'short circuit' between Hegel, with his defence of *Notrecht*, and Kant, the champion of subjective commitment. This makes reciprocal rectification of their conflicting theses possible: the right to live ceases to function as a corrective for the extreme situations engendered by civil society in order to take its place at the heart of a political commitment. On the other hand, put back in its context, the subjective refusal that precipitates this commitment loses its formal, abstract character; it now appears as the product of an underlying antagonism or objective process that links an affirmation of life to revolution. Heine associates himself with the tradition of all those who believe that the revolution must not be called to a halt until the general happiness has been secured. His reference to Saint-Just speaks volumes here, even if he would perhaps have done better to quote Robespierre's uncompromising defence of the 'right to existence', the absolute primacy of the right to live over property rights, and the need for a popular solution to the question of providing all with a vital minimum.[103] Heine does not innocently echo the historical past; his position is, in fact, in profound harmony with the doctrines of Robespierre and Babeuf, which provided the matrix for the rhetoric of the clandestine revolutionary movement under the July monarchy. The same doctrines, quoted almost verbatim, would be explicitly defended at the outbreak of the February Revolution. The 'Manifesto of the Secret Societies',[104] signed by 'forty-eight people, including a group of distinguished individuals who had fought on the barricades,'[105] would forcefully affirm the continuity of the historical current that had its source in 1789 and 1793; it called for the social question to be resolved through 'the application of the principles contained in the Declaration of the Rights of Man'. But 'the first Right of Man is the right to live! Let there be no more poor people under the Republic!'

Although Heine's 1833 text was not published until after his death, all indications are that the conclusions he drew in it were, in his view, of fundamental importance. They formed the basis for 'one of Heine's key positions (bread, revolution, the right to live), positions that were as spontaneous as they were stable'.[106] Thus it is hardly surprising to see that he restates these conclusions, virtually word for word, in many different texts; indeed, down to his last writings, they helped him define the meaning he gave to his life, which he refused to dissociate from his political combat. The most telling statement of these positions is, no doubt, the one in the 1855 preface to *Lutetia*,[107] in which – after a long, dialectical oscillation that has troubled more than one reader, but holds no surprise for anyone who has followed Heine on his *flâneries* – he finally rallies to communism.

The first moment of this dialectic, the moment of immediacy, is dominated by the feeling of 'nameless grief' that comes over the poet when he thinks 'of the destruction with which the victorious proletariat threatens [his] verse, which will sink into the grave with the whole ancient romantic world'.[108] He knows that this world is in any event doomed to disappear; this knowledge sustains the permanent ambivalence that is appropriate in someone who – borrowing an expression coined by a critic – calls himself a '*romantique défroqué*'.[109] 'Yet, despite this,' Heine goes on, 'I publicly confess that this Communism, which is so inimical to all my interests and inclinations, exerts a magic influence on my soul from which I cannot defend myself . . . two voices in its favour move my heart.' The first is 'that of logic' – Hegelian logic, of course (this at the very moment when, in a contemporaneous text, 'Confessions', Hegel is violently repudiated); it is a 'terrible syllogism that holds me in its bonds', because, since there is no refuting the premises on which it rests, one has no choice but to 'accept all its consequences'. '"All men have the right to eat"'; the poet can therefore only 'cry': 'It has long been judged and condemned, this old society! Let it suffer what it deserves!'.

The conclusion to this first syllogism justifies inverting the image that had earlier served as a metaphor (albeit one already tinged with irony) for the destructive potential of communism; it culminates in a word-for-word restatement of a Latin phrase adopted by Kant: 'And blessed be the grocer who will make cornets of my poems for snuff or coffee for the poor honest old women who perhaps in this our present unjust world must do altogether without such comforts. *Fiat justitia, pereat mundus!*'. The second moment, that of particularity, is thus the moment of radical subjective refusal precipitated by an impossibility that is inherent in the existing social order.

The transition to the third moment is made possible by a reference to the unconditional nature of the Kantian imperative. This third moment is not a unity that has once again taken the form of a singularity, as Hegelian logic suggests it should be, but the very opposite, in line with what the lithography of Robert's painting has already taught the *flâneur*. It is explicitly identified here as the insurmountable nature of the antagonism, and thus the imperative need to take up a position within the either/or division that derives from it:

> The second imperative voice which ensnares me is far mightier and more demonic than the first, for it is the voice of *hate* – of the hate which I feel for a party whose most deadly enemy is Communism, and which from this common ground is our common foe. I speak of the party of the so-called representatives of nationality in Germany, of those false patriots whose love for their native land consists only of idiotic aversion to all foreign or neighbouring races, and who day by day pour out their hatred for France.[110]

The communists, then, make up the most advanced wing of the revolutionary democratic movement, the biggest loser in the 1848 revolutions. Yet despite the historical defeat of 1848, exacerbated by Heine's own personal suffering, the poet can die in peace; the victors may have won a battle, but the task ahead of them is a formidable one. Heine's last words, as it turned out, constituted a promise of revenge, the only 'consolation' before he descended into the silence of the tomb:[111] 'now, as the sword falls from the hand of the dying man, I feel myself consoled by the conviction that Communism, when it meets them in its way, will give them the *coup de grâce*, though it will be no blow with a club, but a crushing under the giant's foot, as one treads on a vile worm'.[112] From the defence of the right to live to the defence of communism, Heine's career offers, in miniature, a striking résumé of the trajectory of the whole democratic revolution, from the Jacobins down to Marx – the greatest of 'the most capable minds and the most energetic personalities in Germany',[113] and the principal addressee of these last confessions, which have the ring of a political testament.

From tragedy to comedy: The impossible historical repetition

What it means to throw in one's lot with the revolution and stand up for
the rights of the present can be described differently: it means combating
everything which, in a present weighed down by the past and straining
towards the future, draws things back towards the past, and thus hinders
the process that raises the present to the level of its concept. One's
attitude towards the past must therefore be twofold: rejecting the amnesia
of the powerful and the passion of the multitude, one has to reflect upon
the past to understand the present that has issued from it; but, to prevent
the obsessive return of old figures, one also has to reaffirm the primacy of
the present: 'but I would like to contribute as much as possible to the
intelligence of the present, impartially, and seek the solution of the
stormy, noisy enigma of the day in the past. Salons lie, graves speak the
truth. But ah! the dead, those cold reciters of history, speak in vain to the
raging multitude, who only understand the language of passion.'[114] It is a
question, then, of gathering up the discourse of the dead and preserving
the truth it contains. One cannot speak of earlier generations without
attending to their language and their voice – the voice that unveils the
'enigma of the day', or, rather, endlessly defers this unveiling, for the 'last
word' is always uttered in the mode of the 'not yet' so as to remain faithful
to the promise.[115]

One must, then, gather up the words of the dead – not in order to
bring the dead back to life, but so that they may rest in peace, lest they
become spectres haunting the present, or the helpless victims of the
victors' opprobrium: 'though the swords of the enemies grow duller day
by day, and though we have already conquered the best positions, still we
cannot raise the song of victory until the work is perfected. We can only
during the night, between battles, when there are armistices, go forth with
the lantern on the field of death to bury the dead. Little avails the short
burial-service! Calumny, the vile insolent specter, sits upon the noblest
graves.'[116] If history is to progress, the dead must, as it were, die twice.
The moment of their 'real' death must efface itself before that of a
'symbolic' death secured by the preservation of their discourse, a process
that rehabilitates them in the eyes of the living even while it frees the
living from the obsessive fear of their spectral return. The question of
repetition thus proves inseparable from that of mourning, memory and
spectrality. The stake is to spare the living, the men of modern times,
from enduring the fate of the 'overcunning Master Merlin', 'who,
entwined in his own magic, lies word-chained and self-banned in the

grave';[117] it is to invent (to hold to the terms of this allegory) a disenchantment that is not simultaneously a re-enchantment,[118] a modernity that culminates neither in closure nor in the revival of regressive mythologies, nor, again, in the paralysis of a new iron cage.

In what follows, then, I shall have a great deal to say about death and the dead. For Heine's relationship to time mobilizes a politics of the memory, a politics founded on the idea of solidarity between the generations, the debt that binds them, and the final catastrophe or 'universal bankruptcy' that constantly threatens to swallow them up:

> But there are worse debts than financial ones, left by our ancestors for us to clear. Each generation is a continuation of the others, and is responsible for their deeds. The Scripture says: 'The fathers have eaten sour grapes, and the children's teeth shall be set on edge.' There is a solidarity among successive generations; indeed, the nations that succeed one another in the arena share such a solidarity, and in the end the whole of mankind will liquidate the assets of the past – perhaps through a universal bankruptcy.[119]

To borrow a phrase from Lukács, the 'calling to account' constitutes one of the central problems of historical drama, which always involves an inaugural crime and the spectral return of the dead, the very symptom of a time of crisis and temporal dislocation.[120] On the other hand, we would do well to keep in mind what distinguishes this dialectic of memory and the work of mourning from rememorizing in the Benjaminian sense. Benjamin's concern is to seize, in the sudden flashing-up of an ultimate instant – that of utter catastrophe or emancipation – the time of the now [*Jetztzeit*] contained in each image of the past.[121] In Heine's case we must rather speak of the preservation of the past as a condition not for rememorizing, but for forgetting it. To progress, the course of history must be reflected one last time; it must mourn the now-superseded figures of its consciousness. The spirit of each of the peoples that succeed one another in the 'arena' of humanity has to assume the debt of intergenerational solidarity before passing the torch on to the next, until the ultimate failure – or redemption. Heine's messianism is more Hegelian and, no doubt, more closely akin to the historicism that Benjamin criticizes; but it is also more receptive to a practice of history – that is, to a political practice which involves something more than waiting expectantly for the event that will bring parousia.[122]

In fact – and this is hardly surprising – the idea that repetition is the distinctive sign of the progress of reason in history also has its origins in Hegel. It features in a text on the murder of Julius Caesar, an event to which Heine often alludes.[123] This text draws a parallel between Rome's transition from republic to empire and France's transition from monarchy to republic, between Caesar's fate and Napoleon's: 'In all periods of the world, a political revolution is sanctioned in men's opinions when it repeats itself. Thus Napoleon was twice defeated and the Bourbons twice expelled. By repetition, that which at first appeared merely a matter of chance and contingency becomes a real and ratified existence.'[124] Repetition occurs so that the necessity and objectivity of an event may be *recognized*; this recognition by historical consciousness is required to ensure the transition of spirit to a new figure of its externalization. Repetition is the symptom of a transitional period and, simultaneously, the condition for its success, that is, for realization of the transition to a higher totality. If it is an illusion, it is a necessary illusion, mandated by the ruse of historical reason.

But what, precisely, transpires in the *entre-deux* of the transition, that is, in the transition of the transition, between real and symbolic death, between the first and second departure of the Bourbons, or, more exactly, between two revolutions – in their *entre-deux*? Heine repeats an observation of Hegel's which, in post-Napoleonic Europe, also counted as common sense, especially in the press of the day. Hegel had noted that the spectacle offered by the *theatrum mundi*[125] had switched genres: (revolutionary) tragedy had given way to comedy.[126] In a brief but crucial passage of *The Philosophy of History*, he calls the Restoration of the Bourbons a 'fifteen years' farce'.[127] With its semblance of a return to absolutism, sprinkled with concessions to constitutionalism (the *Charte*) – in short, with its hypocrisy and absurd pretensions – this farce provides a perfect example of the 'prosaic state of affairs in the present' that the *Aesthetics* describes for us: bourgeois society and the concomitant form of individuality emerge with the decline of the 'heroic age' of absolute monarchs and aristocrats, which had been dominated by individuals who, by themselves, had incarnated all law and morality. Hegel thus admirably captures, by way of a contrast with traditional subjectivity, the 'modern' doublet of a finitude that simultaneously grounds the sovereignty of the modern Subject.[128]

This order collapses at the moment of out-and-out struggle, when the individuals who come into conflict – including those whose sights are trained on the past – acquire genuinely tragic stature. This is the moment of the French Revolution or the Peasant Wars. But when a heroic figure 'still proposes to maintain itself as the sole legitimacy and as the righter of wrong and helper of the oppressed in the sense that chivalry did, then it falls into the ridiculousness of which Cervantes gave us such a spectacle in his *Don Quixote*'.[129] Thus Hegel contrasts Cervantes' hero with the protagonists of Goethe's historical dramas (Goetz von Berlichingen and Franz von Sickingen),[130] who, while incarnating a principle that has become 'obsolete' and is doomed to perish, bear witness, in the context of the Peasant Wars, to the real collision between the feudal order and modern society. Hence there is something still authentically tragic about them.

But the 'ridiculousness' of a Don Quixote or the Restorationist 'farce' are expressions of a division that is internal to comedy itself. Each is already a self-parody of comedy, or, more precise, a comedy unaware that it is one, a comedy devoid of comic (self-)consciousness, clinging to what has become the purely formal, outward semblance of the forms of the past. It is as if this comedy were protesting desperately against the need to make the transition from one of these three forms to the next; ultimately, this protest figures as a burlesque realization of all of them. The question nevertheless arises as to why the historical moment of tragedy should give way to that of comedy – why, in other words, the one is said to follow the other within a teleological sequence, where the commonsensical assumption would no doubt be that the two genres are contemporaneous, and belong to one and the same configuration of the spirit of the age.

To make sense of the order in which these moments of historical consciousness emerge, we need to turn to the *Phenomenology of Spirit*.[131] Epic incarnates a narrative discourse, the *Dasein* of representation, which, from its very inception, is shot through with irresolvable contradictions: its middle term, the world of the heroes, is mediated less by the world of the gods (the sphere of a still abstract universal) than by that of the bard (the sphere of the nascent singularity who represents the truth of the epic moment). The hero seems to be suspended between his destiny and the bard's representation of it; he is tossed endlessly back and forth between the abstract movement of an event or of time, and the narrative discourse that articulates it. This discourse is external to its contents, sustained by the singularity of a bard who is external to his own narrative. Already, the shadow of tragic sorrow and tragic weakness hangs over the actions of the heroes.

Viewed from another angle, however, the independence of the world of the gods, far from establishing their superiority, is a form of detachment from the real action. Ignoring the labour of the negative, destiny floats above the action as the 'irrational void of necessity'.[132] The activity of the Olympians therefore begins to seem futile, as if it were empty gesticulation devoid of any real content – a 'ridiculous superfluity'. At the other extreme, epic narrative is undermined by its comic aspect. The epic unwittingly calls for a new form of thought that will transcend it by developing the requisite mediations for the totalization of human action. As a higher, non-narrative discourse of representation, tragedy marks the necessary transition from the empirical existence of representation (epic) to its in-itself. Now the heroes themselves speak before auditors who are also spectators, and whose consciousness will, in the form of the chorus, be reflected or reduplicated in the dramatic representation itself. Moreover, the heroes are 'personified' by real people in the action of the play: as a *character*, the actor is not external to his *persona*.

Thus, according to Hegel, tragedy rises above the ambiguity of epic, with its dissociation of language and content. It does so, however, only at the price of new contradictions. To be sure, confronted with the double division in which spirit now comes on the scene – a division between divine and human law (the family/state dichotomy) and knowledge and non-knowledge (the ambiguousness of the oracle) – the hero recognizes the necessity of their reciprocal relationship in Zeus, the sole figure to embody the substance. But this recognition remains one-sided: it is not shared by the chorus, whose consciousness, the limited consciousness of the spectator, oscillates between terror and compassion. Hence it is a recognition that falls short of a true unification of the Self, the unification of destiny and the substance. The unity of the actor and his role (his *persona*) begins to disintegrate; the self-consciousness of the heroes breaks free of the constraints imposed on it from without. It becomes irony – that is, a consciousness that plays with the *persona* by simultaneously asserting and dropping its claim to represent the fate of the gods. This is the moment of comedy, the moment that Heine would later claim was the best suited for depicting his time: the moment of the greatest possible separation between a universality drained of its content (the gods reduced to mere 'clouds') and the singularity, embodied in a particular figure, which affords itself the absurd spectacle of its rupture with the universal order.

Nevertheless, Hegel adds, there is a certain reconciliation at work in comedy: thanks to its ironic ambiguity, a unity of sorts is once again established between actor, *persona* and spectator. Self-consciousness contemplates, in thought, the dissolution of all essentiality, which it can now claim to master: hence the familiar feeling of 'well-being' and 'release of tension' that comedy affords. It is with a gay serenity, even with a certain jubilation, that, in comedy, Spirit overcomes its earlier inner discord.[133] After the Romantics – especially Friedrich Schlegel, with his praise of irony – Heine was to exalt this serenity, the virtues of 'merriment', and the lion-like mask of irony[134] – at least in so far as it comprised a transitory stage without which it would be impossible to overcome the *misère* of the present and attain a genuinely new form. He would deliberately ignore the Hegelian critique according to which such serenity gives rise to a singular, absolutized Self who becomes the source of a new mythology, the culminating point of 'religion in the form of art'. For Hegel, this bloated Self, which is purely destructive in its most radical, ironic form, pushes the possibilities of representation to their limits; there, in the name of the ironic genius of the individual, representation becomes the negation of any possible concrete content.[135] From this point on, the forms of the alienation of Spirit must be sought, says Heine's former teacher, in revealed religion, which is beyond representation. The perfectly happy consciousness of comedy is in fact an unhappy consciousness that does not know it is one because it has not yet undergone the experience of the loss and 'the grief which expresses itself in the hard saying that "God is dead" '.[136] The pure concept, the pure self-consciousness containing, as its subordinate moments, all the figures that have preceded it (in the religion of art), can come into the world only after a passionate wait, and its passion is always mingled with pain and nostalgia for what must disappear.

No doubt it is on this point that Heine once again parts company with Hegel – but in a way that is still Hegelian. For Heine, the comedy of the present does not announce an advance beyond representation through a (new?) revelation, but a division within representation itself. That, indeed, is what Heinean irony would seem to signify. Faced with the comedy of a present that refuses to acknowledge its own comic character, and, as a result, only succeeds in redoubling it, sinking into the most ordinary sort of absurdity in the process, the ironic consciousness responds with mockery, a distanced repetition of the world, a destructive reconstitution of it on the grand stage of illusion.[137] Unbridled subjectivity embraces the comic present, recognizing in its negativity the vital forces that are straining to break free: it becomes aware of its own ephemeral character. In this way, it arms itself against ridicule: it avoids taking itself too seriously, and so manages to sidestep the Romantic pitfall that Hegel had pointed out (an abstract, pretentious negation of all content). Through its playfulness, it avoids the gratuitous narcissism heavily laced with nihilism that typifies Romanticism. It seeks to contribute to the self-transcendence of the transitory moment of the present, a self-transcendence which heralds the passage from burlesque comedy to genuine tragedy: a new revolution – or rather, as we have seen, the resumption of a single revolutionary process, whose embers were simply waiting for the right moment to flare up again.

That, in any event, is how Heine perceives the historical moment incarnated by the France of the July monarchy: the reign of the bourgeoisie spells the end of the heroic period of which the Napoleonic epic represented the last moment of glory, the final poetic gleam.[138] Political life at times resembles a 'masquerade', and at other times a carnivalesque spectacle.[139] Indeed, is the era of Louis-Philippe not that of the cartoon, the satirical newspaper, and vaudeville? Yet beneath its humdrum surface – and, as it were, unbeknown to its mediocre protagonists – there appears the new face of the tragedy which, in the brief interval of a desperate insurrection, once again moves to the centre of the historical stage:

> it is to be noted that that phase of history is past when the deeds of individuals stand boldly forth: races, parties, the masses themselves are the heroes of modern times: modern tragedy distinguishes itself from the ancient in this respect, that now the chorus acts and plays the leading parts, while the gods, heroes, and tyrants, who were once the true actors, have fallen to the level of mediocre representatives of the will of parties and popular action, and are employed for mere loquacious reflections as presidents at dinners, deputies, ministers, tribunes, and so on.[140]

These lines obviously capture the radical transformation of the experience of history wrought by the French Revolution: modernity is, irrevocably, the age of the masses, the real protagonists of history. Their appearance on the scene has overcome the split between the spectatorial consciousness and the consciousness (divided in its turn) of the heroes. Yet it has not done so in the manner of the ironic subject, by imagining itself to be above the level of all contents, but by changing, if not the stage, then at least the play. There can no longer be any question of leaving it to others to write (and produce) this play. History has become a 'mass experience':[141] events have lost their 'natural' or 'isolated' character, and earlier forms of consciousness have become obsolete. Whatever its trajectory, its successes and failures, the French Revolution has cut the time of history in two.

As for the Revolution's birthplace, France, a country of concrete action, not mere representation, there can be little doubt about the repercussions this event will have on its future,[142] and, by implication, the future of all Europe. Addressing not only the short-sighted French bourgeoisie, hopeful that the fortifications it has thrown up around Paris will be enough to protect it, but also absolutist regimes convinced that the worst is now behind them, Heine prophesies a new cycle of revolutions and wars on a continental scale, a battle between the classes in which 'there will be no question of nationality or religion'.[143] Yet the 'great question' that he asks in the letter to Varnhagen cited above continues to torment him: a new revolution may well be all but certain, but what room does this leave for the 'help of individuals', in particular the 'help' of a poet and fighter? No doubt their role is to prepare for this eventuality, and to prepare themselves for it.

Once again, Heine explicitly and energetically assumes the legacy of the French Enlightenment as a vast movement of intellectual and moral reform, contrasting it with everything that would thrust intellectuals back into a position of docile submission to the established order – with everything, in other words, that is reminiscent of the German situation: 'but I cannot refrain from declaring the truth, that the writers of the last century were the men who did most to cause the outbreak of the Revolution, and who determined its character. I praise them for this as one praises a physician who brings about a rapid crisis, and allays by his skill the illness which might have been deadly.'[144] This remark should be given its due weight: in Heine's view, the mission of Enlightenment intellectuals was not to initiate the revolution, which would have occurred in any case, but to determine its character – or, at least, to shape it in such a way as to preserve it from absurdity or gratuitous cruelty.[145]

It is worth emphasizing that Heine is not urging intellectuals to play a moderating role here – his position stands out sharply against the reigning 'moderantism' of the period, since he holds that a revolution, even an enlightened one, is necessarily 'bloody' and tragic[146] – but, rather, to bring the revolution into closer conformity with its principle, or, better, its concept, in order to preserve it from any temptation to historical regression. The fact that there was a measure of resentment in the attitude of the leading figures of the French Enlightenment basically changes nothing in this respect – no more than the fact that their mission may well have been accomplished thanks to a ruse of reason, not a pure act of the will. The essential point is that their struggle was both necessary and just. Moreover, it has by no means come to an end: 'even to this hour,' Voltaire and Rousseau 'still spiritually lead and rule the French race'. What is more, the opposition between these two figures provides a metaphor for the partisan struggle that punctuates both the revolutionary process itself and the forces currently embodying it. If Robespierre was 'the incarnation of Rousseau', and Voltaire triumphed in the guise of Thermidor, the Directoire and Talleyrand, 'Rousseau's party', for its part, lives on in the working-class faubourgs of Paris and the camp of the now virtually clandestine republican forces.[147] A few years later, this revolutionary continuity with the Year II is still in evidence. Witness the red (blood-red) thread that connects the writings of Robespierre, Marat and Babeuf, reprinted in pamphlets sold for 'two *sous*', to the works of Cabet or

Buonarroti – a thread which appears again in Heine's apocalyptic description of the same faubourgs,[148] in whose near-subterranean obscurity, in an atmosphere reminiscent of Dante's inferno, the pariahs of bourgeois society tirelessly forge the weapons with which to wreak their coming revenge.

But we cannot leave it at that. However the experience of 1793 is assessed, any consciousness that has been arrested at this stage of historical development and is therefore content merely to quote this past, to maintain a mimetic relationship with it, is, for Heine, regressive; outstripped by history, it has fallen behind the demands of the present. In the face of the relationship that the revolutionaries of 1789 and 1793 maintained with a mythologized Antiquity, Hegel had already felt the need to defend the 'life and freedom of the present', the uniqueness of each historical moment: 'nothing can be shallower than the oft-repeated appeal to Greek and Roman examples during the French Revolution'.[149] Heine, for his part, observes that the same mistake is repeated whenever the revolution is treated as a past to be held up as an idol or a fetish:

> It is folly when people now, to excite to zealous imitation of the man, carry about plaster casts of Robespierre; and it is folly when people would invoke again the language of 1793, as the *Amis du Peuple* are doing, and acting thereby, without knowing it, as retrogressively as the most zealous champion of the old *régime*. He who gathers the red flowers which in the spring have fallen from the trees, and would stick them again with wax to the boughs whereon they grew, acts as foolishly as the one who plants cut and faded white lilies in the sand. Republicans and Carlists are plagiarists from the past . . .[150]

This plagiarized revolutionary past then becomes a comfortable costume, the object of a cheap nostalgia; fashion can quote it just as it can quote any other reified element. We already find Büchner's Robespierre accusing his Dantonist enemies of 'parod[ying] the sublime drama of the Revolution, so as to discredit it by calculated excesses'.[151] But by Heine's time the parody resides at another level, defined by the '*gilets à la Robespierre*' that have 'come back in fashion among the republican youth in Paris today',[152] as Gothic paraphernalia had before them.[153]

The cannibalization of the past by the present is doubtless symptomatic. It signals a period of crisis, the chasm between an advance of Reason in history (thanks to which it becomes possible to quote this past) and a state of consciousness that in fact represents a retreat before both the demands of the present and the subversive charge contained in the 'original': 'strange and horrible curiosity that often urges men to gaze into the tombs of the past! This curiosity is excited at certain extraordinary periods, at the close of an epoch, or immediately before a catastrophe.'[154] At the risk of sowing confusion as to the precise nature of his own views,[155] Heine criticizes the republicans of *his* day for – in a nutshell – retreating to positions behind the revolution which they claim to be pursuing. He finds fault with them not despite, but precisely because of a fidelity to 'the letter' of the revolution that violates its 'spirit'. To put it as simply as possible: a *gilet à la Robespierre* and Robespierre's *gilet* are two very different things! Heine's letters of 1840–42 put a finer point on it: it is the narrow-mindedly political republicans of the 1830s and early 1840s who drive a wedge between the political and the social, not their putative ancestors of the Year II. They fail to see that while the newly dominant forces may still be hostile to the republic – Heine refers to them as 'the money aristocracy', in the tradition of the *sans-culottes* and the socialist and communist literature of the day, and, later, as 'the bourgeoisie' – their overriding concern is to defend private property, the real backbone of the existing order.[156] The enemy of this order no longer goes by the name of 'republic', but is now known as 'communism'; more precisely, it is no longer a 'republic of the former kind', but a republic as the 'form under which a new and unheard-of reign of proletarians could come about'.[157]

No doubt the orthodox Babouvists who made up what was by far the biggest contingent in the communist movement under the July monarchy squarely addressed the social question. They were, however, mired in the Year II in another sense: they clung to the levelling egalitarianism that was basic to the doctrine of the *sans-culottes*,[158] without taking into account the new needs of individuals who had thrown off traditional ties, and of societies that were now more than mere subsistence economies.[159] Heine criticizes both the Babouvists and the republicans for divorcing the social from the political and equality from freedom: both parties, he argues, drain the unified movement of revolutionary democracy of its content. It is out of a desire to remain *faithful* to the 'great watchword of the Revolution, uttered by Saint-Just, "Bread is the people's first right"', that Heine reinterprets it as a demand for a 'democracy of terrestrial gods, who are all equally magnificent, equally holy, and equally happy'; a democracy without 'sans-culottes, or thrifty citizens, or bargain-basement presidents',[160] which rejects 'a general equality of cookery, wherein the same Spartan black broth shall be boiled for us all'.[161] In other words, 'wiping poverty off the face of the earth' has to go hand in hand with 'restoring to their proper dignity the poor people disinherited of happiness, genius scorned, and beauty ravished, as our great masters have said and sung'.[162] The right to beauty is an integral part of the right to live, of an affirmation of life in its totality and vital fullness. But it is still predicated upon the right to eat, which it can by no means replace, for 'food is the most important thing'.[163] Heine is among those who understand very well that life is above all a 'fight for the crude and material things without which no refined and spiritual things could exist'.[164]

This two-sided definition of Heine's position aroused controversy in his lifetime, and continues to do so today. His *frère ennemi* in exile, Börne, the other leading figure in the German democratic opposition, openly accused him of aestheticism, and of playing a political double game. Heine had, as it were, put aesthetics in command and, with his inflated poet's ego, was waging a struggle on two fronts: against absolutism on the one hand, but against Jacobinism and the democratic camp on the other. He delighted, said Börne, in 'playing the Jesuit of liberalism'.[165] It is true that Heine's dialectic occasionally cultivates ambiguity for ambiguity's sake, and that many of the countless masks this complex personage wore could only have disconcerted the virtuous Börne. Heine does, in fact, sometimes exhibit a markedly aristocratic disdain – in the 'lofty' sense of an aristocracy of the spirit, of course – for the revolution and the backwardness of the 'masses'.[166] But this is only a transitory *persona*, a 'moment' inserted into a deliberately twisted syllogism that seeks to define the conditions under which it will become possible to overcome this situation and turn the self-transformation of the masses into a reality. As Lukács would later put it: 'even if with a tragic cleavage of spirit' reflecting that of an entire age, Heine 'affirm[s]' the 'perspective held out by the new period in human development';[167] he refuses to descend to the level of an apologist for a declining society awash in resentment and nostalgia.

But much more is at stake. Heine did not restrict himself to espousing his times down to their very contradictions; or, rather, precisely because he was steeped in those contradictions, he was able to detect their most advanced tendencies. The political and theoretical positions he adopted did not simply reflect his social status as a poet who was attentive to high society and frequented a number of Parisian salons. As a Jewish-German *émigré* intellectual, he could move – with varying success, it is true – in circles at both ends of the social scale. Thus his *Philosophy and Religion in Germany* saw its first publication in French in François Buloz's very bourgeois *Revue des deux mondes*; but it was *simultaneously* released in German in the very clandestine periodical '*Die Geächteten*', the Paris organ of the *Bund der Geächteten* [League of the Banned], the main political organization of the German *émigrés*, in which writers and journalists who had fled Prussian despotism rubbed shoulders with artisans belonging to the large community of German workers living in Paris.[168] The *Bund* was to be transformed, after a number of splits and endless internal debates, into, first, the League of the Just (1836–47), and then the Communist League (1847–52), for which a pair of Rhinelanders quite as famous as Heine would one day write a certain *Manifesto*.

It is therefore hardly surprising that the poet's arguments are not as remote as they appear to be from the real debates raging not only in the democratic camp in the broad sense but, more particularly, in the contemporary revolutionary and workers' movements (which, it should be recalled, were far from spontaneously coinciding or converging).[169] Heine's 'pantheistic' critique of the Spartan egalitarianism of the *sans-culottes* is one clear indication of this. Indeed, even in the period when Babeuf and his associates were planning their 'conspiracy for equality', the question of 'luxury' had, as in the Enlightenment (here too, it was Voltaire versus Rousseau), been a subject of bitter debate. Thus Sylvain Maréchal had included, in his 'Manifesto of the Equals', a sentence about the disappearance of the arts for the sake of real equality ('let all the arts perish, if necessary, as long as real equality remains to us');[170] it met with the disapproval of the Babouvists' secret directory, which had, because of its objections to this sentence, refused to authorize public distribution of Maréchal's text.[171]

The debate flared up again in the early 1840s, at the very moment when Heine was writing his dispatches for the *Augsburger Zeitung*. In a finely honed argument, Théophile Thoré, a former *carbonaro*, radical democrat, and partisan of 'socialization' who was nevertheless an anti-Babouvist, criticized Babeuf, whom he contrasted with Robespierre, for professing a leveller's conception of equality as well as a millenarian vision of history based on the belief in a final revolution.[172] Richard Lahautière replied for the neo-Babouvists,[173] insisting that an unbroken line of descent led from Rousseau through Robespierre to Babeuf, while reformulating the Babouvists' conception of equality: they defended, said Lahautière, not uniformity, but the idea that everyone had an equal right to happiness and a decent existence. He conceded, however, that it was necessary to update the obsolete features of the doctrine, which he did not regard as 'the last word on human progress'. Revision was in order, precisely, on the questions of 'the arts and luxury' (they were not to be suppressed, but made accessible to all) and personal dictatorship, which, thanks to the emergence of a 'strong, enlightened' people, had become superfluous: dictatorship could be replaced by a vigorous expansion of democracy.

For the revolutionary French democrats, as for the German *émigrés* (especially in Paris) who closely followed these developments, one's position on the Babouvist version of communism and, more generally, the heritage of 1793 – represented what was quite possibly the central issue of the day. For this issue condensed questions of programme (what was the relationship between the question of the form of government and that of property?), strategy (a conspiracy aimed at imposing a new 'dictatorship' of the kind advocated by Babeuf/Blanqui? a gradualist road to power? the mobilization of non-political means?), organizational forms (secret societies, non-political workers' associations, the creation of communities), and symbolic references (should one burn Robespierre? Babeuf? Rousseau? Saint-Simon?). The path blazed by Heine, among others (of his German contemporaries, I will mention only Büchner), but more by Heine than the others, was that of a revolutionary continuity aiming at something other than a 'repetition' of the 1789–93 period, which would have been doomed to failure from the outset. It was a path which, while it assimilated past experience, had necessarily to include a self-critical moment if it was to divest itself of all vestiges of a mimetic relationship to the past. No doubt this also explains why Heine shares, with Büchner, the strange fate of those victimized by interpretations which treat 'the profound self-criticism of the democratic revolution' as 'directly counter-revolutionary'.[174]

The politics of the name

It was not sheer happenstance that the work of Heine, who never – to put it mildly – had the reputation of an activist athirst for contact with the masses,[175] should echo the debates then raging in the most advanced sections of the French working-class movement. Nor is this quasi-spontaneous echo to be explained exclusively in terms of the unique trajectory of France's German émigré circles, although it was one of the decisive moments of that trajectory, and had a formative influence on it, rooted as it was in a profound understanding of the European crisis caused by the revolutionary break. The possibility that the old order could be revived was quite as illusory as the notion that the events of the 1789–99 period could simply be repeated. The revolutionary process, which was irreversible, had not been finished; it had merely been interrupted. But the revolution could not be continued before it had engaged in a self-criticism implying renunciation of both amnesia and mimesis. And, notwithstanding the reservations expressed in Heine's writings of 1840–42 about the levelling tendencies of a type of communism still heavily influenced by Babeuf – reservations which, incidentally, would be considerably attenuated in his late work (where communism is treated as a strictly German phenomenon)[176] – the poet believed that communism (and this is the crucial point) was what the internal self-criticism of the revolution would ultimately bring about.

The emergence of communism is the event that throws historical time out of joint, radically reordering the relationship between past, present, and future. Hence the importance of the name 'communism', which Heine would later boast that he had introduced in Germany, and even beyond its borders. For Heine, this act of naming was the secularized version of an originary gesture charged with the messianic force that traverses the present and opens on to the future.[177] In other words, the politics of the name was sustained by the force of the rupture condensed in the act of naming. Communism was an 'event' because this name alone aptly designated the *antagonism* of bourgeois society:

> Then, the fearful wheel [of the revolution] would start to move again, and this time we should see an antagonist appear who might well be the most terrible of all who have yet entered the lists with the existing order. This antagonist is still preserving his terrible incognito; he resides like a needy pretender in the *souterrain* of official society, in those catacombs where among death and decay new life is sprouting and budding. Communism is the secret name of the dread antagonist setting proletarian rule with all its consequences against the present bourgeois time. It will be a frightful duel. How will it end? No one knows but gods and goddesses acquainted with the future.[178]

Communism, then, surges up from this truly spectral place – between death and life, broad daylight and the darkness of the 'catacombs' – in order to hoist itself on to the great stage of history, where it is destined to play a major role.[179] Even the revelation of its 'secret name', which draws it into the light, bears the marks of an *entre-deux*, the ambiguity of something revealed but also hidden; at the very moment when communism steps undisguised into the light of day, it also remains 'incognito', an eternal 'gloomy hero' of the impending tragedy, for 'the proper of a proper name will always remain to come. And secret.'[180] The last word can only be a word which defers, and defers in order to be able to state the promise of the event and affirm its coming, its ad-vent: 'The last word has thus not been said, and here is perhaps the ring to which a new revelation can be joined.'[181] The event 'communism' simultaneously and irreducibly partakes of the order of a reappearance [*réapparition*] and recommencement of an already well-known history ('the fearful wheel of the revolution would start to move again'); but also of a future – or, rather, of something to come [*d'un avenir, ou plutôt d'un à-venir*]. As such,

it is unknown, 'secret', and therefore open-ended, for it is wholly dependent on a 'frightful duel' whose outcome remains unknown.

The 'gods and goddesses acquainted with the future' seem to remain
stubbornly silent. Their silence, however, by no means prevents mortal
men from 'giving their cue' to this actor who is capable of elevating the
comedy of the bourgeois parliamentary system to the level of 'modern
tragedy', and thus of transforming the 'secret rehearsals' of its role into a
full-length play.[182] Yet the text of this play cannot be written before it is
performed on stage [la 'représentation'], nor can it be the work of an
author different from the actors who interpret it. At the same time as,
from within, it deals a blow to the categories of representation, communism deals a blow to the categories of the philosophy of history. In this
sense, the fact that Heine's contemporary Büchner makes the revolutionary event that has already occurred into the subject matter of a play
(whose dialogues and ending are determined in advance: Büchner, taking
his premisses to their logical conclusion, draws his material directly from
historical sources, such as collections of speeches or the works of Thiers
and Mignet) represents perhaps the most extreme form of experimenta-
tion with the limits of the categories of historical representation. The
upshot, let us note, is the complete spectralization of Büchner's characters: from the moment of their appearance [apparition] on stage (the
'real' stage, that of the theatre, that is, that of illusory repetition), Danton,
Robespierre and the other protagonists are already, always-already, their
own ghosts, voices that come to us from the tomb, one last time – which
is, however, never the last time; which constantly defers its end.

Of course, there is nothing original about treating the emergence of
communism as a decisive event. From the first, Heine's contemporaries
were alert to the peculiar success of this name, which, precisely, 'enjoyed
a resounding success', in Pierre Leroux's words, from the moment it
reappeared in public (at the banquet of Belleville).[183] This is because
'communism' immediately exhibited a radical novelty, a feature that
distinguished it from the common run of the social and political doctrines
which mushroomed under the July monarchy. Contrary to Saint-Simonianism, Fourierism, positivism, or even socialism – and, above all, to
Bonapartism, which Heine held to be communism's real rival (in 1832,
he said: 'this name [Napoleon] is the deepest word of adjuration among
the people')[184] – communism had neither father nor mother: 'it doesn't
bear anyone's name', as Comte would say in 1848 (see below). It was the
product of a radically secular act of naming in the sense that it was an
authentic creation of the people, the result of a collective effort. Let us
take up the thread of Leroux's argument where we left it: 'it was the

people, or a few writers from the ranks of the people, who discovered the name communism. The word enjoyed a resounding success. Communism in France is comparable to Chartism in England. I myself would prefer the word communionism, which reflects a social doctrine based on brotherhood; but the practical-minded people, which always goes straight to the goal, has opted for communism to designate a republic in which equality would hold sway.'[185]

In an age obsessed with the burden of its dead and the legacy bequeathed it by previous generations, the emergence of the new name heralded a rupture in the relationship to the past. Communism had been freed of the repetition-compulsion characteristic of the family romance or the phantoms of the past; it had not, for all that, lost its memory. Indeed, it renewed its ties with a 'spirit', the 'revolutionary spirit' of 1789/1793, coming forward as its true – or even its sole – heir. Heine takes up the Judaeo-Christian opposition of the body (or letter) and the spirit, affirming the primacy of spirit; but he modifies it in the process, turning it to his own ends.[186] Now it is the parallel with the other, rival name, Napoleon's, which gains new relevance. Heine believes that a secularized Bonapartism – one that does not look for Napoleon's resurrection but remains faithful to the 'spirit' of the name, to nothing but the 'heritage of the name' – still has a future.[187] The question of the name is bound up with that of 'incarnation', of the body (or flesh) that the ghost lacks: the future cannot truly be freed from the dead weight of the past, even while it perpetuates its 'spirit', unless it manages to rid itself of the *belief* in this ghostly 'non-body' that keeps 'coming back to haunt the living' in the guise of an ineliminable residue lodged at the heart of the real.

Heine, as I have said, was not the only one to have been struck by the singular destiny of the word 'communism'. On the eve of the 1848 Revolution, Comte, too, took note of it. He saw in this name a collective creation, the fruit of a historical necessity, and considered it serious competition for what he himself was proposing in this period, a 'fundamental coalition between philosophers and proletarians'[188] united around positivism: 'communism, which does not bear anyone's name, is not at all the by-product of an exceptional situation. We must rather see in it the spontaneous progress, rooted in feelings rather than reason, of the true revolutionary spirit, which today tends to be primarily preoccupied with moral questions, and to treat political solutions, in the true sense of the word, as secondary.'[189] Comte even admitted that communism was 'the only movement that is today capable of posing and pursuing, with irresistible energy, the most important question'[190] – that is, the social question. Moreover, the key to the success that he predicted for positivism resided in 'positivism's basic ability to resolve the main social problem better than communism'.[191] That success alone could, 'today and in the years to come ... save the West from any serious attempt to establish communism'[192] by ensuring the pre-eminence of 'moral means' over the 'political means' to which, despite everything, the communists remained attached.

We are now better able to appreciate the very special, highly atypical position that Heine defended in the pre-1848 political and ideological conjuncture, his borrowings from Saint-Simon notwithstanding. The term 'antagonism', which he no doubt took from the Saint-Simonians (although we should not forget its distant Kantian roots),[193] did not frighten him as it did Comte or Saint-Simon's disciples. These thinkers mentioned antagonism only in order to subordinate it without delay to some other, supposedly more basic principle, in whose light antagonism appeared as an aberration and a source of malfunction. As partisans and artisans of the 'social', their sole motivation for bringing up antagonism was to seek the means of overcoming it, so that they could move on as quickly as possible to something else (universal harmony, industrialism, association, etc.). In contrast, Heine's position and his agonistic conception of life consign to the realm of illusion all hopes of resolving 'the great modern crisis'[194] by developing the appropriate social technologies, whether Fourierist (the system of the phalansteries) or Comtean (the reorganization of society by way of the creation of a new spiritual power).

At a time when approaches aimed at warding off a communist victory were proliferating, and the therapeutic vision of the 'social' as a means for defusing contradictions was rapidly gaining ground, Heine calmly prophesied that 'the dispersed family of Saint-Simonians and the whole general staff of Fourierists will go over to the growing army of Communism', amending the discourse of 'crude demands' with 'the creative word'.[195] In the final analysis, Heine is at antipodes from what would later be called the 'spirit of the '48ers': a spirit steeped in the 'humanitarian' – or 'humanist' – credo (at the time, these two adjectives were much in vogue among the French and the Germans, respectively), inhibited by its political 'moderantism', and inclined to seek social harmony and the peaceful resolution of social antagonisms. It is no exaggeration to say that the spirit of '48, which provided the common denominator for most of the political doctrines that belong to the period before the February Revolution, would become the official doctrine of the provisional government that issued from it. It lent the interlude dominated by the ''48ers' its characteristic air of 'consensus', which was soon swept away by the proletarian blood shed in June and the ruling element's implacable desire for revenge.

For it should not be forgotten that the spirit of '48, however moderate and peaceful it might appear, provoked the 'great fear' of the opposing social bloc.[196] From the revolt of the Lyon silk workers through the strikes, abortive assassination attempts, and insurrections in Paris, to the peasant revolts of 1846–47, the seeming calm of the Orléanist reign betrayed signs of growing fragility. Increasingly, the apprehensions of the possessing classes were focused on the name 'communism': in the political/journalistic language of the period, there is nothing particularly original about the famous evocation of the 'spectre that is haunting Europe', which has come down to us in a text which, although it has now acquired legendary status, was all but ignored during the quarter of a century following its publication.

Whether it was an object of desire or abhorrence, the name 'communism' and the paths along which it spread were highly revelatory of the fundamental tendencies of the period. In the aftermath of the February Revolution, on 17 March, employing a tactic that had a glorious future ahead of it, the National Guard barred the way before the first (peaceful) demonstration by the Paris workers against the provisional government; the Guardsmen carried out their actions to deafening cries of 'down with the communists' or 'throw the communists into the river'.[197] That there was nothing subversive about the proletariat's peaceful and rather ill-defined demonstration made no difference; the mere fact that it had occurred was enough to arouse the deep-seated fears which the spirit of unanimity prevailing in February strained to deny. Less than three years later, at a time when hardly anyone was still willing to defend the regime, which had come to be regarded as ineffectual or even as a hindrance by the ruling elements who had succeeded in crushing the Paris proletariat, the enemies of the revolution would, once again, brandish the threat of the 'red spectre'. In the newspaper that bore this name (it was called, to be precise, *Le spectre rouge de 1852*), a journalist named Romieu denounced the danger represented by both the radicalized peasants and the 'millions of proletarians enrolled in the cause of hatred'. His conclusion was that matters had come to such a pass that 'the army and the army alone can save us'.[198] Should there be any need for further evidence of the peculiar way the 'name communism' functioned, we might note how its spectrality attested its ambiguous relationship to the symbolic order, to which it both belonged (as a name that aspired to the role of master-signifier, the name of names) and was irreducibly alien.

For, behind 'communism', there did not necessarily lurk real and/or representable communists but, rather, the reality that bourgeois society had to repress in order to forge a satisfactory representation of itself: the real of antagonism.

Exorcizing the spectres

Heine's obsession with the past was not his alone. He shared it with an age torn between the fashion of *gilets à la Robespierre* on the one hand and, on the other, fascination for the name 'Napoleon' and nostalgia for the imagery of *fleurs de lys* and royal purple. He once described his native city as follows: 'Düsseldorf is a town on the Rhine; 16,000 people live there, and many hundreds of thousands more lie buried there.'[199] The generations of the dead bear down on the living with all their weight, and return to haunt the present – in the mode of the spectral apparition. They come to demand, not vengeance, but that their words be saved from perdition ('graves speak the truth'), and that the work of mourning be fully accomplished. In other words, they come to demand that they be forgotten (but not that the living forget that they have forgotten them).

A vast gallery of spectres peoples Heine's work; it seems capable of endless proliferation. But not all spectres are alike; the task before Heine consists in making distinctions – sometimes very subtle, shifting distinctions – between these various apparitions, and in playing them off against each other. If nothing real lacks its spectral dimension, taking a political position implies, by its very nature, intervening on the 'spectral battlefield'.

The France/Germany opposition makes it possible to draw a first, and fundamental, spectral dividing line. In the country that has already undergone the experience of the revolution:

> most of the French looked into the graves of the past merely with the intention of picking out an interesting costume for the carnival. In France the Gothic fad was simply a fad, and it served only to heighten the pleasure of the present. The French let their hair flow down long in medieval fashion, and at a casual remark by the barber that it is not becoming, they have it cut off short together with the rest of their medieval ideas. Alas, in Germany it is different. Perhaps just because in Germany medievalism is not completely dead and putrefied, as it is in France. German medievalism is not lying mouldered in its grave; on the contrary, it is often animated by an evil spirit and steps into our midst in bright, broad daylight and sucks the red life from our hearts.[200]

We must, then, pick out the 'phantoms' among the spectres – those figures which have loomed up out of a past that has survived its own death and is therefore not entirely 'past', even if, from the rational point of view, it is entirely *passé*. These unsettling or even frankly alarming creatures, who never tire of plotting against a present they try to reduce to an extension – or, better, repetition – of the past, have made Germany their favourite haunt. As always, Heine calls on the full range of Romantic imagery here too, even as he perverts it and turns it against itself in order to ridicule both the medieval airs affected by the German Romantics[201] and the parody version of the Middle Ages that continues to hold sway in their spectral country. For the German Middle Ages, although equally the stuff of parody, are so in a way that differs sharply from the spirit which animates the light-hearted, carnivalesque French vogue of the Gothic. German medievalism is a 'nauseating' parody acted out by ridiculous hams,[202] for it is completely oblivious to the fact that it is comic. Like Hegel's Restorationist 'farce' (i.e. the France of Louis XVIII and Charles X), this parody, in all its absurdity, is simply a comedy which does not know that it is one, and therefore stubbornly insists on taking itself seriously. The reason is that true comedy would not be tolerated by the absolutist Prussian regime; if a modern Aristophanes were to venture into its dominions, he would promptly be clapped behind bars.[203]

Germany is thus not merely a country haunted by phantoms; it is, in the true sense of the word, a *phantom country*. Caught fast in the mustiest sort of absolutism, it 'phantomizes itself', as it were, for it is quite simply not of the present; it plays no part in the present moment of universal history. It is immeasurably backward, for it lacks even the consciousness of its backwardness: its present is France's or even, perhaps, all Europe's distant past, and its phantoms are hardly even spectres, but, rather, living corpses that give off a 'smell of putrefaction' wherever they go. Indeed, one can tell that a phantom is German by its wickedness and its disgusting stench; the German Middle Ages, which are 'not lying mouldered in the grave', are 'animated by an evil spirit'.[204] Theirs is the odour that hangs tenaciously about the dead who are unaware that they have died,[205] the dead who stubbornly insist on living on, clinging to something less than life or, rather, to an anti-life, while continuing to suck the blood of the present.

France appears to be the very opposite: a country that has succeeded in exorcizing its phantoms, a country in which, basically, the father has been murdered and his debts have been settled. The dead are well and truly buried there, and a community, culture, and '*new life*' have sprung up; one feels that 'there great deeds are dimly developing and unknown gods revealing themselves'.[206] In short, France, a country that has *already* gone through a revolution – or, if you prefer, a country in which the revolution has already truly begun – is distinguished by the fact that its past is, precisely, a revolutionary past, a past that has abolished the past and lives, in a word, in a self-referential time, the incarnation of a break with historical time. Such is the paradox of the modern temporality whose effects Heine will attempt to capture. Spectrology makes it possible to grasp the most important of them. Exit the phantoms, spectres of the past:

> How could a Frenchman be a ghost, or how could ghosts even exist in Paris! In Paris, the foyer of European society! Between twelve and one, the hour that has been allotted to ghosts from time immemorial, the full stream of life is still roaring through the streets of Paris, in the opera the thundering finale is just sounding, out of the Variétés and the Théâtre-Gymnase come streaming the merriest groups, and the boulevards are thronging with rollicking, laughing, bantering crowds, and everybody goes to the soirées.[207]

Even the Parisian night is luminous and radically anti-Romantic; it is the very opposite of its German counterpart, lost in dreams and echoing with the clanking of its ghosts. In Paris, the night is only an interminable twilight, an infinite prolongation of the moment in which the Hegelian owl takes flight. To its sorrowful hooting, which evokes wisdom even as it augurs the helplessness before the phantoms' return that wisdom implies, Heine opposes, in a now-famous image,[208] the vibrant call of the Gallic cock, which dispels 'the feverish dream',[209] puts the Prussian eagle to flight, drives off the spectres of the past, and heralds a dawn that is always new.

Paris may well be the 'Pantheon of the living', and lack all 'ghostly dignity'; yet the new god who holds sway over it is named money ('the rule of the money-god, who is the father and mother of all');[210] and for the moment, the action played out on it, pending the 'mighty actions' to come, is at the level of the light comedy of the Parisian boulevards – a far cry indeed from the tragedy of the *ancien régime* or the Napoleonic epic: 'Even under the Empire the heroes of Corneille and of Racine could expect the greatest sympathy when they played before the box of the great Emperor and a pit full of kings. Those times are past; the old aristocracy is dead; the throne is now nothing but a common wooden chair covered with red velvet; and today the heroes of Paul de Kock and of Eugène Scribe reign in their place.'[211] The gaiety of Paris springs from a world in which authority, its attributes and symbols, have been radically desacralized. Thus the throne is just an ordinary wooden armchair, an idea that the people in arms was to translate into practice during the February revolt: it contented itself, in an act that mimicked the rituals of carnival,[212] with publicly burning a piece of furniture. The crowds of 1789 or 1793 would have opted for more drastic methods.

This is because, in France, the king has *already* been beheaded; the emergence of the constitutional bourgeois monarchy of the House of Orléans only confirms that the sovereign figure of *Homo sacer* is now well and truly dead. He had been symbolically decapitated before the blade of the guillotine fell, and was put to death by what was itself a secularized instrument of execution, the guillotine having suppressed the ancient ritual.[213] This lent the execution of the last of the kings by divine right a foretaste of comedy. It was the very opposite of the execution of Charles I, a true tragedy that unfolded in conformity with the traditional ritual of the executioner and the axe, leaving behind, perhaps, a traumatic residue that haunted Cromwell all his life.

Indeed, Cromwell's case is of special interest from a spectrological standpoint. Heine's Cromwell spends sleepless nights before making up his mind to open the dead king's coffin. Yet it is not spectres that he fears but, rather, the 'real daggers of his enemies'. As for the scene in which the coffin is opened, one that recurs in Heine whenever he wishes to evoke the ghosts that haunt the sleep of despots together with the terrible end that awaits them,[214] the poet gives precedence to the 'more democratic legend': he has Cromwell contemplating the mortal remains of Charles I in broad daylight, calmly and even with humour,[215] qualities that enabled him to 'fell . . . calmly . . . the royal oak . . . that had once reached out its branches so proudly over England and Scotland'.[216] Nevertheless, even in this de-dramatized French version, the killing of the king causes a shock: it is a symbolic amputation – or even castration[217] – that ultimately signifies the decapitation of the mystical body which once united the sovereign to his subjects.

Something of the ancient mode of execution has survived in the new ritual, after all; an act of this kind never occurs without awakening a feeling of anguish closely akin to the castration anxiety called up by the executioner's axe under the *ancien régime*.[218] As Isabelle Kalinowski points out: 'the disappearance of the executioner is premised on the disappearance of the belief that sacralizes him', which certainly takes more time than the guillotine does. *Homo sacer*, Heine repeatedly says,[219] is nothing in the absence of a shared belief in the transcendence of his substance; conversely, he cannot really be killed until this faith disappears, along with the rituals that accompany it, especially the ceremonial surrounding the person of the king. In other words, the guillotine is a necessary condition, if only because it abolishes ceremony;[220] but this condition will be sufficient only if it is accompanied by the labour of mourning for the King as symbolic Father.

It is on this double condition that the historical consciousness can free itself of the double curse that haunts (or, in the French case, haunted) the dark night of despotism: the authority of the name and the spectre of the executioner. Once again, the France/Germany opposition is relevant: it brings two avatars of the 'spirit of the people'[221] face to face. The 'royalism' of the Germans consists of respect for existing authority, a feeling that expands to take in the person who represents it, becoming 'confidence' and cultural 'attachment' as a result. Because France, in contrast, is 'in its very being republican', its natural tendency is to reject all the forms of transcendent authority that escape popular control – all the more so when what is involved is personal authority attempting to drape itself in the prerogatives of the 'great name', a pale substitute for the attributes of *Homo sacer*:

> Since I have studied the French Republicans in their writings, as in their lives, I recognise everywhere as a characteristic sign that distrust of persons: that hatred of the authority of a name. It is not a petty narrow yearning for equality which makes these men hate great names – ah, no! – they fear that those who bear them will use them against freedom; or else by weakness and yielding may allow others to misuse them. For this reason so many great and popular heroes of liberty were executed, because it was feared that in a time of peril they might in perilous circumstances make bad use of their authority.[222]

The way is thus open for the 'secret names' borne by new conspiracies, whispered by spectres come from the future. . . .

The same holds for the couple formed by the king and the executioner, who play alternating roles in the inexorable circle of despotic repetition: the executioner incarnates the initial violence which founds the king's authority, but also, by virtue of the taboo that attaches to him, the ongoing denial of the original crime, in consequence of which it is, inevitably, repeated. In the opening scene of the poem 'Sir Olaf',[223] king and executioner stand side by side, both wearing the same purple garb, ready to strike down the knight who has violated the established order. In 'The Knave of Bergen',[224] the executioner, after seducing the duchess, is dubbed a knight by the duke, who thus reveals the criminal origins of his own nobility in the very gesture that symbolically transfigures them. These origins are still present; they are passed on from generation to generation, and the only possible way that an authority of this kind can legitimize itself is by repressing them.

A new act of violence is required to break out of this perverse dialectic. The despots are haunted by the spectre of the executioner who will chop off their own heads; they know that any child, any 'workman's child', may one day perform this task, wielding the axe in his turn.[225] But the poet also knows that the revolutionary act he dreams of is dogged by a shadow,[226] that of the axe brandished by the spectre who dwells in his thoughts[227] (and is not a '*revenant*', a ghost from the past). The end of despotism is necessarily 'tragic and bloody' – as was, on a spectacular scale, the French Revolution. Revolutionary violence reproduces, up to a certain point, the violence of despotism, for it both responds to and replicates it [*car elle en fournit la réplique*], even while it provides a necessary condition for abolishing it. This is the Jacobin theme of the 'dictatorship of freedom'; Büchner, too, reveals its tragic core when he put these words in Robespierre's mouth:

> They say that the Terror is an instrument of dictatorship and that our Government therefore resembles a dictatorship. Granted! but only as the sword in the hand of Freedom's heroes resembles the saber with which the satellites of tyrants are armed. If a tyrant rules his brutish subjects through terror he is, as a tyrant, justified; destroy the enemies of freedom through terror and as the founders of the Republic you are no less justified. The Revolutionary Government is the dictatorship of freedom against tyranny.[228]

In establishing a new order, revolutionary violence makes it possible to settle the issue by *founding*, through a creative act rooted in the 'vacuum' of the situation, a *new* legality; yet it leaves a traumatic core behind, an irreducible gulf out of which phantoms continue to surge up.

As the lovely parable of the 'Memoirs' makes clear, it is only by lifting the taboo, an act which presupposes the symbolization of the murder of the King, that one can break out of the circle of oppression and rid history of the executioner's spectre. Sir Olaf, forced to marry the king's daughter, soon falls victim to the executioner's axe and, like all modern knights (despite his medieval armour: spectres, it is true, often wear armour . . .), manages only to 'conquer a grave'.[229] But the poet, by kissing the executioner's daughter, discovers the 'two passions to which he was to devote the rest of [his] life: the love of beautiful women and the love of the French Revolution'.[230] Of course, emancipating history from the phantoms of the past proves an arduous, if not impossible, task: do *revenants* not always begin by coming back? Does not the illusion under which Büchner's Robespierre labours consist in thinking that it is possible to do 'away with them' because 'only dead men never return?'[231] He was quite right – except that their spectral doubles continue to haunt the living. Does not the Bourbon Restoration provide an example of such spectral revenge? Of course, 'one fine morning in July, when the Gallic cock crowed, the ghosts were compelled to disappear'.[232] But twenty years later, there could be no ignoring the fact that the apparitions of Marie-Antoinette's ghost had not ceased. In *Romancero* (1851),[233] it is the spectral return of the rituals of the *ancien régime* that signals the return of her ghost to the Tuileries palace. It would not be going too far to read this poem – written after the defeat of 1848 but before Louis Bonaparte's *coup d'état* – as evidence of Heine's fear (which proved well-founded) that the palace of the Tuileries would again become the seat of a dynastic power. If, as we read in the last stanza, the sun, 'when he sees that ghostly crew ... turns away in fright',[234] this is because, against the ruins of the republic in its death agony, one can already make out the outlines of a new, farcical repetition of the past, the paper-mâché empire of Napoleon III. . . . A failure? Undoubtedly, if you think that the bourgeois society that was created by the Revolution (and did everything in its power to bring the Revolution to an end) continues to repress the constitutive violence of its founding moment, the bourgeois secularization of authority notwithstanding.

Yet the failure is only partial: these spectres of the past bear the mark of a profound dissymmetry. Unlike the German spectres, whose anachronism is in harmony with the German present, the French phantoms have themselves been beheaded: ghostly bodies without heads, they are incapable of 'seeing' the living.[235] In the absence of the 'visor effect',[236] spectres are mere parodies of themselves, survivals of survivals; they are, in other words, spectres devoid of spectral consciousness,[237] archaic, absurd relics whose return is authorized only by the historical retreat that followed the brutal suppression of the 1848 uprisings. In fact, as we have seen, Louis XVI and Marie-Antoinette had already been decapitated in the symbolic order before their heads were chopped off by Dr Guillotin's machine; their beheading was ultimately the work of the thinkers of the Enlightenment, as the late collection *Romancero* reminds us one last time.[238] Without a doubt, Heine seeks to achieve the same guillotine-effect through his political writings and, still more, through the power of his satire, his *Witz*, and the cruelty of his irony.

But Heine's task, as he conceives it, is not confined to helping to exorcize spectres. The poet is well aware that no reality, past, present, or future, lacks its spectral lining [*doublure*] – or rather, as he puts it, its 'ghostly dignity'. There certainly are – to cite only these examples – French and even Parisian spectres other than those of decapitated kings. The essential task is to distinguish the different kinds, and, above all, to play some off against others; that is, to shift the lines of demarcation, always moving and unstable, on the field of 'spectral battle'.[239] To do so, one must set out from a 'blank space', that of political intervention itself, always subject to the temptation of representation. It is subject, as well, to the contingencies of the struggle: the crushing defeat of 1848 – or, more exactly, the trauma to which it gave rise – no doubt explains why, in the view of the altogether Heinean Marx who drew up the balance sheet of defeat called *The Eighteenth Brumaire*, the field of spectral battle as such seems to vanish, its internal distinctions blurred in a history become nightmare.

In fact, the interminable but by no means fruitless quest for emancipation from the phantoms of the past can be understood only in the light of the reception reserved for spectres of another kind: those that come from the future; a future that is, to be sure, sustained by memory, but one whose countenance remains forever unrecognizable behind its masks. We would do well to meet the gaze of these spectres, for they do indeed have one: at times it is ironical; at other times it radiates the calm and the humour of Cromwell standing before the corpse of Charles I.[240] At least three spectral figures of this type cross paths in Heine's work, though not, as it were, 'in person': poetry, communism and Judaism. Yet all three are in secret communication, tied to one another by the same messianic thread.

At first sight, it may seem odd to find poetry included in this typology. By virtue of the position it takes in favour of life, its exaltation of the senses (at least before the 'Nazarene' turn of the years in which the poet was bedridden), and the secret affinity it continues to maintain with the ancient gods, Heine's poetry presents itself as the first of the 'counter-phantoms'.[241] Yet even before illness buried him in his 'mattress-grave', Heine had imagined his own spectralization in another mode, halfway between the gaiety of Paris, with its frivolous, bourgeois gods, and the irony of the German poet, convinced of his superiority to the comic spirit of the French:[242]

> I myself, though a German, if I were dead and should go haunting at night here in Paris – I could certainly not maintain my ghostly dignity if, let us say, one of those goddesses of frivolity who know how to laugh so delightfully to your face came running to meet me at a street corner. If there were really ghosts in Paris, I am convinced, sociable as the French are, that they would seek each other's friendship, even as ghosts, they would soon form ghost clubs, found a café for the dead, publish a newspaper for the dead, a Paris *Revue for the Dead*, and there would soon be soirées for the dead *où l'on fera de la musique*. . . . I would just make arrangements to be buried in Père Lachaise so

that I could go haunting in Paris between twelve and one. What an exquisite hour! You German fellow countrymen, if after my death you come to Paris and catch sight of me here at night as a ghost, don't be alarmed. I will not be spooking in the dreadfully unhappy German manner; I will be spooking for pleasure. In all the ghost stories that I have read the ghost usually has to haunt the places where it buried money. As a precaution, therefore, I am going to bury a few *sous* somewhere on the boulevards. Until now I have only cast my money to the winds in Paris, never buried it under the pavement.[243]

The terrible experience of the 1848 defeats, for which Heine's own suffering and physical decline, with their Christlike overtones, were to serve as an allegory, shattered this vision of gay Parisian ghosts, and even ghost clubs joined in a well-intentioned plot against the living. Immobilized by his illness, sharing a common fate with the vanquished, the poet identifies with Lazarus; he presents himself as a spectre, a living corpse who refuses to rot away in his 'mattress-grave': 'in 1847 . . . I still had some flesh on me and some paganism in me, and I had not yet been emaciated down to a spiritual skeleton now awaiting its final dissolution. But do I still really exist?'.[244] Heine now compares himself to his 'colleague Merlin',[245] the sorcerer who falls victim to his own spells and plots. His urban grave, he says, in which he hears 'not a single green leaf rustling', but only the din of the city ('early and late I hear only the rattling of carriages, hammering, scolding, and strumming on the piano'),[246] reminds him of the 'tolling grave' of the magician of Brozeliand. But, if his grave is less 'harmonious', it is because life, Parisian life, manages to steal into it after all; and Heine, unlike Merlin, never stops hatching new plots. His years of extreme physical suffering were productive ones, especially in terms of poetry. If *Romancero*, with its vision of historical collapse, is 'an account of the crisis of modern lyricism' (Jean-Pierre Lefebvre), the fact that Heine wrote it at all attests to his continuing belief in the mission of poetry, its capacity to articulate this unprecedented experience, and save the discourse of the vanquished from perdition.

Even in this state, like a leper shaking his Lazarus rattle to announce his approach, the poet can still imagine a 'whistling, merry' Germany one day acclaiming his work.[247] Only his heart is broken, *Romancero* echoes back; the weapons of poetry are still unbroken, the other fighters 'close ranks', watching and waiting, as he too did, for the redemptive event.[248] The poet 'dies one last time, unambiguously naming those who will resurrect him, his brothers-in-arms'.[249] The pact that unites him and them provides another token of their fidelity. The preface to *Lutetia*,[250] written four years after *Romancero* appeared, unveils the true countenance of these fighters, and names them once again: only the communists, says Heine, are capable of giving the victors of the day, the nationalist, anti-democratic party that now rules all Europe, 'the *coup de grâce*', the 'fatal blow' that will 'crush' them. Until then, their spectral – even infernal – presence will continue to haunt the massive European reaction, announcing its approaching end.

The figure of the Promise answers to more than one name. Another form of expression runs through Heine's work: Judaism. There can be no question about its 'ghostly dignity'. In *The History of Religion and Philosophy in Germany*, the Jewish people is called a 'ghost-nation',[251] a guardian of memory and also, as *Ludwig Börne* would spell out, of messianic hope: 'this German liberator, perhaps the same one that Israel is waiting for ... O dear Messiah, awaited with such longing!' But this Messiah – whose physiognomy is re-created for us, not without irony, in the description of the 'great rabbi Menasse ben Naphtali of Cracow' – is doubled, undergoing a spectralization in his turn; during the 'terrible days' that followed the July Revolution, the clanking of the golden chains that bind the rabbi's hands begins to sound strangely like the clanking of the phantoms of, perhaps, Barbarosssa, the false Messiah of Teutomaniac nationalism. How, then, is one to distinguish between the two? Heine's answer is that this is a question of time, of the right [*juste*] time, which will also be the time of the just: 'Oh! do not fail us, lovely Messiah, you who want to save not Israel alone, as the superstitious Jews believe, but all suffering humanity! Golden chains, do not break! Bind him fast a little while longer, so that he does not come too early, the savior and King of the world!' But does not the Messiah always come 'too early', at the moment when the golden chains choking the hope of liberation are broken, when time bursts open and is divided in two?[252]

In any event, it is clear that, for Heine, although the future is far from being a homogeneous, empty time, not every moment is 'the strait gate through which the Messiah might enter'.[253] This, no doubt, is because Heine, unlike Benjamin, does not reduce historical development to a single, unending catastrophe; in his view, something irreversible occurred with the experience of the French Revolution and the disenchantment of the world. It is true that the threat of disaster hangs permanently over history – the more so since the forces of liberation have now come upon the scene 'in person'. To combat this danger, however, one needs to consider the period and the conjuncture from their tactical and strategic angles, among others. To recognize the rose in the cross of the present, one has to be able to discern the point where the line of life can break the circle of repetition, the point at which one's partisan position intersects a certain configuration of objective spirit, making possible the irruption of the new, its breakthrough and actual advent.

This is a game – or, more exactly, a struggle; and no guarantees are offered in advance. It is a game in which error can be costly; but it is the game of modern politics, which requires that one abandon the terrain of an ontology of history, even a negative one. In the case of France, Heine fears an 'untimely triumph of the proletarians',[254] who have been too profoundly swayed by the primitive egalitarianism of the earliest Babouv-ist/communist doctrines (this text takes explicit aim at the 'preachers of a republic à la Babeuf'). The risk is that such a triumph will be 'of short duration', that it will merely serve as a prelude to a new Thermidor. No doubt Heine also believes, as we shall see, that the 'German road', on which the religious reformation precedes both the philosophical reform/revolution and the future sociopolitical revolution, can provide the right order, the one that will forestall undesirable complications. But he also knows that a wager of this sort is undecidable, in the true sense of the word: 'only our last descendants will be able to decide whether we deserve praise or censure for elaborating our philosophy first and our revolution only afterwards'.[255] Nothing allows us to transcend the partisan position immanent in life, and the revolution as an affirmation of life, so as to eliminate the risk any wager implies. History decides only after the event. In the case of 1848–49 Germany, everyone knows what it decided.

Yet, after the defeat, Heine once again turned to Judaism to name the irreducible promise. By way of a reference to the poet Yehuda ben Halevy, he once again united poetry, the spiritual quest (the real Yehuda ben Halevy was a court poet active at the height of the Arab-Andalusian period; towards the end of his life, he abandoned Spain and secular poetry to go and live in Jerusalem), and the messianic element. With one last twist of Heine's dialectical irony, however, this messianic element was incarnated in something very much of this world, something very material, even materialist, if not banal: *schalet*, Heine's favourite dish,[256] which Jews eat on the Sabbath. It is the only source of perfect happiness for Prince Israel, whom an evil spell changes, for the rest of the week, into a dog: '*Schalet, shining gleam from Heaven,/ Daughter of Elysium! – / Schiller's ode would sound like this if/ He had ever tasted schalet.*'[257] Schalet 'transfig-ures' [*verkläret*] the eye of the prince, who personifies the fate of the ghostlike people and exposes the falseness of the ancient gods and their diabolic sensuality.[258] But the fact remains that schalet is . . . a dish, and that, as always when Heine refers to food in his work,[259] so here too he is, one last time, thumbing his nose at spiritualism (as the parodic reference to Schiller's 'Ode to Joy' indicates) – this at the very moment when the poet announces his newfound faith in a mysterious 'personal God'. Thus Heine reaffirms the 'right to eat' that he had always defended,[260] a right that constituted one of his two main reasons for ultimately rallying to communism. Judaism accordingly represents the point of convergence of all the figures of Heine's messianism: a 'weak' messianism in the sense that it is tempered by historicist elements and strategic considerations, yet a strong messianism after all, in that it preserves – under the most appalling conditions, when the reaction, by crushing hope, had offered the sharpest possible refutation of any teleology of historical progress – the splinter which, piercing the time of the now, opens on to the poetry of the future.

The other German road: Revolutionary democracy

The anti-Staël

If one were asked to choose just one name to represent the history of the cultural interrelations or 'transfers'[261] between France and Germany, one would surely choose Heine's. At any rate, that choice seemed the obvious one to this German poet from Paris who systematically refused to mention the name of a translator in the French editions of his works, and who, indeed, took on a double identity after moving to France: should we say 'Henri' or 'Heinrich' Heine? – or should it be 'Harry', his secret name, that of his childhood and Jewish heritage?[262] Behind the name 'Heine', in any case, lies an entire lifetime constructed around a 'mission' that Heine did not hesitate – and this in his most conspicuously atheistic text – to commend to the protection of 'Providence': it consisted in promoting reconciliation and mutual understanding between France and Germany.[263] When the poet drew up the definitive, legally binding version of his last will and testament, he proudly affirmed that he had successfully accomplished this mission, his 'great task in life'.[264]

But we must immediately single out the features that identify Heine's as a distinctive position within the multifaceted Franco–German transfer that was literally constitutive of modern German culture. To put it rather summarily: where the poet's predecessors 'culturalized' a political reality, Heine – one might say: the name 'Heine' – functioned like a system for permanently (re)politicizing the cultural tradition thus constituted. A Schiller, reacting spontaneously to the end of the Jacobin experiment,[265] saw no other way to preserve the achievements of the Enlightenment and the French Revolution than to make them part of Germany's purely intellectual special mission. In contrast, Heine offered a political reading of German thought and culture, one which sought, by extracting its revolutionary kernel, to pave the way for a more than merely intellectual revolution that would put an end to Germany's social, political and national backwardness.

This at least partly explains the divisive charge – rather unusual for an author who, by all rights, should long ago have been elevated to the ranks of the revered classics – that Heine's name has had in German history right down to our own time. Heine divides.[266] For he attempted 'what no other German writer of comparable stature had dared to do before him: he participated, actively and intensely, in public affairs'.[267] Despite the game of dissimulation that he had to consent to play in order to be allowed to address a German audience, he made no bones about his basic intentions, attacking the spirit of accommodation and 'moderantism' that was deeply ingrained in the intelligentsia of his country. He was incapable of defining his mission without immediately evoking its political objective: he intended to 'destroy these national prejudices that despots so well know how to turn to their account,'[268] and 'frustrate the plots of the enemies of democracy, who exploit national prejudices and animosities for their own uses'.[269] Thus intransigent defence of the French Revolution and uncompromising hostility to Teutomaniac nationalism constituted the foundations of the Franco–German alliance Heine envisaged.

Hence his attachment to Napoleon – not the 'liberticide Napoleon, the hero of the 18th of Brumaire'[270] who was a mortal enemy of freedom and 'truthless to his mother, the Revolution', nor the Catholic convert, but the 'gonfalonier of democracy', whose troops 'made up the holy legions who defended the cause of the Revolution'.[271] Here Heine confronted, head-on, the founding myth of the German national movement (including the 'liberal' version promoted by the *Burschenschaften*), according to which the anti-Napoleonic wars were 'wars of liberation'. In Heine's opinion, the German princes had simply exploited these wars to promote the ends of a rigid absolutism: 'an attempt was made to arouse public spirit among the Germans, and even the most exalted personages began to talk of German nationality, of a *common* German fatherland, of the unification of the Christian Germanic tribes, of the unity of Germany. We were ordered to be patriotic, and we became patriots – for we do everything our rulers order us to'.[272] The Teutomaniac nationalists never forgave him for such remarks; the mutual hatred between them and Heine was inextinguishable – the more so, as we shall see later, in that Heine not only refused to concede them exclusive rights to the national idea, but was determined to contest their cultural and political hegemony over the cause of German unification.

Inevitably, then, Heine's path crossed that of the intellectual Egeria of the liberal, anti-democratic, anti-Napoleonic French camp, Germaine de Staël. Thanks to her *Germany* [*De l'Allemagne*],[273] de Staël had held an undeniably powerful[274] monopoly over the French access routes to German culture for two decades following the publication of the volume. Beginning with the very first edition (1835) of his book of the same name, Heine chose to include a 'frank admission' in the preface: 'I have constantly had in view the work of this grandmother of doctrinaires, and it is with the intention of making reparation that I have given to my book the same title.'[275] Much more was at issue than is suggested by the polemical barbs in Heine's 'Confessions' (which appeared twenty years after the first edition of his *Germany*), aimed, in particular, at de Staël's 'hatred' for Napoleon – a kind of frustrated, inverted love which, according to Heine, was 'the soul of *De l'Allemagne*'.[276] Of course, Heine's *Germany* also mentions de Staël's connivance with the leaders of the European reaction and the Bourbons, who had been carted back to France by the occupying armies of the Holy Alliance. It also dwells on the role of August Schlegel and the rest of the Romantic coterie, who danced attendance on de Staël, and were her unique source of information, which was partial in both senses of the word. Heine's aim in revealing de Staël's sources to the French public was to foil her basic strategy, which consisted in deliberately creating a climate of confusion that, as it were, allowed her to smuggle the now nationalistic and reactionary message of German Romanticism into the camp of the French Romantics, who had rather quickly rallied to the 'party of progress'.[277] In the book proper, Heine couches his polemics in more moderate terms: when de Staël writes without benefit of an intermediary, he says, her 'book is good, even admirable'; but 'the instant' that, under the influence of Schlegel and the 'coterie', 'she encourages . . . certain ultramontane tendencies which are in direct contradiction to her Protestant enlightenment, her book becomes wretched and unbearable'.[278]

Heine's criticisms go deeper when he presents de Staël's imaginary Germany as a set of fantasies that she projects on to the country because of her own political commitments in France – which, to be sure, are once again ascribed to her hatred for Napoleon.[279] Like Tacitus' *Germania*, which is merely an oblique discussion of Rome,[280] de Staël, says Heine, constantly discusses France in her book – except that her own country appears 'in absentia', negatively, via the selective, one-sided image of its neighbour to the east, suddenly endowed with all the virtues that the

Grande Nation supposedly lacks. *Germany* is indeed that, but it is a great deal more besides; de Staël's book, informed by a political project from beginning to end, represents an out-and-out attack on the ideas of the Enlightenment and the French Revolution. What Madame de Staël seeks in the depths of the German soul is, above all else, something to set over against the French Revolution and the 'materialism' and political rationalism that paved the way for it, even if what is involved is only a *supplément d'âme*, an indispensable complement to action, not a model to be imitated as such. In her dualistic schema, the 'enthusiasm' engendered by the contemplative, speculative tendencies of the soul is called upon to sustain (and amend) 'character', whose natural tendency is to take decisive action for freedom.[281] Freedom is embodied in England,[282] the beacon of liberalism and a pillar of the counter-revolutionary coalition. Enthusiasm by itself is insufficient; care must be taken lest the Germans, for whom politics is something radically alien, 'introduce metaphysics into business'.[283] For there is no mistaking the fact that German spiritualism, with all its speculative purity, simply proves that it is impossible to find a rational foundation for the goals of human action, and testifies to the dangers of any universalistic enterprise. Hence the incredible 'reading' (one hardly dares use the term) of Kant as a defender of the founding role of 'sentiment' and a very traditional 'doctrine of the faculties'.[284]

From the Romantics, Madame de Staël takes the great anti-revolutionary credo: the revolt against materialism, the sciences, and the 'tyranny' of reason, all of them attributed to 'the era of pride', that of the Enlightenment, which is accused of destroying 'the prospects of the imagination', 'the terrors of conscience', and 'every belief of the heart',[285] and accordingly blamed for the disenchantment of the world. Hence the exaltation of sentiment as 'the primitive fact of the mind' and guarantor of its 'sublime identity', which is jeopardized by the heartless 'labors of anatomy' effected by analysis and argument.[286] An irrational conception of action, traced back to the inner strength of 'character' and the capacity to make decisions,[287] stands as the corollary to this defence of feeling, especially enthusiasm, the feeling typical of the German soul. England is, precisely, a 'free nation', as opposed to rationalistic France, blemished by the 'black spot' of materialism, which inevitably breeds the 'darkness' of revolution.[288] It is true that England gave birth, with Hobbes and Locke, to materialist, anti-moral (utilitarian) doctrines; but the task of applying them was, without exception, left to France, and the task of refuting them to Germany.[289] At present, however, England combines enthusiasm with character, decision-making capacity with reflection. This is why, 'animated by a determination holy and terrible', it is able to lead all the countries of

counter-revolutionary Europe in the war effort. It is most significant that
de Staël's spiritualist exaltation of peaceful Germany, of the marriage of
'sentiment' and 'character', should culminate in an encomium to war[290] –
counter-revolutionary war, of course; it thus reveals the true objective of
any and all attempts to aestheticize the political,[291] including those
dripping with mawkish sentimentality.

It will have become clearer why, even putting aside conjunctural
considerations, Heine had no choice but to confront de Staël's work. His
Germany meets the challenge she throws down: to outline an overall
approach to German culture that is radically different from hers. To her
exaltation of spiritualism, Heine replies by revealing the 'grand secret' of
German philosophy, its revolutionary kernel: a critique of religion that
culminates in atheism. Against her vision of a drowsy Germany lost in
dreamy contemplation and pure speculation, it pits the revolutionary
traditions of German national history, rooted in the Reformation, Luther's
activity, and the Peasant Wars. To her notion that Germany's mission is to
provide the cultural cement for a European alliance against the French
Revolution, Heine responds by drawing a rigorous parallel between
Germany's intellectual development and the different stages of that
Revolution. Indeed, his argument peaks in a prediction of the coming
German revolution, which will not merely prolong that of 1789–93, but
outstrip it, thanks, precisely, to Germany's long intellectual revolution.

Heine's anti-Staël thus becomes a means of giving systematic expression
to the theme of a radical alternative to the dominant road in Germany. It
served a whole generation as a Bible of subversion, and dealt a serious
blow to the Romantics' domination of intellectual relations between
France and Germany. It is hardly an exaggeration to say that Heine's anti-
religious, revolutionary interpretation of Hegel and German thought in
general marks the true beginnings of the Young Hegelian movement.[292]
We may take the ideologue of the Bismarckian reaction, Heinrich von
Treitschke, at his word: Young Germany, said Treitschke, especially its
emblematic figure Heine, although they did not 'intervene directly in
Germany', helped to 'shake the bases of state, Church, and society and
pave the way for the Revolution of 1848'.[293]

A national-popular narrative

Heine had worked out his riposte to Madamme de Staël even before he
began to compose the essays assembled in *Germany*; the essence of it is
to be found in his version of the grand Hegelian narrative of the history

of German philosophy. This narrative enabled him to treat as inextricably interlinked two phenomena that de Staël, like other counter-revolutionary thinkers, strove at all costs to hold apart: the German national tradition and the revolution. Like Hegel, Heine continues to locate the founding moment of this tradition in Luther's Reformation, which he deemed to be the dawn of a 'new age', as he would say in a roughly contemporaneous autobiographical sketch: the Reformation not only gave birth to 'a liberal religion', but was 'the point of departure for the German revolution'.[294]

However, in a very Romantic evocation of German legends and tales, Heine situates his narrative's point of departure well before the moment of the Reformation.[295] The persistence of an age-old, pre-Christian religious tradition, which began to play a fundamentally ambiguous role when it was intertwined with Christianity, could of course foster pantheism and the 'pandemonic',[296] but it constituted a foundation that was particularly resistant to spiritualism of a 'Nazarene' cast. This is a good example of what Georg Lukács refers to as Heine's way of preserving, 'in modern form, the popular traditions of the German Enlightenment and Romanticism'.[297] Heine's synthesis builds the truth contained in these popular traditions into a founding narrative that thereby acquires historical depth and, in a certain sense, the legitimacy that comes from having roots in a national culture: as such, it is in a position to challenge the hegemony of the narrative constructed by reactionary Romanticism.

Let us, however, again consider Luther's inaugural act, which Heine regards as authentically revolutionary. Its significance is twofold. On the one hand, Luther 'was at once a dreamy mystic and a practical man of action. His thoughts had not merely wings, but also hands; he spoke and acted. He was not merely the tongue of his age, but also its sword.'[298] In a word, he was both 'the most *German* man in our history'[299] and a 'complete man'.[300] Luther therefore constituted an event in German history, for he lifted the curse inherent in the rupture between an overdeveloped theory and an anaemic practice. In breaking with traditional authority, that of the institution and the Letter, he firmly tied the destiny of the new religion to that of reason, 'acknowledged . . . as the supreme judge in all religious controversies. Thus arose in Germany', Heine adds, 'what is variously called intellectual freedom or freedom of thought.'[301]

But Luther went still further. He not only dared to unify theory and practice, but also violated a second taboo deeply anchored in the German tradition. He was unwilling to see freedom of thought granted to only a handful of people living and working in closed circles (for example, scholastics who conducted their disputations in Latin in the medieval universities); he carried debate into 'the market-place', where men could now hold 'disputations ... in the German vernacular, without fear or unease'.[302] Heine thus connects – with Luther's translation of the Bible serving as the link – the very creation of the national language with the emancipatory gesture that established this 'religious democra[cy]'.[303] Luther's gesture – which was not always distinguished by its delicacy, and sometimes even exhibited a 'plebeian crudity' akin to Danton's, or that of 'a preacher on the Mountain'[304] – was well and truly the equivalent of a 'religious revolution'; and revolutions, as everyone knows, 'are not made with orange-blossom'.[305] Indeed, Heine, like Hegel, had already conceived the idea that there was an internal link between the revolution/religious reformation and the peasant uprisings in England[306] and, especially, Germany. While he does point to certain circumstances which tend to excuse Luther's 'disreputable' condemnation of the German peasants, he nevertheless clearly affirms that 'Christ, who died for the equality and brotherhood of mankind, did not reveal his Word to serve as the tool of Absolutism, and Thomas Münzer was right and Luther in the wrong.'[307] He goes on to recall the martyrdom and mass killings inflicted on the peasantry after its rebellion was put down, repeating, with each horror he evokes, 'they were in the right'. But the peasants' sacrifices were not in vain, for, 'in the year of grace 1789, the same strife began in France for equality and brotherhood, on the same grounds, against the same class in power';[308] this revolt, Heine admits, was not pursued to the end, but neither was it crushed, as it had been in Germany. He makes much of the parallel between the Reformation and the French Revolution, going so far as to compare Luther's sermon to a 'battle-hymn', a 'Marseillaise of the Reformation' that heralded other battles and the advent of a new revolution. 'Perhaps', he adds, 'we shall soon need the fierce old words for similar struggles.'[309]

But the religious Reformation and philosophy were linked from the start: that, as Hegel had already shown, was the distinctive feature of the German Enlightenment. A 'daughter of the Protestant church' and 'one of the most important results' of the freedom of thought won in the Reformation,[310] German philosophy repeated the emancipatory gesture of the defrocked monk who defied papal authority and the reigning theology of his day. This, moreover, was why people's attitudes towards Protestantism tended to reveal their political preferences, and why the transition to reactionary, anti-democratic and pro-feudal positions went hand in hand with a retreat towards Catholicism that could take the extreme form of conversion.[311] Heine's presentation of the history of German philosophy, although it respects the rules a work of 'popular' philosophy is supposed to follow, is nevertheless far more than a simple popularization of the Hegelian vision of things. It exhibits – as Jean-Pierre Lefebvre points out – a 'modern point of view'[312] that treats philosophy as a discipline with essentially political stakes. Thus Heine pursues two objectives at once. He sets out to show the sense in which German philosophy truly represents an intellectual revolution that is in every respect the equal of the French Enlightenment and the French Revolution, and naturally convergent with them; even more importantly, he shows that this revolution heralds another that will not be confined to the intellectual sphere, and will outstrip its French antecedents.

The revolutionary kernel or 'secret' of German philosophy is contained in a single word, pantheism: 'no one says so, but everyone knows this: pantheism is the open secret in Germany'.[313] Such is the essential lesson that Heine carried away with him from his student days in Berlin. They had been significantly marked by an episode that occurred late in the *Pantheismusstreit*, a public confrontation between Hegel and the reactionary current, with Schleiermacher at its head, over pantheism and the critique of religion.[314] Pantheism, rooted in the pre-Christian tradition, represented the true alternative to the spiritualism defended by Madame de Staël and the Romantics. That is, it made it possible to avoid the materialism/idealism dichotomy by displacing the question, transforming a purely philosophical debate on the origins of knowledge (doctrines according to which there exist a priori ideas versus those which say that knowledge derives from experience and the senses) into a confrontation between two social systems, spiritualism and sensualism, the second of which (thanks to Spinoza) was gradually evolving out of pantheism. In short, in Germany, the authentic – and formidable – adversary of spiritualism, the 'iniquitous presumption of the spirit which . . . tries to crush matter',[315] was pantheism, an identification of God with the world that culminated in the self-consciousness of the human species; it was not materialism, or the bastardized variant of it known as deism.

To pit pantheism, the authentic German tradition, against rationalism (although Leibniz and Spinoza were products of the Cartesian school), the French Enlightenment (to which Lessing had firmly bound the German *Aufklärung*) or the French Revolution was to fall victim to a misconception, at the very least: 'the political revolution based on the principles of French materialism will find supporters, not opponents, in the pantheists; but supporters who have drawn their convictions from a deeper source, from a religious synthesis'.[316] If one took the political revolution (above all, as we shall see, the politico-social revolution) as one's yardstick, then there was nothing for it but to acknowledge that pantheism (and, consequently, the German tradition) had taken the *lead* over materialism (the French tradition).[317] Heine states this in three different ways. To begin with, he suggests the idea that pantheism, drawing on 'a deeper source', a 'religious synthesis' which he held to be a form of the popular spirit, is at opposite poles from materialism's characteristic abstraction (a philosophical tradition cut off from the life of the people) and one-sidedness (contempt for the spirit). In this conception of a 'world-view' that can satisfy the demand for totality, we plainly have a secularized equivalent for the Hegelian idea of a revolution preceded by a religious reform.

Moreover, on the properly political level, pantheism makes it possible to adopt, but also to go beyond, a fundamental principle of the French and, indeed, any other revolution: 'the great watchword of the Revolution, uttered by St.-Just, "Bread is the people's first right", runs in our version, "Bread is the divine right of man". We are not fighting for the human rights of the people, but for the divine rights of man.'[318] In other words, pantheism makes it possible (see above) both to transcend the crude egalitarianism and the levelling preached by the Jacobins/*sans-culottes*, and to resolve the social question that was posed by the French Revolution but then left in suspense because the Revolution remained unfinished. It is Heine's belief, as we have seen, that communism will ensure that the revolutionary programme is concretely superseded in this way as soon as it ceases to be an exclusively French affair and becomes an essentially German one. In the final reckoning contained in his autobiographical 'last will and testament', he gives the German communists full marks for their theoretical development. He numbers himself among their precursors, since, with his *Germany*, he served as a bridge between 'the proletarians' and 'the most advanced intellects, the philosophers of the great school'.[319]

Finally, Heine points to a third factor: the existence of a messianic element in pantheism, which helps to explain why it has outstripped materialism. Pantheism is Germany's 'open secret', just as communism is the 'secret name' of the antagonism that traverses the bourgeois order. Pantheism is an open secret because it is – and, in a certain sense, always will be – something to come. Its spokesmen are invested with a prophetic function. But the two great men among them – Luther and Lessing, the initiator of the Reformation and the artisan of the German Enlightenment – did no more than announce a third Messiah, the veritable Messiah whose coming will be the sign that the moment of emancipation is at hand: 'Yes, there shall come a third to accomplish what Luther began and Lessing continued ... the third liberator [will come].'[320] Here Heine takes up an idea developed by the second liberator, Lessing, who divided human history into three ages. The first began with the ancient covenant, sealed by Moses; the second with the new one, brought by Christ; the third age is that of the self-education of the human race, which is still awaiting its Messiah.

But, Heine adds, this Messiah will not be a philosopher, a new Lessing. Rather, he will be a new Luther, a man who will bring the tidings of a new alliance between thought and action – a complete, thoroughly German man. Heine's verdict brooks no appeal: 'our philosophical revolution has come to an end. Its great circle was closed by Hegel.'[321] If he invests the concept of revolution with something of its old, cyclical significance here, it is in order to round off his argument about 'the end of philosophy': German philosophy has now reached its limits, for it has developed all the mediations by virtue of which it had, with Hegel, arrived at its concept. Now it must make room for the revolution *tout court*, which it has simultaneously accompanied, prepared and anticipated.

The cycle of German philosophy (but we should perhaps, respecting Heine's metaphor, call it a spiral)[322] is characterized by a progressive movement which, in its turn, comprises an alternation of revolutions and restorations, acts of rupture but also compromises, tragic and comic moments which can punctuate the career of one and the same thinker, and find their culmination in Hegel's grand system. Take, for example, Kant: Heine pays tribute to the *Critique of Pure Reason* as the dawn of an 'intellectual revolution' whose importance rivalled that of the French Revolution; he celebrates the day it was published as 'deism's twenty-first of January', and credits the book itself with toppling 'the keystone of the intellectual *ancien régime*'.[323] The *Critique* dealt a fatal blow to religion: thanks to it, the heavens were emptied of all transcendence, while, on earth, one could detect only a faint echo of the last rites being administered to 'a dying God'.[324] Kant was Robespierre's rival in intellectual terrorism and Republican virtue. But 'by heaven! there is another play to be performed. After tragedy comes farce.' Kant, who has 'so far' 'played the tragic part of the most inexorable philosopher ... stormed heaven and put the entire garrison to the sword' – Kant 'distinguishes between theoretical reason and practical reason, and with the latter, as though with a magic wand, he restores to life the corpse of deism, which theoretical reason had killed'.[325] Like Luther in the face of the peasant rebellion, Kant retreats behind the results of his own critique, offering his faithful, pious acolyte Lampe the consolation of seeing him turn down the path of compromise and concession.

Thereafter, the trajectory of German philosophy is subject to a rep-

etition compulsion: 'not only Herr Joseph Schelling, but also Fichte and
Kant, in a certain sense, may be accused of apostasy'. 'The initiator dies
. . . or becomes a renegade'[326] – such would appear to be the curse under
which German thought labours. Fichte, too, began as an atheist; with his
'Appeal to the Public', he defied the taboo of self-censorship and the
'limited publicity' allowed to the intelligentsia.[327] But it was not long
before he too, like so many others, took the path traced by his intellectual
master, the sage of Königsberg. Similarly, a number of different Goethes
coexisted in the same personage: 'the ministerial Goethe with his concili-
ations and his prudent reticences',[328] the pantheist who advocated political indifferentism and aesthetic contemplation of the world, the
unrelenting adversary of Nazarene spiritualism and the critic of the
Romantic reaction (Heine called Goethe's anti-Romantic polemic 'Goethe's eighteenth Brumaire'), the 'enemy of the Cross' whose 'majestic
form was never contorted by Christian contrition', and the man Schlegel
thought to belittle by describing him as 'a pagan converted to Moham-
medanism' because of his fascination with the Orient.[329]

Hegel represents both the most fully developed synthesis of this oscillation and also the moment when the contradiction bursts into view,
opening the way for a new moment of historical development. That is why
Heine wavers in his judgement of his former teacher, even if we leave
aside the very problematic (because, in a certain sense, still Hegelian)[330]
repudiation of Hegel which, under the impact of the 'Nazarene turn',
appears in Heine's last texts. At certain times (in the early 1830s) Heine
describes Hegel as an 'eclectic', a partisan of the golden mean, 'the
Orléans of Philosophy',[331] and at other times (early in the following
decade, with a touch of self-criticism for the youthful severity of his earlier
judgement)[332] as the true champion of freedom whose message, because
it was formulated 'in such muddily-scholastic terms, so entangled in
perplexing clauses', was accessible to 'the initiated' alone.[333] Let me add
that the earlier judgement, delivered at a time when, in Europe, the
citizen-king still seemed to embody the hopes raised by July 1830, is less
pejorative than it appears to be. Hegel is never identified as a Restoration
thinker; and even when Heine criticizes him for having, 'like Herr
Schelling . . . provided some very disturbing justifications for the existing
order in church and state', he carefully distinguishes Hegel's intentions,
principles, and even the effects of his activity from those of people such
as, precisely, Schelling, who 'twist like worms in the ante-chambers of an
absolutism which is both practical and theoretical' and 'forg[e] . . . fetters
for the mind'.[334]

Yet the fact remains that, with Hegel, philosophy's historical mission has come to an end. Its limits are comparable to those of the Orléanist compromise, the fruit of an abortive revolution, the ultimate mediation preceding and, in a certain sense, preparing new political upheavals. The Hegelian moment appears as the last one in which the contradictory tendencies in philosophy – Kant's Jacobins, Fichte's Bonapartists, and aristocrats *à la* Schelling – could coexist, while preserving what still could be preserved of their truth content and emancipatory charge.[335] Thereafter, philosophy either becomes 'idle and useless shadow-boxing' – the business of a handful of reactionary thinkers who preach 'metaphysical abstractions' to young Germans, encouraging them 'to forget the most pressing demands of the age' and rendering them 'unfit for practical life'[336] – or overcomes its separation from practice and becomes politics, henceforth casting its lot in with that of the German revolution.

That is clearly what is happening in Germany, according to Heine. At the moment when philosophy passes on the torch, it can legitimately say: 'Mission accomplished'. The big – and the only – difference between the Germany which confronted the first French Revolution, as Fichte describes it in a 22 May 1799 letter to Rheinhold, and the Germany which has felt the repercussions of the *Trois Glorieuses*, does not reside in anything remotely resembling a retreat on despotism's part – here Heine sees only a 'melancholy resemblance to the most recent condition of Germany'. The 'single point of difference', he says, lies in the fact 'that during the former period the spirit of liberty flourished among the learned, among poets and men of letters generally, whereas nowadays this spirit finds a far more ready utterance among the active masses, among artisans and tradespeople'.[337] Philosophy is in the process of moving beyond the abstraction of the Enlightenment; it is negating itself by becoming practice and becoming 'people' – indeed, a people of workers and artisans (and thus, tendentially, a 'people-class'); and it is doing so not in the sense of an imaginary identification of the intellectuals with the people, but in the continuity of a political practice that links the fight for intellectual emancipation with the popular struggle for freedom.

Paraphrasing the passage in which Fichte hails the French Revolution, Heine writes: 'German philosophy is a matter of importance that affects the entire human race, and only our last descendants will be able to decide whether we deserve praise or censure for elaborating our philosophy first and our revolution only afterwards.'[338] Like any political enterprise, the German road to revolution carries its share of undecidability, for reasons having to do with the indeterminate nature of all struggle. But, in so far as anyone can hazard a judgement, Heine's is favourable at the moment when he writes *On the History of Religion and Philosophy in Germany*: 'I rather think that a methodical nation like ourselves had to begin with the Reformation; only then could we transfer our attention to philosophy, and only after completing our philosophy could we turn to the political revolution. I find this sequence very reasonable.'[339] It would appear that 'reasonable' should be construed here in the narrow sense of 'corresponding adequately to a certain rationality immanent in history'. Owing to the long preparation carried out by the Reformation and by philosophy, the spirit of the German people has reached a level of self-consciousness that puts it at the head of the European peoples, and thus at the forefront of historical development.

Germany's extreme backwardness is thus dialectically transformed into a head start; the France–Germany relationship has been turned around. It is Germany which now finds itself on the threshold of a new historical moment, a new tragedy that will succeed to the farce of the bourgeois epoch. Whence, as we shall see, the greater radicalism – or, rather, *genuine* radicalism – of the German revolution: 'a play will be performed in Germany, compared with which the French Revolution will seem a mere inoffensive idyll'.[340] But the Heinean dialectic holds many more surprises in store. Far from culminating in a joyous apotheosis, the book called 'On the History of Religion and Philosophy in Germany' ends in a warning, addressed to the French, about what to expect in the event that Germany should be 'freed'. In the drama to come from the other side of the Rhine, in this tragedy of the future, familiar figures suddenly loom up, phantoms whose presence continues to trouble their heirs. Will the curse of the past, the burden of the dead, overtake the living at the last moment, transforming that ultimate moment of redemption into the last moment of the Apocalypse?

Waiting for dawn: The German revolution between dream and reality

Like everything else that came from across the Rhine, German thought could not exist without its spectral double; or let us say, rather, that it was unable to avoid its own spectralization – all the more so in that, in this somnolent country, thought wore a nocturnal aspect from the outset, that of the dream whose work, precisely, accompanies sleep. If, as we have already seen, the French – and especially the Parisian – night is virtually indistinguishable from day, alive with joyous activity and sparkling colour, the German night appears, in contrast, decidedly lunar; it is wholly given over to dreaming, the German activity (but in what sense?) *par excellence,* the veritable national pastime.[341] It concentrates within itself all the ambivalence, the inner reversibility, and the disruptiveness typical of the association of dream images.

Heine pushes the Hegelian metaphors of the moments of night and day as far as they will go; or, rather, he bends them to his purposes through inversion and distantiation, as usual. Dawn is the moment of freedom; dusk is the moment when, after the labour of reason, the owl of Minerva takes her flight to observe a life-form from on high at the very moment when it begins to go into decline. But what happens *after* dusk? What is the status of the night, of the nocturnal but also the diurnal dream, and, consequently, of the *entre-deux* represented by dawn and dusk? These questions comprise one of the basic themes of Romanticism, from Novalis's 'Hymns to the Night' to the second act of *Tristan*.[342] The theme takes on new significance with Heine. 'What did we do last night?', the poet wonders, and answers:

> Yes, we dreamed, in our German fashion; that is, we philosophized. True, not about matters which concerned us immediately or which had just happened; no, we philosophized about the reality of things in and of themselves, about the ultimate grounds of existence, and similar metaphysical and transcendental visions, while the bloody spectacles performed by our western neighbour sometimes disturbed us, nay, even irritated us, since not infrequently French bullets whistled their way straight into our philosophical systems and swept away whole shreds.[343]

Mere idle reverie, an anodyne escape from reality, a flight from the sound and the fury of history? Matters are not that simple, says Heine, adding:

> It is strange yet true that the practical activity of our neighbours on the other side of the Rhine has a unique elective affinity with our philosophical dreams in complacent Germany. By merely comparing the history of the French Revolution with that of German philosophy one might be led to believe that the French, who had so much real business on hand, for which they had to stay awake, had asked us to sleep and dream for them, and that our German philosophy is nothing but the dream of the French Revolution.[344]

The rest of the passage pursues the parallel, which we have already mentioned, between the phases of this dream and those of reality.[345]

In *Germany*, the parallel between German philosophy and the French Revolution is taken up again and developed at length; but, in the process, it is given a new twist. This time the comparison is favourable to German thought: 'this book [the *Critique of Pure Reason*] ... initiated an intellectual revolution in Germany which offers the most remarkable analogies with the material revolution in France, and *must strike the profound thinkers as equally important.* It develops in the same phases, and the most curious parallelism exists between the two.'[346] German philosophy is not merely a dream; it is a revolution in itself, one that prepares and announces another. The dream is wholly invested by the function of anticipatory consciousness immanent within it. It is therefore surrounded by all the ambivalence of a projection that is at once desired and feared, nightmarish and liberating. Heine's tone now turns resolutely prophetic, even apocalyptic, in a twofold sense: it is the tone of revelation, but also that in which one foretells a terrifying event:

> When you hear the thunder and crashing, you children next door, you French people, then take care not to meddle in the work that we will be accomplishing in Germany; or else it might be the worse for you. . . . Do not laugh at my advice, the advice of a dreamer. . . . Do not laugh at the visionary who expects the same revolution to occur in the phenomenal realm as has happened in the realm of the mind. Thought precedes action as lightning precedes thunder. German thunder, of course, being German, is not very agile, and rolls along rather slowly; but it will arrive in due course, and when you hear such a crash as has never yet been heard in the history of the world, then you will know that German thunder has finally reached its goal.[347]

Let us recapitulate. What, to begin with, is at stake here? Heine has gone back to Hegel's question, that of the relationship between Germany and France construed as the relationship between theory and practice. France stands for action, or even sheer activity; Germany is the land of 'tranquil theory' evoked by Hegel, so peaceful that it may be said to have quite simply fallen asleep. But to sleep is to dream; and, as Heine uses it, the term 'dream' condenses all sorts of ambiguities. Mere speculative dreaming as opposed to action, the German dream is also the dream nourished by this action itself. It is quite as if France, absorbed by the urgent need to act, had delegated to Germany the task of elaborating the theory of its actions. German philosophy may be a dream, engendered by its unbridgeable distance from the world of action; but it is a *dream of revolution* in both senses of the phrase: a dream which the *real* revolution will itself have dreamed with the aid of the thinkers across the Rhine; and, as well, a dream of a revolution to come – an anticipation, in thought, of a German revolution.

The function of German philosophy as defined by Heine thus turns out to be very similar to that of Ernst Bloch's 'daylight fantasy'.[348] Contrary to the nocturnal dream, dominated by a chaotic flood of images that surge up from a remote past and are subject to the censorship – relaxed, but not abolished – of the Unconscious, the daydream, rich in images of freedom that elude the censorship of the Ego, is orientated towards communication with others, transformative action, the ambitious desire for a better world. ' "Reverie",' Bloch declares, 'unlike the usual nocturnal "dream", can possibly contain marrow and, instead of the idleness or even the self-enervation which certainly are to be found here, a tireless incentive towards the actual attainment of what it visualizes.'[349] No, the owl of Minerva does not necessarily take wing at dusk; she 'wants to glimmer with red dawn'.[350] That is why the daydream has, for Bloch, the anticipatory function characteristic of thought and theory: it is 'that dream of a matter in nature and history which the matter has of itself and which belongs both to its *tendency* and to the settlement of its *Totum* and *essence*'.[351] The contents of this dream, quite unlike the disguised, transformed contents of the nocturnal dream, already belong to the future; it 'comes itself out of self- and world-extension forwards',[352] helping us to discern a 'not yet' that clears the path to the future.

Heine, setting out from the same tissue of metaphors, comes to the same conclusion when, discussing 'the somnambulist' historian Michelet, he once again dons the mask of an officially acknowledged confidant of Hegel: 'My great teacher, the late Hegel, said to me once: "If anyone had ever written down the dreams which men had dreamed during a certain period of time, one might gather from those dreams a very accurate picture of the spirit of that time." Michelet's French History is such a collection of visions – a dream-book. . . . In fact, to describe that age of somnambulism, there was needed just such a somnambulist as Michelet.'[353] Are we to conclude that, as in Bloch's teleology, a concept like that of the spirit of the times, of which the dream is finally only one manifestation among others, guarantees, for Heine too, that the actual course of events will correspond to the 'dream-book', whether the book's authors know it or not?[354] Here, doubtless, we should limit the analogy between Heine and Bloch: the ambivalence of the *nocturnal* dream clings to Heine's philosophy-dream of revolution.[355] To the very end, it continues to bear the marks of its distance from practice, moving within the celestial spheres of speculation; in this respect it is not very different from visions of a religious kind. Its very content makes it a gratifying dream of the reappropriation of freedom and power, a dream of the future; yet it is a dream of the future constantly haunted by its other, the nightmare of an apocalyptic eruption of uncanny, archaic forces. The ghosts of the past mingle with the spectres of the future; only a political intervention is capable of separating them, or, rather, of productively shifting the lines of demarcation.

We would perhaps do better to speak of a 'secret affinity' than of a 'ruse of historiography' here. The first of these two phrases is Heine's; he uses it to account for the correspondence between the intellectual sphere which is the most speculative and apparently the most remote from all practical considerations, and the deepest, and often most deeply hidden, tendencies of an age. The phrase occurs in the course of a lovely allegorical description of a shell (representing German thought) which continues to echo with the sounds of the sea (the French Revolution) even when it is far from it:

> This phenomenon [of secret affinity or communion at a distance] reminds me of those large sea-shells sometimes placed as ornaments on the mantel-shelf, which, however distant they may be from the sea, at once begin to murmur when the hour of flood-tide arrives and when the waves are dashing against the shore. When the revolutionary tide began to flow in Paris, that great human ocean, when its waves surged and roared amongst you here, German hearts across the Rhine were resounding and murmuring in response.[356]

Nothing guarantees that those who obey this murmur will meet with success, and we soon find Heine evoking the tragic fate of first-generation German republicans such as Georg Forster or Andreas Riedel, forced to choose between the *misère* of exile and the obscurity of a prison cell. Moreover, no one could guarantee – the exile Heine was well placed to say so – that the fate of the democrats of the next generation would be much different from that of their predecessors.[357]

Yet, Heine notes, something *has* changed in Germany since the day when the first Jacobins were waging their desperate struggles. July 1830 had greater impact on the other side of the Rhine than 1789 did,[358] the smaller scale of the July Revolution notwithstanding; to convince oneself of this, one need only compare the festival of Hambach Castle (1832) with the Wartburg festival (1817), or, in the realm of direct action, Büchner's attempted insurrection (1834) with the assassination of Kotzebue (1819). In the immediate aftermath of the Hambach events, Heine wonders, with amazement: 'Can it be true that the silent land of dreams has begun to live and act? Who could have imagined it before July 1830?'.[359] He points to Hambach as proof that the German soul is alive, or, rather, has attained self-consciousness, even if the body it dwells in is 'sleep-bound'. Hambach showed, not that the struggle for a German republic would succeed, but that it would continue: 'I am certain that when we shall long have decayed in our graves there will be strife in Germany, with word and sword, for the Republic. For the Republic is an *idea*, and Germans never yet abandoned one till they had fought it out to its last consequences.'[360] Although Heine would subsequently shower the organizers of the Hambach assembly with sarcasm for their cowardice, he nevertheless considered the event a missed occasion for a 'general uprising' in Germany.[361] Its rather inglorious outcome notwithstanding, Hambach was a turning point, for it confirmed that the nationalistic, Teutomaniac, anti-democratic tendency was in the minority (Heine had always considered it to be the absolute enemy within the German national movement itself).[362] For the first time, in the 'struggle . . . for German unity' – 'the only progressive idea that this early opposition movement [of the type responsible for the events at Wartburg] has brought to market'[363] – revolutionary democracy has a chance to take the upper hand. Hambach was a victory of spirit over the 'phantom' of the past; it was the victory of 'French liberalism' – that is, of democracy – over the 'narrow-minded Teutomania' of the old Germany, quick to burn books and throw itself into military exercises with a vengeance.[364] Now that this moral victory has been won, it is only a matter of time before the German revolution breaks out.

For Heine, the only question about the future runs as follows: 'Thus, since we [have] successfully come full cycle in philosophy, it is natural that we now are proceeding into politics. Will we here follow the same course? Will we open our course with the system of the *Comité du salut public*, or with the system of the *Ordre légal?* These questions fill all hearts with trembling, and whoever has something precious to lose, be it only his own head, whispers timidly: "Will the German Revolution be a dry one, or a red and wet one?".'[365] As for the answer, it not only runs counter to Madame de Staël's thesis, but also flies in the face of the pre-1848 Romantic spirit generally. According to Heine, it is precisely the idealism of the German tradition which breeds radicalism and revolutionary intransigence of the sort that makes all the admirers of a drowsy Germany peopled with introverted musicians, peaceful thinkers, and retiring aesthetes blanch with horror.

Even more clearly in the German than in the French case, philosophy, says Heine, is a factor that tends to radicalize the political struggle: 'although the German revolution will follow Kant's critiques, Fichte's transcendental idealism, not to mention the philosophy of nature, it will not turn out any milder or gentler for that. These doctrines have assisted the development of revolutionary forces which are only waiting for the day when they can burst forth and fill the world with horror and admiration.'[366] The philosophers – at any rate, the heirs to the great idealist tradition – will one day be called upon to play a role of the highest importance, a role in which they will display greater energy and zeal than the French Jacobins. That day will see the emergence of Kantians who are as devoid of piety for the phenomenal world as Kant was towards God; they will ravage the soil of our European life mercilessly with swords and axes in order to root out the last vestiges of the past. Armed Fichteans will appear on the scene, whose fanatical wills cannot be restrained by either fear or selfishness; for they live in the spirit and defy matter, like the early Christians, who likewise could not be overcome by physical torments or physical pleasures. Indeed, in a social upheaval such transcendental idealists would be even more inflexible than the early Christians; for the latter endured earthly torments in order to attain to the bliss of heaven, while the transcendental idealist regards the torments themselves as mere illusion and is inaccessibly entrenched behind his own ideas.[367]

For Heine, thought is not merely *flatus voci*; it is eminently concrete, and owes its existence to real practices seeking adequate expression: 'the most advanced intellects, the philosophers of the great school . . . go from doctrine to deed, to the last aim of all thought, and formalise the programme'.[368] Thought necessarily accompanies a 'historical process which one can only know when one has learned how it ends, so that its end seems to be its result. . . . Thought may seem to precede the real, but this is only because the real is historical.'[369] Heine's storm metaphor should be taken literally: we see the lightning before we hear the thunder, although, in reality, the two spring from the same source at the same time. This explains how Heine could conclude even before the Hambach festival, simply from his observations of intellectual trends, that the outbreak of the German revolution was a certainty, not a matter of hypothesis: 'sooner or later the revolution will begin in Germany; it is already there as an idea, and the Germans have never abandoned an idea, or even a variant – in this thorough country, everything is carried through to the end, however long it takes'.[370] Historicity, which grounds the parallelism between thought and action, also explains why they are contradictory. In other words, there is no thought/revolutionary action without a spectral dimension, or, to be more precise, there is no thought that does not unfold in the shadow of an implacable battle between spectres, whose outcome can be decided only by a political intervention.

'Take heed, then,' Heine admonishes his French readers; 'you have more to fear from a liberated Germany than from the entire Holy Alliance with all its Croats and Cossacks.'[371] The phantoms of the past, 'the old stone gods', the Berserkers (half man, half bear), and the god Thor himself, brandishing his mighty hammer, 'will arise from the forgotten ruins and wipe from their eyes the dust of centuries'.[372] The colours of the German revolution seem to be at the opposite end of the spectrum from those of the dawn announced by the cry of the Gallic cock. Far from retreating before the new light, the phantoms of the past seem all the more impatient to wreak their revenge on the living. Germany, Heine warns, is still obsessed with its feudal, obscurantist past, whose focal point is hatred for the French Revolution, the deepest source of German national feeling. Germany prefers to live surrounded by the ghosts of the past, and stubbornly refuses to forget, as the French typically do.[373] As the hour of the German revolution draws near, there is great risk that the vast energies pent up throughout this long period of political and practical inertia, certain to burst forth the more powerfully after their long sleep, will be captured by an anti-democratic, Gallophobe nationalism. There beckons, in that case, the gloomy prospect of a Franco–German war that will sound the knell of the European democratic revolution.

Heine speaks again, especially in *Ludwig Börne*, of the ambiguity of the German revolution, which will have to confront, simultaneously, the tasks of sociopolitical transformation and the national unification of the country. His fear is that the Teutomaniac current, encouraged by the spirit of the times, will once again (he alludes to the experience of the *Burschenschaften*) infiltrate even the ranks of the revolutionaries, take a real hand in their struggle, and, after momentarily blurring the battle lines, confiscate the victory and channel popular energy in the direction of a reactionary nationalism. In that case, 'these incantations, a mix of ancient superstition and demonic subterranean powers, [will have proved] more powerful than all the arguments of reason'.[374]

Heine clearly sees that, in the German case, revolutionary democracy will be called upon to confront a formidable adversary *within* the revolution itself – an adversary who is all the more dangerous in that he has proved capable of manipulating the mass movement in the interests of the dominant, thus turning the revolution against itself. In a country in which the overthrow of the *ancien régime* and the process of nation-building coincide, nationalism is situated precisely in the void into which the faltering revolution could plunge, to become the most destructive of counter-revolutions. Heine responds not with an abstract cosmopolitanism that would shirk the historical task of national unity, but with his own concept of patriotism, his own version of national symbolism, and his own definition of Germany's special mission in the world. It consists, he says, in putting an end to absolutism and Prussian domination, and resuming the work of the French Revolution. But this time the objective must be to track it 'to its last hideaway', raise it to the level of the political, social and cultural *totality*, and extend it to Europe and the rest of the world.

'Universal Democracy', which will take up the battle with poverty, the negation of beauty, and, simultaneously, the subjugation of the human spirit, forms the sole horizon worthy of the German revolution. Moreover, as the example of Alsace-Lorraine suggests, it offers a far more reliable guarantee for German national integration than the wars of conquest unleashed by the absolutist powers. Germany's freedom is conceivable only in a world that has itself been 'redeemed'. In the preface to *Germany: A Winter's Tale*, Heine provides what is doubtless the most striking description of this freedom:

> Rest easy: I will never surrender the Rhine to the French, for a very simple reason: the Rhine belongs to me. Yes, it belongs to me, by inalienable birthright; I am the free Rhine's much freer son; my cradle stood on its shores; and I do not see why the Rhine should belong to anyone other than its native children. Above all, the Prussians' claws have to be pulled out; after attending to this task, we will choose, by universal suffrage, some honest lad who has the leisure required to rule an honest, hard-working people. Alsace and Lorraine, to be sure, I cannot annex to the German dominions as easily as you do; for the people of these lands hold fast to France on account of the rights they won through the French Revolution, the laws of equality and free institutions, which are very agreeable to the bourgeois mind, even if they leave much to be desired as far as the stomachs of the great masses are concerned. However, the people of Alsace and Lorraine will rejoin Germany when we finish the great work the French have begun – Universal Democracy! When we surpass them in deeds as we have already done in thought; when we rise to the heights required by the farthest consequences of that thought; when we destroy servitude down to its last hideaway, Heaven; when we wipe poverty off the face of the earth; when we restore to their proper dignity the poor people disinherited of happiness, genius scorned, and beauty ravished, as our great masters, the thinkers and poets, have said and sung, and as we their disciples want to do – yes, then not merely Alsace and Lorraine, but the whole of France will fall to us, the whole of Europe, of the world – the whole world will become German! Of this mission of Germany and its universal sway I often dream when I walk under the oak trees. This is *my* patriotism.[375]

When he learned of the outbreak of the 1830 July Revolution, Heine once again wondered: 'And Germany? I do not know. Will we at last make good use of our oak forests, that is, build barricades for the liberation of the world?'[376] Some ten years later, as he was finishing his poetic account of what was to be his last visit to Germany, at a time when the death spasms of absolutist repression augured its imminent end, Heine turned his gaze towards the rebellious German proletarians in Silesia, whose uprising had just been brutally crushed by the uniformed rabble of the Prussian army. In their 'somber eyes' that spill 'no tears of grieving', he discerned the true face of the revolution to come.[377] And even if the winding-sheet ultimately served to shroud those who had been weaving it to cover the corpse of the old world, we can still hear the click-clacking of their looms, so skilfully captured and amplified by Heine's art that it became 'the German workers' *Marseillaise*' (Alexandre Weill).[378] It admonishes us to remain vigilant.

3

Moses Hess, Prophet of a New Revolution?

As a Jew and a Rhinelander, Moses Hess shared with Heine, and also with Marx, a background that 'naturally' placed him in the Germany whose eyes were turned towards the heritage of 1789: a Germany in which the music of the drum major Legrand, although it had certainly been drowned out by the beating of the Prussian drums, was never altogether silenced. It was in prolonging the echo of that music *sui generis* that the France/Germany mediation gradually modulated into translation,[1] the concrete application of a theoretical programme which, for the first time – apart from the messages smuggled past the censors in Heine's letters, or a diffuse Saint-Simonianism perceptible among Hegel's disciples – took seriously the French conception – but it would perhaps be better to say the French invention – of the 'social': 'social-ism'. This transformation of mediation into translation, the indispensable condition for access to the universal, took the form, so to speak, of the repetition, on a grand scale, of an activity with which Hess was already familiar, for he had had to translate the traditional Jewish education of his childhood and youth into German.[2] It was an interminable task if ever there was one – one which, moreover, he attempts to theorize, from his earliest works on, in a way that is not without interest.

Hess's objective was not to defend the cause of Jewish civil rights in the tradition of his Enlightenment predecessors, or even to demand, as Mendelssohn had, that the Jews be granted the status of *producer*.[3] Rather, it was to assign the Jews an active role in universal history, so that they might rise from the position of juridical subjects and members of civil society to that of subjects of history. For Hess, the role incumbent on the Jews was essentially that of a 'spur': they were 'the ferment of the Western world', and their 'vocation' had 'always been to impress the characteristic of movement on it'. This movement, this endless wandering, was wholly sustained by messianic hope, which was, however, common to both Jews and Christians, for their two religions had suffered a common decline in a world abandoned by God.[4] It fell to the present to accomplish the prophet's classic task: to revive hope, redeeming it from the pettiness and abstraction into which it had progressively fallen among Jews as well as Christians.

Did Hess, then, do nothing more than translate the traditional messianic message into the language of the philosophy of history? A comparison with his main Hegelian pre-text, *The Philosophy of History*, will quickly bring out the effects of the displacement that his work on it produced. Hegel, of course, assigned the Jews an important place in the development of world spirit, but it scarcely differed from the one that the *grand récit* of Christianity also authorized: thanks to the Jews, spirit had attained to an early form of self-consciousness which had separated it from nature, and made an historical conception of the world possible. But although the Jews had initiated the break between East and West, their contribution was, said Hegel, limited by the exclusiveness of their religion; their representation of God was marred by 'national individuality and a special local worship'.[5] For Hess, in contrast, if the Jews' mission in universal history no longer occupied the central place it once had, it had by no means come to an end: their active role of mediation, spiritual ferment, and the restoration of hope still mattered to the present. In other words, Hess inflected the universal-historical scheme in order to bring it into relationship with the present, *his* present – in order to reinscribe his own trajectory, and his community's along with it, in that of the human race.

Thus, from the first, Hess's translation proceeds in a number of different registers – political and religious, French and German, Christian and Jewish, philosophical and social. It moves in two directions at once: it is a transposition of the celestial message to the earthly level, but it is, at the same time, a spiritualization of earthly struggles. With Hess, the revolution becomes, all at once, a secularized soteriology, a new name for parousia, the final step towards complete humanization of the world, and a figure in the prophetic discourse which proclaims its sacralization. The revolution is imminent; for that very reason, it is all the more unthinkable in any mode other than that of spiritualist allegory or transposition into the terms of a theological universe. And yet, as if to underscore the paradoxes inherent in non-contemporaneousness, it is precisely at the heart of this 'archaic' universe, dominated by the nexus between politics and religion, that the first systematic attempt was made to provide a German translation of English and, especially, the most advanced French post-revolutionary thought: the science (or, perhaps, the new religion) of the 'social', whose apostles were Fourier and Saint-Simon. Hess was to displace the dilemmas of the German road on to this new terrain: could the 'social', he would ask, serve to reconstruct the kind of unity between the political and the religious capable of sustaining messianic hope? Did it designate the ground on which the emancipatory content of German philosophy could shed its speculative nature in order to become, at last, concrete? And what was its relationship to revolution? Was it the harbinger of a new one or, rather, the principle that would make it possible to *avoid* a new one, and thus a means of re-establishing the pre-eminence of a German road?

Following Hess's career between 1841 and 1844 will allow us to home in on the answers he gave to these questions from a particular angle, determined by the effects of the 1842–43 political crisis, which (at least in the view of broad sectors of the oppositional intelligentsia) dispelled all illusions about the reformability of the Prussian regime. This will throw the specificity of Hess's trajectory into relief: setting out from a project of democratization conceived as political-religious reform, Hess evolved towards what may accurately be called, in the strictest sense of the term, a socialist humanism underpinned by a Feuerbachian anthropology. Yet this evolution reflects, in exacerbated form, not so much a radicalization as the ambivalence haunting a project of emancipation which – in its permanent, but distant, confrontation with the revolutionary event – was animated by both the fascination and the profound anxiety that that event called forth. Hess wanted to go beyond the narrow horizons of speculation and compromise towards political action and the organized forms of the workers' movement; yet he ended up trapped within an even narrower speculative horizon, in a kind of religion of Man that was ultimately quite similar to its Saint-Simonian original and, politically, just as impotent as the reformism of classical philosophy. Hess reproduced the limits of the German road at the very moment when he was straining to transcend them; he thus revealed that it was not viable. And his aporetic radicalization was not simply the reflection of an individual trajectory; the development of the most advanced segments of the German democratic movement, well beyond the circles of the intelligentsia, shows this clearly enough. A symptom of the crisis, the discourse of the communist rabbi also contributed to exacerbating it.

'We Europeans . . .'

'We Europeans are dissatisfied and avid for revolutions':[6] Hess's version of the triarchical schema should be examined in the light of this phrase.

Let us begin by noting the tense that Hess uses, the present. Invoking Cieszkowski, he explicitly declares that his ambition is to shift the Hegelian totalization of universal history towards the future – in Hegel, according to Hess, this totalization takes the past as its basis – and to shatter its principle of closure by opening it up to free action: 'philosophy has so far only referred to what exists, to what has been and has become, not to what will exist; German philosophy, especially in its last, Hegelian phase, may therefore be termed a philosophy of the past'.[7] Thus the philosophy of history yields to Historiosophy. From the study of the past, it turns towards the future, venturing boldly into the promised land of action, the conscious, free and voluntary action that will gradually bring all historical time under its sway: 'we are entering a new world, the world of the absolute action of spirit'.[8] This action is thus clearly described. It is the absolute action of *spirit*, the unique substance that actively constitutes the world; it is *absolute* in that subject and object are already fully mediated in it; and it is, finally, the *action* of spirit because it gives expression to the sovereignty of consciousness and the free will on its way to fulfilment: 'only unfree action, the *fact*, is simply followed by consciousness, whereas consciousness precedes the free *act* . . . it is, precisely, [the will] that gives rise to conscious, sustained action; without it, there could be no genuine freedom and no ethical life'.[9] From the outset, it is plain that the philosophy of action, in its attempt to go beyond the 'suprasensuous, abstract form'[10] of Hegelian universality and the inwardness of reflective consciousness, in fact retreats behind both towards a conception in which the world is constituted by the activity of consciousness and the will – towards, that is, Fichte, as Cieszkowski had explicitly said.[11] 'The living seed of the future' is highly likely to yield only generalities and a formal knowledge that will hardly get beyond the Kantian distinctions of practical reason, as is indicated by the opposition the passage just quoted sets up between fact and action, freedom and necessity.

In making the dialectic of self-consciousness that of a full, unified subject, however, Hess's philosophy of action does not simply drag Hegel back towards Fichte and Kant at the point where it no doubt imagines it is being most faithful to him. Persuaded that he is at his most innovative when he shifts the dialectic on to the new terrain of the future, Hess in fact reduces it to a traditional teleology, converting the philosophy *of* history into a philosophy *about* history,[12] a 'historiosophy' that is actually a theology tailored to fit the problematic of German idealism. At first sight, to be sure, historiosophy's 'discovery' of a third temporal axis would appear to have its origins in a fundamental Hegelian principle which it merely extends: the primacy of the present.[13] As is well known, the

Phenomenology of Spirit defines time as 'the existent Notion itself' [*der daseiende Begriff*],[14] the concept in its unmediated existence; the corollary is that the concept is, in its empirical and temporal determinations, contemporaneous with itself at any given moment in its self-development. The essence of the totality is reflected in the time of history before returning to itself and moving on to the next moment, thus pursuing the endless progress of the Idea. All Hegelian time is suspended from the present, a fully expressive present straining towards the accomplishment of its immanent purpose, which is legible in its very depths.[15] It is an eternally restless present, always 'about to', for it is haunted by the imminence of a future [*d'un à-venir*]. The eminently Hegelian category of 'transition', as we have seen, takes its place, precisely, here.[16]

Hess, however, proceeding very differently from a Heine, who fought for the rights and the freedom of the present, proposes to broach the question of the future; he was the first to take this path, preceding even Cieszkowski.[17] This is the pivotal point in his argument:

> The Hegelian concept trails after the historical facts; in no way, whether prophetic, mystical, or speculative, does it provide a ground for them. Doubtless Hegel believes that there is reason in history, but it is merely unconscious reason. However, if reason does not ground history as conscious reason, as spirit, but only as nature, where in history is there a sacred act of the spirit? Because Hegel utterly failed to recognize the essence of free action, he could not, with the best of intentions, associate it with any period of the past.[18]

Nor, *a fortiori*, any period of the future, we may add. In sum, Hess criticizes Hegel because the 'ruse of reason' in history has a strictly *ex post facto* character that can never be reduced to conscious manipulation of means in the service of ends pre-existent to its own activity, and in no case allows us to predict the course of historical development, which is subject only to the immanent unfolding of its own contradictions. Lukács has shown that in thus seeking a priori, strictly logical-conceptual knowledge of the future, Hess severs the philosophy of history from the present,[19] regressing, as a result, to a position behind that of Hegelian realism. The operation is the more costly in that the results it yields in terms of knowledge of the future amount to a few abstract generalities, a *mélange* of speculative deductions and utopian projections that are the more deeply enthralled to the empirical immediacy of the present for seeking to escape it at an imaginary level.

In the final analysis, Hess takes issue with the Hegelian dialectic for being something other than a religious discourse of a prophetic type, capable of *predetermining* the future in accordance with the schemes of a

teleology as simple as it is purely formal.[20] In Hess, the mission of
philosophical 'speculation', after the historical mediation represented by
the advent of Christ, is merely to play the part that had once fallen to
prophecy.[21] Sacralizing the totality of history does not, however, mean
reviving an outmoded relationship to the sacred, and so sparing oneself
the 'mediation' and 'reflection' due to rational thought; rather, it consists
in reducing history to its essence, the primacy of the free, self-conscious
action that Hess credits with making all history, past, present and future.
The philosopher of action accordingly draws a double border line; it
separates him from the 'supernaturalists' on the one hand and the
'rationalists' on the other.[22] The supernaturalists, disappointed by Hegelianism and 'speculative reason', reject mediation and the freedom of the
spirit in order to seek refuge in the arms of Restoration theology,
'immediate' Romantic faith, or Schelling's irrationalism. In contrast, the
rationalists – that is to say, the Hegelian left – glorify freedom of the spirit,
but reject the primacy of consciousness and thus the 'sacred' nature of
action, which they reduce to a mere 'secular' reality, intelligible only *ex
post facto*. They cannot conceive of a form of 'positive' freedom distinct
from mere *theoria* and the endless practice of criticism.

In fact, says Hess, the sacralization of universal history is possible only
if one sets out from the present, from the moment when the free activity
of spirit is recognized as a 'manifestation of speculative reason'.[23] Such
recognition is, in turn, made possible by a third and ultimate revelation,
which divides historical time into past and future;[24] it was the joint work
of the French Revolution and its prophet, Spinoza. The sovereignty of this
speculative/revolutionary present also makes it possible to name the arena
in which the absolute action of spirit has already been reflected and is
destined to be pursued: Europe, which alone has been charged with a
universal mission. Indeed, Europe presents itself as a double body, like
Christ's: an organic body, with its living, interdependent members, and a
body endowed with a suprasensuous unity, a perfection that makes it an
image of reconciled totality.[25] Like the state in Hegel, Europe embodies
the divine on earth; one must take literally the parallel between the
triarchy and the holy trinity, between Europe's historical mission and the
life of Christ, his passion, death, and resurrection included:

> Europe is a holy sanctuary ... there is no other land like it on earth! Like
> Christ, its model, Europe has sacrificed itself for mankind. It has had to drink
> deeply of the cup of sorrows. It is still livid, and the blood still trickles from its
> wounds. – But, in three days, it will celebrate its resurrection! ... One More
> Day like the first two, and Christ's victory in the history of the world will have

been achieved! Roman-German Europe is the chosen continent and stands under God's special protection ... it is the apple of God's eye, the center from which the destiny of the world is directed.[26]

The triarchical schema – and, through it, the universal-historical schema in general – stand out in clear relief in the light of the Eurocentric premiss on which they rest. The theatre of universal history barely extends beyond the borders of this 'Roman-German Europe' – if, indeed, the function of a concept like that of a 'universal history' is not precisely to (help) draw such borders.[27] The conception of a 'humanity' that is one and yet internally hierarchized only *seems* paradoxical; such abstract universalism is typically founded on systems of distinctions (East and West, but also the normal and the pathological, gender and class differences) constituting so many unthought premisses or obscure implications that continue to haunt and destabilize it from within. From the triarchical point of view, the unity – or, rather, unification – of the human species can be organized only around its European centre, in accordance with a twofold centripetal movement that proceeds from the extra-European (I should perhaps say 'infra-European') world towards Europe,[28] and, within Europe itself, from the periphery to the core constituted by the basic triad – England, France and Germany. With its global ambitions and its place in the action of spirit, Europe appears as a spiritualized Rome and, simultaneously, a universalized earthly Jerusalem.

Within the triadic nucleus itself, Hess, exactly like Hegel and Heine, attributes a decisive role to the France–Germany relationship, which he places, like them,[29] under the sign of the German Reformation: 'the essential tendency of the present resides in the interaction between German and French freedom'.[30] The third period of world spirit begins with the French Revolution: 'the year 1789 introduced the ethical principle into human life', an ethics that is action itself, 'self-conscious, productive action, the element of the future'.[31] Its representative man is Spinoza, 'man *tout court*, the prototypical figure of modern times',[32] the one who comes after Adam and Christ – the first man and the last prophet – to hasten the advent of a new world. Just as Christ brought the age of the prophets to an end (the period of natural spirit) and opened the age of mysticism (the period in which the heart dominates the activity of spirit), so Spinoza brought mysticism to an end[33] – took it, that is, to its term, carried it to its conclusion, and transformed it into speculation – and inaugurated the absolute action of spirit. Of course, ever since Hegel, it had been commonplace to treat Spinoza as a beginning. But Hess 'inverts' the Hegelian vision; for if Spinoza is a beginning for Hegel, he is, precisely, *only* a beginning. As a Jew, he incarnates the inaugural moment of the separation of East and West, but remains haunted by the Eastern world. In posing the absolute as the unique substance, Spinoza perfects the original discourse while remaining trapped within the horizon of an immobile, rigid being. He cannot, says Hegel, conceive of substance as subject, as an opening towards spirituality and activity; he takes up a position short of the 'principle of the Western world, the principle of individuality'.[34] For Hess, in contrast, Spinoza provides the perfect illustration of his definition of the active, modern role that devolves upon the Jews. Where the author of the *Logic* sees the source of an insurmountable limitation, Hess sees a principle of opening at work. Spinoza's constitutive relationship to the modernity inaugurated by the French Revolution exemplifies, in Hess's view, the transition between the Jewish principle – perpetual mediation, the expectant wait – and access to the universal by way of the self-movement of history.

If, on the other hand, Hess follows Hegel in magnifying the place of the French Revolution in universal history, he is also quick to emphasize its limits: 'The French Revolution was a *revolution in ethical life*, neither more nor less. Standing halfway between religion and law, spiritual and material concerns, it served to mediate truth and reality'.[35] The year 1789 made it possible to realize, concretely, the principle of freedom that the German Reformation had attributed to thought, but this realization itself went only halfway; it was left unfinished, or, rather, barely begun. Indeed, it only scratched the surface of the old order, contenting itself with 'challenging antiquated customs': 'the changes it wrought in the old laws and institutions were insignificant; for one thing, they did not last, and for another, they were not thorough enough'. In a word – *pace* Heine – 'it is a dangerous mistake to interpret the French Revolution as a political-social revolution'.[36] If the Europeans are *still* 'dissatisfied and avid for revolutions', that is because this new principle, the political-social principle, awaits its realization; and because the day of this realization – the third day of Europe's resurrection – is now at hand. The new principle irresistibly carries us towards the third pole of *The European Triarchy*:

> Europe has already gone through two revolutions because it did not peacefully yield to the modern spirit. . . . A third revolution lies in store for it. It will complete the work of the modern spirit begun with the German Reformation. It will be the practical revolution *par excellence*, the one that will not merely have a greater or lesser, a *relative* impact on social life, as was the case with the previous revolutions, but, rather, an *absolute* impact. The English revolution will be to the French as the French was to the German.[37]

The triarchical schema now appears in a new light. The third pole is England,[38] which realizes the dialectical totalization of the other two moments: the German – spirit, speculation; and the French – the will, and also ethical life in the sense of *Sitten*.

Across the Channel, a new kind of freedom is on the historical agenda: 'just as *German* freedom has been completed by *French* freedom, so both, after their mediation has been achieved, will in their turn be completed by a third type of freedom that is already budding in *England*'.[39] A synthesis *in actu* of the historical development that preceded it, the new revolution will be total, or, more precisely, *absolute*; it will correspond fully to the new stage in the action of spirit. Nothing can, a priori, elude its grasp; it will not confine itself to the level of preliminaries, like the German revolution, or stop halfway, like the French. But – a point Hess labours – this absoluteness means *radicalness*, not wanton destruction or irrational negativity.[40] The new revolution is radical because nothing, neither nature nor tradition, can now legitimately thwart the autonomous action of spirit; Hess calls on the revolution not to fear the spirit that animates it.[41] Radicalness plainly signifies a consummated break, a critique of existing traditions and standing authorities that leaves no stone unturned, a critique that is consubstantial with the modern condition, in which the world is divested of all transcendence, condemned to instability and 'deathly anguish', 'abandoned and left to its own devices'.[42] Only the immanent action of its spirit can 'found its existence'; the premiss for such action is, of course, 'daring' (in this connection we are reminded of Danton's famous maxim), the permanent restlessness and avidity of spirit; yet it is not arbitrary adventure or arbitrary disorder, an unleashing of destructive negativity, but the emergence of a sovereign consciousness that has reflected the totality of historical development within itself. Neither cyclical return to a past stage nor nihilistic cataclysm, the political-social revolution gives birth, no doubt painfully, to a new – and better – life; it is the rebirth [*re-naissance*] and re-righting of a divided, convulsive world.

From the 'social' to the state

Hess does not content himself with adopting Hegel's conception of a historical dialectic that issues in a new, radical principle; he proposes to provide it with its concept, which he takes from French theory, especially Saint-Simon, and translates into German after first projecting it into English: the social. He is aware that, in doing so, he is setting himself apart from the rest of the German intellectual opposition, as the classification that figures in *The European Triarchy* shows. It breaks the oppositional intelligentsia down into three groups. Hess identifies the political-social tendency, that of the 'English Germans', with the left wing of Young Germany; he includes himself – along with Börne, Gutzkow and Ludolf Wienbarg – in this group, which by itself makes up the left of the oppositional spectrum. The centre is represented by the 'French Germans', who have not gone beyond defending the principles of the French Revolution; Heine, whom Hess – curiously – considers to be more distant from the social tendency than Börne, is identified as the leading figure here. This clearly reflects the impact of the charges of duplicity that Börne levelled at Heine during the dispute that pitted him against the leaders of the German *émigré* community in Paris.[43]

As for the left wing of the Hegelian school – Feuerbach, Ruge, David Friedrich Strauß, *et al.* – which Hess castigates, earlier in the text, for its rationalism and one-sided understanding of the action of spirit, it is unceremoniously placed to the right of the two preceding currents. Hess's assessment of it may seem to contradict the more positive assessments of it sprinkled throughout the *Triarchy*, but, in any event, it testifies to his desire to 'shake up' Hegelianism, whose heirs and epigones have passively assimilated the doctrine of their master, he says, as if it were 'a miasma floating in the atmosphere'.[44] It would be interesting to know in what category Hess would have put Marx, who is absent from the list (he had only just earned his doctorate at the time). There can be little doubt about the answer: he would surely have located him on the right, in the company of the Berlin Young Hegelians with whom Marx was associating during this period. Thus Hess would have placed Marx at a far remove from the political-social tendency, but also from the 'centrism' he imputes to Heine and the 'French' current. Had the same classificatory schema been applied to Engels, it would just as surely have yielded the opposite result: the category 'English German' seems to be made to order for Engels, who initially declared himself a supporter of Börne, established ties with Gutzkow, and, to crown it all, set out for Manchester after an overwhelming encounter with Hess, who would later boast that he had converted Engels to communism. However that might be, it would appear that when, a year after publication of *The European Triarchy*, the bourgeois liberal stockholders of Cologne's *Rheinische Zeitung* turned Hess down for the post of editor-in chief of the paper because they considered him too radical,[45] their own reasoning hardly differed from his!

What was this principle which was so new that it seemed capable of profoundly reshaping the intellectual and political landscape? From Saint-

Simon and his school, Hess took the idea of the 'social', or of 'social-ism', defined as the great alternative to liberal individualism, but also as an antidote to revolution: a means of winding up the revolution that had already taken place, and preventing others from arising in its wake. Beginning with his first book, *Letters from an Inhabitant of Geneva to his Contemporaries*, published in 1803, Saint-Simon had indeed suggested a new answer to the question that had been haunting people's minds since 1789, and all the more intensely after the Year II: how to 'finish' the revolution – with all the ambivalence attached to the word (bring the revolution 'to its term' and/or have done with it once and for all).[46] To be more precise, Saint-Simon had shifted the terms of this question by reformulating it as follows: how was one to go about forging a new social bond? Simply asking the question meant relativizing the radical character of the revolution.[47] The unprecedented 'crisis' sparked off by the French Revolution had at all costs to be resolved by way of its transformation into a 'transition',[48] the emergence of a new principle distinct from the political – and superior to it. The sequence revolution–crisis–transition is crucial in Saint-Simon, in that it provides a foundation for the meaning of contemporary history. The category of transition consequently serves both to designate the cause of the crisis and to ensure that it will be overcome; it fuses the descriptive, the analytic, and the normative.

As a project for the reunification of a society riven by antagonisms, the invention of the social announces the transition, in Saint-Simon's terms, from the 'critical state' of society (the state of crisis represented by absolutist wars of conquest, but also from revolution and criticism in the metaphysical, legalistic spirit of the Enlightenment) to the 'organic state' (a state of affairs organized by industrialism, and therefore peaceful and 'positive'/scientific in spirit). In this perspective, the 'organic state' is understood as resulting from the conscious reorganization of society, from the triumph of the industrial principle, which removes the obstacles to transparency and unity (namely, the anarchy created by the market and the unrestrained play of competing egos) by producing, literally, the stuff of the social bond, where 'social' adequately corresponds to its essence (the constitution of a social bond) and inner purpose (labour, social production).[49] This new 'secular power' goes hand in hand with a no less thorough reorganization of the 'spiritual power' of society. From Saint-Simon's 'new Christianity' to Comte's 'positivist catechism' and Owen's 'rational religion', establishing and propagating a new religion compatible with and even inherently required by the power of science and reason is an integral part of the social project: there can be no social bond in the absence of a 'spiritual' bond, a feeling of belonging to a

united community, and a new ethics that is completely at odds with
liberal individualism and egoism. In the *Triarchy*, this idea takes its place
within a vast historical sequence governed by the action of spirit, of
which it is said to be the culmination. The themes of conscious organization, transparent community, and the organic model ensure a quasi-
natural communication between the French and German traditions; this
provides further confirmation of the philosophical and metaphysical
status of the new principle. Saint-Simon, for his part, had put heavy
emphasis on the philosophical coherence of his undertaking, going so
far as to identify philosophy as the new 'constituent power' of society.[50]
Thus the social becomes the new name for an ontological ground; the
'science' of the social, for its part, becomes the legitimate heir to philosophy, or even its most recent avatar.

Following the indications given by Heine, and situating himself in the
field opened up by the 'Franco–German transfers' of the period,[51] Hess
promptly carries out the translation of the new principle revealed by
Saint-Simon into the language of the philosophy of history. The association Hegel–Saint-Simon is made to stand for the union of France and
Germany, philosophy and the accomplishments of 1789, theory and
practice: 'If with Hegel, as with Germans in general, it is the spiritual side
of things which prevails, the practical side of things has found its representative in France. The relationship between the Germans and the
French, which we have already described, reappears for all to see in their
native sons, Hegel and Saint-Simon.'[52] On the conceptual plane, this
means that the social, reduced to its essence, designates the site where
society reveals itself to itself, in the perfection of an originary unity that
has at last been restored: '*perfection is unity; human society, to reach its goal,
need only be internally united*'.[53] As the truth of society, the social is nothing
other than 'human society', the advent of 'social man',[54] who 'masters
events, directing the course of them with his mind and heart'.[55] Once
internal unity is achieved, the wait for the future will come to an end,
inaugurating the true reign of free, conscious action and, with it, the
supersession of all existing divisions.

Hess's response to the objections of a hypothetical liberal interlocutor
reveals a great deal about the presuppositions underlying this fantasy of
unity and perfection. Let us first attend to the liberal arguments as they
are summed up in the *Triarchy*:

> Who will want to live in your society, since you want to suppress all virtue and
> all free activity? Without oppositions, all life would cease; without competition,
> all effort would cease. Indeed, in your social order, supposed to have reached

the highest possible level, further progress is inconceivable. For men are goaded onward by the separation of their interests and by everything else that opposes them to each other; that is what makes them active, inventive, and productive. In your order, freedom perishes; your paradise is a Cockaigne, your people are automatons! . . . Who, moreover, will stand surety for your society itself? Who can ensure that your supreme leaders, who will in any case have concentrated enormous power in their hands, will not finally become a closed cast, with the result that the separation of property that you fear will reappear, more extreme than ever before?[56]

To this by no means caricatural argument, which weaves together the pluralism of interests, competition, social efficiency, and freedom, Hess can respond only in abstract or even theological terms, by repeating the Name of names and running down a list of the attributes of its essence. The Social, as unity and harmony *per se*, will conduct men towards a religion of Love, the unique and absolute substance of the social *bond* [*lien*] (or of the social as bond).

Love guarantees, to begin with, the irreversibility of the new social order: 'the rule of such a [reconciled] order . . . presupposes too high a degree of intellectual love among mankind to leave room for fears that, where this love had once established its rule, the power of evil could ever return in force'.[57] Second, love, the law of the human species that is immanent in each of its members, guarantees not merely the compatibility of order and freedom,[58] but their reciprocal mediation at the heart of a new totality – a higher totality combining the substantial unity of the social order and its absolute freedom to create and re-create forms that are adequate to its content. Thus the universal reconciliation of the human species, a revelation of its own truth through history, cannot come about without the corresponding reduction of the social relationship to a pure bond, a religion in the sense of *relicare*, which unites individuals in something that can only be Christian love: a 'spiritual bond that should tie the members of human society to one another', in Saint-Simon's terms.[59] The progress of world spirit and the realization of the autonomy of the human species – humanism and the philosophy of history – converge on the infinite reign of the One, the God Who is Love: 'the religion *par excellence*, Christianity, is by its nature the eternal religion of love. Christianity, in the mind and spirit of its founder, is reconciliation . . . *God is love*, Christianity teaches. And love is the soul of everything; it unifies everything; love is religion in the broadest sense.'[60] Thus it is by an internal necessity, by virtue of the ontology which grounds it, that the political-social principle takes the form of a new religion. The Anglo–Franco–German alliance which *The European Triarchy* and its author have in view is placed, in its entirety, under the banner of an alliance/alloy of the political and the religious that will become both a constituent element of Hess's socialism and a bond linking him to the other socialist theoreticians of his day.

But how is this new principle to carve its path through history? More concretely, what are the real obstacles and the sources of contradiction that the age puts in the way of the realization of reconciliation? It turns out that they are of different kinds in each of the three poles of the triad. There is a 'practical' opposition between the money aristocracy and pauperism in England, a 'moral' opposition between spiritualism and materialism in France, and a 'spiritual' opposition between Church and State in Germany. At first sight, as we have already observed, *The European Triarchy* seems Anglocentric: social-political freedom is the synthesis of the two other kinds, and England is said to have assumed, in the course of the nineteenth century, the place that France had held in the eighteenth. This idea that England will take over France's role acquires its full significance from the moment Hess declares that England has also become the only truly revolutionary nation. In Europe, as we have seen, it is the English who stand poised on the verge of a revolution – but a new type of revolution, more radical than anything yet seen. Their country is the only one in which social antagonism is intense enough to provoke a revolutionary outcome. What is more, Hess is concerned to change the prevailing image of the English national character, allegedly absorbed in business and the art of making money, and therefore remote from any tradition of struggle and revolt.[61] Hence he contests the Gallocentric cliché to the effect that France has an eternal monopoly on political and popular uprisings in Europe.

But it must be said that this defence of a hypothetical English revolution remains highly abstract, despite the lyricism with which Hess presents it; it is more a formal product of his 'fundamentalist triadism'[62] than a political perspective concretely bound up with the actual tendencies of the day. To throw this gap in the argument into relief, we need to attend to one essential point: the sole existing, truly operative agent of reconciliation that *The European Triarchy* theorizes and defends as such is *the state*. And the state *ipso facto* leads us back towards Germany, and the meanders of the labour of spirit. Thus all the indications are that England, far from representing the instance of the totalization of historical development, finally serves only as a (no doubt obligatory) detour for spirit, eager to return to itself – that is to say, to the most universal, and therefore the most 'European', country in Europe: Germany.

Defending the 'German road'

There can be no doubt that, in *The European Triarchy*, the state is the figure of concrete universality; the state alone is capable of transcending the one-sidedness and abstraction of both the atomized subject and the rival totalizing institution, the Church. Hess unreservedly endorses Hegel's critique of natural law and 'abstract rationalism', which he, too, blames for the 'unacceptable aberrations' and 'ruthless tyranny' of the Terror.[63] He also refuses to ascribe to a subjectivity counterposed to state power the founding role that liberalism assigns it. For Hess, both these roads, their divergences notwithstanding, lead to the same result: they perpetuate a state of division. They create a rupture between the unifying action of the state and the conditions required for its realization.[64] Hess tolerates no a priori limit, and in particular no legal limit, on state power. The power of the state is in principle absolute; the power it actually wields is determined solely by whether it corresponds adequately to the spirit of the age.

The state thus emerges as the one and only vehicle of the grand reconciliation, the historical agent charged with realizing the promises of the religions, as of all other previous stages of the activity of spirit:

> Once the Church, the clergy, doctrine and dogma have accomplished their task, there still remains a broad field for Christian activity, the state – the ground not merely for spiritual, but for all human activity. The Church could only offer people bliss; the state should offer them happiness. The Church could take only spirit into consideration, the state should consider the whole human being. The Church's position was such that it had no choice but to maintain an opposition between body and spirit, truth and reality, the here-below and the beyond, the present and the future, etc. In the state, in contrast, the future is the present, the beyond is the here-below, and so on. For the promises of the Church are fulfilled in the sacred state, just as those of Judaism were fulfilled in the Christian Church. What belonged to the future for the Church thus belongs to the present for the state – what it was only given to the Church to behold and reveal in the spirit, it is given to us to realize.[65]

The eternal present in which this philosophy of the future culminates is thus nothing other than the eternal present of the state, architect of the grand reunification of the human species.

Secularizing religion means, therefore, sanctifying the state, organizing its organic fusion with the totality of social life – in other words, reunifying social life by raising it to the level of the state. The supersession of religion is its realization, which itself turns out to be religious: 'Christian-German idealism has fulfilled its mission. Time has loosed the bonds of the Church in order to create associations in the form of states, associations that embrace, protect, promote, and sanctify all life.'[66] The separation of Church and state can only be temporary; it is doubtless necessary in order to cut the ties between the state and particular religions, but it is altogether untenable from the standpoint of the 'absolute unity of social life'.[67] For Hess, as for Saint-Simon or Comte, there can be no question of universal reconciliation without a reconciliation of minds parallel to the reconciliation of interests; and, in both cases, it is up to the state to accomplish the mission of unifying secular authority and spiritual authority. The task of the post-Revolutionary period is no longer to dissolve the bond between the political and the religious, but, quite the contrary, to bring about its 'absolute' realization. Annulling the divorce between religion and nature – that is, fully concretizing religion – leads logically to the proposal to create a state religion.

With this, we are at the heart of Hess's argument in *The European Triarchy*. What are we to understand by state religion? Two responses would appear to be out of the question from Hess's standpoint. To begin with, the aim is in no sense to perpetuate, or return to, a pre-Revolutionary state of affairs, that is, an official religion: no particular religious denomination should be maintained in, or promoted to, the rank of a state religion. Such a tie between one particular religion and the state would be, as we have seen, contingent and extrinsic; it would merely reproduce the division between existing religions, and thus intensify their antagonisms. On the other hand, Hess also rules out any solution that would involve superseding these religions 'from below', that is, through the creation of a new 'popular religion' capable of competing seriously with the established churches, and giving practical expression to the measure of hope that each of the existing religions contains. Yet he has at his disposal a model that suggests what such an enterprise might look like – the sequence established by Hegel and developed by Heine: Reformation–Peasant Wars. In Hess's estimation, however, the court of history has pronounced a negative verdict on the matter. It is true that he occasionally envisages the 'state religion' in an agonistic mode, appealing, for example, to the 'best forces in Germany' to defeat their 'adversaries', a 'race of crippled pygmies that has not grown with the times'.[68] 'Consciousness will easily strike down, with its mighty arm, all the dwarfs,' he declares – without, however, telling us just who actually incarnates this omnipotent consciousness. At all events, it is not the 'multitude', which falls short of the level of development that 'world spirit' has attained, and consequently cannot serve as the vehicle of the new principle.

Obviously delighted at being able to turn a traditional anti-Jewish argument against itself, Hess notes, in this context, that the attitude of the Jewish people, which is incapable of grasping the import of Christ's message, of recognizing this truth as its truth, is by no means exceptional; indeed, it provides the model for the masses' relationship to the new figure that spirit has assumed in the world. Such is the tragedy of non-recognition: Christianity's inner truth resides in the abolition of the contradiction between celestial and terrestrial life. Because Christians do not realize this, they continue to despise the here-below (and to live in the midst of contradiction). The truth stands before them (Luther), but they fail to recognize it, leaving the contradiction unresolved.[69] Luther's failure simply repeats Jesus'. In an alienated world, such recognition has become impossible: spirit cannot return to itself; the dualism is irreducible. What is exemplary in the Jewish experience is the failure of the prophetic discourse which, Hess believes, was already given its supreme form by Christ.[70]

Moreover, in a certain way, the failure is insurmountable. No help can be expected from revealed religion, new or old, in going beyond the antagonism between existing religions and progressing towards their reconciliation. That task falls to the state religion which must be created on the twin bases of Spinoza's proposals for a '*credo minimum*' – prescribing justice and charity while ensuring obedience – and the 'true religion', rooted in widely shared notions, in which love will replace obedience. The dualism that appears here is inherent in the political-religious reform which Spinoza describes in the *Tractatus Theologico-Politicus*, and which continues to vex interpretations of that work;[71] through it, the entire question of the masses' relationship to political action and the state is effectively posed. As is well known, Spinoza carefully distinguishes between the *fides catholica*, which is required to secure the obedience of the masses and is under the dominion of the imagination (of superstition and the fiction of a God), and rational religion, a religion of the understanding based on notions of the second kind. However, Spinoza seems to hold – and this is the crux of the matter – that *fides catholica* is both irreconcilably opposed to rational religion and, at the same time, a propaedeutic for it; hence the question as to whether the multitude can be freed from the grip of superstition and sad passions remains undecidable.

Hess's position reproduces this oscillation by way of an opposition between a formal and a substantive definition. On the one hand, the state religion is presented as the common denominator between the different religions, a sort of moral law centred on precepts of love. It is the general container, purged of all particularities, which allows the plurality of religions (with their superstitions) to coexist; the state is to see to it that this religion is disseminated and taught.[72] On the other hand, the state religion does not comprise only moral laws; in a certain sense it is the one 'true' religion, because it is the discovery of the truth immanent in each particular religion, the revelation of the essence of religion. It makes it possible to assign the existing religions their real place, thus ensuring their peaceful coexistence; but it also encourages visions of their dialectical supersession – which involves making existing particularisms 'more flexible', and effecting an ongoing mediation between the various denominations while respecting the individual conscience.[73] In the first case, nothing more is at stake than the imposition of a moral form guaranteeing public order; in the second, the aim is to reach the standpoint of the absolute, the absolutely religious state incarnating the unity of social life as a whole.

Hess's dialectical reformulation of Spinoza's proposals allows him to pinpoint what is at stake in them:[74] they link the reform of the state, its 'sanctification', to the 'sacralization' of the social bond, in the movement of a transformation that is internal to religion. As Chapter 19 of the *Tractatus Theologico-Politicus* points out, the *credo minimum* acquires 'force of law' only when those who hold political power[75] make respecting it a matter of obedience to state law, which is in turn created through the collective practice of democracy. Thus the moral law that prescribes love for one's neighbour, which results from the self-criticism of the religious passions and of the destructive attitudes engendered by superstition, is the accomplishment of the laws governing the body politic; everyone can now legislate for himself, while respecting others and associating with them in a common respect for the legislation that applies to all. The institutions of civil law can then operate without recourse to a transcendent, coercive Authority – or, more exactly, while radically diminishing the transcendence inherent in all authority. The law thus paves the way for its own supersession, and therefore for the 'true religion', divested of all fictions of a personal God and located beyond the heteronomous order in which the morality of the *credo minimum* continues to be articulated. In turn, the pacification of the political community makes possible the coexistence of – and even discussion among – the various religious denominations, but also between those who remain prisoners of the imagination (while practising the *fides catholica*) and those who have attained the highest level of knowledge and intellectual love. In this sense, Hess's proposal may be understood as a process of intellectual and ethical (*sittliche*, like the French Revolution) reform which, via the dialecticizing agency of a 'state religion', combines the supersession of existing religious antagonisms with the secularization of the state itself, at once condition and result of the reactivation of the reformist road. This, then, would be the point at which complete sacralization undergoes a transformation in its turn, becoming a higher form of secularization.

The proposal radically to recast the political–religious complex, while organically reunifying it, is at the heart of the triarchical system. For Hess, this is the mission of an age, his own, which he invites us to construe as post-Revolutionary, in the strict sense of the word. The dissolution of the ties between politics and religion very systematically carried out by the French Revolution was no doubt inevitable, and even salutary, in so far as it exposed, once and for all, the contingency and one-sidedness of the 'religious State' under the *ancien régime*, the emptiness of the official religion, and the 'false unification' of social life. But this divorce between politics and religion is not, as such, viable: it could even lead to the annihilation of both the state and the socio-spiritual bond, the *relicare*, reducing them to a 'state of anarchy' synonymous with 'total regression'. In short, we need to know how to terminate a revolution without giving up what it has achieved, in order to put an end to the concomitant 'momentary suspension of state power' as quickly as possible, and then proceed down the road to orderly freedom.[76] This is another road – it involves rehabilitating the state,[77] that is, bringing it up to 'the level of its times', leading it to self-consciousness (the consciousness of its 'sacredness'), and resolutely orientating it towards reform.

Thus the triarchical schema is turned around once again. At first sight, it would seem to be the supposedly pre-revolutionary England which, slipping into the role once played by France, anticipates Europe's future. But it turns out that Germany is already in advance of the two other terms of the syllogism. The centrality of the *religious*-political moment is the key to understanding this reversal of the model in Germany's favour. For, thanks to the invention of the social, Hess's version of the triarchy functions both as a reaffirmation of the primacy of spirit and as a way of transcending the limits that the Hegelian system imposed on it. The 'new world' we are entering is that of the 'absolute activity of spirit';[78] it embraces both nature and history, so many 'regions' that Hegelian philosophy, which fails to move beyond the moment of the subjective activity of spirit, 'can touch on, but not penetrate'.[79] But if, in principle, no region is exempt from its activity, the fact remains that spirit has chosen to take up its abode in a particular place: Germany. The German people is the 'most universal', and thus the 'most European', in Europe: 'the Germans *should* rather exhibit a universalistic tendency, since that which is most characteristic of them, spirit, is universal in nature'.[80] Accordingly, the supposedly revolutionary English situation can appear only as a national particularity; as in the Reformation period, the country that is truly ahead of the others is the land of Luther and the philosophers. In this way, the two mainstays of the legitimation of the German road are revived: the specific essence of which Germany is said to be the guardian, and the central position assigned to this essence in the progress of the world. Moreover, both are defined through constant contrast with the French Revolution. The fact that Germany's specificity is defined as its greater universality, and its centrality, in consequence, as a temporal lead, does, it is true, allow Hess to get the better of the Romantic, Teutomaniac tendency, but hardly takes us beyond the framework of the German ideology: 'the German nation cannot wallow in complacent, vain national pride. Precisely because it is the *first* to have taken up the struggle of modern times, the sole attitude worthy of it is to respect the particularities in the life of other nations, which merely follow it. Those who are puffed up with patriotic pride are not the true Germans. The Germans *should*, rather, exhibit a universalistic tendency, since that which is most characteristic of them, spirit, is universal in nature.'[81]

A specialist of the universal, Germany is defined as the land of the philosophers – not, in the manner of Madame de Staël and the Romantics, *qua* the incarnation of a 'soul' which is divorced from and even inimical to reason, but in the sense already defined by Schiller's immediate reaction to France's 'revolutionary excesses': as a nation charged with a philosophical mission based on the universal precepts of reason, education, and culture, and of benefit to all humanity: 'it remains . . . our mission to extend the foundation on which the modern period is based, intellectual freedom. We must continue to develop, ever further, ever more concretely, the idea of a united, free human race, the idea of humanity.'[82] No doubt Hess does preserve the universalistic aim, and the possibility of establishing a rational foundation for human goals, that Romanticism stubbornly sought to destroy. But at what price?

In fact – and it is in this sense that Hess may be said to adopt a Schilleresque position[83] – this pedagogical and spiritual mission, even as it preserves the achievements of the German Enlightenment and the French Revolution as its internal objectives, transfers them, via their 'spiritualization', to a sphere ruled by a different principle. In this sense, it serves not as a propaedeutic for or complement to the revolution but, manifestly, as a substitute for and totalizing alternative to it. For, as we are beginning to see, what is really at stake in the European/universal ambitions of the triarchical approach lies in Germany itself. In a notice that serves as the epigraph to *The European Triarchy*, Hess declares that German philosophy has 'fulfilled' its mission – it has 'led us to absolute truth' – and sets himself the task of 'realizing' this truth.[84] Doing so requires overcoming the one-sidedness of the Hegelian left, helping philosophy, which has lagged behind 'life', to catch up with it, and even, 'if possible', re-establishing philosophy's anticipatory function.[85] The stated objective is to go beyond the principle of the freedom of spirit alone, to follow France's example and wage a real struggle rather than remain in one's study like 'Germany's greatest men, from Kant and Schiller to Goethe and Hegel', who merely 'celebrate[d] the [French] triumph *intellectually*'.[86]

Yet the fact remains that this way of going beyond mere spirit still leads, as we shall see, to spirit; that is, it leads to a higher stage in spirit's immanent development, the 'absolute action [of spirit]'. Reality is still absorbed by the movement of thought, and the 'realization' of philosophy remains, now as before, philosophical.[87] Internal to philosophy, it is nothing more nor less than the necessary figure of its new departure, and heralds the advent of a new philosophy, the philosophy of action, whose task is precisely to spare the Germans the horrors of a revolutionary upheaval, while ensuring that they will benefit from the achievements of revolutions past (France) and to come (England):

> The opposition that issued in the French Revolution, the divorce between spiritualism and materialism, never reached a revolutionary level in Germany. The philosophy of action must fully make up for this; Germany will thus be able to appropriate the results of the French Revolution peacefully. We shall experience something of the kind during the future revolution. We do not say that the opposition between pauperism and the money aristocracy, or between spiritualism and materialism, does not exist or has never existed in Germany; but we do say that it is not and will not become so acute as to provoke a revolutionary upheaval. The opposition between . . . the spiritualist and materialist ethic has reached a revolutionary level only in France, just as that between Church and State has reached such a level only in Germany.[88]

From the Young Hegelian vantage point, then, overcoming one-sidedness does not mean abandoning the terrain of 'spirit' but, rather, opening it to new determinations, helping it to overcome its negative, hypercritical tendency, and raising it to the level of its times, which mandates a full reconciliation with life. Karl Gutzkow, the leading figure in the Young Germany movement, does not traduce Hess's position when, in his review of *The European Triarchy* (entitled 'The Philosophy of Action'), he says: 'given the situation in Germany, action could still only have an intellectual character; it had to limit itself to preparing people men's minds for future actions'.[89] When the philosophy of action has accomplished its mission – but is that not what it is already doing? – Germany will at last be 'in its own time', contemporaneous with its own times. Its position, past *and* to come, as a mere spectator of the revolutionary event does not in any way curtail this possibility. Quite the contrary, in fact:

> But everything cannot and should not happen at once. It is only after the fundamental idea of modern times has completely permeated life that freedom will in its turn become authentic, full-fledged freedom. And everything can and should happen only in the right place. Our German districts seem as little destined to be the theatre of the future revolution as they were to be that of the last. Yet Germany will reap the fruits of both: it will peacefully appropriate the results of both the English and the French revolutions. It must, however, have a right to these treasures; it cannot reap without having sown. Germany has that right; it has sown where it reaps! – Germany has laid the foundations for the building of the future, and, as architect, is still present to extend its foundations ever further, as the needs of the day dictate . . . Germany relates to the root of our times as to something that is intimately its own: it had to struggle with itself in order to be born again at the *spiritual* level![90]

At last we have the solution to the riddle: Germany is not behind the times, or, more exactly, it only seems to be; its backwardness is, unbeknown to itself, a lead!

There can be no further room for doubt: the function of the triarchical schema, as enriched and redesigned by Hess, is to reinforce the German road. One by one, Hess rehearses its basic themes: the revolution is all very well and good, but it is the business of our dear neighbours. We Germans are already beyond all that agitation; our mission is and remains the freedom of spirit, whether absolute or active; for us, the education of humanity is, and will be, a surrogate for revolution; it is both motivated by the reforms, and a motivation for them. Germany alone is radical, for it concerns itself with the foundations of things and with the future, bringing together origins and ends. The German road – in its Hessian version as well, which claims to represent the extreme left of the intellectual and political spectrum – turns out to be inextricably bound up with faith in the potential of state-led reformism, a reformism whose only concrete base of support in Germany is Protestant Prussia. Thus it is not at all surprising to (re)discover, in *The European Triarchy*, a ringing endorsement of the reformist tendencies of the Prussian state in its clash with the Catholic Church over the question of civil marriage – a position that was, it is true, shared by all democratic intellectuals – as well as an appeal addressed, in what is literally the form of a prophecy, to the same state, exhorting it to return boldly to the path of reform and concede nothing to the clerical party, which is made to bear all the blame for the reactionary about-face in German policy. It is clear, says Hess, that

> a certain religious party has had political influence in the state which exercises the greatest influence on Germany's intellectual culture [Prussia]; all the misfortunes we have suffered may be charged to its account. . . . How noble the Prussian government would appear if . . . it had not for a single moment strayed from the path of light, and never been unfaithful to the spirit to which alone it owes its power! But we prophesy that it will certainly return to the true path soon, and will no longer endanger its own and Europe's well-being. Not for nothing will Europe have shed its heart's blood in the Thirty Years War and the last war![91]

Undoubtedly, there is a certain artifice at work in these resounding phrases, a measure of tactical calculation as well as something of the style called for in periods in which writers must contend with censorship. The essential point, however, lies elsewhere. For, from Kant and Fichte to Hess, and even the Marx who edited the *Rheinische Zeitung*, the ambiguity involved was a constitutive feature of discourse as such.[92] Hess's position does not resolve it, but reveals the fragile, unstable point around which it turns. In this, it is hardly innovative: the constraints imposed by the censorship and the weight of the absolutist state are, as it were, 'internalized' here, woven into a theoretical argument that consequently oscillates between massive denial of the revolutionary event and an enduring fascination for it. Hess's reformism by no means entails a rejection of the political in favour of the pure introspection of 'spirit', or a simple logico-conceptual leap into utopia.[93] Quite the opposite: it offers a rhetorical base for the rather precise political-cultural strategy elaborated in the last two chapters of the *Triarchy*. The guiding thread of this strategy is provided by Hess's new grounding of the relationship between politics and religion: emancipation of ethical life [*Sitten*] through the establishment of civil marriage, a crucial achievement of the French Revolution and a weapon in the struggle against the Catholic party regrouped around the archbishop of Cologne; and the establishment of 'perpetual peace' among the various religions through the propagation of a state religion. These proposals for reform are accompanied by an emotional plea for the emancipation of the Jews, presented as a veritable 'barometer' for measuring the prevailing 'level of intellectual freedom'. Hess thus sketches the contours of a top–down reform that he places under the twin banners of a 'necessary return to Spinoza'[94] and the internal transformation of religion, for 'the German

people has assimilated religion *in succum et sanguinem*'.[95] The action of the
state is to be at the centre of this reform, for 'the supreme power of the
state will always be required to regulate the spiritual, the physical, and the
ethical in society'.[96]

The Prussian state is thus invited to abandon the politics of the *juste-
milieu* – which consists in making concessions both to Catholicism and to
the most conservative Protestant currents: a brand of politics basically
prompted by a reaction to the French Revolution. Hess calls on Prussia to
take up the tradition of Frederick II, without fear of 'offending the
intellectual rabble'[97] or the natural inclinations of a 'populace' quick to
applaud any anti-Semitic measure.[98] In any case, 'the multitude has always
been uncultivated; power, however, is based not on the multitude, but on
intelligence. Intellectual love has always been the lawgiver.'[99] Hess's return
to Spinoza is in keeping with the standard intellectualizing and elitist
interpretations of the 'intellectual love' and access to the third kind of
knowledge professed by the author of the *Ethics*. Fear of the masses,
reputed to be backward and easily manipulated by reaction and counter-
revolution, haunted the pages of the *Tractatus Theologico-Politicus*; it reappears in *The European Triarchy* in the form of the gulf that separates an
ideal, 'humane society', duly equipped with historical guarantees, from
the 'unlearned multitude'[100] that weighs down upon the present.

As the title of Chapter 4 of the *Triarchy* ('Germany and France. Our
Present; or, the Free Act') indicates, however, the proposed reform will
simply bring Germany up to the level of the present, helping it to catch
up with France's *Sittenrevolution*. The crucial task still remains, the final
moment in spirit's advance towards the total reunification of humanity:
the future. And the principle informing this future is the political-social
freedom that has yet to be achieved; it is embodied by England, and its
imminent realization necessarily implies a revolutionary outcome. Indeed,
if English freedom is the embodiment of the future towards which the
(English) present is straining with its every fibre, German freedom is, in a
certain way, already beyond it: is it not German freedom which is
preparing to appropriate, peacefully, the achievements both of the revolutions that have already been carried out (in France) and of those that
have still to be made (in England)? And is not German freedom the *only*
freedom that can legitimately claim to do so? Does this appropriation not
presuppose a sovereign point of view – the philosophical point of view, to
give it its right name – all the more absolute in that it is supposed to be
capable of accurately assessing not only the achievements of the past, but
also the potential achievement of the future? Does the place from which
this gaze looks out upon the world not represent, in a certain sense, the

'future of the future', the locus of the true triarchical totalization *in actu*, which the philosophy of action is already striving to realize? The *Triarchy* concludes by standing the schema that constituted its starting point (Germany = the past, France = the present, England = the future) on its head; it turns out that, in reality, the past is the French Revolution, and the future English revolution is actually a sort of present; while the German road is the 'true' future – the 'rose in the cross of the present', to make use of the mystical image of the preface to *Elements of the Philosophy of Right*. Germany's present now appears in its true light: already – but I should perhaps say always-already – *after* and, in that sense, *beyond* the revolution.

Radicalization or flight to the front?

The optimism of *The European Triarchy* and its defence of the German road no doubt reflect the reformist illusions typical of the period that preceded the authoritarian turn of 1840. The difference in tone between the 1841 book and Hess's writings of 1842–45[101] indicates just how profound the shift triggered by the political regression of the beginning of the decade really was. By unambiguously dashing hopes that he would liberalize the Prussian regime, Friedrich Wilhelm IV succeeded only in rapidly deepening the crisis, in a double sense: eliminating any possibility that the regime might reform itself, he made it inevitable that its contradictions would burst into the open; but, by the same token, he destabilized an opposition whose entire strategy had been predicated, precisely, on the calculation that out-and-out conflict could be avoided. The practical impotence of the democratic movement was now patent, and contributed to exacerbating the crisis in its turn. It is in this twofold extension of the crisis that we should seek the explanation for the fact that the German road now began to run amok: once the way to compromise or reformist gradualism had been barred, the intelligentsia's internal debates increasingly took the form of a retreat disguised as a philosophical offensive, giving a very peculiar tinge to what some were to call 'the putrescence of the absolute spirit'.[102] Yet we shall see that this oscillation, despite what seems to be its extreme abstraction, provided an echo chamber for the very real tendencies then traversing broad strata of German society, and even affecting the core of the working-class movement.

Hess responded to the new rigidity of the absolutist regime by becoming more radical – or so it would appear at first sight. In the articles he published in the *Einundzwanzig Bogen*, the triarchical schema is replaced by the canonical diptych comprising France and Germany. But, unmistakably, the emphasis is put on the elements of rupture with the past. France, Hess argues, must have done once and for all with the limited, one-sided principles of 1789, and move towards nothing less than the negation of the concept of the state. The concept of the 'political-social' put forward in the *Triarchy* now breaks up into its constituent parts: the 'social' turns *against* the political, staking a claim to its own truth in the form of 'anarchy', a reflection of the harmony of the community that renders all political authority superfluous.

To this anti-statist – or, more precisely, anti-political – radicalization, the German counterpart is a proclamation of atheism, which Hess presents as the authentic contribution of the spirit of classical philosophy. Anarchy and atheism are inseparable in so far as 'religion and politics stand and fall together'; they are both necessary expressions of the same historical state of separation, opposition and domination. No less than the heavenly representation of earthly realities, political representation is synonymous with servitude and mystification;[103] the true modern Church takes the form of 'the Christian State', 'the modern ... "free" state, as it actually exists in France, England, and North America'.[104] The task of the present is to expose, 'relentlessly and with a single blow', 'the lies of religion and politics. ... religious dualism, the heavenly politics, is a product of reflection, dichotomy, and misfortune – as is political dualism, the earthly religion'.[105] Hess adopts a conclusion that the thinkers of the social, particularly the Saint-Simonians, had reached before him: '*at the level of principles*, the form of government ... is a matter of indifference'; this is so even if 'the positive state based on the rule of law, as it has existed, to some extent, in North America since the latter half of the previous century, and in Europe since the French Revolution, represents ... an advance over the feudal, theocratic, and despotic ... state'.[106] The break with liberalism – but also with republicanism – goes hand in hand with a certain political 'indifferentism', which was to resurface during the debate over 'true socialism'. How, indeed, was it possible to imagine – except by leaping into utopia, as the first socialists had – that a transformation of social relations, even a non-revolutionary one, could ignore the question of the form of government – this in a Europe dominated by the alliance between the altar and the throne? If, as Hess thought – to some extent rightly – the shift in the political winds confirmed by the Wilhelmine regime's failure to liberalize created favourable conditions for the spread of his social doctrine, the same shift made it even clearer – and for the same reasons – just how far removed Hess was from anything resembling a practical perspective.

Hess provides this anti-liberal/anti-political radicalization with a speculative framework by means of a new act of translation. The criticism of religion initially inspired by Fichte and Bauer provides the first model, in the texts Hess published in the *Einundzwanzig Bogen*, for the critique of the political and the transition towards the social. Beginning with 'Über das Geldwesen' ('On the Essence of Money' [late 1843/early 1844]) and in 'The Last Philosophers' (early 1845),[107] Hess's language becomes more and more like Feuerbach's; but this Feuerbachian rhetoric is displaced on to a different terrain. The republican Feuerbach is Feuerbachianized in his turn: the state and politics – which, in his view, embody concrete universality and a living realization of the human essence – are demoted to the level of surrogates for religion in an alienated, upside-down world. The transposition of religious reform into political reform, assiduously promoted by Feuerbach, is also displaced: it becomes the self-unveiling of the political as the social. For, according to Hess, the root causes of atomization and the separation of individual men from their species-being are to be sought in civil society.

The fleshless idealism of the modern Church, the state, is simply the inverted image of the spiritless materialism that rules civil society, and of its secular religion, money. Bourgeois man is a Christian on Sundays, but for the rest of the week he keeps faith with the religion of the animal or animalized world, the worship of the Golden Calf: if this commercial 'world knows how to revere the Church and God as its *Sunday meal*, so must it also take into account the stock-market and the cult of wealth (money-making) as its *daily bread*'.[108] Bread and, it must be added, wine – that is, holy blood, the quest for and consumption of which become, in a kind of perverted communion among egoists, the true source of enjoyment in this fallen world.[109] For Hess, the breaking of all communal bonds is synonymous with a relapse into a state of nature, one that reflects an inversion of the biological order as defined by a *Naturphilosophie à la* Feuerbach. Now it is the animal who is the truth of man, rather than the opposite;[110] and the animal has itself relapsed into savagery, as a result of a kind of second inversion, so that man can no longer contemplate a reflection of his own essence in the beast – in particular, the image of one of his three attributes, the *heart*. This experience of the fall of the human species has culminated in a historical situation of lawlessness – a Hobbesian state of nature – in which the alienation of the species is reproduced in a 'horizontal' mode, through the play of the activity and interaction of subjects emancipated from premodern ('vertical') relations of dependence. Under these circumstances, social exchange becomes mutual exploitation, 'the war of each against all'; men subordinate all their relationships to the imperatives of bourgeois society, which tends to make animals of them.

Juridical universalism, the universalism of the Declaration of the Rights of Man, sanctions equality between atomized individuals as well as the predatory freedom required for survival in the maelstrom of generalized competition; it is the conscious form of, and justification for, the negation of their human essence:

> The mutual exploitation of men ... will now be carried out consciously and willfully. Privileged plundering comes to an end; *arbitrary acts of violence* are now *universal human rights*. The rights of man are now identical to those of all human animals, that is, the rights of all isolated and so-called 'independent' and 'free' individuals toward the alienated essence of all; here, the war of all against all is *sanctioned*. The solemn declaration of 'The Rights of Man' is the solemn declaration as to why all beasts of prey have equal rights. They have equal rights – as the 'Constitutions' of the 'free States' say – because they are autonomous and free beings, because they, as Egoists, as 'independent individuals', are now *recognized* and legally *acknowledged*.[111]

Such is the great limitation common to both liberalism and the French Revolution: they have remained at the level of abstraction, which is an inverted figure of the universal (= the human essence) divorced from the individual (who lapses into particularization) and opposed to reality. Thus the Revolution 'allowed the dualism to remain'; it 'really allowed everything to remain as it had been. ... Its freedom and equality, its abstract rights of man, turned out to be just another form of slavery.'[112] The rights of man do not allow one to go beyond the limits of the liberal state.

However, Hess's criticism of the rights of man remained – at least in his texts of 1842–43 – *internal*, in the sense that it criticized those rights in the name of their internal truth, the inseparability of equality and freedom. Disalienation, the emergence of true community, and the realization of man's humanity are conceivable only as an affirmation of the 'absolute' inseparability of freedom and equality.[113] Human emancipation *realizes* legal and political emancipation considered from an 'absolute' standpoint, one that overcomes the particularism and one-sidedness inherent in bourgeois society. In other words, it plunges the essence of the legal-political into the element that corresponds adequately to it, the unification of *social* life and the transcendence of the divisions internal to civil society, both of which are conditions for the realization of the essence of the human species. Not without a certain lyricism, Hess goes so far as to place (again, in his texts of 1842–43) the whole of his struggle, in its most radical dimension, under the banner of freedom and equality: 'What we want is something brand new, something that has never existed before. We must first begin to develop it. *Freedom* and *equality* are beautiful words. We have fought for them, we have sacrificed for them, and it is for them that we want to be resurrected, so that we can stand up and fight once more!'[114] While this position is first stated in the texts of 1842–43, the fact remains that it is perfectly consistent, as we shall see, with the work of Feuerbachian inspiration in which Hess calls for the negation/realization of philosophy *and* religion, inverted yet totalizing, authentic reflections of the human essence. In other words, the problematic of the *realization* of philosophy[115] or religion, while it proposes to negate both in so far as they are phenomena severed from social life, nevertheless does not entail an *exit from* philosophy or religion but, rather, the 'philosophization' or 'sacralization' of social life as a whole. Thus it is merely a philosophical exit, a passage towards a new philosophy (the philosophy 'of action' or of the 'social'), the gesture of accomplishment immanent in philosophy, in all philosophy.

An-archy and atheism explode the concepts of the political-religious and the political-social forged in *The European Triarchy*. There is no longer any question here of a state religion and a transformation of ethical life under the guiding impulse of an enlightened state reformism. In 'world history', the concept of the state has already been 'superseded'; it is a sphere that lacks concrete reality. Because they have not understood this, and continue to cling to the 'fiction of their "rational state"', the Young Hegelians have become, quite simply, 'reactionaries' in practice; they have even retreated behind the principles of liberalism, and are incapable of supporting any movement of *concrete* democratization.[116] The proof is their refusal to endorse elementary liberal demands for the emancipation of the Jews, or reform of the educational system[117] – a refusal based on an apparently ultra-subversive line of reasoning which is in fact typical of the German manner of neutralizing political questions.[118] The Young Hegelians are, moreover, 'philosophers', representatives of the modern 'clergy' whose religion is concretely embodied in the state; whereas humanism, for its part, confines itself to abstractions and the realm of pure theory. These 'theoretical egoists' who look down with 'contempt' upon the 'base mass'[119] are merely a late, particularly conspicuous symptom of the German situation, which is itself an exaggerated expression of the general tendency of the age, marked by the divorce between theory and practice and the development of the first at the expense of, and as a substitute for, the second. The upshot is a very German product, namely, a combination of doctrinaire radicalism and a growing disinclination for action that takes extreme form in the Young Hegelian unworldliness of a Bruno Bauer.

The terms of the problem, then, are clear: the goal is to overcome the gap between theory and practice, revolutionary France and contemplative Germany, Fichte's atheism and Babeuf's communism. It will be necessary simultaneously to do away with the inwardness of thought, 'to turn the sharp edge of the sword of thought toward the outer world',[120] and to move beyond philosophy towards action. Hess intends his proclamation of a break with the past to be radical in the extreme: the aim is to 'touch the igniting flame . . . to the structure of the old society', and 'allow nothing to remain of the old plunder besides activity'.[121] The crisis has to ripen until it arrives at its logical term. 'We now live', says Hess, 'in this reforming or revolutionary time',[122] and it is now a well-known fact that 'without revolution, no new history can begin'.[123] But resolving the crisis requires overcoming all the binary oppositions left intact by (the) previous (r)evolution, in order to arrive at a new *unity*, 'the real *principle* underlying the modern orientation in thought, whether French or German'.[124]

From 1843–44 on, this new unity is grounded in the Feuerbachian demand to transcend the separation between man and his species-being, the source of the division and conflict that dominate social life. But only socialism can legitimately claim to embody this movement of unification, because it restores social life to its truth, which is, precisely, its unity, centred on its subject, Man – but a Man who corresponds to his species-nature:

> Species-man can exist only in a society in which all men can educate themselves, realize themselves, and lead an active existence. This contradiction will be resolved only by socialism, which takes the realization and negation of philosophy seriously, sets aside philosophy as well as the state, and writes no philosophical books about the negation of philosophy. Socialism does not simply assert that philosophy must be negated as mere doctrine and realized in social life; it indicates *how* this is to be done.[125]

To negate philosophy, then, is to 'abolish' it, to *realize* that of which it is the 'anticipation', 'the unity of all social life', that which philosophy itself, as the modern religion, has inherited from its past forms: religion *tout court*, as well as the state, the modern Church, which continues to represent its form of existence. These forms are irrevocably past and *passé*, for in their present state they destroy their inner truth and are transformed into their opposite: an element that no longer anticipates but is hostile to the future.[126] But the fact that they are vehicles of this negative dialectic mandates their own abolition.

As we can already begin to see, the idea that Hess's thought underwent a radicalization has to be sharply qualified. The lines of continuity with the *Triarchy* are not hard to make out: they converge in a single *anti-political* conception, inseparable from an ardent longing to return to the One. Viewed in this perspective, the *Triarchy*'s reformist state was already positioned beyond politics; it was immersed in the 'social', which was elevated in its turn to the level of a new principle of unification – hostile to liberal individualism – of a world torn apart by the law of the market and capitalist accumulation. The postulate – which Hess took from Saint-Simonian or Fourierist French thought – that there exists an 'essence' of the 'social' as *unity*, founding bond, (egalitarian) principle of order within freedom, explains the pre-eminence that he accords to 'social-ism' – a pre-eminence over liberalism, of course, but also over *communism*, and thus, as we shall see, over *revolution*. Communism's detractors notwithstanding, Hess regarded it as essential to 'grasp the concept of communism in all its acuteness and profundity', that is, in the light of the constitutive bond that it establishes between equality and freedom;[127] but this was only the better to account for the dialectical *supersession* of communism: 'German philosophy has already transcended the idealism of Fichte, just as French socialism has transcended the communism of Babeuf.'[128] Both – Fichtean atheism, with its whiff of nihilism, as well as the Babouvists' crude egalitarianism – have overcome their one-sidedness. But the same applies to equality and order without freedom in Saint-Simon or, conversely, to Fourier's excessive libertarianism.

Hess can therefore present the kind of socialism he envisions as the realization of the whole human essence and the sole possible means of closing the gap between the individual and the species: 'this contradiction will be only resolved by socialism'.[129] 'Social man' and 'species-man' are one and the same; this is plainly what Feuerbach, 'the last of the philosophers', anticipates (consider his watchword 'the whole man');[130] although, according to Hess, he does not succeed in theorizing the historical, super-individual conditions for realizing their identity. The position that Hess ascribes to Feuerbach before going on to criticize it is exactly the opposite of the position Stirner ascribes to him. In Stirner's view, Feuerbach slights the individual ego in favour of the species.[131] For Hess, in contrast, '[Feuerbach] anticipates the social man, the "species-man", the "essence of man", and takes it that these essences are self-consciously present in the individual. What a philosophical fraud and a bit of modern state sagacity this is, since species-man can exist only in a society in which all men can educate themselves, realize themselves, and lead an active existence.'[132] This, we should note, is a curious reading of Feuerbach, whose conception of the relationship between individual and species should, rather, be approached in terms of the misrecognition that gives rise to alienation. Moreover, the author of *The Essence of Christianity* holds that alienation can be overcome only at the level of the species and, consequently, of the history of the species, not at the level of the individual, who bears the marks of his finitude. The proof *a contrario* is that a particular individual could incarnate the species in its plenitude, freeing himself of all finitude, only as the result of an 'absolute miracle, a violent suspension of all the laws and principles of reality; it would, indeed, be the *end of the world*. . . . *Incarnation* and *history* are absolutely incompatible.'[133] It would appear, however, that Hess's reading of Feuerbach is not attributable to an error but, rather, dictated by strategic considerations: Hess needs to put a certain distance between himself and Feuerbach in order to establish the originality and credibility of his humanist socialism, which is in fact quite similar (see below) to the communism of love professed by the author of *The Essence of Christianity*.

The definition of what can only be called, in the strict sense, a socialist humanism is worked out at the three closely interrelated levels on which Hess's discourse unfolds: they concern the relationship to philosophy, the subject that his discourse is intended to interpellate, and finally, where these two levels converge, the (re)definition of the German road.

Let us begin with philosophy. It very quickly became apparent that socialism's negation/realization of philosophy was itself – if the reader will forgive this pleonasm – essentially philosophical. To be sure, Hess says that one has to supersede philosophy in order to go over to action (and socialism). In his writings of 1842–43, however, the expectation is (the same holds for praxis in Cieszkowski) that the transition to action will be realized by the activity of *spirit*: spirit is essentially activity, for it points back to the effectuation of the originary act by which the subject, the 'I', is constituted. This act is nothing other than the act of *recognition* by which the subject overcomes its inner division and recognizes that 'the image in the mirror', in which it re-presents itself for itself, 'is its own'.[134] By this originary act, the subject-spirit constitutes itself and the world, or 'life' in its entirety, which is the speculary object of this specific attribute of man's.

The self-creation of spirit[135] is perpetual change, the transformation of all external determinateness into self-determination, a means of access to self-consciousness; it is an absolutely free process that is subject to no a priori limits, an infinity *in actu.* To limit it, to cancel the recognition of any form of determinateness as free activity of the spirit – something private property does by inverting the relationship between the representation of spirit and spirit's being-for-itself – leads to 'standing the world upon its head', turning the relationship between spirit and the result of its activity upside down.[136] In its immanent movement, spirit abolishes this unfreedom and does away with the autonomization of property, while subjecting it to its conscious self-determination. Morality, a consequence of the accomplishment of the free activity of the spirit, is thus revealed to be inseparable from community, just as equality is inseparable from freedom. Setting out to reverse the inwardness of reflection and the divorce between theory and action, Hess ends up producing a spiritualist activism, a new philosophy that he continues to call – in 1842–43 as in the *Triarchy* – a 'philosophy of action' (it was to become 'social philosophy' from 1843–44 on), an attempt to provide a philosophical foundation for socialism. Summoned to turn over a new leaf and become socialists, the so-called 'last philosophers' have no reason, when all is said and done, to feel out of place in Hess's world.

But the same holds for the socialists, for this attempt at philosophization takes place *within* the thought of the social and of social-ism. It proffers social-ism its genuinely philosophical substance, defined as the proposal to bring society (back) towards its essence or its ontological truth: *unity*.[137] The relation between this unity and its true element, the social, is restored, but in a way which goes beyond the egalitarian or religious abstractions that marked the earliest forms of its historical emergence – the Reformation (with its offspring, German philosophy) and the French Revolution. This is the significance of the Franco–German intellectual alliance that Hess steadfastly promoted, as had Heine before him: 'the true *principle* behind the French orientation in thought is more profound [than equality]. Truth, which manifests itself on the one hand as subjective freedom and on the other as objective equality or justice; truth, whose essential feature is *unity*, is the veritable principle underlying the modern intellectual orientation, whether French or German.'[138]

The 'socialist' supersession of egalitarianism has a precise strategic function in Hess: it distinguishes him from 'monkish, Christian' Babouvist communism and, in the process, from any connection with plebeian elements or the *sans-culottes*. More precisely – to use the term that came to replace those just mentioned – it purges Hess's communism of its *proletarian* associations. A comparison with Heine[139] should make it easier to grasp the significance of Hess's posture. Like Heine, Hess employs the reference to communism – but, above all, to socialism – as a means of taking his distance from the egalitarian problematic of the *sans-culottes*. Unlike the poet, however, he privileges unity (not antagonism: hence the primacy of socialism in Hess, whereas Heine makes the opposite choice) and the human species (not the working class, the natural base of support for communism in Heine). In a polemical attack on Lorenz von Stein,

whose book on French socialist and communist theories was fast becoming
the standard introduction to the subject in Germany, Hess criticizes him
for one-sidedly emphasizing equality to the detriment of freedom (and
the reciprocal relation between the two); and, in the same breath, for
insisting on 'the relationship between communism and the proletariat':
'repeated *ad nauseam*', this is, says Hess, 'the only vital thing about
communism that Stein can see'.[140] Stein 'completely separates real socialism from communism' in order to play the one off against the other, and
'thinks that he has accounted for everything with his pitiful category of
égalité'.[141] Stein is guilty, then, of a twofold error. First, he takes notice of
the communitarian claim only in its most primitive, 'materialist' form, the
tendency to bring about equality by pulling all forms of enjoyment *down*
to the same level: that is, the Spartan communism of (generalized)
penury. Stein sees nothing but the 'negative', 'destructive' aspects of the
movement; they serve as his 'bogeyman'. However, he persists in ignoring
– and this is his second mistake – communism's 'positive content', namely,
its intention to restore unity and its desire for 'reconciliation' between, in
particular, antagonistic classes.[142]

As a 'practical ethic' that seeks to abolish all abstract oppositions,
socialism plainly seeks to take up a position *above class* – not, like the
'centrist Hegelian' von Stein, *between* classes, in the sense of an *entre-deux*,
a solution of the '*juste-milieu*' that would in any case represent a premature
(and vain) attempt at reconciliation. Hess, like the Young Hegelians,[143]
declares war on 'mediation', that is to say, the politics of accommodation
so well represented by Hegel. Doubtless he is now no less hostile to the
political-social-religious reform that he himself had proposed earlier.
'Above class' signifies something else: it means 'at a higher level of truth',
a level more 'essential' than the classes and their struggle – for it concerns,
precisely, 'essence'. In order to reach this level one must, of course be
willing to go through a moment of struggle. Socialism is struggle, but
struggle between '*principles*', not classes; it is a struggle by and for self-
consciousness. As a philosophy of the social question, socialism is raised,
without concession, to the level of the self-consciousness of 'spirit' or, in
more Feuerbachian terms, of the 'essence', 'social humanity', or 'human
society'. We no longer find Hess sighing – as in the *Triarchy*, or like the
incorrigible Bauer – over the backwardness of the 'masses'. But the fact
remains that the struggle is directly inscribed in a narrative that anticipates
its own end. And, above all, the existing struggle – or, rather, struggles –
are simply the manifestation of something that runs deeper: the struggle
between principles, the activity of spirit returning to itself as it surmounts
all the obstacles to its self-determination. In other words, the struggle is

merely the phenomenal manifestation of Spirit's irresistible march towards the One. Subsequently, this march becomes, in Feuerbachian terms, a process of disalienation, men's reappropriation of their essence and human powers, the full development of their productive capacities; but the overall scheme is not seriously disrupted as a result.

To put this more precisely, let us return to the France–Germany dichotomy that is central to the texts Hess published in the *Einundzwanzig Bogen*. In so far as it is a philosophical supersession of philosophy, socialism undoubtedly appropriates all that the French current has achieved; but, in the final analysis, it is only in order to reaffirm the pre-eminence of the German road:

> Today, the obstacles that the philosophy of action has to overcome are nowhere greater than in our own country. We are still suffering from that universal medieval illness, with its oppositions of theory and practice, politics and religion, the here-below and the beyond. And yet the philosophy of action can take its principle only from Germany. Only where philosophy in general has reached its culminating point can it transcend itself and go over to action. The opposition between the here-below and the beyond, which has come about only in and through spirit, can, in principle, be overcome only in and through spirit.[144]

And the activity of spirit, its irresistible advance towards self-consciousness, solves the 'riddle of history', the problem of how to progress beyond the status quo. This dénouement signals the advent of something which, though radically new, can be known in advance, thanks to the categories of the philosophy of action. 'Morality', our old friend from the German Enlightenment, is, in Hess's writings of 1842–43, a name for the last stage in spirit's march towards self-determination. It is the moment of absolute unity in which idea and action, liberty and necessity, morality and community converge:

> Freedom is morality; it is above all the fulfilment of the law of life, of spiritual activity, as much in the narrow sense, by which the act is called idea, as in the broader sense, by which the idea is called act, with clear consciousness of this law. Thus it is fulfilment, not as natural necessity or as determination by nature, as was the case for all living creatures until now, but as self-determination. Without this morality, no state of collectivism is conceivable; but also, no morality is conceivable without collectivism. The riddle drawn out of the closed circle of slavery can be solved by the spirit, and by the spirit alone, through the progress of the dialectic, through its history. History has already broken through the closed circle of slavery. The revolution is the break from captivity, from the condition of bigotry and oppression in which the spirit found itself before it became self-conscious. But ... this anarchy only broke through the limits

imposed from the outside, without progressing further to self-determination or self-limitation, to morality. The revolution is still incomplete, and it knows that it is still incomplete. Even so, the anarchy could not stay as it was at the beginning, and has in fact not stayed that way. *And as we, the children of the revolution, move on from it forward into morality, the riddle is thus being solved.*[145]

We have come full circle. A declaration of rupture with what is most unbearable in the German situation, the divorce between theory and practice, has been transformed, in a standard move, into a literal reiteration of the discourse that consecrates this very situation and, more than ever, makes it impossible to go beyond it. The promise of a breakthrough becomes a simple variation on the initial theme: the revolution is splendid, but we Germans have already transcended it, in a present straining with its every fibre to reach the imminent future towards which morality points the way. But morality is precisely that category which is inconceivable unless it is distinguished from politics, which it is supposed to guide from on high.[146] Hess's objective is to show that bypassing the revolution is equivalent to surpassing it; he means to trace the contours of a German road that is, to be sure, not antithetical, but nevertheless distinct from and, in a sense, even superior to the French example. Towards the mid-1840s, this road seemed – to Hess and, no doubt, to the great majority of German intellectuals, as well as the German democratic movement – both impracticable and impossible to avoid.[147] Radicalization led them to reject the reformist solution; but radicalization also led towards the void – or, rather, to a quasi-instinctive retreat before the void it had itself created, and, ultimately, to withdrawal into the categories whose supersession it had announced. This was 'the unending melody'[148] of the German road, the oscillation between the terms posed by the antinomies of practical reason *à la* Kant.

In fact, the crisis intensified as people stepped further and further back from the yawning gulf to which it pointed. Hess offers a striking illustration of this retreat. It amounts to a confession: 'Atheism and communism! Let us examine this sapling. The thing about it that most frightens people is its apparent lack of roots in any solid earth.'[149] A radical gutting of the transcendent signifier, an abolition of any originary foundation, the revolution, Hess concedes, awakens legitimate fears. But the philosopher strikes a reassuring note. The terrifying absence is only 'apparent': it is immediately incorporated into a vast dialectical development of which it simply represents the first moment, which is destined to be promptly surpassed.

This process is without a priori limits, but it is not without an (inherent) end purpose [*fin*]. In other words, what seems to have been lost in terms of foundations is immediately recovered in terms of finality. An-archy, a synthesis of atheism and communism, does indeed appear to be the 'annihilation of all determination', but in fact it is simply a rejection of all external limitation – a negation, not of freedom, but of anything that tends to impede spirit's progress towards self-determination. That, decidedly, is what 'makes it sound much less dreadful'.[150] In this first form of freedom, however, a direct consequence of the revolution, the 'free individual', incapable of rising to the level of self-determination, ends up trapped in the appearance of absence, which he perceives as sheer indeterminateness, the absence of all limitation. Anarchy then changes into its opposite, becoming the intolerable domination and coercion (the Terror) which trigger a movement back towards external limitations (property and differences between individuals). The subjectivists (the Babouvists and the partisans of the Terror) can issue as many moral condemnations as they like (by crying 'treason'); the fact remains that there is something necessary about this revenge of objectivity, as Restorationists such as Saint-Simon, Fourier and Hegel understood perfectly well – at the price of a 'misunderstanding of the essence of revolution' and the placing of new limits, quite as extrinsic as those imposed by their predecessors, on the self-determination of spirit (personal authority in Saint-Simon, material property in Fourier, Being in Hegel). Hence the 'return to the point at which revolution emerges' observable in both Germany and France: 'the Restoration king was driven out, the Restoration philosopher, Hegel, died of cholera'.[151] The new point of departure cannot be a simple repetition of the old. It opens on to a new synthesis which is qualitatively superior to the one that preceded it: objectivity *without* the restoration, anarchy *with* self-consciousness – in a word, Proudhon *and* Feuerbach. The result is a community reconciled, but without revolution – reconciled by association and love.

It is time, then, for the forging of syntheses. Once again, the revolution is behind us – this is the truth of the *Trois Glorieuses*. Indeed, Hegel's death is the equivalent of the July Revolution; such is the truth of the preceding truth. The German road is legitimized once again; the historical antinomy of practice and theory is resolved in favour of theory. While Hess may describe Hegel as a 'Restoration philosopher', his analysis simply prolongs, and cannot but prolong, the conclusions at which Hegel had arrived in *The Philosophy of History*: social philosophy, or socialism, represents the latest and ultimate stage in the immanent development of philosophy. To overcome the crisis, Hess's socialism is constructed as an alternative to the revolution.

The 'religion of love and humanity'

If the radicalization visible in the texts Hess published in the *Einundzwan-zig Bogen* quickly sinks back into the ruts of the German ideology, the fact remains that it announces a transformation of his theoretical system [*dispositif*], one that becomes manifest in 'On the Essence of Money': Feuerbach now begins to play an increasingly preponderant role in Hess's work. The theory of alienation and of the human species gradually displaces the spiritualist activism of Hess's early texts. The stakes of this repudiation of 'Spirit' are nothing less than Hess's relationship to philosophy: his texts of 1844–45 give the 'last philosophers', Bauer, Stirner, and Feuerbach combined, their marching orders, although he does not rule out the possibility that all three will soon be 'resurrected' as socialists. His tone is more vehement, almost terroristic, in 'The Essence of Money': 'they dream of infinite progress and can see it ending in no other way . . . than with the *death* of some lifeless phantom they call "Spirit". They too, the philosophers, are among those who can imagine no reality other than the bad reality that currently exists . . . they themselves are an essential, integral part of this old, bad reality that is on its way to extinction.'[152] Together with their predecessors and competitors, the theologians and priests, they are sorry figures, 'antediluvian creatures'.[153] They are beyond redemption, and have no place in the community of the future. Hess's is a Platonic Republic turned inside out: it will expel not the poets, but the guardians, whether they go by the name of philosophers, scholars, priests or politicians.[154] The truth of which they were only recently the vehicles, the truth of the social, has now taken up residence elsewhere, leaving only speculative corpses in its wake, mired ever more deeply in error and superstition.

As we have seen, this migration of the truth results not from a change of terrain but, rather, from a rearrangement of the terrain itself – the philosophization of the social under the banner of humanism. The definition of the social in organicist terms is now carried out systematically, appearing in the form of the 'social body' whose 'life' is labour or an 'exchange of productive vital activity':[155] 'the fact is that everything that lives works'.[156] Productive exchange brings *two* 'bodies' into play, two strictly homologous organisms:[157] the human and the social. The relationship between them is a *mirror*-relation – '[men] relate to the social body as a whole the way the different bodily members and organs relate to the body of a particular individual';[158] but it is a *centred* mirror-relation: the big organism constitutes the 'vital medium' for the small one – or, to be more precise, 'the medium of exchange of any creature's productive vital activity, its inalienable means of existence'.[159] Consequently, the social medium realizes the human essence, the true centre of this relationship; as in Feuerbach, it is intersubjective. Hess calls this medium 'men's intercourse' [*Verkehr*], and he defines it from the outset in a poietic mode that makes the tendency towards totalization stronger than it is in Feuerbachian intersubjectivity, with its originary experience of sexuality: 'men's intercourse does not *originate* in their essence; it *is* their *actual* essence, that is, both their theoretical essence, their concrete vital *consciousness*, and also their practical, concrete vital *activity*'.[160]

This intersubjective essence is both originary and final; history is conceived as that which makes it possible to link the one to the other, the ideal to the foundation, by way of a vast, tragic sequence, which deploys in its plenitude – but at the price of untold suffering and destruction – the capacity of the human species. 'On the Essence of Money' restores the contents of this 'tragedy of cosmic dimensions' for us.[161] The contradiction between the individual and the species grows more acute; social existence is completely alienated; the last act will soon begin. The final reconciliation, 'that Promised Land ... our eyes can already reach', will (re-)establish unity between the individual and the species, and produce harmony between the individual and the social body, human nature and productive exchange. The road to this reconciliation passes by way of a *conscious reorganization* of all human activity, especially work. Only *organized* work is a free activity; like the 'Spirit' of the now-defunct philosophy of action, it obeys only its own determinations, having freed itself of all external limitations and arrived at full self-consciousness. The social world now corresponds adequately to the subject; henceforth it will be the medium in which the subject realizes his essence, experiencing this correspondence as enjoyment [*jouissance*]. Through this fusion of the dialectic of the human essence and the philosophy of history, Hess provides a philosophical foundation for the socialist project as a project of social reunification, the restoration of the constitutive truth of human existence – via its conscious organization.

Conscious organization of society does not imply the use of the political, voluntarist means of the Revolutionary Year II. Proceeding 'by decree' is out of the question. Hess is very emphatic on this point, even in texts such as *Kommunistisches Bekenntniß* [Communist profession of faith], written after the uprising of the Silesian weavers and the ensuing popular agitation, in a context in which an open clash with absolutism seemed increasingly likely, if not inevitable. For Hess, the deepening crisis takes the form of a mounting internal tension between predictions of an imminent upheaval and exhortations to greater patience. This growing tension is the unmistakable indication of a theoretical 'deadlock'. On the one hand, we are told that 'the last hour of the animal social world will soon have sounded. The mechanism of the money machine has ground to a halt; in vain do our politicians of progress and reaction strive to keep it turning.'[162] On the other hand, at the very moment when the first wave of working-class mobilizations in Germany seems to be confirming this prophecy, prudence and moderation gain the upper hand. To the question 'can people today establish a communist society right away?', the answer is no:

> They can only lay the groundwork for the creation of a communist society.... Above all, we must make present-day society aware of its deplorable state and of the fact that a better fate lies in store for it, so that the desire for humane conditions, the desire to free ourselves of the servitude in which we find ourselves, will be aroused in the majority of men. But, once every force capable of resisting improvements has been eliminated, we must, first, abolish the useless state institutions that squander men's energies in the service of despotism.[163]

Thus the basic argument for gradualism runs as follows: people must be changed before circumstances can be, for the first change is the precondition and the premiss for the second. To the classical aporia of political philosophy – good governance presupposes people who are capable of it, and the opposite is equally true – Hess responds like a good Enlightenment thinker, according priority to education: 'sudden, violent abolition of prevailing property relations would inevitably have negative consequences. Reasonable property presupposes a reasonable society, which in turn presupposes socially educated people, so that a sudden transformation of unorganized property into organized property is unthinkable.'[164] But if Hess's answer is apparently quite traditional, its premisses are less so; for altering property relations, abolishing money – in a word, transforming social relations – is not the same thing as laying down new laws. Rather, making such changes amounts to subordinating the question of law to another, that of the conscious reorganization of society, which provides, simultaneously, the yardstick for justice and truth.

To transform social relations is neither to do violence to them from without, nor, above all, to reason in terms of a radical break. Rather, it is to restore their truth from within, to realize their essence, that is, their founding intersubjectivity: unity, harmony, and reciprocity. It is the identification of this transformation with the gradual revelation of the social itself and the supersession of everything (extrinsic by definition) that perverts it which provides the theoretical foundation for Hess's belief in the virtues of education, heightened consciousness, and what he calls the 'groundwork' for the creation of a communist society. To put it more straightforwardly, social reorganization as a means of access to unity and transparency – here Hess, as we might expect, appeals to the Saint-Simonian idea of 'administration' – is inextricably bound up with a disavowal of the idea of rupture:

> Prevailing property relations will *gradually* be transformed into communist property relations when the aforementioned measures are implemented. The value of money will diminish in proportion as that of human beings increases. The value of human beings will then *necessarily* rise until they have become invaluable, and the perverted value of money will *necessarily* fall until it has become the total absence of value in proportion as the organization of society, set in motion by the *administration*, gains ground on wage work, gradually eclipsing it; in proportion, again, as the socially raised and socially educated younger generation reaches maturity and begins to carry out all social tasks.[165]

Thus socioeconomic relations will necessarily be transformed as they progressively give way before the restored plenitude of the human essence. . . .

If this essence is nothing other than the 'intercourse' between people, its reappropriation, for individuals who are deprived of it in bourgeois society, can be understood only as a tautological affirmation of its constitutive truth, the intersubjective bond itself, the essence of the essence of humanity – namely, Love. Hess's socialism becomes communism in very Feuerbachian fashion, via this identification of the essence of the human species, and the reconciled community of the future, with love.[166] Conversely, as the externalization of this essence, the social medium, the world where productive human activities are exchanged, is also love, although it fails to recognize itself as such because of the alienating inversion that characterizes it. Indeed, everything is love, including the natural-sensuous world regarded from the standpoint of the *relationship* that we establish with it: 'what comes from love? The entire creation, or the universe, which is eternal and infinite, and unfathomable, like love. . . . love creates without end; where the effects of love are not felt, everything begins to disintegrate.'[167] In order to restore unity and realize communism, love need only recognize itself as such; it is enough for this revelation to take place (through education and dissemination of the true message). More precisely (a more moderate version), since the two processes are coextensive, they unfold by degrees; but one necessarily entails the other. We must therefore take affirmations like the following very seriously: 'we need now only *acknowledge* the light of freedom and rid ourselves of the night watchmen so that all of us may joyously join hands'.[168] Ultimately, nothing can prevent humanity from emerging from the cave, which it will do despite the guardians, as a result of the autonomous development of the human species.

More than ever, Hess's communism – like that of all the social thinkers of the period, from Saint-Simon through Comte to Owen – presents itself as a new religion. It is a natural religion, a religion of the 'heart' and 'reason', of 'love and humanity', at once a 'fulfilment of the Christian religion' and a refined form of it.[169] Hess's social philosophy sets out to accomplish the task that Feuerbach had assigned to the reform of philosophy: that of becoming itself through its self-transformation (= reform), that is to say, of becoming religion in order to seize the place that religion occupies.[170] The following passage, about the author of *The Essence of Christianity*, applies, *mutatis mutandis*, to the one who assumed his mantle: 'the true "ground" of [Feuerbach's] thought *is what he presents as its consequence*: his ideal of a communism of love and his conception of the revolution as disclosure, as "the open confession of the secrets of his love". The revolution as confession (so that the sole means of political action is the form of demystification known as disclosure, i.e., books and articles in the press) – that is what he has in mind.'[171] This should doubtless be amended to read that the communism of love *takes the place of* the revolution, or is a transubstantiation of the revolution which results in its transformation into the communism of love.[172] The rights of the German road are restored; hence the air of familiarity, the 'weakness' which – as Engels would later put it – enabled Feuerbachianism and 'true socialism' to 'spread like a plague in "educated" Germany from 1844 on'.[173] This new version of intellectual and ethical reform, distinguished from the political practice that it purports to replace, is addressed to the whole human species, regardless of national or religious distinctions, which have already been swept aside by the level of development that the human essence has reached.[174] It transcends class boundaries as well, for the individuals who make up the human species, capitalists no less than proletarians, are, says Hess, victims of universal alienation: they are all robbed of their humanity, debased by money and relations of competition and mutual exploitation. And all can be saved by 'acting for one another', acknowledging the bonds of love that unite them in their intersubjective 'intercourse', and putting an end to the kind of conflict that is rooted in misrecognition and the inverted existence typical of bourgeois society.

Of course, Hess is not unaware of the existence of the class struggle, nor is he ignorant of the fact that, however universalistic his communism of love might claim to be, his readers are mainly proletarians. He is sometimes even led to pronounce a 'we' that is a class we, a 'proletarian' we; but he invariably covers it over with an 'everyone' embracing both capitalists and proletarians, an 'everyone' that is synonymous with the 'human species', and transcends class differences.[175] It would, however, be a mistake to think, on the basis of a literal reading of the sharply polemical formulations of the *Communist Manifesto*,[176] that ethico-political socialism, especially Hess's, was an expression of the 'class essence' of the German petty bourgeoisie, and therefore foreign to the workers' movement.[177] Again, on a more general level, the sarcastic gibes we find in *The German Ideology* should not make us forget that Marx and Engels were capable of more discriminating judgements – capable, too, of publishing them – concerning the significance of the post-Hegelian philosophical debate in Germany, even in the ranks of the workers' movement. For example, in *Herr Vogt* (1860), Marx notes that 'the various phases undergone by German philosophy from 1839 to 1846 were followed with the most lively interest in these [German *émigré*] workers' societies'.[178]

In the case before us, the lively interest would appear to have been mutual: from the moment of his arrival in Paris as a correspondent for the *Rheinische Zeitung* (late in 1842), Hess assiduously frequented the circles of the French as well as the German *émigré* workers' movement in Paris, and also cultivated his relations with the socialist and communist theoreticians, serving as their intermediary with Germany through both his writings (especially his dispatches to the *Rheinische Zeitung*) and his personal contacts.[179] To quote Auguste Cornu, his role obviously consisted in 'establishing a connection between Weitling's doctrines, which had wide currency in German working-class circles, and the philosophical radicalism of the Young Hegelians'.[180] He soon became a militant in various working-class organizations, in which his texts served as a basis for discussion so often that he has been called 'one of the leaders' of the 'circle of communist workers' among the German *émigrés*.[181] Thus Hess 'discovered the proletariat' well before others, notably Marx. Yet this discovery did not seriously affect his theoretical system; indeed, it gave new impetus to his ethical-humanist flight to the front.

But there is still more to be said here. As we see from the debates that a text such as 'Communist Confession of Faith' provoked among the Parisian sections of the League of the Just,[182] which later became the Communist League, Hess's political tendencies – much more than those of Marx or of Hess's own former collaborator, Engels – reflected the state of mind actually prevailing in the workers' movement of the day. Moreover, this held true for much longer than is generally admitted[183] –

indeed, right up to the eve of the revolutionary upheaval. The 'Confession of Faith' – part of which was published in December 1844 in the Paris *Vorwärts*, followed by full publication in 1846 in the review of the Rhineland partisans of 'true socialism' – left a deep impression on the Paris leadership, and on rank-and-file members of the League of the Just. Even *after* the League's first congress (June 1847), in its most critical period, when an intense internal struggle was raging over the theoretical and political tendencies of the German working-class organization, now rechristened the Communist League, the theses that the organization adopted were still very much 'in phase' with Hess's views.[184] Witness the statutes of the League, and, above all, the 'Entwurf des kommunistischen Glaubensbekenntnisses [Communist profession of faith, draft]'. This text, the fruit of a compromise, was written by Engels; yet a sizeable portion of it (essentially the first six questions and answers) reflected the standpoint of the organization's leaders who, at the time, were obviously more sympathetic to Hess's version of communism than to a revolutionary theory of class struggle.[185] Thus the 'Profession of Faith' defined the objective in terms of the organization of society and collective property; pointed out the essential role of 'principles' – such as the quest for universal happiness – that were present in 'the minds and hearts of all men', and did not 'require proof'; and identified means of action that came down to 'enlightening and unifying the proletariat'.[186] A bitter debate flared up around this draft; significantly, in the course of it, Hess succeeded in bringing the Paris sections of the League to adopt a text that was similar to – even identical with – his own profession of faith.[187] This drew a response from Engels that took the form of yet another profession of faith – known today as 'Principles of Communism', although at the time the accepted title was the same as that of Hess's text.[188] The procedures to which Engels had to resort to secure adoption of his counter-draft 'behind the back of the communities [the League's rank-and-file structures]',[189] so as then to be able to present it to the London leaders of the League as a text representative of the standpoint of the Paris sections, shows that the rank and file remained loyal to the positions defended by Hess, or, at least, resistant to Marx and Engels's innovations – unlike the 'middle-level leadership'. Hence a good deal of artifice and acrimonious debate was required, both before and during the *second* congress of the League, to bring about the change of direction which resulted in the decision to commission Marx and Engels to write the *Communist Manifesto*.

Even a cursory comparison of the two competing 'professions of faith' of 1847 (Engels's versus Hess's) is enough to give us a clear idea of the issues at the heart of the conflict. The main bone of contention was the question of humanism: class struggle or dialectic of the human essence; revolution or ethical sermonizing and peaceful propaganda. Engels aims his anti-humanistic polemic in two directions. First, he stresses the *discontinuity* of the historical-social subject – that is to say, the *modernity* of the proletariat and its struggle. This struggle, he argues, cannot be reduced to that of the dominated classes which existed before the proletariat,[190] or, *a fortiori*, to any conceivable human essence that is assumed to enfold all of them in the process of its self-realization. This irreducibility re-emerges at the rhetorical level. Just as there is no essence pre-existing history that can establish continuity between the proletarian class struggle and the class struggles of the past, so communism is not the fulfilment of the Christian religion; it is not a new religion that expresses the truth of the human species' ongoing existence for itself through, and thanks to, its suffering, and so on. It is theory 'alone' – if one can put it that way – which teaches us 'the conditions for the emancipation of the proletariat;[191] this excludes any principle that would transcend the struggle for proletarian emancipation.

As for the social and historical conditions of that emancipation, they are identified with those of the revolution. This is the second dividing line between Engels's position and socialist humanism. Engels dismisses the illusions of a 'peaceful road' to socialism that would ignore the violence exercised by the possessing classes, for he treats the problem of the revolution apart from all moral presuppositions and from any choice that depends on the free will of an ethical subject.[192] Rather than indulging in prophecies of the revolution's imminence, he raises the question of its contemporary relevance, in its strategic, programmatic, national (German) and international dimensions.[193] It should, however, be pointed out that Engels's account of this debate, long regarded as authoritative, was written many years after the event; and that its author – lapses of memory aside – may well have been rather too eager to demonstrate a 'natural' convergence between the workers' movement and the new theory that he and Marx were then beginning to hammer out. Against Engels's version, I must stress that Hess gave ground only after a long confrontation, a theoretical and ideological struggle rather than the 'quiet revolution' Engels describes in his 1885 text.[194] Moreover, the positions Hess defended had a formative influence on the most advanced wing of the German workers' movement throughout an entire period. This fact alone suffices to show that the question of the 'German road' and the concomitant ideology do not derive from an 'essence' – in this case, a 'class' rather than a 'human' essence – that is allegedly characteristic of the German bourgeoisie or petty bourgeoisie and its intellectual representatives, an 'essence' of which genuine socialists rid themselves upon 'discovering' the proletariat.[195] Confronting the crisis without drawing back in the face of the massive rupture it provoked was, rather, a matter of theoretical and political intervention – a radical intervention, in that it refused to continue to obstruct the work of the antagonism immanent in the real.

4

Friedrich Engels Discovers the Proletariat, 1842–1845

As we have seen, Hegel – and, *a fortiori*, the Hegelian left – considered England a *politically* archaic country with a strong whiff of nostalgia for the feudal past about it; they had a correspondingly low opinion of English political culture. This by no means prevented them from calling attention to Britain's *economic* modernity, which found its theoretical expression in English economics, 'one of the sciences which have originated in the modern age as their element', as Hegel says in *Elements of the Philosophy of Right*. Political economy, he goes on, had grasped the principle informing civil society [*die bürgerliche Gesellschaft*] – namely, the rationality of *labour* as a *mediation* between the particular – the satisfaction of individual needs – and the universal – the relation obtaining between these different needs and the means of satisfying them.[1] For Hegel, to be sure, this form of rationality, together with the sphere of civil society in which it develops, belongs to the categories of the understanding, and thus cannot replace the political criterion. Authorizing the development of the internal mediations of the highest sphere, the state, it is itself destined to be superseded by the active realization of reason in the state.

As Marx points out in his Paris manuscripts (the '1844 Manuscripts'), Hegel alone speaks from the 'standpoint of modern political economy', for he establishes the anthropology of labour on concrete foundations, treating the self-production of the human species as an active relation which, by externalizing man's species-powers, makes man as he exists the product of his own labour. Yet – contrary to a common assumption – to say so is not exactly to sing Hegel's praises – at least, not in Marx's estimation. Marx acknowledges that 'the outstanding achievement of Hegel's *Phenomenology*' is to have grasped species-man as this self-creative process; but he makes it clear from the outset that his objective is to examine 'in detail Hegel's one-sidedness and limitations'. 'Hegel's standpoint', he grants, 'is that of modern political economy. He grasps *labour* as the *essence* of man – as man's essence which stands the test.' In the next breath, however, he criticizes the *one-sidedness* of this conception: Hegel 'sees only the positive, not the negative side of labour'. What he neglects is the negativity of labour, the 'bad side' that enables it to progress, the reality of alienation and the limits that alienation puts on man's develop-ment: 'labour is *man's coming-to-be for* himself within *alienation,* or as *alienated* man'.[2] As for the philosophy that culminates in the Hegelian system, it is merely the reflexive consciousness of this alienation, a purely speculative, formal and abstract transcendence of the limits alienation imposes. Nevertheless, the acuity of Hegel's observations on history tran-scends, as usual, the one-sidedness of his purely conceptual argument; §189 of the *Elements of the Philosophy of Right,* just cited, establishes a close relation between the viewpoint of political economy and the 'mass relationships and mass movements [*der Massen*] in their qualitative and quantitative determinacy and complexity'. In other words, Hegel sees that the effects of the viewpoint of the masses, affirmed once and for all by the French Revolution, are now beginning to make themselves felt on the grounds staked out by political economy.

At the point where Hegel's thought, political economy, and the mass movements of the day intersect, we find someone of particular importance to the further course of our discussion: Friedrich Engels. Engels was certainly not the first to pursue an internal critique of the brand of economics that professed to represent 'socialism' and/or the positions of the dominated classes. The Ricardian left had set out on this path before him, as he himself would later acknowledge.[3] Engels, however, rather like Heine or Hess, shuttled back and forth between different theoretical and national cultures – as, say, a Thomas Hodgskin did not, whatever his other merits. The young German whose first direct experience of English life came late in 1842, when he began working in Manchester, the British city that then ranked as both the industrial capital of the world and a centre of working-class agitation, already had to his credit several years of intense intellectual activity in his own country.

Thus he had published reviews, poems and essays on the German liberal and national movement and the condition of the working class; he had also dabbled in composition and the theatre[4] and mastered no fewer than six languages (by the age of nineteen). His hunger for knowledge was, in the true sense of the word, encyclopaedic. 'Self-taught' and, above all, 'a "travelling-agent" in philosophy', as he liked to repeat,[5] he was steeped in Hegel and profoundly marked by the new spirit of Heine, David Friedrich Strauß, and Feuerbach. Early on, as testimony to his boundless admiration for Börne, he had served public notice of his 'radical, resolute democratic tendency', carving out a unique place for himself among the mass of publicists 'associated with Young Germany';[6] and, also early on, the political acumen of his literary and philosophical interventions had caught the public eye. From the outset, he wrote under the banner of a 'fusion of Hegel and Börne', an image that emblematized 'the German spirit', the 'political practice' born of the French Revolution, and 'the unity of thought and action'.[7] In 1841–42, his polemical ardour, mobilized in defence of the achievements of Hegelianism, was directed first and foremost at Schelling, the key figure of Restoration thought.[8] It is significant – because it indicates both the strategic importance of Engels's choice, and his pioneering role – that when Marx tried, more than two years later (in vain, as it turned out), to persuade Feuerbach to collaborate with him on a journal and other publication projects, he proposed that they should take to the field against Schelling. 'An attack on Schelling', said Marx, 'is indirectly an attack on our entire policy, and especially on Prussian policy. Schelling's philosophy is Prussian policy *sub specie philosophiæ*.'[9]

Engels's talents and interests were even broader than all this suggests. In many ways he was a typical product of German Romanticism, with ties to Karl Gutzkow,[10] the leading figure of the Young Germany movement: he devoured Goethe's complete works, took a passionate interest in Mendelssohn's oratorios and Beethoven's symphonies, and translated Shelley.[11] He learned to 'speak English' very early on, at a time when Marx's still rather narrow horizons took in little more than the typical Prussian and Rhenish concerns, confining him to clashes with representatives of the Hegelian left and run-ins with the absolutist censorship. Establishing himself in the city that was then the beacon of the Industrial Revolution, Engels would soon develop his English well beyond the language of political economy and business that used constantly in his professional life. We should note that just before leaving Germany for Britain, he made an acquaintance who was to have a decisive influence on him: Moses Hess would later boast that he had converted Engels to communism, and doubtless also won him round to the view that England had a special, 'social' mission.[12] Indeed, Engels's work down to *The Condition of the Working-Class in England* consistently bore Hess's stamp whenever he 'spoke German'.[13]

The Engels who arrived in the hub of the capitalist world was, then, a young communist from one of the many small, sleepy Rhenish towns that had so far taken only their first faltering steps towards industrialization. A man with no time to lose, he soon turned the historical lag [*décalage*] exemplified by his own situation and German background to good use, transforming it into a privileged vantage point from which to observe this new world. His taste for love-affairs with women outside his own social class, combined with his political sensibility, gave him direct access – as we shall see, 'direct' certainly does not mean unprejudiced – to the world of the proletariat. But we should not allow his rich experience and zest for life to divert our attention from what matters most. The interest that Engels holds for us is not simply biographical; even less is it anecdotal; it is, in the full sense of the word, theoretical. It is too often forgotten that Engels – or, at any rate, the young Engels – was an original thinker, intellectually more advanced in certain respects – particularly as a result of his experience in the family enterprise and his long stays in England – than the other members of the Young Hegelian movement, Marx not excepted. No doubt Marx would have been the last to quarrel with this judgement. Had he not chosen, in 1844, to commend only three Germans – the troika Weitling, Hess and Engels – for their '*original* works of substance' in socialist theory?[14] Yet this recognition hardly testified to a spontaneous convergence of views. Engels's originality, as we see, does not consist in – or, more precisely, cannot be understood as – a more or less successful 'anticipation' of Marx's trajectory. Indeed, my hypothesis is rather the opposite. It is to the extent that Engels's theoretical intervention is fundamentally distinct – or even divergent – from Marx's that it becomes intelligible; this holds until the moment of his 'true' encounter with Marx, which dates from the period when they co-authored *The German Ideology.*

With Engels, the 'English road' is no longer an abstract reference serving a purely instrumental function (as model or counter-model) in arguments whose real concern lies elsewhere. It loses the formal character it still had in Hess's scheme of things, acquiring the texture of a lived experience with very precise stakes: the *critique* of political economy and the relationship this critique bears to a newly emergent social force, the working-class movement. We can go still further. As the revelation and defence of a new system [*dispositif*], called the 'social', for identifying and managing the contradictions spawned by the emancipation of bourgeois society, the English road, as Engels saw it, could well turn out to be the road of the future, the most advanced pole in the triad described by Hess, and the long-sought alternative to the limited 'French' road – that is to say, to the *unity* of the revolution and the political. But in order to fulfil that role, this English experience would have to be translated into a German idiom that remained as indispensable as ever. If we are to understand the contribution made by Engels – not only as a pioneer of the social sciences and, especially, of their construction of a novel way of *looking* at the working-class world, but also as a theoretician of 'true socialism', a field in which Hess's convert rapidly rivalled his teacher's powers of insight – we have to position ourselves, precisely, among the shifting terms of our European topography: Engels transforms the self-criticism of the revolution into circumvention of the French road via an Anglocentrism painstakingly translated into the language of German theory. He thus provides 'true socialism', a product of the typically German intellectual and political situation, with what Lukács calls its missing link, a link defined in relation to English classical political economy.[15]

So we will be examining, in the pages that follow, a specifically Engelsian trajectory. It is not only different from the one traced by Heine and Marx, but antithetical to it – or, at any rate, an *alternative* to it. This Engelsian – or, more precisely, Hesso–Engelsian – anthropological matrix ('socialist humanism' in the narrowest, virtually etymological sense of the term) underpinned both Engels's 'scientific' work and his interventions as an 'activist'. At what was, to be sure, primarily the conceptual level, but also in the very concrete struggle for control over the earliest organizations of the *émigré* German workers' movement, socialist humanism was the main source of opposition to the theoretical and strategic propositions that assigned primacy to the political, whether they did so in the 'old-fashioned', purely 'French' way (represented by neo-Babouvian communism) or followed the new, 'Franco–German' road that Heine – and, more systematically, Marx – were then in the process of exploring.

All this, of course, was before Engels's encounter with Marx: not the first encounter, which took place in Cologne and was not a great success, although that was soon forgotten in the afterglow of Engels's successful meeting with Hess, but the 'true' encounter, that of the years in Paris and Brussels, during which Marx and Engels teamed up to write *The German Ideology* and then the *Communist Manifesto* – an encounter consecrated by the struggle against 'true socialism' that the two men would henceforth carry out in tandem. If the young Engels – whose positions were very close to Hess's and a very long way from Marx's – interests us in his own right, part of the reason is that he can help us to explain an apparently paradoxical circumstance: although posterity has gone on *ad infinitum* about what distinguishes the 'young' from the 'mature' Marx, only Engels seems to have gone through a 'youthful' period in the true sense, a period of the sort that one must subsequently acknowledge to have been a defeat so that one can put it behind one and go on to become one's real self – in Engels's case, Marx's Other. Engels, it is worth recalling, was never sparing with self-critical clarifications of the historical record. As far as he is concerned, in any event, the critique of German philosophical socialism cannot be termed an '*unacknowledged* self-critique'.[16] Engels's declaration in later life to the effect that 'for a time, we were all "Feuerbachians"' is well known.[17] Here, admittedly, he is referring to a whole generation (including, explicitly, Marx). But a text that dates from a period just after the major turn of 1844, and is contemporaneous with his polemical attack on his own earlier positions (1846), is more explicit:

> Among all the pompous phrases now loudly proclaimed in German literature as the basic principle of true, pure, German, theoretical communism and socialism, there has so far not been a single idea which has grown on German soil. What the French or the English said as long as ten, twenty and even forty years ago – and said very well, very clearly, in very fine language – the Germans have now at last during the past year become acquainted with in bits and have Hegelianised, or at best belatedly rediscovered it and published it in a much worse, more abstract form as a completely new discovery. *I make no exception here of my own writings.*[18]

Thus the original, French or English, had lost nothing of its interest or beauty; the translation, on the other hand, had to be revised from one end to the other. But to say this is already to begin telling another story – or, more precisely, it is to let another story begin to unfold by bringing its premises out into the open.

THE 'ENGLISH CONDITION':
THE *ANCIEN RÉGIME* PLUS CAPITALISM?

Germany – England

A number of texts with emblematic titles – 'The Condition of England', 'Letters from London', 'Outlines of a Critique of Political Economy' – set the stage for the monumental *Condition of the Working-Class in England*, a key work in the intellectual history of socialism. These texts bear witness to the shock that Engels's first stay in England caused him. The posture he adopts in them is strongly reminiscent of Heine's: addressing a German public, Engels invites it, above all, to take the measure of the distance separating it from 'advanced' Europe, and points out some methods by which it can 'catch up'. As an attentive first-hand observer of the political and social reality of the capitalist metropolis a decade after Heine, he rejects the English model in the poet's wake, and in the very same terms.

'Is there any other country in the world', the correspondent for the *Rheinische Zeitung* wonders,

> where feudalism retains such enduring power and where it remains immune from attack not only in actual fact, but also in public opinion? Is the much-vaunted English freedom anything but the purely formal right to act or not to act, as one sees fit, within the existing legal limits? And what laws they are! A chaos of confused, mutually contradictory regulations, which . . . are not in accord with our times.[19]

Whereas some of his contemporaries – notably Tocqueville – were so fascinated by the dynamism of a bourgeois society which had managed to avoid a revolutionary rupture *à la française* that they held it up as a veritable exemplar for the rest of Europe, Engels puts the emphasis on England's political backwardness and the anachronism of a state 'which sees only arbitrary rule in freedom and is up to the neck in the Middle Ages'.[20]

Of course, we should not overestimate either the import or the originality of this initial critique. The 1842–43 articles are not *The Condition* of 1845 or even the 'The Outlines' of 1844. They do not push their analysis of the situation to the point of challenging the separation between the economy and politics, 'civil society' and 'the state', a separation that grounds the liberal approach and allows it to reconcile – at least in the case of lucid liberals like Tocqueville – an unvarnished description of oppression in the factory (which nevertheless remains, in the view of the French aristocrat, a 'civil/private' affair with no political implications) and a paean to the English freedom that must be ascribed, in Tocqueville's estimation, to its political laws.[21] Yet even before Engels begins to analyse the despotism bound up with the condition of the working class, he finds confirmation for the Hegelian or Heinean critique in his first direct experience of the reality of advanced capitalism: his account dwells on England's archaic political system, which, he says, is not simply a picturesque vestige of the past, but the index of a constitutive feature of English society that is, in its turn, the *result* of a historical process: the non-revolutionary nature of the English road – or, rather, the radically unfinished nature of England's attempt to make a 'bourgeois-democratic revolution'. In other words, the non-revolutionary English road is synonymous with *less*, not more, 'formal' freedom, for it has culminated in a political culture and a tangle of institutions that are fundamentally hostile to democracy or the 'principle of freedom', as *The Condition* later puts it: the rigid opposition to universal suffrage and popular sovereignty; the gulf between Britain's political representation and the mass of the people, so wide that it can end up corrupting the country's representatives; the excessive weight of the aristocracy in British institutions; and the antiquated English legal system. In short, Engels emphasizes the omnipresence of those features of the *ancien régime* under whose protective aegis an economic order based on capital flourishes. He homes in on the point around which this archaic system revolves: a belief in the adaptability of the legal and institutional edifice of the monarchy, which enables the archaic British system to accommodate the reality of the bourgeois world without risking a break with the established order.[22]

This political backwardness was reflected, as the young Rhinelander soon realized, in Britain's no less striking intellectual and cultural backwardness. 'Deaf and blind to the signs of the times', the rigidly conservative English intelligentsia has even managed, says Engels, to ignore the great progressive thinkers of its day, including the Englishmen among them (such as Shelley and Byron); its narrow-mindedness redounds to the benefit of the proletariat, which has, in contrast, been quick to appropriate their thought. Although he had by now become a permanent resident of Manchester, Engels had no intention of settling into a stodgy provincialism and abandoning what was most fecund in the German point of view, its theoretical and critical potential. As his writings attest, the ambivalence constitutive of the German intelligentsia, whose radicalism was completely lacking in England, did not by any means escape him.[23] On the one hand, he attributes Germany's intellectual hypertrophy to the working classes' absence from the social and political scene; this is responsible, he says, for the gulf between the intelligentsia and the world of practice. On the other hand, he does not deny that the German intelligentsia has attained a level of theoretical development that is incomparably superior to the English intellectual *misère* – except in the field of political economy, although he considers even English economics to be both deficient and already on the decline. This intellectual *misère* directly reflects the counter-revolutionary rigidity of the English political system, much as 'the enlightened' character of sections of the German elite comes at the price of its fathomless sub-political archaism. Here England and Germany are caught up in a play of mirrors which, as we shall see, is fraught with consequences when it comes to the attitudes of their respective bourgeoisies.[24]

Proud of the fact that he knew how to 'speak German', the decidedly impetuous Engels spent only a few days in his new place of residence before tackling the new social questions head-on. He threw himself into the task with a sense of the concrete that contrasted sharply with the theoreticism of the 'last philosophers' (Hess). The letters that he dispatched to Marx's *Rheinische Zeitung* revolved, from the outset, around the following problem: what were the prospects for the workers' movement in the immediate aftermath of the failed Chartist uprising of August 1842? His second letter, dated 9 December 1842, begins, significantly, like this: 'Is a revolution in England possible or even probable? This is the question on which the future of the country depends.'[25] Influenced by Hess's tripartite schema, Engels takes matters up just where Hegel left them,[26] and asks the same questions. One is struck, upon reading these texts, by the extraordinary optimism – revolutionary optimism, needless to say – that his responses exude.

The type of argument Engels employs was to enjoy extraordinary success in the later history of the workers' movement. It runs as follows: although its dominant classes are blind to the fact, England is torn apart by conflicting material interests. Free trade has merely given free rein to the contradictions of the economy; a new crisis of overproduction is inevitable, and will unfailingly bring unemployment, pauperization and riots in its wake. The crisis will lead to a radicalization of the working class, stripping it of the legalistic illusions that had put a damper on its actions in the summer of 1842.[27] The revolution, necessarily violent, is therefore as inevitable as the crisis, and its victory is assured: 'There cannot fail to be a general lack of food among the workers before long, and then fear of death from starvation will be stronger than fear of the law. This revolution is inevitable for England.'[28] Given what the future holds, Engels is struck by the English bourgeoisie's lack of consciousness[29] and its refusal to make concessions, manifestly related to England's political and intellectual backwardness. Rather than talking about a 'lack of consciousness', one should perhaps talk about a bourgeoisie that has no 'unhappy consciousness', and is incapable of grasping the split between antagonistic interests in their internality.[30]

In other words, the English bourgeoisie has not had to confront the event known as revolution – either directly (the cutting edge of the guillotine) or even on the strictly intellectual plane (the cutting edge of Kant's concepts). Its improbably archaic character, which is attributable to its amalgamation with the aristocracy, is thus transformed into its opposite. As Heine had seen during his stay in England in 1828, and exposed for all to see in a merciless portrait, Britain's aristocratic/ bourgeois elite, detached from its time and place, was the very opposite of a bourgeoisie exercising a 'national/popular' function;[31] the so 'typically British' cultivation of the archaic was in fact nothing more than the ceremony[32] indispensable to the emergence of an ahistorical, if not already post-historical, consciousness. Now, Engels argues, pursuing the argument, the proletariat must accomplish, unaided, the mission of overcoming England's non-contemporaneousness with its times, by bridging the gulf that separates the country from the political experience of the Continent.

Several months later, in a new series of letters, the 'Letters from London', destined for publication in the *Républicain Suisse*, Engels's conception of the role incumbent upon the working-class movement has come into clearer focus. The tendency he now regards as dominant is the inexorable polarization of the contradictions between the two opposed classes. The proletariat, at the very bottom of society, appears, precisely because of its dire poverty, as the exclusive guardian of historical progress. Engels manifestly assigns it a Christlike role; the dialectic thus established is reinforced by the parallel he draws with another revolution, the one carried out by the early Christians (such references were a legacy of Engels's Pietist youth, on which he would continue to draw throughout his life). Even if the word as such does not figure in his text, Engels suggests, through his use of biblical language, that the proletariat is the class which will *redeem* mankind by struggling for its earthly salvation.[33] The prospect of social emancipation is thus explicitly presented as a transfer of the hope for salvation to this world, a commonplace in the socialist discourse of the day: 'it remains true: blessed are the poor, for theirs is the kingdom of heaven and, however long it may take, the kingdom of this earth as well'.[34]

Impressed by the English workers' effort to educate themselves, the existence of a parallel circuit of clubs (such as the Halls of Science), courses in reading and writing, and the diffusion of extremely varied publications, Engels contrasts the proletariat's cultural progress with the intellectual mediocrity of the British bourgeoisie.[35] He also contrasts that mediocrity and its corollary, the purely proletarian make-up of the English revolutionary movement, with the composition of the German movement, which appears, so to speak, as its inverted image.[36] The German movement, set apart by the heavy participation of a radicalized intelligentsia that is simply not to be found in England, has no real popular base, and therefore lacks the active, straightforwardly practical character of its English counterpart. For it is the English movement that announces a revolutionary situation: the action of 'the lower classes', the 'uneducated', offers the only real 'portent of a great revolution' such as is a 'feature of every revolutionary epoch'.[37] Thus, one touch at a time, Engels paints a portrait of the proletarian class as a community completely isolated from the other classes of capitalist society, possessed of its own culture and unencumbered by religious or bourgeois influences. Chartism embodies the purity of a 'class-based' political movement: it is an expression of the proletariat and the proletariat alone. The legalism exhibited by its leadership during the uprising of summer 1842 already numbers among its lost illusions, or, at least, soon will; as for the manifestly religious cast of its Sunday assemblies, more reminiscent of church services than political rallies, Engels barely touches on the matter, and immediately downplays what little he does say by underscoring the anti-religious tenor of the speeches made at these gatherings.[38]

It should be stressed that Engels's vision of the English proletariat is an imaginary construct. Nothing about Chartism is less certain, for example, than the 'purity' of its working-class orientation, as Engels's predecessor Heine had already observed. This applies both to the movement's sense of itself and to its real class make-up. The same is true of its legalism, which was deeply rooted in its 'political' ideology, one that had very little of the 'social' about it (unquestionably a paradoxical phenomenon from Engels's, or Hess's, point of view). This must be admitted by anyone who recognizes the exclusively political character of the key demand of the 'People's Charter': the demand for universal suffrage. The real discourse of the English workers' movement of the 1830s and 1840s did not set proletariat against bourgeoisie so much as it contrasted the 'working classes' with the 'idle' and their tool, the state, which was hostile to universal suffrage and promoted a despotic 'class legislation' (the Poor Laws, anti-union repression, and so on).[39] This was a standpoint shared by the first socialist critics of political economy, especially Hodgskin, for whom the contradiction between 'labourers' (including not only 'journeymen', but also 'masters, planners, contrivers, etc.') and 'capitalists' – that is, the idle who appropriated profits – had to be resolved in favour of 'productive industry' and property rights based on 'justice'.[40]

Beyond their idealized – and idealist – representation of the real workers' movement, which is all of a piece with their markedly eschatological tone, these texts merit attention for another type of argument, which is in fact presupposed by the one we have just examined. Engels's letters reveal – and this is anything but a mere detail – a fundamentally *dualistic* vision of modern society, which is depicted as driven by contradictory interests that are anchored in the objectivity of economic relations, and underlie the endless struggle between the different *classes* that make it up. To these classes correspond, term for term, the competing *political parties*: 'It is well known that in England parties coincide with social ranks and classes.'[41]

However, Engels does not content himself with affirming the primacy of material interests, for that, in his estimation, would be to confine himself to the banally 'materialist', English viewpoint, which is hemmed in by the constraints of 'immediate' social practice and the narrow horizons of political economy. As soon as it is posited, this binary schema is dialecticized; the third term is reinjected into it, but, at the same time, projected into the future. Material interests are thus grasped from the German standpoint; in other words, they are relocated within a conception of things that belongs to the philosophy of history, that of a historical teleology with a progressive orientation, which posits a new, dialectical type of relationship between (political) principles and interests.[42] Principles are not detached from but, rather, based on material interests, which are transformed into instruments, conscious or unconscious, of their realization.[43]

This ruse of history, the result of a self-rectification of the English road via German mediation, confers a new character on the coming revolution: it will no longer be political, but *social*. But those who make the revolution are likely to remain blind to its novelty, unless – so, at least, one may assume – they manage to adopt the lofty perspective of Hegelian philosophy: 'this revolution is inevitable for England, but as in everything that happens there, it will be interests and not principles that will begin and carry through the revolution; principles can develop only from interests, that is to say, the revolution will be social, not political'.[44] In thus posing the 'social' as a determinant moment including and, by the same token, going beyond the political, Engels does not simply adopt Hess's thesis while transposing it to the terrain of concrete analysis; rather, he assigns it its true meaning. It must be emphasized that by the standards of the German radical intelligentsia, this was an original procedure at the time Engels was writing (autumn 1842, winter 1842–43). The intelligentsia in question includes Marx, who had only just begun to address the problems of civil society, to which his attention had been drawn by thefts of wood in the Mosel valley; preoccupied by his philosophical confrontation with the work of Bauer and Hegel,[45] he was, by his own admission, rather remote from the working-class movement, and socialist or communist theories.[46]

The status of critique: Hegel in Feuerbach

Engels's originality comes even more clearly to the fore in 'Outlines of a Critique of Political Economy', written in late 1843/early 1844. By subjecting the categories of political economy to a systematic critique, this 'brilliant essay' – according to Marx, who was profoundly influenced by it[47] – opens up new theoretical perspectives. We would do well, then, to determine its status, or, more precisely, the standpoint from which it is written. To begin with, Engels's critique is characterized by its pervasively moral tone, which – notwithstanding its currency in a period rife with Romantic and 'humanitarian' critiques of capitalism – ought not to be written off as a simple expression of the indignation that contact with the bourgeois industrial world aroused in its author, even if his hot temper certainly accounts for a great deal. Thus, from the beginning to the end of the 'Outlines', political economy and capitalism are denounced as 'a developed system of licensed fraud', 'born of the merchants' mutual envy and greed' and 'bear[ing] on its brow the mark of the most detestable selfishness'.[48] Trade is described as 'legalised fraud', in line with its 'immoral nature'; landownership is called 'robbery'; and competition is branded the 'deepest degradation of mankind'.[49]

Engels does not, however, remain on the plane of mere external denunciation; he attacks the premises and moral objectives of political economy on their own ground. More precisely, he challenges the basic principle according to which political economy is constituted as an autonomous discourse through inclusion in the overarching rationality of moral philosophy,[50] not exclusion from it. At the ethical level, Engels's manifest intention is to establish himself as the anti-Adam Smith. From the very first, he takes direct issue with the fundamental assumption underlying Smith's whole conception of social development; it is justified in Smith's most famous work, as is indicated even by its title, *The Wealth of Nations*. According to Smith, 'the accommodation of an European prince does not always so much exceed that of an industrious and frugal peasant, as the accommodation of the latter exceeds that of many an African king, the absolute master of the lives and liberties of ten thousand naked savages'.[51] In a less lyrical but more densely argued style, Smith tries to prove that, in the nations which are making 'progress' towards 'opulence' (Western Europe and North America), those in which capital accumulation is proceeding at a steady rate and whose wealth is consequently increasing, wage-earners and the poor have, at the very least, less to complain about than do their counterparts in the countries that 'are stand[ing] still' or 'go[ing] backwards' – that is to say, the pre-capitalist societies whose destiny is, basically, to be colonized.[52] This vision subtends the whole of Smith's historical account, a veritable liberal theodicy centred on the 'natural' emergence of capitalism, the object of the third book of *The Wealth*. Its title is significant: 'Of the different Progress of Opulence in different Nations'.[53]

For Engels, in contrast, the 'natural' result, as it were, of the accumulation of capital is not the general welfare but, rather, deepening poverty and the most extreme polarization of conditions at opposite ends of the social scale. He contests the category of 'national wealth' and, consequently, that of the 'national', 'political' or 'public' economy, which mask, behind their illusory universality, the rule of private property and the oppression of those who do not own any:

> The term national wealth has not only arisen as a result of the liberal economists' passion for generalisation. As long as private property exists, this term has no meaning. The 'national wealth' of the English is very great, and yet they are the poorest people under the sun. One must either discard this term completely, or accept such premises as give it meaning. Similarly with the terms national economy and political or public economy. In the present circumstances that science ought to be called *private* economy, for its public connections exist only for the sake of private property.[54]

This destruction of the public sphere is by no means the prelude, in Engels's opinion, to the acquisition of new liberties. Political economy's claim to represent a doctrine of freedom and moral progress is self-contradictory: behind the 'free-trade system' and the suppression of the mercantilist systems instituted by absolutism – which was ready to go to war to defend them – a new monopoly is emerging, that of property; a new servitude, that of relations founded on competition; a new type of violence, that of colonial rapine; and a new despotism, that of wage-slavery.[55] The liberal economy's dissolution of all forms of community – including the family,[56] the last refuge of *Sittlichkeit* – fosters not peace and freedom, but novel forms of oppression, the physical and moral degradation embodied in the factory system, and an 'internalized' state of war, diffused throughout the whole of the social body.

Yet Engels's critique does more than turn the pacificatory, emancipatory and moral pretensions of political economy against their source. Beyond a doubt, his originality and the novelty of his approach reside in the fact that the discursive object 'political economy' is subjected to an *anthropological* critique of Feuerbachian–Hegelian inspiration, accompanied by a historical and sociological vision that is brought to bear on the economists' discourse, its status, and its links to the development of capitalist relations. In the same period, Hess was pleading, in 'On The Essence of Money', for 'the right use of Feuerbach', defined as 'the application of [his] humanism to social life';[57] Feuerbach's God, in other words, should be replaced by Money, and *The Essence of Christianity* by *The Essence of Money*. Against this background, Engels's 1844 'Outlines' reinjects Hegel into the attempt to establish a humanist foundation for socialism; thus this text provides an early example of the 'Hegel in Feuerbach' that Althusser discusses in connection with Marx's *1844 Manuscripts*. Engels's standpoint is, very precisely, that of an integral humanism – in other words, Feuerbach as revised by Hess – which 'rises above the opposition of the two systems' of economic thought (mercantilism and liberalism), and, 'proceed[ing] from a purely human, universal basis', 'assign[s] to both their proper position'[58] – that is, the point of view that will provide them with the foundation they lack.

But Engels goes further still: he extends (and 'dialecticizes') the humanist critique to the categories bourgeois society mobilizes in reflecting on its own practice, categories which are thus made to deliver up their secret from within: human alienation. In other words, Engels essays an immanent critique of the main categories of political economy, with a view to showing that the fact that they lack an adequate (i.e. anthropological) foundation fosters their internal division, the consequence of an abstract, one-sided opposition that is blind to its own premises, and accordingly incapable of overcoming antagonism:

> The eighteenth century, the century of revolution, also revolutionised economics. But just as all the revolutions of this century were one-sided and bogged down in antitheses – just as abstract materialism was set in opposition to abstract spiritualism, the republic to monarchy, the social contract to divine right – likewise the economic revolution did not get beyond antithesis. The premises remained everywhere in force. . . . It did not occur to economics to question the *validity of private property*. Therefore, the new economics was only half an advance.[59]

Once it is put in the context of a historical process comprising the different stages of capitalism and the revolutions that have punctuated it, the evolution of the categories of economics acquires both a meaning and a goal: it announces that economics itself will be superseded. Engels associates this event with a total – and thus a social – revolution; it will coincide with the realization of history's immanent goal, the full humanization of the natural and social world. Trapped within the categories of the understanding, political economy – just like the French Revolution – falls short of the dialectical *Aufhebung* and, therefore, of true concrete universality, which is represented by the realization of the human essence (not the state), the 'great transformation to which the century is moving – the reconciliation of mankind with nature and with itself'.[60]

Measured by the yardstick of the humanist critique, economics appears as an *inverted* world, whose main category, value, is 'abstract', alienated, internally divided, and dominated by a derivative factor, price: 'thus everything in economics stands on its head [*so steht alles in der Ökonomie auf dem Kopf*]. Value, the primary factor, the source of price, is made dependent on price, its own product. As is well known, this inversion [*Umkehrung*] is the essence of abstraction; on which see Feuerbach'.[61] This leads on naturally to the religious metaphors that cast economics as an illusion, a belief system which spawns its own priests, doctrinal disputes, tribunals and prophets: 'for the sake of this ridiculous illusion [the mercantilist dogma that it was necessary to achieve a favourable trade balance] thousands of men have been slaughtered! Trade, too, has its crusades and inquisitions.'[62] Mercantilist dogma will be subjected to the onslaught of the liberal Reformation, led by the '*economic Luther*, Adam Smith',[63] who will establish the objective laws of private property.

For Engels, Smith's political economy represents a genuine advance, a historically necessary stage reflecting the *objectivity* of capitalist development.[64] Engels's critique has nothing to do with advocacy of a 'moral economy of the crowd' based on the traditional norms governing transactions in pre-capitalist societies,[65] or a defence of the 'republican' vision of a Sismondi, rooted in the confined world of the Italian or Swiss city-states; much less is it a plea for pre-Smithian economic theory, either mercantilist or physiocratic. That, indeed, is why Engels does not hesitate to accentuate the *dynamism* of the system, as is attested by his frequent use of the term 'industrial revolution', a Saint-Simonian term that liberal and even radical English critics long avoided for fear of weakening the 'front' opened jointly with the aristocracy, with its politico-economic line of defence (the voting system based on the poll tax and the protectionism of the Corn Laws).[66] For Engels, in contrast, the recognition that political economy represents a scientific advance which breaks with the empiricism and national narrow-mindedness of the mercantilist system does not in any way blunt the critical thrust of his discourse, in so far, precisely, as the 'revolutionary' industrial world of which political economy is the expression makes it possible to reach a higher level of universality, and put matters on 'a purely human basis'. Through the play of its own inner contradictions, political economy reveals this world's internal limits, and sets the stage for its overthrow. For 'just as theology must either regress to blind faith or progress towards free philosophy, free trade must produce the restoration of monopolies on the one hand and the abolition of private property on the other'.[67]

Political economy is accordingly called upon to choose: it must either become a straightforward apology for the only truly monopolistic regime, based on the private property of a minority; or it must yield to the critique of the 'English socialists', who 'have long since proved both practically and theoretically that [the opponents of private property] are in a position to settle economic questions more correctly even from an economic point of view'.[68] Indeed, the emergence of a *laissez-faire* society, and of enterprise freed from mercantilist constraints and feudal archaisms, was quite as necessary as is the advance which will 'go beyond the economics of private property',[69] a development that the socialist and working-class critique has already announced.

Thus Engels reinserts capitalism based on free competition, along with its theoretical self-consciousness, political economy, into a historical dialectic, a philosophy of history capable of putting political economy's own account of social development back within a more comprehensive sequence that is assigned its *telos*: the realization of the human essence. For one cannot expose the inverted/alienated nature of the economy/economics without thereby 'outlining', as the title of the essay modestly suggests, a method for 'standing it back on its feet'. This inversion of the inversion is presented both as a consistent development of the dialectic internal to the economic categories and, simultaneously, as a necessary resolution of historical antagonisms. It aims to bring out the hidden presuppositions of political economy, and to go beyond their unmediated character, advancing from the presupposed to what is posed by the internal movement of the concept – to, that is, the higher form of the concept's restored unity. This is how Engels proceeds with the first 'category established by trade', value. Its division into real value and exchange value, and the 'violent' opposition between the two faces of value, each the prisoner of its one-sidedness,[70] make it impossible to formulate an objective determination of value independently of the give-and-take of competition. The imaginary denial of the division by the two terms of the contradiction, each of which claims to represent the totality by itself, stands value 'on its head', making it dependent on its own product, price.

Political economy moves, precisely, within the limits of this alienated world, in a desperate quest for a Feuerbach of its own.[71] If it were to find one, value would no longer be posed one-sidedly, but as a *relation*, or – to be more precise – as the relationship between production costs and utility; in that case, the opposition between the two aspects (between real utility and its determination, between this determination and the freedom of the owners/exchangers of goods), would be clearly visible. It is private property, the real presupposition for this exchange, the property that was there all along behind the division (and its ineffective denial), which is thus called into question, as well as the language it spontaneously speaks, that of political economy.

Besides private property and the divisions it causes (separation of the human activity of production from its natural conditions; the division of this activity into labour and capital), their basic consequence, competition, is also at stake here. Competition appears as an implacable dissolvent; it extends its dominion over all social relations, which it transforms into a series of blind clashes between interests entrenched in their particularity. It is responsible for the constant fluctuation of prices, for supply and demand – for, in a word, a generalized social disorder, with the many crises and the impoverishment this disorder brings in its wake. All moral values are destroyed by the atomization of individual interests, which makes any form of conscious control over the results of individual activity impossible. The reality of competition is a far cry indeed from the spontaneous, optimal order described by Adam Smith and celebrated by his liberal epigones as a combination of individual forces which, albeit unintentional, always yields a positive result (and is endowed with tremendous powers of expansion).

Accordingly, the truth of competition is *crime* rather than general prosperity. Crime appears as the necessary consequence of an order exposed as the disorder of an already declining society driven by a literally self-devouring logic. This disorder is responsible for a new kind of servitude to which the formally equal individuals who have been emancipated from traditional 'vertical' constraints now subject each other, in accordance with a dynamic that leads inexorably to mutual aggression and mutual destruction. Such a society not only produces crime, but also trivializes it, making it one more activity among others, governed, like the rest, by the prevailing laws of supply and demand, competition, and demography. Hence one may talk about a veritable economy of crime, at once an image and an integral part of the normal functioning of the global economy.[72] Crime therefore becomes more than a derivative effect of the subordination of the whole of social 'life' to the self-destructive rationality of capitalism; it serves as a kind of litmus test which reveals the real effects of that subordination.

To eliminate it, and abolish competition, social relations must be completely overturned. Only if all the members of society collectively decide how much to produce – this is Engels's one positive indication as to what the 'beyond' of an economy based on private property might look like – can the Gordian knot of value be cut. Competition will disappear at the same stroke: 'if the producers as such knew how much the consumers required, if they were to organize production, if they were to share it out amongst themselves, then the fluctuations of competition and its tendency to crisis would be impossible'.[73] *Conscious organization* of the economy is the condition *sine qua non* for forging a new unity between the activities of society and the human species: 'carry on production consciously as human beings – not as dispersed atoms without species-consciousness [*Gattungsbewußtsein*] – and you have overcome all these artificial and untenable antitheses'.[74] A schema that is fundamental to the socialist tradition is laid down here;[75] it makes the abolition of competition (between individuals and productive units) the touchstone for the reorganization of society, or, rather, for the creation of a 'true' society by way of the generalization of conscious organization. Capitalism is identified with a state of permanent anarchy and disorder, and contrasted with the different kind of society that is destined to replace it, which is defined in terms of voluntary association, the re-establishment of the sovereignty of species-consciousness, and the assumption by a reunified subject of conscious control over the whole of social life. After Feuerbach – or, rather, to complement Feuerbach – Engels appeals to Fourier[76] and Owen: an index of the utopian dimension inherent in any exercise of this kind, which proffers a description/prefiguration of the future by tracing the figure of a community capable of unifying reason, human nature, and the historical process.

The inevitable revolution

In the 1844 'Outlines', the splitting [*Spaltung*] of labour into wage-labour and capital initiates a dialectical development for which the category of value has already provided the model. The break-up, due to private property, of an original unity sets off a cascade of divisions affecting both labour (the separation of labour from its product and conditions) and capital (a division between profit and original capital, a distinction within profit itself between interest and profit in the strict sense); it multiplies the effect of 'irrationality' [*Unvernünftigkeit*] inherent in the original division. The alienation of labour and interest-bearing credit form the two ends of a chain that soon partitions all mankind into hostile classes. Class antagonism can only grow more intense, creating the conditions for its reversal, that is, the reunification of the human species via the abolition of private property:

> all these subtle splits and divisions stem from the original separation [*ursprüngliche Trennung*] of capital from labour and from the culmination of this separation – the division [*Spaltung*] of mankind into capitalists and workers – a division which daily becomes ever more acute, and . . . is *bound* to deepen. . . .

If we abandon private property, then all these unnatural divisions disappear. The difference between interest and profit disappears; capital is nothing without labour, without movement. The significance of profit is reduced to the weight which capital carries in the determination of the costs of production; and profit thus remains inherent in capital, in the same way as capital itself reverts to its original unity with labour.[77]

Things will come full circle – humanity will return to itself – only at the price of ruptures, crises and revolutions, not in linear fashion. The 1844 'Outlines' permits Engels to base the prognosis made in his previous letters on a more precise analysis of economic relations. The coexistence of pauperization and the concentration of wealth, as well as the exacerbation of the contradictions between classes, are phenomena which occur with the regularity of the 'law of nature' that governs the trade cycle: 'it is obvious that this law is purely a law of nature and not a law of the mind. It is a law which produces revolution.'[78] Because this law is 'natural', in contrast to the intellectual character of other kinds of laws (for example, the laws of conscious control that govern socialist society), its operations escape the conscious attention of those involved; it reflects the pure objectivity of socioeconomic relations. Its ultimate consequences go unnoticed by the apologists for capitalism, in particular the economists among them: the crises of overproduction, 'which appear as regularly as the comets', plunge the mass of the existing proletariat into extreme poverty, driving an ever growing number of small capitalists into its ranks as well.

The overriding tendencies of the social dynamic are conducive to the *exacerbation* and, at the same time, the *simplification* of class antagonisms: a proletariat whose numbers are constantly increasing confronts the thin layer of those who concentrate an ever-greater amount of property in their hands: 'each successive crisis is bound to become more universal and therefore worse than the preceding one; is bound to impoverish a larger body of small capitalists, and to augment in increasing proportion the numbers of the class who live by labour alone, thus considerably enlarging the mass of labour to be employed (the major problem of our economists) and finally causing a social revolution such as has never been dreamt of in the philosophy of the economists'.[79] Thus the social revolution is presented not as the result of a sudden act of force or a violation of history, but as the ripe fruit of a system sapped from within, whose basic harmony the economists, willing to admit nothing more serious than the existence of temporary fluctuations, desperately and vainly seek to demonstrate.

As a resolution of the contradictions inherent in socioeconomic relations, Engels's revolution acquires an objective character that distinguishes it from the voluntarist visions which had very wide circulation in the revolutionary movement of the day[80] – and, by the same token, from their mirror-image, the counter-revolutionary 'conspiracy' theories. But the objectivity of the revolutionary phenomenon ties it in with a rather strictly mechanistic determinism that has, moreover, a strong teleological tinge. The sequence crisis/revolution serves to guarantee the correspondence between the ripening of economic conditions and the attitude of the proletariat, which is left with no choice but to engage in a general confrontation. This is a new figure of the ruse of reason. What is more, it requires, as its necessary complement,[81] the intervention of a Subject invested with a messianic function, a subject that is omnipotent because it is free of all ideological contamination, one that embodies the reflexive consciousness of the species, *Gattungsbewußtsein*. Thus there emerges, just below the surface, a dichotomy that was to enjoy a long and bright future: the dichotomy between revolution based on 'objective' necessity and revolution stemming from the revolutionary agent's growing 'consciousness' of its mission. The two terms of this dichotomy converge, ideally, in the postulate of the *imminence* of the revolutionary moment.

As we can see from the two groups of texts that frame the 1844 'Outlines' – the series of articles 'Progress of Social Reform on the Continent' (November 1843), and another series published in *Vorwärts* in August–September 1844 – Engels's idea of the imminence of a new kind of revolution intersects, from the outset, Hess's 1841 schema – and for good reason, since Engels explicitly recognizes Hess as the first prophet of the new revolution in his country. The question of this imminent revolution is posed in terms of the trajectory specific to each of the three countries in the triarchy, as national particularities dictate (economic practice in the case of England, political practice in that of France, philosophy in that of Germany). But the fact that all three trajectories culminate in the same point indicates that we are looking at a general process of accession to concrete universality. The complementary national roads taken by the social revolution make up for each other's deficiencies: thus they avoid contingency and one-sidedness in order to establish the social revolution as the true figure of universality, the culmination of the historical process in the totality of its development, the 'necessary conclusion, which cannot be avoided to be drawn from the premises given in the general facts of modern civilisation'.[82] There is no contradiction, then, between concrete universality and the national-popular, but – quite to the contrary – a necessary inference from the one to the other. This theme, which Heine developed at length, is familiar to us by now.

Let us begin with the German variation on it. The event here consists in the encounter of two tendencies: on the one hand, the spread of communist ideas among the working classes, due essentially to Weitling and immigrant workers in France; and, on the other (Engels treats the second aspect in greater detail), the transition to communism of the most advanced representatives of German philosophy, the Young Hegelians – or, more precisely, some of them. Engels dates this transition quite exactly (he says that it began in August 1842), highlighting the pioneering role played by Hess and his letters in the *Rheinische Zeitung*, as well as the subsequent conversion of some of the leaders of the philosophical party (Marx and Herwegh, but also – an obvious error on Engels's part – Ruge). The strength of this 'philosophical communism', like its contribution from a universal point of view, resides precisely in its deep implantation in the national tradition.[83] This implantation, which is due to philosophy's role in the formation of the German nation, makes German communism particularly resistant to the repression brought to bear on it: as 'a *necessary* consequence of [Young-Hegelian] philosophy',[84] itself an authentic product of the whole German tradition going back to the Reformation, it is virtually indestructible.

In France, the contradiction that undermined the principle of political freedom for a long time has now, says Engels, come to light, leaving the French with a choice between a new kind of servitude on the one hand, and freedom and authentic equality on the other: 'both these consequences were brought out in the French Revolution: Napoleon established the first, and Babeuf the second'.[85] Engels paints a well-informed picture of the socialist and communist currents in France: his very Hessian reading of Fourier[86] is flanked by an assessment of Babouvism and neo-Babouvism that is very much on the mark. He has an acute understanding of the role of Babouvism as the historical source and intellectual matrix of communism – including even that 'other and more powerful communism' that blossomed in the aftermath of the revolution of 1830. But he perceives French communism's limits as well: although it is true that it raises the social question, which no mere change of regime will suffice to resolve, it also betrays its political origins. As is attested by the ascendancy of democratic and republican slogans, the heritage of the great Revolution continues to weigh heavy on its heirs.

Only Proudhon and his *What is Property?*, which Engels considers 'the most philosophical work, on the part of the Communists, in the French language', are spared this criticism. Engels adopts Proudhon's conclusions: like Hess in the essays collected in his *Einundzwanzig Bogen*, he comes out in favour of 'anarchy', and rejects all forms of government, democracy included; he goes so far as to endorse the very liberal Proudhonian argument about the inviolability of the principle of *individual* responsibility even where it runs counter to that of majority rule.[87] As Engels is addressing politically very moderate English readers[88] – in, moreover, an Owenite newspaper, *The New Moral World* – his remarks are doubtless partly motivated by tactical considerations. By depreciating the political, he also seeks to minimize the differences between France and England in order to 'sell' communist doctrine to a public that would most certainly have been put off by its republican or violent features. But more is involved, as we can see from the articles Engels subsequently published in *Vorwärts* for an audience of 'outsiders', the German *émigré* community in Paris; for these articles radicalize his anti-political stance.[89]

Without disavowing his earlier positions, Engels completely changes their thrust, repeating certain of Hess's formulations of 1841 in what is virtually their original form. Appearances notwithstanding, he now says, it is England which is in the forefront of the revolutionary development of world history: 'the significance of the English in recent history is less conspicuous and yet for our present purpose it is the most important'.[90] This importance stems from the fact that the English are representatives of the *social*, a synthesis of 'the Christian spiritual principle' of the Germans – religion and the Church – and 'the Ancient materialist principle' of the French – politics and the state. Before achieving this synthesis, the English had to contend with the contradiction between the two, owing to their twin origins, French and Germanic;[91] but they succeeded in externalizing this division, transforming it into a 'source of energy' and objectifying it in the form of practical activity. Simultaneously preoccupied with concrete activity and the salvation of their souls, simultaneously religious and irreligious, the English turned towards industry, trade and colonial conquest. Thus they struck out on the road of an

> upheaval which is all the more momentous the more quietly it is brought about, and . . . will therefore in all probability attain its goal more readily in practice than the political revolution in France or the philosophical revolution in Germany. The revolution in England is a social one and therefore more comprehensive and far-reaching than any other. . . . The only true revolution is a social revolution, to which political and philosophical revolution must lead.[92]

Moreover, for Engels, who is willing to avail himself of anything on offer when it comes to refuting received opinion, it is simply false to say that England is *politically* one revolution behind France. Indeed, one might almost maintain the contrary, since 'the English revolution of the seventeenth century provides the exact model for the French one of 1789'. The parallel, developed in great detail (Cromwell = Robespierre + Napoleon; the threefold division Gironde/ Montagnards/Hébertists and Babouvists = Presbyterians/ Independents/Levellers), is further substantiated by its 'in both cases ... rather pitiable' result, one that is limited by the exclusively political character of these two revolutions.

Britain's lead is thus strictly correlative with the 'anti-political' implications of the fact that it is a fundamentally 'social' country. As Engels uses the word, 'social' – at least when considered from the standpoint of immediacy – designates a very special sort of disconnectedness and generalized atomization, a kind of autonomous, extremely efficacious individual activity that nevertheless lacks all political unity, is blind to its own premises, and has not attained to the self-consciousness of the species: 'France's actions were always national, conscious of their entireness and universality from the start; England's actions were the work of independent coexisting individuals – the movement of disconnected atoms – who rarely acted together as one whole, and even then only from *individual* motives. . . . In other words, only England has a *social* history.'[93] Of course, this history is still unaware of itself, external to itself, subjected to the abstraction of money and the alienation into which man has been plunged by the results of his own activity, which dominate and enslave him. The bourgeois universe is that of a 'complete perversion' of all human relations. Yet this upside-down world is working towards its own overthrow; in itself, it is merely 'the last necessary step towards the free and spontaneous association of men'.[94] Its internal fragmentation, manifested in class division, the emergence of a modern proletariat, and the increasingly intense 'fight of the poor against the rich', is setting the stage for a human emancipation that will transcend the narrow, one-sided horizon of politics and the French model.

It is not a question, then, of either repeating or negating 1789. The goal is, rather, dialectically to supersede it, to traverse that historical moment, pursuing the struggle within the limits of 'democracy by itself', but with a view to going beyond it towards a new type of democracy, social democracy.[95] Is the choice still between a new kind of democracy and a form of social organization beyond democracy, as the essay published in the *New Moral World* proclaimed? Nothing, in fact, allows us to say that Engels's position on this question has changed, inasmuch as social democracy is here merely posited as a moment of *transition* towards socialism, and, therefore, towards the *abolition of the political* and all forms of democracy: 'but democracy by itself is not capable of curing social ills.

Democratic equality is a chimera, the fight of the poor against the rich
cannot be fought out on a basis of democracy or indeed of politics as a
whole. This stage too is thus only a transition, the last purely political
remedy which has still to be tried and from which a new element is bound
to develop at once, a principle transcending everything of a political
nature. This principle is the principle of socialism.'[96] Thus, if one had to
point to a difference from the 1843 text, it would not lie in the anti-
political aspect of the later article, since Engels's anti-political stance
remains remarkably constant,[97] but, rather, in a terminological shift –
from communism, to which Engels basically referred in discussing France
for the Owenite newspaper, to socialism, which is undeniably associated
with the idea of the centrality of the English road. It is true that the
borderline between the two is, at the very least, blurred for Engels, who
does not hesitate to range Proudhon with the communists. The effect of
this subtle shift, however, is quite striking: Engels takes up the problematic
of the *transition* again, in the course of a teleological argument that makes
socialism the end of history, the ultimate moment in the development of
a human race which has at last attained the plenitude of its social being.

Tilting the main axis of the triarchy towards England, a move that is
intimately bound up with the ongoing depreciation of the political in
favour of the social, has, in its turn, the effect of throwing a new light on
the question of the right *political* form, in the proper sense of the word.
Once again, the English case is revelatory. The picture Engels draws of
the British political regime is, to begin with, more finely shaded than in
the 1842–43 letters: now Engels is ready to admit that 'the fear of
despotism and the struggle against the power of the Crown came to an
end a hundred years ago; England is undeniably the freest, in other
words, the least unfree, country in the world, not excepting North
America, and the educated Englishman consequently has about him a
degree of innate independence such as no Frenchman, to say nothing of
the Germans, can boast of'.[98] But the eulogy very plainly ends where the
virtues of individual freedom do; for, in the public sphere, the rights
granted on paper are hollow. According to Engels, the freedom of the
press is as dependent on the state authorities as it is in Prussia (which is
saying a great deal!); the police impose severe restrictions on the right of
assembly; and the rights of association and *habeas corpus* are, in actual
practice, prerogatives of the rich, for only the rich dispose of the means
required to ensure that they are enforced. Thus, point for point, Engels
overturns the liberal schema, which exalts English political freedom and
quietly assigns the more questionable aspects of British life to the private
sphere. Paradoxically, however, he does so only in order to endorse that

schema all the more firmly when he declares that England is ahead of France as far as revolutionary development is concerned. He observes, of course, that the monarchy plays a fundamental and increasingly important role in the political imagination 'of the English', including – we need only recall his 1843 remark on the constitutional stance of English socialists – the English proletarians. He even speaks of the 'loathsome cult of the king as such'; but all that is involved here is, precisely, a cult, the worship of a fetish devoid of any real substance, or of a magic word that is wholly self-referential (like 'God') and consequently empty.[99] Thus the court ceremonial of the British monarchy functions, says Engels, as a hyperbolic metaphoricization of the theology peculiar to political forms, democratic forms included. It is an alienated reality, an inverted image of social relations that has survived its own death, which makes it easier to decipher and 'stand back on its feet'.

Depreciation of the political and depreciation of the ideological go hand in hand. Engels purely and simply denies that the political illusion generates real effects; his analysis completely neglects the stabilizing and integrative function of the monarchy – even in the working class – as well as the role it plays in sustaining an imperial nationalism and a political culture that are simultaneously Francophobe, anti-democratic, and hostile to any and all manifestations of the revolutionary spirit. Under these conditions, he can indeed affirm that the 'social' English road skirts the pitfall represented by the question which continues to preoccupy the French, their communism notwithstanding: that of the political regime. The English can, Engels claims, skip, as it were, the stage of a 'simple' republic in order to go directly to the stage of social democracy and socialism. Hence he can serenely defend the incredible – if not absurd – position according to which the British working class, despite its extreme political moderation, support for the constitutional monarchy, and avowed aversion to violence, is closer to a revolutionary victory than a proletariat steeped in the experience of several recent revolutions, prepared to undertake radical action at the drop of a hat, and possessed of a political culture unrivalled in Europe – namely, the French proletariat, which collectively invented communism. If Engels did not thus stand things on their heads, however, the entire 'dialectic' of the political and the social, with its powerful teleological bent, would be called into question. There could be no better illustration of the confusions into which a certain German discourse led the man who nevertheless showed himself to be the most concretely political of all our Rhenish publicists and intellectuals – or, at any event, the closest to the gargantuan forces that all of them expected to overthrow the existing order.

THE PROLETARIAT: 'POPULATION' OR 'CLASS'?

The Condition of the Working-Class in England attributes to the class it is about an image and a status whose impact on the tradition of the workers' movement is no doubt equalled only by the scant attention that the book's theoretical premises have hitherto received. It seems as if the only real questions put to this fundamental work bear on the accuracy of its descriptions or the political predictions accompanying them – as if there were no need to ask what, in the same text, authorizes and, indeed, indissolubly combines a 'positivist' and a 'historicist' critique. Yet it requires no great acumen to trace this characteristic combination back to its unique premiss, which is simply the *anthropological* premiss that informs everything Engels says. The task is all the easier in that the author unveils the elements constitutive of his vision, with a candour bordering on naivety, in the first pages of the book (the dedication and preface). While he dedicates *The Condition* 'to the working-classes of Great Britain', thereby conflating his dedicatee and the object of his analysis, he does not pretend to speak in their name, or to adopt 'their' viewpoint in the narrow sense of the term (their viewpoint as a class), but, rather, claims to raise it to a higher level in order to reveal its true content: it is the viewpoint of *Mankind*.[100] The identity of the book's dedicatee, author and object – that is to say, of the subject and the object of knowledge – can be established only at the level of the human species. 'Man is the truth of the proletarian', because, *by virtue of his very inhumanity* (the consequence of his dehumanization), the 'proletarian is the man in man'; he reveals what is most human in man, and can consequently lead (us) to man's truth (which is ours as well).[101] This is one way of formulating the anthropological postulate which attests that Engels's book belongs to the discursive matrix of the 'human sciences' and, more generally, modern humanism.

The status that *The Condition* assigns the working class provides an exemplary instance of what Michel Foucault calls the empirico-transcendental doublet: the twofold division that constitutes man as the grounds of his own finitude. Hence the oscillation inherent in a discourse that presses the claims of the empirical on the plane of the transcendental; hence also the repression that makes up an integral part of this operation (which takes place in the mode of the always-already: it is a failure before it begins, and can be endlessly repeated). Engels's ambition – of which he serves notice in the preface, via a semantic coup which makes the words 'propertyless', *'working man'*, and 'proletarian' synonymous[102] – is to establish a perfect *continuity* between the analysis of the 'condition' of the working class – or, rather, of the 'working population' – and that of the class as 'the labour movement'; in other words, between the empirical worker, a product of his proletarian condition, and the worker 'as Human Being', engaged in a struggle against that very condition and, accordingly, conceived as a champion of 'our common cause, the cause of Humanity'.

This dualism, as our examination of *The Condition* will show, surges up again and again, becoming the source of an irreducible instability; Engels's text is condemned to making endless attempts to resolve it. Its effects emerge with full force when, at the end of his account, Engels broaches a very delicate point, on which the fate of the revolution depends: the relations between species and class – the One of the human essence, in what is assumed to be the imminence of its emergence, and the unbearable effects of antagonism, which continue to haunt all Engels's evocations of a reconciled humanity.

From the 'social' to 'socialism': The great romance of organization

As an inquiry into Manchester's working-class world, *The Condition* belongs to a body of literature that was growing by leaps and bounds in Europe in the 1830s and 1840s, thanks, for the most part, to the efforts of doctors and men of letters who were also convinced social reformers. The broad range and narrative qualities of this literature, as well as the solidity of the research on which it was based, showed early on that it would make an important contribution to the nascent 'human sciences', especially 'the science of the social'; here 'social' designates both that which constitutes man's essential being and that which makes knowledge of it possible, a founding principle that was simultaneously normative and epistemological. *The Condition* was, then, a work in a new 'scientific' genre contemporaneous with the stunningly rapid expansion of the industrial world. It took its place squarely within a species of discourse that proposed to study the object lodged at the heart of the social: the 'population', considered as an aggregate composed of discrete units, that is, legally free and equal individuals no longer bound by traditional ties. These individuals were atomized and autonomous, yet determined, whether they knew it or not, by the objective circumstances that shaped their condition: the new social circumstances spawned by the Industrial Revolution. For Engels – who was not simply an investigator seeking to gather empirical data but, rather, an authentic pioneer of the 'social sciences' – 'society' presented itself from the first as a fragmented, unintentional yet total order, lacking an outside; it was an irreducible, determinant reality in the life of individuals, but it was also a mobile, expansive reality,[103] a set of vital forces that were closely bound up with population movements and had to be regulated and augmented.[104]

In *The Condition*, the moralist who produced the texts that had so far appeared under Engels's signature, such as the 'Letters from London' or the 1844 'Outlines', yields to the *physiologist* or observer (who was by no means neutral, as we shall see; but it must be borne in mind that this was a feature common to all the pioneers of the 'social', which was, inextricably, an object of knowledge and a normative ground). This observer observed social facts, especially social 'evils', which he approached as 'natural phenomena' wholly independent of the individual will; for, in this respect, individuals merely constituted *passive* material that was subject to the play of circumstances. Take Engels's perception of the alcoholism that wreaked havoc among the proletariat:

> It is morally and physically inevitable that, under such circumstances, a very large number of working-men should fall into intemperance. . . . Drunkenness has here ceased to be a vice for which the vicious can be held responsible; it becomes a phenomenon, the necessary, inevitable effect of certain conditions upon an object possessed of no volition in relation to those conditions. They who have degraded the working-man to a mere object have the responsibility to bear.[105]

Much the same thing held for crime, 'the result of a law of Nature' comparable to the one, formulated by Réaumur, which governed the transformation of matter from the liquid to the gaseous state:

> Under the brutal and brutalising treatment of the bourgeoisie, the working-man becomes precisely as much a thing without volition as water, and is subject to the laws of Nature with precisely the same necessity; at a certain point all freedom ceases. Hence with the extension of the proletariat, crime has increased in England, and the British nation has become the most criminal in the world.[106]

This explains the assertion – which is surprising in some respects, yet typical of the analytic of finitude – to the effect that 'English socialism, i.e., Communism, rests directly upon the irresponsibility of the individual.'[107] The individual's 'irresponsibility' constitutes her essential nature; it allows us to acquire knowledge of her, and so makes possible the freedom of the 'irresponsible' individual. This is the substance of Owen's theory of character.[108] We would be perfectly justified in calling Engels an Owenite in this connection; let us not forget that the manager of the spinning mills at New Lanark liked to present himself as the inventor of the true 'science of society' – as the indefatigable promoter, not of a utopia, but of an eminently concrete *social technology*, a *social engineering* (based on science) that was entirely rational because it was adapted to the new circumstances created by the Industrial Revolution.[109] The panoptical model inevitably comes to mind here; as E.P. Thompson notes: '[Owen] was in one sense the *ne plus ultra* of Utilitarianism, planning society as a gigantic industrial *panopticon.*'[110] And let us not forget, either, that Bentham, as Engels himself points out – and as Heine had noted before him – was held in high esteem within the workers' movement.[111]

Thus the epistemic foundation common to social-ism and socio-logy resurfaces. The two were similar, as the semantic history of the words confirms,[112] both in their conception of social relations – the idea that individuals are *conditioned* by external circumstances – and in their political objectives: the elaboration of *social technologies* designed to treat (more or less radically, depending on the variant) the collective 'pathologies' and the chaos into which the first capitalist revolution, the so-called 'industrial' revolution, had plunged European societies. In other words, both social-ism and socio-logy sought to anticipate, and contribute to, a reorganization of the whole gamut of social relations, with a view to making them more harmonious and transparent to themselves.[113] If socialism presented itself as always-already 'scientific', the 'science of society' had to vie with it for control over this terrain.

Rather than engage in the canonical – and reductive – exercise of contrasting 'science' with 'utopia', we would perhaps do better, for the reasons just evoked, to examine the constitutive bond between thought about the social – social-ism and socio-logy – and the utopian tradition. Classical utopia has been defined as the 'great romance of the state',[114] a narrative of the conditions under which individuals fully coincide with their essence as subjects of law. Modern or 'social' utopia re-organizes this juridical anthropology, which is internal to the state's administrative apparatuses, in order to put it to work as a system for the production of individual and collective 'life', of 'population' and 'society'. It does so by generalizing the schema of social organization – or, rather, thanks to the production of the social (or the 'social bond', the social as bond) through organization.[115]

Contrary to the affirmations of liberal critics, then as now, the great romance of organization is not inherently 'totalitarian' – or, at any rate, no more so than the modern state as such, the liberal state included; no more so, if you prefer, than Bentham's panopticonism. For, just as the classical utopians suggested that 'one can and at a certain level [even] must (no proponent of natural law would deny this) ignore private property in order to think the relationship between the state and the subjects of law'[116] and in order to neutralize (at the imaginary level) the obstacles thwarting the ideal functioning of state sovereignty,[117] so modern utopians propose to ignore, at a certain level, not property, but competition and the market (and, secondarily, the vestiges of premodern society represented by the patriarchal family, the established Church, and so on) in order to think the ideal relationship between modern state apparatuses (the family, the school, asylums, and so on) and individuals and populations.

In a word, the narrative system – and critical charge – characteristic of utopian discourse served to reveal and to regulate, from within, the concrete functioning of the real social technologies elaborated by the various systems of state power. These social technologies played an active part in the rationalization of governmental practices, that is to say, in the elaboration of the 'governmentality' (Foucault) typical of the capitalist state. Jurists were accordingly replaced by social engineers, in particular by the managers of the apparatuses of an emergent bio-power (from the factory and workhouse to the medical or prison system). In Engels's terms, they were the new philosophers of the industrial age.[118] This explains why the favourite themes of the so-called 'utopian socialists' – sometimes dismissed as oddities extrinsic to the project of social reform – unmistakably belonged to the discursive regime of bio-power, whether one considers its political anatomy of the body or its application of the bio-politics of populations. Witness the principle of the *series* in Fourier, the founder of the 'societal mechanism' (an instrument ideally adapted to regulating the movements and events affecting populations); Owen's unflagging interest in physical education, phrenology, and the regeneration of the human race (the title of one of his major works is *The Revolution in the Mind and Practice of the Human Race*); Saint-Simon's government by the 'elite of producers', technocrats charged with administering society the same way one manages things; and so on.

Thus the utopian narrative was constituted not as power's irreducible other, but as its obverse, the formal neutralization of the obstacles standing in its way; in short, it was constituted as an imaginary apolitical space into which any transcendent power could be projected. Yet its effects were absolutely real: utopian discourse hewed closely to a practice internal to the system of power, serving as a brake, a self-control mechanism, a means of automatic, permanent adjustment of the modalities in which power was exercised. And, as *The Condition* attests, utopian discourse was *constitutive* of the theoretical enterprise that Engels helped to found:

if that discourse is 'superseded' in his text, it is a supersession which implies the 'negation/realization' of utopian social science in the 'new science' of a socialism that has reached maturity.

What is more, Engels never disavowed his close, complex relationship with Owen (whom he had known personally), as we can see both from the high praise lavished on him in *The Holy Family* and *Anti-Dühring*,[119] and by Engels's lifelong fascination for his social engineering, 'technical competence', and 'practical approach'. Indeed, with this in mind, we would do well to re-examine the entire conception of a socialism defined as the antithesis of market-based competition and capitalist 'anarchy' – a conception detailed in *Anti-Dühring*, which, as is well known, was of fundamental importance to the doctrine and discourse of the Second International.[120] For the moment, let us simply note that this discourse was built up around the theme of *organization* as the essential form of social life, together with its corollaries:[121] the idea that the economy should be planned, that society (assumed to be homogeneous) should be subject to conscious control, and so on. I should add that these themes are not original to Engels, even if he helped to make them part of the 'common sense' of the socialist movement (and, above all, helped to transform them into tenets of Marxist 'orthodoxy'), but are, rather, commonplaces 'of the nineteenth century, speaking, like a ventriloquist, through him'.[122]

Let us, however, return to the relationship between Owen and Engels, our sole focus here. The culminating point of this ambiguous filiation was doubtless reached with Engels's 1888 revisions to the Third Thesis on Feuerbach. They provide an exemplary illustration of his approach to the 'materialist doctrine concerning the changing of circumstances and upbringing' – which, however, forgets that 'circumstances are changed by men', and that 'the educator must himself be educated'. At stake in this rewriting of Marx[123] was nothing less than the Marxian definition of revolutionary practice [*revolutionäre Praxis*] in its absolute immanence to the development of social relations and their antagonisms, as a 'coincidence of the changing of circumstances and of human activity or self-change [*Selbstveränderung*]'.

The way Engels goes about correcting certain phrases – or, more precisely, 'putting them under erasure' – does, it is true, associate Owen with the materialist doctrine criticized at the beginning of the Third Thesis[124] – which would appear to indicate that Marx is taking his distance from Owen. But, more importantly, Engels also seeks to attenuate the radically immanentist character of Marx's definition by replacing 'revolutionary' with 'radically innovative' [*umwälzende*], while purely and simply deleting 'self-change'.[125] With these modifications, he lent his immense authority to the predominance, within the workers' movement, of classically dualistic conceptions and their corollary, a pedagogical, state-centred conception of the relationship between theory and the real historical process, the party and the class. Engels's emendations tip the emancipatory project in the direction of the rhetoric of power, of 'those who know', and of apparatuses that reproduce the structural features of the capitalist division of labour. We should recall that well before Stalin came up with his famous maxim, 'the cadres decide everything', the executor of Engels's estate (and, consequently, of Marx's), Karl Kautsky, observed that 'no reasonable person would want to begin building a house before his whole plan had been finished and approved of by people competent to do so'.[126] Such statements were by no means exceptional; they entered into the common sense of the officials of the Second International and of their understanding of Marxism, as is shown, for example, by the following sentence, which occurs in a letter from Guesde to Marx: 'Like you, I contest the idea that we can establish what we have set out to simply by destroying what exists, and I think that, sooner or later, leadership has to come from above, from those who "know more about things".'[127] It is a great pity that Marx's response to Guesde has not been found.

A physiologist in the big city

Let us now consider the representative themes of Engels's inquiry. The chapter titles of *The Condition* speak for themselves: 'The Great Towns', 'Competition', population movements ('Irish Immigration'), the social division of labour and its effects ('Single Branches of Industry', 'The Agricultural Proletariat', etc.). The sociological gaze,[128] omnipotent and resolutely medical, comes into its own here. It diagnoses, on the basis of the symptoms that appear within its field of vision, the diverse 'pathologies' afflicting 'the social body': 'the great cities have transformed the disease of the social body, which appears in chronic form in the country, into an acute one, and so made manifest its real nature and the means of curing it'.[129] As for the remedies, Engels does not seem exactly averse to administering shock treatment. The diseased body will have to be purged if it is to be restored to health, even if this means subjecting it to a bleeding:

> the course of the social disease from which England is suffering is the same as the course of a physical disease; it develops according to certain laws, has its

own crises, the last and most violent of which determines the fate of the patient. And as the English nation cannot succumb under the final crisis, but must go forth from it, born again, rejuvenated, we can but rejoice over everything which accelerates the course of the disease.[130]

The prospect of change is inseparable from crisis, but the transition leading beyond the crisis has yet to be described.

Powerfully buttressed by the reports of various commissions of inquiry, the *medical* gaze underlies the obsessive attention lavished on the 'physical and moral state' which specifies the 'condition' of the working-class. The workers' physical state, to begin with: *The Condition* treats constantly of bodies, their strength (or weakness), and the combinations and relationships established between them. From the outset, these relationships are emblazoned with the mark of class division. Lengthy descriptions aim to force the bodies of the proletarians into the categories forged by the medical gaze; their sensitive frames bear the scars and suffer from the pathologies caused by manual labour. Certain themes recur again and again: deformity (workers are short, malformed, mutilated in various ways),[131] disease (which is directly linked to living and working conditions), and emaciation – in sum, a state of chronic attrition of the forces of the proletarian body that can, moreover, be passed on by heredity. An obsession with height and weight, and the fear that the industrial work regime is stunting and levelling *Homo sapiens*, are central to the representation of workers as a distinct (sub-)race. Engels even quotes an industrialist who fears that 'the operatives of Lancashire would soon be a race of pigmies'.[132]

As for the 'moral' condition of the proletariat, Engels's account of it revolves around five constantly recurring variables: the proletarians' (very low) educational level; the two 'pleasures' in which they characteristically overindulge (alcohol and sex); their (lax) attitude towards religion; and the situation of the family (marked by dissolution and the reversal of traditional roles). In the vicinity of these variables there appear, in the background, the figures of the delinquent and the criminal, even the monstrous criminal.[133] There can be no doubt that Engels's gaze faithfully trails in the wake of the systems of 'population' control which were extended to the lower classes at the beginning of the nineteenth century:[134] the rapid expansion of prisons and the invention of the 'delinquent' (together with the complementary figure of the 'monstrous criminal'); control of the birth rate (if it is imperative for Engels to mark his discourse off from Malthus's, this is because their two positions confront each other, at least in part, on the ground of the same discursive regime); the organization, with a view to the 'moralisation of the poor classes', of the 'canonical' family, which the Industrial Revolution threatens to destroy (especially as a result of the reversal of the 'natural' roles of men and women, the source of a powerful fantasy about a generalized social depravity).[135] All this is to be accomplished by medical and legal control of sanitary conditions, deformities, perversions and other physical or mental pathologies, with an eye to augmenting the vital forces of both the individual body and the collective body known as the 'population', or even 'society'. Hence the 'sexualizing' thrust of Engels's descriptions.

Engels's discourse is unmistakably inscribed within the system of 'power over life', or 'bio-power',[136] whose deployment fostered the re-organization of knowledge that came about with the emergence of the 'human sciences'. The two faces of his text, anatomico-pathological and anatomico-political, concern the individual and the bio-political body of the population, which determine the nature of the two principal, eminently complementary procedures used to 'situate' the proletariat: the subjection of the proletarian body – notably by way of its sexualization[137] – and the racialization of the workers as a social group. Engels's descriptions of proletarian bodies reflect, in very telling fashion, the ambivalent feelings of contempt and fear elicited by both physical labour and the extreme physical and symbolic violence engraved on the flesh of those subjected to the mechanization of factory work. As Étienne Balibar has pointed out, the capitalist division of labour, especially in so far as it takes the form of a division between mental and manual labour, 'changes the status of the human body (the human status of the body): it creates *men-bodies* whose bodies are body-machines; they are fragmented and dominated, utilized for an isolable function or a movement; their integrity is destroyed, but they are simultaneously fetishized; their useful organs are subject to both atrophy *and* hypertrophy'.[138] Hence the metaphoricization of this destruction of super-exploited bodies: it engenders images of the 'degeneration' and 'enfeeblement of the body', as well as abiding fantasies about a regression towards the animal state, which, as we shall see, are obsessively projected on to that segment of the proletarian population which condensed all these marks of the subhuman: the Irish immigrants. These men-bodies appear in Engels's text as the bearers of a precocious and unbridled sexuality,[139] whose imaginary exuberance – which, once again, stirs up obscure feelings of fascination and repulsion – reflects a fetishistic sexualization of this subhuman body, a sort of permanent reversibility of its weakness into 'bestially' superhuman strength. The animal metaphors, particularly of scenes of collective copulation stimulated by the heat of both the bodies and their surroundings, are especially suggestive.[140]

Sexualization is part of a discursive ensemble that strains to make class differences permanently *visible*, eliminating the opacity surrounding the somatization of the proletarian 'condition' and exposing it, in its entirety, to the clarity of the sovereign gaze. Engels's criticism of the big city, developed in analyses that were innovative in their day (his strolls through the Manchester of the years 1842–44 rank, with Heine's earlier London excursions, among the first major *flâneries* of modern literature),[141] is highly significant in this respect. The urban spatial structure, he complains, makes the working class invisible, while simultaneously establishing the primacy of the visual that makes this invisibilization visible: 'I have never seen so systematic a shutting out of the working-class from the thoroughfares, so tender a concealment of everything which might affront the eye and the nerves of the bourgeoisie, as in Manchester.'[142]

Not only is the big city the place where individuals are atomized as a result of the creation of new spatio–temporal matrices (the theme of the lonely crowd[143] and its correlatives, the figures of the *flâneur* and the criminal, appears in Heine, Engels and Poe before finding full-blown expression in Baudelaire); it is also an obstacle that is simultaneously erected and surmounted by the new system for delimiting the visible and the invisible. The city is no longer the 'world within a world' represented by the pre-industrial and largely precapitalist city of the Classical age, 'a different world' and 'difference itself become a world';[144] it is a veritable Second Nature,[145] lacking (at least tendentially) an outside, an all-encompassing universe that has abolished difference amid the selfsameness of the spatio–temporality of Capital. This accounts for Engels's transformation of the cityscape of the traditional urban utopia. In the classic city, as Marin has shown, the coexistence of the bourgeois universe and that of absolutism, the City and (in close proximity to it) Nature, confronts the gaze with a plurality of non-congruent spaces; the result is that a city map, as such, can function as a utopian diagram. Engels's typically modern Manchester, in contrast (as we shall see when we come to discuss his map of the city), is an authentic 'dystopian' figure, the experience of a loss, the result of the destruction of a past still present in his native Wuppertal (Nature, the past). It is a negative utopia that has become a Second Nature (the 'urban jungle') and is haunted by its dark inversion (see below), which cannot be represented on any map: the destruction of the destroyer, the end of the city, the vision of the city as ruin (the First Nature's revenge on the Second) become the only possible (anti-urban) utopias.[146]

*

Engels's description of Manchester is organized around a map; it allows our gaze, which is thus identified with the author's, to roam freely through the city. The map of Manchester and its surroundings[147] makes it possible to organize a 'guided tour' of the city[148] around a visual support that is immediately legible and offered up to the boundless sovereignty of the gaze. The Manchester represented here appears as the classic type of a city fashioned exclusively by capitalist accumulation. It is a grey, homogeneous space stretching the length of the major thoroughfares for the circulation of goods, productive flows, and the work-force (streets, canals, the railway), a sprawling space that *lacks any representable outside* (nothing on the map assigns limits to the city as such, and Engels forewarns us, in his description of the 'environs', that they will eventually be transformed into extensions of the downtown working-class neighbourhoods). Significantly, the only features represented figuratively are the barracks (a dotted line and a few black rectangles indicate where they stand) and the commercial district (distinguished from the rest of the city by cross-hatching). The only elements described in the same code as is used for the statements of the 'guided tour' are set off in a space next to the map that does not really belong to it (the legend): mentioned here are the Stock Exchange, the Workhouse (and its extension in the paupers' burial ground), the names of bridges or poor neighbourhoods, and two churches identified as 'remnants of the old pre-manufacturing Manchester',[149] the sole remaining markers of a temporality different from that which holds sway in the metropolis.[150]

But Engels does not only provide the reader with a cartographic, two-dimensional representation of the city. He plunges into it, travels the length and breadth of it, collecting the stuff of its urban physiology, which comprises – it is this link between the gaze and the experiential field that is constitutive of the medical literature of this period and, indeed, of its literature *tout court*[151] – a physiognomy and a characterology, elements that are indispensable for establishing the political anatomico-pathology of the proletariat. The new regime of visibility and narration is not limited to what the eye can see. It implies a type of proximity (already suggested by the images of the crowded big city and its anonymous masses) that inspires profound ambivalence, a physical contact that Engels both desires – because, without it, he cannot penetrate to the depths of the city and drag what lurks within the social/urban body to the surface – and fears, for it confronts him with the spectacle of the poverty, deformity and filth of the bodies that the same gaze closely pursues.

We could doubtless put what causes what the other way round, in so far as it is precisely the threatening aspect of physical contact which makes

PLAN OF MANCHESTER AND ITS SUBURBS

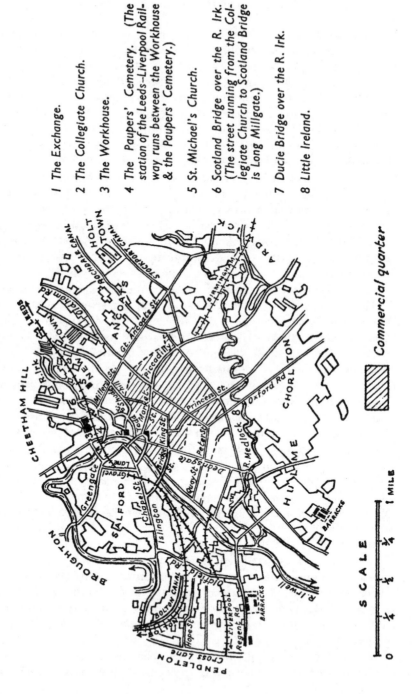

1 The Exchange.

2 The Collegiate Church.

3 The Workhouse.

4 The Paupers' Cemetery. (The station of the Leeds–Liverpool Railway runs between the Workhouse & the Paupers' Cemetery.)

5 St. Michael's Church.

6 Scotland Bridge over the R. Irk. (The street running from the Collegiate Church to Scotland Bridge is Long Millgate.)

7 Ducie Bridge over the R. Irk.

8 Little Ireland.

[///] Commercial quarter

SCALE

0   ¼   ½   ¾   1 MILE

it aesthetically fascinating and desirable, whereas the fact that it is a necessary means of acquiring knowledge can itself become a cause of dread.[152] London's crowds – which Heine could still compare to a 'rushing stream of faces of living men', and contrast with a cityscape dominated by death (the 'stone forest of houses')[153] – take on a truly spectral dimension for Engels: his book is haunted by the image of the proletarian bodies, already half in the grip of death, which the bourgeoisie does everything in its power to sweep from its field of vision. Engels strives to free himself of this spectre by bringing it into the light of day, and by shedding light on what is thus revealed. In his dedication 'to the working-classes of Great Britain', in which he addresses the workers directly, he says: 'I wanted to see you in your own homes, to observe you in your every-day life, to chat with you on your condition and grievances, to witness your struggles against the social and political power of your oppressors'; and he declares that he is 'glad and proud' to have done so.[154] But in the rest of his book, the spectral ambivalence looms up again; the tone is less lyrical, and often dominated by morbid images, while the gaze is haunted by the fearful, repulsive spectacle that unfolds before it, invading every nook and cranny of the realm of experience.

Of the big city and its inhabitants, *The Condition* offers an in-depth vision, an 'essential section' that reveals the 'other side of the picture'; it peers into the dark corners of the working-class slums, the maze of interlinked inner courts devoid of light and air, and plunges into the sweltering hells of the factories and mines. In this respect, too, it is situated within the discursive matrix that emerged in the course of the first half of the nineteenth century. Constitutive of the new regime of visibility, the discovery of the 'depth' of the body and its tissues by the medical gaze (the anatomico-pathology of Laënnec and Bichat) is contemporaneous with the discovery of the urban space by the Heinean *flânerie*, and the realistic or detective novel.

Lodged in the folds of this three-dimensional structure, the 'passages' in fashion in the 1840s formed intermediaries between inside and outside, just as the serialized novel transforms 'the boulevard [into] a dwelling for the *flâneur*; he is as much at home among the facades of houses as a citizen in his four walls'.[155] The stethoscope might be defined as the medical equivalent of the passage, while the doctor's 'quick appraising glance' parallels that of the realistic novelist. Both are haunted by metaphors of unveiling, penetration to the depths, and the projection of a three-dimensional space on to a flat surface: 'the problem, then, is to bring to the surface that which is layered in depth; semiology will no longer be a *reading*, but the set of techniques that make it possible to

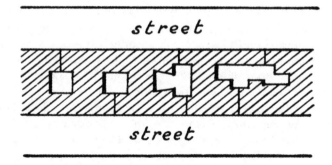

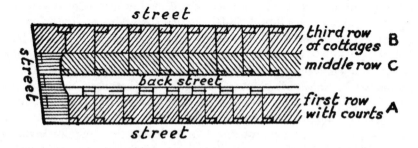

constitute a *projective pathological anatomy*. . . . The anatomico-clinician's gaze has to *map a volume*; it deals with the complexity of spatial data which for the first time in medicine are three-dimensional.'[156]

There is a patent structural similarity here to Balzac's approach, as described by a friend of Baudelaire's, Hyppolite Babou: 'when Balzac breaks through walls to give free rein to observation, people listen at the doors, creep along peering over fences, make little holes in the wall, train their opera glasses, at night, on the silhouettes that dance behind lighted windows far in the distance; in short, they behave, as our English neighbours in their prudery put it, like police detectives'.[157] Thus this gaze is in no sense the prerogative of a handful of specialists; relayed in more or less popularized forms by an immense literature, including 'literature' in the narrow sense of the word, it spread through broad social strata, becoming part of the 'sensibility' of the time.

It therefore comes as no surprise that Marx, in a chapter of *The Holy Family*[158] which constitutes one of his unfortunately rare sallies into the analysis of 'mass culture', should linger, at considerable length, over a wildly popular specimen of the serialized realistic novel, Eugène Sue's *Les Mystères de Paris*. 'Depth', in the sense of a narrative technique, is, precisely, the main theme of Marx's discussion of Sue's novel. It so happens that a year earlier, the same work had been favourably reviewed by Engels, who praised its 'forceful' description of 'misery and demoralization', and took its concern with the social, as well as its depiction of lower-class characters, as proof that 'the style of novel writing has undergone a complete revolution during these last ten years'.[159] *The Holy Family* – a few pages of which, incidentally, were written by Engels – was to strike a very different tone. Marx directs his polemical fire and his sarcasm at both the platitude of Sue's explanatory schemas – a banally 'materialist' social psychology – and the excessively speculative 'depth' of its Young-Hegelian German critic, who redoubled the hypostatization of 'mystery' by equating it with the omnipotent activity of consciousness. One would be hard pressed to come up with a more accurate description of the political stakes of this kind of populist representation of the people, endemic in the literature of the period; it constituted a formative influence on the 'spirit of 1848' with which Marx never ceased to settle accounts.

From class struggle to race war (and vice versa)

In the anatomico-pathology of *The Condition*, the categories used to classify the working-class population are those typical of the social science of the day: the proletariat is treated as a distinct 'class', but also as a distinct 'race', 'people', and even 'nation' different from the bourgeois 'class', 'race', 'people' and 'nation'. This idea is developed in two divergent yet related senses, depending on whether the emphasis falls on the traits that derive from the proletariat's 'condition' or its class character, that which constitutes it in opposition to the dominant classes. In the first case, we are dealing with a 'race . . . robbed of all humanity, degraded, reduced morally and physically to bestiality'.[160] In the second, Engels proffers us a strictly binary schema that casts the proletariat in a distinctly more favourable light: bourgeoisie and proletariat clash as if they were two opposed communities altogether alien to one another – as if, in other words, they were hostile peoples or even nations. Here the radical reference functions metaphorically (in the mode 'as different as if . . .'):

> the working-class has gradually become a race wholly apart from the English bourgeoisie. The bourgeoisie has more in common with every other nation of the earth than with the workers in whose midst it lives. The workers speak other dialects, have other thoughts and ideals, other customs and moral principles, a

different religion and other politics than those of the bourgeoisie. Thus they are two radically dissimilar nations, as unlike as difference of race could make them, of whom we on the Continent have known but one, the bourgeoisie. Yet it is precisely the other, the people, the proletariat, which is by far the more important for the future of England.[161]

Engels's ambivalence is in fact the constitutive ambivalence of the discourse on the race struggle; it attests to the transformations that that discourse underwent in the first half of the nineteenth century.[162] This version of it, contemporaneous with that of Disraeli's 'two peoples',[163] has roots in a very old discursive stratum – of radical-popular provenance in its English variant, but aristocratic in the French variant espoused by Boulainvilliers. It presents race struggle as a struggle between foreign entities, possessing different origins and speaking different languages, although the notion of race, immediately coded in terms of social groups, was assigned no stable biological meaning and was often associated with the (more or less fictive) historical rupture of an 'invasion' – Norman in the English case,[164] Frankish in the French. By Engels's time, however, the status of this discourse was changing: from an oppositional discourse underpinning a thoroughly agonistic vision of history, it was in the process of becoming the dominant discourse, and would soon be integrated into the systems of bio-power.[165] Once that shift had taken place, it was no longer a question of a confrontation between separate races whose antagonism stemmed primarily from their different geographical origins, but of a division within one and the same race, traceable to the emergence of a sub-race or sub-humanity whose degeneration represented a threat for the whole 'race' or 'society'. Of course, the biological retranscription of the older discourse was not accomplished at a single stroke. Hybrid forms sprang up, one of which is attested by a passage from Carlyle quoted – favourably – by Engels.[166] This passage illustrates the telescoping of the two strata, in which the old motif of the oppressed native Saxon, typical of English radicalism, is juxtaposed with the modern vision of the 'savage', 'degraded', bestial Irish immigrant. A 'national bane', the Irishman takes the place formerly attributed to the Norman lord.

Working in a similar – if not, indeed, the same – register, Engels finds himself at no great distance from Carlyle. For Engels, too, this very special segment of the proletariat concentrates within itself, hyperbolically, all the racial characteristics of the class. This, moreover, explains why it can be recognized on sight; a quick appraising glance, especially if the senses of hearing and smell are also brought into play,[167] is enough to tell whether someone is Irish (and, I am tempted to add, paraphrasing Jean

.Genet, what the colour of his skin is).[168] To these unmistakable identifying marks (a Celtic physiognomy and accent, monstrous uncleanliness,
drunkenness), we may add Engels's description of the Irish national
character, which is just as rich in stereotypical images: the Irishman has a
'cheery care-free temperament' and a 'southern facile character',
although his 'crudeness' 'places him but little above the savage,' and
'makes him incapable of sharing ... enjoyments' more 'humane' than
drunken stupour, and so on.[169] The immigrant working-class population
is thus a *metonymy* for the problems posed by the proletariat-as-population
– for its heterogeneity, its fluctuating nature, the contradictory imperative,
which Engels very clearly perceives,[170] to stabilize a part of it (basically in
big industry, which requires orderliness and discipline) while destabilizing
the conditions of reproduction of the class as a whole by holding open
the possibility of a new wave of proletarianization, in order to maintain a
constant tendency to super-exploitation. For such is plainly the basic
tendency, the essential 'open-endedness' of the capitalist mode of production, as *The Condition* suggests and Marx's analyses in *Capital* were later to
prove:[171] not 'average' exploitation but super-exploitation, even at the
price of the physical non-reproduction of labour-power and the destruction of entire 'populations'.

Thus the immigrant proletariat appears as the proletariat of the
proletariat, the most exploited, degraded, and bestialized segment of the
'race' of workers. Engels presents us with an outrageously overdrawn
portrait that comes close to being an expression of pure and simple
hatred: 'these people having grown up almost without civilisation, accus-
tomed from youth to every sort of privation, rough, intemperate, and
improvident, bring all their brutal habits with them among a class of the
English population which has, in truth, little inducement to cultivate
education and morality'.[172] The Irish are said to have imported 'filth and
drunkenness', 'the custom of crowding many persons into a single room',
and a 'new and unnatural method of cattle-raising in cities':[173] pork-
raising. Indeed, dire poverty, uncleanliness and crowding have contributed to making them more and more like pigs.[174] In an approach
strikingly similar to Carlyle's,[175] Engels even sounds the theme of the
foreign invader, whose roots in radical-popular English ideology went
deep (Saxon natives versus Norman aristocrats) – but he does so only to
turn it against the 'weak' or the weakest of the weak. The 'pressure' due
to the presence of these specimens of a particularly degraded sub-
humanity, systematically reduced to the level of beasts, contributes to
'degrading' the English proletariat as a whole, downgrading its living and
working conditions and depressing its wage levels.[176] The degradation of

the Irish is passed on hereditarily, leading to an apparently terrifying result: the creation of 'a population strongly mixed with Irish blood'.[177]

Engels's attitude towards the Irish proletariat is marked throughout, however, by a highly characteristic, unresolved ambivalence.[178] It is as if the biologizing retranscription of the earlier discourse about race war includes moments of reversibility at which an older discursive stratum resurfaces. The immigrant as 'savage', a familiar character who symbolizes the pre-civilized period in the narratives of natural law, accordingly acquires some of the characteristics ascribed to the 'barbarians' in an older aristocratic discourse: vim and vigour, bravery, and the triumphant freedom enjoyed by an individual who stands outside (rather than coming before) a 'decadent civilisation' – which it is his historical mission to destroy.[179] If England is to recover, 'born again' and 'rejuvenated', from the 'social disease' afflicting it, the 'course of the disease' will have to be 'accelerated' in order to precipitate the 'final crisis'. 'And to this the Irish immigration further contributes', Engels adds, 'by reason of the passionate, mercurial Irish temperament, which it imports into England and into the English working-class.' The Irish and the English are to each other much as the 'Latin and the Germanic peoples'; and 'the mixing of the more facile, excitable, fiery Irish temperament with the stable, reasoning, persevering English must, in the long run, be productive only of good for both'. A new world will arise from the ruins of bourgeois civilization.

What is more, Engels is no stranger to the poetry of ruin that haunts the modern gaze on the city and bourgeois society; this is the subtext of his description of Manchester. Walter Benjamin evokes 'the archeological view of catastrophe' and the accumulation of ruins from which the modern gaze views the present. Thus, in the case of Baudelaire – but this is something we have already seen in Heine – it is the 'idea of the decrepitude of the big city [which] is at the basis of the permanence of the poems which he has written about Paris'.[180] Michel Foucault calls attention to the nineteenth century's penchant, from Goya to Delacroix or Baudelaire, for discoursing on death, especially once the medical gaze has emerged.[181] For his part, Engels – who certainly possessed a thoroughly Romantic temperament, although he was little inclined to melancholy, and even had a whiff of vitalism about him – has Hegelian affinities: the morbid images of corpses and the spectacle of social decomposition represent, for him, only a transitory moment in which the struggle between life and death sets the stage for the advent of a new, higher form of life. *Anti-Dühring*, or the manuscripts collected posthumously in the *Dialectics of Nature*, say precisely that:[182] life is contradiction; it is that which resists death. 'Living means dying,' Engels writes, in terms very similar to those Claude Bernard ('life is creation'; 'life is death') or even Bichat ('life is the set of functions that resist death')[183] had employed before him.

Death is contained 'in embryo' in life, is immanent in it, is the condition of its productivity. The same holds, in Engels's estimation, for that wellspring of social pathologies known as the urban form of life, as long as it is viewed from the standpoint of its demise, of its effacement in the sands of a time emancipated from the nightmare of historicity. Faithful, in his youth, to certain ideas of Owen's and Fourier's, to whose authority he quite explicitly appealed, Engels would never cease to dream of the disappearance of cities and a mode of distributing populations over a territory that would eliminate urban concentrations as such.[184] This, in its turn, was doubtless not unrelated to his somewhat *völkische* predilection[185] for the 'barbarians', especially the Germans, conquerors of 'a dying civilisation' and a 'dying Europe', for their 'vitality' and their regenerative mission: 'But what was the mysterious magic potion with which the Germans infused new vitality into dying Europe? ... It was not their specific national qualities ... but simply – their barbarism, their gentile constitution. ... All that was vital and life bringing in what the Germans infused into the Roman world was barbarism. In fact, only barbarians are capable of rejuvenating a world labouring in the throes of a dying civilization.'[186] No doubt this argument has a polemic thrust, directed as it is against 'our chauvinist historians'; it puts the emphasis not on the qualities – although Engels acknowledges them – of the 'highly gifted Aryan tribe ... in the process of all vigorous development' characteristic of the Germanic peoples,[187] but, rather, on the virtues of their 'barbarian' social organization, depicted as communalist and democratic. Yet it is situated on the same discursive grounds, and would appear to have in common with the historians of *Blut und Boden* an image of 'barbarian society' that makes it a synonym for 'vitality' and 'regeneration', 'bravery' and 'freedom'.

The battlefield

The idea of race struggle provides the matrix for Engels's discourse on class struggle, moulding each of its many sedimented layers. But we would do better to speak not of evenly layered strata but of non-contemporaneous, telescoped levels, whose interaction produces unexpected combinations, such as the Carlylean amalgam which associates the archaic figure of the virtuous native Saxon with the modern, biologizing vision of the enemy incarnated in the sub-race of immigrant proletarians. In Engels's formulations, what survives of the older discourse is, of course, the idea that there exists an antagonism between classes/races/peoples that must be conceived of in terms of *war*, or, more precisely, 'social warfare'.[188] This discourse on the war of the races was capable of generating a historical narrative cast entirely in agonistic terms, distinct from the narrative developed by the theologians, or the theoreticians of natural law. Obviously, this was what made it possible and, in the final analysis, necessary – since such discourse is always-already invested with 'class' connotations – to rewrite the discourse of race war as a theory of class antagonism. Foucault emphasizes that 'the rhetoric of the war between the races has had the function of a counter-history'; he adds that 'the idea of revolution . . . is inseparable from the emergence and existence of the practice of a counter-history', and goes so far as to say, in an extreme formulation, that 'racism is, literally, the rhetoric of the revolution, only turned upside-down'.[189] Naturally, Engels is not the only one to whom this remark applies; when Marx needed an agonistic narrative schema, in the very text in which the proletariat first appears in his work, he, too, fell back on the schema of race struggle, together with the Master and Slave dialectic.[190] As we can see from his second address on the Franco–German War (September 1870) before the General Council of the International Working-Men's Association, the notion that wars between states (and thus, at least indirectly, class conflicts) might be transformed into 'race wars' (pitting the Teutonic peoples against 'the combined Slavonian and Roman races)'[191] never ceased to haunt Marx's vision of the European revolution.[192]

But the notion of war does not only function as a metaphor: it also shapes Engels's basic conception of the confrontation between antagonistic social groups, which is conceived of as a clash between symmetrically opposed armies or camps that are fundamentally separate, so that only a face-off on the battlefield can bring them into contact. The 'days' of insurrection that punctuated the French Revolution, like the barricades thrown up during the *Trois Glorieuses*, provide a concrete and very commonplace illustration of this schema, which is basic to the revolutionary (and also, doubtless, counter-revolutionary) 'sensibility' throughout what Hobsbawm calls the 'Age of Revolution' (1789–1848), and even thereafter. It is well known that the 'General' – as Engels was nicknamed by his friends, especially the Marx family, after he published his analyses of the Franco–German War – was interested in warfare to the end of his life.[193] But if he had high military ambitions, it was above all as a strategist[194] of what he thought of as an army of the proletariat, or of the proletariat armed. Beyond the importance of the properly military aspect of politics, his imaginary rank reflects a highly militarized conception of politics, that is, of the class struggle, particularly of the party-class, which he frequently refers to as the avant-garde of the proletarian army.

With Engels's strategic turn in the 1880s and 1890s,[195] the idea of insurrection yielded to that of the war of position. But this, too, is a military concept. Engels's turn merely breathed new life into the earlier schema, confirming the importance of the function exercised by the proletariat's military leadership. A protracted war of position calls, after all, for the creation of a much firmer and more disciplined (the key word) military structure than does an isolated uprising:

> [In 1848,] the masses, sundered and differing according to locality and nation-ality, linked only by the feeling of common suffering, undeveloped, helplessly tossed to and from enthusiasm to despair; today the *single* great international army of socialists, marching irresistibly on and growing daily in number, organisation, discipline, insight and certainty of victory . . . this mighty army of the proletariat has still not reached its goal, [is] far from winning victory by *one* mighty stroke, [but] it has slowly to press forward from position to position, in a hard, tenacious struggle. . . .[196]

Reversing but also extending the discourse of the race struggle, the model of social warfare in its Engelsian version – the theory of the 'two peoples' – provides a very effective anthropological and sociohistorical foundation for a certain vision of the proletariat. This model, already in evidence in his writings of 1842–44, makes the proletariat a class standing outside bourgeois society, ontologically distinct, as it were, from the dominant class, and immunized in advance against the various forms of ideological 'contamination' (which necessarily come from without). Engels declares the proletariat to be free of religious, moral, political and even national prejudices – all of which he attributes, in the context of the mounting polarization between social classes, to the bourgeoisie alone.[197] This is a theory of the *tabula rasa*; the people or race of workers provides a clean slate for the inscription of revolutionary ideas.

Nevertheless, while it seems to rest on a simple binary schema, the model of war takes, from the first, a twofold form that hews closely to the folds of the empirico-transcendental. The social war certainly is, in essence, a face-off between the two great classes of society, but it is also, and immediately, a 'war of each against all' that pits individuals against each other and saturates the body of society with a destructive conflictual-ity that it is impossible to control. Stirner's phenomenology of egoism and mutual exploitation, once stripped of its subversive pretensions, seems to Engels – much as it did to Hess in his roughly contemporaneous essay 'The Last Philosophers' – to provide a particularly faithful reflection of the modern condition, characterized by the swirling, random movement of atomized individuals in perpetual collision:

> The social war, the war of each against all, is here openly declared. Just as in Stirner's recent book, people regard each other only as useful objects; each exploits the other, and the end of it all is that the stronger treads the weaker under foot, and that the powerful few, the capitalists, seize everything for themselves, while to the weak many, the poor, scarcely a bare existence remains. . . . Everywhere barbarous indifference, hard egotism on the one hand, and nameless misery on the other, everywhere social warfare, every man's house in a state of siege, everywhere reciprocal plundering under the protection of the law, and all so shameless, so openly avowed that one shrinks before the consequences of our social state as they manifest themselves here undisguised, and can only wonder that the whole crazy fabric still hangs together.[198]

There is an oscillation between the two different representations of the 'social war' evoked here: Engels depicts classes in pitched battle and, at the same time, a generalized 'anomie', to anticipate a terminology that was to appear somewhat later. On the one hand, in other words, the idea of *fragmentation* is taken to an extreme (the atomistic schema); on the other, the opposing forces are *structured* as much as possible around the schema of a binary confrontation. Would reference to a Hobbesian model make it possible, if not to overcome this instability, at least to diminish it?

The situation is more complicated. The language that Engels, Stirner and Hess use to evoke the 'war of each against all' does indeed have a Hobbesian ring, and the problematic at work here is reminiscent of Hobbes's version of a common representation of the 'state of nature'. However, the reference to the author of *Leviathan* is in fact only indirect. Engels – exactly like Marx at roughly the same moment, as well as a good many other virulent critics of the 'egoism of interests' in modern society – repeats Hobbes's phrase about the state of nature with an eye to reorientating the fundamentally dualistic schema of the struggle between races/classes towards the idea that an 'infinitely proceeding division of society' (Marx)[199] reduces it to a hotchpotch of competing groups. On this point, then, we must look to Hegel and his critique of the atomism of interests, the false infinity exuded by a civil society that is the victim of its uncontrollable inner fragmentation. Especially relevant is a paragraph from *Elements of the Philosophy of Right* that everyone[200] had in mind at the time: the famous passage in which Hegel calls 'civil society' 'a field of conflict [*Kampfplatz*] in which the private interest of each individual comes up against that of everyone else'.

Engels's 'social war' is not a struggle for recognition *à la* Hobbes, a struggle that traverses society horizontally and is carried out exclusively on the terrain of representation and of signs, far from all real flesh-and-blood combat.[201] In Engels' opinion, civil war is not an embodiment of the absolute anti-political state projected in *Leviathan*; quite the contrary, it is the highest goal of the political, the moment in which politics, manifesting itself in its purity, creates the conditions in which it can be superseded. Civil war does not prepare the advent of its radical Other in the form of a pacified civil state by way of the voluntary founding act that constitutes a sovereign power; rather, it sets the stage for its own *dialectical transformation* into a higher (and final) form of class war, civil war – that is to say, precisely that which can never legitimately found a sovereign power, according to Hobbes. In other words, the Engelsian equivalent of the 'state of nature' does not augur a sudden transition, effected by fiat, towards a state of non-war that corresponds to the constitution of state sovereignty; rather, it underwrites a process of self-transcendence of war which passes, in obedience to an internal necessity, through a moment of extreme intensification of the existing antagonisms prior to a final reconciliation. Engels's schema of social struggle thereby offers a way out of the Hegelian aporia (entitlements for the poor or exportation of the contradiction via colonization) as to the issue of the conflict that rends civil society from within. Thus it saves the proletariat, whatever the unbearable precariousness of its condition, from the status of *Pöbel* (rabble), the status of a population that is in excess however one looks at it, and forever incapable of constituting itself as a subject (and therefore *always* only a step away from turning into its double, the threatening 'mob', an agent of pure destruction and social chaos).

Instead of either a Hobbesian mechanism of the passions, which guarantees the pre-eminence of the instinct for self-preservation (i.e. the absolute nature of the fear of death), and thus necessitates a pact of sovereignty, or of a confession of impotence before the irruption of a kind of pure negativity *à la* Hegel – alternatives that reflect one and the same dread of mass movements – Engels offers his reader a teleological narrative with a prophetic function: under the sign of the inevitable, it weds the figures of Catastrophe (economic collapse) and Parousia (the proletarian insurrection). Very precisely at their point of junction, Engels situates the growing polarization between classes. It is an objective product of economic relations, and – by virtue of its destructive effects – a concrete prefiguration of the coming cataclysm; it is simultaneously a means of

gradually bringing the empirical state of the class struggle into conformity
with the ideal-typical situation of a confrontation between two armies. To
all intents and purposes, then, mapping the model of war on to the realm
of the 'social' invests the latter with a peculiar instability, which the
resources of Engels's dialectical narrative are immediately mobilized to
overcome: 'in this country, social war is under full headway, everyone
stands for himself, and fights for himself against all comers. . . . And this
war grows from year to year, as the criminal tables show, more violent,
passionate, irreconcilable. The enemies are dividing *gradually* into two
great camps – the bourgeoisie on the one hand, the workers on the other.
This war of each against all, of the bourgeoisie against the proletariat,
need cause us no surprise, for it is only the logical sequel of the principle
involved in free competition.'[202] It seems that nothing can stop this
process of gradual clarification and generalization, identified with the
'development of the nation' itself[203] – an irresistible 'evolution' announcing a terrible dénouement from which the English bourgeoisie continue
to avert their eyes.

But does it go without saying that this is what will happen? The
permanence of the 'war of each against all', precisely, gives us reason to
doubt it; for, from within the model of war, it breeds uncertainty on two
crucial points. To begin with, the very principle motivating this war,
competition, causes disparities or even divisions within the proletariat.
These spring up not merely between individuals, but also between class
fractions (Irish immigrants versus the English, industrial versus non-
industrial workers, etc.). What is more, they are far from being merely
transitory. Thus Engels's reflections on wages and their tendency to
fluctuate around a shifting, complex 'average' paves the way for a description of the fragmentation of the proletariat in the face of the always
differential effects of competition. But how can we envisage the working
class as an army ranged for battle if certain obviously non-functional
divisions are rife within it? It is all the more difficult to do so in that –
here is our second point – the effects of competition seem, on the whole,
to have a far more deleterious effect on the cohesion of the proletariat as
a class (and, after a fashion, as a race) than on that of its adversary, the
bourgeoisie.[204] The war is by no means fought out on equal terms, in
particular because the bourgeoisie has a monopoly on state power – or,
in other words, because of the patent asymmetry between working-class
association and the strength of the state. Thus the two aspects come
together in such a way as to cast doubt on the symmetry between the two
'camps' that the model of class (or race) war presupposes. Rather than a
concept, this model accordingly tends to become a kind of ideal-typical

situation – or, more precisely, to take on a transcendental function; its discourse subsumes empirical contents whose transcendental premisses it reveals.

Tertium datur?

Is this a truly original view of historical development? We should note that the notion of social polarization, a simplification of class contradiction, is directly bound up with the fundamentally binary schema of a struggle between races/classes, especially as it was employed by socialist thinkers in the 1830s and 1840s. As early as 1795, Babeuf – who, we might mention in passing, invented the term 'working class'[205] – defined the 'political revolution' as an 'open war between patricians and plebeians'; this open war was simply the most recent episode in the 'perpetual war' that began with the total dispossession of the plebeians by the patricians.[206] It was Saint-Simon who introduced into scholarly discourse the concept of a specifically modern, dualistic and antagonistic division of society, even if he considered the state of affairs he thus described to be eminently regrettable.[207] In the early 1840s, the Fourierist Victor Considérant, adopting some of the Saint-Simonians' analyses, formulated a very explicit theory of the tendential polarization of the social classes, identifying the new dominant class, defined with precision as the exclusive proprietor of the means of production and trade, as a new aristocracy:

> Society tends to be ever more distinctly divided into two great classes: a handful of people who own everything or almost everything and are the absolute masters of the whole of the realm of property, commerce, and industry, and the overwhelming majority, who own nothing, live in an absolute collective dependence on those who possess capital and the instruments of labour, and are forced to hire out their arms, talents, and strength to the Feudal Lords of modern society for a precarious and constantly falling wage.[208]

The essential point is that, in a certain sense, this dichotomous vision merely *inverts* the liberal idea of 'a democratic social state', exemplified by Tocqueville's American vision. That idea is synonymous, not with the absence of differentiation (the opposite tends to be the case), but with the circulation and maximal mobility of the attributes of social rank; and, on a more pragmatic level, with the expansion of a stabilizing middle class.[209] All these factors, it is assumed, ward off the transformation of modern social stratification – that is to say, *class* division – into a hierarchy like that of the *ancien régime*, with its distinctions among closed orders

[*Stände*], castes, or even races[210] – or forestall the inevitable revolutionary dénouement, should it in fact *be* inevitable.

The scenario sketched out in *The Condition*, or in Victor Considérant's *Manifesto* (but does not Considérant's *Manifesto* anticipate the scenario we find in the other one?), echoes Tocqueville's, adopting its basic terms (a binary social situation most assuredly leads to revolution) while turning its argument upside down. Tendentially – we are still following Engels – liberal society proves just as compartmentalized and divided as the society of the *ancien régime*: the confrontations between its two classes/peoples is conceived on the agonistic pattern used to describe and name social struggles in societies dominated by the aristocracy and absolutism. Can we not push the paradox a little further, and say that this inclination to envisage the confrontation between the classes of bourgeois society on the model of the confrontation typical of precapitalist societies is an example of the superimposition of old attitudes and mental habits on new realities, on both sides of the line between dominant and dominated? Whether we take the language of popular protest (which advocated struggling against the new 'money aristocracy', that is, pursuing the revolution until genuine equality had been achieved – a fundamental theme of Babouvism and the *sans-culottes*),[211] or the vision of the dominant (which, in the case of liberals like Tocqueville, sought to avoid, precisely, the transformation of the new dominant class into a neo-aristocracy, and, in the case of the Social Darwinism–Nietzscheanism of the anti-1789 tradition, aimed, on the contrary, to form a new elite on the model of a caste), 'the persistence of the old régime' (Arno Mayer) is constitutive of the specifically European tradition, which is itself deeply beholden to the French experience. In a certain sense, the French Revolution, by virtue of its fundamental contribution to the autonomous activity of the subaltern classes (and, no less, by virtue of the reaction it elicited from the dominant classes, which had been permanently traumatized by the 'Great Fear' of 1793), firmly established an understanding of class antagonism that bore the marks of its origins in the society of the *ancien régime*.

No doubt that is also one of the reasons for the lag between, on the one hand, the revolutionary orientation *constitutive* of the French working-class movement, which claimed to be the sole heir to the sociopolitical subject of Year II, tying the social question to that of a change in the regime from the outset; and, on the other, English movements like 'Chartism', which steered clear not only of the central feature of *social* antagonism (the class opposition between capitalists and proletarians), but also of the *political* demand for any change in the regime involving more than the question of universal suffrage. Engels, however, carried away by the anti-political ardour that inspired his excessively optimistic vision of the English situation, was blind to the existence of this lag, even if the common sense of the day had it that a new revolution could begin only in France. Some three years later, he was to be a stupefied witness to the collapse, without a real fight, of what remained of the (supposedly) most advanced proletarian movement in Europe, at the very moment when the whole continent was swept up in a revolutionary storm, and the red flag was galvanizing the energies of the direct heirs to what was supposedly the narrowly 'political' Year II. In 1845, to be sure, *The Condition* had held open the possibility that England might evolve in a different direction. . . .

Revolution without a revolution?

In Chapter 6 of *The Condition*, which is about 'labour movements', Engels attempts to work out a systematic solution to the problem posed by the need to move from the empirical proletarian, observed in the objective reality of his condition, to the ideal proletarian, elevated to the status of 'Man', the living embodiment of the universal qualities of the human species. Thus this chapter has a strategic function in the theoretical system at work in Engels's book; this function is marked at the end of the previous chapter by a shift in the speaker's position. From a discourse *on* the class, we move to a discourse *of* the class, the discourse it utters about itself in the course of its constitution as a collective force: 'let us see what *they* say of [their condition]'.[212] In other words, we move to the level of the discourse that enables the proletarians, the victims of reification and the stultifying effects of capitalism, to rejoin the ranks of the human species, whose reunification is synonymous with concrete negation of the existing order: 'the workers, treated as brutes. . . . are men so long only as they burn with wrath against the reigning class'.[213] One of the dramatic high points of *The Condition*, the section on 'labour movements', strives to hold the terms of the empirico-critical doublet constitutive of the book's theoretical humanism together by asking – and answering – a now classic question: how is the transition from a 'social category' or a 'working-class population' to something like a workers' 'movement' to be achieved?

In *The Condition*, this question is couched in the following terms: how does the worker become a Man? There is little doubt about the result as such; the process of humanization seems to be well-nigh complete, as the dedication 'to the working-classes of Great-Britain' attests: 'I found you to be *Men*, members of the great and universal family of Mankind, who know their interest and that of all the human race to be the same. And as such, as members of this Family of "One and Indivisible" Mankind, as Human Beings in the most emphatical meaning of the word, as such I, and many others on the Continent, hail your progress in every direction and wish you speedy success.'[214] The workers are not only becoming men, they are becoming the most humane of men, the best representatives of the good qualities of the species: generosity, solidarity, kindness, and nobility of soul.[215]

What, according to Engels, makes this leap possible, even necessary? His argument is developed on two different levels, which intersect in the idea that the condition of the working class is a temporary one – in the sense that it cannot be sustained and is, indeed, all but impossible: 'this ... state of things ... cannot and will not last. The workers, the great majority of the nation, will not endure it.'[216] It cannot be sustained, to begin with, because it is subjectively intolerable. The worker rebels against the extremity of his condition; the duty to struggle is born of the fact that this intolerability exists: 'the working-man is made to feel at every moment that the bourgeoisie treats him as a chattel, as its property, and for this reason, if for no other, he must come forward as its enemy. . . . he can save his manhood only in hatred and rebellion against the bourgeoisie'.[217] The strength of Engels's argument, which is highly reminiscent of Heine's affirmation of the right to existence, surely lies here:[218] he describes a subjective refusal that is not dependent on an overarching moral imperative because it is the expression of an impossibility that is internal to existing social relations, an immanent expression of their antagonistic character.[219] The universality of the human species to which Engels refers loses its abstract quality, for it is no longer an essence that precedes itself but the result of a constitutive process, set in motion by the particular struggle against its particularization.

How can this revolt be transformed into collective practice and a movement of the class as a whole? The answer is contained in a single word: *association*, the species-activity of the proletariat. The word had served the revolutionary movement as a rallying cry since Babeuf, who, in the tradition of the *Social Contract*, treated it as equivalent to 'citizenship'.[220] It is in the common struggle to win (back) their rights that the associated constitute themselves as such, establishing, by this act of self-determination, the domain of the common, mutual recognition, and association as the truth of politics.[221]

The theme of association brings us to the heart of the specificity of the political. This specificity implies the autonomy of its subject: politics is the business of the people constituting itself as a people. For Engels, the constitution of the proletariat (the 'people in the people') as a class coincides with its struggle for *association*, which is simultaneously the means and the end of the movement of the class (the term 'association', as Engels uses it, also covers the idea of 'labour union', which, as such, is absent from the German text, except in the form of the English term 'trade union'). Moreover, it is no accident that the words 'mass' [which we find in its French form, *masse*, in the original German text] and 'power' occur in the book only once each, when Engels defines the immediate purpose of association:[222] to endow the workers with an existence as a collective force seeking its basic rights (the regulation of wages through *negotiation*) *in confrontation with* the capitalists. In the process of doing so, however, the associations transcend the limits of mere 'economic struggle' – to use a term that begins to make sense only after the emergence of a split between 'political' and 'economic' struggles. In Engels's view, in 1845, the trade unions are anything but 'trade-unionist' (in the pejorative sense of a narrow-minded, economistic consciousness later described at length by Lenin in *What Is To Be Done?*). On the contrary, they attack the existing social and economic system at its root, competition.[223]

The syllogism can accordingly be taken to its conclusion. Despite their limits, the associations *necessarily* lead the workers to an understanding of the need to abolish competition in general, and thus radically to transform social relations. This is the premiss which makes possible the affirmation that the economic struggle (for higher wages) and the political struggle against bourgeois domination are of the same order.[224] Association guarantees the seamless continuity that runs from present attempts to organize the class through the revolutionary rupture down to the future communist society: 'if the competition of the workers among themselves is destroyed, if all determine not to be further exploited by the bourgeoisie, the rule of property is at an end ... the moment the workers resolve to be bought and sold no longer, when ... they take the part of men possessed of a will as well as of working-power; at that moment the whole Political Economy of today and the laws determining wages are at an end'.[225] The dialectic of the concept of association generates effects that dissolve its political character: initially posited as a figure emblematic of politics in its specificity, it is transformed into its opposite and, as such, announces the end of the political under the reign of a reconciled humanity.

'Association' thus reveals the truth of 'organization', which is the foundation of the 'social'; the essence of association is situated beyond the realm of the political, in the transparency and harmony of a rationally organized 'true society'. Hence the constitution of the working-class movement, as well as its political maturation, do not require any specifically political practice, for the movement's political practice is conflated with the organization of the class, while its further organization is ensured by the constant exacerbation of the contradictions engendered by class polarization. For the same reasons, it becomes impossible to conceive of any notion of 'organization' that does not function as the absolute Other of 'competition' – in other words, is different from, much less antithetical to, that of working-class association.

In the realm of political action, Engels does not by any means propose to create a new tendency or party different from those already in the arena; he argues for the combination – or, rather, fusion – of the existing tendencies of the workers' movement. This is the condition for their mutual rectification:

> The working-men's movement is divided into two sections, the Chartists and the Socialists. The Chartists . . . are the more backward, the less developed, but they are genuine proletarians all over, the representatives of their class. The Socialists are more far-seeing, propose practical remedies against distress, but, proceeding originally from the bourgeoisie, are for this reason unable to amalgamate completely with the working-class. The union of Socialism with Chartism, the reproduction of French Communism in an English manner, will be the next step, and has already begun. Then only, when this has been achieved, will the working-class be the true . . . leader of England. Meanwhile, political and social development will proceed, and will foster this new party, this new departure of Chartism.[226]

Thus the revolutionary orientation of the workers' movement is synonymous with its unification, which is, in a certain sense, guaranteed in advance by the course of 'political and social development', independently of the shifting conjuncture and the outcome of internal struggles.

This thesis weighs heavy on Engels's analyses of the different proletarian or socialist currents in England. The *social* nature of Chartism and the elimination of petty-bourgeois elements from it (in Engels's words, its 'purely proletarian' character) are no longer taken for granted, as they are in the 1842–43 Letters. Yet because they are inherent in the very *nature* of Chartism, they appear soon enough as the result – imminent, if not already achieved – of a development that was present in embryo from the beginning: 'therein lies the difference between Chartist democracy and all previous political bourgeois democracy. *Chartism is of an essentially social nature*. The "Six Points", which for the Radical bourgeois are the beginning and end of the matter, which are meant, at the utmost, to call forth certain further reforms of the Constitution, are for the proletarian a mere means.'[227] The assumption is that the radicalization of Owenite socialism and its 'fusion' with the workers' movement are inevitable. (Social) Owenism can thus be productively played off against Chartism (with its penchant for the political). But the opposite is also possible: the radical nature of proletarian Chartism can be played off against the reformism of the socialists, who are out of touch with the real movements.[228]

Engels's optimism about the social, anti-bourgeois character of the English movement reflects the privileged place he assigns to England within the European triarchy. This Anglocentrism is in fact nothing more than the expression/metaphoricization of the relationship between the political and the social revolution already postulated in his writings of 1842–43. The *Condition* confirms the analyses developed in the *Vorwärts* articles; England is plainly on the revolutionary road as a result of the 'industrial revolution', which, as in Saint-Simon, fulfils the same historical mission as the French political model. It even 'forces' the workers to 'think and demand a position worthy of men'.[229] Engels lays great stress on this point: the English road is not 'less' revolutionary than the French or the German: 'the industrial revolution is of the same importance for England as the political revolution for France, and the philosophical revolution for Germany; and the difference between England in 1760 and in 1844 is at least as great as that between France under the *ancien régime* and during the revolution of July'.[230] Capitalist development and the development of the conditions for social revolution are of the same nature. The political situation and the balance of forces do not make any real difference; they can at best delay or hasten the inevitable day of reckoning.

The political backwardness of a country that has not experienced its 1789 is by no means an impediment. Indeed, it is, potentially, an accelerating factor: the English revolution will confront social questions and the problem of private property directly, without – as in France – focusing its energies on the question of the political regime. In other words, a political revolution can be dispensed with; here *The Condition* endorses one of 'true socialism's' fundamental theses. What is more, Engels pauses long enough to take issue with the prevailing notion that the English proletariat is lacking in revolutionary spirit, allegedly a French monopoly. The sum and substance of what he says is that appearances are deceptive; the two proletariats are equally radical, and differ only in the way they wage their fight:

It is said on the Continent that the English, and especially the working-men, are cowardly, that they cannot carry out a revolution because, unlike the French, they do not riot at intervals, because they apparently accept the bourgeois *régime* so quickly. This is a complete mistake. The English working-men are second to none in courage; they are quite as restless as the French, but they fight differently. The French, who are by nature political, struggle against social evils with political weapons; the English, for whom politics exist only as a matter of interest, solely in the interest of bourgeois society, fight, not against the Government, but directly against the bourgeoisie; and for the time, this can be done only in a peaceful manner.[231]

The English workers' indifference to political matters is accordingly interpreted as the sign of a maturity and radicalism *greater* than those of their French counterparts. The proof of this radicalization is the English propensity to strike, described at length in *The Condition.* Engels's assumption is that strikes will lead automatically to a revolutionary dénouement; they 'are the military school of the working-men in which they prepare themselves for the great struggle which cannot be avoided', 'the strongest proof that the decisive battle between bourgeoisie and proletariat is approaching', 'the pronunciamientos of single branches of industry that these too have joined the labour movement'.[232]

In many respects, the young Engels's 'Anglocentric' theory of revolution appears to be the result of a blindness that was all the more serious in that it afflicted few of his contemporaries, for whom the idea that London (or Manchester) might replace Paris as the capital of the revolution seemed far-fetched, to say the least.[233] But it must also be said, in Engels's defence, that all Europe had trembled at the thought that summer 1842 might bring a Chartist insurrection; at the time, even the very 'French' Heine had been overcome by a rare access of pro-English feeling.[234] Moreover, the rapid upgrading of the repressive arsenal at the disposal of the English state, proportionate to the 'great fear' that had seized the dominant classes in Britain at the thought that 'continental' revolutions might 'contaminate' England[235] (let us note that the English repressive apparatus proved very effective indeed in 1848), shows that the threat had been taken seriously.

The fact remains that Engels's predictions about the future development of the British workers' movement were promptly (less than four years after *The Condition* was published) contradicted by the course of events: after the summer 1842 defeat (whose consequences turned out to be much more serious than Engels had thought), its Chartist component, far from asserting its 'social' character and purely proletarian make-up, went into a period of decline that was briefly – and only very partially –

interrupted by the echo that the 1848 'continental' revolutions found in Britain (the failure of the April 1848 Kennington Common rally). The English workers' movement's refusal to raise the question of the political regime turned out to be a sign of 'political' as well as 'social' backwardness, and contributed significantly to its acceptance of bourgeois politics, even at the level of ordinary economic struggle (the exclusion of unskilled workers from the trade unions), throughout a period that ran down to the late 1880s. As the British historian Tom Nairn points out:

> The backwardness or non-radical character of political life and aspirations signified permanent *im*maturity: the resigned absence of certain necessary conditions for *any* revolution. . . . A mounting indifference to 'merely political' considerations did not indicate passage beyond the level of radicalism to something greater – to a real socio-economic transfiguration springing from 'class'. It signposted the contrary – long-term retreat below that level and resigned acceptance of never getting there, to the land of authentic popular sovereignty, equality and freedom (as distinct from estate-liberties).[236]

Furthermore, Chartism did not in any sense 'fuse' with Owenite socialism, which took an ever greater distance from anything that smacked of the workers' movement.

All in all, it would appear that at the very moment when *The Condition* was prophesying an imminent social revolution – and even suggesting that it would break out before the economic crisis expected for 1853 – the English workers' movement had already entered a phase of deradicalization that was to last for several decades, transforming it, until the emergence of the new unionism, into a corporatist trade-union apparatus and a political appendage of the Liberal Party. Subsequently, on a number of different occasions, Engels reconsidered the evolution of the English situation *after* 1848,[237] accurately singling out its essential features: he highlighted the proletariat's political and ideological subordination to the bourgeoisie, hypothesized that the working class had been 'bourgeoisified', or that a 'labour aristocracy' had sprung up as a result of British capitalism's imperial role, noted the existence of proletarian support for colonial policy and the spread of racist attitudes among the working class, and so on. But he offered no real explanation (apart from the fluctuations of the business cycle) for the disparity between his predictions and what actually occurred in the period that drew to a close in 1848 – that is to say, for the fact that *there was no* English 1848. In contrast, what had been brewing on a Continent supposedly mired in an archaic political struggle was an authentic revolutionary storm, whose tragic outcome would have a decisive impact on developments down to the end of the century.

Engels's error cannot be attributed to simple miscalculation or lack of foresight; it was the necessary consequence of a theoretical system whose premisses short-circuited his analysis of the real working-class movement. Here it is instructive to compare him to Marx, even after the 'true' encounter between the two men in 1844. From the first text (written late in 1843) in which he looked to the proletariat as the main actor in the coming revolution, Marx privileged the Franco–German axis and, of its two components, identified Germany as the chosen land of 'radical revolution'. In contrast, Engels, in a later text (1847), continued to peg the chances for a successful revolution to the level of a country's economic and, above all, industrial development. Hence he maintained his Anglo-centric vision, affirming, very logically, that '[the communist revolution] will . . . be slowest and most difficult to carry out in Germany, quickest and easiest in England'.[238] Yet the *Manifesto of the Communist Party*, co-authored by Marx and Engels on the eve of the 'real' revolutions of 1848, *does not mention* England in connection with social revolution. Indeed, the tendency runs the other way: the most significant passage on England is one in which Chartism is discussed as an example of a 'workers' political party'[239] that succeeded only in wresting *concessions* from the bourgeoisie (the law on the ten-hour working-day) and turning its internal contradictions to advantage. Rejecting economistic, anti-political Anglocentrism, the *Manifesto* reaffirms Marx's position of 1843–44, while reformulating it: 'the Communists turn their attention chiefly to Germany, because that country is on the eve of a bourgeois revolution', which 'will be but the prelude [*unmittelbares Vorspiel*] to an immediately following proletarian revolution'.[240]

In the final analysis, Engels's socialist humanism shows that it is impossible to forge even a *concept* of politics that is adequate to this revolution whenever it is assumed to be inevitable. For lack of such a concept, Engels's narrative becomes prophecy, relapsing into all the ambiguities and impasses of the philosophical posture. It announces the Good News of a Revolution that is an apocalypse in both senses of the word: an announcement of the end of the world, or of *a* world, and a revelation of the imminent Presence, of the establishment of a divine kingdom on earth. But Engels, in keeping with spectral logic or haunt-ology,[241] constantly wavers between heralding a revolution associated with a cataclysm and the desire to exorcize it, in accordance with the classical logic of prophetic discourse, which consists in brandishing the threat of punishment in order to provoke a reaction to the spread of evil. Here, in exaggerated form, we find the ambivalence constitutive of the German road: Engels predicts the revolution with the tranquil assurance of a physiologist, and a conviction authorized by the scientific knowledge of its laws; but it is impossible to say whether he does so to hasten its advent or to issue a last warning to the dominant class, summoned to abandon its suicidal indifference and carry out reforms, even at the eleventh hour.

In the introduction to *The Condition*, Engels denounces 'the scornful smile which [the English bourgeois] assume when any one begins to speak of the condition of the working-class ... upon a soil that is honeycombed, and may any day collapse, the speedy collapse of which is as certain as a mathematical or mechanical demonstration'.[242] The gathering threat is a terrible one, he warns, for the 'wrath which before too long a time goes by, a time almost within the power of man to calculate, must break out into a revolution in comparison with which the French Revolution, and the year 1794, will prove to have been child's play'. As this day of wrath is on hand, 'it is high time ... for the English middle-class to make some concessions to the working-men who no longer plead but threaten and demand; for in a short time it may be too late'.[243] In this light, Engels's repeated assertions to the effect that it is impossible to find a peaceful resolution to the crisis sound less like a rallying cry than an ultimate warning addressed to the powerful to induce them to choose, however late in the day, the path of concessions and reforms.

If, despite all, the battle breaks out, those who turned a deaf ear to the appeals for reform will only get what they deserved: 'if, up to that time [the coming crisis of 1853], the English bourgeoisie does not pause to reflect – and to all appearance it certainly will not do so – a revolution will follow with which none hitherto known can be compared. The proletarians, driven to despair, will seize the torch which Stephens has preached to them; the vengeance of the people will come down with a wrath of which the rage of 1793 gives no true idea.'[244]

In the key pages containing his conclusion, Engels considers the implications of the dilemma 'reform or revolution' for the question of the violent nature of the process, but also – this aspect seems to be inseparable from the first – its bearing on its class dimension. With a purely proletarian revolution he associates the terrifying, simultaneously fascinating and repellent imagery of sheer destruction, of the unleashing of blind violence – in a word, of the victory of the modern barbarians described throughout *The Condition*: the proletarians. Yet, as we have seen, he seems rather to doubt that any reformist initiative can come from the upper classes, although he does not exclude that possibility outright. Moreover, he rules out the eventuality of, as it were, a moderate revolution of the kind the Gironde attempted, deeming it incapable of preventing a subsequent radicalization. He therefore turns towards the dominated, in the hope that the spread of socialist and communist theories among the working class will exercise a *moderating* influence on the revolution.[245] His assumption is that the expansion of the audience for these theories will make people, especially workers, more civilized; but that, secondarily, it will also give pause to certain elements of the bourgeoisie, prompting them to join the ranks of the social movement and contribute, albeit only in auxiliary fashion, to tempering its proletarian ferocity and concomitant penchant for violence.

This might seem a strange sort of wager, given what Engels says elsewhere about the radical nature of communism. Yet there is a logic to it. For Engels, socialism and communism are situated above the antagonism between bourgeoisie and proletariat, beyond the division of humanity into opposing classes. They represent the standpoint not of the worker but of Man; not of class particularity but of concrete universality; not of antagonism but of its dissolution in the final reconciliation of humankind. In other words, they represent the absolute standpoint of Feuerbachian humanism, applied to social realities and to history:

> The revolution *must* come; it is already too late to bring about a peaceful solution; but it can be made more gently than that prophesied in the foregoing pages. This depends, however, more upon the development of the proletariat than upon that of the bourgeoisie. In proportion as the proletariat absorbs socialistic and communistic elements, will the revolution diminish in bloodshed, revenge, and savagery. Communism stands, in principle, above the breach between bourgeoisie and proletariat, recognises only its historic significance for the present, but not its justification for the future: wishes, indeed, to bridge over this chasm. Hence it recognises as justified, so long as the struggle exists, the exasperation of the proletariat towards its oppressors as a necessity, as the most important lever for a labour movement just beginning; but it goes beyond this exasperation, because Communism is a question of humanity and not of the workers alone.[246]

Here we come back to Hess's lessons, along with the main themes – sometimes stated in the very same terms – of the 'true socialism' – Feuerbachian humanism applied to the social question – that *The German Ideology* and the *Communist Manifesto* subject to a withering (self-)critique. More generally, a certain Romantic spirit of the day, eminently characteristic of the 'generation of 1848' (at least on the Continent), breathes from these pages: a spirit inclined to seek social compromise, to which even certain sections of the dominant classes were predisposed, tormented as they were not only by fear, but also by a form of unhappy consciousness in the face of the trauma caused by industrialization.[247] We need to dwell on this point, against an entire interpretative tradition that includes – and may well even be confined to – the Marxist tradition. *The Condition* attests the 'discovery' of the proletariat in the sense in which it was 'discovered' by the 'inquiries' into the 'condition of the working-class' that mush-roomed in the first half of the century in close conjunction with the political purposes of their authors (who were generally sympathetic, in France, to socialist tendencies),[248] not as it is defined in the theoretical universe constructed much later by the analyses we find in *Capital.* This 'discovery' takes place, from first to last, under the banner of socialist humanism; Engels, in so far as he was involved, left no doubt on this score.[249] No doubt his candour explains both the leading role he later played in the struggle against 'true socialism', and also why he felt the desire to include, in the 1892 German edition of *The Condition*, a self-critical note on humanism.[250] But, more broadly, this German variant of Romantic humanism takes its place within the emergent discourse on 'man' and 'the social', with its scientific (and also post-philosophical) pretensions. It is organized around the empirico-critical doublet that underpins all these discursive formations; the impossible yet endlessly repeated attempt to reduce it to unity lends them their characteristic instability.

In the closing pages of *The Condition* – which are caught on the horns, precisely, of the dilemma 'reform or revolution' – we find a particularly exacerbated instance of this constant oscillation. According to what Engels says here, the struggle would proceed 'very peacefully' if 'it were possible to make the whole proletariat communistic before the war breaks out'. On the other hand, we know that only struggle – and perhaps only across-the-board struggle, can bring the whole proletariat into the communist ranks. Engels's peaceful solution comes down to wanting the results of the revolution before the revolution, or even without the revolution. The oscillation inherent in the argument is sustained, and intensified, right down to the last sentence of the book, which sounds more like an ultimate warning addressed to the bourgeoisie than a call to insurrection: the peaceful solution seems impossible from now on; the contradictions are only growing sharper; soon 'the war-cry will resound through the land', and '*then* it will be too late for the rich to beware'. It follows that it is not yet too late, although there is no time to lose: 'meanwhile, I think that before the outbreak of *open*, declared war of the poor against the rich, which has now become inevitable in England, there will be enough intelligent comprehension of the social question among the proletariat, to enable the communistic party, with the help of events, to conquer the brutal element of the revolution and prevent a "Ninth Thermidor"'. The two-headed spectre of the Terror and Thermidor, the infernal couple of revolution and counter-revolution that haunts German philosophy, appears, very logically, at the heart of these hopelessly irresolvable aporias, revealing the fundamental 'hitch' in the argument; it looms up out of the gulf separating the actually existing proletariat from Humanity reconciled, ordinary battles from revolutionary apocalypse, business-as-usual from the Day of Salvation.

Hardly has it been called up than the revolutionary spectre is conjured away, driven back into the shadows, invited to take to its heels; the cataclysm is imminent, but it can be avoided on condition that. . . . But it will take time to create this condition as well, and that time is sorely lacking. To make matters worse, the requisite condition can be created only with the help of 'events', and one is hard pressed to see how these events could do anything but hasten a dénouement that is, in any case, 'ineluctable' – and so on.

The *Condition* closes with this scene of exorcism. Incidentally, the last touches were put to the manuscript under very curious circumstances: its author and Moses Hess were on a joint lecture tour in the small towns of the Wuppertal,[251] where, far from the jungle of the English cities, the two comrades conquered edgy – but at the same time, no doubt, fascinated – audiences of cultivated bourgeois who were typical representatives of the peculiarly German phenomenon known as philosophical socialism. Engels's Elberfeld speech of 15 February 1845 gives us an idea of what was said in the exchanges that took place during these lectures: 'social revolution' is 'the necessary result of our existing conditions',[252] especially *competition*;[253] both free trade and protectionism are basically incapable of providing the necessary remedies (since Engels's audience was most certainly very bourgeois, most of his lecture is devoted to this last point). The social revolution is presented, from the very beginning of Engels's talk, as 'the open war of the poor against the rich'; it cannot but 'go for the thing itself [and] grasp the evil by the root'.[254] Hence only the 'proclamation of the principles of communism', truly radical principles, makes 'real social reform' possible.[255] As this last term ('social reform') suggests, 'the peaceful introduction or at least preparation of communism' turns out to be the '*one* means' of avoiding 'the bloody solution of the social problem'.[256] Let us 'contribute our share toward humanising the condition of the modern helots', and create 'for *all people* such a condition that everyone can freely develop his human nature'; let us renounce the mere 'semblance' of selfish enjoyment by giving free rein to the inclinations of 'reason and the heart'; let us, in a word, 'really . . . bring into being' 'real human life with all its requirements and needs'[257]

– such was the course of action which Engels ardently urged upon the 'gentlemen' (he was presumably addressing an all-male audience) of Elberfeld and the surrounding region.

In the light of the barbarity which broke over this region and the rest of Europe after the hopes raised by 1848 had been dashed, Engels's sermon seems like the last glimmer of an age in which the respectable society of the proto-industrialized cities of the peaceful Rhineland could still allow themselves the luxury of putting the world to rights (in words!) well into the wee hours of the morning, in the company of a scion of one of the best families of the region, flanked, it is true, by a rather disreputable Jewish journalist.[258] Strange conspiratorial scenes, where, amid the euphoria inspired by the knowledge that absolutism was in an advanced state of decay, and at a time when the effects of the antagonism between capital and labour were only just peeking over the horizon – a horizon dominated by the country landscape, church steeples, and the figures of the aristocrats and bureaucrats of the *ancien régime* – it was still possible to believe that philosophy had maintained its power to exorcize spectres, and that the reiteration of its own confession of impotence possessed, after all, a kind of healing power.

5

Karl Marx: From the Public Sphere to Revolutionary Democracy, 1842–1844

A few months after the inglorious collapse of the 1848 revolutions, when the order of the day was resigned abandonment of all hope that the revolutionary movement could be rekindled, Engels wrote to Marx: 'emigration . . . is a real SCHOOL OF SCANDAL AND MEANNESS . . . an institution which inevitably turns a man into a fool, an ass and a base rascal unless he withdraws wholly therefrom'.[1] Did he have a premonition that their exile was just beginning, and would henceforth form the inescapable horizon of their lives? However that may be, statements like this one have to be understood as the words of the vanquished, and are directly attributable to the trauma of defeat. In this respect, Marx's second exile is the very opposite of his first, which lay on the other side of the divide represented by the débâcle of 1848. For when Marx settled in Paris, in autumn 1843, he no more had an air of defeat about him than did Heine in the immediate aftermath of the July Revolution, although he was deep in the midst of the political and theoretical crisis sparked off by the prohibition of the *Rheinische Zeitung*. He meant his first exile to be resolutely offensive, like Heine's: it would allow him to work towards a political and cultural alliance between France and Germany, an indispensable condition for the success of a new revolutionary wave in Europe that would be more extensive and more radical than the previous one. What is more, the new revolutionary upheaval, as Marx saw matters at the time, would not be long in coming. For however strange, even incomprehensible, it may seem to us today, such, on the eve of 1848, was the main feature of an experience shared by the community in which the generation of adoptive Parisians who had emigrated from Germany or elsewhere found itself evolving: the *émigrés* were convinced that they were witnessing a mass upsurge which the old order was straining its every fibre to hold in check. The most optimistic (or pessimistic, depending) lived in daily expectation of revolutionary upheavals. Thus, when one of the most prominent representatives of the *émigré* community, the Russian Alexander Herzen, affirmed that 'the emigration is the first sign of a revolution in the making',[2] he was merely stating a truth widely regarded as self-evident (by, among others, the networks of police agents working in the service of all the autocrats of Europe).

It is, however, possible that, in thus emphasizing the break represented by 1848, I am succumbing in my turn to the 'retrospective illusion' that often dominates biographical and, more generally, historical narratives: it consists in interpreting an event in the light of what came after it. Is there any need to repeat Althusser's warning about histories composed 'in the future anterior',[3] that is, projective histories in which one figure of self-consciousness stealthily takes the place of its predecessor, thereby investing events with an illusory 'meaning'? On the other hand – as has been pointed out by one of Althusser's former collaborators, Alain Badiou, whom I follow here – any interpretation of history – or, more precisely, any interpretation of history that also constitutes an intervention in it – must plainly accommodate this retroactive dimension. Indeed, it is only in consequence of an *ex post facto* decision to bring an interpretative intervention to bear on an earlier event that the event is recognized *as* an event, as a radical opening invested with a dimension of irreducible contingency and undecidability.

Yet I could also state the situation the other way round: as radical opening, an event is constituted only retroactively: on condition, as it were, that one has always – or, rather, always-already – adopted the standpoint of the event itself. Thus the event results from an intervention and an interpretative wager which consists in drawing out its trajectory and, from the perspective so offered, attempting to discern its consequences, determine what relation they bear to it, and even examine its traces in the present. Such is the case even if those traces can be recognized and accounted for as such only from the vantage point offered by the interpretative decision itself; in this sense, Althusser's warning is still valid. Thus we are caught between the opening of a historical situation on the one hand and, on the other, the 'always-already' of the intervention-interpretation which recognizes it for what it is, but can be discerned only retroactively. It would seem to follow that the sole means of guarding against the illusions of (retro)projective history consists, precisely, in boldly accepting the future anterior as the proper tense for political interpretation.

This hypothesis comes down to naming the 'event Marx' by examining the conditions of an encounter between an intellectual trajectory and a historical conjuncture – by trying to discern or, rather, work out the consequences of the break that encounter produced, as well as the openings it made possible. The sequence of events we shall be examining unfolded over a period of less than three years: from late 1841 to winter 1844. In the course of it, a young doctor in philosophy who had set his sights on an academic career after briefly nursing hopes of literary fame became, instead, a journalist and public activist caught in a running battle with the Prussian censorship; he later went into exile and adopted communist positions. These two moments formed the starting and finishing points of a number of different 'transitions': from the stuffy atmosphere of the small towns of the Rhineland to what Marx himself called the 'capital of the new world';[4] the Paris which, thanks to Heine, the younger German generation had already discovered; from the status enjoyed by the editor of a prestigious newspaper financed by a fraction of Cologne's respectable bourgeoisie to that of an exile scraping by on allowances from friends while chipping away at his family's modest savings; from the clubs frequented by the Rhineland's enlightened middle classes to the meetings held in the less reputable cafés on the outskirts of the French capital (in particular, the *Barrière du Trône* on the southeastern edge of the city), where the German or French artisans and workers who made up the core of revolutionary Paris met and talked.

The pivotal event in the young Marx's trajectory comes into focus against the backdrop of a *crisis* that we can date to 1843. It was a twofold crisis, both personal (Marx's marriage, tensions in his family, the dashing of his hopes for a career, the near-certainty that he would suffer a decline in social status, and, finally, his departure for France), and intellectual (Marx's withdrawal to Kreuznach as a stage in the redefinition of his relationship to Hegel). In a more general sense, this crisis was also political. The Prussian regime's recent authoritarian turn, while it had succeeded in briefly throwing the government's adversaries off balance, could only lead to a rapid exacerbation of existing contradictions: it was more a desperate bid for survival than a successful attempt to regain the initiative. Marx punctuated this sequence of events with a number of key texts: his letters to Ruge; the writings he produced at Kreuznach in 1843, including a manuscript (hereafter 'the Kreuznach manuscript') containing a critique of Hegel's *Elements of the Philosophy of Right*; and, finally, 'On the Jewish Question', a text that he almost certainly finished in Paris. These writings are framed, on the one hand, by Marx's 1841 doctoral dissertation and the articles he contributed to the *Rheinische Zeitung*, and, on the other, by the first work Marx wrote in exile, sometimes called the

'1844 Introduction' to the 'Contribution to the Critique of Hegel's Philosophy of Law'.

This is the set of texts I shall be examining to test the political interpretation that forms my working hypothesis: under the impact of the crisis of 1843, Marx, who had until then been a representative of a radical strain of the reformist tendency known as 'Rhenish liberalism', rapidly went over to the revolutionary camp. The prospects for a German and European revolution, regarded as the sole task worthy of the times: such was the event that Marx would henceforth attempt to theorize, the statement whose bearer he would become. Presiding over this abrupt shift was a single question that will serve as our guiding thread here: the question of how to repeat the emancipatory act of the French Revolution in order to put an end to Germany's *ancien régime* – how, that is, with the 'German *misère*' as one's starting point, to take up a position on the trajectory of this founding event, and accede to the universality of the new world-historical moment. Marx agreed with a whole generation of German democrats about what the givens of this problem were; but he tore it from the context created by the previously proposed 'solutions', in an act of rupture that represented a literally unprecedented political-theoretical break with the past. This was what distinguished him from all the other leading figures of the democratic opposition (Ruge, but Engels and Hess as well), and brought him close to Heine. However – to paraphrase a remark that he himself made in a letter to Freiligrath[5] – if Heine was a poet, Marx was a 'critic': that is, a theoretician.

Whatever the standard account of the formation of Marx's thought may – in its different and, indeed, conflicting versions – have to say on this point, Marx's theoretical break was predicated on a political break, and cannot be understood unless this is borne in mind. It was not the passive reflection of a conjuncture, or simply a way of adapting to its subsequent twists and turns, but an active response to events, a process of political-theoretical redefinition. Yet this process had nothing of a triumphal march (or even a slow progression) towards the truth about it, for it proceeded thanks only to its own failures, constantly displacing the limits it continued to run up against. It is in this sense that it can indeed be called a 'break'. Thus Althusser was right to admit, in the texts he wrote to 'rectify' his initial positions, that Marx's political break preceded and conditioned his epistemological break; but Althusser went only half-way down the path that he opened up.[6] For if the 'break' is political, it cannot be reduced to the discovery of a 'class essence' (here, a proletarian class essence) supposed to pre-exist it. Nothing suggests that the 'humanism' of a Weitling, a Hess or the young Engels, or even 'liberalism' (in its

German-Rhenish version, at any rate), was specifically 'bourgeois' or 'petty-bourgeois', that is to say, *external* to the workers' movement. Quite the opposite:[7] this humanism was the fountainhead of the 'common sense' of the workers' movement in Marx's day. Conversely, Marx's very particular (and, as we shall see, highly paradoxical) 'proletariat', which he first names in the 1844 'Introduction', can be understood only in a political sense: 'proletariat' is the right name, discovered at last (and substituted for 'Third Estate', 'people', '*sans-culotterie*', etc.), for the antagonism immanent in modern society. This presupposes that the question of emancipation is decided *in and through* antagonism, in and through the deployment of its immanent effects, rather than in the external, overarching context of a 'reconciliation'. In the intellectual climate that prevailed before 1848, the political approach that such a presupposition implies was anything but self-evident; indeed, it was that of a tiny minority.

I should add that my redefinition of the Marxian break as a political break bound up with the crisis of 1843 is based on a very precise reading of Marx's relationship to Hegel. *Pace* the interpretations which set out to reduce the specificity of the young Marx's trajectory by dissolving it into the collective trajectory of the Young Hegelian movement – whether with an eye to applauding Marx's early views or, on the contrary, in order to contrast them with the direction his thought took after *The German Ideology*[8] – it is, in my view, the *substantial* nature of Marx's relationship to Hegel which sharply differentiates him from the rest of the Young Hegelian movement, and functions as the veritable *conceptual operator* of the break. It is true that when Marx became a Hegelian, in around 1837, the Hegelian school was already officially in crisis, riven, since the 1835 publication of Strauß's *The Life of Jesus*, by internal divisions charged with political significance (a 'right', a 'left' and a 'centre'). In a certain sense, it was already too late, by then, to appeal to anything that could claim the mantle of Hegelian orthodoxy,[9] so that Marx's – or any other contemporary thinker's – relationship to Hegelianism was necessarily problematic, stemming as it did from an appropriation of the system as mediated by others. But the fact remains that the distinctive character of the early Marx's approach was palpable from the moment he made his entry on to this fragmented scene: with, that is, his 1841 doctoral dissertation.[10] Indeed, if my hypothesis is correct, Marx turned Hegel against himself; he elaborated a Hegelian critique of Hegel. That, needless to add, is the only way to radicalize the process of Hegelian thought, and blaze a path to a Hegel beyond Hegel.

FIGHTING FOR FREEDOM WITH PINPRICKS

The 'party of the concept'

At first sight, discoursing on the difference between the philosophy of nature in Democritus and Epicurus seems like the kind of comfortable academic exercise tailored to the ambitions of a young man with his sights set on a university career. Marx dedicated his doctoral dissertation to his future father-in-law, '*Geheimer Regierungsrat*' Ludwig von Westphalen, presenting it as 'the preliminary to a larger work' which would treat 'in detail the cycle of Epicurean, Stoic and Sceptic philosophy in their relation to the whole of Greek speculation'. The greater scope of the future work, he added, would make it easier to achieve the 'strictly scientific' form that the subject called for, while eliminating the somewhat 'pedantic' air of the thesis.[11] We thus stand firmly on the ground of the history of philosophy here, and seem to be worlds apart, even at the level of purely speculative struggle, from the audacious frontal attacks that Ruge, Bauer or Hess launched on Hegel, religion, and the ideology of the Prussian state in the same period.

But let us not be fooled. It is not out of mere literary coquetry that Marx places his work under the banner of Prometheus – 'the most eminent saint and martyr in the philosophical calendar' – and his hatred of the gods (απλω λογω τυζ παντας χθαιρω θεουζο). Marx intends his revaluation (a highly critical one, as we shall see) of the philosophies of late Antiquity, which fare poorly in Hegel's version of the history of philosophy, as a two-edged sword. Against Hegel, Marx proposes to rehabilitate these philosophies, centred on a subjectivity freed from the terror of the gods, as 'the key to the true history of Greek philosophy'. At the same time, *with* Hegel, he dwells on the many misadventures of this subjective freedom, which ultimately finds itself cut off from the movement of the world. In other words, Marx's detour through Democritus and Epicurus not only served as a way of acquiring academic respectability, but also allowed him to have his say in the debate then raging in German intellectual circles. At the heart of this debate was the relationship between philosophy and the world as it appeared after Hegel's death. Marx shared the Young Hegelians' thirst for 'action',[12] and, like them, defended philosophy's radical autonomy and critical function over against all existing forms of authority, especially the Christian–feudal state embodied by an increasingly hidebound Prussia. Despite his ties of friendship to Bruno Bauer and other members of the Berlin Circle at that time, however, he struck out on a path that diverged from the one taken by historiosophy *à la* Cieszkowski, or a philosophy of self-consciousness *à la* Bauer.

To leave us in no doubt as to where he stands, Marx inserts, at the end of the first part of his dissertation, a paragraph in which he drops his mask, as it were, and spells out what is at stake in his text. To begin with, he rejects the critique of Hegel then dominant among the Young Hegelians. Popularized above all by Bauer,[13] this critique turned on the idea that Hegel had made a 'compromise', and accordingly drew a dividing line between an 'esoteric', radical Hegel on the one hand, and an 'exoteric', conservative Hegel on the other. A critique of that sort, Marx explains, is a moral critique that makes judgements on the basis of a criterion external to its object.[14] If, he goes on, it refuses to grasp its object from within, it is because it is still prey to the illusions of the unmediated consciousness, for which an inner, essential inadequacy is reflected, precisely, in an inverted manner, as a form of exoteric consciousness. A moral critique of this kind reproduces the illusions of the subject, here Hegel himself, for whom the apparent compromise has nothing to do with the principle of the system as such, which, in his view, only *seems* to have been compromised, but is in fact not affected at all: 'Suppose', objects Marx, 'that a philosopher has really accommodated himself, then his pupils must explain *from his inner essential consciousness* that which *for him* himself had the form of an *exoteric consciousness*'.[15]

In other words, moral criticism cannot establish a genuinely critical relationship to the Hegelian system; it cannot 'construe [Hegel's] essential form of consciousness', grasping it as a figure determined from within, and, consequently, surpass it. It gets bogged down in phenomenal consciousness, and so fails to maintain an organic relationship to the system, falling back into a pre-Hegelian position as a result. Its mirror-relation to the Hegelian system simply reduplicates the mirror-relation to the world into which this system relapses when it becomes an 'abstract totality'. Criticism should accordingly strive to show that the division of consciousness into the 'exoteric' and the 'esoteric' stems from its illusion that there exists a relationship of externality between the system's essential principles and their phenomenal manifestations. In other words, criticism must challenge the very notion that the system has a core hidden away somewhere beyond the reach of exoteric consciousness, one perfectly indifferent to its divagations.

Marx does not, however, restrict himself to criticizing Hegel's epigones. His description of their trajectory and methods positions them within the very movement by which philosophy 'becomes worldly', showing that the moment they embody is a necessary one. It is defined as a moment of reflection or division internal to the theoretical position itself, which has been cut off from worldly reality. The task of philosophy is accordingly defined as essentially *critical*, in a resolutely Hegelian sense;[16] it is to 'measure the individual existence by the essence, the particular reality by the idea' – in other words, to remove any obstacle that would come between the real and its concept, blocking realization of the concept. This bears emphasizing: from the outset, criticism is based, in Marx's work, on a rejection of the kind of moral denunciation that confronts empirical reality with a norm, the 'is' with the 'ought'; at the same time, Marx rejects the position of the transcendental subject. He is determined to restrict criticism to the plane of immanence, and to take part in the self-transformation of the real; his critique situates its understanding of its own position, too, at that level.[17]

But the form in which philosophy finds its immediate realization also proves to be contradictory. In turning outwards, towards the world, philosophy undergoes the experience of its own loss, recognizing its own inner weakness in the object it criticizes: criticism's ultimate objective, the becoming-philosophical of the world, is simultaneously a becoming-worldly of philosophy. This is certainly the strong point in Marx's argument, and the most Hegelian point as well: it is here that we find Marx at the furthest possible remove from any Young Hegelian temptation to take a narcissistic pleasure in the critical act. The transition towards philosophy's 'truth', the realization of that 'truth', entails an experience of its loss: philosophy is dissolved into the network of its mediations. It does not lose itself in the sense that it makes an illusory flight towards non-philosophy – that is precisely the error for which Marx criticizes the party of 'positive philosophy' *à la* Schelling, as we shall see. What is lost is philosophy as an isolated activity, existing in itself and surveying the world from on high.

This moment of loss manifests itself as a new division within philosophy itself. The consciousness turned towards the world finds its counterpart in the consciousness that turns against philosophy, picturing the emancipation of the world of non-philosophy as an emancipation of consciousness *from* philosophy itself. Curiously, however, this doubling takes the guise of an opposition between philosophical tendencies, which becomes, in its turn, a struggle between two parties. The 'loss' of philosophy thus means that it can henceforth appear only as the result of a partisan struggle; all attempts to go back to a state of affairs short of a struggle between parties (or to make an imaginary move 'beyond' such struggle), notably by hiding behind 'a philosophical giant of the past', can only produce the effect of 'comical contrast' characteristic of insignificant historical moments.[18]

The correlate of the first of this pair of opposed tendencies – the kind of criticism that consists in 'turning-towards-the-outside of philosophy' – is the 'liberal party' or 'party of the concept': that is to say, the union of Hegelianism (or one fraction of it) with the anti-absolutist opposition. The correlate of the second is the 'positive philosophy' professed, with increasing success in the late 1830s and early 1840s, by Hegel's arch-enemy Schelling, hauled out of retirement by the Prussian regime after the death of the very liberal Gans, and given Gans's post at the University of Berlin in an effort to counter the influence of Hegelianism. From the moment of his Munich lectures of 1827–28 – and with renewed vigour from, in particular, the mid-1830s on – Schelling subjected Hegel's dialectical rationalism to a ruthless critique, in the name of a defence of the empirical, contingency, finitude, and the irreducibility of the real *qua* 'existent'. Schelling sought to locate the origins of philosophy in non-philosophy, in the 'positivity' of the existent; his thought was at the opposite pole from the 'negative' rationalism that reduced the world to its logical structure, or to concepts. Reason, said Schelling, must accept its own limits by acknowledging the positivity of that which is radically external to it ('external' in fact meant 'transcendent'), and can be apprehended only by an act of pure will stemming from the divine will, which is unconditional and unconstrained by any law. Reason can be apprehended, in a word, only in the mode associated with creationist theology and a personal God.

Although Schelling himself was the *bête noire* of the liberal intelligentsia in general, and the Hegelians in particular,[19] and although his positive philosophy was closely allied to the official personalist theology of the Restoration, his teaching nevertheless had its moment of glory (a relatively brief one, it is true) in *Vormärz* Berlin, making headway even in certain circles of the Hegelian left.[20] It is not hard to detect the traces it left in the critique of Hegel's philosophy carried out in the name of 'sensuous positivity' by Feuerbach, who, in Schelling's wake, challenged the claim of Hegel's system to generate its own beginning.[21] Similarly, we can find traces of Schelling in Cieszkowski, whose 'historiosophy' heralds, in the name of the 'will' and 'action', the advent of the true unity of thought and being at a higher, 'absolute' stage of the activity of the spirit.[22]

According to Marx, only the party of criticism, which has turned outwards, that is, towards politics (he calls it the 'liberal' party),[23] is also, precisely, the party of the concept: this party alone, 'despite its inner contradiction', is capable of attaining the consciousness 'of both its principle in general and its goal'. If the party of criticism makes it possible to advance towards self-consciousness, and 'achieves real progress', it is because it acknowledges that the labour of the negative is its own internal determination. It makes it possible to surpass the system by grasping it from within and drawing it towards the concept – it is in this sense that it is, concretely, the 'party of the concept'. Conversely, in its mystical flight towards immediate certainty and a non-philosophical foundation, positive philosophy not only proves incapable of surpassing the abstract system against which it has turned, but *ipso facto* condemns itself to actualizing that system's successive moments – without, precisely, being aware of the fact.

Faithful to Hegel, Marx perceives the limits and one-sidedness of the critical-liberal party:[24] absorbed in 'making the world philosophical', it tends to neglect the 'becoming-worldly' of philosophy, its integration into the real world, which implies grasping its objectivity. Such is the thrust of Marx's critique of Epicurus as well, especially of the Epicurean notion of the *clinamen*, often ignored by critics who are bent on reducing Marx's Prometheanism to a philosophy of the subject. It is true that 'we have been set free' by Epicurus, but his freedom is that of abstract, singular individuality. His world appears as a place indifferent to what occurs in it; it is a far cry from the Aristotelian physics of space with its prime mover. It is subject to the rule of chance and the kind of abstract possibility that 'is not interested in the object which is explained, but in the subject which does the explaining'.[25] Epicurus' explanatory method 'tends . . . to negate all objective reality of nature';[26] his physics has more to do with a semiology of nature that opens on to an ethics.[27]

Unlike Hegel's critique – which conflates Epicurus and Democritus, and makes the two of them together the counterpart to Stoicism – Marx's restores the specificity and internal consistency of the doctrine of the Garden: the law that expresses the declination of the atom from the straight line '*goes through the whole Epicurean philosophy*',[28] and it is here that the key to Epicureanism must be sought. Defined as pure form, as a negation of all relativity and all relation to other existents, the atom is an object that has immediately to negate all relative existence in order to be able to relate only to itself. It can do so only if it abstracts from its relative existence, the straight line, by swerving away from it. Similarly, Marx continues, 'the entire Epicurean philosophy swerves away from the restrictive mode of being wherever the concept of abstract individuality, self-sufficiency and negation of all relation to other things must be represented in its existence. The purpose of action is to be found therefore in abstracting, swerving away from pain and confusion, in ataraxy.'[29]

Thus the *clinamen* and repulsion represent '*the first* form *of self-consciousness*', the form which perceives the other only as pure singularity: 'for man as man to become his own real object, he must have crushed within himself his relative being, the power of desire and of mere nature'.[30] Epicurus' gods, the ideal incarnation of abstract individuality, swerve away from all that exists, from the world as such; indifferent to it, they impassively abandon it to its own devices. Is the philosopher who casts his lot with the party of the concept condemned to share their fate?

We can clarify our discussion somewhat by comparing Marx with another, equally atypical figure of the Young Hegelian movement, Moses Hess. Seeking to carve out a place of his own in the political-philosophical sphere, Marx took up a position diametrically opposed to Hess's. Hess had criticized the Young Hegelians for their 'rationalism' and one-sided insistence on intellectual freedom, which sacrificed the 'sacred' character of free, self-conscious action.[31] Their negativity, he maintained, made it impossible for them to conceive of 'positive' grounds for freedom; it condemned them to *theoria*, that is to say, the endless repetition of the critical act. As we know, for the same Hess, the Hess of *The European Triarchy*, the total 'sacralization' of social activity that is authorized by the positive foundation of freedom ultimately leads to a reconstruction of the politico-religious instance through establishment of a state religion – before yielding to an anthropology of Feuerbachian inspiration that culminates in a secular religion of universal love.

Conscious of the Hegelian left's one-sidedness and penchant for hermeticism, Marx struck out on an entirely different path: he joined the radically critical party, turned his back on the sacred for good and all, and recognized that division and conflict were both his own essential concerns and the condition for all historical development. Instead of the critique of religion so dear to the Young Hegelians, he opted, from the outset, for the kind of criticism that was most closely tied to the world, political criticism – that of the terrestrial sphere in which Epicurus' Garden, too, was located. At the same time – poles apart from Hess in this respect as well – he continued to call for the sharpest possible break between religion and the state, the focal point of modern politics.

Non-contemporaneousness in the Rhineland

But just what kind of a 'world' did criticism find itself confronting as it set out to forge its arms? It was, needless to say, the Europe of the period following Napoleon's defeat, the Europe of the Holy Alliance, still in the grip of reaction, yet already shaken by the revolutionary wave of the 1830s (the *Trois Glorieuses* in France, the Belgian Revolution and the Italian uprisings). But, first and foremost, Marx's world was the world of the Rhineland, a very peculiar province of the Kingdom of Prussia; hence I need to say a few words about the state of the province at that time.

The exceptionality of the Rhineland went back to the nineteen-year-long French presence there (1795–1814), as a result of which the province was undoubtedly the part of the German Confederation that was most deeply and enduringly affected by the French Revolution. Under the French, the position of big landed property had been seriously undermined and the privileges of the *ancien régime* abolished, together with the legal and administrative impediments to the accumulation of capital (the corporations, for example). The introduction of the Napoleonic Code had guaranteed equality before the law and the right to a public trial, the principal gains of this period; notwithstanding repeated attempts at 'Prussification' of the law, these forms of legal protection were maintained throughout the *Vormärz* and, indeed, right up to the early twentieth century. The heritage of 1789 continued to hold a central place in the political and cultural life of the province, not least in the everyday consciousness of the working population: was not the annual meeting that the veterans of Napoleon's army held to honour the memory of the victor at Austerlitz a major event in the life of Cologne?[32] Again, it was to cries of 'Long live Napoleon!' that the workers and artisans of Cologne and Elberfeld rose up in August 1830 to demand the abolition of excise taxes, higher wages, and access to elementary-school education;[33] while further south, in Mainz and Darmstadt (Hessia), French flags made their appearance, sometimes even in the hands of soldiers![34]

All this, no doubt, goes a long way towards accounting for the specificity of 'Rhenish liberalism', the 'liberal party' that Marx identified with the party of the concept. Its dominant tendency was, to be sure, moderate, and did not go beyond advocating a 'top–down reformism'; yet it was committed to universalistic conceptions of freedom and equality that sharply distinguished it from its English cousin. Did not the merchant David Hansemann, a leading light among Cologne's liberal bourgeoisie, go so far as to exclaim in 1840: 'the Rhinelanders now give pride of place to the ideas of equality and the omnipotence of the state, ranking them higher than freedom itself'?[35] In this context, a Heine, who continued to pay homage to Napoleon as the symbol of anti-absolutism, or a Marx, who in 1842 blasted liberal England as the 'proof on a big historical scale' that freedom had become synonymous with the '*assujettissement*' of the multi-tude, look like partisans of a radical variant on a basic democratic liberalism common to the whole opposition rather than independent agents or isolated figures – much less representatives of a revolutionary current (which was nowhere to be found) distinct from the 'liberal party'.

For this reason, and in view of the real economic dynamism that made itself felt with the establishment of the 1835 Customs Union [*Zollverein*], historians usually depict the Rhineland of the *Vormärz* as a region that was fully integrated, both socially and economically, into the modern world;[36] this is how they explain the 'overdevelopment' of the Rhenish intelligent-sia, whose representative men included not only Heine but, a generation later, Hess and Marx. A more complicated version of this thesis – based, moreover, on a certain reading of Marx – has it that the situation in the Rhineland bore the marks of an opposition between a mature civil society and an archaic, authoritarian Prussian state which put severe external constraints on it. The corollary is that Marx was, theoretically and politi-cally, the natural product of this opposition, of which, the argument runs, the 1848 revolution represented the culmination.

This vision of a modern bourgeois Rhineland comparable to mid-nineteenth-century New York, according to an authoritative specialist on the question,[37] must be seriously questioned and qualified. To a great extent, it is a distortion born of the historiographical illusion that Arno Mayer analyses,[38] an illusion bred by too exclusive a focus on the innova-tive forces that herald the dawn of a new society and the resultant neglect of older, more permanent features; and also, no doubt, by our fascination for retrospective interpretations of historical situations, which explain the beginning of a story in terms of its outcome. Capitalism did ultimately triumph in the Rhineland, bringing all social relations within its compass; but the fact is that the old order did not simply subsist as a kind of residue. It was very successful at holding the new forces at bay, managing to re-establish its dominance, at the price of certain adjustments, through-out an entire historical period.

In this respect, the Rhineland of Marx's birth had much more in common with the society of the *ancien régime* than is commonly supposed. Politically speaking, this is self-evident; the Rhineland was, after all, part of the kingdom of Prussia, with its medieval assemblies dominated by the nobility, its Prussian bureaucracy and censorship, and, crowning the whole, a powerful and extremely reactionary Catholic Church. As for the socioeconomic situation – admittedly more complex – its archaic features were still quite conspicuous in Marx's day: despite a nineteen-year-long French presence and the profound traces it had left in its wake (especially, as I have said, the advantages that came with the adoption of Napoleonic law), the Rhineland presented the picture of a massively rural, parochial little world, sprinkled with quiet, conservative towns (including a few nascent industrial centres such as Aachen or the Wuppertal).[39] It was a world in which big and still powerful landowners existed side by side[40] with a commercial and financial bourgeoisie that invested more heavily in real estate than in productive enterprise,[41] a landholding peasantry that still comprised a large majority of the population, a bloated artisan class, and a few small pockets of capitalist production of an overwhelmingly pre-industrial kind (the *Verlagssystem*).

The Rhineland looks less like an enclave of modernity in a Germany struggling to emerge from the obscurity of feudalism and absolutism than a society immobilized by ossified social relations and racked by a profound crisis; it was a veritable concentrate of the various kinds of backwardness separating Germany from its own present. The break-up of precapitalist relations, albeit by no means complete, had nevertheless proceeded far enough to provoke a mass pauperization[42] that traumatized the lower strata of society (from the peasantry through the artisans to the workers) and provoked disarray and a sense of helplessness even among the upper classes and the intelligentsia. A modern legal system coexisted with a state apparatus which, casting the gains of the Stein–Hardenberg reform period to the winds, stubbornly defended absolutism and the bases of the feudal order. An intelligentsia nourished on French ideas and classical philosophy rubbed shoulders with a powerful and predominantly reactionary clergy – especially in the case of the Catholics, who formed the majority of the province's population. An enlightened or even radical press that sought to address a cultural elite coexisted with typically premodern forms of political action: carnival societies, religious heresies, and so on, the whole awash in an ocean of peasants – who, it is true, were not always passive, as is attested, in particular, by their increasing readiness to engage in 'illegalities' in the Foucauldian sense (for example, the theft of wood).

In short, the *Vormärz* in the Rhineland, more reminiscent of 1789 France than of the England racked by the Chartist general strike in the summer of 1842, represented an exacerbated form of German non-contemporaneousness in pre-1848 Europe. The chronic social crisis, which occasionally became acute, went hand in hand with a political and ideological crisis. The Prussian state found it increasingly difficult to fulfil its role of social leadership/domination; the measures it took to re-establish social order usually succeeded only in exacerbating existing contradictions. As Jonathan Sperber emphasizes: 'at different times during the *Vormärz*, political life would break through the official limitations surrounding it and become, however briefly, and to however limited an extent, a mass politics. Repression invariably followed these incidents, but not before they revealed the depth of social and political tension, mobi-lized segments of the population for political action, and provided a cadre of potential future activists with training in mass political leadership.'[43] Of course, the actions undertaken by the government succeeded in neutral-izing the forces hostile to it, at least temporarily; but they also exposed the fragility of the social bloc sustaining the *ancien régime*, and, above all, left no room for attempts to implement reformist policies to defuse the crisis. Hence a German particularity: the fiercely uncompromising attitude of the absolutist regime simply enhanced the Rhine Province's sense that it stood apart from the rest of the kingdom of Prussia, while the crisis, with its social and political origins, further vitiated Prussia's claim to German national leadership. The Rhineland was clearly undergoing a crisis of hegemony that could only deepen under the rule of the Romantic Friedrich Wilhelm IV.

From civil society to the state

In turning outwards, towards worldly realities, philosophy-become-criti-cism had immediately to confront this social formation in crisis, heavily dominated by an alliance of social forces of the kind typical of the *ancien régime*. If we take this fact as our starting point, we can make sense of the intellectual and political strategy to which Marx intended to harness the 'party of the concept'; for anyone who wishes to develop a strategy needs first to define his objectives, and, to that end, identifying the adversary is the first item on the agenda. Criticism accordingly took as its main targets the three pillars of the existing order: an aristocratic caste that clung fiercely to its privileges, a Prussian regime that was rapidly regressing towards the 'Christian state', and the reactionary ideologues who legiti-mized the perpetuation of absolutism. It was above all the partisans of Romanticism, among whose number Marx included the theoreticians of the Historical School of Law, who drew his fire. As he saw it, the Romantic principle was not merely nostalgia for a vanished world, but the defence of an actually existing social and political order, the *ancien régime*,[44] undertaken at the very moment when that order had become cognizant of the threats hanging over its future.

Marx meant to turn one very precisely identifiable weapon against the Holy Trinity that constituted the German – and, especially, Rhenish – *misère*: the achievements of the Enlightenment and the French Revolution, which he summons his readers to assume and defend *en bloc*. To avoid all misunderstanding, let me point out here that this is the explanation for his frequent and insistent references to a tradition encompassing Machiavelli and Kant, Spinoza and Hobbes, the work of the Convention and Benjamin Constant. The significance of these references is inseparable from the strategic use to which Marx put them. Thus his homage to Kant does not in any way indicate adhesion to Kantianism in the strict sense; it is, rather, a defence, in the words that Marx here borrows from the early Görres, of 'the *German theory* of the French revolution' against 'the German theory of the French *ancien régime*'[45] represented by the Historical School of Law and its attempted destruction of any and all rational foundations for moral values. Similarly, Marx does not cite the names of all the classics of modern political philosophy, from Machiavelli through Spinoza to Hegel, out of a desire for doctrinal totalization but, rather, as a way of evoking an intellectual modernity thanks to which it has become possible to theorize the call for a secularization of politics.[46] He means to present a contrast capable of bringing out the regressive spiral into which the Prussian state was being drawn in the mistaken belief that it could resolve the crisis confronting it by abandoning the rationalism of the reform era for the model of a patriarchal authority with strong clerical overtones.

Bearing this in mind, we need to distinguish Marx's defence of the universality of the concept 'man' from his subsequent recourse to Feuerbachian anthropology. For the journalist and publicist who wrote for the *Rheinische Zeitung*, the reference to man in his universality was first and foremost a weapon in the struggle against the 'Christian state' of which the Romantic King Friedrich Wilhelm IV dreamt, and which the ideologues of German conservatism legitimized. This, incidentally, explains the sharply anti-Romantic thrust of the passages Marx devotes to the subject. In Marx's conception, the 'Man' of the French Declaration of Rights names the most radical of the perspectives held out by the French Revolution, one that neither the American Revolution nor the 'Glorious Revolution' realized: the American Revolution accepted slavery; the 'Glorious Revolution' appealed to the authority of a legacy bequeathed it by tradition.[47] For it was the universalistic radicalization of the concept of man which delegitimized all forms of inequality and all 'natural' subordination of one man to another. It provided freedom with its true content, which was inseparable from equality and diametrically opposed to any conception of 'liberties' understood as accretions of special privileges conferred upon certain individuals (or classes) by virtue of purely external, accidental particularities unrelated to men's common reason and being. Conversely, to sacrifice, as the Romantics did, 'the universal freedom [and reason] of human nature' on the altar of a 'natural' hierarchical order incompatible with any rational grounding of moral values was, in Marx's opinion, not only regressive, but perfectly illusory; those who sought refuge in the 'miraculous and the mystical', only to end up in religion's embrace, were, fundamentally, simply reacting to the trauma provoked by the crisis of an order that had itself become incomprehensible and inconceivable, that is, 'natural' in the Hegelian sense of 'notionless' [*Begrifflos*].

Marx emphasizes the non-self-coincidence inherent in Romantic consciousness, which mistakes its real nature in conceiving of itself as a continuation of, or a return to, the premodern world. In reality, it is nothing more than an anti-modern reaction, which, though it is certainly regressive and potentially barbaric, is nevertheless part of modernity itself, and, in a certain sense, dependent on and subordinate to it – 'infected by this century', as Marx puts it.[48] Its Christian ideal is not a return to the totalizing faith of the Middle Ages, but a political instrumentalization of religion whose moving spirit is counter-revolutionary *ressentiment*. The characteristic feature of Romanticism is a state of permanent frustration: in the depths of its vivid imagination we find an ample residue of 'polemical bitterness impregnated with political tendencies'. The 'modern knight' Friedrich Wilhelm is not a new Barbarossa but his ghostly double, at once comic and dangerous, and his reign is 'the time in which ghosts and witch trials are *legitimate*'.[49]

By putting the main line of demarcation where it does, this basically political interpretation of the Enlightenment heritage functions from the outset as an appeal to the critical party to break through the narrow bounds of a critique focused on religion or on settling accounts with Hegel, to contest, instead, the intellectual and cultural hegemony of the forces sustaining the *ancien régime*. That, concretely, is what the *Rheinische Zeitung* set out to do under Marx's lead, as Sperber points out: 'under his direction, the newspaper played down theological speculation, while covering business and political news in detail'.[50] In fact, the enhanced role that Marx assigned the critical party – which implied, as we shall see, its transformation into an authentic 'national/popular' party – went well beyond a simple redefinition of who the enemy was. Essentially, it required that the paper develop its activities so as to transform them into a struggle for the real democratization of society and the state. It was not enough to contemplate, *à la* Bruno Bauer, the deepening crisis while awaiting the inevitable redemptive cataclysm[51] that only the 'terrorism of theory' could hasten. Taking its stand on the ground of partisan struggle, philosophy now rejected all *attentisme*; it assumed the historical mission of the French Revolution, becoming the 'organizing soul'[52] behind the real forces struggling for democratization one step at a time. Thus, in order for criticism to 'become worldly' and lose itself in its concrete realization, as the programmatic language of Marx's doctoral dissertation suggested it should, it had, after naming its foe, to choose its arms, even if it did not conceive of itself as 'armed critique' – or, rather, precisely to the extent that it did not wish to appear as such.

No doubt the fact that Marx's philosophy (and not just Marx's) now made its 'appearance in the newspapers'[53] had more than a little to do with his search for a career alternative as his prospects for an academic appointment faded and then, with Bauer's dismissal (March 1842), vanished altogether. But it also reflected a shift in the political situation, a desire to profit from the small window of opportunity opened by the Prussian regime with the enthronement of Friedrich Wilhelm IV. The new 1841 censorship instruction bred many illusions; Marx was, without a doubt, one of the few not to have shared them. Indeed, in his 'Comments on the Latest Censorship Instruction'[54] – an article prudently published in Switzerland in Ruge's review *Anekdota* more than a year after it was written – Marx calls the 1841 ordinance more backward, in certain respects, than its 1819 predecessor, which had itself been quite draconian. He clearly perceives, behind the apparent relaxation of restrictions, the new face of Wilhelmine absolutism, which had characteristically abandoned rationalist principles (since these might serve as reminders of Prussia's reformist traditions) for the ideal of a Christian state: a *mélange* of paternalism and the Romantic dilution of objective/legal norms in the miasma of 'personal relations', that is to say, the favourable disposition of despotism and its agents. But, Marx says, the fact remains that this new instruction, which does recognize 'the value and need of frank and decent publicity', serves notice of the new king's willingness to adopt a tolerant paternalistic attitude, and avoid systematic recourse to repressive measures. It also proves that the principles he invokes to justify his decisions are contradictory, and attests to the increasingly open character of the crisis. Thus Marx observes, in his conclusion, that 'the Prussian writers stand to *gain through the new instruction*, either in *real freedom*, or in freedom of *ideas*, in *consciousness*'.[55] Later, writing to the *Oberpräsident* of the Rhine

Province, he would not hesitate to make tactical use of the wording of this instruction – although a certain irony can also be detected between the lines of his letter – in a last-ditch effort to save his newspaper, which was under attack by the censors.[56]

To be sure, the question of the free press transcended job or career considerations, just as it transcended tactical political concerns. Or let us say, rather, that its importance stemmed from the fact that it made it possible to combine both with a basic Enlightenment demand that Kant had already formulated: the demand for the creation of a public space or sphere as a means of carrying out permanent intellectual and political reform. In Kant's estimation, publicity [*Publizität*] is the vehicle for the moralization of politics; it is the condition for gradual progress towards freedom and a state based on the rule of law, of which the Republic represents the fully realized form.[57] In line with the maxim which affirms that 'all actions affecting the rights of other human beings are wrong if their maxim is not compatible with their being made public',[58] every act is subject to the test of publicity, which determines whether it is valid, that is, both morally free and necessary. In this way, the ethical categorical imperative is made to mediate the transcendental maxim of constitutional law – 'act in such a way that you can wish your maxim to become a universal law (irrespective of what the end in view may be)'.[59]

Thus the public sphere, in its Kantian version, makes it possible to wed morality and the law while respecting the distinction between them, as well as to bring constitutional and civil law into communication: the 'persons' of civil law become the 'citizens' of constitutional law, attain their majority, and take an active part in public affairs. Publicity has, first and foremost, a critical function; it is a concrete, quasi-institutional embodiment of philosophy. As an institution that both monitors public affairs and constantly proposes change, publicity is led to demand its autonomy *vis-à-vis* the state, as well as to serve as one of the permanent organs assuring its rational functioning. To put it more concretely: the process of publicity makes it possible to do away with the opacity and the cult of secrecy that dominate in the antechambers of despotism, but it also rules out any critical activity that would go beyond the bounds of the law, and seek to overturn established authority. Hence its ambition to present itself as a substitute for revolution and an embodiment of the German road to modernity and freedom.

As we saw in Chapter 1, Kant puts various empirical limits on the constitution of this public space, granting only intellectuals and the middle classes access to it. The autonomy he confers upon intellectuals, the key to the system as a whole, comes at the price of a defensive rejection of any kind of illegal activity and any extension to the lower classes of the forms mobilized for interpellating persons as citizens. But the Marxian problematization of the public space does not merely reject these compromises, which nothing in the rest of the system justifies. In this case, too, Marx traces matters back to the principle informing the system as a whole, and he fully endorses Hegel's critique of the relationship that Kant establishes between politics and morality.

In other words, Marx was to adopt the standpoint not of morality [*Moralität*], but of objective morality or *Sittlichkeit*, a concept designed to overcome the split between norm and reality, internal, ethical law and external, juridical law, systematic deduction and historical genesis. *Sittlichkeit* implies a rejection of the illusion of a founding practical-juridical intersubjectivity conceived as a relation between free wills, which Hegel had denounced as a merely formal representation confined to the level of immediate existence; it displaces the point of departure by showing that it is a point of arrival as well, the result of the self-activity of Spirit. Thus the standpoint of *Sittlichkeit* emerges as that of free existence, of the will of Spirit realizing the unity of subjective and objective good. Law finds its culmination in the element of *Sittlichkeit*, in an objective framework which is the product of the activity of Spirit, and in which the individual's mode of existence no longer appears to be determined by subjective choice, but rather stems from an order that contains the conditions of its organization and operation within itself. That order itself comprises three moments: the family, civil society and the state, 'an absolute and unmoved end in itself, [in which] freedom enters into its highest right'[60] – the crowning moment in the development of objective Spirit.

How is the question of the public sphere posed in this context? For Marx, unlike Kant, the public sphere is not the arena in which politics is gradually subsumed under a metapolitical instance of a juridical-moral type. Restored to its place in the process by which *Sittlichkeit* is constituted, the public sphere is, of course, situated in civil society, the contradictory form out of which the idea of the state will emerge. The heart of the problem lies here, in the 'transition' from civil society to the state; it is by returning to this problem again and again that Marx elaborates his critique of Hegel's solutions to it. From the articles he wrote for the *Rheinische Zeitung* to the essay in the *Deutsch–Französische Jahrbücher* in which he announces that he has rallied to the proletarian revolution – it was entitled, significantly, 'Contribution to the Critique of Hegel's Philosophy of Law. Introduction' – Marx never ceases to confront what appears to him to be the constitutive enigma of modern politics: how is it possible to make the 'transition' from bourgeois society to a form of state power which has been stripped of its hegemonic function and the attributes of transcendence?

Let us recall, to begin with, the *paradoxical* aspect of Hegel's problematic – paradoxical, at least, if one subscribes to the liberal conception according to which the 'state' and 'society' are two mutually limiting spheres, each external to the other. In *Elements of the Philosophy of Right*, civil society is simply 'the external state'. The relations it establishes between its members develop in externality: they presuppose the separate existence of individuals who are independent yet bound to each other, unbeknown to themselves, by non-conscious and, what is more, largely counter-intentional forms of interaction.

The idea of the state is nevertheless at work in civil society – which is why it is an external *state* – without, however, attaining self-consciousness – which is why it is still only an *external* state. The ties between individuals, expressions of the universality present in this relationship, escape the individuals' notice and control, imposing themselves as a blind necessity which dominates them from on high. Only with the moment of the state will these relations be grasped in their internality, as products of the free activity of Spirit. But it is only by passing through the contradictions of civil society that the idea of the state can be actualized. The state clearly 'emerges' from civil society, from the contradictory relations of interdependence through which the idea of the state makes its way, in order to 'emerge', in its turn, beyond externality.

To put the matter somewhat differently: civil society is nothing other than the state, but it is 'the state . . . of the understanding',[61] which thinks that there is something beyond itself that is, precisely, the Absolute of the state. Kant's problematic of the public sphere provides the exemplary instance of this illusion that civil society entertains about itself: blind to its own state substance, the activity of a public sphere dissociated from the state claims to regulate the functioning of the state from a standpoint external to it. In fact, it has no choice but to oscillate between accepting the reality of state power, which it can then serve only by offering it a new type of legitimization, and negating it (and therefore negating itself as well, to the extent that it has been authorized in advance) when the state stands in its way. Similarly, to present the law, by way of the public sphere, as the subordination *in actu* of politics to morality is to ignore the moment of *Sittlichkeit* – in order stubbornly to maintain the claims of a founding intersubjectivity. In both cases – and, as we can easily see, for reasons that run much deeper than the social psychology of the German petty bourgeoisie[62] – Kant's thesis about publicity appears to be a confession of impotence rather than a road, even a reformist road, leading to the subversion of absolutism.

Can we conceive of a different problematic that preserves Kant's achievement – the critical attitude – while going beyond it? Putting his faith in the free press, Marx answers that we certainly can, if we take the question of the 'transition' from civil society to the state seriously – if, that is, we refuse to pose it in terms either of a subordination of politics and the state to a metapolitical instance, or of a gradual pacification that compensates for the divisions of civil society. In other words, this transition must be grasped as nothing other than the movement of civil society in the immanence of its own contradiction. The free press then appears as the long-sought mediation for the process by which the state comes into being, emerging as strictly coextensive with the process by which the whole range of political and social activity is democratized.

Positioned between the family and the state, civil society effectively represents the difference of the system of *Sittlichkeit* at the moment of its division and differentiation.[63] The individuals who were united in the family now become 'private persons who have their own interest as their end',[64] who pursue a 'selfish end'.[65] The moment of civil society is thus that of the division or negativity which breaks the natural totality of the family down into its constituent parts. But it is, precisely, as a specific difference that civil society constitutes itself as the mediation for the entire process of *Sittlichkeit*, presenting itself as the moment of the 'reflection' or reduplication of an object in the relationship that binds it to its mirror-image.

This process of division originates in need, which takes a social form, that of a system of needs. It is prolonged in the division of labour, a remarkable arrangement that allows individuals to fulfil, unawares, a function that transcends them, even if they think that they are only pursuing private goals. However – and this is the crucial point – both the 'system of needs' and the organization of society in 'estates' [*Stände*] and corporations, an organization that has its roots in the division of labor, function as instances of *recognition*: they enable individuals to recognize the web of external connections in which they are inserted. Recognizing need, in turn, makes it possible to transcend its immediate, natural character, and to introduce an element of universality through an understanding of its social character: such recognition 'spiritualizes' need. This is not by any means to say that Hegel proposes to meet people's demands for bread and butter with courses on the dialectic (quite the contrary: he defends, as we have seen, the right to a decent existence).[66] It simply means that need (the need for food or anything else) is no longer represented as sheer particularity; in other words, it means that its insertion into a global – social and cultural – system of needs is recognized as such. Similarly, the fact that an individual belongs to an 'estate' [*Stand*] and a corporation 'spiritualizes' the particularity of his social function in so far as he participates freely in a system of solidarity and shares a state of mind, that is, a culture. These make possible a twofold recognition:[67] from the point of view of the individual, the recognition of the rational content of the law [*Gesetz*], which is thereby posed as such [*gesetzt*]; from the point of view of the social totality, the recognition of the individual's right to security and protection.

The originality and coherence of Hegel's thesis about the 'transition' from civil society to the state bear emphasizing: the state 'emerges' from the representation of the *Stände* and the organized corporations, not from the 'police' or the corps of civil servants, who also make up part of civil society. The state thus relays and realizes the demands posed by the various forms through which society constitutes itself; it is in this sense that Hegel intends to locate the deduction of the state in the strict immanence of the contradictory form represented by the moment of civil society. In this perspective, the transition from society to the state marks Hegel's break with the 'natural', paternalistic model of authority: he proceeds in strict opposition to those who, in their yearning for the traditional order, trace society back to the family, and exalt patriarchal authority as the general source of all authority. For Hegel, the individual constitutes himself as such by tearing himself away from the natural totality of the family, and rising, by way of the mediations of civil society, to the level of the state. Similarly, in contrast to the anachronistic projections of the ideologues of Romanticism, it is because they base themselves on the development of the different forms of consciousness, the free consent of the individual, and the recognition of the universal concept of man that the modern *Stände* and corporations can be distinguished from the straightforward identification of the individual with his social status characteristic of the medieval world.

Between the individual and the totality, then, civil society puts a number of sub-systems that form so many mediations by means of which the rational content of the social order is recognized by the independent agents who make it up. It is through these mediations that society 'makes the transition' to a higher moment of its development, the state. The dividing-line separating Marx from Hegel is determined, precisely, by this question of mediations: even before the systematic exposition that Marx makes in the Kreuznach manuscript, the *Rheinische Zeitung* articles on the free press present themselves as an implicit but unmistakable critique of Hegel's solution to the problem of the 'transition'. For Marx, there is nothing to be gained from the organization of society into 'estates' [*Stände*] or corporations. Ensconced in their particularism, desperately defending the privileges of the *Stände*, above all those of the aristocracy,[68] these relics of a feudal past are incapable of rising to the standpoint of the law and its universality. Their very existence is incompatible with citizenship; it hinders the creation of truly representative institutions and the recognition of the principle of popular sovereignty. The *Stände* are sham mediations, through which the contradictions and conflicts characteristic of the absolutist regime are perpetuated.

Similarly, it is clear to Marx that, among the existing 'estates' or classes, the estate represented by the civil service can by no means lay claim to a privileged access to universality, Hegel's thesis about the 'universal estate' notwithstanding.[69] The form of consciousness typical of this class is the bureaucratic spirit, and this spirit is condemned to reproduce the split between the existing state and civil society. By what only *seems* to be a paradox, the most classic of liberal distinctions, the one that distinguishes active citizens from the others, is reproduced within the forms of consciousness found at the heart of the absolutist state: monopolization of active citizenship by the administration and its agents; mistrust of the people, who are supposed to lack the 'state *frame of mind*'; the cult of the *arcana imperii*; and bureaucratic knowledge.[70] Indeed, Marx even shows that the bureaucratic fantasy of total control over society changes into its opposite. The refusal to take public opinion into account culminates in an inability to deal with the root causes of problems; this is true however well-intentioned the bureaucracy – that is to say, independently of the moral judgement one may make of it. If the administered pose a problem, then it is necessary to change the administered – to 'change the people', as the poet was to put it; such is the inevitable upshot of the bureaucratic principle. Bureaucratic management goes hand in hand with aggravation of the crisis, particularly the social crisis.[71] The bureaucracy is an illusory mediation, a rationalizing instrument that negates itself; it is in fact sustained by the separation between the state and civil society, which it can only reproduce in its turn, plunging ever deeper into a 'false infinity'.

The fact that the bureaucracy is impotent and the *Stände* are archaic seems to point to an ineluctable conclusion: every attempt to solve the problem of the 'transition' from civil society to the state without democratization is illusory, and doomed to failure. The advent of a *sittliche* state is synonymous with the gradual conquest of democracy, with the democratic renewal of all forms of social activity. This is what the system of the free press, which the *Rheinische Zeitung* sought to illustrate by example, would set out to show.

The system of the free press

Marx's thinking about the press, like his own practice as *de facto* editor-in-chief of the *Rheinische Zeitung*, is organized around the three axes that establish the general contours of a nascent public sphere: the question of language and style, the role of philosophy, and the organization, properly speaking, of the free press as a (sub-)system included within the process of *Sittlichkeit*.

The question of language and style allows Marx to define the political stakes of his enterprise from the outset. Whether the authorities and the intellectuals can find a *modus vivendi* depends to a very large extent on the trade-off between censorship and self-censorship, on the existence of a shifting, ambiguous space delimited, first, by external constraints (which the authorities reserved the right to impose) and, second, by the integration of such constraints into the very form (and limits) of public discourse. We have already seen how Kant, for instance, defended himself against the accusations levelled by the champions of order: he explicitly declared his preference for a purely speculative language meant for the ears of a minority, and simultaneously cultivated a 'style' rich in allusions, one that played on multiple meanings and linguistic ambiguities.[72] But Kant also held that such dissimulation had to respect certain limits. Thus his opposition to the clandestine diffusion of texts in any form, one of the clauses of the pact founding the public sphere, ruled out anonymous publication and imposed, in the form of a certain threshold of self-censorship, an impalpable limit on all discourse conducted outside the private sphere. In addition, it reinforced the exclusion of the subordinate classes from a public sphere reserved for the possessing classes and 'thinking men'.

One of the main features of the 1841 Prussian censorship instruction consisted precisely in shifting the balance between censorship and self-censorship. The authorities recognized the legitimacy of the public sphere and acknowledged that citizens had a right to criticize, but demanded, in return, that they express themselves with 'seriousness' and 'modesty', especially – a restriction that went beyond those contained in the tyrannical ordinances of 1819 – when it came to anything that had to do with religion. But this is exactly the point that Marx is not prepared to concede, even if the terms of the compromise on censorship are renegotiated. The demands put on style, he says, strip away the last vestiges of objective legality in which the rules on censorship might drape themselves; they restore the censor to a position of omnipotence, once again making his subjective dispositions the only possible criterion of judgement. This is a procedure by which 'even lettres de cachet could be set to music';[73] it shows just how self-contradictory any attempt to devise a legal rationalization for the practices of absolutism is. These legal pretences are in fact only a pretence of legality which, in accordance with the Romantic inspiration to which the new king ostentatiously laid claim, banish even the semblance of objective/legal norms, replacing them with a mystical veil made up of 'personal' virtues and relationships. For legal guarantees, the new decree substitutes the censor's 'benevolent attitude'; it is fashioned in the image of the king's 'love', and is supposed to take the place of the constitution that the regime stubbornly refused to promulgate. Such, in the final analysis, are the very traditional screens behind which the impersonal apparatus known as the Prussian administration seeks to occult its arbitrary rule. Only when censorship is abolished can legal norms be formally and substantively restored. At that point, a press law providing an objective framework for freedom of expression will replace a system whose ultimate objective, whatever variant of the system happens to prevail in a given time and place, can only be to restrict such freedom.

To hasten that day, Marx sounds the call for a stylistic offensive that will exploit the resources of ironic gaiety and the mask, in the tradition of a Goethe (mentioned by name) and a Heine (never cited, yet constantly evoked). Only ironic mimicry can expose the ludicrousness and arrogance of official seriousness and modesty: 'I treat the ludicrous seriously when I treat it ludicrously, and the most serious immodesty of the mind is to be modest in the face of immodesty.'[74] But Marxian irony has no intention of retreating into the obscurity of allegory; quite the contrary, it associates wit with light. Its gaiety and high colour contrast sharply with the grey-on-grey imposed by the absolutist regime, inviting the kind of frank public discussion that disdains the sham of self-censorship and 'moderantism'. Even philosophy, as we shall see, is urged to drop its customary jargon and 'speak German', in order to attract an audience among a public that has become coextensive with the 'people' as a whole.

Yet the party of criticism cannot, in Marx's view, throw caution to the winds. To make progress possible under prevailing conditions, it has to accept the principle of a restriction on publicity. It is on the question of the *name* that it can consent to certain compromises. German journalists, says Marx, are fated to 'remain nameless in *saecula saeculorum*;[75] pointing the paradox, he adds that 'anonymity is an essential feature of the newspaper press'.[76] The mask of anonymity or the pen name has a depersonalizing effect that fulfils a twofold function. For the public, it serves notice that the arguments a writer develops are not to be regarded as subjective opinions; thus it focuses debate on the matter at hand and the internal logic of a line of reasoning, rather than the empirical individual who happens to be speaking at a given moment.[77] For the person wearing the mask, of course, it offers additional protection, but here, too, what is at stake is a freedom that soon takes on an objective existence in the public sphere. If the authorities decide to react, they are forced to take the newspaper itself to court in the person of its publisher. They thus betray their desire to attack, not just a personal opinion, but the free press as an institution. Conversely, if they refrain from resorting to repression, they legitimize, not a particular point of view, but the function of the press as such in public debate. Respecting the principles he lays out here, Marx himself, like most other editors, remained a faceless publicist in this period. All the articles he published in the Rheinische Zeitung appeared anonymously; the only time he ever 'signed' a piece, it was – tellingly – as 'a Rhinelander'. Marx would later express surprise that any Germans 'even had names' at this time.[78] The question of the name would crop up again once he no longer considered himself bound by the terms of the compromise – because, quite simply, the compromise had fallen apart. He would then, reversing his previous position, prioritize the injunction to come forward in person as the author of anything he wrote.[79] Pointing to the public collective 'confession' that grants access to self-consciousness, he would write: 'in order to secure remission of its sins, mankind has only to declare them for what they actually are'.[80]

Undeniably, the call for anonymity represents a break with the practice, advocated by Kant, of making one's judgements public. Although the 'depersonalization effect' does not go to the extreme of clandestine diffusion of the written word, it represents a radical break with the vision of the philosopher as a master of his discourse who enlightens the public and the prince with his wisdom. It would, indeed, be inconceivable without an institution – the free press, precisely – whose basic principle more or less requires that one give up the detachment and contemplative attitude typically required by intellectual work. It is impossible to take an active part in producing a newspaper or journal, to say nothing of managing and editing one, while leading the 'mechanically ordered, almost abstract . . . existence'[81] of the sage of Königsberg.

Thus philosophy's new function turns out to be inseparable from a new type of practice and even a new style; all three are reflections of a new political conjuncture, which Heine had already identified with an 'awakening of political life' in Germany.[82] 'The public' had become 'eager to see the Leviathan itself' at a time when it was becoming increasingly obvious how onerous the burden of censorship was; 'it was precisely then that philosophy made its appearance in the newspapers'. It had long 'remained silent in the . . . face of . . . self-satisfied superficiality', faithful to the 'long years of study by genius', the 'hard-won fruits of self-sacrificing solitude', and 'the unseen but slowly exhausting struggles of contemplative thought' – in short, to everything that official criticism 'boasted . . . it would blow away like soap-bubbles . . . by means of a few hackneyed newspaper phrases'. But although philosophy 'had even *protested against the newspapers* as an unsuitable arena', it had at last been forced 'to break its silence', and 'become a newspaper correspondent'. In this way, says Marx, it made its way 'into salons, priests' studies, editorial offices of newspapers and court antechambers'. It is only in this way that 'philosophy becomes worldly and the world became philosophical'.

According to Marx, the party of criticism has now taken possession of the whole field. It is no longer one system struggling against others, but 'philosophy in general in relation to the world'. Internally, by its content, philosophy has, of course, always represented 'the intellectual quintessence of its time'; but when this internal content meets an external manifestation adequate to it, it enters into 'contact and interaction with the real world of its day', becoming 'the philosophy *of* the contemporary world', the philosophy in which the contemporary world is reflected and attains to self-consciousness.[83]

To accomplish this transformation, philosophy has to recognize its internal divisions and the struggle animating it as an integral part of itself. But this struggle takes the form of a struggle between parties. For 'without parties there is no development, without demarcation there is no progress'.[84] In becoming worldly, philosophy dives into the fray and pursues its activity in the thick of it; the cries of its enemies, auguring its triumph, announce 'the life of its ideas, which have burst the orderly hieroglyphic husk of the system and become citizens of the world'.[85] Philosophy affirms its civic-mindedness by participating actively in the construction of citizenship, by taking up a position at the centre of the public sphere and becoming the 'living soul of culture'. It thereby breaks with its earlier situation, in which, to elude the censorship, it had 'ceased to speak German' and resorted to expressing itself 'in incomprehensible mysterious words because comprehensible words were no longer allowed to be comprehended'.[86]

Philosophy openly assumes its point of view: it speaks on behalf of all humankind. Like the revolutionary proclamation of equality/liberty, the concept of 'human nature' or 'human society', directly bound up with 'human rights', designates, as we have seen, not an anthropological Absolute, but an indispensable rallying point in the struggle to strip absolutism of the transcendent trappings it asssumes in presenting itself as a 'Christian state'. In the universalistic concept of man, as in the radical rejection of all forms of inequality and 'natural' hierarchy guaranteed by a transcendent order, Marx sees the culminating point of modern political philosophy's attempt to secularize politics. He borrows Kant's metaphor of the Copernican revolution to describe this movement of emancipation of the political sphere. If we examine them closely, the scientific, philosophical and political revolutions turn out to be internally linked:

> Immediately before and after the time of Copernicus' great discovery of the true solar system, the law of gravitation of the state was discovered, its own gravity was found in the state itself. The various European governments tried, in the superficial way of first practical attempts, to apply this result in order to establish a system of equilibrium of states. Earlier, however, Machiavelli and Campanella, and later Hobbes, Spinoza, Hugo Grotius, right down to Rousseau, Fichte and Hegel, began to regard the state through human eyes and to deduce its natural laws from reason and experience, and not from theology.[87]

In his confrontation with the partisans of the German-Christian state – theologians, Romantics, or 'positive' philosophers – Marx even moves beyond the intellectual horizons of modernity; in the name of a defence of reason, he lays claim to the tradition of philosophy *tout court*, including ancient philosophy, which he evokes by naming the founder of dialectics and the first anti-Platonist: 'Recent philosophy has only continued the work begun by Heraclitus and Aristotle. You wage a polemic, therefore, not against the rational character of recent philosophy, but against the ever new philosophy of reason.'[88]

Even in this polemical context, however, Marx distinguishes his strategic defence of rational thought, the modern autonomy of the political, and the heritage of 1789 from a continuist vision of things. His idea of politics and the state is that of 'the more ideal and profound view of recent philosophy', the philosophy of Hegel, which marks a departure from the way 'earlier philosophers of constitutional law [constructed] the idea of the state'. He puts the emphasis on Hegel's critique of the diverse attempts to confer a foundational role upon subjectivity. In simultaneously rejecting naturalism, contractualism, and even abstract rationalism, Hegel, he says, does not set out from 'the reason of the individual', which cannot pre-exist social relations, but from 'social reason'; he constructs the idea of the state by 'proceed[ing] from the idea of the whole'. The state is accordingly conceived as a 'great organism' that unites the objective and subjective conditions for the realization of freedom.

In an overwhelmingly monarchical and absolutist Europe, however, such an encounter between the state and its concept remains remote: 'but if some European states are in fact based on Christianity, do these states correspond to their concept and is the "pure existence" of a condition the right of that condition to exist?'[89] Hence criticism's task consists in recognizing the mediation that interposes itself between the immediate existence of the state and its concept. In fact – this is the meaning of the immanent movement that enables empirical reality to attain effectivity – mediation is already at work: it operates, from within, upon the moment of immediacy, shattering its apparent unity.

As a publicist working for the *Rheinische Zeitung*, Marx devoted his theoretical and practical efforts to winning recognition for the idea that a free press is the defining feature of civil society. Only a free press makes it possible to free the 'transition' from civil society to the state from the trammels of the false infinity of bureaucratic relations and the ossified particularisms of the *Stände*:

> In order to solve this difficulty, therefore, the rulers and the ruled alike are in need of a *third* element, which would be *political* without being official, hence not based on bureaucratic premises, an element which would be of a *civil* nature without being bound up with private interests and their pressing need. This supplementary element with the *head of a citizen of the state* [*staatsbürgerlich*] and the heart of a citizen is the free press. In the realm of the press, rulers and ruled alike have an opportunity of criticising their principles and demands, and no longer in a relation of subordination, but on terms of equality as *citizens of the state* [*in gleicher staatsbürgerlicher Geltung*]; no longer as *individuals*, but as *intellectual forces*, as exponents of reason. The 'free press', being the product of public opinion, is also the creator of public opinion.[90]

Although Marx makes use of the Feuerbachian metaphors of the head and the heart,[91] he soon turns them, dialectically, to his own ends. The free press is a mediation because the fact is that the two counterposed moments of membership in the state – the moment of civil society and the moment of 'politics' in the sense of *Staatsbürgerlichkeit* – converge *in* the free press, not in some bureaucratic-monarchical Absolute. But the free press cannot play its mediating role unless it is willing to live with the consequences of this split, to accept conflict and internal division: the critical function of the press establishes a sphere of equivalent positions, a genuinely civic [*staatsbürgerlich*] sphere in which confrontation and debate between opposing viewpoints become possible. The contending parties can achieve mutual recognition only if they engage in such face-to-face confrontation: the private interests of the members of civil society acquire legitimacy, but come to realize their limited nature; while the administration and government, for their part, can assume their role only if they concede that they are each but one of the agencies of the *sittliche* state, and that their claims to exclusive representation of the life of the state are illegitimate. Indeed, the conflict between civil society and the particular agencies of government constitutes part of the 'system of the understanding', the moment of the external state, defined, precisely, as the moment of division.

However fierce it may be, the struggle between one of these state agencies, the censorship authority, and the mediating instance, the free press, now ceases to be regarded as a corrosive element which threatens to destroy the realm of public affairs. Quite the contrary: once it has been restored to its place within the process by which the external state surpasses itself, this struggle appears as the veritable driving force behind it:

> To condemn the popular press is to condemn the political spirit of the people.... the struggle against something that exists is *the first form* of its recognition, its reality and its power. And only struggle can convince both the government and the people, as well as the press itself, that the press has a real and necessary right to existence. Only struggle can show whether this right to existence is a concession or a necessity, an illusion or a truth.[92]

The moment of division and negativity is also that of the duplication of an object confronted with its own mirror-image, and brought to recognize it *as* its own: hence Marx's frequent use of terms involving the idea of reflection. Because it functions like a reflexive system, a system of self-address or a kind of public confession, the free press holds up the people's own image before it, raising it to the level of the totality. The press is a concrete embodiment of the spirit of the people, the *Volksgeist.*

> The free press is the ubiquitous vigilant eye of a people's soul, the embodiment of a people's faith in itself, the eloquent link that connects the individual with the state and the world, the embodied culture that transforms material struggles into intellectual struggles and idealises their crude material form. It is a people's frank confession to itself, and the redeeming power of confession is well known. It is the spiritual mirror in which a people can see itself, and self-examination is the first condition of wisdom.[93]

The moment of reflection, in fact, operates as a dialogical system that brings together the two moments represented by the constitution of the subject and its entry into the objectivity of the system of *Sittlichkeit*, a people becomes a people only by establishing a relationship between itself and its own image. Conversely, only the existence of the public sphere enables the government to extricate itself from the 'false infinity' of solipsistic, repressive official discourse:

> It is the *censored* press that has a *demoralising* effect. . . . The government hears only its own voice, it knows that it hears only its own voice, yet it harbours the illusion that it hears the voice of the people, and it demands that the people, too, should itself harbour this illusion. For its part, therefore, the people sinks partly into political superstition, partly into political disbelief, or, completely turning away from political life, becomes a *rabble of private individuals.*[94]

We have now gained a better understanding of the displacement to which Marx subjects Hegel's conception of the society/state 'transition'. For Hegel, as is well known, it falls to the corporation to forestall the transformation of the people into a rabble – both through the cultural role it assumes, and also by propagating an attitude ('honour')[95] that tends to bind the members of a society together. On the other hand, as Hegel explains in *Elements of the Philosophy of Right*, there can be no incarnation of a people's spirit and culture prior to the moment of the state. Marx transfers these determinations from the state to the mediation internal to civil society, thus clearing the space which the public sphere is called upon to occupy. As a result, the activity of the free press, the 'work of the press' – which consists in concretizing truth – becomes the means of attaining the standpoint of the social totality.[96] For both Marx and Hegel, the truth of a moment of the constitutive process resides in its very form, in the path by which a given result is reached.[97] Indeed, this truth, as it unfolds, takes the form of the loss of the object as a pure given, the experience of its dissolution into the network of mediations which restores the totality for us at the very moment when it disappears in the recognition of the insurmountable gap between the object and its own concept.

The form adequate to the free press is therefore fundamentally *expansive*: the press is called upon to constitute itself as a veritable system freed of all a priori constraints on its self-activity, and capable of recapitulating within itself the whole process of *Sittlichkeit*. It thus becomes a living organism whose various branches and sub-branches, with their differentiated functions, comprehend all the manifestations of the spirit of the people. Uniting the particular and the universal, theory and action, the press prefigures the great organism of the democratic state:

In the natural development of the popular press, each of the different elements which determine the nature of this press must first of all discover for itself its *specific* form of development. Hence the whole body of the popular press will be divided into different newspapers with different complementary characteristics, and if, for example, the predominant interest of one is in political science, that of another will be in political practice, or if the predominant interest of one is in *new* ideas, that of another will be in *new* facts. Only if the elements of the popular press are given the opportunity of unhampered, independent and *one-sided* development and of achieving independent existence in separate organs, can a 'good' popular press be formed, i.e., one which harmoniously combines all the *true* elements of the *popular spirit*.[98]

By making its entry into the newspapers, by becoming a 'newspaper correspondent', philosophy assumes its critical mission; it 'becomes worldly' by rising up, in and through its division, against a world that is itself internally divided. The press, for its part, becomes a popular press in struggling to establish itself as the system of the free press in the face of all the obstacles the state puts in its path; one might almost say that the press – and, through its mediation, philosophy – 'become the people', a people that 'really' thinks and acts 'as a people'. Philosophy and the press speak the people's language, and give voice to its hopes and passions (even its excesses); they are simultaneously the 'audible voice of the country' and the figure of the 'truly political'. An expansive principle, their development, like the life of the people, is an endless process of becoming, subject to no a priori limits. That is why philosophy and the press appear as the historical fusion of the party of criticism and the national/popular party, whose twofold mission – the two aspects of which must under no circumstances be separated – is national unity and the overthrow of absolutism: 'the *popular* character of the free press ... the historical individuality of the free press ... makes it the specific expression of its specific popular spirit'. This is what 'the speaker from the princely estate' cannot accept; he 'demands ... that the press ... should revolve around certain individuals instead of around the spiritual heavenly bodies, the nations'.[99]

Thus the free press becomes the organizing centre of the national/popular historical bloc in its struggle for cultural and political hegemony against the forces supporting the *ancien régime*. Accordingly, the aporias of Kant's concept of *Publizität* vanish all by themselves: the expansiveness of the public sphere, the moving spirit behind the democratization of the social totality, is inseparable from the 'becoming-state' of the historical bloc, and poles apart from anything resembling the subordination of politics to an external/transcendent principle. At the same time, this expansiveness is a manifestation of the spirit and life of the people as such, of the self-constitution of the people as people: any empirical restriction on this process that would reproduce the distinction between passive and active citizens becomes inconceivable, and radically incompatible with the very foundations of the *sittliche* state.

As they collapse – and they collapse 'into themselves', not into a transcendent absolute – Kant's aporias take Hegel's inconsistencies with them: the *sittliche* state cannot be defined as the 'absolute and unmoved end in itself [*absoluter unbewegter Selbstzweck*]', the 'divine will as present spirit, *unfolding* as the actual shape and *organization of a world*'.[100] The organism of the state, a living product of all the mediations that make it up, is to be understood as an incessant production of new life, a movement that unifies social life by acknowledging the constitutive role of its internal differentiation. What disappears as a result is the state as abstract universality and power exercised from above; Marx regards it as an 'association of free human beings who educate one another,'[101] and subordinates its activity to the rational, public forms of its existence. Thus he rids it of those elements of transcendence that continue to obscure the Hegelian vision of things. This rectification – the displacement that Marx effectuates within Hegel, and, via Hegel, within political philosophy in general – has at least two distinct aspects. It makes the transition undergone by civil society synonymous with a process of permanent democratic reform of the full range of social activities. This reform process consequently defines its own end, the rational state, as that of an organism animated by an unceasing movement towards democracy, a living organism in the sense that it constantly produces new life.

A crucial consequence follows from these two displacements. The state – and, more broadly, the political arena – do not, in the first instance, consist of institutions, even if, strictly speaking, nothing falls outside the purview of institutions, and it is critically important to transform them. The *sittliche* state is by no means the first and last subject of politics, for it emerges as a result of the operation of mediations that permanently subject the immediate unity of social life to the test of its immanent negativity.[102] Above all, politics involves practices, expansive practices with no a priori restrictions. Constantly eluding the control of institutions, they transform the relations between all the different spheres of social activity: the political is not of the order of that which institutes, or of the constituent,[103] but of the order of constitution. Democracy is nothing other than the result of the constitutive process that permanently refounds social life; it is therefore itself to be understood as the result – which is always unfinished, and can always be arrived at again – of democratization.

We have seen that the free press occupies a pre-eminent place in this process, as the catalyst of hegemony and protagonist of the movement that seeks to win the battle of democracy via a process of permanent reform. No doubt its enemies have understood, better than its partisans, that it functions as the party of the national/popular bloc in all but name. Hence the vehemence of their attacks, which contrast sharply with the lukewarm defence put up by the advocates of the free press:

> Apart from the catchwords and commonplaces which fill the air, we find among these opponents of press freedom a *pathological emotion*, a passionate partisan-ship, which gives them a *real*, not an imaginary, attitude to the press, whereas the *defenders* of the press in this Assembly have on the whole *no real relation* to what they are defending. They have never come to know freedom of the press as a *vital need*. For them it is a matter of the head, in which the heart plays no part.[104]

Such is the paradox of the situation of the Rhineland: over against the tenacity and obstinacy exhibited by the absolutist regime and its social base stand the 'moderantism' and compromising attitude of the 'half-hearted' bourgeois liberalism that dominates the historical bloc. Marx makes no secret of his mistrust of a 'liberal opposition' that flaunts its inability to defend the most elementary democratic demands: 'The *liberal opposition* shows us the level of a political assembly, just as the opposition in general shows the level of development that a society has reached. A time in which it is philosophical audacity to doubt the existence of ghosts, in which it is regarded as a paradox to oppose witch trials, is the time in which ghosts and witch trials are *legitimate*.'[105]

Marx repeats, almost verbatim, something we have already heard Heine say: German liberalism, too, is shaped by Germany's backwardness, in a country in which the ghosts of the *ancien régime* continue to hold sway. Unlike its French counterpart in 1789 (the reference to the Germans' lack of 'heart' quoted a moment ago does double duty as a coded allusion to their lack of French spirit), the German – and, especially, Rhenish – bourgeoisie refuses to adopt a 'civic-minded' stance, failing to do anything more than defend its particular interests as one of the 'estates' [*Stände*] of civil society. This accounts for the weakness of its attachment to the free press. Its inability to establish itself as a national/popular class has given rise to the specifically German phenomenon of a liberalism characterized not only by its moderation but, more damningly, by its political *impotence*. 'if we now look back on the press debates as a whole, we cannot overcome the dreary and uneasy impression produced by an assembly of represen-tatives of the *Rhine Province* who wavered only between the deliberate obduracy of privilege and the natural impotence of a half-hearted liberalism'.[106]

Hence the free press faces a twofold task. It must promote everything that can contribute to sapping the domination of the forces of the *ancien régime*, while simultaneously struggling to shift the balance of power within the national/popular bloc in favour of consistently democratic positions. Is this a single-handed combat? The editorial success of the *Rheinische Zeitung* strongly suggests the opposite. Indeed, even if the paper can be considered a precursor, it took its place, from the moment it was launched, within a larger movement that saw the radicalization of one fraction of Rhenish liberalism from 1842 on. Exemplified by the activism of a Franz Raveaux among Cologne's lower classes,[107] this radicalization was the sign of a split that grew increasingly obvious as 1848 drew near: it set moderate liberals apart from a radical-democratic grouping more favourable to mass actions and not unwilling to look to popular mobilizations for support.

Volksgeist and revolution

It proved quite difficult to wage a struggle on two fronts – or, rather, to break up the immediate unity of the front in order to transfer the forces on it elsewhere, according to the battle plan advocated by Marx and carried out in practice by the *Rheinische Zeitung*. In 1842, Rhenish radicalism was still in its infancy; in any case, throughout the *Vormärz*, the radical tendency represented a small minority, and was only loosely organized. Caught between an absolutist regime that was never loath to show its claws, and the weakness of the oppositional forces, the mediating activity of the free press ran the risk of finding itself confined to a realm of abstractions. Events soon showed that Marx's political wager rested on a double condition, both empirical and conceptual. At the empirical level, Marx's position could obviously be sustained only if the Prussian state granted the press a certain margin for manoeuvre. But, as we shall see, if the 1841 censorship instruction did indeed usher in a period during which the authorities refrained from taking overtly repressive measures, this period lasted little more than a year. Again, at a more theoretical – yet related – level, Marx's proposal to resolve the problem of the 'transition' from civil society to the state by promoting expansion of the public sphere was explicitly conceived as a process of permanent democratic reform. Although the ultimate objectives of the methods preferred by Marx the public activist were radical (the goal was democracy, not constitutional monarchy or mere guarantees of individual rights), the principles informing them were reformist: respect for the established legal order and confidence in the possibility of gradual change were among their essential features. Hence the need for tactical retreats, without which, Marx thought, it would be impossible to avoid lapsing into the practical impotence of a hyper-radicalism which was as abstract as it was purely verbal (concretely, the hyper-radicalism of the Berlin *Freien*), and which, indeed, complacently celebrated its detachment from real political practice. 'Such a clear demonstration against the foundations of the present state system', Marx wrote to Oppenheim about the essays published by the *Freien*, 'can result in an intensification of the censorship and even the suppression of the newspaper. It was in this way that the South-German *Tribüne* came to an end. But in any case we arouse the resentment of the many, indeed the majority, of the free-thinking practical people who have undertaken the laborious task of winning freedom step by step, within the constitutional framework, while we, from our comfortable armchair of abstractions, show them their contradictions.'[108]

Thus the only possible form of 'practical action' is that which aims to win freedom step by step, 'within the constitutional framework'. *Nolens volens*, Marx accepts the limits put on political activity in the Prussian Rhineland, which Sperber describes as follows: 'political organization might be tolerated, provided it was informal in nature and local in scope; political agitation was sometimes allowed, provided it was addressed to a limited and upper-class audience; political dissent was permitted, provided it was moderate in form and expressed with the consent of the authorities'.[109]

It will be said that there is nothing particularly original about all of this. Unless Marx had been willing from the outset to opt for clandestine action, prison or exile, he obviously had to accept, like everyone else, the constraints imposed by the situation and the prevailing balance of forces. He had no choice but to settle for one or another variant on the 'German road'. His originality *vis-à-vis* his contemporaries, however, resides in the fact that he gave theoretical expression to his method, right down to its very aporias and contradictions. Thus his tactical moves were subordinated to strategic choices, and these were rigorously embedded in the vast syllogism that offered a solution to the Hegelian riddle of the transition from society to the state. In this sense, Marx's rupture with the Berlin *Freien*, though it did not simply follow from the critique of abstract freedom elaborated in his 1841 dissertation, or from his overall strategy for the public sphere, was nevertheless perfectly consistent with both. Thus it originated in a different approach to political action, not in the fact that Marx was more radical than others, or – as the canonical version of the young Marx's trajectory has it – had thrown in his lot with the opposing class.[110]

On a strictly conceptual plane, Marx's method rests on the idea that the contradictions of civil society can be 'resolved' at a higher level, that of the ethical, democratic state. This is clearly the sense of the dialectical 'transition' in question here. All the ambiguities of this process are concentrated in a single world; 'spiritualization' is the essential task with which the principal mediation, the system of the free press, is charged: 'what makes the press the most powerful lever for promoting culture and the intellectual education of the people is precisely the fact that it transforms the material struggle into an ideological struggle, the struggle of flesh and blood into a struggle of minds, the struggle of need, desire, empiricism into a struggle of theory, of reason, of form'.[111] To be sure, we have seen that for Hegel, whom Marx simply echoes here, 'spiritualizing' a 'material' need such as the need to eat does not mean tempering it – nor, *a fortiori*, abolishing it or imagining that one can satisfy it by listening to sermons or reading philosophy books. It means *recognizing* that it belongs to a 'system of needs' and, consequently, to a culture which confers upon it its universal character and objectivity. In this sense, 'spiritualizing' the material struggle would mean integrating it, via the mediation of the free press, into a network of more extensive social connections that would make possible self-reflection and a recognition of certain 'forms' and 'ideas' through which the material struggle can re-present itself while breaking free of the immediate constraints that have begotten it.

The transition to the moment of the state, a fully conscious and free entity, is the sign that this spiritualization has been brought to its term. According to Marx, a 'modern state' that 'corresponds to its concept' can – and must – rise above the particularism of socioeconomic interests, those of the possessing classes included – not by negating them from a position outside them, but by relativizing them and restoring them to their proper place.[112] This implies legal/constitutional recognition of customary rights and, more generally, of the justice of the 'rightful urge' of the 'poor class'.[113] But such recognition cannot be guaranteed without the involvement of the free press, which makes the voice of the suffering classes heard in the public sphere, and puts socioeconomic questions at the centre of political debate: 'it alone', says Marx of the role of the press in the economic crisis of the Mosel region, 'can make a particular interest a general one', since 'it alone can make the *distressed state* of the Mosel region an object of general attention and general sympathy on the part of the Fatherland'.[114] In other words, the press makes it possible to recognize the political nature of economic problems; it reveals the intimate ties between 'economic question[s]' and those bearing on 'internal and external policy'.[115] For Marx, there is a basic incompatibility between the principle of publicity and the absolutization of private property, which cannot proceed in the absence of the 'appropriate form, that of secret procedure'.[116] Thus the law emerges as a space of conflict within which it is possible to affirm the priority of the standpoint of the 'poor class', for, in the final analysis, only the pre-eminence of the poor is compatible with modern legal rationality, which it anticipates from a historical-genetic point of view.[117] Hence, as Marx sees it, there is no contradiction whatsoever between the formal universality of the law and the legal privilege enjoyed by the special customs of the lower classes, for if this universality is to become concrete, it must evolve out of conflict and, confronted with the basic asymmetry that divides the law into the customary law of the poor and the non-law of the privileged, must recognize in the processes of its formation (i.e. in the work of 'formalization' characteristic of the juridical instance) the political nature – the 'politically overdetermined' nature, one might say – of the law. To put it differently: the realization of the law, as a process of production of rational/universal norms, passes by way of the self-recognition of the constitutive conflictuality that confers upon the law its function of investing social practice with a political purpose.

Politics, posited as a movement of democratization of the full range of social activities, thus makes it possible to confront the internal contradictions of civil society by tapping the emancipatory potential of a legal system that is receptive to the gains made by the lower classes. This point is crucial. Faced with the social question, Marx places himself in the tradition of the French Revolution and the project of a 'popular political economy' defended by the Robespierreans, the urban *sans-culottes*, and the most radical wing of the peasant movement: a project centred on subordinating property rights to the right to existence.[118] If Marx subscribes to Hegel's critique of the natural law tradition, as well as his conception of law as recognition of a juridical order whose rationality is that of things themselves, he also affirms, in the tradition of Year II of the Revolution, the necessity of subordinating the economic to the political in order to protect the rights of the lower classes and overcome socioeconomic inequalities – both by legal means and also by establishing an economic and political democracy.[119] 'The question', says Marx in rejecting the claims of the representatives of the big landed property-owners, 'can be summed up in a few words: Should landed property criticise and be master over political intelligence or should it be the other way round?'[120]

Thus Marx adopts a position that is diametrically opposed to the 'social-ist' conception defended, notably, by Engels and Hess – a conception that seeks in the 'social' a new, radically anti-political principle of cohesion and harmony.[121] This explains why he keeps his distance from the socialist and communist theories of his day, which he takes for 'dogmatic abstrac-tion[s]',[122] even if he credits them with identifying the 'undeniable collision' of the period, and articulating the 'troubled conscience'[123] that has overcome modern society – an anguish he confesses to sharing.

Marx's idea of democracy, as a process of complete democratization subordinating the socioeconomic to the political, is inconceivable without the finality of a state which embodies objective morality:

> In a true state there is no landed property, no industry, no material thing, which as a crude element of this kind could make a bargain with the state; in it there are only *spiritual forces*, and only in their state form of resurrection, in their political rebirth, are these natural forces entitled to a voice in the state. The state pervades the whole of nature with spiritual nerves, and at every point it must be apparent that what is dominant is not matter, but form, not nature without the state, but the nature of the state, not the *unfree object*, but the *free human being.*[124]

Let us note that here, too, Marx quite spontaneously echoes the formula-tions of Saint-Just, for whom, in economic matters, the 'established Republic' has an obligation to 'embrace all relations, all rights, all duties, and confer a common appearance on all parts of the state'.[125] But Marx adds something specifically 'German' – precisely the activity of 'spirit'.

The spiritualization of the material struggle coincides, for Marx, with the 'political regeneration' – that is to say, the democratization – of all social activities; it designates the victory of the 'free man' over feudal man, who was reduced to the status of an 'unfree object' or animal. Thus Marx takes the French Revolution – because of the unprecedented expansion of the public sphere, especially the press, that it made possible – as the model for a simultaneously material and spiritual revolution. Hence the idea of a revolutionary press does not seem at all far-fetched. Marx seizes on the example of the Belgian Revolution of 1830 to sketch its basic features:

> In France it was not freedom of the press but censorship that made for revolution. But leaving this out of account, the Belgian revolution *appeared* at first as a spiritual revolution, as a revolution of the press. The assertion that the press caused the Belgian revolution has no sense beyond that. But is that a

matter for blame? Must the revolution at once assume a *material form?* Strike instead of speaking? The government can materialise a spiritual revolution; a material revolution must first spiritualise the government. The Belgian revolution is a product of the Belgian spirit. So the press, too, the freest manifestation of the spirit in our day, has its share in the Belgian revolution. The Belgian press would not have been the Belgian press if it had stood aloof from the revolution, but equally the Belgian revolution would not have been Belgian if it had not been at the same time a revolution of the press. The Revolution of a people is *total*, that is, each sphere carries it out in its own way; why not also the press as the press?[126]

Thus it is a particular figure of spirit, the *Volksgeist* or 'spirit of the people', which encompasses both the material and the spiritual struggle, and makes it possible to overcome the split between them. The fact that the press faithfully follows the life of the people inevitably makes it an active participant in the revolution, inasmuch as the revolution represents the crowning expression of the *Volksgeist*; conversely, the fact that the revolution is 'total' makes the revolutionary press one specific modality of a phenomenon which embraces the whole of social life. But is Marx's argument tantamount, once we have made the detour (*censure oblige!*) through the Belgian case, to an implicit profession of faith in a press that is a 'midwife' of revolutions? A few sentences scattered through the *Rheinische Zeitung* articles – sentences that evoke, in 'coded' fashion, struggles which are far from being purely intellectual – can indeed create that impression.[127]

However, Marx's position is less clear-cut than a hasty reading might lead one to believe. To be sure, against the partisans of the *ancien régime*, he justifies the revolutionary role played by the press at certain historical moments – the reference to the Belgian case here serves as a synecdoche for all revolutions. But, by the same token, the importance of that role is downplayed by way of its subordination to a figure of Spirit, the *Volksgeist*, which a people can only rarely claim to incarnate. In other words, while it is true that a press in conformity with its concept could be nothing but revolutionary in the France of 1789–93 or the Belgium of 1830, it is not necessarily so in Germany in 1842. For the same to hold for contemporary Germany, one would have to assume, first, that the process of Spirit was passing through a new revolutionary moment, and, what is more, that it had fallen to the German people to give this moment concrete form. In short, one would have to assume that a German revolution was the order of the day, that this revolution had been recognized as the rose in the cross of the historical present.

It is quite possible, however, that the genius of the German people is something else entirely. The historical foundations for freedom of the press in Germany are to be sought in German 'literature' and 'intellectual culture', as well as in the special role the country has to play in the intellectual field.[128] Marx does, it is true, say that 'one form of freedom governs another just as one limb of the body does another'.[129] But interdependence does not by any means rule out a hierarchization of these freedoms, any more than it rules out hierarchization of the members of the body. Thus, according to Feuerbach, the source of all these organicist metaphors, while it is necessary to bear in mind the union of the 'head' (the German, masculine, reformist, 'spiritual' principle) and the 'heart' (the French, revolutionary, feminine and sensualist principle), the pre-eminence of the head is constantly presupposed: it alone is *active* in the true sense (i.e. 'masculine', in this androcentric metaphorical scheme), since the 'agitation' contributed by the feminine-revolutionary principle is associated with 'passion' and emotion, which are divorced from spirit (and those who embody it, the German philosophers).[130] Marx would appear to be saying the same thing when he affirms that 'the emancipation of the brain' – which he identifies with the free press, the sole concrete figure of the activity of spirit – takes precedence over 'the emancipation of arms and legs' – that is, the 'trades'.[131] Certainly, he is quick to point out – and it is here that the significance of the identification between the 'head' and the press lies – that such emancipation has to quit the 'firmament of the imagination', where the 'German liberals' place it, to take its stand on 'the solid ground of reality'. But the fact remains that the emancipation of the head re-establishes the pre-eminence of the labour of spiritualization and, with it, of the philosopher-journalist.

In Belgium, the revolution 'spoke before striking'; but, in the end, it struck. In Germany, on the other hand, 'speaking' might make it possible to forgo 'striking'. Indeed, the free press appears as the sole – and, given the seriousness of the crisis, the last available – means of avoiding revolution. Marx turns the argument of its detractors against them: rather than the free press, it was censorship and all the other restrictions imposed on 'speaking' that brought about acrimonious divisions; by blocking the process of mutual recognition between the government and the people, these restrictions made the government an instrument of repression, and left it the prisoner of its own monologues, while transforming the people into 'a rabble of private individuals' seesawing between passivity and blind revolt.

It was not out of merely tactical considerations, then, that Marx appealed to the Prussian government to return to its earlier reformist course, or that he insisted on the national, 'German' nature of the liberalism professed by the *Rheinische Zeitung* – though we would do well to bear in mind just how little room for manoeuvre he had. When, in November 1842, he wrote to the *Oberpräsident* of the province, Von Schaper, on behalf of the newspaper's shareholders, Marx still thought he could save the *Rheinische Zeitung*, as the *personal* letter he wrote to Oppenheim in late August testifies; by the same token, he continued to hold open the possibility of finding a reformist solution to the crisis. To preserve such slivers of a public sphere as already existed, and were indispensable to anyone who had set himself 'the laborious task of winning freedom step by step', it was necessary to make concessions, even at the price of a break with former allies tempted by a radicalization as abstract as it was untimely.[132] There was nothing at all absurd about Marx's calculation: Von Schaper, who had already stepped in on a number of occasions to curb the impulses of the most zealous of the Prussian censors, did in fact win a reprieve for the paper. But it was to be the last.

Warmed by this very fragile success, Marx went so far as to argue that the principle of representation by 'estates' [*Stände*] would be transcended as a logical consequence of 'the consistent and comprehensive implementation of the fundamental institutions of Prussia';[133] in support of his thesis, he recalled the modernization of the Prussian administration and army carried out during the reform period.[134] He regarded these reforms as so many steps towards an organic, self-conscious state that would gradually leave the irrational principles of feudal institutions (especially representation by estates) behind. He therefore invoked the 'free creations of the spirit of the Prussian state', even admitting the existence of truly representative institutions, notwithstanding the bureaucracy's increasing rigidity and absolutism's edgy defence of the existing order.[135] Similarly, the hope for a peaceful resolution of the economic question, which Marx expressed again the first time he took a public stand on communism,[136] was, rather than a mere concession to the censors' scissors, an indication of how close Marx's positions were, *on this point*, to those of 'true socialism', and particularly of Moses Hess (a letter from whom provided the pretext for the polemic with the *Augsburger Zeitung*).

Despite its theoretical originality and political richness, Marx's strategy for democratization, deduced from the dialectical resolution of the society/state transition, leads back, like the strategy of many others, to the vicinity of the German road. The revolution is legitimate, but it is other people's business; the mission of 'spiritualization' incumbent on Germany will allow it to escape the horrors of the revolutionary hell even as it reaps the benefits of revolutionary gains; thanks to state reform, stimulated by the practical philosophy that has invested the public sphere, it will prove possible to resolve existing contradictions peacefully and productively, and so on. In a word, if the place Marx occupied was unique, it nevertheless lay squarely within the realm of what he would later call 'the German ideology'.

THE ROADS OF EXILE

The ship of fools

> I do not undertake to insure the ship of fools.
> Karl Marx[137]

The respite that the Prussian absolutists granted the *Rheinische Zeitung* in autumn 1842 proved brief, shattering the last remaining illusions as to the possibility that the Prussian state might set out on a reform course.[138] Von Schaper, *Oberpräsident* of the Rhine province, had so far succeeded in restraining the censors' zeal; now, however, his efforts would prove insufficient. The dismissal of Bruno Bauer from the University of Bonn in March 1842 was a clear sign of the Prussian regime's renewed intransigence, sparking, in reaction, 'a profound political and ideological radicalization among dissident intellectuals'.[139] Beyond a doubt, the year 1842 marked a turning point in the crisis, and would soon be perceived *as* such. Tellingly, a few months into 1843, Bauer published a massive polemical work entitled *The Rise and Fall of the German Radicalism of the Year 1842*.[140]

From early October 1842 on, repressive measures followed one another in swift succession. Carl Grün, one of the future representatives of 'true socialism', lost his post as editor-in-chief of the Mannheim *Abendzeitung*. A few days later, Dr Witt was relieved of his responsibilities at the *Königsberger Zeitung*, the leading liberal paper in northern Germany. In the meantime, on 9 October, Friedrich Wilhelm IV had issued a Cabinet Order requiring the presidents of the provinces and the censorship ministers to declare their opposition, in the press, to publications which 'gave a distorted picture' of reality, and 'corrupted' readers. On 10 November, Von Schaper wrote to the Minister of the Interior to say that the tendency of the paper Marx had edited since the summer of 1842, the *Rheinische Zeitung* (whose readership in the province was growing by leaps and bounds),[141] 'was increasingly negative'. The mounting repression peaked in December 1842–January 1843, when the poet Georg Herwegh was expelled from Prussia and the Leipzig *Allgemeine Zeitung* was banned. Finally, on 21 January 1843, in the wake of a series of articles by Marx in the columns of the *Rheinische Zeitung* on the condition of the Mosel vine-growers, as well as his attacks on Russian despotism, the decision was made to shut down the paper. To crown it all, in March 1843 the government also banned Arnold Ruge's review, the *Deutsche Jahrbücher*, thus stifling the last of the major free voices in the kingdom of Prussia.

Marx, already worn down by his interminable guerrilla war with the censors, was relieved – if not delighted – when he learned this news. In an early 1843 letter to Ruge, he said:

> In the suppression of the *Rheinische Zeitung* I see a definite *advance* of political consciousness, and for that reason I am resigning. Moreover, I had begun to be stifled in that atmosphere. It is a bad thing to have to perform menial duties even for the sake of freedom; to fight with pinpricks, instead of with clubs. I have become tired of hypocrisy, stupidity, gross arbitrariness, and of our bowing and scraping, dodging, and hairsplitting over words. Consequently, the government has given me back my freedom.[142]

Thus ended the period of fighting for freedom with pinpricks. But the government would have to pay a high price for its victory. It thought it had scored a triumph by silencing every dissident voice; in reality, it had committed an act of the sort that could only foment rebellion among an intellectual and political generation that had doubtless merely been looking for an acceptable compromise. Henceforth, the popular protest movements would be unable to steer clear of direct confrontation with the representatives of the absolutist regime. The uprising of the Silesian weavers and the Cologne riots would both confirm that, from 1844–45 on, the social and political crisis was entering a pre-insurrectional phase.

The dissident intelligentsia would have to pay an equally heavy price. By eliminating the rare remaining forums for public expression, the government had left the reformist project that inspired the intellectuals, Marx included, no room for manoeuvre. Thus the crisis of hegemony besetting the alliance of social forces that supported the *ancien régime*, matched as it was by a strategic crisis in the opposite camp, had soon reached boiling point, as is confirmed by all the convergent exposés of Prussian despotism, whether Marx's, Feuerbach's, or Ruge's. The result was drastically to limit the range of possible responses to the crisis. One consisted in giving up political activity for the haven of pure speculation, while waiting for the redemptive event that would come along to resolve the crisis; this was the path taken by the Young Hegelians in Berlin and also, in a way, by Feuerbach. An alternative, for those who put no faith in the illusions of the omnipotence of spirit, was withdrawal into a critical pessimism, a choice that came down to relinquishing all hope of political change; Ruge was to adopt this stance. There was, finally, a third option: an authentic radicalization that refused to abandon the ground of political practice, while duly noting that it was impossible to pursue the political struggle on German soil.

The correspondence between Marx and Ruge during this period provides an exemplary reflection of this deadlocked situation, in which the play of contradictions seemed to be incapable of crystallizing real alternatives. The crisis of the absolutist regime had reached the point of no return; the 'German *misère*' was exposed for all to see; but at the same time the *misère* and the impotence of those who had hitherto struggled against it also came to light. The resulting situation was, then, an extreme one, by virtue of the impossibilities it revealed, the void it created, and – not least – the solitude to which it condemned all those who attempted to think out, let alone work out, a practical solution for which the premises were utterly lacking. In this sense, Germany in 1843 resembled Machiavelli's devastated Italy or the Germany which, dismembered by the Napoleonic conquest, had led Hegel to exclaim '*Deutschland ist kein Staat mehr*'.[143] For the 'freedom' which Marx describes as something that the attitude of the Prussian government had 'given him back' was by no means a return to a freedom he had once enjoyed; it was not a reassuringly familiar landscape briefly obscured by the compromises for which political struggle called. This 'freedom' was in reality the freedom of an unpredictable new situation fraught with risk, and it took the form of separation, division and solitude.[144]

For Marx, as for others before – and, still more, after – him, solitude was to take the acute form of uprootedness known as exile. It is surely no accident that in Marx's case, political crisis went hand in hand with personal crisis, intensifying the separation from his earlier self which the new conjuncture provoked. During his first trip abroad, a voyage to Holland which he set out on in March 1843 in a kind of dress rehearsal for his departure for Paris, Marx took the measure of the upheaval exile would bring. In a letter to Ruge, he talks about an 'inverted revelation' (but, he is careful to point out, 'a revelation for all that')[145] inspired by a comparison between his native land and Holland, the only country on the Continent which had managed to hold absolutism at arm's length (the 'Dutch anomaly'[146] that had prevailed since Spinoza's day).

The revelation in question is shame – shame before the abhorrent spectacle of Prussian despotism. Such shame does not, however, leave those overcome by it the prisoners of an unhappy consciousness. It is, rather, the statement of an impossibility as well as a revolt in the face of the intolerable, of the kind that quickly modulates into inner conflict:

> You look at me with a smile and ask: What is gained by that? No revolution is made out of shame. I reply: Shame is already revolution of a kind; shame is actually the victory of the French Revolution over the German patriotism that defeated it in 1813. Shame is a kind of anger which is turned inward. And if a whole nation really experienced a sense of shame, it would be like a lion, crouching ready to spring.[147]

This, then, is the real substance of the revelation to which shame served as a prelude: the imminence of the German revolution. The last words of the letter say this still more plainly: Germany's 'fate' is 'the impending revolution'. Before discovering the proletariat, before forging the concepts of his theory of history, Marx makes the leap; he is virtually the only one in the democratic German opposition to do so, with the exception – a crucial exception, to be sure – of Heine.[148] But this amounts to saying that, like all acts of rupture, this new stance – which, it bears emphasizing, is *political* – appears from the outset in a highly paradoxical light. Marx's revolutionary political position is not the fruit of a free choice among several 'positive' possibilities, for it proceeds, literally, from an impossibility: it is the production of a new possibility. *A fortiori*, it is in no sense a mere reflection of external conditions – the result, say, of a slow, laborious 'reform of the understanding', or of adaptation to an altered external environment.[149] Rather, it surges up out of a contradiction and a struggle that divide even individuals from themselves ('a kind of anger which is turned inward', says Marx), confronting them with possibilities that pre-existed their consciousness; this is so even if the typical task of revolutionary politics consists precisely in re-elaborating these possibilities by playing on their internal contradictions in order to generate new possibilities. This re-elaboration is pursued, not in contemplative serenity, but in the heat of battle; there are no guarantees as to its outcome, and there is no eliminating the measure of undecidability that attaches to it. The revolution is the 'springing lion', the *salto mortale* of which Kant had already spoken.

In other words, commitment to the cause of revolution is not one available 'option' among others, a choice made by a rational agent or the result of an act of free will; it is a production of alternatives that emerge from the rejection of an imposed solution, and also from an impossibility. For if shame was already a revolution, Germany was at antipodes from it, entangled as it was in the comedy of an absolutism in decline. Yet the question before Marx was well and truly that of a *German* revolution, not a revolution of which Germany had, since Kant, been merely a benevolent spectator and 'spiritual' guide. To describe this backwardness, Marx combines a theatrical metaphor with another image that haunts the Western tradition, that of the *stultifera navis*:

> The comedy of despotism that is being played out with us is just as dangerous for [Friedrich Wilhelm IV] as the tragedy once was for the Stuarts and Bourbons. And even if for a long time this comedy were not to be looked upon as the thing it actually is, it would still amount to a revolution. The state is too serious a thing to be turned into a kind of harlequinade. A ship full of fools could perhaps be allowed to drift for quite a time at the mercy of the wind, but it would be driven to meet its fate precisely because the fools would not believe this. This fate is the impending revolution.[150]

Shame, the budding awareness of the comedy of the *ancien régime*, is a revolution in itself; yet it seems that the same could be said of shamelessness and unthinking absorption in the comedy. Marx echoes the post-Hegelian commonplace about the transformation of tragedy into comedy or, rather, farce (comedy without comic awareness), and goes on to draw his conclusions about the transitory or even unsustainable character of the German situation. Like a ship of fools, Germany, too, is sailing towards its destiny; its journey is its transition [*passage*], with the difference that the madmen's destination, unlike Germany's, appears to be well known in advance.[151] Is what we have here a reductive interpretation of the schema of the ruse of history, regarded as a naive teleology which guarantees a dénouement that must inevitably come, independently of the consciousness (i.e. the unconsciousness) of the actors? So it seems – if we ignore the economy of the text in which Marx's remarks are embedded. But once we take that economy into account, we are led in a different direction altogether. For, as Marx takes pains to point out, he finds himself aboard a barge, the *Trekschuit*, which is making its way across Holland. It is, then, precisely because he, too, is on the threshold of an exile for which the voyage through Holland serves as a preamble, because he is a passenger *par excellence* – that is to say, a prisoner of his passage – that he can recognize the German ship of fools as his own, at the very moment when he steps off it.

Marx himself is in the situation of the madman who, caught in his floating prison, 'cannot and must not have another prison than the threshold itself'.[152] That is what makes the miracle, the '*inverted* revelation', possible – like the 'tail wind' which drives the ship of fools before it. Was not water supposed to purify the madman, and transport him to

the shores of the other world? What the revelation in question here
heralds is not the quietist's wait for the redemptive event; in a certain
sense, that revelation augurs itself, its own revelatory character, that is, its
anticipatory function. In other words, the *event* represented by the
inverted revelation is a product of the chance encounter of heterogeneous
factors which, amid the solitude of a voyage, have all come together on
board the *Trekschuit*; as such, it is symptomatic of the imminence of the
revolution, which consequently appears – to the consciousness capable of
grasping its historicity, of 'posing', retrospectively, its premises – as a
'fate'.

The impending revolution is not arrival at the Absolute of a history
that unfolds in utter indifference to the peregrinations (in the literal
sense of the word, in the case at hand) of consciousness. Rather, it is the
moment when everything suddenly changes direction, when consciousness
grasps that the Absolute is nothing other than its own forward movement,
the culmination of which will then appear as its inevitable consequence.
Marx's *stultifera navis* thus says the same thing as Heine's storm metaphor.[153] Just as the bolt of lightning precedes the thunder, although they
derive from a common source, so the revelation Marx has aboard the
boat announces its imminent landing on the far shore. In both cases, it is
the historicity of the real – Marx's revelation is ultimately nothing other
than thought's new awareness of its own historicity – which justifies the
parallel between dream and reality, thought and action, and assigns them
their mission: the imminence of the revolution does not have the status
of a positive prediction of a 'natural' development but, rather, designates,
first and foremost, the *emergency* of the moment. In other words, the
revolution appears 'imminent' in the movement which reveals that the
conditions for it are lacking. These conditions must therefore be *created*.
The process of their creation begins the moment they are perceived and
enunciated as such.

The balance of Marx's correspondence with Ruge backs up this line of
argumentation. There is no exaggerating the importance of these texts,
which were later published in the *Deutsch–Französische Jahrbücher*, and are
thus more than a private correspondence: they provide a first-hand
account of a veritable turning point, a 'new life',[154] a point of entry into
the 'new [world]'[155] towards whose shores the ship of fools is insensibly
drifting. Upbraiding Ruge for yielding to despair, Marx contends that
hope is given only to those who are willing to cross the desert of despair,
and goes on to draw the conclusion that in a situation of 'void' – that is
to say, a situation in which all possibilities are open – to act politically and
acquire the political understanding that can be found only among the

people is a way of trying to avoid 'catastrophe'.[156] Hope is not, then, simply the opposite of despair. It issues from it; it comes from turning despair back upon itself.

Criticism, which includes self-criticism as a moment inherent in its process, will from now on have no choice but to be radical; it must become '*ruthless criticism of all that exists*, ruthless both in the sense of not being afraid of the results it arrives at and in the sense of being just as little afraid of conflict with the powers that be'.[157] To this end, criticism must above all avoid opposing the 'is' to an abstract ethical 'ought', and shun utopian projections such as those of the various communist systems.[158] Rather, it must learn to recognize, in the immanence of the real, both the 'ruptures' which shatter its immediate unity and the contradictions that it can neither tolerate nor overcome as long as the 'old system' remains in place. Only on this condition can criticism confront 'existing reality' with 'true reality' – with an understanding of the underlying tendencies of the real world, which it helps raise to the level of the concept. In so doing, it goes to the source of the principal difficulties confronting the democratic movement, which are above all *internal*.[159]

In an extremely confused situation, in which the 'social reform' movement is teeming with nostrums and visionary schemes, this, says Marx – who is eager to make it plain that he has not fallen victim to the doctrinal fever endemic to critical situations – is the only possible definition of theory's anticipatory function – and it is a direct descendant of the Hegelian thesis about the rationality of the real. The lack of an 'exact idea [about] what the future ought to be' 'is precisely the advantage of the new trend': 'we do not dogmatically anticipate the world, but only want to find the new world through criticism of the old one'.[160] Once again, then, Marx rejects the three most deeply entrenched conceptions of political action: that which sets out to ground politics on an ethical imperative, but also those which subordinate it to a programme, or to the realization of a utopian plan that pre-exists the contradictory movement of reality. This is a constant in Marx's thought; there is obviously a profound continuity between his rejection of communism in the letters to Ruge and the famous, specifically Marxian redefinition in *The German Ideology*: 'Communism is for us not *a state of affairs* which is to be established, an *ideal* to which reality [will] have to adjust itself. We call communism the *real* movement which abolishes the present state of things.'[161]

The answer to 'the question of "whither"' in fact consists in a displacement of the question itself: the goal is not an immutable beyond, and is to be found only on the path that consciousness follows in order to reach it. Did not the 1841 text on censorship already announce that 'truth includes not only the result but also the path to it'?[162] But this is a path strewn with obstacles, which consciousness, if it is to progress, must learn to recognize as obstacles of its own devising: 'The reform of consciousness consists *only* in making the world aware of its own consciousness, in awakening it out of its dream about itself, in explaining to it the meaning of its own actions.' Dream precedes action, for, as in Heine, the dream is a dream *of* the world itself, participating, with all its ambiguities and confusions, in the movement of emergent consciousness that it merely anticipates: 'Hence, our motto must be: reform of consciousness not through dogmas, but by analysing the mystical consciousness that is unintelligible to itself, whether it manifests itself in a religious or a political form. It will then become evident that the world has long dreamed of possessing something of which it has only to be conscious in order to possess it in reality.'[163]

In a certain sense, then, the movement, for Marx, takes priority over the goal. But it does not do so in the sense later defined by Bernstein, for whom the goal was nothing and the movement all.[164] A conception of that sort dissociates, precisely, the goal from the movement; in its refusal to understand that the goal is immanent to the movement, it is simply the inverted – and pale[165] – reflection of doctrinaire utopianism and program-matic dogmatism. The new consciousness which Marx means to help bring about does not result from a 'natural' development of the world, nor is it the constitution of the world by a consciousness that recovers its originary freedom in the purity of a founding moment. It presents itself from the first as a 'clarification . . . to be gained by the present time of its struggles and desires',[166] a clarification whose precondition is that one take sides in a struggle which has always already begun. There can be no critique without such commitment, and no commitment without real struggle: 'nothing prevents us from making criticism of politics, partici-pation in politics, and therefore *real* struggles, the starting point of our criticism, and from identifying our criticism with them. In that case we do not confront the world in a doctrinaire way with a new principle: Here is the truth, kneel down before it! We develop new principles for the world out of the world's own principles.'[167]

The 'becoming-worldly' of criticism depends, as is now evident, on a specific encounter. That is, criticism cannot become concrete unless it encounters its 'point of application'; otherwise, it can only deviate towards the 'critical criticism' of the Berlin *Freien*. Marx clearly names this point of application: politics. It is in this precise sense that his path coincides with Ruge's throughout the year 1843. Marx and Ruge make convergent 'self-criticisms of liberalism'; both its *impotence* as well as its 'apolitical' (and fundamentally Kantian) character.[168] Taken in itself, the argument is not particularly original: the accusation of '*powerlessness*' is a well-worn commonplace in the polemics that raged within the various currents of Young Hegelianism in the period of its decline. Moreover, it would hardly be going too far to interpret this kind of polemical rhetorical fury – of which the very prolific Bauer[169] offers a particularly striking example – as a kind of ritual exorcism of the spectre that had been haunting the nights of German philosophy since the day the sage of Königsberg revealed his 'enthusiasm' for the revolution: the spectre of impotence.

In fact, the true radicalism of Ruge's and Marx's critique resides less in the rhetorical force of the denunciation of liberalism and the *juste-milieu* than in their refusal to exempt *themselves* in any way from their own critical diagnosis. In other words, Ruge's and Marx's critiques are also self-critiques which shun the complacency steeped in nihilism that was the stock in trade of the Berlin circle. For Ruge, liberalism is not even a 'party', an active force in the real world; it is an amorphous mass of decent feelings that never moves beyond contemplation. Marx's more precise critique dissects the 'idealist' illusion of the liberals, from which he himself, as we have seen, had not always been altogether exempt: the liberals were convinced that they could rechannel the ambitions of the young king, Friedrich Wilhelm IV, who had proclaimed his desire to subject the monarchy to a Romantic renewal, in the direction of democratic reform, and even the founding of a Republic. The conclusion is obvious – and it counts as a personal self-criticism: the reformist road is impracticable. 'That is the unsuccessful attempt to abolish the philistine state on its own basis; the result has been to make it evident to the whole world that for despotism brutality is a necessity and humanity an impossibility. A brutal relationship can only be maintained by means of brutality.'[170]

Both Marx and Ruge maintain that the liberal opposition has failed to overcome its congenital defect – its spectatorial attitude, or an inclination to withdraw into the inner realm. This failing was inscribed in the very moment of its constitution: contemporary Germany, and the liberal tendency that grew up in tandem with the process of German state-formation, emerged out of a confrontation with the French Revolution, in a climate of repression that foreclosed the possibility of democratic development for a long time. Cut off from the world of practice, taking refuge in a 'good will' that refused to reflect on its own premises, liberalism has merely reinforced the 'apoliticism' of the German situation by giving it the bad conscience of the petty bourgeoisie, the notorious

German 'philistinism' [*Spießbürgerlichkeit*]. Philosophy is the one field in which the Germans have risen to the level of the present; German philosophy therefore deserves to be saved, on condition that it abandons its narcissistic self-contemplation and is fully secularized. Ruge talks about 'dissolving' philosophy,[171] whereas Marx was later to talk about the 'supersession' [*Aufhebung*] of philosophy, understood as its suppression/realization;[172] but both thinkers agree that philosophy must be transformed, from within, until it has become an active political party: 'the cause must be grasped by the roots; that is, only philosophy can attain and grasp freedom ... the transcendence of liberalism is possible only by the dissolution of the old sense of superiority and powerless self-seclusion of philosophy, only insofar as all minds with talent and fire are directed to the one, great, infinitely profitable purpose of causing the breakup of boneheaded philistine consciousness and the engendering of a living, sensitive, political Spirit'.[173]

The order of the day was thus to forge *political* understanding – in other words, to wage an open struggle for democracy. Moreover, as the time had come to drop all pretence and declare mankind's sins 'for what they really are',[174] the struggle for democracy implied the overthrow of absolutism and the establishment of a German Republic. To drive the point home, Ruge proposed 'the dissolution of liberalism into democratism' shortly before following Marx into exile;[175] Marx, for his part, said that 'free men' were necessarily 'republicans', and did not hesitate to invoke the Greek *polis* as the model for a 'democratic state', the only form of community that could realize human freedom.[176] The reference to the universal concept of man, which the French Revolution had pushed to the forefront of the historical stage, constitutes the very horizon of democracy. In his correspondence with Ruge, Marx alludes to Feuerbach's critique of religion, but he does not give the concept of man the specifically Feuerbachian meaning that he would later assign it (especially in the *1844 Manuscripts*) – namely, that of a generic essence to be reappropriated.[177] For the moment, Marx's point is not about putting an end to alienation, but about the conquest of liberty, which he conceives as a process of emancipation from all relations of servitude and subordination.

The reference to man is therefore inseparable from the reference to inhumanity, the 'political world of animals', and the 'consistent system' 'engendered and shaped' by 'centuries of barbarism'.[178] Hence Marx contrasts 'the human world of democracy'[179] with the 'dehumanized world' of the *ancien régime*, in which absolutist despotism and relations of servitude based on natural 'inequalities' persist. Monarchy is the incarnation of this dehumanized world; to prolong its existence is to continue to treat men as if they had not yet come of age. Overthrowing the monarchy is the only way out of the German comedy: 'for a king there is only *one* situation which is ridiculous and only *one* which is embarrassing, and that is abdication from the throne'.[180] *Ipso facto*, any attempt to resolve the crisis which, like 'true socialism', ducks the question of a change in the political regime, its institutional forms included, is dismissed out of hand.[181] Marx's self-critical rejection of liberalism must not be confused with anything resembling indifference to the world of politics; for Marx, it is unthinkable that a German revolution should fail to assign a central place to the battle for democracy, including its institutional forms, even if democracy is not simply – or even mainly – a matter of institutions (we shall return to this point in a moment). Without a doubt, this commitment to democracy puts a permanent dividing line between Marx's thought and socialist doctrines, and, beyond that, is the source of a permanent cleavage within the German workers' movement.[182]

Thus far, Marx's and Ruge's self-criticisms are largely convergent. It is no accident that the frontiers separating both Marx and Ruge from the partisans of an 'anti-politics' (the Berlin Young Hegelians[183] or the 'true' socialists) coincide, or that the project to collaborate on a review (the future *Deutsch–Französische Jahrbücher*) was conceived at this moment. Nevertheless, even before Marx and Ruge fell out in 1844, their main areas of disagreement were apparent.[184] For Ruge, the sovereign people of the democratic state constitutes a unified whole which supersedes (in the sense of an *Aufhebung*) social divisions. Once the 'crudeness' of the rights habitually invoked to maintain the boundaries between the social estates [*Stände*] has been denounced, says Ruge, 'it is only narrowness of mind to continue to give weight to these boundaries', which are 'illusory' in themselves, except for those which separate 'the knowers' from 'the ignorant' (a proviso that says a great deal about Ruge's world-view).[185] Marx sees things very differently. In the 'old system' of philistinism and generalized servitude, he detects the beginnings of new ruptures provoked by 'the system of industry and trade, of ownership and the exploitation of people'. These ruptures are anything but illusory; indeed, Marx affirms that they are literally insurmountable and unbearable within the limits of this system. Thus the antagonisms of the modern world, those which divide bourgeois society from within, *sunder* mankind into 'the animal world of philistinism which passively and thoughtlessly consumes' and 'suffering human beings who think', 'thinking human beings who are oppressed'.[186] In the union of the last two components of humanity, that is, theoreticians and the disinherited multitude – I am tempted to say 'true humanity' – Marx sees the condition for the long-awaited emergence of 'the product that the present time bears in its womb'.[187]

The political implication was twofold. On the conceptual plane, to begin with, Marx continued to hold that the political state was the place where the contradictions of civil society could be dialectically overcome, in line with his analyses in the *Rheinische Zeitung*. But whereas Ruge confined himself to the level of an abstract universality indifferent to the conflicts that traverse society, simply treating the modern state as synony-mous with the embodiment of human freedom, Marx contended that the 'political state expresses, within the limits of its form *sub specie rei publicæ*, all social struggles, needs, and truths'.[188] In the divergence between the state's inner purpose and its existing conditions, he saw the driving force behind a movement of democratization capable of abolishing the existing social order.[189] Moreover, this divergence was constitutive of the modern state as such, like the movement of democratization rooted in it. To highlight the difference between his *political* approach and those of the various socialist schools, Marx stressed that 'it is precisely the political state – in all its *modern* forms – which, even where it is not yet consciously imbued with socialist demands, contains the demands of reason'.[190]

In other words, 'rule by man' – that is, democracy – and 'rule by private property'[191] are contradictory, while 'specifically political questions' – for example, the transition from a system of assemblies of social estates [*Stände*] to representative institutions – express this 'difference' *sub specie rei publicæ*. Carried through to its full term, and generalized to the entire range of social activities, the democratization of political 'forms' (in the sense of 'institutions') transcends its own limits.[192] Indeed, says Marx, attaining its 'true significance' even amounts to its 'defeat', after which it becomes the principle animating a global reorganization of social rela-tions: access to the truth of the object implies the experience of its loss or dissolution in the whole set of mediations that make it up. To posit democracy as democratization, a transition from the 'specifically political form' of the representative system to the 'generalised form' that 'brings out its true significance', is to posit the primacy of processes and practices over institutions.[193] Political understanding can rise to a position of command over civil society only if it is posited as a transformative power immanent in social practice. As we have seen, the same principle governed Marx's approach in the preceding period as well. But there is a difference, and it is crucial from a strategic standpoint. Whereas the *Rheinische Zeitung* pinned its hopes on an expansion of the public sphere through develop-ment of the free press, so as not to have to begin by posing the 'specifically political' question of a change in regime, the letters to Ruge contend that it is necessary to begin with, precisely, the 'specifically political' question of representative institutions. In a word, the letters affirm that it is necessary to challenge the monarchy openly – on the understanding that, carried through to the end – that is, to the 'generalised form' of democracy – the process constantly exceeds this initial, institutional moment in order to contest 'rule by private property'.

Marx's insistence that democratization could resolve the contradictions internal to civil society – which has been described as a 'return to Hegelian "realism"'[194] – had another strategic consequence. When the question arose as to which real forces could provide the radical party in Germany with its base of support, Ruge, as we have seen, simply answered 'the people'; in his view, the work of criticism had made it possible to overcome all the social distinctions that divided it from itself. Marx, for his part, introduced an additional, critically important distinction: the petty bourgeoisie did not have a monopoly on the pettiness and philistinism of the petty-bourgeois spirit, for the German bourgeoisie was quite as thoroughly contaminated by them, and consequently incapable of leading a democratic revolution:

> The mistake which people made for a time was to attach importance to the desires and thoughts that would be expressed by the king. This could not alter the matter in the slightest: the philistine is the material of the monarchy and the monarch always remains only the king of the philistines: he cannot turn either himself or his subjects into free, real human beings while both sides remain what they are.[195]

'Exploitation' and 'domination' – which form, as Marx spells out in this letter, 'a single conception'[196] – draw dividing lines which, *pace* Ruge, are not easily effaced by criticism of the principles legitimizing the *ancien régime*.

This is how Marx begins to explore a political horizon broader than that of the French Revolution – at least if one considers the French Revolution, from the standpoint of its result, as a 'bourgeois' revolution that barely made a dent in the rule of property – whereas Ruge is content to make abstract references to the principles of 1789.[197] It follows, in Marx's estimation, that the fate of the democratic revolution in Germany rests wholly in the hands of an alliance made up of 'suffering human beings who think' and 'thinking human beings who are oppressed' – in the hands of a people that is precisely *not*-whole, and consequently acquires something of the character of a people-class, the exact nature of which remains, for the moment, enigmatic.

Hegel beyond Hegel

Before casting him out on to the roads of exile, the crisis of 1843 took, with Marx, what may seem like a paradoxical form, although it is in fact one rather typical of moments of rapid historical change: withdrawal into the solitude of his study. It was essentially from his father-in-law's study in Kreuznach that Marx bade his intellectual farewell to Germany. As we might expect, the exercise soon evolved into an (initial) settling of accounts with Hegel that also had Marx drawing up a balance sheet of the French Revolution – as if the intimate link between that seminal event and the philosopher who had revealed its theoretical import had to be demonstrated yet again, at the very moment when Marx was situating both Hegel and the Revolution within their limits.

The Kreuznach manuscript retraces this experience of limits. On the verge of a departure which, he knew, might well prove final, Marx returned to the scene of the crime – Hegel's unsuccessful attempt to solve the problem of the transition from civil society to the state – with an eye, as it were, to tracking Hegel down. In a paragraph-by-paragraph commentary on the core section of the chapter on the state in *Elements of the Philosophy of Right*, he sought to ferret out its secret weak point with the resolve typical of a last look. What he learned in the course of this attempt, which dates from the same period in which he wrote the letters to Ruge, was to be reworked and expanded upon in texts he would publish later in the *Deutsch–Französische Jahrbücher* ('On the Jewish Question'; 'Contribution to the Critique of Hegel's Philosophy of Law. Introduction'). This, no doubt, is why Marx considered the work he did in Kreuznach to have been nothing more than an exercise pursued for his own private purposes. The manuscript thus provides a fascinating – and revealing – glimpse behind the theoretical scenes of the dramatic political and existential shift then under way.

A Feuerbachian Marx?

The point of departure, which is also a self-critical result, is simply stated. It is no longer enough to propose alternatives to Hegel's mediations; the time has come to grasp things by the root and find out in what sense, and why, the paths taken by the Hegelian 'transition' from civil society to the state fail to provide a way out of the 'German *misère*'. In his reading of Hegel, Marx was to proceed as a consistent Hegelian, inverting Hegel and incorporating, in this inversion, Feuerbachian notions that seemed to him to offer useful springboards for a critique – but in a way that is still fundamentally Hegelian. Contrary to what most commentators suggest,[198] the Feuerbachian elements (the notion of 'species' [*Gattung*]; the 'trans-formative' method, that is, the inversion of subjects into predicates) are not simply transferred to a new domain[199] – politics rather than religion – but transformed as a result of their integration into a conceptual appara-tus that seeks to push the internal limits of the Hegelian system beyond themselves. That, for example, is how Marx treats the concept of 'species', as we shall see: instead of being reduced, as in Feuerbach, to a founding intersubjectivity incarnated in the originary, absolute experience of sexual love, species in Marx takes on a new meaning as it is pressed into the mould of the Hegelian notion of the 'life of the people'. Similarly, the inversion of subject into predicate is no longer a way of devaluing mediations and moving towards 'immediate sense certainty'; in a manner that is utterly alien to Feuerbach, it serves as a lever which enables the dialectical process to continue after breaking free of the bad abstractions that block its development in Hegel.

In other words, while Marx makes use of Feuerbach's criticism of religion, he does not adopt the analysis put forward in *The Essence of Christianity*, according to which religion is proper to man, the object that contains the totality of his essence and consciousness, but must be 'stripped of its veils' if its inner truth is to be exposed to view (a truth which is itself the whole truth of the human essence, and so on). Above all, while Marx recognizes, in the modern state, the expression of a form of political alienation, he does not make the state into something that is simply unreal, an inverted projection of the human essence which, in turn, has effects on social life (effects that go unexplained in Feuerbach). Grafting the Feuerbachian analysis of alienation on to the Hegelian notions of 'abstrac-tion' and 'representation', he seeks to explain the specific mechanisms that lead to the autonomization of political power. He essays a critique of *modern* politics, in so far as modern politics establishes a relation to the world very different from the one maintained by the theological-political complex of the *ancien régime* – even while he continues to retain something of its transcendence. Marx's critique seeks to trace matters back to the foundations of the new sphere, unprecedented in human history, which encompasses the bureaucracy, the legislature, and the representative system.[200] I should add that, by the time Marx joined the *Rheinische Zeitung*, he was already convinced that it was necessary to turn from the criticism of religion to political criticism.[201] He makes this plain enough in the letters to Ruge, which are contemporaneous with the

Kreuznach manuscript. While 'religion, and next to it, politics, are the subjects which form the main interest of Germany today', he writes, religion merely represents 'a register of the theoretical struggles of mankind': what must be criticized at present, 'the political state', will henceforth serve as 'a register of its practical struggles', as an expression of 'all social struggles, needs and truths'.[202]

If Marx brings Feuerbach's criticism of religion to bear on something other than its original object, it is, precisely, because he seeks to ferret out the elements of transcendence – more exactly, to use the term that recurs from one end of the manuscript to the other, the 'mystic elements' – in the Hegelian conception of the state, with a view to detecting its inner flaw. For, just as (to anticipate the formulations of the 1844 Introduction) 'the *ancien régime* is the *concealed deficiency* of the modern state',[203] so an element of transcendence continues to weigh heavily on the vision of the state developed in *Elements of the Philosophy of Right*. This element is insistently referred to as 'logical mysticism' in the Kreuznach manuscript. It is, says Marx, still religious, and its persistence explains why Hegel stubbornly maintains his '*uncritical, mystical* way of *interpreting* an *old world-view*', drawn straight from the *ancien régime*, 'in terms of a new one'.[204] But this regressive interpretation ultimately only reveals the truth of the modern state itself, in as much as it betrays its 'concealed deficiency', 'the thorn in [its] flesh'.[205] Hegel's failure to resolve the problem of the transition from civil society to the state reflects the inability of the modern world derived from the French Revolution to overcome the separation between society and a state that continues to retain something of the monarchy's transcendence. Thus the typically German lag between theory and sociopolitical reality serves, so to speak, as a chemical indicator of modernity's internal contradictions.[206] A critique of the mysticism of Hegel's political philosophy is not only the logical extension of the ongoing battle against the absolutist Christian state, but also a propaedeutic for the criticism of modern politics, in the same sense in which 'the criticism of religion is the premise of all criticism'.[207] But there is a difference: 'for Germany the *criticism of religion* is in the main complete',[208] whereas the criticism of the state has not even begun.

Just what does Hegel's failure consist in, according to Marx? In the fact that Hegel ceases, precisely, to be a Hegelian when, within the system of *Sittlichkeit*, he arrives at the moment of the state after working through those of the family and civil society. In other words, he fails because he is unable to honour his promise to proceed dialectically – to reconstitute the 'logic of the thing itself' – and, accordingly, to deduce the state from a civil society grasped in the strict immanence of its internally contradictory movement. In fact, Hegel approaches matters the other way round: 'the so-called "actual idea" (mind as infinite and actual) is presented as if it acted in accordance with a specific principle and with a specific intent. It divides into finite spheres; it does this "so as to return into itself, to be conscious of itself"; and this it does indeed so that what comes to pass is precisely what exists. At this point the logical, pantheistic mysticism becomes very clear.'[209] Instead of proceeding from the presupposed to the posed – that is, from the family and civil society to the state – Hegel poses these presuppositions as the result of the activity of a hypostatized Subject[210] that descends to the level of their finite existence only in order to contemplate the infinity of its own activity. The plane of immanence is thus abandoned in favour of an a priori idea, whose imaginary internal activity constitutes the world:

> Family and civil society constitute *themselves* as the state. They are the driving force. According to Hegel, they are on the contrary produced by the actual idea. It is not the course of their own life which unites them in the state; on the contrary, it is the idea which in the course of its life has separated them off from itself. Indeed, they are the finiteness of this idea. They owe their presence to another mind than their own. They are entities determined by a third party, not self-determined entities.[211]

The state ceases to be the result of a labour of mediation internal to the social totality; it acquires an ontological-logical substantiality, becoming an Absolute that is indifferent to the movement constitutive of reality, which, moreover, it pretends to dominate.

Hegel's 'deduction' of the state cannot be anything more than the semblance of a deduction, one which sets out from abstract generalities, not specific differences within the spheres of *Sittlichkeit*. The dialectical syllogism is stood on its head: rather than attaining concrete universality via the divisions engendered by the self-negation of the particular, Hegel begins with abstractions decked out with the attributes of the universal and derives the particular from them: 'the transition is thus derived, not from the particular nature of the family, etc., and from the *particular* nature of the state, but from the *general* relationship of *necessity* to *freedom*'.[212] The dialectic becomes a method external to its object, and enters into relation with the real only in search of a set of examples that can serve to illustrate its speculative developments. Thus it degenerates into a scholastics of the concept, which Marx explicitly compares to the theological demonstrations of the 'mystery' of the Holy Trinity.[213] Hegel is unable to produce the specific concept of the constitution, for his 'point of departure is the abstract idea, whose development in the state is the *political constitution*. What is therefore being treated here is not the political idea, but the abstract idea in the political element.'[214] Marx's conclusion, encapsulated in a well-known phrase, is that, in Hegel, 'not the logic of the matter, but the matter of logic is the philosophical element. The logic does not serve to prove the state, but the state to prove the logic.'[215]

It is hardly an accident, then, says Marx, that this state is none other than the actually existing one. The other side of Hegel's logical mysticism is merely submission to an empirical reality cloaked in ideal, abstract determinations: the result of 'this inversion of the subjective into the objective and of the objective into the subjective . . . is that an *empirical existent* is uncritically accepted as the actual truth of the idea; for it is not a question of bringing empirical existence to its truth, but of bringing truth to an empirical existent, and so what lies to hand is expounded as a real element of the idea'.[216] Because he turns the method that leads consciousness to the truth of process upside down,[217] Hegel is unable to bring the movement immanent to the real to its concept; instead, he relapses into a pre-critical posture in his attempt to effect a speculative transfiguration of the existent. 'In this way,' Marx adds, 'the impression is produced of something mystical and profound.'[218] The hyper-speculative autonomization of the universal, reduced to a transcendent Absolute, proves inseparable from what might seem to be its opposite, an uncritical empiricism that legitimates the existing order.

This empiricism – or, more precisely, this inversion of speculation into empirical reality, and vice versa – finds its extension in the places in which, according to Hegel, the universal is realized – the mediations that are supposed to solve the problem of the transition from civil society to the state. These are the bureaucracy, the legislative power in its relation to the constitution, and the mechanisms of political representation – in a word, the three pillars of the modern state. In the course of his analysis, Marx discovers a new facet of Hegel's logical mysticism in all three. Just as speculative hypostatization goes hand in glove with a trivial empiricism, so the spiritualization to which it subjects reality finds its counterpart in subordination to the 'crass materialism'[219] inherent in the existing order: the arrogance of the bureaucracy and the private property that becomes the true religion of the state. Once again, a critique of Hegel's political philosophy turns out to be inseparable from a critique of modern politics.

The bureaucracy as a system of power/knowledge

Let us begin our discussion with the bureaucracy. Pursuing the analyses he had published in the *Rheinische Zeitung*, Marx paints a disenchanted picture of the 'universal state', which, in Hegel's view, transcends the multiple interests of the 'estates' [*Stände*] of civil society. He regards the state, simply, as a particular corporation, the 'corporation of the state', 'a particular, closed society within the state'.[220] By dint of its very closure, which unites it with the essence of the corporatist spirit, the bureaucracy constitutes itself as the mirror-image, within the state, of the corporations of the other *Stände*; these, too, are caught up in a process that is supposed to lead them towards the state, although it in fact tends to promote their own bureaucratization. Whence the deep – albeit secret – solidarity between the existence of the bureaucracy and the organization of civil society in corporations; both are based on the suppression of 'real political life', that is, of democratization.[221]

Far from transcending the division running through civil society, the bureaucracy duplicates it by internalizing it within the state. It thereby creates a new split: that between bureaucratic knowledge and real knowledge, the knowledge of the people, which, by yet another inversion, is 'de-realized', that is, radically negated by the bureaucracy. The bureaucracy may be a corporation, but it is not a corporation like any other, for, by virtue of the real position it occupies in a 'hierarchy of knowledge' set up by the political state, it lays claim to embodying the general interest. It is not so much the straightforward projection of an alienated essence as an autonomized representation or real abstraction, inasmuch as it is a product of the separation of civil society and the state. This illusion may be 'imaginary', but it is also, Marx points out, 'practical'.[222] He adds that Hegel takes at face value precisely the bureaucracy's self-representation – the 'bureaucratic illusion' in so far as it is an integral part of the 'illusion of the state' – and lends it the semblance of a speculative foundation. To be sure, the bureaucracy transcends the particularism of interests only 'formally', in the manner of a categorical imperative, a consequence that would contradict its own premises if this formalism did not take itself for its own end and profess to attain the universal. The way it really functions thus reflects the separation between the material and formal principles at the basis of the political state, a separation which it reproduces, while endowing it with material form and, at the same time, the requisite supplement of ideality: 'since this "state formalism" constitutes itself as an actual power and itself becomes its own *material* content, it goes without saying that the "bureaucracy" is a web of *practical* illusions, or the "illusion of the state". The bureaucratic spirit is a Jesuitical, theological spirit through and through. The bureaucrats are the Jesuits and theologians of the state. The bureaucracy is *la république prêtre*'[223] – and, one might add, the state's theological supplement even if the state in question happens to be a republic.

Exemplifying the usurpation of social knowledge by one particular corporation, a usurpation exacerbated by its strict internal hierarchization, the bureaucracy appropriates the essence of the state, treating it as though it were its own private property – for it is the existence of private property which constitutes the real precondition for its own power. The principle informing this bureaucratic power resides both in the cult of secrecy, a direct consequence of the closed nature of the corporation, and in the worship of authority, the sole defence against those who might attempt to penetrate the mystery by force – that is to say, in the present case, the people, bearer of the true 'significance of the state' considered as the manifestation of its public existence. By particularizing the state and cutting it off from all forms of publicity, the bureaucracy transforms its spiritual principle into 'crass materialism, the materialism of passive obedience, of faith in authority, of the mechanism of fixed and formalistic behaviour, and of fixed principles, views and traditions'.[224] Crass materialism, then, cannot function without the symbolic supplement of an Authority that guarantees the sublimity of its principle (which is itself founded, let us not forget, on 'secrecy'), making it a veritable element of closure extended to the whole of social life. Identifying with the state, a veritable concentrate of power/ knowledge, the bureaucracy represents a permanent factor which tends to devalue public opinion and political spirit as a manifestation of the life of the people; it is, in short, a negation of everything that is democratic.

None of this is without consequences for the Hegelian conception of the state, which everywhere posits that 'the question as to what constitutes the State is one of advanced science, and not of popular decision'.[225] Here the Hegelian inversion of speculation into empirical reality, and vice versa, takes the form of an idealization of the bureaucracy and an empiricization of 'public consciousness'.[226] 'Forgetting' that the real state cannot claim to be 'the objectification of the *political attitude*', Hegel treats it as 'a finished thing', and identifies it with the government, that is, in the final analysis, the bureaucracy. This 'amnesia' is not the fruit of a simple logical error; it is, rather, an eminently political symptom of the fact that Hegel's thought is permeated by the spirit of the Prussian bureaucracy.[227]

Legislative power as constitutive power

Consequently, the bureaucracy is merely an illusory mediation between civil society and the state, an instrument of domination that absolutizes the capacities of a political formalism cut off from its real content. From time to time, however, Hegel makes the opposite – or, rather, inverse – mistake (we are still considering Hegel's mystical inversion of himself): he treats the material content as an absolute, isolated, here too, from its formal, conscious determinations. This occurs when he denies the legislature the legal right deliberately and formally to modify the constitution, or, *a fortiori*, to create another. The point is crucial: Marx, via an 'extraordinary combination of Spinoza and Rousseau',[228] does not take 'legislative authority' to refer to an already legitimate authority operating within the framework of a constitutional separation of powers, but, rather, to the power which creates the constitution, any constitution, and pre-exists it as it pre-exists the 'actual, empirical, established legislative authority'.[229] This authority is the 'representative of the people, of the will of the species', and this will is absolute. It has 'made the great, organic, general revolutions'; it is 'unqualified'; and it rests on the presupposition that, in principle, the 'movement of the constitution' is identical with its 'real bearer, the people'. Marx goes so far as to equate this authority with the political state as a whole,[230] radically subordinating the institutional level to that of constituent practices. Recapitulating the lessons of the French Revolution in a few lines, he spontaneously reproduces 'the master-principle governing Jacobin discourse'.[231] We have now left the field of the philosophy of law behind, and have come to the heart of the question of the political considered as a transformative, constitutive power,[232] the expansive capacity to reconstruct the real – a capacity, subject to no a priori limits, from which all constitutional and legal norms derive.

Hegel, says Marx, cannot resolve the 'antinomy' handed down to him by the tradition of constitutionalist thought: the 'collision' between legislative power considered, on the one hand, as the 'power to organize the universal . . . the power of the constitution' that 'reaches beyond' and 'subsumes it'; and, on the other, as a 'constitutional authority' 'subsumed under the constitution'.[233] His attempt to overcome this antinomy consists, to begin with, in exempting the constitution from 'direct determination' by the legislature, even though the constitution is the legislature's 'presupposition'. But this presupposition is condemned never to be 'posed'. At best, Hegel allows for indirect determination by the legislative power, which can partially and only gradually influence the lawmaking process, depending on circumstances independent of its will. 'In the nature of things and circumstances', the legislature can thus do 'what, from the nature of the constitution, it ought not to do. It does *materially* and *in fact* what *formally*, *legally*, and constitutionally it does not do.'[234] But this patently contradicts the Hegelian definition of the state as the 'highest presence of freedom', the absolute realization of the will and self-consciousness. Hegel simply displaces the antinomy of constitutionalism. The constitution is posited as pre-existent to the constitutive process: its development, which cannot accede to self-consciousness, contradicts its appearance, which remains unchanged.[235]

Behind these logical inconsistencies in Hegel, it is not very difficult to make out the political stakes – which are, quite simply, the question of revolution: 'Certainly, entire state constitutions have changed in such a way that gradually new needs arose, the old broke down, etc.; but for a *new* constitution a real revolution has always been required.'[236] But revolution is just what Hegel, learning the lessons of the French Revolution, wishes to avoid, in order to substitute for it the 'small revolutions' that can be undertaken on the government's initiative. These can, as easily as not, prove to be 'retrograde revolutions' or 'reactions':

> The legislature made the French Revolution; in general, wherever it has emerged in its particularity as the dominant element, it has made the great, organic, general revolutions. It has not fought the constitution, but a particular, antiquated constitution, precisely because the legislature was the representative of the people, of the will of the species. The executive, on the other hand, has produced the small revolutions, the retrograde revolutions, the reactions. It has made revolutions not for a new constitution against an old one, but against the constitution, precisely because the executive was the representative of the particular will, of subjective arbitrariness, of the magical part of the will.[237]

From this point on, matters are clear: Hegel is the theoretician of 'revolutions from above' as opposed to revolutions *tout court*, and this inversion breeds all the others. 'To invert Hegel' – or, if you prefer, to reestablish the proper relation between subject and predicate – is to take the opposite position. The right to make revolution is unconditional, for it alone establishes right; it alone can deliver political forms of their abstraction, and bring them into conformity with the life of the people: 'posed correctly, the question is simply this: Has the people the right to give itself a new constitution? The answer must be an unqualified "Yes", because once it has ceased to be an actual expression of the will of the people the constitution has become a practical illusion.'[238] In 'standing the Hegelian dialectic back on its feet', Marx was not so much borrowing

Feuerbach's transformational method as taking up a political position,[239] one that was intended to translate his new awareness of the imminence of the revolution into the language of philosophy. In a notebook that dates from his Kreuznach period, and is exactly contemporaneous with his manuscript on Hegel, Marx, glossing an essay of Ranke's on the Restoration in France, makes the point even more explicitly: 'in general, it is to be observed that the transformation of the subject into a predicate and the predicate into a subject, which puts the determined in place of what determines it, always portends an imminent revolution. And not only on the revolutionary side of the fence.'[240]

Of course, the political constitution is not the whole of a people's life, but only a partial expression of it (Marx calls it a 'compromise' or 'accommodation') that reflects a given state of the relationship between the political state (institutions) and the non-political state, or the sphere of social relations. This explains why it takes the form of a contract.[241] Similarly, 'legislative authority' becomes a 'metaphysical state function' as soon as it is divorced from the power of the executive, which attributes to the legislature the 'theoretical energy' of the popular will, distinguished from the 'practical' energy that the executive arrogates unto itself.[242] As we shall see, it is 'true democracy' which, by transcending and enveloping the political state, makes it possible to reorganize the relations between the two spheres, and to resolve the problem of the transition from civil society to the state while giving this transition its true name: revolution. In the course of writing his manuscript, Marx abandoned the standpoint he had adopted in the *Rheinische Zeitung*, which was identical to the one he had expressed in his letters to Ruge: in the Kreuznach manuscript, the political state has ceased to be the expression of 'all social struggles, needs and truths'. The dialectical process is now radicalized: the political state is but one of its moments, which, as the logic of the dialectic dictates, can attain its truth only at the price of its 'loss', of its disappearance as a fixed entity isolated from the internal labour of the mediations of the social totality.

But does this necessarily entail abandoning the political for the social, as a certain *doxa* would have it?[243] The answer is no, and in a double sense. To begin with, the political state 'disappears' only in so far as it is a separate entity, a power that has been rendered autonomous and claims to represent the totality. It is 'dissolved' into the constitutive processes of 'true democracy'. The twofold priority defended by Marx – that of democratization over democracy, and of practice over institutions – is taken to its logical conclusion by 'true democracy', which redefines politics in terms of constitutive power, or the expansive power to transform the real.[244] In other words, Marx is not in any sense an 'inverted liberal' who predicts the absorption of politics by a civil society restored to the transparency of its basic principle; he is a thinker of the eminently political conditions constitutive of its expansiveness, of the abolition of the separation between the (merely) political state and civil society.

What form does the question of institutions and the political constitution (in the strict sense) take in this context? Like Hegel, Marx is careful not to hold out a ready-made constitution, but he does indicate what the informing 'principle' of any constitution should be. In 'true democracy', the constitution ought to present itself as a form compatible with its own transformation, divested of all transcendence, and cognizant of its own limits. Its principle is 'movement': it should always be subject to emendation by its real bearer, the people. Here, then, we have a new priority, that of 'constitutionalization' over the constitution (in the narrow sense); it is derived from the primacy of the constituent process (in the broad sense) over institutions. The *process* of redesigning the constitution as it unfolded during the French Revolution, rather than one or another specific constitution, provides Marx with his historical reference.[245] The identity – it can be termed an 'identity of essence' – which he establishes between the 'legislative authority' in an Absolute, constitutive sense and the French Revolution, that 'great, organic, general revolution' (legislative power is precisely the power to 'organise the universal'),[246] leaves no room for doubt on this score.

Representation as political abstraction

While Marx defends the French Revolution, here as always, against anything that would turn the clock back to an earlier time – in this case, the Hegelian compromise – he is also intent upon establishing its limits, some of which Hegel had already grasped. For Marx, there is a term-by-term relation between Hegel and the French Revolution, whether Hegel retreats to positions behind it or advances beyond it; that is why the critique of Hegel is, once again, inseparable from that of the Revolution, and vice versa. More precisely, Marx's critique of Hegel is morphologically equivalent to his critique of the Revolution: just as he criticizes Hegel for his inconsistencies, so his analysis of the French experiment accentuates the fact, not that it was 'bourgeois', but that it remained *incomplete.* Moreover, Marx's explanation as to why the Revolution was left unfinished would provide the matrix for a further displacement of the political in his thought, thanks to which he would, taking its internal limits as his point of departure, reach a new understanding of it.

This is shown by Marx's discussion of the question of political representation. As in his analysis of legislative authority, so here, too, he quickly moves beyond the framework of an abstract legal discussion. The great merit of the French Revolution, he says, is that it created representative institutions based on universal suffrage and the equality of all citizens before the law, and this advance is irreversible. To grasp both its import and its limits is, *ipso facto*, to define the contents and aims of any new revolution, which will have to take matters up where the preceding revolution left them.

For, says Marx, the French Revolution did not, any more than Hegel, resolve the problem of the transition from civil society to the state – and Hegel had already understood its failure to do so, in the constant lag that separated him from the event even as it bound him to it. However, whereas *Lectures on the Philosophy of History* emphasizes the 'spiritual' or cultural aspect of the revolutionary experiment[247] (no Reformation [*Réforme*] had preceded this revolution, which developed in externality), Marx shifts his own analysis towards the nexus between the social and the political. Moreover, his verdict has a very different ring to it: although the French Revolution, because it was left unfinished, failed to resolve the problem of the transition, it nevertheless did make it possible to pose it – the point is crucial – in the right terms. Indeed, 'only the French Revolution completed the transformation of the *political* into *social* estates, or changed the *differences of estate* of civil society into differences of social life which are without significance in political life. With that the separation of political life from civil society was completed.'[248] This could just as readily be put the other way round: in order to shatter the transcendence to which despotism laid claim, the French Revolution also had to shatter the immediate unity between the political and the social on which that transcendence rested, for this unity was the unity of unfreedom. Political representation simply gives direct, frank expression to this act of separation between civil society and the state, the founding act of modernity: 'the representative constitution is a great advance, since it is the *frank, undistorted*, consistent expression of the modern condition of the state. It is an *unconcealed* contradiction.'[249] 'Political representation', Marx adds, 'does not *keep* civil and political life separate; it is merely the *representation of a really existing separation*',[250] which it re-creates, in its turn, in the separation between the abstract, represented people and the real people.[251]

This statement would, however, remain insufficient if Marx did not expand on it in an analysis of the effects of the rupture brought about by the revolutionary phenomenon. By giving full expression to the contradiction between civil society and the state, the French Revolution radically transformed both its terms. To put it differently: dualism was not abolished but, rather, displaced within the space delimited by the two poles of the contradiction. This created a new split between 'man', a member of civil society, and the 'citizen', a member of the state. It is only by 'abstracting' from his condition as man and his insertion into the organization of civil society that the political subject can become a citizen and make his entry into the political community: it is only as a 'sheer, blank individuality' who accepts the fact that the political is divorced from the social that he can take part in the life of the state, which is based on the freedom and equality of its citizens. The state, the result of a process of abstraction, constitutes itself as an abstraction: it is a merely political state, a contradictory form of community that is confronted from the outside by a civil society which the atomism of private interests has torn apart. For if the political state is an abstraction, it is a *real* abstraction: '[the current notion of the state] is also atomistic, but it is the atomism of society itself. A "view" cannot be concrete when its *subject*-matter is abstract. The atomism into which civil society plunges in its *political act* follows necessarily from the fact that the community, the communistic essence [*das kommunistische Wesen*] in which the individual exists, is civil society separated from the state, or that the political state is an *abstraction* from it.'[252] This abstraction produces, in its turn, real effects: by virtue of its representative character, the modern state establishes a new division between the represented and their representatives, the represented and the real people; it reflects the atomism of particular interests and contradicts the substantial expression of the life of the people. The political state is 'abstract' in the sense suggested by the etymology of the word; it appears as the residue or 'precipitate' of the constitutive movement by means of which civil society transcends its own limits to attain political existence, while leaving its internal differences intact, or, rather, transforming them into mere 'differences of *social* life' 'without significance in political life'.[253]

The state is incapable of substantially affecting the contents of civil society, for it is, precisely, a product of civil society's abstraction from itself. Hence the state can overcome social differences only in imaginary ways, in the heaven of the equality that prevails between the subjects of law.[254] Separated from social life, political life becomes a secularized religion rather than a secular politics – 'the ethereal regions of civil society'[255] – claiming, in its turn, to represent the universal, and give form to the life of civil society as a whole. This is the source of the political illusion, which is not merely a lag internal to consciousness, but the counterpart to the state's real abstraction or existence as the autonomized power of society.

Hegel rises to the level of the French Revolution by grasping the import of this separation and posing it as a contradiction.[256] But he completely fails to recognize the mediations which would allow him to resolve the contradiction. Worse, in stubbornly defending the system of representation by estates [*Stände*], at the price of multiple logical and empirical convolutions, he makes it impossible to recognize even the preconditions for these mediations. Characteristically, he cannot so much as 'name' the object of the controversy (a representative constitution as opposed to a constitution based on estates). Indeed, he attempts to 'cobble together' a modern solution out of the stuff of the *ancien régime*.[257] he wants the estates of civil society to operate like the immediately political estates of the Middle Ages, and therefore makes them expressions of the separation of state and civil society, as well as their identity. Rather than producing a mediation, in the dialectical sense, he simply falls back on an intermediate solution, 'composite mixtures', frameworks for negotiation between wills separated in advance.[258] Thus he proceeds inconsistently with his deepest intuition: the contradiction at the origins of the modern separation between the state and civil society.

Hegel turns a blind eye to the necessity of political abstraction, to that which makes it the true foundation of modern politics. The reason for this is simple, and brings us back to the same reasons that led him to devalue 'legislative authority': 'in the modern sense, in the sense expounded by Hegel, the political-estates element is the *separation of civil society from its civil estate* and its *distinctions, assumed as accomplished*'.[259] But, in order to 'pose' and 'accomplish' this self-separation, civil society must literally take leave of itself, undergo a 'transubstantiation', 'jump over a chasm', as Marx reminds us. In a word, it must undergo a revolution. It is, naturally, at this point that Hegel begins to draw back: 'it is here, however, not a question of a gradual *transition* but of a *transubstantiation* and it is useless to refuse to see the chasm to be jumped over, which the jump itself demonstrates'.[260] The degeneration of the dialectic into an evolutionary gradualism becomes apparent from the moment Hegel sets out to detach the constitution from the process leading up to it: namely, the activity of the 'legislative authority'. Hence it is only logical that it should reappear when it is a question of understanding the 'political act' 'into which civil society plunges'[261] as a revolutionary act, as the moment in which the legislature begins to act as a constituent power.

Hegel's 'accommodation'[262] to German political realities thus places him, to begin with, in a position on the far side of the historical achievement of the political revolution – or, if you prefer, of the revolution to the extent that it remains merely political. This explains his wilful blindness to the sense in which the principle of elections, representative institutions, and universal suffrage represent, despite their limits, a historical advance. Hegel's distrust of the legislature, the agent of the revolutionary process, prevents him from seeing that the demand for the 'greatest possible *generalisation* of *election*' to the legislature, its full reappropriation by civil society, reflects an effort, however limited or self-contradictory, to make political reality and social reality coincide, and thereby to overcome the dualism that keeps society and state separate. But only elections, with the suppression of all restrictions on the franchise and voter eligibility, make it possible to establish a '*direct* relation of civil society to the political state – a relation that is not *merely representative but actually exists*'.[263] Thus Marx, who in this respect places himself in the tradition of the Rousseauist critique of representation,[264] draws a crucial distinction between, on the one hand, the unlimited franchise and the electoral principle, which are universally valid, and, on the other, political representation as a form of reproduction, within the state, of the separation of the political state from civil society.

Viewed in this light, the existence of representative institutions is a compromise solution, the only possible form of participation in a political state in so far as it remains a power separate from civil society; it is the abolition of the political state within its own limits.[265] It is an abstract form – in the sense that, through this form, by posing its political existence as its true existence, civil society ends up abstracting itself from itself. But it is an abstract form that calls for its own supersession. The process leading to universal suffrage (the French Revolution and the struggles for electoral reform in England: it should be borne in mind that Marx wrote the Kreuznach manuscript only a few months after the Chartist uprising of summer 1842) entails a demand for the abolition of the separate existence of civil society, and thus also for the abolition of the political state and representative institutions; it reflects the tendency to transcend this separation within the limits of political abstraction itself.

Marx was never to waver on this point. In the language of 'On the Jewish Question', this means that political emancipation is well and truly a form of human emancipation, the most advanced form possible 'in the hitherto existing world order', and that the possibility of human emancipation can be raised only on the basis of political emancipation, as an internal rectification of the movement leading up to it.[266] In the *Commu-*

nist Manifesto, Marx and Engels express the same notion by saying that it is impossible to imagine the emancipation of the proletariat before 'winning the battle of democracy', synonymous in its turn with 'raising the proletariat to the position of ruling class'.[267] A quarter of a century later, we again find the same general idea in Marx's recognition that the constitution of the Paris Commune was a 'thoroughly expansive political form', 'a political form at last discovered under which to work out the economic emancipation of labour'.[268]

The origins of permanent revolution: 'True democracy'

The Kreuznach manuscript, the first fruit of the 1842–43 crisis, represents a moment of rupture in the formation of Marx's thought: here political criticism is transformed into a criticism of the political in a re-examination of the status, sites and limits of modern politics. Within a basically Hegelian conceptual framework, the political is subjected to a crucially important displacement: distinguished from all that pertains directly to the state, it is stripped of the last remnants of transcendence, to appear from now on as a transformative power immanent in the various social practices. In other words, the political state no longer functions as an Absolute, the culmination of the self-constitution of civil society, as it still did in the *Rheinische Zeitung* articles. To return, by inverting Hegel, to the logic of the thing itself, Marx carries the dialectical process through to its full term: the moment in which the political state attains its truth as the democratic state is simultaneously the moment of its loss or disappearance as a distinct entity, the source and mainstay of the political illusion. But this disappearance is synonymous with a displacement of the political, which, redirecting its expansive capacity, emerges as the ongoing democratic refoundation of all the material conditions of the political. These conditions are defined as concrete social activities – the constitution of the life of the people.

This is what the concept of 'true democracy' is charged with expressing: as the vogue for 'calling things by their true names' that took the period by storm had it,[269] democracy was 'true' if it corresponded to its concept – or, rather, if it was swept up in the internal movement that would carry it towards its concept. Plainly, then, 'true democracy' was not primarily defined as either an institutional project or a set of procedures, even if institutions and procedures comprised a part of what it was. True democracy referred to a set of constituent processes that gave condensed expression to the permanent self-criticism of civil society. Marx presented three of its principal modes, which we need to attend to in some detail here: true democracy as a real tendency, as an 'absolute' ('material' and 'formal') capacity for transformation, and as an expansive process, a force drawing bourgeois society beyond its own limits.

Was Marx a Spinozan?

Let us begin with the definition of democracy as the 'truth' of 'all state forms', 'the solved *riddle* of all constitutions'.[270] Here Marx seems to adopt the Spinozan notion according to which the democratic state is 'the most natural' of all, 'approaching most closely to that freedom which Nature grants to every man'.[271] In Spinoza's view, democracy should be understood as an internal tendency at work in all forms of government; it channels the displacement of the relationship between the power of the multitude and the state in a direction that tends to make them coincide. Many commentators have pointed out that Marx adopts Spinoza's conception of democracy.[272] But, if so, he inverts it in the process. Spinoza, who comes up against an aporia – the (im)possibility that a multitude should be capable of self-government[273] – has no choice but to define democracy as a stabilizing element that works upon other forms of government from within, and, consequently, as a limit case without a principle of its own (the *Tractatus Politicus* breaks off, precisely, in the midst of the chapter on democracy). So conceived, democracy would be the one absolutely real political tendency, and, at the same time, the one absolutely utopian form of government. Marx, for his part, cuts the Gordian knot: he simply identifies democracy with the 'genus constitution', and treats all other forms of government as species of this genus.[274] For Spinoza, democracy is inconceivable unless one sets out from its other. Ultimately, it is a kind of perfect aristocracy in which the sovereign assembly tends to expand until it encompasses the whole people,[275] or even a popular monarchy capable of bringing the power conferred upon the king into perfect conformity with the power of the people itself.[276] Marx contends, in contrast, that 'democracy is the truth of monarchy, monarchy is not the truth of democracy. Monarchy is necessarily democracy inconsistent with itself; the monarchical element is not an inconsistency in democracy. Monarchy cannot be understood in its own terms; democracy can.'[277] More generally, 'it goes without saying that all forms of state have democracy for their truth and that they are therefore untrue insofar as they are not democracy'.[278]

If this is so, it is because Marx feels nothing of the ambivalence which makes the masses,[279] for Spinoza, simultaneously the unique source of political power and an object that must be directed and contained in order to ensure the stability of the state. Because of this ambivalence, Spinoza rejects all forms of revolution, which for him is synonymous with the destructive – and also self-destructive – movement of a multitude become an anarchic mob, prey to its sad passions and primitive, superstitious imagination.[280] In contrast, the Kreuznach manuscript defines democracy as the 'self-determination of the people', and at least tendentially identifies it with the political as such, considered as a mode of existence of the 'people' or the 'whole *demos*' reappropriating the totality of its human essence. For, since Spinoza's time, the experience of the French Revolution had left its mark on history – the indelible mark of the masses' intervention in the process by which freedom becomes a necessity. Democracy, a conscious human creation, an emancipation from any determination that seeks to place itself above the activity of the people, embodies the inner truth of the political principle, just as Christianity, in so far as it is the alienated projection of the human essence, embodies the truth of the religions that preceded it.

Democracy represents a fully secularized politics from which the last remnants of transcendence – including, as we shall soon see, the one that erects the political itself into a quasi-religious Absolute – have been eliminated: 'to democracy all other forms of state stand as its Old Testament. Man does not exist for the law but the law for man – it is a *human* manifestation; whereas in the other forms of state man is a *legal* manifestation. That is the fundamental distinction of democracy.'[281] The law, the constitution, and the existing forms of power are human realities. As such, they are susceptible to transformation through human action, which is subject to no limits other than those that are internal to such action, as is demonstrated by the entire history, with its triumphs and defeats, of the revolutionary experience.

Marx's critique of essentialism

Democracy, then, is recognition of the true subject, the one that Hegel's logical mysticism spirits away: namely, real man, the real people. But how should the notions of 'subject', 'man', or even 'species' [*Gattung*] and 'species-being' [*Gattungswesen*] be understood? Some of Marx's formulations might lead us to believe that what is involved here is a pure and simple transposition of Feuerbachian concepts. Thus Marx speaks of the 'communistic [*kommunistisch*] being' within which individual existence unfolds;[282] the alienated expression of this communistic being is represented by the political state. Again, he regards legislative power as the 'will of the species',[283] and makes the gap between essence and existence the driving force behind the movement that brings about democracy. For Marx, what actually exists thus appears as a split between, on the one hand, a generic abstraction, the purely political state which, at the imaginary level, transcends its empirical contents; and, on the other, those contents themselves, born of the division internal to civil society. Does it follow that the people, regarded as the embodiment of the species, is a figure of the One, an originary substance that, identical with itself and wholly unmarked by finitude, provides an a priori guarantee that historical development is meaningful? If this were the case, 'true democracy' would simply be a creation *ex nihilo*, the result of a pure act; while the subject of the political would be a pure self-activity that does not enter into a relation with anything other than itself. We would accordingly have to range Marx alongside Moses Hess and the partisans of a philosophy of action of a Fichtean–Bauerian inspiration;[284] furthermore, the movement of history would be reduced to an evolutionary process necessarily culminating in a revelation of the essence of the state – that is, the full self-presence of the species Man.

It is true that Marx's utilization of Feuerbachian concepts, even if he reworks them, is not without consequences. The temptation to resort to a teleology of the human essence, realizing itself by way of a simplified dialectic of the transition from existence to essence, undeniably functions as a factor of internal instability in Marx's text. If, however, we pay close attention to the crisscrossed concepts brought together in the conceptual apparatus that Marx puts to work here, matters appear in a somewhat different light. To begin with, we need to notice that the species-being in question is not traced back, as it is in Feuerbach, to any kind of originary intersubjective situation; this means that the political, as Marx understands it, cannot be the expression of a communal tie or a pure interhuman bond.[285] Instead of this purity of origins, we find the Hegelian notion of the 'life of the people'.[286] As for the notion of species, it exists only as self-determination of the people, a moment in which the people actually attains its concept. And, whatever we care to say about it, this process – for what is in question is quite clearly a process, not an ecstatic moment or a leap beyond history – implies the existence of an irreducible lag, which, incidentally, invests 'true democracy' with the paradoxical status it has in political thought.

Where does the irreducible opposition between the logic of the concept and anthropological essentialism lie? We have already encountered it in the paradoxical evolution of the state. The dialectician does not, once the political state attains its concept, celebrate the advent of its 'essence', revealed at last; rather, he announces its 'disappearance' or dissolution in the network of mediations that the constitutive process has brought to light. Similarly, when it is a question of determining, in positive fashion, the ultimate human essence, Marx becomes highly elliptical, precisely where Feuerbach (or, in the same vein, Hess) is prolix (see below). It as if this essence melted away just when it is was supposed to appear 'in person'. Indeed, it is the illusion that there exists something like an occulted essence beyond phenomenal existence, something of the order of an abstract Absolute, which the movement of the concept sets out to dispel.

This is evident from the manner in which Marx criticizes, before the fact, the essentialist positions that would gain the greatest currency in his day: he treats them as characteristic of the political illusion. It is precisely when civil society takes itself for a unified whole and hastens to accomplish 'the political act' (which necessarily seems to it to be a 'sensational act', an 'ecstasy'), in order to accede to an 'essential' beyond, that it misses its goal (which consists in overcoming its separation from the state and achieving political existence, its authentic existence). Hence it succeeds only in attaining the abstraction of the purely political state,[287] which is thereby condemned to misunderstand itself: it identifies itself with the life of the people as a whole, professing to master its determinations at the very moment when it is subject to them. Absolutized private property, which holds sway over a civil society liberated from the bonds of the *ancien régime*, becomes the profane religion of the contemporary world, while bureaucratic formalism exercises an imaginary mastery over the antagonisms dividing society.

In 'On the Jewish Question', Marx was to make the same critique, pursuing the analyses of the limits of the 1789–93 experiment that he had begun in the Kreuznach manuscript in order to show that the political emancipation brought about by the French Revolution had, even in its 'terrorist' phase, paid tribute to an illusory belief in the omnipotence of the political – and, we may add, of the 'people' as well, for that was the magic word of the day. In this sense, the Revolution's Jacobin phase and the Jacobin phrase-mongering which 'declar[ed] the revolution to be permanent' could only prolong, by coercive means, the 'sensational act' accomplished at the political level; to go further, it would have had to transcend its own internal limits.[288] Of course, as we have seen, this revolutionary 'failure' was 'necessary'; it represented a 'great advance' – not in the banal sense of a way-station on the road to the realization of a pre-established plan, but because it was only by way of this failure that historical necessity could be constituted. By establishing a representative regime, it produced a '*frank, undistorted, consistent* expression of the *modern condition of the state*', its 'unconcealed contradiction'.[289] It thereby made it possible to *recognize* this contradictory situation, so that the historical imperative to supersede it could emerge. Thus Marx redefined the unfinished Revolution's 'incompleteness': it was not a momentary pause in a linear advance towards an ultimate truth, but a necessity that had been retroactively constituted by the failure of what the Revolution itself took to be its inherent purpose.

The 'people' in a 'true democracy' is thus something more than the abstract 'people' of the French Revolution, because Marx assumes from the first that 'true democracy' is the self-criticism of the merely political revolution and the representative democratic state. The words 'the state is an abstraction, the people alone is what is concrete'[290] should be understood to mean 'the concrete people, the people of "true democracy," is the bearer of the real movement that puts an end to the abstraction of the merely political state, whatever form it may take'. Hence 'true democracy' cannot simply be identified with 'the Republic', for the Republic remains 'merely political': 'the struggle between monarchy and republic is itself still a struggle within the abstract state. The *political* republic is democracy within the abstract state form. The abstract state form of democracy is therefore the republic; but here it ceases to be the *merely political* constitution.'[291]

The Republic goes beyond the limits of abstraction once the content of the state ceases to be external to it. The United States provides the proof *a contrario*: 'Property, etc., in short, the entire content of the law and the state, is the same in North America as in Prussia, with few modifications. The *political* republic is democracy within the abstract *state form*, as is the monarchy here.'[292] This form remains an alienated form, reflecting the division between the political state and civil society. It is a secularized form of religion, not a truly secular politics, and it is heir to something of the transcendence of the theological-absolutist state: 'up till now the *political constitution* has been the religious *sphere*, the *religion* of national life, the heaven of its generality over against the earthly existence of its actuality. . . . *Political life* in the modern sense is the *scholasticism* of national life. *Monarchy* is the perfect expression of this estrangement. The *republic* is the negation of this estrangement within its own sphere'.[293]

Redefining the political

Moving beyond abstraction accordingly implies dispelling the practical illusion that misleads the political state into taking itself for an embodiment of the totality:

> In democracy the political state, which stands alongside this content and distinguishes itself from it, is itself merely a *particular* content and particular *form of existence* of the people. In monarchy, for example, this particular, the political constitution, has the significance of the *general* that dominates and determines everything particular. In democracy the state as particular is *merely* particular; as general, it is the truly general, i.e., not something determinate in distinction from the other content. The French have recently interpreted this as meaning that in true democracy the *political state is annihilated*. This is correct insofar as the political state *qua* political state, as constitution, no longer passes for the whole.[294]

Thus it is by acknowledging its own particularity and becoming aware of its own limits – which requires that it first accomplish the difficult task of radically reducing its transcendent elements: of, that is, reducing the state to its true foundation, self-determination of the people – that the political state opens up a space for the reunification of the formal and material principles. The rest of the passage spells this out: 'in all states other than democratic ones the *state*, the *law*, the *constitution* is what rules, without really ruling – i.e., without materially permeating the content of the remaining, non-political spheres. In democracy the constitution, the law, the state itself, insofar as it is a political constitution, is only the self-determination of the people, and a particular content of the people.'[295]

Thus the encounter between the state and its concept – the self-determination of the people – comes about not when one adds something to the state (which would make it, for example, a totalizing and even tendentially totalitarian super-subject) but, quite the opposite, when one *takes something away* from it: namely, the illusion that it stands above civil society even while claiming to dominate it. Situated within its inherent limits, grasped in the element of its finitude, the state 'disappears' – but only as a separate entity, a fixed, immutable given – in order to dissolve into the network of mediations that constitute concrete universality. Marx defines this disappearance with great precision, situating his own views *vis-à-vis* the 'recent interpretations' advanced by the 'French'.[296] The 'disappearance' of the political state does not in any way signify the pure and simple absence of law, a constitution, or even state institutions – Marx is quite immune to all 'anarchist' temptations[297] – but, rather, a constant effort to decentre that frees juridico-political forms of their 'determinateness' [*Bestimmtheit*: abstract, passive determination] in order to restore their 'self-determination' [*Selbstbestimmung*], defined as the self-determination of the people.

In this sense, the moment of the truth of the state is also the moment of its loss, which clears the way for a displacement of the relationship between 'political spheres' and 'non-political spheres', that is, a displacement of the status of the political itself. But how, then, is this displacement to be understood? Is what is involved here an 'inversion' that would replace the political with the social? Or is it a moment of epiphany that would enable the light of the political principle to penetrate all the spheres of society at once?[298] If we follow the thread of Marx's argument, the position that gradually emerges differs from both alternatives: the displacement in question here is, rather, a transformation of the political that amounts to posing it as a power of transformation. In other words, that which, in its immanent movement, 'precipitated' civil society into a domain beyond its limits (by means of an 'act' that it took for an 'ecstasy' and a revelation of its hidden substance), that which presented itself, precisely, as the Absolute of the political, the merely political state, *was already the political.* Or again: the political is nothing other than the very movement that traces the political back to its material and social conditions, conditions which it is then brought to acknowledge as its own. The political is the permanent self-criticism of a civil society which has become conscious of itself, one which subverts its own limits and posits itself as the power of self-transformation.[299] After democracy as a merely political form comes 'true democracy'. It supersedes the 'abstract' and 'partial' nature of its predecessor[300] by liberating the principle at its core and pushing back its limits, thereby revolutionizing the very foundations of the life of the people, the relations constitutive of civil society. Decentring the political state is tantamount to transcending the separation between the formal and the material principle:[301] the relationship of the political to the non-political is 'inverted' in its turn, the 'non-political' spheres are grasped from within, and their 'content' is subjected to the labour of democratic transformation, which reveals their immanently political character.

Viewed in this light, the 'practice of true democracy' designates an eminently *expansive* process, the self-criticism of a civil society understood as inherently political; it is the threshold above which the politicization of the various social instances and the socialization of the political become coextensive. This is clearly the content of a 'new' revolution which is simply the reflection of the 'old' one upon itself, the political revolution which recognizes that it was not merely political, after all: 'true democracy' forms the horizon of the 'true revolution'. In other words, at the very moment in which he poses, *in their finitude*, the moment of the political state and the political emancipation that emerged from the French Revolution, Marx, like Heine before him, revives the tradition of Jacobin radicalism, the refusal to 'finish the revolution', the idea of a permanent revolutionary process that radically overturns the whole social order. Only by developing an immanent critique of the political state and political emancipation, and by placing himself in the historical movement that the very failure of the Year II made possible, can Marx rise to the historical level of the Jacobin leadership, which he would later seek to conceptualize as that of 'radical' – that is to say, permanent – revolution.[302]

Democracy and the transparent society

Thus the Kreuznach manuscript leads us on to the continent that *Elements of the Philosophy of Right* had already identified as central – namely, the anatomy of civil society. For the moment, however, Marx does not venture on to this new terrain, which was to be the object of the critique of political economy that he would start to work out in Paris in the set of texts known as the '1844 Manuscripts'. He does, however, set out those elements of the 'critique of Hegel's presentation of civil society'[303] that he needs for his present purposes. His starting point is the internal transformations brought about in the estates of civil society when civil society is divorced from political society; he begins, in other words, with the emergence of specifically modern social relations. It was Hegel's belief that the fundamental contradiction of modern society resided in the inherent impossibility of moving beyond the particularity of atomistic objectives; he argued that the consequence was an ever more pronounced polarization between wealth and poverty, ceaselessly reproduced by the play of the system of needs and an increasingly specialized division of labour. He further discerned in this process the formation of a 'class tied to such specializ[ed] and limit[ed] work'; as it sank into poverty, he said, it tended increasingly to become a 'large mass' [*grosse Masse*] and, consequently, a 'rabble' [*Pöbel*], always ready to explode in revolt, and lacking all 'feeling of right, integrity, and honour'.[304] Marx radicalizes Hegel's thesis by showing how the contradiction informing civil society engenders a division that is internal to man's being and an alienated existence that stands the relation between means and ends on its head.

He introduces his argument with the observation that the disintegration of the premodern community has given rise to a social order which,
though fluid as a result of its emancipation from the rigidities of the
ancien régime, is nevertheless fundamentally irrational. It is a profoundly
hierarchical social order which neither politics nor the system of needs
suffices to render intelligible:

> Within society itself, however, the difference was developed in mobile and not
> fixed circles, of which *free choice* is the principle. *Money* and *education* are the
> main criteria. . . . The estate of civil society has for its principle neither need,
> that is, a natural element, nor politics. It consists of separate masses which form
> fleetingly and whose very formation is fortuitous and does *not* amount to an
> organization.[305]

Marx develops the observation far enough to note – without, however,
dwelling on the point or assigning it any particular positive function –
that the pauperized masses that emerged out of the class tied to the
segmented labour process were not a simple, if inevitable, by-product of
the contradiction that saps the foundations of bourgeois society, as Hegel
had thought. Rather, they formed its very basis: 'only one thing is
characteristic, namely, that *lack of property* and the *estate of direct* labour, of
concrete labour, form not so much an estate of civil society as the ground
upon which its circles rest and move'.[306]

Marx says no more on this subject, promising to pursue it later.[307]
Hence we search in vain for the proletariat in the Kreuznach manuscript;
indeed, we do not even find the radical rejection of private property that
is a feature of all of Marx's work beginning with 'On the Jewish Question'.
For the moment, it is the theme of the alienation of the human essence
that holds centre stage. The basic division of civil society leaves the
individual without communal ties (Marx, let us note in passing, had no
great yearning for their return, since he identified them, as we have seen,
with the community of non-freedom), and makes his integration into
society a purely external determination, a private status that he has to
relinquish in order to attain to what is henceforth the sole accessible
communal/human form, the abstraction of the political state. Disconnected from his real, communal being, the individual discovers that his
existence is rooted in contradictory social spheres; the links between them
appear to be accidental and, as it were, optional.[308] The result is not
freedom; rather, the individual is confronted with a disjunction or radical
break between freedom and its real conditions. This break, in turn,
spawns a new inversion: henceforth the separate individual existence takes
itself for its own end, reducing its real contents to the level of a means

and nursing illusions about its limited nature, which it confuses with concrete emancipation.[309] It is in this sense that the liberation of civil society flies in the face of the promise of modern freedom.

A rationalist impulse nevertheless runs through this irrational order. Marx sums it up with a term of social-ist provenance, '*organisation*'. The social-ist tenor of the word (which locates the essence of the social in a metapolitical principle of harmonization)[310] stands out all the more sharply in that it is opposed to the organizational pretensions (Marx speaks of 'organisational forms') that come from on high, from a political state that seeks to dominate (in a necessarily formal manner) the contents from which, as a merely political state, it is separated by its very nature.[311] Has Marx, in his turn, lapsed into the '*grand récit* of organization'? Does he, too, seek to restore, by devising new social technologies, the original harmony and transparency of social relations? A passage in the Kreuznach manuscript would seem to indicate that this is indeed the case; it suggests that the representative character of legislative power will have been transcended once individual activities and species-activities coincide. This would make 'every person ... the representative of every other'.[312] We would thus arrive at a state in which the individual is absolutely immanent in the species – something like a radical reduction of social relations to transparent, harmonious intersubjective relations.

Marx's formulations are admittedly rather elliptical and quite difficult to interpret. After all, even when the legislature is stripped of its representative character and no longer separated from the executive – when both are subject to the incessant constituent activity of the people exercising self-determination – it is destined to remain a part of 'true democracy', like the principle of elections, the law, and the constitution. True democracy is still a *state form*:[313] this most certainly rules out both anti-political readings as well as confusion with the problematic of the withering away of the state, but it is not of much help when it comes to determining the specific content of the practices of democratization typical of true democracy. The first part of 'On the Jewish Question' seems clearer: it culminates in a definition of human emancipation as something which 'will have been accomplished' 'only when man has recognised and organised his "*forces propres*" as *social* forces, and consequently no longer separates social power from himself in the form of political power'.[314] But, here again, one is hard put to say what this recognition/organization of social forces or the political practices it presupposes is meant to include.

All things considered, we can only affirm that Marx, although he falls back on the dialectic of existence and the human essence, nevertheless consistently avoids (although his recourse to this dialectic would normally lead him to do precisely the opposite) anything resembling a systematic treatment, full-scale depiction or positive representation of the concrete universality that he now projects beyond the horizon of civil society and the political state. He offers us nothing comparable, in this respect, to the socialist theoreticians' maniacally precise descriptions, nor does he make long lyrical speeches on 'love' and the universal attraction of Being, of the sort we would expect from a Feuerbach or a Moses Hess.[315] We can perhaps hazard the hypothesis that this stubborn avoidance, this near-total silence, provide, if not the answer to the question, at least the beginnings of a displacement of it. To put it differently, these as yet 'white metaphors' of concrete universality (which, admittedly, are extremely unstable, because they are partially veiled by the massively essentialist language that Marx borrows from Feuerbach) may represent the only available means of evoking a radically open-ended political form that is yet to come, one towards which Marx is still groping his way in the abstraction of a critique of Hegel that he simultaneously intends as a critique of the limited political emancipation actually achieved by bour-geois society. If this is correct, it follows that the reference to the species is haunted by a constitutive instability; that it is a provisional notion subject to progressive destabilization; and that it operates like the spectral trace of a different social logic, one which comes from the future and is yet lodged at the heart of bourgeois social relations. For its part, 'true democracy', defined as the self-presence of the human essence, would be more an appeal (straining only a little, one might say a performative construction) for a democratic political practice that does not yet exist or, more precisely, has not yet been recognized – and cannot yet be 'named' – rather than a stable concept awaiting its systematic presentation. We might push the point and argue that 'true democracy' looks towards a form of political practice – the German revolution – that rears it head against the backdrop of its impossibility, in the void of a Germany in which the atmosphere has become so oppressive that no kind of political initiative is possible.[316] It would thus point to what in fact transpired: the Kreuznach manuscript, a heuristic exercise which Marx never intended for anything other than his own 'private' use, came to a halt precisely on this threshold. It was the trace of one transition, born of the failure of another (the 'transition' from civil society to the state which Hegel thought out and the French Revolution attempted to realize) – the last German signpost on the road to exile that Marx would soon take.

The new world

In late October 1843, Marx left Germany to settle in the 'capital of the new world', Paris.[317] It is easy to imagine the amazement into which the spectacle of the big city must have plunged this not very cosmopolitan native of the Rhineland, capable of writing, only a year and a half earlier, that the hubbub and high society of Cologne (which boasted all of 70,000 inhabitants at the time!) were incompatible with the pursuit of philosophy.[318] Marx reacted to the shock of the big city as other illustrious German *émigrés*, notably Börne and Heine, had reacted before him: by immersing himself in books on the French Revolution, with the intention of writing his own history of the Convention (while also, let us add, studying political economy). Thus, before Marx began to acquire an everyday experience of Paris, he thought of the city as a text, a hieroglyphic in which the history of modernity was inscribed. Indications are that he devoted the first months of his stay to this allegorical existence, far from the tumult of the political meetings and debates of the German *émigrés* – moreover, he abandoned this way of life only 'under duress',[319] in late July 1844, in order to engage in a polemic with Ruge in the pages of *Vorwärts*.[320]

The Marx who disembarked in this new world, then, tried not to wander too far from the shores of the old. That is, the imaginary Paris of the European triarchy, which beckoned to him as it beckoned to every other enlightened intellectual of his day, preceded the real Paris; the *gap* between the two conditioned Marx's encounter with the French intellectual and sociopolitical scene, and constituted the traumatizing core that shaped his first experience of exile. Hence the striking – and paradoxical – continuity between Marx's first Paris period and the solitary retreat into an obscure Rhenish town that had gone before it. In this light, the dogged determination with which he pursued the research programme he had already set for himself – study of the French Revolution and a critique of Hegel, especially of his analysis of civil society, which explains why he now immersed himself in economic works – can be understood only as an attempt to overcome the lag constitutive of this experience that began as an experience of emigration.

There is nothing surprising about the fact that Marx initially limited his practical activities to carrying out the plan, already on its way to realization before he left Germany, to bring out a review with Ruge. Their joint project was modified in only one respect: the *Deutsche Jahrbücher* was renamed the *Deutsch–Französische Jahrbücher*. This change alone indicates

the appeal of a Franco–German political and intellectual alliance, constantly present in the German Jacobins' thoughts, or dreams, from the
time of the French Revolution onwards. The new wave of exiles, whose
leading figures were Marx and Ruge, would at last – or so they believed –
translate this long-cherished project into reality. Despite the failure of
attempts to secure the collaboration of various French thinkers[321] or
celebrated German theorists such as Feuerbach, the *Deutsch–Französische
Jahrbücher* appeared at the end of February 1844. Publication ceased with
the first issue, putting a symbolic end to the extension of Marx's German
activities on French soil.

It was in this one and only issue that Marx was to publish his first
'Parisian' text – 'first' if we do not count his critique of Bauer's pamphlet
on the Jewish question. It may be regarded as a partial restatement of the
conclusions he had reached in the Kreuznach manuscript (especially its
criticisms of the limits of merely political emancipation). The title is
significant, although it bears little relation to the contents: 'Contribution
to the Critique of Hegel's Philosophy of Law. Introduction'.[322] If only by
virtue of the fact that it was published, this text marks an irrevocable
break with the past: a veritable anthology of memorable phrases[323] – many
with a long and glorious future ahead of them – cast in an incisive,
carefully chiselled style that is at once speculative and polemical, this
'Introduction' has all the appearances of a first Marxian manifesto. It
openly announces Marx's shift to revolutionary positions, and heralds the
entrance on to the German philosophical scene of an actor literally
unheard (of) until then, the proletariat. As has been often – and rightly –
pointed out,[324] it draws up an extraordinary, multiple balance sheet that
is both autobiographical and historical. Three trajectories cross in it:
Marx's, his generation's, and that of a national tradition grasped in its
universal significance. Marx's intention was not to tell the story of an
individual conversion to a new cause, but to show in what sense the
question of the German revolution – henceforth inseparable from the
role which, as he now recognized, fell to the new actor on the historical
scene, the proletariat – was, in Hegel's phrase, the 'rose in the cross of
the present'. The revolution was the immanent conclusion to a unique
process that had begun with the Reformation and was now moving
towards a climax, along with the cycle of classical philosophy and the
terminal crisis of absolutism. An individual itinerary and a collective
journey; a singular national history and the destiny of Europe; the past
and the present; theory and practice – all were convened for an unprecedented encounter. The crisis had been turned inside out: it had become
absolutely constructive, opening out on to a radical alternative. The 1844

Introduction resounds like the cry raised by the look-out as the new world swims into view.

'War on the German conditions'

Marx sets the stage with his very first sentence: 'for Germany the *criticism of religion* is in the main complete, and criticism of religion is the premise of all criticism'.[325] 'For Germany': the place in question is, then, Marx's native land, a scene observed from the distance that he has now taken from it. Something has just been carried to its full term there (the criticism of religion), but this something merely forms the immediate precondition for another task, which it merely anticipates. The terminus has already become a point of departure; the new process has been set in motion; it is, in fact, already well under way; there is no escaping it, even – indeed, especially – if one has packed up and left. Nothing for it but to pitch in.

The criticism of religion has, then, been completed, and religion now appears for what it is, a purely human artifact. This simple observation is in itself the acknowledgement of a debt to the Enlightenment and, at the same time, a fresh line of demarcation. For the criticism of religion itself undergoes a division as soon as its fundamental implication has been spelled out. The rejection of a celestial reality – in other words, the criticism of theology – is now a matter of historical record. But to leave matters there would be to regress in the manner of a Bruno Bauer and the Berlin *Freien*, who can do nothing more than ask questions in what remains a theological mode – which is to say, in the final analysis, from the standpoint of the Germano–Christian state. In becoming worldly, irreligious criticism [*irreligiöse Kritik*] is transformed into criticism of the world that gives birth to religion. This is the Feuerbachian schema of alienation, of the inverted projection of the human essence in the form of an imaginary world. Once again, however, Marx both adopts the Feuerbachian schema and, simultaneously, diverts it from its original objective. The human essence in question here, and its division, are more than a matter of consciousness alone: '*man* is no abstract being encamped outside the world. Man is the *world of man*, the state, society.'[326] Alienated consciousness points to something other than itself; it is merely the effect – and, necessarily, a secondary effect – of a contradictory reality.

The conclusion that follows from this is crystal clear: 'the struggle against religion is therefore indirectly a fight against *the world* of which religion is the spiritual *aroma*'.[327] To accept this conclusion is *ipso facto* to confront this world head-on, as criticism 'reflects' its own secularizing movement back upon itself: 'thus the criticism of heaven turns into the criticism of the earth, the *criticism of* religion into the *criticism of* law and the *criticism of* theology into the *criticism of* politics'.[328] Thus Marx returns to his starting point: once again, criticism comes face to face with the world, and it does so in the very particular place known as Germany. But this return has brought a critically important gain, expressed in the form of a double displacement. First, the object of Marx's critique has changed: from religion to law and politics. Second, the domain subjected to criticism has changed: beneath the criticism of German juridical and political consciousness, what is now called into question is the world that has spawned it. This world is nothing other than the German *misère* in the exacerbated form in which it appears in 1843.

A single word is enough to describe it: anachronism. The hands of the German clock have come to a standstill; they point to the hour of the *ancien régime*. Germany's backwardness *vis-à-vis* the historical present is not a mere lag that could be overcome with a little rationalizing boost; it is a yawning gulf, almost an absurdity. The reasons are well known: the German example shows what can become of a nation that has witnessed repeated restorations without ever going through a revolution,[329] a nation that stubbornly persists in producing the regressive cultural forms (the reactionary historicism of the school of legal scholars *à la* Gustav Hugo, national-liberal Romanticism, the neo-mercantilism of Friedrich List's *Nationalökonomie*) that either legitimize this state of affairs or propose equally anachronistic ways of putting an end to it. Civilized conceptual language is not sufficient to describe such anachronism; perhaps that language is no longer even adequate. Criticism, if it is not to remain the prisoner of the anachronism of its object, has to transcend itself by refusing to conceive of itself as 'its own end'. It has to speak the language of the passions, for, as is well known, '*nothing great in the World* has been accomplished without *passion*'.[330] Purged of the last vestiges of aestheti-cism, it will now plunge into the fray. Its very form has become worldly: now the sole objective is to 'strike' the enemy, even 'to exterminate him [*ihn zu vernichten*]'.[331] By gripping the masses, criticism becomes a force, a 'material force' pitted against other material forces in a life-and-death struggle.

To achieve this formal revolution, Marx had a discursive and stylistic apparatus to hand, provided by Heine; he was to make extensive use of it. At least as far as he was concerned, the 1844 Introduction sealed the symbolic encounter of these two major figures of the German emigration. It also coincided with their real encounter, which, as a result of the to-ing and fro-ing that marked the lives of both these exiles, took place somewhat later than might have been expected; when Marx arrived in Paris, Heine was in Germany on what turned out to be his final visit to his native land.[332] In the irony and the profoundly dialectical artistry of the poet's tropes, Marx found, if not weapons *tout court*, then at least weapons that were well suited to radicalizing the critical form that he intended to put to use. The most obvious point of convergence between the two men is to be found in Marx's adoption of Heine's revolutionary (and subtly distanced) interpretation of the imagery of the Romantics and the Hegelian narrative. Germany's present, says Marx, is 'the past of the modern nations', the spectre that reminds them of their still unpaid debt; for even the modern nations have not quite settled accounts with their own past. This is what makes German backwardness contemporaneous, despite everything, with its own times: 'this struggle against the limited content of the German *status quo* cannot be without interest even for the *modern* nations, for the German *status* quo is the open completion of the *ancien régime* and the *ancien régime* is the *concealed deficiency of the modern state*'.[333]

The German spectre looms up out of a scene of historical repetition. We already know what kind of play is acted out on this stage. It is a comedy, the comedy of a despotism that has outlived itself; it stands in the place occupied by the tragedy of the other peoples. It is a truly absurd comedy: its heroes are already ghosts, fluttering about in a vain attempt to escape their own spectrality.[334] The spectacle is a pitiful one, yet the political forces of the Germany to come will gain from it something that will enhance their power: the cheerful serenity that emanates from comedy and induces humanity to part peacefully with its own past. Combined with criticism's passion for negation, this serene cheerfulness is an indispensable source of 'enthusiasm' and 'audacity' – the cardinal revolutionary virtues, and the only ones capable of motivating a victorious struggle against the philistinism and petty-mindedness that are choking the life out of German society.

Marx uses what might seem like an odd term to describe this parochial, self-satisfied attitude: he calls it 'epic'. We should recall that what he has in mind here is not heroic epic but, in the tradition of Hegel's critique of the Homeric paradigm,[335] the breakdown of epic into the kind of fragmented narrative in which every episode reveals the distance between the hero and the subject of the enunciation, between the content and the language in which it is expressed, between the action (which tends to become vain gesticulation) and the abstract destiny that hangs suspended over the world from a position outside it. In short, Marx is thinking of the kind of epic in which the comic spirit has already begun to peep through.

This will remind us of the 'Heine effect', of course, but also of the sense in which Brecht intended *Die Kleinbürgerhochzeit* to be 'epic theatre'. In both cases, the reader/spectator is invited – in Marx, by the theatricality of the text; in Brecht, by theatrical devices in the proper sense – to give up his routine perceptions of the world and to view it as something strange – or even, in the case of the German situation, something extreme and, indeed, literally unbearable in its very mediocrity. Plainly, then, the form of Marx's critique, its stylistic features included, cannot be considered apart from the new relationship to practice that he intends to establish.

It is, precisely, armed with these weapons wrested from the arsenal of the German tradition that criticism has to confront the issue on which its 'becoming-worldly' depends: namely, the relationship between philosophy (especially the philosophy of law and the state) and practice. This new syllogism, like others before it, sets out from a standard Hegelian theme that was practically a journalistic stereotype in the *Vormärz*. We will recognize the first notes of the tune: the Germans have thought – that is to say, have experienced in philosophy and speculation – what other peoples, above all the French, have carried out in practice. But the rest is less familiar: what is changing at present, says Marx, is the palpable, openly affirmed and, at the same time, absolutely constitutive nature of the crisis. What the Germans have gone through 'in thought' is not mere illusion, but their own 'post-history'.[336]

Philosophy's anticipatory function is fully restored. But how are we to conceive its relationship to practice? Marx's answer, like Heine's, is a dialectician's answer, an answer that gives conceptual form to what Heine had worked out in the form of narrative. What presents itself objectively in France as a practical conflict between concrete social and political forces is reflected in Germany, where it becomes a theoretical conflict: criticism, emancipated by the split within philosophy, proceeds to turn against philosophy. But, as we have seen, criticism itself undergoes a split, turning away from the critique of religion in order to become a critique of the real world, society and the state.

Thanks to the crisis, the supersession (*Aufhebung*, of course!) of philosophy is now the order of the day; it presupposes, in one and the same movement, its negation [*Negation*] and realization [*Verwirklichung*]. Its negation, to begin with: the negation of '*hitherto existing philosophy*, of philosophy as such'[337] – that is, philosophy as a reality detached from the world, blind to its own premises, and functioning as if it were an imaginary compensation for the German *misère*. Marx makes much of the bad infinity that has sprung up in this mirror-relation between the real and its philosophical consciousness. As an ideal image, consciousness can play the role of an immediate negation of the real situation by recasting it as a purely speculative activity; nevertheless, as the reflection, however abstract, of a really existing beyond (beyond the Rhine, in the present case), it transforms all notions of realization, of the transition to action, into contemplation of this irreducibly external reality.

To move to the level of practice, we have to smash the mirror and negate philosophy, while bearing in mind that the mirror in question is, precisely, one in which the image of the subject making the critique is also reflected. The resolutely practical party's mistake is that it forgets this; thus it nurtures the illusion that the reality of the German situation has already transcended its philosophical consciousness, that this consciousness is now external to its own subjective position. The illusion of unmediated practice consists in its failure to see how the critical posture continues to depend, for better or for worse – most assuredly for worse, but for better as well – on philosophical consciousness, and that this consciousness cannot be superseded in reality unless its truth content is preserved. 'You demand', writes Marx, with – let us hazard the term – the 'practicist' party in mind, 'that *real living germs* be made the starting point, but you forget that the real living germ of the German nation has grown so far only inside its *cranium*. In a word: *you cannot supersede philosophy without making it a reality* [*ohne sie zu verwirklichen*].'[338] And – drawing once again on Hegel's and Heine's founding narrative – Marx goes on to locate, concretely, the first of these 'living germs' in the Reformation and the activities of Luther, while also mentioning the Reformation's non-spiritual counterpart, the Peasant Wars, the 'most radical fact of German history'[339] before philosophy made its entrance on to the scene. The moment of the negation or loss of philosophy as a permanent object is also the moment – perhaps the only possible moment – of its redemption.

But German philosophy – or, to be more precise, the most advanced form of German philosophy, its veritable apogee in the work of Hegel – is not an idealized (and speculative) image of German realities alone. Or, rather, in order to function as such, it has to become an image of the world; indeed, of the world and its greatest accomplishments. This is what it means to be contemporaneous with the present in theory alone: 'in politics, the Germans *thought* what other nations *did*. Germany was their *theoretical consciousness*.'[340] There is nothing, it will be said, very new about this idea, which had been common coin at least since the first German Jacobins began calling Kantianism the 'German theory of the French Revolution'. Marx, however, takes the syllogism to its logical conclusion: if the premiss is correct, he argues, then the German crisis, whose truth should be sought nowhere else than in its philosophical form, is not a purely German affair, a particularism without interest for the present-day struggle. It is the crisis of the whole modern world which finds its image in the status quo of German philosophy: no doubt this image is distorted, abstract and idealized, but, for that very reason, it is larger than life, as if reflected in (precisely) a convex mirror. In other words, the root cause of the crisis – that is to say, the fact that the revolutionary moment which founds modernity remains unfinished – finds theoretical expression, in a form that is at once both unrecognizable and caricatural, in the contradictions, failures and divisions of the German (in fact, Hegelian) science of law and the state. This explains, incidentally, why the first revolutionary political-intellectual manifesto published by the young Marx bears the title – which at first sight seems strangely speculative – 'Contribution to the Critique of Hegel's Philosophy of Law'.

Let us, however, go back to the syllogism worked out in Marx's text in order to take it one step further. The critical-practical party, which also has its origins in philosophy's internal divisions, can no longer restrict itself to criticizing the illusions of consciousness; since it intends to combat the world that gives rise to them, it must necessarily, in confronting German philosophical consciousness, combat the world of which that consciousness is the reflected form. It must go to the very root of the crisis if it is to recognize it as its own. Moreover, if it is granted that the crisis is simply a sign that the revolution has been left unfinished, then the crisis of this crisis will serve as a reminder that it is not possible to leave the revolution unfinished, in order to create an opening for the revolution that will go to the root of the matter: the radical revolution.

The critical-practical party can now drop its mask and come forward as the radical revolutionary party, the one that grasps the world-historical significance of the German situation and restores its true universality. That universality is nothing other than the recognition of the struggle of the particular against its particularization; consequently, it is also the rejection of any 'abstract' universality, philosophical or theological, which, by confining itself to the plane of ideas, seeks to 'abstract itself' from the struggle – a move that can only confine it to the narrowest sort of particularism. One point, however, remains to be clarified: has the radical, universalizing party ceased to be *German?* Quite the opposite, replies Marx. As a product of the permanent self-criticism of theoretical consciousness, it merely reveals the truth contained in the authentic national tradition: that of the Enlightenment critique of religion, Luther and the Reformation, and the Peasant Wars. Common to them all is a call for radicalism. Marx goes so far as to talk about '*practical* energy' in connection with 'the radicalism of German theory'. He was to speak for the rest of his life in the name of this theory, the only one that seemed to him to achieve the dignity of what one can hardly avoid calling a 'theoretical practice': 'the evident proof of the radicalism of German theory, and hence of its practical energy, is that it proceeds from a resolute *positive* abolition [*Aufhebung*] of religion'.[341]

The most fitting terms that Marx can find to conclude this section of his text are borrowed from Kant:

> The criticism of religion ends with the teaching that *man is the highest being* [*das Höchste Wesen*] for man, hence with the *categorical imperative to overthrow all relations* in which man is a debased, enslaved, forsaken, despicable being, relations which cannot be better described than by the exclamation of a Frenchman when it was planned to introduce a tax on dogs: Poor dogs! They want to treat you like human beings![342]

This is a fine example of Marx's style: the contrast between the two parts of the sentence (almost without exception, commentators ignore the second) produces an irresistible effect of ironic distantiation that tempers the pathos created by evoking the categorical imperative – or, rather, encourages us to see in it less a first-person appropriation of Kantian humanism[343] than a lucid acknowledgement of the debt practical criticism owes the Enlightenment. This acknowledgement comes at the moment in which criticism realizes that its object has changed: from the critique of religion to that of law and politics, and also – let us not forget – from '*man* [as] an abstract being [*abstraktes Wesen*] encamped outside the world', a being [*Wesen*] who is, among other things, that of the categorical imperative *à la* Kant, to 'the world of man, the state, society'.[344]

Let us also note that when he talks about the 'positive abolition' of religion, Marx once again introduces the Hegelian theme of the superiority of the German *Aufklärung* to the French Enlightenment. The suggestion is that the French Enlightenment did not go beyond an unmediated negation of religion, because it was incapable of grasping religion's essential determinations in their internality. The balance of the text confirms this: Marx maintains that Luther and the Reformation set the stage, theoretically and practically, for the moment of German philosophy, and puts the whole of this movement under the banner of the revolution.[345] The historical significance of the Reformation lies in its internalization of the question of faith and religious authority; this was the first step in a secularizing movement that paved the way for a philosophical critique of religion which traced it back to its human roots and freed the people from the bonds of servitude. Accordingly, philosophy's role appears as the inverted image of theology's: whereas the peasant rebellion led by Münzer (the 'most radical fact of German history') was condemned by Luther, allied with the princes he had emancipated from the Church's tutelage, in Marx's day, the 'eve of [the German] revolution', it is the status quo of unfreedom that finds, in philosophy, an adversary worthy of it.[346]

Marx thus rallies to Heine's vision of history, his cosmopolitan and simultaneously national/popular narrative, which treats the Reformation, the Peasant Wars, and the formation of classical philosophy as a single emancipatory sequences.[347] The radical revolution in Germany unmistakably appears as the theoretical and practical culmination of a national history, as the point at which this national history intersects, in a decisive, open confrontation, the development of the other European peoples, and thus as the moment at which the differential temporalities overlap, interrupting the course of events and opening out on to an unprecedented alternative.

The radical revolution

But the new revolutionary moment has so far been defined exclusively in terms of its speculative determinations. What makes it radical? In what sense is it anything more than an abstract promise proffered by a theoretical consciousness whose critical energy is equalled only by the distance separating it from practice *tout court*? It is certainly true, as Marx knows very well, that 'it is not enough for thought to strive for realisation, reality must itself strive towards thought'.[348] 'The arm of critique', he declares in a famous passage, 'must replace the critique of arms, material force must be overthrown by material force; but theory also becomes a material force as soon as it has gripped the masses. Theory is capable of gripping the masses as soon as it demonstrates *ad hominem*, and it demonstrates *ad hominem* as soon as it becomes radical. To be radical is to grasp things by the root. But for man, the root is man himself.'[349] This is an astonishing sentence; it shows that Marx, far from rejecting the importance of 'ideas' (or 'theory') in history, assigns them a leading role, or even, perhaps, makes them history's driving force, on condition – and it is, evidently, this condition which marks his break with idealism[350] – that the 'theory' in question is not a collection of ideas but an *active* principle, a set of *practices*. This signifies, above all, that theory must henceforth consent to confront the *conditions* of its practices, conditions which are *not* theoretical (otherwise this thesis would simply bring us back to a belief in the omnipotence of ideas) and imply a *displacement* of the question of the essence of man, as we can see from the beginning of the 1844 Introduction. Man is the 'root' of man, then, if one assumes that 'man is *the world of man*, the state, society', *considered from the standpoint of their material transformation.*

At this point, let us, pause briefly to sum up what Marx has said so far. How to make criticism radical and how to make it practical are henceforth inseparably linked questions, each of which presupposes the other. Solving them requires going beyond the philosophical form of criticism, which also means going beyond the unreflected character of practice. At least in Germany, this double movement takes place on a new terrain, that of *politics* defined as the construction of a new practice 'that grips the masses': radical revolutionary practice. The break with Young Hegelian 'critical criticism' has been consummated, in so far as 'critical criticism' represents an exacerbated form of the impasses of the German road. So that it does not sink into self-satisfied contemplation of the activity of a 'Spirit' revelling in the distance it has taken from 'vulgar' politics and the multitude, so that it can become an active force, criticism has to take its stand on the ground of the masses, who are the very stuff of politics.[351] In other words, *radical* politics is *mass* politics, in the twofold sense that it is formulated from the masses' standpoint and is part of their own constituent movement.

But hardly has it been evoked than this new ground gives way beneath our feet. The forward movement of the syllogism suddenly grinds to a halt: 'a major difficulty, however, seems to stand in the way of a *radical* German revolution'.[352] What is the nature of this difficulty? The fact that the peculiarity of the German situation, the lag that separates it from its present, leads – since it is reflected within that situation – to the erosion of the notion of practice, if not to its utter collapse. This definition may appear abstract, but it allows us to reconstruct the sometimes only implicit steps in Marx's line of reasoning. The lag between theory and reality is reproduced in the lag separating the state from civil society, which is reflected in its turn within civil society, shattering its apparent unity. Hence we are brought back to our point of departure, the question of the transition from civil society to the state. This time, however, we find ourselves approaching it from the other end – by going back, precisely, to its roots, the world of man and concrete social life: that is to say, the analysis of civil society inspired by *Elements of the Philosophy of Right.*

Let us rapidly recall the central features of that analysis.[353] As a moment of difference, civil society breaks up the immediate unity of human existence, making its externalization possible. The starting point for this process of division is simply *need*, a dynamic concept that connects material, passive (or unmediated, natural) need to the recognition of need, that is, to its insertion into a system of needs by means of which the particular needs of one individual come to reflect those of all the others. The notion of need simultaneously introduces the dimensions of finitude and liberty into social life, via the movement that 'spiritualizes' need by raising it to the level of representation as a socially recognized existence.

With that, things rapidly fall into place. A revolution is not radical unless it puts an end to the separation between civil society and the state – that is to say, unless it simultaneously overcomes the internal division of civil society and the imaginary transcendence of that division, namely, the abstraction of the merely political state. A single sentence summarizes the conclusions of both the Kreuznach manuscript and the polemic with Bauer: it contrasts the 'radical revolution', which can bring about true 'human emancipation', with the 'partial, the *merely* political revolution, the revolution which leaves the pillars of the house standing'. If it is to become effective, this revolution requires 'a material basis':[354] it must be reflected in the formation of a system of needs. There can be no radical revolution in the absence of a rupture within the system of needs, unless new needs emerge along with the recognition of their novelty, that is, the fact that they are not satisfied under the existing system – and, if one means to be radical, the recognition that the existing state of affairs makes it impossible to satisfy them.

In fact, 'radical needs' point less to a positive expansion of the system of needs than to the point at which it breaks down, ceasing to function as a 'system' which ensures the differentiation/integration of the particular within the universal.[355] To this we must add a supplementary, specifically German problem: how can these radical needs appear, if 'partial needs', those that correspond to the merely political revolution, remain unsatisfied? There is no escaping the conclusion that the radical revolution emerges, and can only emerge, against the backdrop of its negation, its own impossibility: 'only a revolution of radical needs can be a radical revolution and it seems that for this the preconditions and ground are lacking'.[356]

Does the German revolution, then, confirm Kant's position, the *salto mortale* which Marx mentions again here?[357] To leave it at that would be to miss the essence of the matter. For Kant,[358] the perilous leap represented by the revolution is a sign, in itself contingent, of the unity of nature and freedom in the history of the human race; but it is a sign whose significance can be deciphered only by a spectator, so that there must always be an irreducible gap between her subjective position and the event. It is this illusion of the spectatorial consciousness that Marx challenges by dialecticizing the *salto mortale* without denying its contingency, despite what is often said. In a certain sense, this leap is what separates the event from itself, for it is the event which, in its absolute contingency, poses its own preconditions in so far as it determines that they were the preconditions for its realization. Necessity is born of contingency, retroactively – it is the recognition of this retroactive effect, through affirmation of its void and the radical impossibility of conditions guaranteeing it in advance, which indicates that the subject cannot remain aloof from a process that occurs in the register of the always-already. The Kantian illusion lies not so much in a vision of the *salto mortale* that must at all costs be 'reduced' through incorporation into a determinist or substantially teleological scheme, as in the notion of a consciousness presumed to observe, from its sovereign (albeit concerned, sympathetic) position, the course and consequences of the great leap.

We can now see more clearly what it means to call the German situation radical. The radicalism of the revolutionary leap emerges from its very impossibility, from Germany's extreme backwardness. This impossibility, however, is doubled in its turn: it becomes radical by making partial leaps and unfinished revolutions impossible. In Germany, in other words, it is already too late for a partial revolution, a merely political revolution, a revolution *in civil society*. This is the other side of the coin: German backwardness rules out the substitution of the particular for the universal that leads to merely partial emancipation. Marx now turns the spotlight on another aspect of civil society, focusing on its internal dialectic: class contradiction.

In France, one and the same mechanism explains the course the revolutionary process has taken, the reason it has remained unfinished, and why it must be resumed: a particular class attains to a hegemonic position and evicts another from it, appearing as the universal class with which all of civil society is called to identify. The revolution surges up when this class – the bourgeoisie, to give it is name – succeeds in representing its particular emancipation as that of society as a whole;[359] and, conversely, when another class – in this case the aristocracy – comes to be regarded as the negation of emancipation as such, the personification of 'the notorious crime of the whole of society'.[360] Hence the outburst of revolutionary enthusiasm that accompanies this double recognition; without it, the revolution would not have been possible. But the same holds for the illusion it trails in its wake: if this class 'emancipates the whole of society', it does so only on condition 'that the whole of society is in the same situation as this class, e.g., possesses money and education or can acquire them at will'.[361]

When all is said and done, we are still in the realm of the particular: the social order has not been shaken to its foundations. Yet the story is by no means over; the French drama continues to unfold, one social class succeeding the next in the role of emancipatory agent until a class emerges that 'organises all conditions of human existence on the presupposition of social freedom'.[362]

Nothing of the sort can be imagined in the case of the prosaic German epic. The German bourgeoisie is incapable of assuming the role its French counterpart played in 1789; it cannot call itself the general representative of society confronting its negative representative – the mainstays of the *ancien régime* – and drum up revolutionary enthusiasm for its cause. Yet its patent cowardice must be chalked up to something quite different from simple subjective weakness. If its consciousness of itself reflects the prevailing mediocrity and philistinism, this is because the nature of the basic antagonism shifted between the moment when the German bourgeoisie made its entry on to the historical scene and the moment when emancipation became possible. German history, indeed, is nothing but the story of this perpetual failure: whenever a new class aspired to a hegemonic position (before the bourgeoisie, it was the princes opposed to the monarchy and the modernizing bureaucrats opposed to the aristocracy), it was already threatened from below by a new dominated class. The impotence of the German bourgeoisie is merely another chapter in this old story, this incessant alternation between the 'too early' and the 'too late'.

German radicalism is decidedly not a matter of free choice. As Marx had already pointed out in his letters to Ruge (which, incidentally, appeared alongside the 1844 Introduction in the sole issue of the *Deutsch–Französische Jahrbücher*), it was the reaction to an impossibility, a radical alternative to a radical crisis: 'in France it is the reality of gradual liberation, in Germany the impossibility of gradual liberation, that must give birth to complete freedom'.[363] Accordingly, the only appropriate response to the German crisis is to seek out the true mediation that is capable of shattering the immediate unity of the real: in short, to acknowledge that the labour of the negative is always-already at work, recognize the new antagonism, and *give it its name*. Only this operation – a veritable *salto mortale* of thought on the order of the performative, rather than the didactic, descriptive or deductive – is capable of identifying the new actor whose entry on to the scene will give a dramatic new twist to the whole plot – a plot which, precisely, has yet to be written.

The paradoxical protagonist

Thus the hour of the *proletariat* has sounded. Marx's definition is so familiar that we sometimes forget how strange it is. Yet that strangeness makes itself felt from the very first words: the '*positive* possibility of a German emancipation' lies with a class that is, precisely, radically divested of all positivity. What status can possibly be ascribed to a class which is not one, which is a dissolution [*Auflösung*] *in actu* of class society? A first answer springs to mind; it figures in Marx's text, and runs as follows: the negativity of the proletariat is merely a positivity that is not conscious of what it is, the positivity of the human essence. In reality, the proletarian is Man, but in inverted form, that of the 'complete loss' of his essence, which prefigures its inevitable 'complete rewinning'.[364] In his conclusion, Marx even goes so far as to place 'the only *practically* possible liberation of Germany' under the banner of '*the* theory which proclaims man to be the highest being [*das höchste Wesen*] for man'.[365]

This is, once again, in the Feuerbachian vein, which Marx laces with Kant whenever he wishes to present it from the historical standpoint that we have already encountered in the Kreuznach manuscript and the polemic with Bauer. It is easy enough to assign this text a posterity, in which *The Holy Family* holds a prominent place;[366] there Marx does indeed lapse into an anthropology built up around the theme of labour and its alienation, attributing an 'essence' and even a 'being' to the proletariat, together with a teleologically guaranteed historical mission. In the 1844 Introduction, however, the proletariat (let us note in passing that Marx speaks only of the proletariat's role in the *German* context) is not defined on the basis of anything remotely resembling the creative essence of labour – a term that is, moreover, conspicuously absent here; the proletariat is defined only 'negatively', in terms of the dissolution, brought on by 'rising industrial development', of the other 'social estates'. Yet we have seen that, in the Kreuznach manuscript, Marx had already recognized in 'the estate [*Stand*] of direct labour, of concrete labour . . . not so much an estate of civil society as the ground upon which its circles rest and coincide'.[367] A ground there may be, but let us note that it is one which gives way beneath this society's feet to reveal the constitutive emptiness at its core. Moreover, we learn nothing else about this essence that is to be 'won back', although we have been advised that it 'is no abstract being encamped outside the world'.[368] No doubt there is, in Marx, a strong desire to fill in the kind of yawning negativity upon which he has just conferred the name 'proletariat'; but, at the same time, there is also something that seems to make this impossible, 'or at least problem-atic', as Marx says about the emancipation of the German bourgeoisie.[369]

From the very first, the proletariat's entry on to the scene has some-thing unstable and paradoxical about it, something which emerges even more sharply when we compare Marx's text with the contemporaneous writings of the very Feuerbachian, very humanist Engels. Plainly, the proletariat as negatively defined by Marx has nothing of the massive empirical presence it has in Engels. It appears at the end of a series of rather abstract syllogisms, enveloped in a philosophical discourse that is a far cry from the social science and the social-ist thought that inform Engels's approach. There is nothing surprising about this lack of 'sociolog-ical' substance. Marx encounters the proletariat at the theoretical and symbolic level before making contact with the real (specifically, the Parisian) workers' movement, because he is looking (literally) for an answer to a pre-existing *political* question (how to conceive the imminent transformation of the crisis into a German revolution). His question is diametrically opposed to the one raised by Engels, Hess and the socialist movement more generally (how to attain to the pacific essence of the social, and thereby resolve the crisis). This bears emphasizing: no episte-mological break or sociological encounter precedes Marx's encounter with the proletariat, or is capable of accounting for it.

In opting for the revolutionary radicalism that led him to discover the proletariat, Marx – like Heine before him, but on a politico-philosophical trajectory that was very much his own – joined the very thin ranks of those who rejected the *juste-milieu* and the conciliatory views characteristic of the 'Forty-eighters'. Even if the term 'communist' is nowhere to be found in the 1844 Introduction, then, Marx's path was bound to cross that trodden by Babeuf's and Robespierre's heirs – that is to say, the path of the French (more precisely, if we include the German *émigré* organiza-tions, the *Parisian*) communist movement, which reached its zenith in this period.

But let us come back to the question of the proletariat. All the indications are that the Marxian proletariat is defined by a radical lack, but also by the desire to overcome it, a desire for 'suture' (to adopt a term used by Ernesto Laclau and Chantal Mouffe)[370] that is confronted with the impossibility of its satisfaction – the last occurrence of, and a final farewell to, a nostalgia for the ontological. Might the proletariat be no more nor less than the reduplication of this initial impossibility within itself? In other words, might the proletariat be, not an inverted figure of totality, but an embodiment of the impossibility of full totality, the absolute movement of mediation, the empty place designating the irreducible gap within the existing order? If so, 'proletariat' names that which prevents the totality from ever achieving closure, for it points, precisely, to the antagonism within the totality, an antagonism that cannot be overcome for as long as that totality develops within its own limits. It designates the element which the totality seeks to negate at all costs, to repress so that it may present itself as such, as a unified totality. Hence the emancipatory dimension of the act that recognizes the proletariat by naming it. The paradox of its definition is thus simply an effect that is inherent in the performative character, and internal to the symbolic order, of the act that presides over its initial appearance.

This second possibility is the only one that can account for the paradoxical status the proletariat has throughout Marx's work. It is, moreover, adumbrated in the text of the 1844 Introduction, in a somewhat enigmatic sentence that usually goes unnoticed. After defining the proletariat as 'the negative result of society', and therefore as a negation of private property, which society 'has made the principle of the proletariat', Marx goes on to draw a surprising parallel: 'in regard to the world which is coming into being the proletarian then finds himself possessing the same right as the *German king* in regard to the world which has come into being when he calls the people *his* people as he calls the horse *his* horse. By declaring the people his private property the king simply states that the property owner is king.'[371]

Here we are clearly at the heart of what can only be called the symbolic function that Hegel had already brought out in his analysis of the monarch as an 'irrational' moment, pure waste, whose authority, entirely dependent on his 'name', is nevertheless indispensable to the totalization of the existing political and social order.[372] Marx adds that the king is precisely the empty subject who, by 'declaring', in the performative mode, that the people is 'his' people (the phrase that follows – 'as he calls the horse *his* horse' – brings out the purely 'formal', that is, symbolically effective, nature of this act even more clearly), confirms the rule of private property. In like fashion, calling the 'proletariat' the negative result of – or antagonistic force immanent in – bourgeois society reveals the void that is constitutive of the existing order, and the fact that it lacks any transcendent 'guarantee', while conferring a performative dimension on the discourse about the 'world which is coming into being'. Proletarian rule is not an ideal state to be realized in the future, not a negative version of bourgeois monarchy; it is that which, in bourgeois society (crowned with a king belonging to the *ancien régime*), confronts that society with its own impossibility, its pure difference.

'Nulla salus sine Gallis'

But what, exactly, will be the proletariat's role in the coming revolution? Can the radical revolution be described as 'proletarian'? Marx says nothing of the sort, any more than he uses the term 'socialism' or 'communism' to designate the content of the transformation he envisages. What is in question resembles not a conversion to a pre-existing doctrine, but an 'encounter': that of philosophy and the proletariat. Marx defines it as the result of a process of self-criticism. Germany provides the setting for this encounter; its temporality is that of a revolution 'which goes to the root of things'; its form is that of the mutual 'abolition' of the two protagonists. Philosophy, we now know, cannot abolish itself without realizing itself [sich verwirklichen]; as Marx spells out at the end of the text, it cannot realize itself without abolishing the proletariat. What of the proletariat: must it, in order to be abolished – or, more exactly, to supersede itself [sich aufheben] – 'realize' itself? An asymmetry springs up between the two terms 'philosophy' and 'proletariat', and Marx carefully refrains from resolving the difficulty. As Georges Labica emphasizes:

> Philosophy . . . will remain consciousness even if, with Marx, at the end of its difficult penitence, it at last succeeds in uttering the name of its own existence, the name 'proletariat'. But this utterance comes with what is perhaps its last breath: Aufhebung, disappearance. Who, however, disappears? The 'Introduction' ends on this exquisite note. The alliance of philosophy and the proletariat is not an equation, it is an asymptote.[373]

Should we, as certain critics do,[374] emphasize this gap, and conclude that Marx's conception of the proletariat in this text remains a 'passive' one, as his adoption of the Feuerbachian metaphor of the head and the heart might seem to suggest? On such a reading, the proletariat would be the 'heart', and the role of the 'head' would, once again, fall to philosophy. But to adopt such an interpretation would be to forget the self-criticism of philosophy carried out in the preceding pages. The philosophy in question here is no longer a detached form of social activity; it has (at least tendentially) become critical practice, a material force that grips the masses; and it designates the theoretical moment of revolutionary political practice. Moreover, from one end of the text to the other, Marx abstains from using the term 'philosophy' to refer to this new mode of intervention by and in the real; rather, he uses the neutral – albeit not antithetical – term 'theory' [Theorie]. Again, if it is true that he echoes Feuerbach's phrase, he utilizes it more as a metaphor than as a concept: in contrast to its function in his articles in the *Rheinische Zeitung*,[375] here it serves less to affirm, as in Feuerbach, the joint primacy of 'spiritual' activity and the German-reformist path than the radical alternative to them: criticism amid the turbulence and imminence of revolution. While we scan the 1844 Introduction in vain for the concept of 'revolutionary practice' [*revolutionäre Praxis*] found in the Third Thesis on Feuerbach, we should nevertheless note that the proletariat is summoned to 'supersede itself' [*sich aufheben*], and that it is not invited to do so under the tutelage of a third party. We would, moreover, be hard put to explain how Marx could retreat to a dualistic conception *short of* the idea of democracy as the 'self-determination of the people' that he elaborated in the Kreuznach manuscript.

The crux may well reside in the fact that the proletariat of the 1844 Introduction, in its alliance with practical criticism, is not so much a preexisting reality that subsequently goes into action to 'make the revolution', assert its leadership of it, affirm its hegemony, and so on, as, in a certain sense, *the revolution itself*, the power of rupture that comes into being in and through the revolutionary process. This is a process in which the proletariat eventually supersedes itself, appearing as the absolute subject of the mediation, the empty place out of which a 'transition' or radical opening can emerge and be realized. The term 'proletariat' names the permanence of the process; by virtue of its irreducible character, its wild, ungraspable nature, it marks the threshold beyond which the revolutionary process can no longer be confined to partial, 'merely political' revolutions that would observe the limits of civil society and the representative state – or come to a standstill. In this sense, the 1844 Introduction makes a crucial innovation by offering the first formulation of the idea of permanent revolution[376] that does not merely echo the discourse of the Jacobins.

This innovation is prolonged by the very status of Marx's text: the radical revolution has already begun, and this text is its (first) manifesto. By naming the proletariat and sealing its alliance with philosophy, the Introduction proclaims that the new world exists. It emerges as the text/act which condenses, in its very utterance, a process that is at once imminent and already under way. It announces a break in historical time, the moment at which the 'not yet' and the 'always-already', a 'too early' and a 'too late', are each transformed into the other, revealing their truth: the impossibility of the 'right moment', of the thing's coinciding with its own time. The revolution *always* comes 'too soon', because it sets out from the constitutive incompleteness of the real; it is the perilous leap, not of the present towards the future (that would still be to conceive it as a simple acceleration of linear time), but of the future into the present, whose essential open-endedness it thereby reveals.

Has the course of events given the lie to Marx's prediction, or, more importantly, robbed it of its anticipatory dimension? Does not the defeat of the revolutions of 1848 confirm the idea that a radical revolution was premature in Germany, or even that it was born of an illusion fostered by Marx's 'obsession' with Germany's backwardness (which, as we have seen, was that of a whole generation, and had nothing of a personal idiosyncrasy about it)? Half a century after that defeat, did not the ageing Engels come to the following self-critical conclusion? 'History has proved us wrong, and all who thought like us. It has made it clear that the state of economic development in the Continent at that time was not, by a long way, ripe for the elimination of capitalist production.'[377]

Engels's version of things is often commended for its realism,[378] but it has a very strange ring to it, reminiscent of nothing so much as history rewritten from the standpoint of the victors. In place of a real history of struggles, with all the attendant contingency and undecidability (which can issue in defeat), it puts a theodicy of the development of the productive forces, which function as a guarantee for the 'ripeness' of 'objective' conditions; at the same time, it remains blind to its own retrospective character. Engels offers us, from within Marxism (incidentally, he was responsible for consecrating that term), the prototype of a narrative in which – to borrow Walter Benjamin's famous metaphor – historical materialism functions like the hunchback puppeteer who hides under the table on which a game of chess is being played, guiding the puppet who makes the moves.[379] When the game is played like that, Benjamin adds, historical materialism always wins. In fact, the 'realism' Engels displayed in 1895 reinforces, in its fashion, the collective repression which German cultural and political life brought to bear on the revolutionary event after 1850, a form of repression exercised even – perhaps above all – by those who had suffered the trauma of the defeat.[380] It is – I may say in passing – altogether characteristic that, in the period of radicalization which followed the October Revolution (before it ebbed in 1923–24), the revolutionary German left felt the need to challenge the ageing Engels's account, while restoring the texts Marx wrote around 1848 to pride of place.[381]

In historical perspective, it is Marx's theses which impress us with their accuracy and their capacity truly to break with the past. To begin with, the mere existence of the revolutionary wave of 1848, surely the most broadly European revolutionary movement in history, shows that Marx's

Marx's statements of 1843–44 about the 'imminence' of the revolution were not mere wishful thinking or the figments of a feverish imagination. Above all, did not the defeat of the 1848 revolution in Germany, due largely to the weakness of the forces dominating the democratic camp, confirm – albeit *a contrario* – Marx's theses as to the impossibility of a partial revolution in Germany and the political insignificance of the German bourgeoisie, with its congenital inability to constitute itself as a 'national-popular' class? In the final analysis, does not the uniqueness – or even the tragedy – of German history consist in the perpetual failure of its democratic revolution and the self-destructive compulsion to reproduce the lag that separates Germany from its own present? If so, then the radical revolution envisaged by Marx was far from an ideal figure functioning, in line with a quintessentially idealist tradition, as a surrogate for an impossible political revolution.[382] Rather, it was an anticipated – or, more precisely, an anticipatory – explanation for this impossibility. In France, the desire to 'finish the revolution' gave rise to the compromise represented by the Republic. In Germany, it came down to smothering revolutionary democracy in the cradle. The upshot was a compromise between the bourgeoisie and the *ancien régime*, followed by the unification of the country amid '*Blut und Eisen*'; the ultimate consequences were militarism, two world wars, and the unimaginable barbarity to which they gave rise.

No doubt there was something disproportionate – almost scandalous – about the idea of a radical revolution in Germany. In the 1844 Introduction, Marx himself acknowledged that the German proletariat was only just 'coming into being';[383] yet a few months later, referring to its first active manifestation (the uprising of the Silesian weavers), he did not hesitate to christen it the 'theoretician of the European proletariat'.[384] But it is also true that the manifesto he wrote for the *Deutsch–Französische Jahrbücher* ended with a modest declaration. Borrowing a metaphor from Heine, Marx wrote that even when 'all inner requisites [for Germany had been] fulfilled', it would nevertheless be the '*ringing call of the Gallic cock*' that would herald the 'day of German resurrection'.[385] In 1843, Arnold Ruge had already written to his compatriots that there could be '*nulla salus sine Gallis*'. And it was in fact in Paris, on 24 February 1848, that the cock crowed.

Less than a month later, on 18 March, Berlin was covered with barricades.

In January 1919, as the *Freikorps* was crushing the Spartacist rebellion in the streets of Berlin, Rosa Luxemburg recalled the failure of 1848, and declared that the 'series of defeats' with which 'the whole road of socialism is covered' were 'the pride and strength of international socialism'.[386] In view of this series of defeats, which has only grown longer since, Marx's hypothesis may well appear to be a fiction, or even the fullest expression of the myth that animated the *Vormärz*. Yet in its very exaggeration, and even in its inaccurate appraisal of the actual relation of forces, it yields up its kernel of truth: it offers us the sole vantage point from which the antagonism inhabiting the real does not disappear from view, the standpoint from which it becomes possible to conceive of radical alternatives, even if they fail.

To use a term of Walter Benjamin's, by restoring the charge of the 'time of the now' that cuts through the experience of history, the Marxian hypothesis is a standing invitation to free ourselves, if only in thought, from the so-called manifest truths of the established order.

Conclusion:
Self-Criticisms of the Revolution

Was the French Revolution ever finished, and, if so, when? This question has been asked for more than two centuries; the positive responses have been accompanied by a profusion of dates, from Thermidor through 18 Brumaire to – for those who regard 1789 as the commencement of a long-term process that culminated in the consolidation of the republic – the Paris Commune. But why, indeed, stop there? Was not Vichy the ultimate revenge of the Revolution's French adversaries? In any event, even more remarkable than the diversity – or, rather, the contradictory nature – of the answers given to our question is the fact that the question itself keeps resurfacing, obsessively, in public debate. This is a clear indication of its continuing relevance to the present. It is as if no political or intellectual conjuncture could define itself in its specificity without measuring itself against this question, the symptom of an unresolved problem that the present is unable to settle and have done with. From *this* point of view,[1] the year 1789 has no equivalent in either the Glorious Revolution (although it closed off a period of upheavals that lasted almost half a century) or the American Revolution, two founding moments in the trajectory of the revolutionary phenomenon and modern politics.

In fact, if the question of the 'end' of the French Revolution has been so insistently posed, this is because, from the very first, the participants in the Revolution and the commentators on it had constantly to confront the question of its unfinished nature – or, in other words, the spectacle of its failure. I should make it clear at the outset that this 'failure' can be measured only against criteria of 'success' or 'failure' that were radically new – or, more precisely, immanent to the revolutionary event itself. The revolution of 10 August 1792 and those of 31 May and June 1793, which opened the way to the Jacobins' rise to power, the Terror, Thermidor, and Napoleon's *coup d'état*, all turned on this question of the 'end' of the Revolution, an end that was as ardently desired as it was stubbornly resisted. The question of the unfinished nature or the end of the Revolution was thus internal to the revolutionary process itself; the fact that it cannot be made to disappear suggests, at the very least, that what began at this unique moment was an unfinished and, in a sense, an interminable history, a history that continued to exceed the effects that it produced. For, as the capital letter suggests, the Revolution is not one revolution among others; it provides the basis on which people have thought and, on the practical level, lived out *all* other revolutions, including the question of their 'end'.

The powerful impact of the recent discourse about the 'end of history' is hardly due to its originality, even less to its author's incredibly, makeshift metaphysics (which none of the great philosophies of history would have dared to exhibit so ingenuously); it is rooted in the simple declaration that, after the collapse of the USSR, 'we cannot picture to ourselves a world that is essentially different from the present one, and at the same time better'.[2] But this kernel of truth had already been extracted from its shell in the 1970s by the 'revisionist' school of French historiography (to be sure, it was presented rather more polemically, as it had not yet been reinforced by the demonstrable reality of the failure of Soviet socialism). 'The French Revolution is over':[3] such was the rallying cry raised by the leader of this school, François Furet. Endlessly outdoing itself in the attempt to rebuild society *ab ovo*, driven by 'mental representations of power' as imperious as they were 'frenzied',[4] and obsessed by a fantasy of original purity, the French Revolution, said the revisionists, should now be considered to have reached its 'end' in both senses of the word. It had come to an end, that of a national trajectory which, under the auspices of liberalism, had 'reconciled'[5] the conflicting terms (monarchical and Jacobin) inherited from the past. Thus Tocqueville's dream of a France rid of the burden of its exceptionalism had come true; the country could now join the community of European nations that had reached political and social modernity without a revolution. But the French Revolution had also – and perhaps above all – come to an end in the sense that the liberal reconciliation in question here exposed the Revolution's real internal 'end', and, in the process, that of any revolution: namely, its 'murderousness',[6] for the 'the two undertakings' – the Gulag and the Terror – are seen as 'identical', and this identity puts 'the issue of the Gulag at the very core of the revolutionary endeavour'.[7]

It is, of course, eminently possible that the omnipotence Furet attributes to what he sometimes calls 'ideology' or 'discourses', and at other times 'mental representations' or 'the symbolic system', the 'project', or even, simply, the 'idea' or 'design', is ultimately no less idealist than the thinly veiled providentialism of the narrative of the 'end of history'. There is nothing particularly new about it, the reader will observe, if she recalls, with André Tosel, that 'it is the classical liberal philosophies of history that have been the most markedly teleological, the most likely to justify the sacrifice of individuals and entire peoples by invoking the nobility of the goal, which was that of (Western) civilization itself'.[8] The 'end of the grand narratives', proclaimed far and wide since Jean-François Lyotard made it postmodernism's chief battle cry,[9] might well, in this case, ultimately mean nothing more than the collapse of any 'grand narrative' offering an alternative to the one favoured by a liberalism that has driven all its rivals from the lists.

Yet however one-sided and, frankly speaking, superficial the phenomenology of the revolutionary process proposed by the 'revisionist' historians may be, it has undeniably succeeded in capturing the *Zeitgeist* engendered by the defeats of the working-class and mass movements in the late 1970s, which Enrico Berlinguer summed up as 'the exhaustion of the propulsive force of October 1917'. In any case, this phenomenology seems better placed to capture the spirit of the age than the absurdly overblown attempts to provide liberalism with an onto-anthropological foundation.[10] For even if we grant that Fukuyama's version of the 'end of history', helped along by the failure of the Soviet regime and the concomitant 'obviousness' that there is no alternative to capitalism, has conquered the mass audience that earlier versions failed to conquer,[11] it is Furet's rewriting of the founding narrative of the French nation which has doubtless already shown that it has the longer future ahead of it. For, precisely because he has managed to produce a grand narrative capable of standing as an alternative to the one handed down by the revolutionary tradition (its most moderate, 'republican' forms included), a narrative that draws together in a single sequence, crowned by the *telos* of a triumphant liberalism, the trauma of the original experience and the happy ending of the self-destruction of French exceptionalism, Furet (together with his disciples) has provided the discursive foundation required by the collective effort to delegitimize references to the Revolution, and thus exclude them from public debate. Rejecting as 'illusory' or even 'murderous' the 'idea' that 'history is shaped by human action rather than by that which is institutionalized [*l'institué*]'[12] – that is, the idea that human beings can experience their history as something other than a more or less naturalized ('institutionalized') *fatum* – Furet takes his place as the veritable anti-Michelet of his day, rather than the anti-Soboul or anti-Mathiez that he himself would have preferred to be. And it is indeed the case that this idea has established its dominion everywhere, under the auspices of an ongoing liberal 'revolution/restoration' (Gramsci).

But does Furet succeed any better than his countless predecessors in what remains, when all is said and done, an attempt to conjure away the spectre of revolution? It is an attempt which, as such, can only offer additional testimony to the stubborn presence (in, precisely, a spectral mode, the mode of that which returns to haunt the present) both of what it is charged with exorcizing and also of the fundamental ambivalence (fascination/repulsion) that it continues to inspire. Here, too, a certain reality principle has not been slow to take its revenge; the emergence, over the last decade in France, of popular struggles and movements referring very conspicuously to the symbols and founding statements of the revolutionary moment has put an end to the dream or the nightmare – depending on one's point of view – of a nation pacified by the managerial skills of Guizot's latter-day champions. The workers' strikes, the chants and the banners of demonstrators, the protest marches of undocumented immigrants struggling for their 'rights', the mass petitions in their support, the refusal to put up with practices of delegation, and even a return to forms of direct action, extralegal or violent forms included, all bear witness to the emergence, or re-emergence, of a 'common sense' of the subaltern classes that harks back, sometimes explicitly, to the discursive matrix of the *sans-culottes*.[13] Indeed, Furet himself was not unaware of this, as we can see from the barely veiled melancholy of his last writings.[14]

What has been said so far is, at any rate, enough to remind us that if the referents provided by 1789–93 have been repeatedly invoked – or 'put to the test', as Jacques Guilhaumou so aptly expresses it[15] – over the long course of popular struggle and revolt, and if the French Revolution anticipates, in a certain sense, all subsequent revolutions, it is above all by virtue of the *constitutive tension* that marks its founding statements, and so makes possible their subsequent reappropriation by the participants in social movements: property rights versus the right to existence; the relationship between liberty and equality; the question of revolutionary war and 'terror', of the nation and cosmopolitanism. The revolutionary event casts this tension in the form of a process; hence, indeed, the irreducible dualism of the categories mobilized to think the revolution, simultaneously both event and process. An expansive process by its very nature, permanently displacing the limits within which some have sought to confine it *ex post facto*,[16] the temporality of the Revolution is in fact pregnant with – indeed, saturated with – the future. Thus it presents itself – to paraphrase Hegel – as the temporality of the becoming-subject of the substance of politics, whatever term is used to designate this substance: *multitudo*, the 'masses', the 'people', or, later, the 'people of the people', that is, the 'proletariat'.

In the post-Revolutionary era, it is no longer possible to put a 'natural' limit, or a limit 'in principle', on the affirmation of a right to engage in politics, or, *a fortiori*, on the universal capacity to do so. The universality in question is, however, a paradoxical one, for it is eminently 'partisan', surging up out of the very negativity characteristic of situations of domination. Freedom, in other words, can now be won only by those who are subjected to unfreedom. We can give a name to this event/process: the democratic revolution, or, again, revolutionary democracy. There can be no democracy without revolution – or rather, as Lukács said in a late work, no democratization [*Demokratisierung*] without revolution,[17] since democracy is not defined primarily in terms of institutions or procedures and still less with reference to the state, but, rather, as the set of practices which constitute mass politics. It is defined, then, in terms of a process, whose radical openness (its unpredictable instability, its indeterminate outcome) nevertheless derives from the *salto mortale* of the revolution as its founding moment, and whose development once again throws up, in its turn, the question of institutions and procedures, while subordinating it to that of practices.

Thus revolutionary time presents itself as the becoming-necessary of emancipation – on the express condition that we understand this necessity not as the manifestation of an a priori meaning or goal, but as the retroactive effect of an event, irreducibly contingent and undecidable in itself, that poses its own presuppositions, thus defining them as the conditions for its realization. The temporality of the process bears the stamp of its unfinished, and therefore reiterable, character – on condition, again, that we seek no cautious calculation behind the fact that it remains unfinished, no wisdom or ruse of reason of a gradualist kind that would put off until tomorrow what cannot be finished today, but, rather, discern in it the *failure* of the revolution coming up against its own limits: in other words, the fact that it misses its mark, in a failure which is as destructive as it is necessary, precisely in so far as it is only when the process is grasped (retrospectively) as such, on the basis of the series of internal determinations which show that it is in fact a 'defeat', that it can begin anew. This, then, is why the self-criticism *of* the revolution – for access to it is reserved for those who adopt the perspective of its defeat [*défaite*], that of the void of the situation attested by this undoing [*dé-faire*] of the revolution – is the very condition for its reactivation, the condition for the 'inversion' of the void into a new opening on to the event.

But something must also be said about the space that this process marks off as it unfolds: the French Revolution and its direct consequences – which can be extended to encompass, at the very least, the Napoleonic Wars – constituted a European event, the event that made it possible to define Europe in terms of something other than an aggregation of dynastic sovereignties, or the cosmopolitanism of the Roman Catholic Church. And that is not all: coming after the establishment of American independence and the formation of 'Atlantic' centres of revolution,[18] and extending, in the phase of its radicalization and at the price of untold contradictions, to the abolition of slavery and the spread of the revolution to the colonies, the French Revolution did not remain isolated. It took its place in a nascent movement of decolonization, and inaugurated a cycle of revolutions on a world scale. Its universality was the concrete universality of an emancipatory force that challenged the world order put in place by centuries of European expansion, colonial pillage, and the slave trade. Its defeat bore down with all its weight on the defeated – from the humiliated Parisian *faubourgs* to the Antilles in revolt; from France's fragile Italian or Rhenish 'sister republics' to those who had secretly agitated for a republic among the English proletariat. That is why the self-criticism of the revolution is nothing other than the process by which it 'became a world': a laborious process that transformed the revolution itself as much as it transformed the world it brought into being.

German Idealism attests that this process of becoming is in no sense linear; it is not the simple extension – not even an irregular, accident-ridden extension – of a principle defined once and for all at the outset. A vast movement of intellectual and moral reform, and of the formation of new groups of intellectuals, Idealism was condemned to anticipate politics, or even to proceed at cross-purposes with it, in a country for which unification in a nation-state remained (in the period that interests us) a remote objective; as a result of the extreme fragmentation of the territory, combined with economic backwardness, culture had played (since Luther's translation of the Bible) a 'hyperinflated' role in ensuring national unification and communication among the various social spheres. As a recommencement of the *Aufklärung* and its inaugural moment in Germany, the Reformation, classical philosophy reflected a world-historical moment that was doubly mediated by, on the one hand, the fact that the revolutionary event had already taken place; and, on the other, by the deferral of its effects, or the 'impossibility' – that is, the constant denegation – of a German revolution, which was no sooner evoked than it was dismissed out of hand.

Philosophy took the form of a reflexive reaction to the crisis inaugurated by the revolutionary event; yet it ended up reproducing its presuppositions, refusing to produce any possibilities other than a reformulation of the *Aufklärung* as 'reformism from above'. From this point of view, as both Heine and Gramsci have emphasized, philosophy even retreated to a pre-Reformation position, which had succeeded (within, to be sure, certain limits) in mobilizing both the 'top' and the 'bottom' of society, the peasantry and sections of the aristocracy and the intellectuals, and then actively incorporating them into a new historical bloc of social forces. In retrospect, Kant's and Hegel's reformist ambivalence looks like the last attempt to maintain the line of the *Aufklärung* – top-down reforms carried out without the participation of the people, combined with relative auton-omy for intellectuals – in a period in which this line had already become untenable. The mobilization of the German princes by the anti-French coalition, the emergence of a profoundly anti-democratic, Francophobe, and spontaneously anti-Semitic nationalist tendency, the extreme agressive-ness of the aristocracy in the face of a mortal threat – all this created radically new conditions, unleashed destructive forces of hitherto unsus-pected dimensions, and intensified the polarization of the situation. Because they had failed to measure themselves against this objective reality, Kant's propositions about 'publicity', or Hegel's about the organic state – to say nothing of Schiller's civic-aesthetic education – looked more like signs of impotence than concrete political interventions, even of a mod-erate, gradualist kind.

Yet the trajectory of German Idealism cannot be summed up as the reproduction of its own impotence and its infinite remoteness from the event, which is the criticism the Hegelian left would later direct at it. Haunted from within by the fact of the revolution, which it made into a founding reference point of modern reflexivity and national culture, Idealism carried the idea of the impossibility of revolution to an extreme; it thereby created a *new* situation. In other words, Idealism's predictable failure led to an exacerbation of the crisis, which now took the *internalized* form of a twofold division between a cultural/intellectual sphere that was 'advanced', in that it had already 'digested' – if not anticipated – the effects of the revolutionary event; and the political and socio-economic reality of a country which was still profoundly marked by the *ancien régime* – and would, to boot, suffer the consequences of the reactionary rigidifi-cation of the princely courts that had joined in the struggle against republican, Napoleonic France.

German theory and culture thus reflected a *twofold* gap: the gap internal to the pair Germany/France (or, if you like, Germany/the French Revolution), which served as a trope for the relation between theory and practice; but also the gap which separated them from their own reality, which then appeared in the guise of the 'German *misère*' of which Heine would speak. Once it had attained self-consciousness, the crisis became unbearable. The intellectual and moral reform promoted by classical philosophy had ultimately – by virtue, precisely, of its political failure – triumphed on its own ground, if only in the sense that it demonstrated the futility of all subjective positions attempting to escape the crisis: the classical illusion that one could remain at an Olympian distance from the event no less than the regressive reveries of the Romantics. Having lost its innocence, German theoretical consciousness could only confirm something that nothing and no one had initially perceived or desired: namely, that the impossibility/denegation of revolution changes into its opposite, the impossibility of non-revolution. More: this development concealed in its depths a founding narrative which made the revolution the very horizon of contemporary reality, and endowed Germany with 'progressive' traditions (the sequence Reformation/Peasant Wars/*Aufklärung* as its culmination), thereby revealing, just below the surface, a revolutionary possibility still more ripe than the one bequeathed to posterity by the French.

From Kant to Marx, the trajectory of German theory described the new space opened up by the revolution once it had been raised to the level of its concept, in the very precise sense that its self-criticism, which conditioned its timeliness, was elaborated in that space. The legacy of classical Idealism – or, if you prefer, its confession of failure, that is to say, the consciousness that the German situation was untenable, unreal or inactual (in the Hegelian sense): this was what the *Vormärz* generation inherited. But Idealism's failure – which, as we have seen, is barely distinguishable from its success (on condition that it is grasped retrospectively, from the standpoint of the self-critical process sustaining it) – was to have a striking impact on the new configuration taken by the German and European crisis in the years leading up to 1848.

Indeed, the 1830s and 1840s marked a turning point in the global situation, shaped as they were by a twofold tendency: from below, a resumption of revolutionary activity; and, in response to it, a more fiercely absolutist reaction on the part of the authorities. More than a warning, the 1830 July Days, which had been preceded and were followed by the emergence of multiple focal points of the revolution in Europe (the Belgian Revolution, the Greek and Serbian wars of independence, insurrections in Italy, unrest in Germany) and beyond its boundaries (especially in Latin America), bore witness to the illusory nature of the restorationist enterprise of the Holy Alliance. In Germany itself, in the wake of the

Hambach festival, the cracks in the power structure became increasingly evident, threatening the fragile equilibrium established during the anti-Napoleonic wars. But it was the attitude of the absolutist state that was chiefly responsible for exacerbating the crisis: every call for change promptly led to a new turn of the screw by the repressive apparatus, which sought to create the impression that it was restoring order and was fiercely resolved to block all change, although in fact it succeeded only in making radicalization inevitable in the long run.

Thus the situation had reached a total impasse. The *Aufklärung*, with its extension in classical philosophy, had ended in failure; the aesthetic age belonged to a past that was dead and gone; as for 'actually existing' Romanticism, it now wore the grotesque, repugnant features of the regime of Friedrich Wilhelm IV. When the king decided to eliminate the last pockets of freedom left to the oppositional intelligentsia and liberal reformism (the press, the publishing industry and academia) the turn the crisis took dictated the production of new possibilities. The only remaining option was that of rupture: finding a way to break out of the situation became, in a certain sense, the shared mission of the generation of Marx, the Bauers, Hess and Engels, which explains the ambiguous 'family resemblance' that links them all – a mixture of bombast and a desire for innovation, frenzied pursuit of the radical and the oppressive sense of being mere epigones.

It was precisely from this crossroads (for which the turn of 1842–43 serves as a sort of natural landmark) that a number of competing – even antagonistic – routes branched out. The first, which falls outside the scope of our study, consisted in repeating, in a hyperbolic mode, the gesture of classical philosophy, of 'criticism', or of spirit confronting the world – all in the name of moving beyond it. This was the Young Hegelian road, 'critical criticism' *à la* Bauer; without the faintest shadow of a bad conscience, theory began to celebrate its divorce from practice. Feverish activism in the world of the press, accompanied by flirtation with literary-journalistic Bohemianism (for which the absolutist regimes displayed a certain tolerance), succeeded to the restlessness of the concept, and the intellectual-as-apostle-of-'criticism' sank into narcissistic contemplation of his isolation and impotence. A veritable fountainhead of the versions of nihilism to come, this sort of Young Hegelianism 'realized' classical philosophy, in its fashion: repeating, in a regressive mode, the very terms of its failure, it exposed the fault-line running through it.

The second road, which I have called that of the 'social' and of 'social-ism', is exemplified by men such as Hess and the young Engels. To appreciate the originality of their trajectory, we must first – as I hope I have shown – cease to consider them in a teleological relationship to Marx (making Hess Marx's 'precursor' and Engels his [eternal] 'faithful right-hand man', or by a simple inversion, his 'henchman'), that is to say, as evolving in a direction determined in advance, with Marx as its *terminus ad quem*. Still more: we must acknowledge the profound contradiction that *separates* them from Marx. The social-ist road, especially in its Hessian–Engelsian variant, attempts to confront the crisis by making a leap beyond politics that is not a form of regression towards the purity of the concept or the 'criticism' cherished by the Young Hegelians, but a search for a new unifying principle lodged within the relations of bourgeois society. The 'social' accordingly appears as the expression of an approach to the revolutionary event that grasps it within its limits; it is the right name for that which the revolution ran up against, exposing it without being able to go beyond it.

It soon becomes clear, however, that this search was short-circuited by a desire for premature reconciliation, which was rather hastily confused with an exit from the ambiguities of the past. The failure of the German road was not fully reflected on; far from being resolved, the ambiguities were simply shifted on to a new terrain. The 'social-ist' self-criticism of politics was transformed into an imaginary neutralization of antagonism in a new Absolute, the 'social'. A secularized figure of transcendence – even, in Hess's case (as in almost all the 'social-isms' of the day), a secularized reconstruction of the politico-religious – the social turns out to be the technology characteristic of the modern period, which aims to reveal the harmonious essence of the life of the community whose concrete emergence it at last makes possible, thanks to its project for the reorganization of society as a whole.

The question of class – or, rather, of *class antagonism* – accordingly functions as a kind of litmus test which reveals this double dilution of the political in the infra-political or antipolitical (the organization of socio-economic exchanges as a way of abolishing the anarchy and competition characteristic of mercantile-bourgeois society) or in the metapolitical instance of the social regarded as a secular religion ('humanist' or 'humanitarian', in the vocabulary of the day). The limit case – which, as such, is paradigmatic – is, of course, that of Engels. The figure of the proletariat that this *flâneur* and physiologist of the English city discovers is pinned to the grid of the objectifying (medical) gaze characteristic of the engineers of the social; the proletarian, who turns out to be a veritable compendium of the debilitating 'pathologies' brought on by industrialization, is constantly haunted by his double, the embodiment of the dangerous class and the symptom of an unbearable antagonism. In the face of this situation, the task that devolves upon this socialism, which pretends to be both scientific and humanist at the same time, is to show the proletariat its essential humanity. This humanity, which the proletariat shares with its class enemy, makes it possible to transcend the split between antagonistic classes; it clears a path for the harmonization of society that can circumvent the trauma of revolution or confrontation on the treacherous ground of the political.

What becomes strictly inconceivable in the context defined by this 'socialist humanism' is the thematization of a working-class politics or a politics of class (i.e. a politics conceived on the basis of the antagonism between capital and labour) as well as a revolutionary-democratic perspective, which is considered to be an illusory diversion alien to the 'social' instance. Once politics has thus been pitched overboard, a space is created for moral preaching addressed to each of the contending parties (exhortations to mutual restraint for the sake of a common humanity); it is borne up by a naive faith that each side can correct the other's errors, and that the various working-class organizations will spontaneously merge. Yet the fierceness of the clashes within the German workers' movement, both before the 1848 Revolution (in the Communist League) and during it, between a 'social-ist' line advocating political indifferentism and resolutely opposing participation in the democratic revolution, and a line à la Marx, linking 'permanent revolution' to working-class hegemony of the bloc of forces supporting revolutionary democracy, show that there was no resolving the massive contradictions stemming from differences that might seem merely speculative.

There was an aggravating circumstance: the German 'social-ist' road appears all the more abstract (in the narrow sense of the word: formed by abstraction, exclusion of the concrete) and impracticable in that it had to do without the basis on which its French or English originals rested: a 'liberal' (by the standards of the day) political compromise à la française (the July monarchy) or the dynamism of capitalist development in Britain. It should also be noted that the denegation of the political by the 'social' produced, in its turn, wholly determinate political effects: at the moment when, in England or France, Owenism and even Saint-Simonianism were exercising a far-reaching influence on the self-organization of the working class, Engels and Hess were attempting to persuade the Rhenish bourgeoisie to demonstrate its humanity. . . . As for the absolutist – especially the Prussian – regimes, which never failed to provide reminders of their existence whenever the opposition pretended to forget it, they hardly seemed convinced that this 'social' sensibility represented a threat, preferring to train their fire on the demands for democracy.[19] This will not seem at all surprising if we bear in mind that most of the representatives of German socialism (from Grün to Gottschalk, and, later, Lassalle) repeatedly endorsed the idea of a 'popular' monarchy, which they preferred to a 'red republic' – even during the 1848 Revolution. Metapolitical radicalization was inverted into a new figure of impotence, even of philistinism.

Heine's and Marx's road was altogether different, for they never lost sight of the red thread that bound democracy to the revolution. Why is Heine a key figure in the evolution of the crisis of post-revolutionary, but also pre-revolutionary, Europe? To begin with, because it so happens that he had occasion to converse with Goethe, Hegel and Marx, and was able to confront modernity's aesthetic task *par excellence*: namely, the break with Romanticism, its religion of art and worship of the individual genius. This was a break that could be accomplished only by, precisely, the 'last of the Romantics', who preserved the radical thrust of Romanticism (its fashioning of a 'popular' language and form, its art of the fragment, its irony and ambiguity) – in short, its anti-Classical edge. Inextricably interweaving aesthetic and political modernity, Heine, living in the capital of the European revolution, forged a new language whose raw material was history, and whose form was intrinsically dialectical.

But Heine interests us in a properly 'German' mode, in that he refuses to dissociate the stakes of the aesthetic from politics quite as firmly as he resists the separation of politics from philosophy. In other words, he interests us because he thinks the effect of the encounter of the French Jacobin tradition in the field of philosophy with the national/popular aspirations revealed (and perverted) by Romanticism. The first to offer a revolutionary interpretation of Hegelianism, he appears as the veritable founder of what the next generation would call the 'Hegelian left', embodying a tendency within it that was distinct from – and no doubt in competition with – that of Strauß (and, later, Bruno Bauer): one that was less concerned with theology and the confrontation, on this ground, with the German-Christian state – in short, a tendency that was less 'Prussian' in that it had turned more directly towards politics and towards France. In secret sympathy with the most radical tendencies of the popular movement, whether French or German, Heine elaborated a cultural project with hegemonic ambitions, and a political project that defined the tasks of revolutionary democracy on the scale of the historico-social totality.

To put it differently: if Heine took up the legacy of Romanticism and classical philosophy, it was in order to confront the riddle of his times from a world-historical standpoint. A Hegelian 'with a French heart' – to echo Feuerbach – he discerned, in a present haunted by the shade of 1789–93 and the tragicomic spectres of its repetition, the possibility of making a *new* revolution, an authentic Franco–German *Aufhebung* of the previous one. This would be an unprecedented revolution; yet it had a long-standing score to settle, for, as the sudden apparition of its ghostly double teaches us, only this revolution could redeem the defeats and humiliations of the past, liberating the present from the threat that the sphinx of its own timeliness held dangling over its head. Heine opened a breach in the crisis which thereby ceased to reproduce its own impossibilities and began to open out on to new constitutive processes.

It fell, however, to the theoretician to raise the alternative to the level of the concept. Marx's trajectory in this short period (he wrote his first Parisian texts barely three years after finishing his doctoral dissertation) may be likened, in many respects, to an accelerated passage down the road travelled by the theoretical consciousness of his day. Setting out from a political Hegelianism bent to the service of a strategy of democratization that played with and upon the authorized (and the conceivable) limits of the German road, the publicist who worked for the *Rheinische Zeitung* responded to the exacerbation of the crisis by making a 'perilous leap' in thought that had its spatial counterpart in his move from Germany to Paris. Elaborating a self-criticism of philosophy (a Hegelianism beyond Hegel) and, at the same time, of politics (the inversion of reformist impracticability into a new revolutionary possibility), he faced up to the unfinished nature of the revolutionary event, arriving at the consciousness of its 'absolute' limits, that is, of the retroactive necessity of its 'failure' to the emergence of something new.

It is true – as the 'social-ist' road affirmed, but as Hegel's analysis of the aporias of bourgeois society had already indicated – that a politics defined within the horizon of the French Revolution cannot *but* confront its own premises (the relations of civil society, the 'social') if it is not to become ineffectual, or even reactionary; yet Marx does not therefore conclude that politics should be abandoned. He demands, on the contrary, that politics be redefined. The transition from a strategy of the public sphere (the Rhenish moment) to that of true democracy (the moment of Kreuznach), and thence to a strategy of the radical revolution placed under the sign of the proletariat (the Parisian moment), is the mark of this twofold movement of a constant redefining of boundaries: confronted with its presuppositions, politics is 'reduced' or resituated within its limits, and stripped of its pretensions to the absolute (whether as a pure act immanent in the life of the community, or as an unlimited capacity of manipulation extrinsic to it), but only in order immediately to emerge in an (always-already) extended and concretely radicalized mode, as revolutionary politics, a reconstruction of the spheres of social life grasped from within, in their articulation as a whole.

Far from dissolving into the social, politics discovers its concept in the event/process of the revolution; yet, in a certain sense, it cannot but miss it. Such is the paradox – too often occluded or misunderstood – of politics in the Marxian sense of the word: that is to say, a politics subject to the condition of the revolution; for the revolution is not, strictly speaking, either 'political' or 'social' (or 'socioeconomic'). It is, rather, that on the basis of which, precisely, the distinction between the political and the social (or the socioeconomic) is made possible, and becomes meaningful: a distinction which, however, ceaselessly cancels itself out in the twofold (revolutionary) process of the 'reduction' (de-absolutization) and radicalization of politics.

This also enables us to account for another of Marx's paradoxes, that of the status of the proletariat, which, as we have seen, he puts at the opposite pole from the sociological positivity of an Engels. To name the 'proletariat', rather than describe its 'condition', and to identify it with the negativity of a non-class which reveals the antagonism inherent in bourgeois society, rather than treating it as a massive empirical fact destined to be absorbed by the ideal figure of human plenitude – what does this come down to, if not to calling, in the performative mode, for a type of political practice that has yet to be constructed and, more importantly, to be thought? Notwithstanding a recurrent temptation to substantialist regression, especially in the direction of the anthropology of labour adumbrated in the Paris manuscripts (the '1844 Manuscripts') and *The Holy Family*, it is because Marx sets out from this *constitutively* political status of the proletariat (which is therefore fundamentally unstable as well, since it is never fixed by the guarantee of an ideal mission) that he can forge the theory of bourgeois society (which later becomes the theory of the capitalist mode of production), on condition that it is thought in its unity with the theory of the revolution – where, in this unity, the political nature of that theory is at stake.

This result heralds an important turn, one of which we, too, must take the measure. The problematic of the radical revolution and the constitution of the proletariat poses politics as permanent revolution; it is the first formulation of this idea that innovates with respect to the language of the Jacobins (which Heine still spoke: the right to existence, the aristocracy of money, etc.) – that of a revolutionary doctrine of natural law and a concept of 'citizenship'. Yet, as we have seen, Marx's formulation is also elaborated in the context of a break with the matrix of the 'social' and 'social-ism', once Marx had become aware of their paradoxes. The theoretical revolution that ensued, from *The German Ideology* down to the critique of political economy, the work of an entire lifetime, would be inconceivable without this inaugural political break.

Marx's communism – on the threshold of which our study comes to an end – is not, then, one form of communism among the others that preceded or, possibly, came after it; it is not simply one more item on the list of the various 'communisms' that have appeared in history since Plato or the Franciscans.[20] This is not to say that the Marxian version of communism represents the ultimate figure of something that had been present in embryo from the very beginning, and, in more or less finished form, throughout the evolution whose culmination it is supposed to be. If Marx's communism continues to qualify as an event, it is quite simply to the extent that it shatters this succession of inert figures following one another in a homogeneous, indifferent time; it is because there is a 'before Marx' and an 'after Marx' which radically reorders – even for us, today – the entire sequence of the figures of communism.

If Marx carries this charge, it is not only because – *pace* the canonical narrative – his trajectory does not follow automatically from one particular figure of communism, the one embodied in 'social-ism', whose aporetic political inscription it is supposed to share. Even if it means choosing, it is preferable, as we have seen, to situate Marx at the opposite pole from a Hess, in the lineage of the communism associated with the tradition of the French Revolution and a Jacobin–Babouvist matrix recast in Hegelian terms, which serves as his guide in his first, 'social' battle over the theft of wood. Rather than an Achilles heel, or the sign of a troubling lacuna, politics is, in my opinion, Marx's *strong point*, the point where his work is at its most open and innovative; it is here that it displays a novelty of the kind which so transforms its object that it never ceases, precisely, to elicit all kinds of resistance from those who strive to return at all costs to the previously existing configuration. Marx was a political actor and thinker *par excellence*, and only became such by elaborating the theory of his practice: in this he was closer to a Tocqueville than to a Proudhon, or to his Young Hegelian contemporaries (whose disappearance from the scene – so different from Marx's continuing presence – was signed and sealed by the revolutions of 1848).

Yet that is not quite all. In a certain sense, Marx was no more 'Jacobin' than 'social-ist', no more 'French' or 'English' than 'German' (or again, no more 'political' than 'social' or, *a fortiori*, 'economistic'), because his trajectory was precisely not based on *adhesion* to one or another of the pre-existing figures of communism. Rather, it opened on to the highly unpredictable event constituted by their *encounter* under the sign of their reciprocal *self-criticism*. Thus it was a trajectory that transformed *all* of them under the impact of the novelty that Marx introduced. In this sense, we should not look behind his intervention for the act of a 'thinker of genius', a thinker who was 'right' where all the others were wrong; we should, rather, look through it to the moment in which the long, slow labour of the self-rectification of the democratic revolution crossed a new threshold.

Marx's act of intellectual insurrection, carried out under the determinate (and extreme) conditions that made it possible 'negatively', as it were (failure, exile, and the concomitant solitude), was an act that took its place in the wider historical experience, the multifaceted development of a radicalization that left its stamp on many different spheres of social life throughout the years leading up to 1848. Yet Marx, by inscribing this experience in the history of philosophy – or, more precisely, in its margins – produced a possibility that has no known precedent: that of communism as the never-ending, self-critical return of the democratic revolution. In this, too, he represents an event: it displays a sign of 'rememoration, demonstration, and prognostication'. And it is only after he has led us to this threshold that, on our own trajectory, we take our leave of him, at the point where the German road forks in two very different directions – one of which opens on to a radical alternative.

Afterword
Interview with Sebastian Budgen
Translated by David Broder

Against the Stream
Sebastian Budgen: It would be useful to begin with a short biographical note. What baggage did you have when you arrived in France, aged eighteen? What were your first experiences, your first encounters? Why did you decide to write the dissertation that would later become *Philosophy and Revolution?*
Stathis Kouvelakis: While I have loved reading since I was a child, I took an interest in Marxism for mainly political, rather than bookish, reasons. My activism began in Greece, during my high school years. Among my generation, that choice was quite widespread. In 1981, I joined the youth organisation of what was called the Greek Communist Party (Interior), which was Eurocommunist in orientation. Althusser was relatively widely read within that political tendency – which was in the minority as compared to the orthodox Communist Party but had a major audience among high school and university students. More widely, in Greece during that era, Althusserian Marxism was in the air, both in militant milieux and among those circles simply interested in intellectual debate. One reason for this was that there was a large audience for the works of Nicos Poulantzas, who was in a sense the official theorist of the Eurocommunist current. He provided a form of political translation of Althusserianism, even as he proposed an original theoretical elaboration.

Arriving in France in 1983, after briefly passing by way of economics, I began my study of philosophy, seeking to deepen my intellectual interest in Marx and Marxism, and to place it within a wider perspective. For some years, I was also active in the Union of Communist Students (UEC)[1] and, above all, in the French Communist Party (PCF), which I left when Pierre Juquin declared his candidacy for the 1988 presidential election – though I ultimately remained quite close to it up till the end of the 1990s.[2] I did all my studies at Paris Nanterre University, where I very quickly entered into contact with Georges Labica, who supervised my dissertation.[3]

I began working on this thesis at the very beginning of the 1990s, and I finished it at the University of Paris VIII in 1998, under the supervision of Jean-Marie Vincent. So I 'hurried slowly', as they say ... Apart from incidental factors, I think the reason why this work took so long was that I was looking to follow my own path. Indeed, it was during these years that I changed my approach to Marx and that I drew away from Althusserianism – albeit without becoming anti-Althusserian.

Could you situate your trajectory in the French context of the 1980s and 1990s, which saw the rapid reflux of Marxism and, more broadly, the end of the multiform radicalization that had marked French society in the wake of 1968?
By the start of the 1990s, and in fact long before that, it had become clear that anyone who chose to work openly on Marx, or from a perspective identifying with Marx, was committing suicide in terms of their academic career. This was particularly the case in philosophy, but not only there; I think we could say the same of any university department. So right from the start, I knew that this choice would come at a heavy cost – and indeed I was not mistaken, either in terms of my own career or those of the handful of people who made comparable choices during that era. From the early 1980s onward, a real wall was erected in the French university and in connected arenas – publishing, 'established' journals, media access – which excluded from the field of legitimate discussion and research subjects any work on (or based on) Marx and Marxism.

I must insist on this point because there is now a tendency to construct a sort of history of ideas in which we emphasize – and, in part, quite rightly so – that the retreat of Marxism is the consequence of the decline of the organisations and regimes that claimed its mantle. What this narrative tends to obscure is that Marxism underwent an extremely methodical purge which combined a powerful element of what Bourdieu calls 'symbolic violence' with an implicit but very effective exclusion from access to any academic position . The result, in generational terms, is that my generation is the least represented in France among the people working within a Marxist framework. Thus the 'original choice' – to use Sartre's term – that lay behind my selection of this specific subject was the choice to reinvent a form of unity of theory and practice: one that would be adequate to a difficult conjuncture, where there was little choice but to learn to swim against the current.

More particularly, this search for theoretical-practical unity meant rejecting the stance, rather widespread among a certain milieu, that juxtaposes radical political positions, or even political engagement, with academic work that respects the framework of institutional legitimacy. For my part, I have never accepted this game of Dr Jekyll and Mr Hyde: I am not a legitimate academic by day and a 'subversive' by night. I have stuck to working on this subject not in spite of the circumstances but because of them – all the while conscious that this means falling out with many people, most importantly the French university as an institution.

Even so, the academic context of this era – the one in which your work is inscribed – is marked by the role played by Georges Labica and the people around him, as they worked to resist throughout their own era.
I think that André Tosel summed it up most judiciously in his text on the 'thousand Marxisms'. He wrote that it is thanks to Georges Labica – his dogged work, his initiatives and his capacity to rally people around himself – that what had been a rout could be transformed into an 'intelligent retreat' that prepared the terrain for an intellectual revival – and perhaps, ultimately, one that was not only intellectual.[4] From my BA onwards, I had the privilege of regularly following the activities of the Marxist research group led by Georges Labica. This group – its core made up of philosophy lecturers at Nanterre University and researchers at the National Centre for Scientific Research (CNRS) – brought together what was, in my view, the greater part of the theoretical work on Marxism being done in France at the time: it was truly its intellectual epicentre. I see this as an exciting adventure that played out in a period – the 1980s – which has been characterized by a lucid cultural historian as a 'great nightmare'.[5]

Georges Labica enjoyed great moral authority, and for me he was a model of political and intellectual firmness, engagement and tenacity in the face of every challenge. He was also a very generous person who never sought to impose his own personal agenda on others, either politically or intellectually; he had a capacity to get very different people working around him, while deeply respecting their distinct personalities. That is a quality I have never found elsewhere, especially in the academic milieu. He did not like talking about himself, and, in my view, he was also someone who took insufficient concern to promote and spread his own work.

Was this group coherent in theoretical terms, or was it already heading towards the fragmentation to which André Tosel referred with his formula, 'the thousand Marxisms'?
We might say that Labica's leadership ensured the regulated and yet productive coexistence of a multiplicity of orientations. Most of the members of the group, or those regularly associated with its activities, were attached to what I would call Althusserianism in the broad sense. Put

another way, they belonged not to the small circle of Althusser's disciples who all came out of the École Normale Supérieure, but, like Labica himself, to a second circle: a periphery of the Althusserian current. Some of them – including Labica – had participated in the journal *Dialectiques*, which had profoundly marked the Marxism of the 1970s. Indeed, it is mentioned as participating as such in the first edition of the *Dictionnaire critique du marxisme* (1982), which was the group's founding act.

So the dominant atmosphere was post-Althusserian but included trajectories that increasingly asserted their own singularity. We should mention the names of Tony Andréani, Jacques Bidet and Jean Robelin, as well as the close relations that always existed between this group and André Tosel, who was based first in Nice, then in Besançon and subsequently – sadly, all too briefly – in Paris. However, alongside this post-Althusserianism, there were also strong personalities that represented very different orientations, such as Jacques Texier, a pioneer of Gramscian scholarship in France; Solange Mercier-Josa, who did essential work on Hegel and the Young Hegelians; and Michèle Bertrand, who produced interesting work on the relation between Marxism, ideology and psychoanalysis.

There were a lot of PhD students gravitating to this group. I myself belong to a cohort of several dozen researchers working, during more or less the same period, under Georges Labica's supervision. The remarkable thing – and this says a lot about the intellectual and political context of those years – is that, within this group, the 'foreigners' were very much in the majority. And when I say 'foreigners', I do not just mean the 'non-French', but researchers who, for the most part, returned to their country of origin once they finished their theses. Among those of us working more explicitly on Marx and Marxism, almost all were 'foreigners', or else atypical PhD students – in general, secondary school teachers deciding to embark on their research at a relatively advanced age. So we saw that the problem of a generational rupture, and of the nonrenewal of Marxism's presence in the French university as an institution, was clearly posed.

One last thing: this group had a rather developed network of international contexts, for the most part in Italy (and that was the legacy of what had begun with *Dialectiques*). At a certain moment, in the 1970s, we could speak of a 'Latin Marxism' around the journal *Dialectiques,* the left-Eurocommunist network around Pietro Ingrao and his circle in Italy, and intellectuals such as Nicos Poulantzas and Christine Buci-Glucksmann in France who brought back to life an arc that had begun with the exchanges between Antonio Labriola and Georges Sorel at the beginning of the twentieth century. But by the 1980s and 1990s, the interlocutors had changed: no longer were they the major intellectuals of the Italian Communist Party, but philosophers like Domenico Losurdo, Alberto Burgio and Costanzo Preve. The group also had a developed array of contacts in Germany, including Wolfgang Haug and Berlin's *Das Argument* group (whose great project, the *Historisch-kritisches Wörterbuch des Marxismus,* was inspired by the *Dictionnaire critique du marxisme*), and in the Spanish-speaking world (I remember Francisco Fernández Buey and Pedro Ribas, in particular).

What was almost totally missing was any opening to the English-speaking world (with the exception of David McLellan). This was certainly a paradox, but it was also an obvious limitation, given that, during that era, the international centre of gravity of Marxism had already shifted towards Anglophone countries. In France at that time, there was almost no recognition of this fact. The reason for this is no doubt to be found in the weight of a network that had, for the most part, come out of the communist intelligentsia of the previous period, but also – despite the very open and interdisciplinary character of the themes addressed – in the essentially philosophical orientation of this group. This explains how the work of the likes of Fredric Jameson or David Harvey could go unnoticed at the very moment that the aura around them was growing at the international level.

Could we characterize this core that formed around Labica as orphans of the left wing of the French Communist Party, dissidents who left the party at the turn of the 1980s and who – to put it briefly – had decided to forget about political activism and reorient their energies towards academic research?

In broad terms, I think that is an accurate assessment, but it is only one side of the coin. Indeed, Labica had understood that the only way to pursue a systematic and collective work around Marx, from the 1980s onwards, was to distance oneself from political apparatuses. In other words, while important theoretical work – with all its limits – had been achieved in militant spaces during the previous period, these spaces now belonged to the past. The only concrete option to guarantee continuity, but also a handover of the reins, was to build something at the institutional (and thus university) level.

All the same, I should emphasize the fact that Labica never lost sight of the contradictions inherent to his approach. Working within the university, he took a resolute stance against any attempt at an 'academic Marxism' amputated of its political and interventionist dimension, submissive to intellectual fashions, or which internalized the dominant criteria for legitimacy. He always railed against attitudes that suggested, 'Let's withdraw into our studies in order to work from some celestial point of view.' Labica fiercely attacked the claim that philosophy's task consists of providing other theoretical practices with their supposedly missing (ethical, ontological, etc.) 'foundation'. He had an uncompromising conceptual ambition to produce a comprehensive theoretical work, including the relatively special-ized aspects which that can entail. But this project was always linked to the questions posed by the conjuncture.

I will mention just one example of this. Owing, notably, to his own personal journey, which strongly intersected with the history of Algeria, Labica was doubtless among the first to understand how important religion and the politics/religion relationship were going to become, starting in the early 1980s. This was a theme which the research group he directed studied for many years, with contributors coming from a broad disciplinary and intellectual spectrum. I think that this is where we should locate the cement for a group that had such diverse orientations: in a form of nonsectarian fidelity to Marxism, and in the rejection of philosophy's superiority to other forms of knowledge and to other social and political practices.

Moreover, Labica himself was a model of the combative intellectual, even if we could not say as much of all the members of the group. He did not hesitate to stick his neck out, including on the political and militant plane, even after leaving the PCF. I remember him being a joint candidate supported by both the LCR[6] and the PSU[7] in the Hauts-de-Seine in the 1986 parliamentary elections. Over the 1980s he was close to the LCR, and he also took part in the initial discussions that resulted in the campaign around Pierre Juquin in the 1988 presidential contest. He then distanced himself from French politics and refocused on anti-imperialism, and especially on Palestine. He was also conscious of the fact that even if he had achieved a 'small miracle' in creating this space for Marxism within a university institu-tion that vehemently rejected it, this was a very precarious gain which was constantly under threat. Indeed, it did not survive his retirement in the mid-1990s.

Marx and Political Theory

How did you put together the research subject that led to *Philosophy and Revolution*?
The question gnawing away at me long before I began working on my thesis was the problematic existence of a political theory – or thinking on the political – in Marx. This question made its mark on me, first of all because it was precisely the object of the debate that was underway at the time I became active as a militant. For the most part, this debate played out in Italy, but it also did so – in a different form – in France, revolving around the interventions of Nicos Poulantzas, Althusser, and Étienne Balibar – not to forget those of the Trotskyist current, in particular Ernest Mandel and Henri Weber. We followed all of this very closely in Greece, especially

because the Greek Communist Party (Interior) was very plugged in to the debates in Italian communism and French Marxism. We were keenly aware that it was, in the last analysis, Norberto Bobbio who had won out in the controversy that he had initiated. And this victory, of course, said a lot about the strategic, theoretical, and even existential crisis which the communist movement was undergoing at that time.

Bobbio's arguments are well known: that there is no theory of the state in Marx and, particularly, that there is no theory of the socialist state. More fundamentally, he argued that there is no conceptualization of the political – in the strong sense of the term – in Marx, beyond some instrumental and reductive considerations on institutions, law and democracy. All of these are supposed to disappear under communism, assimilated to the withering away not only of the state but of the political as such. For Bobbio, the Stalinist regime and its avatars were able to establish themselves precisely on the basis of this absence, or more exactly, this blind spot. That is also the reason why, according to him, the Eurocommunist strategy – itself the heir to the Gramscian approach speaking of a 'Western road' to revolution – was an aporia, with no possible resolution other than rallying to social democracy and the renunciation of any anti-capitalist perspective.

Of course, this debate was at a quite different level to that of the hullaba-loo created in France by the 'nouveaux philosophes', who made out that Marx is directly to blame for the Gulags. Nonetheless, Bobbio's argument did, in substance, amount to saying that, in the last analysis, the roots of Stalinist degeneration and the impasse of the revolution in the West are to be found somewhere in Marx's theory itself, rather than in the logic of historical situations. What I subsequently realized – to my great surprise, I must say – is that during that same period Althusser had come to rather similar conclusions. Certainly, most of these texts were published only posthumously, notably 'Marx in His Limits',[8] but these positions were also quite clearly stated in his last public interventions, in texts like 'At Last the Crisis of Marxism', 'Marxism as a "Finite" Theory' and 'Marxism Today'.[9] Moreover, this explains why the retreat of Marxism in France did not owe simply to the anti-Marxism of our opponents, and thus to the political turn to the right of the late 1970s. It also owed, perhaps more than anything, to a disintegration that affected Marxism from within, particularly in the orbit of the Althusserian current that had been its most dynamic pole – we could even say one with a tendency toward hegemony – during the brief 'golden age' running from the mid-1960s to the turn of the 1980s.

My work was an attempt to situate myself within this debate by readdressing its stakes in a more fundamental way. By 'fundamental' I mean that we could not think in terms of a 'return to Marx' or a return to a 'classical

Marxism' – in other words, to the foundational texts – even if that meant proposing a novel interpretation. Rather, if we were to have any chance of arriving at new results, it was necessary to widen our focus. That meant not only integrating Engels into this narrative in a much more organic way – and Georges Labica's works had utterly convinced me that this was necessary – but, most importantly, transcending any purely 'internalist' study of Marx's texts (or Marx and Engels's texts), even while maintaining a concern for conceptual specificity and philological precision.

Initially, I thought that this meant looking towards the intellectual context that Marx broke out of – which is to say, from among the so-called 'Young Hegelians'. They were not only interlocutors but also rivals on the terrain from which Marx and Engels emerged – even if this 'and' (linking the two) points to a theoretical problem, rather than something that can be taken for granted either theoretically or biographically. I quite quickly realized that because the Young Hegelians were epigones, it was impossible to do without a return to this foundational sequence – namely, the articulations of Kant and of Hegel – that formed this study's point of departure.

At the same time, I became conscious of the fact that understanding these theoretical problems demanded a precise study of the historical conjuncture that the Germans call the *Vormärz*: the period extending from the revolutions of 1830 to the revolution of 1848. Indeed, I understood that if we really want to break with the teleological vision that makes the evolution of Marx's thought an end point, inscribed in advance through the logic of a sequence that is only its anticipation – if we want to understand, in other terms, the emergence of this thought as a real event, as a theoretical revolution in the strong sense of the term, with its dual dimensions of internal necessity and irreducible contingency – then we have to work on these three levels simultaneously. In my view, no study on the formation of Marx's thought had been able to do that or even really set out to do so.

Let's talk more specifically about Althusser, the role he played in your approach, and how you drew away from his interpretation of Marx's thought. First of all, there was a divergence in terms of method. As I said before, I wanted to readdress the question of the formation of Marx's thought by taking a wider view, going beyond a simple study of Marx's own texts. Althusser did not do that, or only did so patchily. His view of the Young Hegelians, and also of Engels's trajectory, remained rather conventional, except in the case of Feuerbach. He showed genuine interest in Feuerbach, but, for reasons owing to his own political-theoretical strategy – namely, the demands of his 'anti-humanist' polemic – Althusser greatly exaggerated Feuerbach's importance to Marx's trajectory.

The outsized place he accorded to Feuerbach correlates to the anti-Hegelian stance that Althusser shared with the protagonists of the French thought of the 1960s. But I thought that it was untenable – mistaken, on both philological and conceptual grounds – to reduce Hegel to an obstacle, an impediment from whom Marx constantly sought to free himself (but, mysteriously enough, never managed to do so – Althusser himself was forced to admit, however grudgingly, that Marx 'returned' to Hegel at the threshold of each theoretical turning point in his work, whether in the case of the *Economic and Philosophic Manuscripts of 1844* or that of the *Grundrisse*).

As concerns the endeavour of 'historicizing' the formation of Marx's thought, we know that this comes up against a double objection of principle in Althusser insofar as it contradicts both the 'scientificity' of theory, as he defines it (against Gramsci's 'historicism' more particularly), and the 'symptomatic reading' of the texts. This form of reading, to which Althusser devoted himself, is a strictly 'internalist' one, caught within the structuralist formalism that was dominant in that era.

Moreover, even if I tried (as should any researcher) to demonstrate some originality, I do not think that my work is a sort of absolute point of departure – once again, in contrast to Althusser. So I was not at all loath to discuss the different theses elaborated on this question, least of all those emanating from thinkers who identify with Marx. I did not seek to reduce these theses to mere 'ideological errors' or – as is most often the case with Althusser – to simply treat them with disregard or silence. The most important among them, polarising the debates from the 1960s onwards, was precisely Althusser's thesis of an 'epistemological break'. In this sense, my work is inevitably post-Althusserian.

This 'break' thesis is fundamental: the whole of the Althusserian approach depends upon it. But Althusser himself evolved, in terms of how he defined it. Initially, he thought of it as an 'epistemological break' in the strict sense, as a passage from the Marx of 'humanist ideology', in his youthful writings – and, on the philosophical plane, an idealism that Althusser saw not as Hegelian but rather as Young Hegelian, closer to Fichte than to Hegel – to the Marx of what Althusser calls 'science'. That is to say, he saw this as a passage to historical materialism, and one which also had a deferred effect on philosophy.

For Althusser, as for the whole 'Marxist-Leninist' tradition, Marx's theory is not limited to historical materialism alone. Rather, it also entails a whole philosophy apart, 'dialectical materialism', which Marx himself, again rather mysteriously, was unable to elaborate or, actually, even to begin working on. Althusser took on the responsibility of doing this in Marx's place. His 'symptomatic reading' of *Capital* tackles this very task through a sort of induction of the philosophy missing from Marx but, in a certain sense, practically present in the fundamental texts of historical materialism. In fact, this was more of a programmatic declaration, which would not produce many results, except a few of Althusser's elaborations in *Reading Capital* (indeed, very interesting ones, even if their relation to Marx himself is, at the least, problematic) on the notion of historical time – or, in that same volume, Balibar's general theory of transition, as well as Althusser's general definition of philosophy as a 'theory of theoretical practice', a sort of hyper-epistemology that the texts on the philosophy of scientists try to put into effect.

Through what he called 'self-criticism', Althusser engaged in a process of rectifying his early 'theoreticist' theses. He said that, despite their will to Marxist orthodoxy, these theses had ultimately ended up within the rationalist framework developed by Bachelard and Canguilhem's French school of epistemology. In his 1970s texts, he argues that what precedes and conditions the epistemological break is a political rupture. Marx takes up the perspective of the proletariat, and that is precisely where we ought to start retracing the theoretical revolution that he authored. So here we have a second Althusser, a 'politicist' Althusser who redefines historical materialism as a 'revolutionary science' and philosophy itself as a 'class struggle in theory'.

Do you concur?

Yes, that was the point of departure of my own reflection, corresponding to the Greek conjuncture I mentioned above. All the same, what struck me as I went along is that the second Althusser is, in fact, an inversion of the first – he does not really change his schema, but simply inverts it. Althusser thus ends up saying that in Marx the political break does indeed precede the epistemological break; but this rectification leads him to the conclusion that Marx was, in the last analysis, an ideologue and that, as such, he was unable to master the consequences of his own discourse. According to the second Althusser, this latter is constructed around gaps, which make up so many insurmountable theoretical aporias (the incompleteness of *Capital*; the absence of any theory of the state, of class, or of ideology; the lack of elaboration on the dialectic; etc.). Indeed, ideology is now no longer seen as simply the anti-science of the earlier texts, but as an implacable subjection mechanism that emanates from an 'interpellating' instance, thought on the model of the Church. We ought to emphasize that this conception is wholly unable to lay claim to Marx's own problematization of ideology, however we interpret it.

Far from being the 'continent of the science of History', as the first Althusser had haughtily put it, Marxism thus corresponds to a 'proletarian ideology' – meaning the workers' organisations' legitimising discourse which would ensure the subjection of their members to the bureaucratic apparatus that makes up their backbone. Marx's scientific and philosophical relevance thus appears as largely fictitious – and moreover, he would be wiped away almost completely in the late Althusser's writings on 'aleatory materialism'. While Marx's practical effectiveness had played a decisive role in the constitution of working-class subjectivity, it was now obsolete. Marxism should be understood as a 'finite' theory in the sense that it plays out within contradictions that reveal its 'finitude', and in the sense that its crisis – long deferred, but ultimately breaking out with the reflux of the 1970s – marks the exhaustion of its effects *qua* concrete form of the 'fusion of the workers' movement and theory'. Here, we are not very far from the wisdom of a Raymond Aron, the 'official' thinker of Cold War liberalism in France, and it is hardly surprising to see the late Althusser accepting the formula 'imaginary Marxism', with which the author of *The Opium of the Intellectuals* had saddled the Althusserian endeavour of the previous period.[10]

The last texts that Althusser published during his lifetime, as well as those that Balibar wrote in their wake, allowed me to get a (partial) measure of the disintegration of Althusser's thought, which was further confirmed and amplified by posthumous publications of his writings. This is particularly true of 'Marx in His Limits', in which the extent of the involution of Althusser's thought becomes manifest.[11] Here, Althusser presents an extremely instrumental vision of the theory of the state in Marx, concluding from this that, in Marx, there is not and there cannot be a theory of the political. He thus converges with the argument of the liberal socialist Bobbio. Reading this text also allowed me to explain the evolution of some of Althusser's disciples, and in particular Balibar, who subsequently continued in this aporetic-'deconstructive' and – let's say it – frankly masochistic vein over the whole period that followed.

What took over from Althusser in your work? Was it one particular author, or a more personal theoretical orientation?
I would hope that it is the second, even if – as I said – it is illusory to think that you are inventing everything anew. In my view, the necessary conclusion was that if the politicist Althusser, who had constituted my original point of departure, led only to an intellectual shipwreck, then it was necessary to start over again. A resolute shift of perspective was necessary in order to be able to historicize Marx; this served not to reduce him to a particular context (and thus sink into a banal relativism), but rather to grasp his singularity and give a full account of the disruption caused by the upsurge of an innovative, properly revolutionary thought. In this book I tried

– within the limits of someone who has had neither a historian's nor a Germanist's training – to follow the *Vormärz* period with a certain degree of accuracy and, ultimately, to understand the degree to which this period was mesmerized by the movement that would break out with the revolutionary wave of 1848. In my view, this constitutes the most important key to understanding the theoretical revolution initiated by Marx.

In so doing, what I in fact rediscovered was a 'historicist' approach to the texts, in the Gramscian sense of that term: an 'absolute' historicism. Having started out as a militant in a party that was Eurocommunist in orientation, I very soon took an interest in Gramsci, even in my high school years. This owed to Palmiro Togliatti's 'thematic' edition of Gramsci's *oeuvre*, which was available in Greece starting in the 1970s. But it is also true that, under the influence of Althusser, I first of all sought out Gramsci the political theorist, a Gramsci who was the precursor, we might say, to the late Poulantzas – the Poulantzas of *State, Power, Socialism*. After that, I began to work more in-depth on both Gramsci's philosophical writings and his – simultaneously philological and historicist – method more broadly. I was also very much pushed in this direction by reading the works of some of the eminent representatives of the Italian school of approaching the texts, like Domenico Losurdo, to which it is worth adding André Tosel's work on Gramsci. We could say that this book – which, as its title suggests, heralds a movement from philosophy to revolution, from Kant to Marx – is a way of reflecting on Gramsci's renowned series of equations 'philosophy = history = politics'.

Looking beyond Althusser, let's talk about some of the other – mostly French – authors and works addressed in this book which were already available when you started out on this work, and against which you defined yourself: in particular, the works of Auguste Cornu, Maximilien Rubel and, later on, Miguel Abensour.

Not all of these stand on the same level. Cornu's works, to start with him, were completely forgotten and, for a very long time, unavailable. In general, they were only known by hearsay, by way of Althusser mentioning them. And things have barely changed since then. I myself read Cornu attentively, and that helped me a lot because he had worked seriously on the Young Hegelians. So he helped me understand the need to situate Marx in this context in order to grasp his particular trajectory. For a long time, the materials appearing in Cornu's four volumes, and especially the long translated excerpts featured therein, were the only texts by some of the Young Hegelians that were available in French. I also discovered that Cornu had taken an interest in Moses Hess, a key figure in my narrative. This latter was not, however, new to me, given that Gérard Bensussan – who was, for a time, a close collaborator of Labica's and co-editor of the *Dictionnaire critique du marxisme* – had already devoted an utterly remarkable book to Hess.

Reading Cornu prompted me to shift the focus of my narrative. But evidently, it was necessary to complete this with more recent works by Germanists and historians, who had innovated considerably on the older works by Jacques Droz on Rhenish radicalism and the first socialist currents. Without providing an exhaustive list, I should nonetheless mention the works of Jean-Pierre Lefebvre and Lucien Calvié, as well as those by Michel Espagne and his team on Heinrich Heine, and the ones by Michel Werner and Gerhard Höhn on the intellectual exchanges between France and Germany. To these, it is worth adding the works of historians of socialist and communist thought: particularly Jacques Grandjonc's works on the notion of communism, but also those of Jacques Guilhaumou and Florence Gauthier on Jacobin thought and the theoretical languages of the French Revolution.

Nonetheless, I ought to mention one further important point, for it relates to the distance I took from Althusser's approach – namely, the approach taken up by Georges Labica. Indeed, Labica represents an attempt to embrace, and even to radicalize, the second Althusser, the politicist Althusser. For Labica – and this is where he fundamentally differs from Althusser – there is no 'Marxist' or 'Marxian' philosophy. Althusser's error was precisely that he reproduced the duality between historical and dialectical material-ism, which in fact came out of the matrix of 'diamat' – the dominant vulgate of the Stalin era. There is only one 'Marxist status of philosophy', and Labica defines it as an 'exit from philosophy', the '*Ausgang*' from *The German Ideology*, which serves as the guiding thread of his interpretation.[12]

We would have to engage in a long discussion on precisely what Labica meant by 'exit from philosophy', insofar as this designates a process marked by a constitutive incompleteness, which thus has to be reiterated. We do not 'exit' from philosophy in the sense that we slam a door behind us, or else we would end up with a positivist flattening of Marxism. But I was not satis-fied with Labica's conclusions, especially because I did not think that he had done enough to problematize the relation between the adoption of a political position and the simultaneously theoretical and ideological terrain of the workers' movement. For him, engagement on the side of the prole-tariat led directly to the revolutionary science of historical materialism, without any specific mediation demarcating this science from the discourses that overwhelmingly dominated the workers' movement at the time.

One of the essential points of my argument is that this process is a lot more tortuous than that; it entails multiple mediations and bifurcations. Marx began from a radical democratism, and he became a revolutionary before he became a communist and set to elaborating the materialist conception of history. Through this transition, he would come to oppose intellectual and militant figures linked to the workers' movement; for a class position is not automatically a revolutionary position, and it does not necessarily lead to a materialist conception of the historical process. More particularly, I try to show that Hess and Engels had entered into contact with the workers' movement before Marx did, without that leading them to communism in a Marxian sense (as a tendency of the class struggle). Their intellectual horizon evolved – in Engels's case, remaining, up to a certain point, within the terms of what was in that era known as 'true socialism'. This was a humanist socialism that explicitly rejected politics, discarding the perspective of a revolutionary overthrow of bourgeois society in favour of a vision of 'the social' and of 'social-ism'. These two terms corresponded to an operation that would restore the integrating essence of social relations – the antidote to the atomization and the antagonizms inherent to capitalist modernity – and which would be capable even of winning the support of the enlightened bourgeoisie.

Towards the end of the 1990s, there was renewed interest in the young Marx in France thanks to Miguel Abensour's book *Democracy Against the State: Marx and the Machiavellian Movement.*
Democracy Against the State is certainly a stimulating and original book. It is an internal reading of the texts, conducted from a liberal – broadly speaking, Arendtian – point of view. More particularly, it addresses the text often referred to as the 'Kreuznach manuscript', in which Marx commented on extracts from Hegel's *Elements of the Philosophy of Right*. Abensour strove to connect a particular moment in the young Marx – the moment of 'true democracy' – to republicanism, such as it was theorized, most importantly, by J.G.A. Pocock and, in a wider sense, by Arendt. That is to say, republicanism as *vita activa*: active participation in the life of the city and in the formation of a subject sharing the foundational values of the political community (liberty, civic virtue, citizenship). However, I think that this view totally overlooks the fact that, for Marx, politics is always constitutively linked to a material transformation of social conditions, even if the terms in which he thought these transformations did evolve. For Marx, political praxis cannot be reduced to a subjective moment, to the affirmation of an autonomy of politics defined by its constituent subject. Marx took an interest in the *Elements of the Philosophy of Right* precisely because it was in this text that Hegel had tried to think through the relations of the state and the sphere of social relations, by integrating the advances made by political economy. The 'true democracy' at issue in the 1843 manuscript on Hegel should thus

be understood as a first approach to politics *qua* endeavour of radically transforming social relations, which Marx defined as the transcendence of the division between the political state and bourgeois civil society.

Abensour tries to salvage a certain moment in the young Marx, but he portrays it in a unilateral way. Ultimately, this corresponds to an even more forceful denunciation of the Marx that followed, on the basis that he had drifted away from this 'Machiavellian moment': that is to say, that he had a kind of flash of theoretical brilliance in his youth but then supposedly abandoned this as he sank into economism, statism and teleological visions of the class struggle.

Abensour's reading is linked to that of another figure often seen as an alternative to Althusser – both at the political level and in terms of textual interpretation – namely Maximilien Rubel, who both published and commented on Marx's works. I know that you are very critical of the work that Rubel did on *Capital*, but did he provide important bearings for the period on which you worked?
No, not really. Rubel had the merit of making available to the French public a certain number of Marx's texts, and of conducting a philological work that did have interesting aspects, even if I think that his mania to publish Marx in the form of digests – or even straight-out eliminate whole chapters of his books – is entirely unacceptable. Nonetheless, contrary to a myth that he himself propagated, claiming that he had completely freed himself from Marxist interpretations of Marx and that he wanted to return to Marx *beyond and against Marxism*, his reading of Marx, in reality, represents a choice that comes from a very specific intellectual tradition which is internal to Marxism. As Lucien Goldmann had already shown, this was the neo-Kantian and ethical reading of Marx upheld by certain Austrian theorists, notably Karl Vorländer and Max Adler.[13] This intellectual tradition has always represented a certain sensibility within Marxism (in the broad sense of the latter), mostly linked to the social-democratic current of German-speaking central Europe – rather embarrassingly for the libertarian Rubel, who mentions this only in an occasional and moreover confused way. I do not think that I particularly had to position myself in relation to Rubel's reading, which I always thought was theoretically weak.

One name that recurs quite often throughout this book – quite surprisingly, for a Marxist – is Michel Foucault. In what sense was he useful to your attempt to think through Marx's intellectual process?
This may appear paradoxical, but Foucault did play an important role in this work, even though it has nothing in common with his vision of Marx

and Marxism. Foucault had what we would rightly define as antagonistic relations with Marxism. He thought of himself as someone setting himself in competition with Marx, as Isabelle Garo very aptly demonstrates in her book.[14] But he positioned himself that way, at least in part, because he was situated on the same terrain.

The Foucault that interested me is Foucault as a theorist of discourses. That seemed relevant when I was examining the juncture between a properly philo-sophical discourse, or a properly philosophical system of discourse, and other types of discursive regimes that emerged in this same era, most particularly those linked to 'the social' or 'social-ism'. That is why Foucault appears most of all in the chapter on Engels. In my view, we cannot understand the young Engels's most important text, *The Condition of the Working Class in England*, with-out studying the way in which it was inscribed within a discourse of 'the social' and reflecting upon the working-class conditions that constituted themselves in this era. To put this another way, the emerging workers' movement's theo-retical literature – to which this book belongs – did not emerge in a vacuum, nor as an immediate expression of working-class experience, but built on exist-ing discourses of both scientific and reforming pretensions which were indis-soluble. These discourses made up the common ground among both the socialists and the 'bourgeois' observers of the working-class condition.

Decentring the Narrative

Now let's turn to the book's structure. You stop at the beginning of 1844, before Marx's great works – before *The Holy Family*, before *The German Ideology* – and before the moment of the revolutionary processes of 1848. What can justify such a choice, from the viewpoint of a wider project on Marx and his political thinking?

My initial intention was to go further – indeed, that is always the case with projects of this type – more precisely, up to *The German Ideology*, up to the moment of the 'break', as Althusser defined it. I had to stop before then. As justification for that, I could mention a lack of time – the extensions – and that was indeed a real problem. All the same, I overran a lot in finishing this work, which took no less than eight years. But the main reason, I think, was one internal to the logic of the book: I stopped at the moment of Marx's texts' publication in the *Deutsch-Französische Jahrbücher* (Franco-German yearbooks). Yet, as the title of this journal suggests – and only one issue would ever appear – this moment represented the logical conclusion of the French-German axis that structures the book as a whole. Of course, I did also include an English dimension, principally by way of Engels, but I would recognize that this is less systematically developed than the French-German axis.

To put that another way, in analyzing these texts from 1843–44, I thought that I had arrived at the end of the demonstration that I was capable of offering at that moment – that of showing how the 'political break' took place and, more precisely, how Marx 'passed' from radical (but reformist) democratism to revolution. I demonstrated how, in this revolution, he recognized – he named and, through this act of naming, contributed to constituting – a new subject unprecedented in the German context, the proletariat, and thereby also posed this revolution as a radical one that would go beyond the French horizon of 1789–93.

In a certain sense, Marx thus brought to a conclusion the sequence that I address in this book. Through this vision – unprecedented, in such terms – of a radical revolution in Germany led by the proletariat, he operated at a junction with Heine. Indeed, this would be concretized for the first time in the *Deutsch-Französische Jahrbücher*, in which Heine published his satirical poem 'Hymn to King Louis'.[15] To follow Marx up till the decisive threshold that is his Parisian moment thus seemed to me to be, if not a conclusion, at least a provisional point of culmination, adequate to the demonstration that I was attempting in this book.

Even so, this journey was not sufficient. I tried to go further in the texts that I wrote subsequently, including my contribution to the collective volume *Marx politique*, in which I tried to show how Marx reflected on the question of political emancipation and its relation with emancipation *tout court*, or with social emancipation.[16] The question formulated in his youthful texts (the abolition of the separation between the state, or the purely political state, and civil society, or more precisely 'bourgeois civil society', *Bürgerliche Gesellschaft*) is picked up again and reworked in later texts, most particularly in his writings on the Paris Commune. There, too, I took a stance against any vision dividing Marx into two periods that have nothing to do with each other. I tried to show, on the contrary, that there are deep threads Marx picks up and reworks from one period to the next, aiming at something that corresponds to a thinking on the political, but a thinking on the political whose terms are profoundly reformulated and displaced.

Could you pursue that work in a second volume?

It would not exactly be a second volume, representing the linear continuation of *Philosophy and Revolution*, but something dealing more systematically with Marx's development beyond the moment of the Franco-German yearbooks – that is, not only the philosophical moment of the Paris manuscripts (the so-called '1844' manuscripts) but also his works at the turning point marked by *The German Ideology* and the moment of the 1848 revolutions. For me, the latter was a profoundly Gramscian moment, in the sense that Marx elaborated a hegemonic strategy for a democratic revolution under the leadership of a radical bloc within which the proletariat fought to conquer a leading position. The challenge consists of working out how the defeat of this strategy opened out onto the critique of political economy and, subsequently, onto what I would not hesitate to call the 'political turn' that Marx took after 1870, starting with the moment of the Paris Commune.

Now let's turn to how you chose which authors to discuss in this book. Why – along with the inevitable Marx-Engels pairing – Heine and Hess, and no one else?

One of my obsessions in writing this book was to succeed in providing a historicization that could restore the singularity of the trajectories of the different actors. This implied breaking with the idea that all these developments had to tend towards Marx. I thought about how I could translate this idea into the structure of the book, and, at a certain moment, I even thought that the arrangement of the different parts could be aleatory, so that you could read them without any pre-established order – a little like Raymond Queneau intended with his *Cent mille milliards de poèmes*. It was Fredric Jameson who convinced me to drop this idea; he told me that I had to adopt a narrative dimension – unavoidable in any theoretical text – and that there necessarily must be some order that would prevail over the other possible ones. That also meant accepting having a certain teleology, as an 'empty form' inherent to the order of the exposition. But it is possible to counter that by introducing ruptures both on the formal level and on the level of content, as a way of refuting the idea that Marx was contained 'in embryo' in everything that went before him.

So even in accepting that the order of the book should be oriented towards the Engels-Marx pairing – indeed, very much a classic one – I still made sure that each chapter was singular: not simply in its content – for it was necessary to study the authors for themselves, and not as more or less incomplete 'precursors' to Marx – but in its very form. I tried to give each chapter a sort of colour, a style of its own, that also played on the analytical tools that each of them mobilized. So to construct the chapter on Engels, I used Foucault; and in the chapter on Heine, I made heavy use of Walter Benjamin.

To better understand how these choices were made, it is better to start with what is missing. Why is there no chapter on Feuerbach?

I thought that in order to shift our perspective on Marx, it was important to reorient it in relation to the fundamental problem posed to an oppositional German intellectual of his time: namely, the problem of the German revolution. Of course, the latter must be understood as just one part of what was playing out more widely in Europe at the time. But here the German angle is wholly decisive. And Marx himself formulated this problem very clearly – although, as I gradually understood as I worked through these materials, he was not the only or even the first person to do so. He went back to the idea that obsessed Kant and Hegel: that while it was the French who *carried out* the revolution, it was the Germans who *thought* it.

This is the original discrepancy between the two situations; and it can be declined in various ways, according to different modalities. Of course, this means the relation of a French practice to a theory that is, paradoxically enough, a German one, developing at a distance from practice – or even in opposition to it. This is also a spatio-temporal problem: the question of how a 'backward' reality, the 'German misery' as Heine called it, was able to articulate itself alongside the 'advanced' French process – indeed, the question of how the realities of these two social formations corresponded to one another amid the entanglement of European geopolitics following the French Revolution. This is also a means of understanding the relations between politics and philosophy, for it was politics that marked the French situation and philosophy that constituted the German speciality.

Of course, a third term, in addition to the France–Germany pairing, was represented by England – which represented capitalist development, but also political economy. Here, we again find ourselves in a landscape that at first glance recalls the 'three sources of Marxism': the harmonious synthesis theorized by Karl Kautsky. This reading would enjoy extraordinary fortune in the workers' movement's self-representation of the emergence of Marxian theory. Yet research into this problem does not bring to light any quasi-spontaneous convergence leading to such a harmonious synthesis of knowledge. Rather, it shows a difficult process involving an irreducible element of contingency, constituted by way of a constant interplay of discrepancies. It was Gramsci who reflected most deeply on this question, which constituted the point of departure for his key concept of 'translation' – the operator of the passage between these three European realities and languages.

What I myself understood – and it was this that led me back to reading Gramsci – is that the terms of the problem had already been posed by Hegel and by Kant, and thus by contemporaries of the French Revolution, simultaneously both close to it and distant from it. These contemporaries had reflected on the nature of the world-historical process that it unleashed, and on the way in which it 'translated' into their own country, namely, Germany. Indeed, here we arrive at the great German paradox: that all these philosophers who embraced the French event nevertheless held firm to keeping it at a distance from the German reality. In other words, the revolution was a great thing, but only for other people – the French. In Germany there would be a different approach – through reforms, preferably 'from above', but in which the philosopher-intellectuals saw themselves being given a specific, strategically important role.

These were the terms of the problem of the 'realization of philosophy', such as the founders bequeathed it to the following generations – and they were what dictated my choices in terms of which authors to foreground. That meant beginning with Kant and Hegel – the necessary point of departure – and then continuing with Heine, because for the following generation, it was he who revived the question of the relationship between Germany and the revolution, and the relationship between Germany and France in particular. I then continued with Moses Hess, for he theorised this 'European triarchy' of Germany, France and England, and played a decisive role in a first effort at the translation of the discourse of French socialism and of political economy into German – and here I mean 'translation' in the Gramscian sense. Finally, I came to the trajectories of Engels and Marx, in all their singularity – which also means in their contingency.

Sure, but to go back to my question: Why not Feuerbach?
This choice had to do with the distance that I took from the Althusserian interpretation. For Althusser, Feuerbach plays a central role – after all, it is the latter that allows him to ground the thesis of a fundamentally humanist young Marx, followed by the rupture that he describes in terms of an 'epistemological break'. In part, I took against this narrative, since I think that Althusser greatly overestimated Feuerbach's influence on Marx – and, indeed, he was not the only one to do so. In fact, Feuerbach occupied a much more 'legitimate' place in the 'orthodox' narrative than did the German thinkers, on account of his 'materialism'. The latter, conversely, were irredeemably cast aside on account of their 'idealism'. We need only read a few pages of Plekhanov – one of the main reference points of the 'Marxist-Leninist' vulgate – to get a sense of this. In my view, Marx was never 'Feuerbachian', properly speaking. To put it briefly, the fundamental problems posed by Feuerbach – the alienation of man in religion, and the search for a materialism rooted in 'sensibility' (*Sinnlichkeit*) – were never Marx's own. What led him to take an interest in Feuerbach was his search for a critical approach to Hegel. Moreover, this rupture had already largely begun, on the basis of his more rigorous, in a sense more 'Hegelian', reading of Hegel himself. And Marx was driven to do so because Feuerbachianism was something diffuse, to which everyone in these milieux became receptive at a certain moment, and to which one could not simply remain external until

such time as one's break with these milieux was definitively consummated. As such, his concomitant interest in Feuerbach should be understood as a 'field effect'. This leads back to the fact that this moment of Marx's journey can only be understood in terms of the Young Hegelian discursive and theoretical terrain.

So I do not at all cast aside the question of theoretical humanism. But what I try to show is that, in order to clearly understand this question, we have to proceed by way of Moses Hess and Engels. They became true Feuerbachians: they were genuine 'theoretical humanists', or in other words, partisans of 'true socialism'. They wanted to remain at a distance from politics, let alone revolutionary politics. They sought to change people's minds through a doctrine of love and social harmony, directly linked to Feuerbachian anthropology. Marx did not at all follow them down this path. Out of that pairing, it was Engels who would join up with Marx, albeit later than is commonly thought.

That does not mean that Engels contributed nothing new to Marx, nor that the exchange between the two did not also run in that direction. But I think that it is vitally important to emphasize that, up to a certain moment, Marx's and Engels's trajectories diverged considerably, and that what – decisively, although not exclusively – separated them was the question of theoretical humanism.

Heine, Hess and Rhenish Radicalism

Let's get to the chapter on Heine, without doubt one of the most unique aspects of this book. You portray Heine as a central figure in this period. I imagine that this was something of a gamble, in that he had largely disappeared from the Marxological landscape, if he ever was truly part of it. What's more, Heine was not a philosopher, and as such he is most of all addressed by specialists in German literature.

It is true that for some time Heine has had little presence in the French intellectual and cultural context. This was not always the case. Indeed, there was a time during which Heine was more of a reference point because he made up part of a cultural and literary canon upheld essentially by communist culture. And, certainly, we can look to relatively recent works of very great quality, notably those of Jean-Pierre Lefebvre, Michael Werner, Lucien Calvié, and Michel Espagne and his collaborators. But as you just mentioned, these never went beyond Germanist circles. Paradoxically, in a certain sense, Heine – a great classic of German culture – is someone who has to be rediscovered, not only in France, but also in other linguistic and cultural areas.

For my part, I have tried to contribute to this rediscovery, restoring not Heine 'the philosopher' – for that he was not – but Heine as an essayist and intellectual, in the strong sense of the latter, for he played a fundamentally important role throughout the *Vormärz* period. This provides a redefinition of the France–Germany relationship – which, for Marx as for his whole generation, was mediated by the figure of Heine. I note that Heine was a man living in exile in Paris from 1832 onwards, when he was already a well-established figure in the German literary and cultural scene. It is Heine who allows us to reformulate the question of Germany's relationship to the revolution, neither as its distancing, 'reforming' translation, nor as a simple repetition – as intended by the German Jacobins, or, in a very abstract sense, the Young Hegelians fascinated by the anti-religious radicalism of the French process. For this reason, he became a central figure in the formation of what we could call a German intellectual radicalism, constitutively linked to the French revolutionary processes, including in the broad sense. He contributed to updating this radicalism by opening it up to the currents that marked his era: Saint-Simonianism, communism, the emerging workers' movement.

For this reason, Heine is an indispensable link in the chain for understanding how the 1840s generation – that is to say, the Young Hegelians, in the strict sense of the term – took form. It seemed to me, and indeed this was an interpretative choice of mine, that it was more important to study Marx in relation to Heine – but not at all in a teleological sense, as these two figures absolutely cannot be reduced to one another – than to study Marx in relation to Feuerbach. If you want to understand how Marx organically attached the political struggle to communism by way of revolutionary democracy, then Heine, rather than Feuerbach, is the important reference point. If you want to understand the transmission of the idea of a German revolutionary inheritance, with its constitutive moments in the Reformation, the Peasant War and classical philosophy – an idea present already in Hegel – then again it is necessary to look to Heine.

I must confess that there is also another reason. Throughout this whole period, during the 1990s, I, like so many others, particularly Daniel Bensaïd, read a lot of Walter Benjamin. I was simultaneously both struck by the way in which Benjamin worked on the nineteenth century – thus including the period that interested me – and intrigued by the fact that Heine had very little presence in his work. In Benjamin, Heine's whole place was, in a sense, preempted by Baudelaire. I thought that this absence was all the less justified, given that there is something very Benjaminian, we might say, in the figure of Heine. A lot of the themes that Benjamin addresses in his *Paris: Capital of the Nineteenth Century* are also found in Heine: exile; *flânerie*, the fragmentary form and the use of irony; the appearance of the big city in poetry; the experience of the defeated revolution and that of a history which, after the crushing of the hopes of 1848, veered towards the nightmarish.

So I sought to shine a light on Heine as a pioneer of the emerging modernity – which is not without consequence for his role in the history I am studying. That is also the reason why I think that the encounter between Heine and Marx – which took place in Paris, at a decisive moment for their respective development – was an epochal encounter, opening up an unprecedented intellectual and cultural possibility: namely, the idea of an encounter between aesthetic, intellectual and political modernities. That promise continues to haunt us, because it remains unfulfilled.

We should also say something about Hess. In the background to the chapter you devote to him, were you thinking about the same thing that I was when I reread it – that is, that there are certain analogies between our own period and Hess's thought: this form of humanism that is full of fine sentiments but is politically completely impotent? Here, should we see an implicit critique of a certain theoretical and political atmosphere that you found in France in the watering down of the French left, in the subsidence of Marxism and in the rise of a rather limper thinking – a sort of vague social-democratic humanism?
It can be read in that way – even if that was not my primary concern. Incontestably, these days there is a particularly diminished – even frankly worrying – form of 'humanism' that impregnates political discourse, indeed not only on the left. We could think of the explosion of 'charity' and 'compassion', a touch of 'soul' or 'ethics' for neoliberal policies; or of 'humanitarian' paternalism, which is very convenient as a means of dressing up imperialist military interventions. Nonetheless, to be fair to Hess, we ought to say that what bears most comparison to his 'humanism' would be something like Pope Francis's virulent condemnation of the 'rule of money', and his talk of rehabilitating 'social cohesion' and 'living together'.

That said – and to get back to Hess – we ought to see how contradictory he was as a figure. Of course, there was this element of sentimental and apolitical humanist socialism, which you mention, and whose consistency I wanted to show. To simplify my thinking, I would say that if Marx were as Feuerbachian as Althusser claimed, he would have become Moses Hess and not Karl Marx. But there are other aspects of Hess that are just as important. The first is that he allows us to understand that being in contact with the workers' movement does not necessarily mean – as I have already said – adhering to revolutionary positons. Exactly the opposite could be the case. We often forget how powerful this sentimental, ethical, and very deeply religious socialism was in the workers' movement of the time. In a certain sense, religion was 'in the air' during that entire pre-1848 Romantic era. Saint-Simoniansm, one of the key intellectual and political movements of that time, conceived of itself as a new religion.

This relationship with religion led me to one of the least apparent, but nonetheless significant, threads in this work: the theme of messianism, which is also present in filigree in the chapter on Heine. Indeed, while there are a lot of things separating Heine and Hess, this is a dimension that links them together, even if their conceptions of messianism substantially differed. Hess sought a reconstruction of the politico-religious nexus by way of humanist anthropology, whereas Heine conceived of the messianic promise as the spectral presence that the defeated generations of the past bequeathed to the present. However, both drank from this same source: indeed, anything else would be surprising among Jewish intellectuals developing in this milieu, a radicalism that was essentially Rhenish. Marx – and we know of his problematic non-relation to his Jewishness – and Engels were also Rhenians; in a general sense, the history in question here was fundamentally Rhenish, before it became a history of exiles. And this thread of Jewish messianism is one of its constitutive aspects.

Should Marx, too, be located within this messianic thread?

It is an old argument, notably advanced by Karl Löwith and, more recently, by Balibar – the latter in reference to my work.[17] For Balibar, the appearance of the proletariat in Marx, in the 1843 introduction to the *Critique of Hegel's Philosophy of Right*, corresponded to a 'messianic moment', attested to by the extensive use of religious metaphors belonging to an apocalyptic and prophetic register. These metaphors expressed the radical turnaround of the proletariat from being 'nothing' to 'everything', with the 'radical revolution' at issue in this text appearing as a sort of re-creation of the world *ex nihilo*. Certainly, religious metaphors were part of the style of the time, and in this sense they correspond to a *topos* that was by no means specifically Marxian. The same is largely true of the conception of religion that this text of Marx's carries forth: as simultaneously both the cry of the suffering creature and its consolation ('the opium of the people').

In my view, there is not much to be gained by taking a lead from metaphors or from the stubborn insistence on assigning a religious origin to each and every political concept. As we know, unlike Engels, Marx never developed an interest in religion; the only threads attaching him to a messianic sensibility were Hess (whom he read and indeed knew personally) and, in a more underground fashion, Heine. In this sense, yes, there is an indirect, mediated messianic element – a Jewish one, but not only that – which corresponds to the specificity of Rhenish radicalism and the general Romantic atmosphere of the period.

But I do not think that this element played a structuring role in the process that led Marx to his 'discovery' of the proletariat. In my view, the latter can only be understood as a solution to the 'enigma' of the German revolution – that of its non-contemporaneity – an enigma that had incessantly haunted thinkers beyond the Rhine ever since the French Revolution. The negative subjectivity of the proletariat came to be at one with a dialectical reasoning, via a sort of deduction – and certainly, a very speculative one, conducted on the basis of examining a historical problem; it was a German translation of the conjuncture with which he found himself confronted. All this distances us, I think, from any 'messianic moment'.

Should We Bury Engels's Legacy?

Now let's get to Engels. Clearly he does not emerge unscathed from this book, especially because of the way in which he dealt with Irish migrant workers in his *Condition of the Working Class in England*. Of course, as you yourself emphasize, this book represents Engels prior to his intellectual encounter with Marx. But what you say is laden with consequences, both for how we address the long – and still ongoing – debate on the relationship between Engels and Marx, the specificities of each man, and for the role that Engels supposedly played in a certain tradition of Marxism against which some seek to define themselves.

In my interpretation, I try to go against the existing critical approaches to Engels which are found in the abundant literature devoted to his role in the elaboration of the theory bearing the name 'Marxism'. And indeed, the latter bears that name thanks, essentially, to Engels. Here, 'critical approach' should be taken to mean everything that stands out from the vulgate according to which Engels was simply Marx's alter ego, the brilliant right-hand man who did us the service of completing Marx's work. Setting aside those who seek to exclude him from the field of study, pure and simple – with Maximilien Rubel at the forefront – most of these approaches aim to criticize or even reject the late Engels's 'philosophical' writings, and above all the idea of a 'dialectics of nature'. Perry Anderson has rightly emphasized that almost all of what he has called 'Western Marxism' is characterized by the rejection of this Engelsian legacy. The critique addressed against Engels also concerns his interpretation of *Capital* – particularly its order of exposition, as well as his role in editing volumes II and III of *Capital*. This critique was recently revived, most significantly by Michael Heinrich, in the wake of the release by Marx-Engels-Gesamtausgabe (MEGA) of the set of Marx manuscripts that Engels used to publish the last two volumes.[18]

Conversely, the tendency with regard to the young Engels is to rehabilitate his pioneering role in the critique of political economy and in the study of working-class realities. It is telling that an 'anti-Engelsian' like Terrell Carver and an 'Engelsian' like Labica agree on this point.[19] The latter strongly advocated for this pioneering Engels, one already standing on the terrain of the historical materialism that was to be constructed. But Labica's argument left me deeply unsatisfied. In my view, he underestimated the extent to which Engels's texts belonged to a type of discourse that was hegemonic in that era: one which reflected on the problems posed by the working-class condition in medical terms, as a 'physiology' of social conditions. For example, an analysis of class realities in racial terms was an integral part of this type of discourse, and, in this sense, it is hardly surprising that we can find some characteristic elements of this in Engels. Obviously, that is embarrassing for the present-day reader, and indeed it also poses a host of problems that we would be wrong to think are now behind us.

So you try to break out of any opposition between a 'young Engels' and a late Engels, as in the model of the opposition between the 'young Marx' and the mature Marx?

I attempted a critical reading of the young Engels precisely because I think that Engels is an original thinker. Among other reasons, I did so because, unlike Marx, he did not come from a university mould, and he had first-hand knowledge of the economic and social realities of England. In this sense, there are a lot of theoretical innovations to be found in Engels, particularly in his first attempts at the critique of political economy and in his analysis of the working-class condition. These remain conditional, nonetheless, on an understanding that his critique was based on philosophical humanism and adhered – on the model of Hess's critique – to the orientations of 'true socialism'.

Indeed, upon reading *The Condition of the Working Class in England*, it is striking to note the extent to which Engels did indeed make up part of this tendency; and this is even more explicit in the conferences he gave together with Moses Hess in Rhenish towns in early 1845. Engels and Hess showed their great moderation – and even their rejection of politics – in seeking to displace the problems posed by the working-class condition and the demands of the emerging working class from the political terrain to another: the terrain of the 'social'. The 'social' was conceived in the manner of Saint-Simon, before being adopted by the French 'social science' of Auguste Comte and Émile Durkheim as a regulating, pacifying principle, defined in terms of 'social cohesion' – to use a terminology that is very much present in contemporary sociology. For Engels, the true contradiction of capitalism was not class antagonism, properly speaking, but the contradiction between the 'social' principle and the money/market duo, wherein the latter was the bearer of chaos, selfish individualism and boundless competition.

Another innovation of Engels's that I tried to emphasize is his thinking on urban space, which developed through his observation of the working-class condition. Henri Lefebvre has already brought this to light.[20] This perspective on the nascent modernity of the nineteenth century is one of the most interesting aspects in Engels, and indeed in Heine. It was not by chance that Engels went on to write on *The Housing Question*, one of the first texts addressing urban problems from the historical materialist viewpoint in any systematic way.

What consequence do these analyses have in terms of the late Engels, his role in the constitution of Second International Marxism, his supposed positivism, and any differences that he may have had with Marx?
When I said that I was taking a stance at odds with almost all of the existing literature, I was referring to the need to restore the young Engels in a critical manner, without thereby sharing in the rejection of the later Engels, and without erasing the originality of his intellectual trajectory – including after the undeniable turning point constituted by his work with Marx. Quite the contrary.

Of course, there are elements of continuity in Engels, but they do not necessarily work in the direction that you suggest, that of a flattening-out of theory. Engels did take an interest in so-called 'utopian' thought in a sustained way, but also, as I just said, in thought on urban questions, on anthropology, on history and, in particular, on religion.

Conversely, other elements of continuity are more problematic. It seems to me that his thinking on the 'social' left traces in the conception of socialism that he later elaborated in *Anti-Dühring*. There, he described socialism as a managed economy, a rational reorganisation of an industrial society; by this he meant a way of transcending the anarchy of capitalist production, but one that nevertheless extended the kind of socialization immanent to the latter. Engels thus did not think in sufficient depth about socialism – or rather, communism – as a new mode of production founded on revolutionized social relations. All this had a decisive impact on the dominant vision of socialism under the Second International.

Nonetheless, I hold in very great esteem Engels the historian – from his studies on the Peasant War, to those on German unification as a 'revolution from above', or on the family and gender relations – despite the limitations (evident to us) of the anthropological material he had available. I think that the late Engels's contribution on questions of political theory and strategy is also original, far from the banally 'reformist' Engels we often see. Jacques Texier demonstrated as much, making the case for a kind of pre-Gramscian Engels.[21]

Nor do I share the horror that most of the 'Western Marxists' have for the late Engels's 'philosophical' writings. We know that they were instrumentalized, particularly by means of the editorial work done for the 'book' *Dialectics of Nature*, where all kinds of pieces were fitted together by the Soviets in order to define the fundamentals of Stalin-era Diamat. In my view, Labica was right to emphasize the essentially reactive character of Engels's interventions, and the fact that they aimed, above all, to oppose the arguments of the likes of Eugen Dühring or Ernst Haeckel – rather than to establish any 'Marxist philosophy'. I also agree with André Tosel where he interprets the texts brought together in *Dialectics of Nature* as a critical reflection on the development of natural sciences.[22] Without doubt, this work is, in many respects, a dated one, and it remains caught in the evolutionist vision that dominated in that era. Nonetheless, it can be read as a contribution to the reflective work that scholars have conducted with regard to their own practice, rather than as the first draft of a logical-ontological meta-discourse (in spite of Engels's tendency to enounce universal 'laws' of dialectics).

That said – and with all the necessary caution demanded by the more precise studies I have not yet been able to undertake – it seems to me that, despite everything, what emerges from Engels as a figure is that in certain ways he remained close to the socialist thought of the nineteenth century, in what we might call its standard version. Without doubt, in Engels, we do not find the powerful singularity of Karl Marx, and sometimes he even tends to reduce some of Marx's innovative aspects. To cite a few examples of this, I think that his way of understanding *Capital*'s order of exposition in logical-historical terms is inappropriate, and that it tends to flatten out the theoretical stakes of this work's structure. Engels also proved a lot more reticent than Marx in breaking with Eurocentrism, as notably indicated by the way he positioned himself in the debate on the revolution in Russia. He did not take seriously the indications that Marx had given in his draft letters to Vera Zasulich, which favoured a non-capitalist road finding a base in peasant communal forms. All this also had a very serious impact on the Eurocentrism – sometimes reaching caricatural proportions – of the Second International.

Marx and Politics Today

Since the book's publication, research on Marx has continued unabated. I am thinking, here, of a series of biographies – especially those by Francis Wheen, Jonathan Sperber and Jacques Attali – as well as a series of meticulous studies on the young Marx.[23] Within this category, we could cite the works of Roberto Finelli, Gareth Stedman Jones, Warren Breckman and Douglas Moggach.[24] In hindsight, does this literature lead you to change your point of view, going deeper into certain aspects, or does this not really change your perspective?

What we realize, after the fact, is that what we wrote was a lot less original than we thought – for the same reasons that we never think all by ourselves. What I take most of all from the titles you mention – to which it is worth adding the French works by Franck Fischbach and Emmanuel Renault – is that even if their approaches are very diverse, there are also telling convergences with what I tried to do in this book.[25] All these books foreground the importance of the Young Hegelian context to grasping Marx's trajectory in all its singularity. Most of them situate this trajectory in relation to the political context and the intersection of the French Revolution with classical German philosophy. In the English-language works – which are the most stimulating, in my view – we find the idea that Marx was a true 'political mind' and that his relationship with Hegel was of a depth that distinguished him from his interlocutors and rivals. Jonathan Sperber's biography – the only one that contributes new elements – works in this same direction, even if Sperber slides into historical relativism and makes Marx into a figure trapped in the nineteenth century. Even someone like David Leopold, coming from the Oxford analytical tradition, has strongly emphasized the fact that we have to approach Marx as a political thinker.[26] So my work should be situated within this wider movement of rereading Marx. All the same, I think that there is still something original about my approach, without doubt corresponding to the fact that it is more linked to the debates in French Marxism – and, more broadly, in 'continental' Marxism, as English-speakers would say. For this reason, strategic questions are more present, and we break out of the framework of an academic discussion among learned readers. And this has not escaped Anglophone interpreters. While recognising the seriousness of my documentation, the author of the review of my book in the journal of the venerable American Sociological Association accused me of 'blurring the distinctions' between, on the one hand, historical research and social science analysis and, on the other, political polemic and the construction of a 'myth' seeking to legitimize political radicalism.[27] Well, I, for my part, totally admit to such 'blurring' – synonymous with politically committed research. I think that Marx would have no problem with that.

To conclude on the political level, there is no doubt that the political and intellectual atmosphere has changed a lot since the 1990s. There is a renewal of work on Marx, who is no longer a pariah figure. But this does not prevent Marx from remaining very relevant as a thinker of defeat – as you emphasize in the final pages of the book. How would you summarize the political dimension of this book, with eighteen years' hindsight?
There is a red thread running through this book: the idea of the constitutive relation between democracy and revolution. We could even say that, to

my eyes, democracy and revolution are – as Spinoza might put it – two modes of one same substance. This 'French' vein in Marx joins up with the central concern of my own political trajectory. The work of Nicos Poulantzas, to whom this book is dedicated, opens out onto a far-ranging critique of the relations between democracy and socialism. This is also the red thread of Gramsci's reflection on hegemony – and indeed of Lukács's thinking, from his famous 'Blum Theses' to the political conclusion of his ontology in his fundamental *Demokratisierung heute und morgen*.[28]

I myself pick up on this question – indeed, trying to renew its terms – because I am convinced of its central importance today. Of course, this is the question left to us by the collapse of the Soviet-style regimes and by the involution of the twentieth-century revolutionary experiences as a whole. But this is also the question posed by the evolution of neoliberal capitalism and by the demands formulated by the popular mobilizations of recent years. Neoliberal capitalism is emptying the idea of democracy of any meaning, even in terms of the very limited democratic frameworks that emerged as victories of the long struggles of the labouring classes. On the other hand, we have seen that, despite their potential for democratic rupture, the recent popular upheavals – from the 'Arab Spring' to the mass movements of the 2010–12 years in Greece and Spain – were unable to deliver real change because they did not challenge the existing economic and social structures. The satisfaction of making even relatively modest gains requires a high level of confrontation with the dominant classes, and with national and transnational institutions like the EU that crystallize the power of the latter. Today, we have to invert Poulantzas's dictum 'Socialism will be democratic or will not be at all.' We cannot defeat the de-democratization carried forth by neoliberalism without posing the questions of the overthrow of capitalism, of the hegemony of the subaltern classes, and thus of the activation of the communist tendency of the class struggle.

The Marx in question in this book is not a Marx of defeat, but the Marx of the 'self-criticisms of the revolution', as the title of the conclusion puts it. This is the Marx who grasped the limits of the revolutionary experience that had begun in 1789–93; he understood that its 'failure' was retroactively necessary, in order to allow for the advent of something new. This is the Marx who conceived of communism as the ever-renewed self-criticism of the democratic revolution. Today, it is true that we might be tempted to invert that argument, making democracy the self-critical moment of communism. But that would be to forget what Lukács formulated in his 'Blum Theses': there is no Chinese wall between democratic revolution and socialist revolution. As Heine said, in a line I have placed in the epigraph to this book: 'The revolution is one and indivisible.'

Notes

Introduction: From Philosophy to Revolution

1. It is announced at the political level in the 'Blum Theses' (1928). *The Young Hegel, The Destruction of Reason*, and *Zur Ontologie des gesellschaftlichen Seins* mark the principal stages in this itinerary.
2. Michel Foucault, *Dits et écrits*, Paris, 1994, vol. 4, p. 685 (hereafter *DE*, followed by the volume and page number). Let us note that the category of *process* features prominently in this text; it is systematized in the twofold definition of the Enlightenment as 'singular event' and 'permanent process' (ibid.).
3. 'I wanted to show how an analysis of this kind [of the state as a relationship of war] is plainly articulated with a hope of, imperative for, and politics of, revolt or revolution. That, not racism, is my basic concern.' Michel Foucault, *"Il faut défendre la société"*, Paris, 1997, p. 76.
4. See 'La grande colère des faits (sur André Glucksmann)', *DE* 3: 277–81.
5. The reference to Kant's text appears in a 1978 discussion of the history of science (see *DE* 3: 431); Foucault takes it up again, in the context that interests us here, in an April 1979 text that appeared in *Le Nouvel Observateur* (*DE* 3: 783) a week after the publication, in the same weekly, of his open letter to the Iranian Prime Minister, Mehdi Bazargan (*DE* 3: 780–82), condemning the executions of members of the opposition and the suppression of basic freedoms by the post-revolutionary regime.
6. *DE* 4: 684. We have an unmistakable indication of this reversal: the text of the 1984 course culminates in a surprising reference to a philosophical filiation that, for the first time, ranges Nietzsche side by side with the Frankfurt School and, even more surprisingly, Hegel (*DE* 4: 688). 'La grande colère des faits', in contrast, peaks in a diatribe against Hegel, who is declared guilty of 'effacing the night of the world', a metaphor for the victims of totalitarian state power (*DE* 3: 281).
7. Alain Badiou, *Le siècle* (forthcoming).
8. Michaël Löwy, *Pour une sociologie des intellectuels révolutionnaires*, Paris, 1976, p. 14.
9. Georg Lukács, *Lenin: A Study on the Unity of His Thought*, trans. Nicholas Jacobs, London, 1970, p. 11.
10. Ibid., p. 13.
11. Ibid., p. 11.
12. 'He understood and explained all events, Russian as well as international, from this perspective – from the perspective of the actuality of the revolution.' Ibid.
13. Ibid., p. 12.
14. 'What is my actuality? What is the significance of this actuality? And what do I do when I speak of this actuality? That, it seems to me, is what constitutes this new interrogation of modernity.' Foucault, *DE* 4: 681.
15. See Georg Lukács, *History and Class Consciousness*, trans. Rodney Livingstone, Cambridge, MA., 1972.

16. See, respectively, Michel Foucault, 'L'expérience du dehors', *DE* 1: 518–39; *The Archaeology of Knowledge*, trans. A.M. Sheridan Smith, New York, 1972, p. 140; 'Le retour de la morale' (interview with G. Barbedette and A. Scala), *DE* 4: 696.

17. 'The coincidence of the changing of circumstances and of human activity or self-change [Engels struck the term 'self-change' when he edited Marx's text] can be conceived and rationally understood only as *revolutionary practice*'. Karl Marx and Frederick Engels, *Collected Works*, 50 vols, London, 1975–2002 (hereafter *MECW*) 5: 7.

18. André Tosel, 'Les aléas du matérialisme aléatoire dans la dernière philosophie de Louis Althusser', *Cahiers Philosophiques*, no. 84, 2001, p. 38.

1   Kant and, Hegel, or the Ambiguity of Origins

1. As Joël Lefebvre emphasizes, Introduction to *La Révolution française vue par les Allemands*, ed. and trans. Lefebvre, Lyon, 1987, pp. 14–18.

2. Hannah Arendt, *On Revolution*, Harmondsworth, 1990, p. 52.

3. Immanuel Kant, 'The Contest of Faculties', in *Political Writings*, ed. Hans S. Reiss, trans. H.B. Nisbet, 2nd edn, Cambridge, 1991, p. 182.

4. Ibid., p. 181.

5. 'The dignity of freedom must come from the bottom up; freedom without disorder can only come from the top down.' Johann Gottlieb Fichte, *Beitrag zur Berichtigung der Urteile des Publikums über die Französische Revolution*, Leipzig, 1922, p. 9.

6. Ibid., p. 24. As Étienne Balibar has shown in his analysis of *Addresses to the German Nation*, the same ambivalence resurfaces in the Fichte who, though still a champion of the republic, had also become an apostle of German patriotism. Sometimes the internal frontier to be crossed is the real frontier of the real territory invaded by Napoleon's armies; at other times it is identified with a frontier internal to consciousness, which is the only possible locus of German national aspirations. Non-violence seems to have been an essential feature of Fichte's patriotism, just as it was an essential part of his Jacobin project of 1793. See Balibar, 'Fichte and the Internal Border: On *Addresses to the German Nation*', in *Masses, Classes, Ideas: Studies on Politics and Philosophy Before and After Marx*, trans. James Swenson, London, 1994, pp. 61–84.

7. Fichte, *Beitrag*, p. 5.

8. Kant, 'Perpetual Peace: A Philosophical Sketch', in *Political Writings*, p. 101. Kant distinguishes the republic, which is radically representative, from democracy, which – referring to Rousseau's conception of it – he assimilates to 'pure', direct, and therefore impossible, democracy. The fact remains that merely mentioning notions like 'republic' or 'the rights of man' was explosive in the absolutist Prussia of 1795.

9. Ibid., p. 118. See also Kant, 'The Contest of Faculties', p. 184n: 'The best way of making a nation content with its constitution is to *rule* autocratically and at the same time to *govern* in a republican manner, i.e. to govern in the spirit of republicanism and by analogy with it.'

10. Kant, 'The Contest of Faculties', p. 186.

11. Kant, 'Perpetual Peace', p. 115.

12. The reading 'societies' or 'cabinets', where one could find the writings of Enlightenment thinkers and French newspapers or journals (notably, *Le Moniteur*), were at the centre of the mushrooming discussions that drew a public hungry for the least scrap of news from across the Rhine. These societies, often with links to Masonic lodges, contributed to the broad diffusion of Kant's writings. They came under heightened surveillance from 1791 on; beginning in 1793, some were forcibly dissolved. See Henri Brunschwig, *Société et romantisme en Prusse au XVIIIe siècle*, Paris, 1973, pp. 46–50.

13. 'On the Continent there were two social structures that left a decisive imprint on the

Age of Enlightenment: the Republic of Letters and the Masonic Lodges. From the outset, Enlghtment and mystery appeared as historical twins.' Reinhart Koselleck, *Critique and Crisis: Enlightenment and the Pathogenesis of Modern Society*, Oxford, 1988, p. 62.

14. Kant, 'The Contest of Faculties', p. 188n.

15. Ibid., p. 187.

16. '*There is a single dangerous misunderstanding regarding the whole of practical Reason*,' warns Gilles Deleuze, 'believing that Kantian morality remains indifferent to its own realization. In fact, the abyss between the sensible world and the suprasensible world exists only in order to be filled.' Deleuze, *Kant's Critical Philosophy: The Doctrine of the Faculties*, trans. Hugh Tomlinson and Barbara Habberjam, London, 1984, p. 39.

17. The first argument cited by Kant, in his response to the very reactionary Woellner, one of the ministers of Friedrich Wilhelm II, is that his book 'is not at all suitable for the public: to them it is an unintelligible, closed book, only a debate among scholars of the faculty, of which the people [*das Volk*] take no notice' (Kant, *The Conflict of Faculties*, trans. Mary J. Gregor, Lincoln, NE, 1979, p. 15).

18. Johann Gottlieb Fichte, *Appellation an das Publikum*, Jena and Leipzig, 1799, p. 40.

19. See the selections from Forster in Lefebvre, *La Révolution française*, esp. pp. 142–5, 156–9, 174–9.

20. Ibid., p. 144.

21. Ibid., p. 143.

22. Domenico Losurdo, *Autocensure et compromis dans la pensée politique de Kant*, trans. Jean-Michel Buée, Lille, 1993, p. 76.

23. Jacques Droz makes this point nicely in his classic study *L'Allemagne et la révolution française*, Paris, 1949, pp. 15 ff. The same point is emphasized in Lucien Calvié, *Le renard et les raisins. La Révolution française et les intellectuels allemands, 1789–1845*, Paris, 1989, pp. 23 ff.

24. See Friedrich Schiller, *On the Aesthetic Education of Man in a Series of Letters*, trans. Reginald Snell, London, 1954.

25. Ibid., p. 35. Let us note, however, that on the same page, Schiller denounces the ethos of the upper classes at least as harshly. Such is the tragedy of the aesthetic position, the solitude that is the lot of the partisan of the Beautiful – a solitude that he transforms into a position from which he can take an Olympian view of society.

26. Ibid., pp. 120 ff.

27. Ibid., pp. 128 ff.

28. Kant, 'Perpetual Peace', p. 125.

29. Ibid., p. 118.

30. 'Moralising politicians . . . try to cover up political principles which are contrary to right, under the pretext that human nature is *incapable* of attaining the good which reason prescribes as an idea. They thereby make progress *impossible*, and eternalise the violation of right.' Ibid., p. 119.

31. 'It may well be the case that despotic moralists, i.e. those who err in practice, frequently act contrary to political prudence by adopting or recommending premature measures, yet experience must gradually bring them out of their opposition to nature and make them adopt better ways.' Ibid.

32. This was one of the major criticisms that Hegel would make of Kant's moral doctrine.

33. Kant, 'Perpetual Peace', p. 126. 'In the principle that the maxims of international right may be incompatible with publicity,' Kant adds, 'we thus have a good indication that politics and morality (in the sense of a theory of right) are *not in agreement*.' Ibid., p. 128.

34. See Kant, 'On the Common Saying: This May be True in Theory, But It Does Not Apply in Practice', in *Political Writings*, pp. 74–6. On the distinction between active and passive citizens, see ibid., pp. 77–9 and *The Metaphysics of Morals: Introduction to the Theory of Right*, in Kant, *Political Writings*, §46, pp. 139–40. Kant is not unaware of the aporia inherent in this practical compromise; in the end, he writes: 'but I do admit that it is

somewhat difficult to define the qualifications which entitle anyone to claim the status of being his own master [and thus the status of active citizen]'. Kant, 'On the Common Saying', p. 78n.

35. See Jürgen Habermas, *The Structural Transformation of the Public Sphere*, trans. Thomas Burger with the assistance of Frederick Lawrence, Cambridge, 1989, pp. 110–12.

36. Hence Kant's insistence that philosophers should neither help to diffuse the literature that circulated 'under the table', as they often did at the time, nor take part in the activities of secret societies, lodges, clubs, etc. (see Kant, 'Perpetual Peace', p. 115; 'On the Common Saying', pp. 85–6).

37. I take this expression from André Tosel, *Kant révolutionnaire*, Paris, 1988, p. 93.

38. Ibid., p. 39.

39. Kant, 'The Contest of Faculties', §8, pp. 188–9.

40. Ibid., p. 186; emphasis added.

41. Cited in Calvié, *Le renard et les raisins*, p. 42.

42. Kant, 'On the Common Saying', p. 86.

43. Kant, *The Metaphysics of Morals*, §52, p. 162.

44. Kant, 'On the Common Saying', p. 82. See also Kant, *The Metaphysics of Morals*, §49A, pp. 143–7.

45. Kant, 'On the Common Saying', pp. 79–82.

46. Ibid., p. 75.

47. Ibid., p. 78 and n.

48. Kant, 'Perpetual Peace', pp. 118–19n. This passage is prudently relegated to a footnote. That the revolutionary phenomenon was something objective and, as such, comparable to a natural upheaval was a commonplace of the pro-republican literature of the day (see Losurdo, *Autocensure*, pp. 120 ff.).

49. Kant, 'The Contest of Faculties', p. 185; emphasis added.

50. See G.W.F. Hegel, *Elements of the Philosophy of Right*, ed. Allen W. Wood, trans. H. B. Nisbet, Cambridge, 1991, §141, p. 185: 'The identity – which is accordingly *concrete* – of the good and the subjective will, the truth of them both, is *ethical life*.'

51. See ibid., §337, p. 370.

52. See ibid., §29 and remark, p. 58.

53. This is forcefully explained in ibid., §135, remark, pp. 162–3.

54. See ibid., §136–40, pp. 163–83. The peregrinations of 'free' subjective consciousness, which is in fact cut off from the conditions of access to objectivity, are retraced in a famous passage in G.W.F. Hegel, *Phenomenology of Spirit*, trans. A.V. Miller, Oxford, 1977, pp. 119–38.

55. G.W.F. Hegel, *Lectures on the Philosophy of World History: Introduction*, trans. H. B. Nisbet, Cambridge, 1975, pp. 76–7.

56. Ibid., p. 81.

57. G.W.F. Hegel, *The Philosophy of History*, trans. J. Sibree, New York, 1956, pp. 446–7.

58. Respectively, Joachim Ritter, *Hegel and the French Revolution*, trans. Richard Dien Winfield, London, 1982, p. 43; Arendt, *On Revolution*, p. 51. For Arendt, who reactivates the old liberal critique of Hegel, he stands convicted of having hailed the French Revolution in its plebeian dimension as, precisely, a social revolution, which, according to her, diverted it from its only legitimate content, the *constitutio libertatis*. As I shall show later, Hegel had every reason to plead guilty to the first count of the indictment, but, equally, to reject any inference from the first to the second.

59. Hegel, *Phenomenology of Spirit*, pp. 355–63.

60. On Hegel's conception of necessity as a retroactive effect, see Slavoj Žižek, *Le plus sublime des hystériques. Hegel passe*, Paris, 1988, esp. pp. 35–42, 111–22.

61. Thus, in the period just before the proclamation of the Empire, Rome's republican constitution was an 'utterly unsubstantial form' (Hegel, *The Philosophy of History*, p. 314); while the pagan Roman world 'no longer possessed anything stable', and 'came to an open rupture with reality' when it succumbed to the Christian 'revolution' (ibid.,

p. 318). Similarly, the Byzantine Empire, torn apart by 'insane' passions, became 'rotten' and crumbled before the Turks (ibid., p. 340). As for the French *ancien régime*, by the eve of the Revolution, it was no more than 'a confused mass of privileges altogether contravening Thought and Reason' (ibid., p. 446). In other words, it continued to exist, but had become inactual, irrational and unreal.

62. Hegel, *The Philosophy of History*, p. 446; emphasis added.
63. The Young Hegelians would subsequently reformulate this idea, wrongly presenting it as a rectification, if not a refutation, of Hegel.
64. An example is provided by the passage in which Tocqueville expresses his disgust at the Enlightenment men of letters who, with their 'abstract and general theories', their love for principles 'based on reason', and their 'new systems', wrested cultural and intellectual hegemony from the aristocracy and played a political role of the utmost importance in paving the way for revolution. See Alexis de Tocqueville, *The Ancien régime*, trans. John Bonner, London, 1988, pp. 110–18.
65. Hegel, *The Philosophy of History*, p. 446.
66. The features of the Reformation that Hegel singles out for attention are secularization and modernity, not religious mysticism of any kind. Ibid., pp. 445–6.
67. Ibid., p. 445.
68. Hegel, *Phenomenology of Spirit*, p. 359.
69. The collision of absolutized particular wills leads to the reign of disposition [*Gesinnung*], which, in its subjective form, appears as virtue and inevitably degenerates into tyranny. Hegel, *The Philosophy of History*, pp. 449–50. See also Hegel's analysis in *Phenomenology of Spirit*, pp. 358–60, where the Terror is presented as the encounter between the singular and the universal in their abstraction, and as the destructive negation of the singular, in its very being, by the universal.
70. Hegel, *The Philosophy of History*, pp. 451, 453.
71. Ibid., pp. 451–2.
72. Hegel, *Elements of the Philosophy of Right*, §258, remark, p. 276.
73. Rousseau's position in political economy has even been characterized, not without reason, as a 'theoretical *jacquerie*'. See Yves Vargas, *Rousseau. Économie politique (1755)*, Paris, 1986, p. 60 and *passim*.
74. See Hegel, *Elements of the Philosophy of Right*, §29 and remark, p. 58.
75. Hegel, *The Philosophy of History*, p. 452.
76. 'The Few assume to be the *deputies*; but they are often only the *despoilers* of the Many. Nor is the sway of the Majority over the Minority a less palpable inconsistency.' Ibid., p. 448.
77. See Hegel, *Elements of the Philosophy of Right*, §303, pp. 343–4; §308, pp. 346–8; §310–1, pp. 349–51.
78. Ibid., §303, p. 344.
79. Commentators often note only the first aspect, the fear inspired by the revolutionary mobs (see, for example, Bertrand Binoche, *Critique des droits de l'homme*, Paris, 1989, p. 90), forgetting that Hegel is thinking at least as much of the opposite constellation, illustrated by the Spanish case: that of mobs instrumentalized by the nobles and clergy. The supposed irrationality of the mob resides precisely in this erratic oscillation between two extreme positions.
80. Hegel, *Elements of the Philosophy of Right*, §258, p. 277.
81. Napoleon made the same mistake when he offered the Spanish a constitution that was 'more rational than what they had before', but foreign to their culture. See ibid., §274, addition, pp. 312–13; Hegel, *The Philosophy of History*, pp. 452–3. I cannot examine the Spanish case at any length here. Let me, however, note that it seemed at the time to be the perfect anti-1789, the model of a successful counter-revolution that had the support of a majority of the people and was capable of mobilizing reactionary mobs at least as dangerous as those to be found in republican France.
82. Hegel, *The Philosophy of History*, p. 420. It is Hegel himself who uses the word 'revolution'

to designate the Reformation: 'the time-honored and cherished *sincerity of the German people* is destined to effect this revolution out of the honest truth and simplicity of its heart'. Ibid., p. 414.

83. This is true, notably, of Haller, whom Hegel showers with sarcastic comments in *Elements of the Philosophy of Right*, §258, remark, pp. 278–81. See Jacques d'Hondt, *Hegel en son temps (Berlin 1818–1831)*, Paris, 1968, pp. 116 ff. It may be said that, beginning with Novalis and his manifesto 'Christendom or Europe' (in *Philosophical Writings*, ed. and trans. Margaret Mahony Stoljar, Albany, New York, 1997, pp. 137–52), defence of a mystic version of Catholicism was an integral part of anti-1789 thought.

84. Hegel, *The Philosophy of History*, p. 425.

85. The key passage runs as follows:

> Thus there was also a secular reform – a change affecting the state of things outside the sphere of ecclesiastical relations: in many places a rebellion was raised against the temporal authorities. In Münster the Anabaptists expelled the Bishop and established a government of their own; and the peasants rose *en masse* to emancipate themselves from the yoke of serfdom. But the world was not yet ripe for a *transformation of its political condition as a consequence of ecclesiastical reformation*. (Hegel, *The Philosophy of History*, p. 419; emphasis added.)

86. Hegel, *The Philosophy of History*, p. 453.

87. See Hegel, *Elements of the Philosophy of Right*, §183, p. 221. This system of mutual dependence, animated by the pursuit of selfish objectives, is described as '*the external state, the state of necessity* and *of the understanding* [*Not- und Verstandesstaat*]'.

88. Ibid., §261, pp. 283–5.

89. Ibid., §194, pp. 230–31.

90. Ibid., §196, pp. 231–2, §199, p. 233.

91. 'The object . . . in civil society in general [*die bürgerliche Gesellschaft*] [is] the *citizen* [*der Bürger*] (in the sense of *bourgeois*). Here, at the level of needs . . . it is that concretum *of representational thought* which we call *the human being*; this is the first, and in fact the only occasion on which we shall refer to *the human being* in this sense.' Ibid., §190, p. 228.

92. At the heart of this 'state of necessity and the understanding' (see §183), the 'abstract moment of the *reality* of the Idea' appears as 'the *relative totality* and *inner necessity* of this external *appearance*'. Ibid., §184, p. 221; emphasis added.

93. Ibid., §197, p. 232.

94. See the famous passage in ibid., §243, p. 266.

95. After examining two frequently proposed solutions to the problem, social aid and full employment, and observing that they simply reproduce the problem, Hegel concludes: 'this shows that, despite an *excess of wealth*, civil society is *not wealthy enough* – i.e. its own distinct resources are not sufficient – to prevent an excess of poverty and the formation of a rabble'. Ibid., §245, p. 267.

96. It does not seem to be going too far to speak of 'ideological state apparatuses', as Jean-Pierre Lefebvre and Pierre Macherey suggest (*Hegel et la société*, Paris, 1984, p. 51) – but in conjunction, here, with something like an anticipation of mutual aid societies and state health insurance.

97. The hysterical yapping of the very liberal M.T. Duchâtel, to cite one example, can help us to form a more exact idea of the prevailing climate and the arguments of Hegel's opponents; see François Ewald, *Histoire de l'État providence*, Paris, 1996, p. 26.

98. Hegel, *Elements of the Philosophy of Right*, §235, p. 261; §241, p. 265; §242, pp. 265–6.

99. Ibid., §127, p. 154.

100. Ewald clearly sets out this diagram, in its original version, as the type of rationality at the basis of a harmonious society (Ewald, *Histoire de l'État*, esp. ch. 1, 'Droit civil', pp. 19–50). He rightly emphasizes the fact that liberal morality and the (inward) sense that one has a duty to perform acts of charity are not a mere *supplément d'âme* for

liberalism, since they are part of its very foundations. They fulfil a simultaneously educative, cultural, ethical and political function: to guarantee the continued existence of the social order, one has to 'sermonize the poor'.

101. Hegel, *Elements of the Philosophy of Right*, §127, p. 154; §230, p. 260; §236, p. 262; emphasis added.

102. Domenico Losurdo, 'Tension morale et primat de la politique chez Hegel', *Actuel Marx*, no. 10, 1991.

103. On the project for a 'popular political economy' and the specificity of the 'peasant road' developed during the French Revolution, the indispensable source is E.P. Thompson, 'The Moral Economy of the English Crowd in the 18th Century', in *Customs in Common*, London, 1991, pp. 185–258.

104. See Solange Mercier-Josa, *Entre Hegel et Marx. Points cruciaux de la philosophie hégélienne du droit*, Paris, 1999, pp. 75–127.

105. Domenico Losurdo, *Hegel et les libéraux*, trans. François Mortier, Paris, 1992.

106. 'Such necessity [*Not*] reveals the finitude and hence the contingency of both right and welfare'. Hegel, *Elements of the Philosophy of Right*, §128, p. 155.

107. Ibid., §189, p. 227.

108. As Ritter points out (*Hegel*, p. 72): 'it has become clear to Hegel in his encounter with political economy that *the political revolution itself and with it its central idea of freedom belong historically to the emergence of the new society; this is its actuality and historical necessity*'.

109. See Eric Weil, *Hegel and the State*, trans. Mark A. Cohen, Baltimore, MD, 1998. Weil's book, first published in 1950, played a pioneering role in the field of Hegelian political philosophy in France.

110.
'Another breach, therefore, took place, and the Government was overturned. At length, after forty years of war and confusion indescribable, a weary heart might fain congratulate itself on seeing a termination and tranquillization of all these disturbances. But ... there remains on the one hand that rupture which the Catholic principle inevitably occasions; on the other hand that which has to do with men's subjective will.... The will of the Many expels the Ministry from power; and those who had formed the Opposition fill the vacant places; but the latter having now become the Government, meet with hostility from the Many, and share the same fate. Thus agitation and unrest are perpetuated. This collision, this nodus, this problem is that with which history is now occupied, and whose solution it has to work out in the future'. (Hegel, *The Philosophy of History*, pp. 451–2.)

111. This is the provocative but stimulating thesis defended by Arno J. Mayer in *The Persistence of the Old Regime*, London, 1981.

112. In an essay on the Württemberg Assembly, Hegel had already lavished high praise on the 'great secular spectacle' of the king offering his people a progressive constitution, while severely criticizing the kinds of resistance put up by the representatives of backward-looking feudal forces. Hegel, 'Proceedings of the Estates Assembly in the Kingdom of Württemberg, 1815–1816', in *Hegel's Political Writings*, trans. T.M. Knox, Oxford, 1964, p. 251 and *passim*.

113.
'The supremacy implied in monarchy is essentially a power emanating from a political body, and is pledged to the furtherance of that equitable purpose on which the constitution of a state is based. Feudal sovereignty is a polyarchy: we see nothing but Lords and Serfs; in Monarchy, on the contrary, there is one Lord and no Serf, for servitude is abrogated by it, and in it Right and Law are recognized; it is the source of real freedom'. (Hegel, *The Philosophy of History*, p. 399.)

114. See Hegel, *Elements of the Philosophy of Right*, §279–82, pp. 316–20.

115. See, for example, ibid., §272, addition, p. 307; Hegel, *The Philosophy of History*, p. 39. Note Hegel's proximity to Hobbes, who defines his Leviathan/state as a 'Mortall God'. Thomas Hobbes, *Leviathan*, ed. C.B. Macpherson, Harmondsworth, 1981, p 227.

116. Hegel, *Elements of the Philosophy of Right*, §279, addition, p. 321. On this point, see Lefebvre and Macherey, *Hegel et la société*, pp. 72–3; Domenico Losurdo, *Hegel et les libéraux*, p. 60 and *passim*.
117. Hegel, *Elements of the Philosophy of Right*, §279, addition, p. 323; §280, addition, p. 321.
118. Bernard Bourgeois ('Le prince hégélien', in *Études hégéliennes*, Paris, 1992) rightly argues that we should not put too liberal a construction on Hegel's conception of constitutional monarchy; Hegel diverges from the principle that 'the prince rules, but does not govern'.
119. Hegel, *Elements of the Philosophy of Right*, §289, pp. 329–30.
120. Ibid., §256, p. 273.
121. Ibid., §272, pp. 305–8.
122. Ibid., §303, p. 343.
123. Ibid., §205, p. 237; §303, pp. 343–4.
124. Ibid., Preface, p. 17.
125. 'It is a dangerous and false prejudice, that the People *alone* have reason and insight, and know what justice is; for each popular faction may represent itself as the People; and the question as to what constitutes the State is one of advanced science, and not of popular decision.' Hegel, *The Philosophy of History*, p. 43.
126. Hegel, *Elements of the Philosophy of Right*, §256, pp. 273–4. See also §182, addition, pp. 220–21: '[civil society's] full development occurs later than that of the state, which it must have before it as a self-sufficient entity in order to subsist'.
127. Ibid., §258, p. 275.
128. Ibid., Preface, pp. 12, 17.
129. On this point, I agree with Jürgen Habermas: Hegel favours 'the revolutionizing of reality without Revolution itself' ('Hegel's Critique of the French Revolution', in *Theory and Practice*, trans. John Viertel, Cambridge, 1988, p. 123). The question is whether the 'secret foundation' of all German philosophy, Habermas included, is not to be sought here.
130. Hegel explicitly raises this possibility (ibid., §295, pp. 334–5); should it come about, he looks to the sovereign to remedy the situation.
131. Hegel, 'The English Reform Bill', in *Hegel's Political Writings*, p. 269; Hegel, *The Philosophy of History*, p. 452.
132. Hegel takes pleasure in comparing the savage cruelty of the British occupation with the (relatively) civilized character of the Turkish conquest ('The English Reform Bill', p. 306).
133. Ibid., p. 325.
134. 'An opposition which, erected on a basis hitherto at variance with the stability of Parliament, might feel itself no match for the opposite party in Parliament, could be led to look for its strength to the people, and then introduce not reform but revolution.' Ibid., p. 330.
135. Hegel, *The Philosophy of History*, pp. 71–2.
136. Ritter, *Hegel*, pp. 62–3.
137. Hegel, *Elements of the Philosophy of Right*, §341, p. 372.

2   Spectres of Revolution: On a Few Themes in Heine

1. Friedrich Engels, *Ludwig Feuerbach and the End of Classical German Philosophy*, MECW 26: 357.
2. Heine attended Hegel's courses in Berlin from 1821 to 1823, notably those on the philosophy of history and the philosophy of law; he also had the opportunity to see the philosopher in the salons of the Prussian capital. On these and related matters, see

Jean-Pierre Lefebvre, 'Heine et Hegel: Philosophie de l'histoire et histoire de la philosophie', doctoral dissertation, University of Paris IV – Sorbonne, 1976, pp. 32–72.

3. Heine, *French Affairs*, trans. Charles Godfrey Leland (Hans Breitmann), *The Works of Heinrich Heine*, London, 1893, vol. 7, p. 94.

4. The fragment 'The Debt' brings together extracts from a text by Cobbett that had been published in his newspaper *The Register*. It explains that the country's debt – and, more generally, the English policies of the past few decades – were the inevitable consequences of a stubborn desire to combat revolutionary France in the hope of driving it to acts of desperation that would ruin the international reputation of the Revolution, and, simultaneously, stop the spread of democratic ideas in England (especially ideas about extending the right to vote). See Heine, *English Fragments*, in *The Sword and the Flame: Selections from Heinrich Heine's Prose*, trans. Charles Godfrey Leland (Hans Breitmann), ed. Alfred Werner, New York, 1960, pp. 460 ff.

5. See Heine, *French Affairs*, pp. 155 ff.

6. In *Ideas – The Book of Le Grand*, it is the drum-major Legrand, a character closely associated with the paternal figure of Napoleon, who teaches the young Heine French, the language of the triumphant Revolution. When he reappears, we find him beating the retreat after the disastrous Russian campaign. See Heinrich Heine, *Ideas – The Book of Le Grand*, in *Selected Prose*, ed. and trans. Ritchie Robertson, Harmondsworth, 1993, pp. 89–143.

7. Heine, *Ludwig Börne, A Memorial*, Book II, trans. Frederic Ewen and Robert C. Holub, in *The Romantic School and Other Essays*, ed. Jost Hermand and Holub, New York, 1985, p. 282; translation modified.

8. 'The emancipation of the people was our great task in life; we have struggled and borne great misery for it.' Heine, 'Confessions', in *Heinrich Heine, 'Confessions' and Leo Tolstoy, 'A Confession'*, trans. Peter Heinegg, Malibu, CA, 1981, p. 42.

9. As is noted by Dolf Oehler, *Ein Höllensturz der Alten Welt*, Frankfurt, 1988, pp. 239–67.

10. Such readings had already been proposed, if not by Hegel himself, then at least by the students and collaborators closest to him, beginning with Gans; see the evidence assembled by Jacques d'Hondt in *Hegel secret* (Paris, 1968) as well as d'Hondt's biography of the philosopher (*Hegel*, Paris, 1998).

11. Lukács points out that Heine was 'the first in Germany to grasp the revolutionary implications of Hegel's philosophy'. Georg Lukács, 'Heinrich Heine as National Poet', in *German Realists in the Nineteenth Century*, trans. Jeremy Gaines and Paul Keast, London, 1993, pp. 95–126, esp. pp. 121–3.

12. A distinction made famous by Engels in *Ludwig Feuerbach*.

13. Strauß's book appeared in 1835. Heine's monograph *On the History of Religion and Philosophy in Germany* was first published in 1834 in *Revue des deux mondes*, and reprinted the following year in the French edition of his works published by Renduel as well as in the second volume of *Salon* [*French Painters*], published in Hamburg by von Campe.

14. Heine, *Ludwig Börne*, partially trans. Frederic Ewen, in *The Poetry and Prose of Heinrich Heine*, ed. Ewen, New York, 1948, p. 394.

15. Heine, *French Affairs*, p. 155.

16. 'Louis-Philippe has forgotten that his Government was born of the principle of popular sovereignty, and now, in afflicting blindness, he would uphold it by a quasi-legitimacy, by alliances with absolute princes, and by a continuation of the period of the Restoration. . . . Louis-Philippe, who owed his throne to the people and to the paving-stones of July, is an ungrateful man, whose apostasy is the more distressing as we perceive day by day that we are grossly deceived'. (Ibid., pp. 45–6)

17. Ibid., p. 110.

18. This is suggested by Ortwin Lämke, 'Heine, *Lutèce* et le communisme. Une nouvelle conception de l'histoire après 1848?', *Revue Germanique Internationale*, no. 9, 1998, p. 93.

19. See below: 'The politics of the name'.

20. See Lefebvre, 'Heine et Hegel, pp. 175–204. Lefebvre pursues the argument in 'Le syllogisme de l'histoire dans le *Romancero*', *Cahiers Heine* [1], Paris, 1975.

21. Lefebvre, 'Heine et Hegel', p. 203.

22. Heine, *Lutetia*, trans. Charles Godfrey Leland (Hans Breitmann), *The Works of Heinrich Heine*, vol. 8, pp. 253–4; translation modified.

23. Ibid.; translation modified.

24. Ibid., p. 257.

25. Ibid.; translation modified.

26. Ibid.

27. Ibid., pp. 253–4.

28. Already, during his London *flânerie*, the 'poor German poet' catches himself *yawning* in front of a shop that sells engravings (Heine, *English Fragments*, p. 431). As we shall see in a moment, Heine had a very special personal relationship to the paintings by Robert in question here.

29. Heine, *Lutetia*, pp. 258–9. The firm Goupil et Rittner, based at 12 boulevard Montmartre and specializing in the reproduction of works of art, was, under the July monarchy, one of the most prosperous businesses of its kind, and also one of the first to expand abroad. The firm that succeeded it after Rittner's death in 1840, the house of Goupil et Vibert, was one of the principal publishers of engravings depicting the 1848 revolution. See Ségolène Le Men, 'Les images de l'année 1848 dans la "République des arts"', in Maurice Agulhon, ed., *Les révolutions de 1848. L'Europe des images, catalogue de l'exposition*, vol. 1, Paris, 1998, pp. 34–7.

30. Heine, 'French Painters', trans. David Ward, in Susanne Zantop, *Paintings on the Move: Heinrich Heine and the Visual Arts*, Lincoln, NE, 1989, pp. 138–43.

31. The impossibility of such inversion is the defining feature of another mode of reproduction, photography, typical of the industrial age. Should we regard this feature of the engraving as a trace of the path followed by those painters who, with the arrival of the daguerreotype, abandoned the realm of art for that of mass reproduction – a path that Robert, a former engraver who turned to painting (as Heine reminds us), followed in the opposite direction?

32. See Walter Benjamin, 'The Work of Art in the Age of Mechanical Reproduction', in *Illuminations*, ed. Hannah Arendt, trans. Harry Zohn, London, 1973, pp. 219–53.

33. See the account by Camille Selden (Elise Krinitz) in H. H. Houben, *Henri Heine et ses contemporains*, Paris, 1929, p. 300.

34. Heine, 'French Painters', p. 140.

35. Heine, *Lutetia*, p. 260; translation modified.

36. Ibid., p. 263; translation modified.

37. In Grandjonc's words: 'the year 1828, which saw the appearance of this book, marked the end of the tunnel for revolutionary democrats and the point of departure for a genuine renewal of communitarian thinking with political aims ... revolutionary democratic thought once again assumed a place of honour alongside the utopian-societal thought of Fourier, mutualist-cooperative thought of Owen, and mystic-individualistic thought of Saint-Simon'. Jacques Grandjonc, *Communisme / Kommunismus / Communism. Origine et développement international de la terminologie communautaire prémarxiste des utopistes aux néo-babouvistes*. Schriften aus dem Karl-Marx-Haus 39/1, 2 vols, Trier, 1989, vol. 1, p. 125.

38. Heine, *Lutetia*, p. 264; translation modified.

39. The suicide of Léopold Robert (1794–1835) elicited countless commentaries at the time, enhancing the aura of mystery surrounding this Romantic painter. He was said to have killed himself because of his hopeless love for Princess Charlotte Bonaparte, wife of Louis-Napoleon Bonaparte's brother.

40. Heine, *Lutetia*, p. 263.

41. Walter Benjamin, 'Central Park', trans. Lloyd Spencer, *New German Critique*, no. 34, Winter 1985, p. 32.

42. Gerhard Höhn, *Heinrich Heine. Un intellectuel moderne*, Paris, 1994, pp. 129 ff.
43. *Pace* Michael Werner, for whom the 'original road' proposed by Heine was defined by 'a permanent to-and-froing between fact and idea, body and spirit, or, if you like, the particular and the general' (Werner, 'Réflexion et révolution. Notes sur le travail de l'histoire dans l'œuvre de Heine', *Revue Germanique Internationale*, no. 9, 1998, pp. 48–9).
44. Heine, *French Affairs*, pp. 159–60; translation modified.
45. 'You know what I mean by social conditions. They are the manners and customs, the doing and letting be done, the whole public as well as private impulses of a race, so far as the predominant view of life is expressed by them.' Heine, 'The French Stage: Confidential Letters Addressed to M. August Lewald', trans. Charles Godfrey Leland (Hans Breitmann), *The Works of Heinrich Heine*, vol. 4, p. 151.
46. See Chapter 1, above: 'Superseding the Revolution?' Let us simply recall that, according to Hegel, 'liberalism as an abstraction, emanating from France, traversed the Roman World; but Religious slavery held that world in the fetters of political servitude. For it is a false principle that the fetters which bind Right and Freedom can be broken without the emancipation of conscience – that there can be a Revolution without a Reformation.' Hegel, *The Philosophy of History*, trans. J. Sibree, New York, 1956, p. 453.
47. Heine, 'The French Stage', p. 152. The tone of this sentence reflects its place in Heine's argument; he means to show that 'it is rather to certain social conditions that comic dramatists owe their superiority in France' (ibid., p. 151); whereas 'the *political* condition of the country is as unfavorable to comedy as to tragedy' (ibid., p. 181).
48. Heine, *English Fragments*, pp. 494–5; translation modified.
49. Ibid., p. 496; translation modified.
50. Georg Büchner, *Danton's Death*, trans. Stephen Spender and Goronwy Rees, in Eric Bentley, ed., *From the Modern Repertoire, Series One*, Bloomington, IN, 1949, Act 1, Scene 6, p. 45. The exact wording of Saint-Just's remark is: 'Those who make revolutions by halves simply dig their own graves'. It occurs shortly before another famous line in the same text: 'the wretched are the lords of the earth; they have the right to speak as masters to those who command them'. Louis Antoine de Saint-Just, *Discours et rapports*, ed. A. Soboul, Paris, 1957, p. 145.
51. Heine, *French Affairs*, pp. 99–100.
52. Ibid., pp. 246–7.
53. 'A German with his thoughts, his ideas, which are weak as the brain from which they come, is at the same time only an idea, and when this idea displeases Government, they send him to prison in a fortress. So they had sixty ideas locked up in Köpenick, and nobody missed them.' Ibid., p. 247.
54.
   'If the English people quarrel with their nobility, it is not on account of social equality, of which they never think, and least of all about civil freedom, which they fully enjoy, but because of pure questions of money; because the nobility, in possession of all the sinecures, ecclesiastical endowments and offices, which are extravagantly salaried, revel bravely and luxuriously, while the greater part of the people, overloaded with taxes, languish in deepest misery and die of hunger. Therefore a parliamentary reform is required. . . .' (Ibid., p. 103)
55. See Chapter 3.
56. Heine, *Lutetia*, partially translated by Frederic Ewen, in *The Poetry and Prose of Heinrich Heine*, p. 780.
57. Heine first *distinguishes* the Chartists from the workers' movement, observing that the former 'represent themselves as a purely political party with a well-defined program, while the factory-workers . . . are only poor day-laborers, who can hardly speak from hunger, who are indifferent to all political reforms and only ask for bread'. He immediately adds: 'But a program rarely expresses the intimate thinking of a party; it is merely its outward badge, a spoken "cockade". The Chartists who profess to limit themselves only to political questions, cherish objectives which are in profound accord

with the unspoken, unarticulated feelings of the hungry workmen; the latter can always take the program of the Chartists as their slogan, without ceasing to pursue their own aims' (*Lutetia*, trans. Ewen, pp. 780–81). Yet, if Chartism and the workers' movement were convergent and mutually reinforcing, there was yet, Heine thought, a real difference between them, especially at the discursive level. This is a view shared by certain contemporary historians, such as Gareth Stedman Jones (*Languages of Class*, Cambridge, 1982).

58. Heine, *Lutetia*, trans. Ewen, p. 781.

59. Heine begins by observing that 'the French Communists have much the same standpoint as the English factory operatives', but adds that 'the former are impelled by an idea, and the latter only by hunger' (*Lutetia*, trans. Leland, p. 337; translation modified). It would seem, then, that the two countries arrived at the same point, but by different paths, France's being more ideological, England's more material (or economic).

60. See Chapter 4.

61. Heine, 'Appel an die Demokraten', in *Historisch-Kritische Gesamtausgabe*, ed. Manfred Windfuhr, vol. 12, part 1, Hamburg, 1980, pp. 467–70.

62. Ibid., p. 289.

63. But, as recent research on 'Franco–German cultural transfers' has shown, Saint-Simonianism also had one of its sources in Hegelianism; figures such as Victor Cousin or the Saint-Simonians Jules Lechevalier, Eugène Rodrigues, Eugène Lerminier and Gustave d'Eichtal played an essential role here. See Michel Espagne, 'Le saint-simonisme est-il jeune hégélien?', in Jean-René Derré, ed., *Regards sur le Saint-Simonisme et les Saint-Simoniens*, Lyon, 1986, pp. 59 ff.

64. As Warren Breckmann notes (*Marx, The Young Hegelians and the Origins of Radical Social Theory*, Cambridge, 1999, p. 198), 'Saint-Simonianism was "in the air" in the early 1830s [in Germany].' On the German reception of Saint-Simonianism and, in particular, Gans's role, see ibid., pp. 158–76, 196–9.

65. For example, in a fragment I have already cited, 'An Appeal to Democrats', Heine tries to adopt a standpoint beyond (so to speak) the conflict that pitted partisans of the monarchy against its adversaries within the ranks of the democratic opposition. In *French Affairs* (p. 260; translation modified), we even find this passage, typical of a defender of the 'German road': 'Yes, one can, without being illogical, wish the Republic might be introduced into France, and, at the same time, monarchism be maintained in Germany. In fact, those whose most heartfelt concern is to preserve the advantages that the democratic principle has secured can easily come to take this view.'

66. See below: 'Exorcizing the spectres'.

67. Heine, *Lutetia*, trans. Leland, p. 323; translation modified.

68. One cannot fail to be struck by the similarity between Heine's language and the terms Marx uses in evaluating the political significance of the Paris Commune: '[the Commune] was a thoroughly expansive political form. . . . Its true secret is this: it was essentially a working-class government, the product of the struggle of the producing against the appropriating class, the political form at last discovered under which to work out the economical emancipation of labour.' Marx, *The Civil War in France*, MECW 22: 334.

69. Heine, *Lutetia*, trans. Leland, p. 167; translation modified.

70. Heine, *French Affairs*, p. 31.

71. Heine, *Lutetia*, trans. Leland, pp. 158–9; translation modified.

72. Georges Labica, *Robespierre. Une politique de la philosophie*, Paris, 1990, pp. 67–8.

73. Heine, *Lutetia*, trans. Leland, p. 156; translation modified.

74. Robespierre, 'Réponse à l'accusation de J.-B. Louvet', in *Écrits*, ed. Claude Mazauric, Paris, 1989, p. 191.

75. See also Robespierre's reply to Petion: 'you criticize it [the Conseil général of the city of Paris] for having prolonged the revolutionary movement beyond its term. What was this term? You do not say: it is probable that it was the moment when they should have

abdicated; with the result that, according to you, the revolutionary movement should last exactly twenty-four hours. You measure political revolutions as one does those of the sun.' Ibid., p. 200.

76. Saint-Just, *Discours et rapports*, p. 127.

77. Babeuf, *Le Tribun du peuple*, no. 36, 10 December 1795, in Babeuf, *Écrits*, Paris, 1988, p. 282.

78. See Grandjonc's study (*Communisme*, esp. vol. 1, pp. 75–82), which establishes the essential role played by the Club du Panthéon, a centre of Babouvist and Robespierrean agitation until it was closed down by the Directory in February 1796. Individuals such as Marc-Antoine Jullien, the first communist orator about whom we have a contemporary written report (1797), and also Buonarroti embodied the link between the doctrines of Robespierre, which represented their intellectual point of departure, and those of Babeuf, to which they later rallied. Babeuf himself was vehemently anti-Jacobin in the Year II, and even briefly supported the Thermidoreans; however, he began to modify his views with his imprisonment in 1795, writing, for example: 'Robespierrism exists throughout the Republic, throughout the class of the far-sighted and the judicious, and, naturally, everywhere amongst the people. The reason is simple. Robespierrism is democracy; these two words are identical: thus, if you put an end to Robespierrism, you are certain to put an end to democracy as well' (Babeuf, *Écrits*, p. 287). On the activities of the Club du Panthéon, see Jean-Marc Schiappa, *Gracchus Babeuf, avec les Égaux*, Paris, 1991, pp. 114–17.

79. Heine, Letter of 1 April 1831 to Varnhagen von Ense, in *Works of Prose*, ed. Hermann Kesten, trans. E.B. Ashton, New York, 1943, p. 308.

80. Georg Büchner, *Briefwechsel: Kritische Studienausgabe*, ed. Jan-Christoph Hauschild, Basel and Frankfurt, 1994, p. 34.

81. Büchner issued his call in *Der Hessische Landbote*, an important document in the history of revolutionary German and European thought. The full text may be found in 'Le messager Hessois', in G.M. Bravo, *Les socialistes avant Marx*, Paris, 1979, vol. 2, pp. 8–20.

82. Heinrich Heine, 'Differing Conceptions of History', in *Selected Prose*, p. 193.

83. Ibid., p. 195.

84. As noted in Lefebvre, 'Heine et Hegel', pp. 108 ff.

85. Hegel, *Phenomenology of Spirit*, trans. A.V. Miller, Oxford, 1977, p. 27.

86. Ibid., p. 6. There follow the examples of birth, sunrise (i.e. the French Revolution) and the growth of the oak.

87. Hegel, too, is haunted by this very modern historical melancholy, born of a sense of the precariousness and endless changeability of the world. See his well-known reflections on the ruins of ancient civilizations in the *Philosophy of History*, pp. 72–3. Even if 'out of death, new life arises', it behoves anyone who meditates upon the forward march of humanity to bear in mind that 'history cuts us off from the finest and noblest' – in short, as Goethe says, 'that nothing endures' (Hegel, *Lectures on the Philosophy of World History: Introduction*, trans. H.B. Nisbet, Cambridge, 1975, p. 32).

88. Hegel, *The Philosophy of History*, pp. 26–7.

89.
'Reason ... is *Substance*, as well as *Infinite Power*, its own *Infinite Material* underlying all the natural and spiritual life which it originates, as also the *Infinite Form* – that which sets this Material in motion.... Reason is the *substance* of the Universe; viz., that by which and in which all reality has its being and substance.... It is the *Infinite Energy* of the Universe.... It supplies its own nourishment, and is the object of its own operations. While it is exclusively its own basis of existence, and absolute final aim, it is also the energizing power realizing this aim; developing it not only in the phenomena of the Natural, but also of the Spiritual Universe – the History of the World'. (Ibid., p. 9)

90. Heine, 'Different Conceptions of History', in *Selected Prose*, p. 196.

91. 'Amid the pressure of great events, a general principle gives no help. It is useless to

revert to similar circumstances in the Past. The pallid shades of memory struggle in vain with the life and freedom of the Present.' Hegel, *The Philosophy of History*, p. 6.

92. Ibid.

93. Heine, Letter of 23 August 1838 to Karl Gutzkow, in *Heinrich Heine's Memoirs, from his Works, Letters, and Conversations*, ed. Gustav Karpeles, London, 1910, vol. 2, p. 73.

94. Many writers have, in the wake of (the young) Thoman Mann's commentary on *Ludwig Börne*, compared Heine to Nietzsche. Such comparisons are commonplace in early-twentieth-century reactionary French readings of Heine (see Elisabeth Décultot, 'La réception de Heine en France entre 1860 et 1960', *Revue Germanique Internationale*, no. 9, 1998, pp. 181 ff.); as a result of the growing vogue for Nietzsche, they began to find favour with other kinds of critics as well. Gerhard Höhn, for example, in his commentary on 'Different Conceptions of History', says: 'in a sentence that could well have been written by Nietzsche, Heine finally adopts the position that life is a value' (Höhn, *Heinrich Heine*, p. 156. See also ibid., pp. 121–3; and Höhn, 'Heine und Nietzsche, Kritiker des Christentums', in Joseph A. Kruse, ed., *'Ich Narr des Glücks': Heinrich Heine 1797–1856, Bilder einer Ausstellung*, Stuttgart, 1997, pp. 357–60).

95. Friedrich Nietzsche, *Beyond Good and Evil*, trans. R.J. Hollingdale, Harmondsworth, 1990, §259, p. 194.

96. See Jean-Yves Mollier, 'La culture de 48', in Sylvie Aprile *et al.*, *La révolution de 1848 en France et en Europe*, Paris, 1998, pp. 137 ff. For example, George Sand, who was close to Heine until 1848, saw in the working class 'the Messiah promised to the nations' who would fulfil Christ's message (cited in ibid., p. 156). Leaving aside the Christian socialism of a Buchez, many socialist theoreticians, from Barbès to Cabet and Leroux to Flore Tristan, shared this vision of Christ as a primitive communist, the bearer of a message of social equality. Moreover, in the imagery of the February Revolution, religious symbols were associated with the symbolism of the republic, and anticlerical outbreaks were the exception rather than the rule among the lower classes. The clergy's general tendency was to seek an accommodation with the new regime.

97. On this subject, see, among other texts, Heine, *English Fragments*, pp. 498–9; *Ludwig Börne, Eine Denkschrift*, in Heine, *Historisch-Kritische Gesamtausgabe*, vol. 2, Hamburg, 1978, pp. 110–11; and *Lutetia*, trans. Leland, pp. 448–50, 463–4.

98. Addressing Jesus, the poet exclaims: 'The censor would have stricken out/ The most offensive section,/ And you'd have not been crucified/ Thanks to his kind protection./ Had you left that Sermon on the Mount/ To be preached by later messiahs, /You'd still have had spirit and talent enough,/ And could have spared the pious./ You scourged the bankers, the changers of gold,/ You drove them out of the temple./ Luckless crusader, now on the cross/ You hang as a warning example!' *Germany: A Winter's Tale*, trans. Aaron Kramer, in *The Theory and Prose of Heinrich Heine*, p. 259.

99. Nietzsche, *Beyond Good and Evil*, §62, p. 88; original emphasis. Nietzsche's evaluation of the sequence Reformation/Peasant Wars/Enlightenment is in every respect antithetical to Hegel's, which Heine adopts as it is; see notes 304, 307 below.

100. Heine, *Ludwig Börne: A Memorial*, p. 271.

101. On the role Nietzsche played in elaborating the reactionary visions of the world (i.e. visions forged in reaction to the Enlightenment, liberalism, science and democracy) that prevailed in the Europe born of the defeat of the 1848 revolutions, see the last chapter of Arno J. Mayer, *The Persistence of the Old Regime: Europe to the Great War*, London, 1981, pp. 275–329.

102. Heine, 'Differing Conceptions of History', pp. 196, 351n.

103. See especially Robespierre's speech of 2 December 1792 on the 'right to existence', and, above all, to bread, in Robespierre, *Écrits*, p. 22. On this aspect of Robespierre's doctrines, see Florence Gauthier, *Triomphe et mort du droit naturel en Révolution: 1789, 1795, 1802*, Paris, 1992, pp. 55–95.

104. See Maurice Agulhon, *Les Quarante-huitards*, 2nd edn, Paris, 1992, p. 128.

105. Ibid.

106. Lefebvre, 'Heine et Hegel', p. 108.
107. Heine, *Lutetia*, trans. Leland, pp. 1–15.
108. Ibid., p. 11; translation modified.
109. This is how he begins his 1855 'Confessions'. The expression was taken from Henri Blaze de Bury. See Heine, 'Confessions', p. 21.
110. Heine, *Lutetia*, trans. Leland, pp. 11–12.
111. A silence which it was Heine's desire that nothing should disturb: 'I forbid that any speech be made at my grave, either in German or French' (Heine, 'Testament', in *The Poetry and Prose of Heinrich Heine*, p. 500): 'Not a mass will be sung for me/ Not a *Kaddish* will be said' ('Commemoration Service', in *Romancero*, in *The Complete Poems of Heinrich Heine*, trans. Hal Draper, Oxford, 1982, p. 643).
112. Heine, *Lutetia*, trans. Leland, p. 13.
113. The 'Confessions' speak of the 'more or less clandestine leaders of the German communists' who are 'great logicians, the most capable of them the products of Hegel's school'; 'the future', adds Heine, 'belongs to them' (Heine, 'Geständnisse', in *Historisch-Kritische Gesamtausgabe*, vol. 15, Hamburg, 1982, p. 143). Yet, apart from 'Messrs. Feuerbach, Daumer, Bruno Bauer, Hengstenberg, and whomever else', none of whom Heine treats very kindly, only two names stand out: that of 'the gatekeeper of the Hegelian school, the wrathful Arnold Ruge' – although Heine surely knows what separates Ruge from communism in general and Marx in particular (the polemic between Marx and Ruge was raging in *Vorwärts* when Heine's collaboration with the paper was at its most intense) – and that of, precisely, 'my more obdurate friend Marx', the only one Heine calls a friend ('Confessions', pp. 51–2). Thus it is Marx who appears, to Heine, to be both the leading figure in the intellectual current that had its source in Hegel, and the leader of the political party to which the future belongs.
114. Heine, *French Affairs*, p. 155.
115. 'The last word has thus not been said, and here is perhaps the ring to which a new revelation can be joined'. Heine, *Ludwig Börne: A Memorial*, p. 268.
116. Heine, *English Fragments*, p. 496.
117. Heine, *French Affairs*, p. 97.
118. I take this idea from Jean-Marie Vincent, *Max Weber ou la démocratie inachevée*, Paris, 1998, esp. pp. 187–8.
119. Heine, 'Memoirs', in *Selected Prose*, p. 312.
120. See Lukács's comments on historical drama in *The Historical Novel*, trans. Hannah and Stanley Mitchell, Harmondsworth, 1981, esp. pp. 116–17.
121. See Benjamin, 'Theses on the Philosophy of History', in *Illuminations*, ed. Hannah Arendt, trans. Harry Zohn, London, 1973, pp. 255–66.
122. We shall come back to the question of Heine's messianism and its relation to Judaism later; see 'Exorcizing the spectres'.
123. For another example, see the poem 'The Ex-Living Man', in *Romancero*, pp. 626–7.
124. Hegel, *The Philosophy of History*, p. 313; translation modified.
125. The theatrical metaphor of spirit's progress in the world is also drawn from Hegel (*The Philosophy of History*, p. 28). Hegel inverts, as it were, the Baroque vision which makes the theatre an *imago mundi*, the vision of a world consisting of ambiguous signs vacillating between reality and illusion, a vision that devalues a history made of sound and fury; he reads the results of the activity of reason in the *theatrum mundi*, and in it alone, with no possibility of any other form of transcendence.
126. According to Agulhon (*Les Quarante-huitards*, p. 12):

> the idea was quite common at the time. Since republicans venerated the great Revolution, and since its rhetoric and imagery had become a part of their culture, it is not surprising that, whether consciously or not, they all bore its marks. Thus one is hard put to name a single critical observer of the men of 1848, from Marx through Proudhon and Louis Reybaud ('Jérôme Paturot') to Gustave Flaubert, who failed to note this air of pastiche.

127. Hegel, *The Philosophy of History*, p. 451. See also Paul-Laurent Assoun, *Marx et la répétition historique*, Paris, 1978, pp. 60 ff. (Assoun's is one of the very few systematic analyses of the Marx–Hegel relationship from this standpoint.)

128. See Hegel, *Aesthetics: Lectures on Fine Art*, trans. T.M. Knox, Oxford, 1975, vol. 1, pp. 193–4.

129. Ibid., p. 196.

130. Let us note in passing that Marx and Engels would later comment on the Goethean model at length in their correspondence with Lassalle about his play *Franz von Sickingen*. The story of Franz von Sickingen, which has left a deep mark on German culture, seems to lend itself admirably to a dramatization of the problems of historical tragedy and, above all, the question 'too early or too late'. On this discussion, see Georg Lukács's very informative text 'Die Sickingendebatte zwischen Marx, Engels, und Lassalle' (in *Karl Marx und Friedrich Engels als Literaturhistoriker*, Berlin, 1947, pp. 5–62).

131. Hegel, *Phenomenology of Spirit*, pp. 439–53.

132. Ibid., p. 443.

133. In his most Heinean text, 'Contribution to the Critique of Hegel's Philosophy of Law. Introduction' (1843–44), Marx would call for the '*serene* historical decision [*diese* heitere *geschichtliche Bestimmung*]' that would make it possible for Germany to rid itself of the petrified figures of its anachronistic present. *MECW* 3: 179; translation modified.

134. On the praise of merriment (but as a necessary step towards preparing a return to the serious): 'But just the weightier the subject, so much the more merrily must we manage it.' Heine, *English Fragments*, p. 481. On the typically German, lion-like nature of the ironical mask, see Heine, 'The French Stage', p 226. Jean-Pierre Lefebvre ('Le ton Heine', *Cahiers d'Études germaniques*, no. 34, 1998, pp. 155–60) has nicely brought out the significance of Heine's defence of Schlegel's irony against Hegel, a position that remained Hegelian even as it took its distance from Hegel.

135. See Hegel, *Aesthetics*, pp. 71–5.

136. Hegel, *Phenomenology of Spirit*, p. 455.

137. In *Danton's Death*, Büchner was to take this logic even further: he made a historical event into the stuff of a 'real' play by staging the event in its entirety.

138. On the Napoleonic epic as the last popular poem, see Heine, 'The French Stage', pp. 192–3.

139. See, for example, the carnival imagery in Heine, *French Affairs*, pp. 130–1.

140. Ibid., p. 283; translation modified.

141. Lukács, *The Historical Novel*, pp. 19–20. Incidentally, Lukács refers here to Heine's *Ideas – The Book of Le Grand*.

142. For Heine's sense of an impending 'catastrophe', see *Lutetia*, trans. Leland, pp. 58–9. As I have already noted, one of the main questions that Heine had posed eight years earlier, in *French Affairs*, concerned the stability of the regime that had emerged from the July Revolution.

143. Ibid., p. 304.

144. Heine, *French Affairs*, p. 190.

145. Ibid.

146. In *Germany* (see below), Heine stresses the fact that the influence of philosophy on every aspect of German life is by no means synonymous with moderation but, rather, the source of a radicalization even more acute than that which marked the French experience.

147. 'Rousseau's party, suppressed since that unhappy day of Thermidor, lived poorly, but sound in mind and body, in the Faubourgs Saint-Antoine and Saint-Marceau, in the persons of Garnier Pages, Cavaignac, and of so many other noble Republicans, who from time to time appear for the gospel of Freedom. I am not virtuous enough to be able to attach myself to this party, but I hate vice too much to ever make war on it.' Heine, *French Affairs*, pp. 192–3; translation modified.

148. The faubourg depicted in both the 1832 and 1840–44 chronicles is the Faubourg Saint-

Marceau (see Heine, *Lutetia*, trans. Leland, p. 51). Let us note in passing that this faubourg held a special place in Heine's imagination, although he doubtless ventured into it only rarely. The poem 'Early Morning' (*New Poems*, in *Complete Poems*, p. 370) is, of all the poems in the section of *New Poems* entitled 'Ballads', one of those most thoroughly steeped in the urban atmosphere; it dramatizes a fugitive encounter between the poet, who is making his way back to his home in the everyday bourgeois world, and an unknown passer-by, an embodiment of the misty, pallid early-morning hours still clinging to the night that envelops the Faubourg Saint-Marceau.

149. Hegel, *The Philosophy of History*, p. 6.
150. Heine, *French Affairs*, p. 80; translation modified.
151. Büchner, *Danton's Death*, Act I, Scene 3, p. 38. Let us note that this play also fiercely satirizes the protagonists of the revolutionary period, especially those of lower-class origin, for imitating Rome.
152. Heine, 'French Painters', p. 129.
153. 'Most of the French looked into the graves of the past merely with the intention of picking out an interesting costume for the carnival. In France the Gothic fad was simply a fad, and it served only to heighten the pleasure of the present.' Heine, 'The Romantic School', trans. Helen Mustard, in *The Romantic School and Other Essays*, p. 124. I hardly need point out that Marx exploits this theme to the full in *The Eighteenth Brumaire*.
154. Heine, 'The Romantic School', p. 2.
155. A risk that he openly acknowledged, as is shown by his polemic with his exiled *frère ennemi* in the democratic opposition, Ludwig Börne.
156. See Heine, *Lutetia*, trans. Leland, pp. 322–3.
157. Ibid., p. 323.
158. Heine systematically attributes this levelling egalitarianism to a 'Nazarene' temperament and an inability to enjoy life. See, for example, the parallel he draws between Robespierre and Louis Blanc in ibid., p. 174.
159. In fact, the France of the July monarchy had left the subsistence economy behind more in theory than in fact; it was still subject to famines that reawakened fears of the *jacqueries*, and even recalled the Great Fear. Such apprehensions were entirely justified, as is indicated by the riots that broke out shortly before the Revolution of February 1848 in Buzançais (in the Indre district), the Western Loire valley, and, more generally, in western France as a whole. See Vigier, *1848, les Français, et la République*, Paris, 1998, ch. 1, 'Buzançais, le 13 janvier 1847', pp. 37–53; André Jardin and André Tudesq, *La France des notables*, Paris, 1973, vol. 1, ch. 9, 'La crise de la fin de règne', pp. 233–41.
160. Heine, *On the History of Religion and Philosophy in Germany*, trans. Robertson, in *Selected Prose*, p. 249; translation modified. Heine goes on as follows: 'You demand simple costumes, abstemious manners, and pleasures without spice; we, on the other hand, demand nectar and ambrosia, purple robes, delicious scents, sensual pleasures, splendour, dances of laughing nymphs, music and comedies'.
161. Heine, *Lutetia*, trans. Leland, p. 174.
162. Heine, Preface to *Germany: A Winter's Tale*, in *Complete Poems*, p. 482.
163. Heine, 'Geständnisse', p. 141.
164. Walter Benjamin, 'Theses on the Philosophy of History', p. 256.
165. See the selection from *Lettres de Paris* that Heine included in *Ludwig Börne: Eine Denkschrift*, pp. 122–7. In the correspondence dating from the period in which the two men were still seeing each other, Börne criticizes Heine both for his political ambiguity and for behaviour out of keeping with his standards of moral virtue. See Börne's letters to Jeanette Wohl in Houben, *Henri Heine*, pp. 73 ff.
166. The most explicit and best-known text in this vein is doubtless the 1855 'Confessions'. See Heine, 'Confessions', pp. 42–3.
167. See Lukács, *The Historical Novel*, p. 29.
168. Jan-Christof Hauschild and Michael Werner, *Heinrich Heine. 'Der Zweck des Lebens ist das Leben selbst'*, Berlin, 1999, p. 294.

169. The associative, communitarian workers' movement, often strongly influenced by Saint-Simonianism, Fourierism, or communism *à la* Cabet, set out to explore a path to emancipation quite distinct from the revolutionary conspiracies of the secret societies and, more generally, the agitation of the republican and neo-Babouvist movements. See Jacques Rancière's historical overview in *La nuit des prolétaires. Archives du rêve ouvrier*, Paris, 1981.

170. 'Manifesto of the Equals', in Albert Fried and Ronald Sanders, eds, *Socialist Thought: A Documentary History*, Edinburgh, 1964, p. 52.

171. Another sentence, libertarian this time, also came in for criticism; it proclaimed that 'the revolting distinction between the rulers and the ruled should at last disappear'. See Grandjonc, *Communisme*, vol. 2, pp. 315–17.

172. Théophile Thoré, 'Babouvisme', in ibid., document 15, pp. 412–15.

173. Richard Lahautière, 'Réponse philosophique à un article sur le babouvisme, publié par Théophile Thoré, dans le *Journal du Peuple* (no. du 24 novembre 1839)', in ibid., document 16, pp. 424–8. Lahautière, according to information assembled by Grandjonc, had ties with certain circles of the German emigrant community, and was probably linked to August Hermann Ewerbeck, a leader of the League of the Banished, the future Communist League (ibid., p. 424).

174. Georg Lukács, *Skizzen einer Geschichte der neueren deutschen Literatur*, Neuwied and Berlin, 1963, p. 97. Lukács refers in particular to Büchner's play *Danton's Death* (ibid., p. 100). On this question, see Elisabeth Décultot, 'La réception de Heine en France entre 1860 et 1960', pp. 167–90.

175. It should be borne in mind, however, that Heine was under rather close surveillance by the police of three European countries (France, Prussia and Austria). See Hauschild and Werner, '*Der Zweck*', pp. 383 ff.

176. Lämke's remarks on this subject are apt ('Heine, *Lutèce* et le communisme', *Revue Germanique Internationale*, no. 9, 1998).

177. 'The communists, who were scattered in isolation in all countries and lacked a specific consciousness of their intentions, learned that they really existed through the [Augsburg] *General News*; they learned on such an occasion their true *name*, which had hitherto remained unknown to these poor foundlings of the old society.' Heine, 1845 Preface to *Lutetia*, trans. Gilbert Cannan and Robert C. Holub, in *The Romantic School and Other Essays*, p. 299; emphasis added.

178. Heine, *Lutetia*, trans. Ashton, in *Works of Prose*, p. 136. This passage alone plainly raises all the problems posed by Derridean spectrology (Jacques Derrida, *Specters of Marx*, trans. Peggy Kamuf, New York, 1994).

179. 'Communism . . . is the dark hero destined for a great, if temporary, role in the modern tragedy.' Heine, *Lutetia*, trans. Ashton, pp. 136–7.

180. Derrida, *Specters of Marx*, p. 17.

181. Heine, *Ludwig Börne: A Memorial*, p. 268.

182. Heine, *Lutetia*, trans. Leland, pp. 301–2.

183. The banquet took place on 1 July 1840. 'The rapid spread of communist doctrines and a communist vocabulary among the people date from this moment and this apparently banal, but in fact major, event.' Grandjonc, *Communisme*, vol. 1, p. 210. On this decisive event, see also ibid., vol. 2, documents 18 and 19, pp. 445–63; Bravo, *Les socialistes avant Marx*, vol. 2, pp. 210–32.

184. Heine, *French Affairs*, p. 68.

185. Pierre Leroux, Letter of 15 September 1841 to George Sand, in Grandjonc, *Communisme*, document 28, p. 518.

186. Heine cites a passage from Lessing: 'who will free us from the more intolerable yoke of the letter! Who will finally give us a Christianity as you would teach it now; as Christ himself would teach it!': Heine, *Religion and Philosophy in Germany*, trans. Robertson, p. 265.

187. 'Yes, for those Bonapartists who believed in an Imperial resurrection in the flesh, all is

at an end. Napoleon is now for them only a name, like that of Alexander of Macedonia or Charlemagne, whose direct heirs died early in like manner. But for the Bonapartists who believe in a resurrection of the spirit, there now blooms the best hope. Bonapartism is not for them a transferral of power by begetting and primogeniture.' Heine, *French Affairs*, p. 355.

188. Auguste Comte, 'Discours sur l'ensemble du positivisme' (1847–48), in *La science sociale*, Paris, 1972, pp. 245–6.

189. Ibid., p. 249.

190. Ibid., p. 250.

191. Ibid., p. 251.

192. Ibid., p. 252.

193. See Grandjonc, *Communisme*, vol. 1, p. 127; vol. 2, pp. 374–5. The term made its appearance as early as 1826 in the Saint-Simonian newspaper *Le Producteur*, and was current by 1829. Charles de Villers, credited with the first attested occurrence (*Le Spectateur du Nord*, April 1798), derived this utilization of the term from Kant.

194. 'To the extent that the great modern crisis is a product of the natural course of events, political organization will increasingly present itself as impossible unless opinions and customs are reconstructed.' Comte, 'Discours sur l'ensemble du positivisme', p. 244.

195. Heine, *Lutetia*, trans. Ewen, p. 830.

196. Vigier (*1848*, p. 34) underscores the impact of 'this social fear that, to the very end, provided the background for this history'; he adds that the leaders of the Bonapartist *coup d'état* followed others in adroitly taking advantage of it. Toqueville's *Memoirs* show, furthermore, that the most lucid spirits among the bourgeoisie had no illusions about the consensus of February and the insipid romanticism that suddenly became fashionable in the period.

197. See Garnier-Pages's account, which I have already had occasion to cite, in Agulhon, *Les Quarante-huitards*, p. 136.

198. See Raymond Huard, 'Renaissance et mort de la République', in Aprile *et al.*, *La révolution de 1848 en France et en Europe*, p. 52. Jacques Derrida is plainly mistaken when he identifies *Le Spectre rouge* as the newspaper of a revolutionary group, and Romieu as a proponent of the *jacquerie* (*Specters of Marx*, p. 116n.). It is worth noting that Derrida adduces this example in criticizing Marx and Marxism for pointlessly turning against itself the schema of the conspiracy and the image of the spectre proffered by the enemy.

199. Heine, *Ideas – The Book of Le Grand*, p. 101.

200. Heine, 'The Romantic School', pp. 124–5.

201. Above all else, according to Heine, the German Middle Ages *smell*, and smell bad. They are still rotting and stink of death. See, for instance, *Germany: A Winter's Tale*, p. 249; 'The Romantic School', p. 124.

202. 'The Middle Ages I'll endure,/ No matter how dark they be – / If only from that hybrid thing/ You'll promise to set us free;/ From that new-fangled chivalry,/ A nauseating dish/ Of Gothic illusion and modern lie,/ That's neither foul nor fish./ We'll shut down all the theaters/ And chase the clowns away/ Who parody the olden times – / O King, we await your day!': Heine, *Germany: A Winter's Tale*, pp. 270–1.

203. 'For the real Aristophanes things would be bad:/ He'd soon be marched before us,/ Clinking his chains and accompanied/ By a huge policemen's chorus'. Ibid., p. 296.

204. Heine, 'The Romantic School', p. 125.

205. In Heine's opinion, his German contemporaries are, above all, vampires:

> You could die without even noticing. Indeed, many of you have long been dead and buried, and your true life is only now beginning. If I contradict such madness, people are cross with me and scold me – and, terrible to tell, the corpses leap up at me, and abuse me, and their odour of decay offends me worse than their insults. (Heine, *Religion and Philosophy in Germany*, trans. Robertson, p. 268)

206. See Heine's hymn to this 'Paris ... Pantheon of the living' in Heine, *French Affairs*, p. 94. Heine's is the mirror-opposite of Hegel's vision of Rome as a 'Pantheon of all deities, and of all Spiritual existence', for Hegel's is an empty, abstract Pantheon, a collection of idols that have been drained of their inner spirituality (Hegel, *The Philosophy of History*, p. 107).

207. Heine, 'The Romantic School', pp. 96–7.

208. The metaphor of the cock or rooster as a harbinger of popular revolt runs through the whole of Heine's work. See, for example, Heine, *French Affairs*, p. 372; or *Germany: A Winter's Tale*, p. 273. As Heine was composing *Germany: A Winter's Tale* (in the winter of 1843–44), Marx finished the Introduction to his 'Contribution to the Critique of Hegel's Philosophy of Law' with this sentence: 'When all inner requisites are fulfilled, the *day of German resurrection* will be proclaimed by the *ringing call of the Gallic cock*.' Marx, 'Contribution to the Critique of Hegel's Philosophy of Law. Introduction', *MECW* 3: 187.

209. Heine, *Germany: A Winter's Tale*, p. 516.

210. Heine, 1855 Preface to *Germany*, trans. Charles Godfrey Leland (Hans Breitmann), *The Works of Heinrich Heine*, vol. 5, p. xxx.

211. Heine, 'The French Stage', p. 202.

212. See the account by Countess Marie d'Agoult (alias Daniel Stern) in Agulhon, *Les Quarante-huitards*, p. 45, and the engraving that illustrates this episode, as well as Le Men's comments, in *Les révolutions de 1848. L'Europe des images*, pp. 54–5.

213. See the horrified reaction of Barbarossa's ghost to the poet's facetious description of the guillotine: 'The King, you say! And his royal Queen? / Strapped! Onto a plank! / That goes against all etiquette / And all respect of rank!' Heine, *Germany: A Winter's Tale*, p. 268.

214. See Heine, 'The Romantic School', pp. 123–4.

215. Heine's commentary comes in response to two of the genre paintings that Delaroche exhibited at the 1831 Salon. Heine, 'French Painters', p. 151.

216. Ibid.

217. 'My regular coachman, an old *sansculotte*, told me that when he saw the king dying he felt "as if one of his own members were being sawed off" [members, the Member? S.K.] He added, "it gave me a pain in the stomach and the whole day I shied away from food".' Heine, 'French Painters', p. 149; translation modified.

218. In Heine's 'Memoirs' (pp. 330–31), a text shot through with fantasy images, a couple consisting of an executioner and a witch ('the Göcherin') are reputed to perform castrations; Heine's description of the castration scenes leaves nothing to the imagination.

219. Ibid., p. 137.

220. This is the meaning of the reply, cited above (see note 212), that Barbarossa's ghost makes to the poet in *Germany: A Winter's Tale*.

221. Hence the use of formulations such as the (royalist or republican) 'essence' or 'nature' of a people. See, for example, Heine, *French Affairs*, pp. 269–70.

222. Ibid., pp. 271–2; translation modified. For readers of the day – and, indeed, for any attentive reader of Heine – this is a perfectly transparent, albeit implicit, critique of Bonapartism.

223. Heine, 'Sir Olaf', *New Poems*, pp. 370–72. The fact that this poem dates from 1839 shows that the dialectic of the despot and the executioner antedates the texts written in the wake of the 1848 defeat (the 'Memoirs' and the poems collected in *Romancero*).

224. Heine, *Romancero*, pp. 570–71.

225. This is the theme of the poem 'Charles I' (ibid., pp. 575–6).

226. This spectre, unlike the Roman lictors, is always 'standing in back of me'; it is the shadow which the figure exposed to the light cannot escape: 'I am your "lictor"; with shiny axe / I follow close behind / On all your travels – I am the deed, / The offspring of your mind.' Heine, *Germany: A Winter's Tale*, p. 246.

227. This is what this spectre says to the poet: 'I am no scarecrow, no ghost of the past / Out of the grave arising; / And I am no friend of rhetoric, / Do little philosophizing. / I'm of a practical character: / The calm and silent kind. / But know: I'll carry out, I'll do / All that you've had in mind. / And even though the years go by, / I find no satisfaction / Till thought becomes reality; / You think, and I take action. / You are the judge; the headsman am I, / Who stands and awaits your will; / And whether your judgment be right or wrong, / Obediently I kill.' Ibid., pp. 245–6.

228. Büchner, *Danton's Death*, Act I, Scene 3, p. 38.

229. Heine, 'French Painters', p. 126.

230. Heine, 'Memoirs', p. 336; translation modified.

231. Büchner, *Danton's Death*, Act I, Scene 6, p. 48.

232. Heine, *French Affairs*, p. 372; translation modified.

233. See Heine, 'Marie-Antoinette', in *Romancero*, pp. 576–7.

234. Ibid., p. 577.

235. One might, for example, compare the Emperor Barbarossa's majestic spectre, a symbol of Teutomaniac nationalism, its armour as perfectly well preserved as the black–red– gold of the emperor's German flag, with the decapitated, ludicrous ghosts haunting the Tuileries. See, respectively, *Germany: A Winter's Tale*, XV and XVI, pp. 263–9; 'Vitzliput- zli', in *Romancero*, p. 601.

236. 'This thing meanwhile looks at us and sees us not see it even when it is there. A spectral asymmetry interrupts here all specularity. It de-synchronizes, it recalls us to anachrony. We will call this the *visor effect*: we do not see who looks at us.' Derrida, *Specters of Marx*, pp. 6–7.

237. 'Yet, strange to say, I almost think/ Not one of them knows she is dead/ Nor realizes quite positively/ That she has lost her head./ It's empty posing, as of yore,/ For affectation's sake – / It's ludicrous and eerie too,/ These headless curtseys they make.' Heine, 'Marie-Antoinette', in *Romancero*, p. 577.

238. 'The French Revolution did this, with/ Its doctrines unholy, unclean;/ It's all the fault of Jean-Jacques Rousseau,/ Voltaire, and the guillotine.' Ibid.

239. Derrida accuses Marx of obsessively exorcizing spectres, like his adversaries, because he is haunted by a metaphysics of presence, a vision of the normal that associates it with fullness and transparency. This criticism does not seem to me to apply either to Marx or to Heine, both of whom indefatigably demolish that kind of ontological nostalgia. The accent both put on exorcizing phantoms – on the desire to free oneself from the past so that something new can finally come into existence – should itself be histori- cized: as Fredric Jameson notes in his essay on *Specters of Marx*, 'one reply to Derrida's fundamental critique of Marx lies in this particular conjuncture, namely that Marx may be more sensitive to the essential malevolence of the past and the dead than anything that can be found in the prototypical situation of mourning and melancholia as *Hamlet* archetypically configures it' (Jameson, 'Marx's Purloined Letter', in Michael Sprinker, ed., *Ghostly Demarcations: A Symposium on Jacques Derrida's* Specters of Marx [London and New York, 1999], p. 58).

240. Heine, 'with eyes like stars that shone with strange insistence', *Germany: A Winter's Tale*, p. 494.

241. See Isabelle Kalinowski, 'L'histoire, les fantômes', *Revue Germanique Internationale*, no. 9, 1998.

242. On the contrast between German irony and French comedy, see Heine, 'The French Stage', pp. 225–6.

243. Heine, 'The Romantic School', p. 97.

244. Heine, 'Postscript to the *Romancero*', p. 693. See also, in the same collection of poems, 'Forest Solitude' (pp. 615–19) and 'Meeting Again', in which the poet and his com- panion figure as 'two faded ghosts' running wild among the dead (p. 644).

245. Heine, 'Postscript to the *Romancero*', p. 693. On the Merlin allegory, see Heine, *French Affairs*, p. 97.

246. Heine, 'Postscript to the *Romancero*', p. 693.
247. Heine's 'Confessions' concludes with this image. Heine, 'Confessions', p. 73.
248. 'In vigil day and night, I could not sleep/ Like all my friends in my own tented squad . . . / My wound's are gaping wide – A post's unmanned! – / One sentry falls, another takes his part – / And yet I fall unvanquished, sword in hand – / The only thing that's broken is my heart.' Heine, 'Enfant perdu', *Romancero*, pp. 649–50.
249. Lefebvre, 'Heine et Hegel', p. 203.
250. See Heine, *Lutetia*, trans. Leland, pp. 1–15 and my analysis above.
251. 'Like a ghost guarding a treasure that was entrusted to him during his life, this murdered nation, this ghost-nation sat in its dark ghettos and preserved the Hebrew Bible.' Heine, *Religion and Philosophy in Germany*, trans. Robertson, p. 230.
252. Heine, *Ludwig Börne: Eine Denkschrift*, pp. 110–11.
253. 'This does not imply, however, that for the Jews the future turned into homogeneous, empty time.' Benjamin, 'Theses on the Philosophy of History', p. 266.
254. See Heine, *Lutetia*, trans. Leland, pp. 194–5; translation modified.
255. Heine, *Religion and Philosophy in Germany*, trans. Robertson, p. 291.
256. See the account by Moritz Oppenheim, which bears on the year 1831, in Houben, *Henri Heine*, pp. 71–2.
257. See 'Princess Sabbath', in *Romancero*, p. 653.
258. 'Schalet is God's bread of rapture,/ It's the kosher-type ambrosia/ That is catered straight from Heaven;/ And compared with such a morsel/ The ambrosia of the pagan/ Pseudogods of ancient Hellas/ Who were devils in disguise, is/ Just a pile of devil's *dreck*.' Ibid., p. 654.
259. See, for example, the recurrent descriptions of mutton with Teltower turnips in Heine, 'The French Stage', p. 143; or 'small salted anchovies' in *Deutschland, ein Wintermärchen*.
260. See above: 'The revolution as the right of (and to) life'.
261. On the problems associated with the use of this term, see Michel Espagne and Michael Werner, Introduction to the special issue of *Revue de synthèse*, 12, no. 2 (1988), 187–94; Espagne, *Les transferts culturels franco-allemands*, Paris, 1999, esp. ch. 1, pp. 17–33.
262. See the lovely passage about this threefold interpellation in Heine's 'Memoirs', pp. 321–4.
263. Heine, *Religion and Philosophy in Germany: A Fragment*, trans. John Snodgrass, London, 1882, p. 19.
264. Heine, 'Confessions', p. 42.
265. Schiller's *On the Aesthetic Education of Man* was written between June 1794 and October 1795; the first nine letters (which date from September and October 1794), the most overtly political, can be read as a contemporary commentary on the end of the Terror regime.
266. Let us simply cite, among the most recent chapters in this story, the polemics that raged for nearly a quarter of a century (1965–88) around the proposal to name the university in Düsseldorf, Heine's native city, after the poet. On the polemics that have marked Heine's reception in Germany, see Joseph A. Kruse, '200 Jahre Heinrich Heine: Wirkung, Ruhm und Kontroversen', in '*Ich Narr des Glücks*', pp. 3–17.
267. Höhn, *Heinrich Heine*, p. 14.
268. Heine, *Religion and Philosophy in Germany*, trans. Snodgrass, p. 19.
269. Heine, 'Testament', p. 500.
270. Heine, *French Affairs*, op. cit., vol. 2, p. 85.
271. Heine, 'Waterloo. Fragment', in *Historisch-Kritische Gesamtausgabe*, vol. 15: 187–8.
272. Heine, 'The Romantic School', p. 21. Heine goes on to contrast the French version of patriotism, which he says is universalistic, with German patriotism, which 'contract[s] the heart just as leather contracts in the cold', and is narrow-minded and hostile to the idea of European citizenship.
273. Germaine de Staël-Holstein, *Germany*, trans. O.W. Wright, vol. 2, New York, 1871, hereafter referred to as 'Staël, *Germany*'.

274. As is attested by Sainte-Beuve's reaction to the publication of Heine's book: 'Heinrich Heine', reprinted in Heine, *De la France*, ed. Gerhard Höhn and Bodo Morawe, Paris, 1994, pp. 403–4.

275. Heine, *Religion and Philosophy in Germany*, trans. Snodgrass, p. 7.

276. Heine, 'Confessions', p. 27.

277. On this point, see Michael Werner, 'La réception de Heine en France', *Cahiers d'Études germaniques*, no. 34, 1998, pp. 13–14.

278. Heine, 'The Romantic School', p. 2; translation modified.

279. *Germany*, vol. 1, p. 239.

280. Heine, 'The Romantic School', p. 2.

281. See Staël, *Germany*, p. 362.

282. Ibid., p. 369.

283. Ibid., p. 230.

284. Ibid., pp. 157–80. Here are two suggestive sentences: 'Kant is very far from considering this faculty of sentiment as an allusion; on the contrary, he assigns to it the first rank in human nature' (p. 167). 'Kant, who seemed to be called to conclude all the grand intellectual alliances, has made the soul one focus, in which all our faculties are in contact with each other'. Ibid., p. 172.

285. Ibid., p. 254.

286. Ibid., p. 118.

287. Ibid., p. 362

288. 'Neither Locke nor Condillac knew the dangers of the principles of their philosophy; but very soon this black spot, which was hardly visible in the intellectual horizon, grew to such a size as to be near plunging the universe and man back again into darkness'. Ibid., p. 138.

289. Ibid., p 131.

290. In a note to the second edition – the censors destroyed the first – Madame de Staël explicitly says: 'by this phrase . . . [about the 'sea which bathes their rocks', the proud 'banner of their country', etc.] I have been trying to designate England; in fact, I could not speak of war with enthusiasm, without representing it to myself as the contest of a free nation for her independence.' Ibid., p. 369.

291. 'All efforts to render politics aesthetic culminate in one thing: war'. Benjamin, 'The Work of Art in the Age of Mechanical Reproduction', p. 243.

292. As has been suggested by Höhn (*Heinrich Heine*, p. 90) and Lefebvre ('Heine et Hegel', p. 281).

293. Cited in Antonina Vallentin, *Henri Heine*, Paris, 1956, p. 188.

294. Heine, 'Notice biographique à l'adresse de Philarète Chasles, 15.1.1835' in *Sämtliche Werke*, vol. 15, Hamburg, 1982, p. 103.

295. Heine, *Religion and Philosophy in Germany*, trans. Robertson, pp. 210–17.

296. The word is Heine's (*Religion and Philosophy in Germany*, trans. Robertson, p. 217).

297. Lukács, *Skizzen einer Geschichte*, p. 98.

298. Heine, *Religion and Philosophy in Germany*, trans. Robertson, p. 224.

299. Ibid.; original emphasis.

300. Ibid., p. 225.

301. Ibid., p. 227.

302. Ibid.

303. Ibid., p. 226.

304. It is precisely this 'plebeianism of the spirit' in Luther, this anti-aristocratic revolt, which Nietzsche found intolerable: 'the Lutheran Reformation was, in its whole breadth, the indignation of simplicity against "multiplicity". . . . Today it is easy enough to see how in all cardinal questions of power Luther's disposition was calamitously myopic, superficial, and incautious. He was a man of the common people who lacked everything that one might inherit from a ruling caste; he had no instinct for power [*Macht*].' (See Friedrich Nietzsche, *The Gay Science*, trans. Walter Kaufmann, New York, 1974, §358, pp. 310–11.)

305. Heine, *Religion and Philosophy in Germany*, trans. Robertson, p. 231. Admittedly, this is a point on which Heine is more or less in agreement with de Staël, who describes Protestantism as a 'revolution prepared by ideas', and sees Luther as 'the most German' of 'all the great men produced by Germany': in him, 'the courage of the mind was . . . the principle of the courage of action' (Staël, *Germany*, pp. 293, 294). Thus Heine is not wrong to identify Madame de Staël's Protestantism as a factor working to attenuate her reactionary orientation.
306. See the parallel drawn between the Peasant Wars and the English Revolution in Heine, *English Fragments*, pp. 493–8.
307. Heine, *French Affairs*, pp. 186–7. This is the exact opposite of Nietzsche's position. For Nietzsche, Luther's conduct was dictated by his *resentment of the aristocracy*. Nietzsche accuses him of having a destructive fury fuelled by self-hatred (Luther was 'a man who, [finding] it impossible to be a monk, pushed away the dominion of the *homines religiosi*, and thus . . . himself made within the ecclesiastical social order what in relation to the civic social order he attacked so intolerantly – namely, a peasant rebellion' (Nietzsche, *The Gay Science*, §358, p. 312). Moreover, the section from which this passage is taken is entitled, significantly, 'The peasant rebellion of the spirit' (ibid., pp. 310–13). Nietzsche, too, establishes a continuity between Protestantism and the Revolution; but he does so, of course, only in order to reject both in disgust (ibid., §350, pp. 292–3).
308. Heine, *French Affairs*, pp. 187–8; translation modified.
309. Heine, *Religion and Philosophy in Germany*, trans. Robertson, p. 232.
310. Heine, 'The Romantic School', p. 24; Heine, *Religion and Philosophy in Germany*, trans. Robertson, p. 227.
311. Heine cites the cases of the (alleged) conversions of Friedrich Schlegel, Ludwig Tieck, Novalis, Zacharias Werner, Adam Müller, etc. Heine, 'The Romantic School', p. 23. Tieck and Novalis did not, in fact, convert; they contented themselves with defending an idealized image of medieval Christianity. See Novalis's essay 'Christendom or Europe' (in *Philosophical Writings*, ed. and trans. Margaret Mahony Stoljar, Albany, NY, 1997, pp. 137–52), a veritable manifesto that sums up what the Romantics had to say on the question. Novalis's exaltation of the feudal order and his fervent admiration of the papacy had been enough to alarm even the usually unexcitable Goethe.
312. Lefebvre, 'Heine et Hegel', p. 52.
313. Heine, *Religion and Philosophy in Germany*, trans. Robertson, p. 250.
314. See Lefebvre's powerful demonstration in 'Heine et Hegel', pp. 52 ff.
315. Heine, *Religion and Philosophy in Germany*, trans. Robertson, p. 238.
316. Ibid., p. 249.
317. Heine's positive evaluation of the pantheistic moment antedates the turn that the Young Hegelians made in the 1840s, when pantheism and the Protestant Reformation were more or less completely identified with the mysticism and egoism of bourgeois society. It is in this sense that Marx, repeating a commonplace of the day, denounces Hegel's 'logical, pantheistic mysticism' (Marx, 'Contribution to the Critique of Hegel's *Philosophy of Law*', *MECW* 3: 7). Faithful, nevertheless, to one facet of the Hegelo-Heinean narrative, he continued to invoke the emancipatory content of the Reformation, particularly in his 1844 'Introduction' (see Chapter 5). On the anti-pantheistic turn of the 1840s, see Warren Breckman, *Marx, the Young Hegelians, and the Origins of Radical Social Theory*, Cambridge, 1999.
318. Heine, *Religion and Philosophy in Germany*, trans. Robertson, pp. 249, 351n.; translation modified.
319. See Heine, 'Letters on Germany', *The Works of Heinrich Heine*, vol. 5, pp. 221–2.
320. Heine, *Religion and Philosophy in Germany*, trans. Robertson, p. 261.
321. Ibid., p. 289.
322. See Heine, *Ludwig Börne: A Memorial*, p. 273.
323. Heine, *Religion and Philosophy in Germany*, trans. Robertson, pp. 265–6.
324. Ibid., p. 266.

325. Ibid., pp. 276–7; translation modified.
326. Ibid., p. 288.
327. See Heine, *Religion and Philosophy in Germany*, trans. Snodgrass, pp. 139 ff.
328. Ibid., p. 134.
329. Heine, 'The Romantic School', pp. 30, 37, 44. It is worth pointing out that what Goethe's reactionary contemporaries regarded as a betrayal of sacrosanct Western values is taken by contemporary criticism to be an archetypally 'orientalist' vision that constructs a mythical, aestheticized Orient reflecting a world-view shaped by colonialism. The classical reference here is Edward Said, *Orientalism*, New York, 1979. See pp. 154–5 for a discussion of Goethe and his *Westöstlicher Diwan*.
330. See Lefebvre's commentary on the text of the 1855 'Confessions' in 'Heine et Hegel', pp. 9 ff. In condemning Hegel – i.e. the pantheistic, atheistic point of view – Heine uses 'the same very Hegelian formulas he used in 1844', merely 'inverting' them in his own fashion.
331. Heine, 'Introduction to Kahldorf Concerning the Nobility in Letters to Count M. von Moltke', trans. Frederic Ewen and Robert C. Holub, in *The Romantic School and Other Essays*, p. 246.
332. Heine's Preface to *France*, a text distinguished by the 'unprecedentedly' vehement tone (Gerhard Höhn) in which it exposes the reality of the German situation, doubtless represents this 'ultra-left' critique of Hegel at its height. Heine, *French Affairs*, p. 20.
333. Heine, *Lutetia*, trans. Leland, p. 453.
334. Heine, *Religion and Philosophy in Germany*, trans. Robertson, p. 87; translation modified.
335. 'Indeed, if one sees Kant as the terrorist Convention and Fichte as the Napoleonic Empire, then one can see Herr Schelling as the reactionary Restoration which followed.' Ibid., p. 289.
336. Ibid., p. 291.
337. Heine, *Religion and Philosophy in Germany*, trans. Snodgrass, pp. 143–4.
338. Heine, *Religion and Philosophy in Germany*, trans. Robertson, p. 291.
339. Ibid.; translation modified.
340. Ibid., pp. 292–3.
341. Heine delights in poking fun at the purely speculative, even chimerical, German soul. See for example, *Germany: A Winter's Tale*, pp. 246–7.
342. 'The holy, unspeakable, mysterious Night . . . is eternity.' *Hymns to the Night. Spiritual Songs*, trans. George MacDonald, London, 1992, p. 18. As if in echo, Wagner's Tristan says: 'mid the daylight's idle fancies, he has only one longing, a longing for the holy night, where forever, solely true, love and rapture [*Liebeswonne*] await'. Richard Wagner, *Tristan und Isolde*, trans. Stewart Robb, New York, 1965, Act 2, Scene 2, p. 17.
343. Heine, 'Introduction to Kahldorf Concerning the Nobility', p. 245.
344. Ibid., pp. 245–6.
345. Ibid., pp. 246–7.
346. Heine, *Religion and Philosophy in Germany*, trans. Robertson, pp. 265–6; emphasis added.
347. Ibid., p. 292.
348. Ernst Bloch, *The Principle of Hope*, trans. Neville Plaice et al., London, 1986, vol. 1, esp. ch. 14: 'Fundamental distinction of daydreams from night-dreams: Concealed and old wish-fulfilment in night-dreams, fabulously inventive and anticipatory wish-fulfilment in daylight fantasies' (p. 77 and *passim*).
349. Ibid., p. 88.
350. Ibid., p. 93.
351. Ibid., p. 95. Bloch, however – concerned to keep his distance from both Freudian theory, which radically diminishes the sovereignty of the Ego, and Romanticism, which places a high value on the interior dream-world of the Night – elaborates a notion of the waking dream divested of all ambivalence and internal reversibility. In other words, his notion of the dream is itself dream-like. In reality, Bloch needs a concept that one-sidedly valorizes the dream so that it can be assigned its place in the Subject's ongoing

development, and a world endowed with purpose by a dialectic of essence and an Aristotelian teleology of matter (see ibid., p. 206 and *passim*). See Jean-Marie Vincent's critical remarks in *Critique du travail*, Paris, 1987, ch. 2, 'Ernst Bloch: l'utopie concrète et le piège de l'ontologie', pp. 39–56.

352. Ibid., p. 99.
353. Heine, *Lutetia*, trans. Leland, pp. 435–6.
354. This is, notably, Jean-Pierre Lefebvre's view, which he develops in a commentary on the same text: 'insofar as fantasy is one of the forms in which the spirit of the times manifests itself, Michelet writes historical history after all: this is the ruse of historiography'. 'Heine et Hegel', p. 121.
355. Already in Novalis, night marries desire with death, pleasure with the death drive. See, for example, the well-known lines in 'Longing after Death' [*Sehnsucht nach dem Tode*] in Novalis, *Hymns to the Night*, pp. 22–4.
356. Heine, *Religion and Philosophy in Germany*, trans. Snodgrass, p. 144.
357. 'We young ones shall not forget these songs, and some of us will one day teach them by heart to grandchildren yet unborn; but many of us will have rotted by that time, some in the prisons of home, some in the garrets of exile.' Ibid., pp. 145–6.
358. As is emphasized by Lukács, *Skizzen einer Geschichte*, p. 97.
359. Heine, *French Affairs*, p. 263 (chronicle of 16 June 1832).
360. Ibid., p. 266.
361. 'Only in that period, during the days of the Hambach festival, could a general uprising have been attempted in Germany with some chance of success'. Heine, *Ludwig Börne: Eine Denkschrift*, p. 78.
362. Ibid., p. 83.
363. Ibid., p. 84.
364. Ibid., p. 83.
365. Heine, 'Introduction to Kahldorf Concerning the Nobility', pp. 246–7.
366. Heine, *Religion and Philosophy in Germany*, trans. Robertson, pp. 291.
367. *Ibid.*, pp. 291–2.
368. Heine, 'Letters on Germany', pp. 221–2.
369. Lefebvre, 'Heine et Hegel', p. 275.
370. Heine, Letter of 1 March 1832 to Johann Friedrich von Cotta, in *Säkularausgabe*, vol. 21, ed. Christa Stöcker, Berlin and Paris, 1970, p. 31.
371. Heine, *Religion and Philosophy in Germany*, trans. Robertson, p. 293; trans. modified.
372. Heine, *Religion and Philosophy in Germany*, trans. Snodgrass, p. 160.
373. Heine, *Religion and Philosophy in Germany*, trans. Robertson, p. 293.
374. Heine, *Ludwig Börne: Eine Denkschrift*, p. 97.
375. Heine, Preface to *Germany: A Winter's Tale*, p. 482; translation (of the Preface to the German version) modified in the light of Heine's preface to the French version.
376. Heine, *Ludwig Börne: A Memorial*, p. 281.
377. See Heine, 'The Silesian Weavers', in *New Poems*, p. 544. This poem was published in *Vorwärts* in July 1844, when the polemic between Ruge and Marx on the relationship between the political and social revolution was getting under way in the same newspaper. The poem, which circulated very widely and sometimes secretly, became one of the founding texts of the German workers' movement. In an 11 July 1847 letter posted from London, K.M. Kertbeny informed Heine that, every Friday, the German Communist Association of the *West End* read it as its 'opening prayer' (cited by Höhn, *Heinrich Heiner*, p. 333n.)
378. Ibid.

3 Moses Hess, Prophet of a New Revolution?

1. On translation, especially the translation of French revolutionary discourse into the language of German philosophy, see Engels's remarks in *The Holy Family*, *MECW* 4: 19–31; and Jacques Guilhaumou's comments in 'Le jeune Marx et le langage jacobin (1843–1846)', in Lucien Calvié, ed., *Révolutions françaises et pensée allemande*, Paris, 1989, pp. 105–22.
2. Raised in the tradition of Talmudic exegesis, Hess never attended a German school. Up to the age of twenty, his German was shaky; his native language was Yiddish.
3. However, Mendelssohn uses this term to mean both business activities and the activities of the learned, enlightened Jews for whom he himself doubtless furnished the model. The business practices he had in mind were of the kind that Marx and Hess would later describe as 'sordid Jewish practices'; they came to represent, for both men, the *summum* of the degradation of the Jews and their involvement in the alienation of bourgeois, Christian society. See Moses Mendelssohn, 'Du salut des juifs', in Gérard Raulet, ed., *Aufklärung. Les Lumières allemandes*, Paris, 1995, pp. 159–63.
4. Moses Hess, *Die europäische Triarchie* [hereafter *ET*], in *Philosophische und sozialistische Schriften, 1837–1850*, ed. Auguste Cornu and Wolfgang Mönke, Berlin, 1961, p. 130.
5. Hegel, *The Philosophy of History*, trans. J. Sibree, New York, 1956, p. 195.
6. *ET*, p. 108.
7. Ibid., p. 82. See August von Cieszkowski, *Prolegomena zur Historiosophie*, Hamburg, 1981, partially translated as *Prolegomena to Historiosophie*, in Lawrence S. Stepelevich, ed., *The Young Hegelians: An Anthology*, Cambridge, 1983, pp. 57–89.
8. *ET*, p. 77.
9. Ibid., p. 83.
10. Ibid., p. 79.
11. See Cieszkowski, *Prolegomena to Historiosophie*, p. 71. On the significance of this return to Fichte, see Georg Lukács's classic study 'Moses Hess and the Problem of Idealist Dialectics', in *Political Writings*, London, 1972, pp. 185–7.
12. The phrase is taken from Georg Lukács.
13. On the privilege of the present in Hegel, see Louis Althusser's remarks in Althusser and Étienne Balibar, *Reading Capital*, trans. Ben Brewster, London, 1970, pp. 113–14 and *passim*. Oddly enough, Althusser echoes the Young Hegelians almost verbatim: 'the ontological category of the present prevents any anticipation of historical time, any conscious anticipation of the future development of the concept, any *knowledge* of the *future*'. Ibid., p. 95.
14. Hegel, *Phenomenology of Spirit*, trans. A.V. Miller, Oxford, 1977, p. 27.
15. There can be no doubt that the following sentence from *The Communist Manifesto* should be read in the light of the Hegelian conception of the present: 'In bourgeois society, therefore, the past dominates the present; in Communist society, the present dominates the past'. Marx and Engels, *The Communist Manifesto*, *MECW* 6, p. 499.
16. Hegel, *Phenomenology of Spirit*, pp. 6–7. Hegel gives the examples of birth, sunrise (i.e. the French Revolution), and the growth of the oak.
17. Hess's first book, *Die heilige Geschichte der Menschheit. Von einem Jünger Spinozas* [The sacred history of mankind. By a disciple of Spinoza], in which he develops his critique of the Hegelian philosophy of history, was published in 1837, a year before Cieszkowski's *Prolegomena to Historiosophie*.
18. *ET*, pp. 86–7.
19. Lukács, 'Moses Hess', p. 188.
20. The prophetic dimension of Hess's discourse seems to have escaped Lukács's attention.
21. *ET*, p. 84.

22. Ibid., p. 87.
23. Ibid., p. 90.
24. 'In a more specific sense, however, the French Revolution constitutes the dividing line between the past and the future.' Ibid., p. 116.
25.

> Europe, as it is already beginning to emerge before our eyes, is the concrete fulfilment of the Christian idea of the kingdom of God. The kingdom of God will yet be realized on earth, down to its seemingly most superficial moment. Not even the "New Jerusalem" with its splendours will be wanting. . . . We are not yet in the habit of regarding Europe as a whole, as an organism – and yet nothing is more important or profitable for us than this way of considering the matter. (Ibid., p. 103)

26. Ibid., p. 102.
27. The epigones sometimes seem bent on outdoing their Master's Eurocentrism; but it may be that, in their naivety, they simply reveal it for what it is. See, for example, Cieszkowski's crude paean to colonization as a means of promoting the spiritual growth of the colonized and the moral refinement of the colonizer (Cieszkowski, *Prolegomena zur Historiosophie*, p. 30).
28. See *ET*, pp. 93–4, which rehearses the main themes of Hegel's *The Philosophy of History*. As we have seen, Hess's account departs from Hegel's only as far as the role of the Jewish people is concerned.
29. In a diary entry dated 1 January 1836, Hess mentions having read *On the History of Religion and Philosophy in Germany*, the first part of Heine's collection *On Germany* (cited in Gérard Bensussan, *Moses Hess, la philosophie, le socialisme*, Paris, 1985, p. 46). Hess quotes this work in *ET*, p. 87, in a passage which emphasizes the contradictory nature of Hegel's enterprise.
30. Ibid., p. 94.
31. Ibid., pp. 116–17.
32. Ibid., p. 90. This, of course, is a Spinoza refracted by Heine, Hegel, and the *Pantheismusstreit*. Witness Cieszkowski's interpretation of the Spinozan thesis of parallelism in terms of the mirror-relation ('everything is reflected in everything else') between microcosm and macrocosm (Cieszkowski, *Prolegomena zur Historiosophie*, pp. 46–7).
33. 'Only fully accomplished mysticism is speculation. Spinoza is the first truly speculative mind, the fully accomplished mystic.' *ET*, p. 91.
34. *Hegel's Logic*, trans. William Wallace, Oxford, 1975, §151, p. 214.
35. *ET*, p. 117.
36. Ibid., pp. 117–18.
37. Ibid., p. 120. Notice the slippage, highly characteristic of the Hegelian vision of things, between the terms 'reform/Reformation', when it is a question of the German Reformation, and 'revolution'.
38. The idea of an alliance with England had been dear to Saint-Simon, the thinker who provided a conceptual foundation for the new principle which Hess believed England embodied (see Henri de Saint-Simon, *La Pensée politique de Saint-Simon*, ed. G. Ionescu, Paris, 1979, pp. 97 ff., 117 ff.). Saint-Simon put the Franco-English alliance at the centre of a 'reorganization of European society', the title of a book he published in 1814 (*La réorganisation de la société européenne*). His project also included Germany, which he thought would face a revolution in its turn if the reorganization of Europe did not produce results in time (ibid., pp. 88–104).
39. *ET*, p. 95.
40. Ibid., p. 121.
41. 'Hardly have we begun to act independently than we take fright at our own spirit.' Ibid.
42. Ibid.
43. Although Hess was a faithful reader of Heine's work, he was somewhat more favourably disposed towards Heine's adversary; thus he accuses Heine of 'rail[ing] in an undigni-

fied way against Börne', whereas he merely observes, in a more neutral tone, that Gutzkow 'rails against' Heine. Ibid., p. 118.

44. Ibid., p. 82.

45. On this episode in Hess's life, see Auguste Cornu, *Karl Marx et Friedrich Engels—leur vie, leur œuvre*, Paris, 1958, vol. 2, pp. 6–7.

46. Reproducing the ambiguity of the watchword 'finish the revolution', Saint-Simon occasionally presents the 'industrial cause' as a return to 'the real goal, the truth, of the revolution' (whence the importance of the term 'Industrial Revolution', which he coined). This was a goal that the metaphysicians and jurists who led the industrial revolution obscured with their juridical-political speculations, which only reflected, Saint-Simon affirms, their insatiable appetite for power. Yet, a few lines further on, he describes the 'industrial cause' as distinct from the 'interests of the revolution', whatever they may be; the 'industrial cause', he adds, is above all distinct from those political (anti-monarchical) interests, apart from a shared opposition to the restoration of big landed property (Saint-Simon, *La pensée politique*, p. 173).

47. See ibid., pp. 110–11. See also Saint-Simon, *Lettres d'un habitant de Genève*, in *La Pensée politique de Saint-Simon*, p. 79, on the necessity/possibility of putting an end to the crisis provoked by the revolution of 1789.

48. In *Catéchisme des industriels*, Saint-Simon's only response to the question of how 'to describe the present state of matters in politics' is contained in the following sentence: 'Here, in few, is the essence the answer to your question: THE PRESENT AGE IS AN AGE OF TRANSITION' (*La Pensée politique de Saint-Simon*, p. 199).

49. Émile Durkheim has nicely brought out the continuity between the founder of the thought of the social and the socialist current in general (*Socialism and Saint-Simon*, ed. Alvin W. Gouldner, trans. Charlotte Sattler, London, 1959, pp. 207 ff.). After associating himself with this tradition, Durkheim offers his famous definition of socialism not as a transformation of property relations, or, *a fortiori*, the relations of production, but in terms of a deliberate (and unifying) reorganization of the economy and, consequently, 'society' as a whole (ibid., p. 21).

50. Saint-Simon, *Catéchisme des industriels*, p. 178.

51. See Michel Espagne, 'Le saint-simonisme est-il jeune-hégélien?', in Jean-René Derré, *Regards sur le saint-simonisme*, Lyon, 1986, pp. 45–71.

52. *ET*, p. 148.

53. Ibid., p. 153.

54. Ibid., p. 154.

55. Ibid., p. 148.

56. Ibid., pp. 154–5. Some debates go back further than one might think!

57. Ibid., p. 155.

58.
> The greatest freedom is . . . conceivable only amid the greatest order, just as the greatest order can subsist only amid the greatest freedom. For freedom, as has already been shown in these pages, is autonomy. But a being is not autonomous unless it can obey its own laws; and as the supreme law of humanity – love, both intellectual and actual love – is also the law of each and every one of its members, freedom and order will never clash as long as people respect this law of love. (Ibid., p. 156)

59. Cited in Dominique Dammame, 'Saint-Simon', in F. Chatelet, O. Duhamel and E. Pisier, *Dictionnaire des œuvres politiques*, Paris, 1998, p. 733.

60. *ET*, p. 112.

61. 'Wherever the stakes are humanity and concrete progress, the English people is to be found in the forefront of the struggle!' Ibid., p. 104.

62. The phrase is Gérard Bensussan's (Benussan, *Moses Hess*, p. 18).

63. *ET*, pp. 125–6.

64. Ibid.

65. Ibid., p. 113.
66. Ibid., p. 115.
67. Ibid., p. 134.
68. Ibid., pp. 133–4.
69. Ibid., p. 131.
70. From a different point of view, this is what brings Christ down to the level of the ordinary, making him no more than a prophet: whence the 'Jewish' aspect of Hess's attempt to translate Christianity into other terms.
71. See, simply by way of example, Gilles Deleuze, *Spinoza: Expressionism in Philosophy*, trans. Martin Joughin, New York, 1990, pp. 289–301, esp. p. 395n. 6; Étienne Balibar, *Spinoza and Politics*, trans. Peter Snowden, London, 1998, pp. 25–49; and 'Spinoza the anti-Orwell: The Fear of the Masses', in Balibar, *Masses, Classes, Ideas*, trans. James Swenson, London, 1994, pp. 3–37; Alexandre Matheron, *Le Christ et le salut des ignorants chez Spinoza*, Paris, 1971, pp. 144 ff.; André Tosel, *Spinoza ou le crépuscule de la servitude*, Paris, 1984, pp. 245–57.
72. This is what Hess calls 'practical Christianity', something that others, he observes, condemn as 'religious indifferentism' (*ET*, pp. 133–4). Without seeking conflict with existing denominations, the state is urged to promote this practical Christianity – not through professions of faith, but by including it in the school curriculum (ibid., p. 142).
73. Ibid., p. 133.
74. In what follows, I adopt André Tosel's dialectical, Gramscian interpretation (see his *Spinoza ou le crépuscule de la servitude*, pp. 233 ff.), the one that best lends itself to my purposes.
75. Baruch Spinoza, *Tractatus Theologico-Politicus*, trans. Samuel Shirley, Leiden, 1989, p. 280.
76. 'The revolution, although its objective is to raise supreme authority to the appropriate level, can realize its purpose only by taking the grave risk of momentarily suspending state power.' *ET*, p. 133.
77. As Auguste Cornu points out:

> for Hess as for the Young Hegelians, the ultimate goal of History remained the transformation of the state; but, by the state, Hess meant the social organization of a country more than its political organization. He conceived the state as a superior sort of Church whose mission was to serve as a kind of spiritual and material bond among men. (Auguste Cornu, *Moses Hess et la gauche hégélienne*, Paris, 1934, p. 40)

78. *ET*, p. 77.
79. Ibid., p. 80.
80. Ibid., p. 160.
81. Ibid.
82. Ibid.
83. On Schiller, see Chapter 1 above: 'Politics between a foundation and the *salto mortale*'.
84. *ET*, p. 77.
85. Ibid.
86. Ibid., p. 145.
87. On this point, see Gérard Bensussan's fine demonstration (Bensussan, *Moses Hess, passim*), which unfortunately fails to consider the specifically political consequences of Hess's approach (in fact, they form its real premisses).
88. *ET*, p. 160.
89. Cited in Cornu, *Moses Hess*, p. 46.
90. *ET*, pp. 159–60.
91. Ibid., p. 139.
92. Thus I disagree with Gérard Bensussan, who thinks that this ambivalence is a mere 'ruse' intended to beguile the censors (Bensussan, *Moses Hess*, p. 34).

93. This is where Lukács's critique reaches its limits, at least to the extent that it bears on Hess before his 1843 'radicalization'.
94. *ET*, p. 135.
95. Ibid., p. 144.
96. Ibid.
97. Ibid.
98. Ibid., p. 143.
99. Ibid., p. 154.
100. Ibid.
101. In what follows, I shall be referring mainly to the following works by Hess: 'Socialismus und Communismus' (hereafter SC), in Moses Hess, *Philosophische und sozialistische Schriften, 1837–1850*, ed. Auguste Cornu and Wolfgang Mönke, Berlin, 1961, pp. 197–209; 'Über das Geldwesen' (GW), in ibid., pp. 329–48; 'Kommunistisches Bekenntniß in Fragen und Antworten' (KB), in ibid., pp. 359–68 ;'The Philosophy of Action' (PA), trans. Ronald Sanders, in Albert Fried and Sanders, eds, *Socialist Thought: A Documentary History*, Edinburgh, 1964, pp. 249–75; 'The Recent Philosophers' (RP), trans. Lawrence S. Stepelevich, in *The Young Hegelians*, pp. 359–75.
102. Marx and Engels, *The German Ideology, MECW* 5: 27.
103. SC, p. 202.
104. RP, pp. 361–2.
105. PA, pp. 256–7; translation modified.
106. SC, p. 207.
107. The translation of the title of Hess's essay, *Die letzten Philosophen*, translated as 'The Recent Philosophers' in Stepelevich, p. 359, is modified here and throughout.
108. RP, p. 369.
109. 'In the alienated life of the social body, in *gold*, the commercial world enjoys its own alienated existence. The *thirst for wealth* of the mercenary world is the *bloodthirstiness* of the beast of prey.' RP, p. 368; translation modified.
110. 'It is true that man is the truth of the animal, but would the life of nature, would the life of man itself be perfect if animals did not exist independently?' Ludwig Feuerbach, 'Towards a Critique of Hegel's Philosophy', in *The Fiery Brook: Selected Writings of Ludwig Feuerbach*, ed. and trans. Zawar Hanfi, Garden City, NY, 1972, p. 55.
111. RP, p. 369; translation modified.
112. PA, p. 261.
113. 'Only through absolute *freedom*, not only of "labour" in the more restricted, parochial sense, but also of all human inclinations and activities in general, is absolute *equality* or, rather, the community of all imaginable "goods" possible, just as, conversely, freedom is conceivable only within this community.' SC, p. 206.
114. PA, p. 275; translation modified.
115. As Gérard Bensussan rightly points out, it was in this period (centred on the pivotal year 1843) that Hess's 'theoretical path crossed that of Marx and Engels at this precise point [the *Aufhebung* of philosophy]' (Bensussan, *Moses Hess*, p. 91).
116. Those whom Hess describes as 'Hegelian rationalists' (or 'rationalist politicians') 'are liberals only in a sphere that lacks reality, that can have no reality. . . . Whenever they descend to the level of real life, [the rationalist politicians] become reactionary . . . they want their "rational state"; but as this state is a fiction, they do not really want *any* liberal principles at all' (SC, pp. 208–9). See also PA, pp. 264 ff.
117. SC, p. 209.
118. Thus it is in the name of a *strict atheism* that Bruno Bauer objects to granting equal rights to 'Jews *qua* Jews' for as long as they cling to their particular religion and community. Indeed, Bauer goes still further: he holds that the Jews, by virtue of 'their attachment to their law, their language, and the whole of their being', are 'responsible for the oppression that they have suffered', and that the enduring nature of their 'being' (Bauer examines its origins in the Scriptures at length) has cut them off from

the movement of history and the 'historical peoples" struggle for emancipation. Only if they sacrifice this 'being' and their 'chimerical, stateless nationality' by becoming atheists together with the Christians can they profess to 'participate in the real business of the people and the state, sincerely and without secret reservations' (see Bauer, *Die Judenfrage*, Braunschweig, 1843, pp. 4, 61). Thus the 'critique' that claimed to be the most scathingly radical could perfectly well serve as a vehicle for the most shopworn stereotypes of traditional anti-Semitic rhetoric. Hess can quite rightly contend that 'the Young Hegelians, paradoxical as it may sound, are still caught in the trammels of the theological consciousness' (PA, p. 264).

119. RP, pp. 361, 363–4.
120. SC, p. 198.
121. PA, pp. 263–4.
122. RP, p. 363.
123. PA, p. 267.
124. SC, p. 204.
125. RP, p. 363; translation modified.
126. PA, pp. 256–7.
127. SC, p. 206.
128. PA, p. 273.
129. RP, p. 363; translation modified.
130. 'What is the very theme, the kernel of [*The Essence of Christianity*]? It is nothing other than the overcoming of the split into an essential and unessential I – the deification, that is, the presentation, the regarding of the whole man from head to foot.' Feuerbach, '*The Essence of Christianity* in Relation to *The Ego and its Own*', trans. Frederick M. Gordon, *The Philosophical Forum* 7, nos 2–4 (1977), p. 83.
131. Feuerbach replies in the passage of '*The Essence of Christianity* in Relation to *The Ego and its Own*' cited in note 130.
132. RP, p. 363; translation modified.
133. Feuerbach, 'Towards a Critique of Hegel's Philosophy', p. 57.
134. PA, p. 249.
135. 'Activity is, in a word, self-creation, the law of which is perceived by the spirit as a result of its own act of self-creation.' Ibid., p. 251.
136. See PA, pp. 273–4.
137. It is this ontological dimension of the 'social' that is obscured in Cornu's account of Hess's thought, which he is consequently inclined both to overestimate (when he makes Hess Marx's predecessor in the invention of the social; see Cornu, *Moses Hess*, pp. 2, 108) and to underestimate (when he straightforwardly contrasts [ibid., pp. 91, 103] Hess's 'moral' or 'utopian solution' with Marx's 'social solution', thus ignoring the intrinsically normative, and also metaphysical, thrust of the concept of the 'social').
138. SC, pp. 203–4.
139. See Chapter 2 above: 'The politics of the name'.
140. SC, p. 205.
141. Ibid.
142. SC, p. 206.
143. Compare Bruno Bauer's diatribes against the politics of the *juste-milieu* implemented by the July monarchy (Bauer, *Die Judenfrage*, p. 56), his defence of 'a cruel theory, inventive in its cruelty' that 'takes everything to a peak and to the point of extremity', as contrasted with the healing, soothing power of 'ordinary life' (ibid., p. 62), his dismissal of the 'band of mediators' who claim to represent the people within the framework of the Christian state (ibid., p. 56), and so on.
144. SC, pp. 197–8.
145. PA, p. 274; emphasis added.
146. See Chapter 1 above.
147. That is why we cannot agree with Gérard Bensussan when he says (Bensussan, *Moses*

Hess, p. 94) that Hess's essays of 1842–43 contain 'the outlines of a *strategy*', although 'neither its stakes, nor its objectives, nor its means of action' are defined. That is rather a lot for a strategy, even one that exists only in outline, to be missing.

148. According to Adorno, this is an exemplary manifestation of the pitfalls of a bad infinity. See Theodor W. Adorno, *In Search of Wagner*, trans. Rodney Livingstone, London, 1981, p. 54.

149. PA, p. 269.

150. Ibid.

151. Ibid., pp. 270–71; translation modified.

152. GW, pp. 331–2.

153. Ibid., p. 332.

154. Ibid., p. 347.

155. Ibid., p. 330.

156. Ibid., p. 359.

157. 'What holds for the bodies of small entities also holds for those of big ones, and it holds for the unconscious *heavenly* bodies, as they are called, as well as for the conscious bodies known as *social* bodies' (GW, p. 330). Here Hess takes up one of the great themes of idealist philosophy, one that is rooted in cosmological narratives and mystical visions: the principle that man is a microcosm of the social/natural whole.

158. Ibid.

159. Ibid.

160. Ibid., p. 331.

161. Bensussan, *Moses Hess*, p. 114.

162. GW, p. 348.

163. KB, p. 364.

164. KB, p. 365.

165. Ibid., emphasis added.

166. According to Feuerbach, only love can transcend the finitude of human existence (*Principles of the Philosophy of the Future*, trans. Manfred H. Vogel, Indianapolis, IN, 1986, p. 53). There is no 'practical and organic' transition between object and subject, the subject and his species-being, the individual and the community, other than love, that is, Christian love 'take[n] ... at its word' ('*The Essence of Christianity* in Relation to *The Ego and its Own*', p. 90). This is because 'Feuerbach only treats the essence of man in society – he is a social man, a *communist*' (KB, p. 91).

167. KB, p. 367. Feuerbach expresses precisely the same idea when he makes love 'the true ontological proof of the existence of an object apart from our minds' (*Principles of the Philosophy of the Future*, p. 53), infinity *in actu* (see note 166 above).

168. GW, p. 333.

169. KB, p. 366.

170.
> Philosophy steps into the place that religion had occupied. This means, however, that a totally different philosophy replaces all previous philosophy. ... Should philosophy be able to replace religion, it must, qua philosophy, become religion. This means that it must, in a way suited to its own nature, incorporate the essence of religion or the advantage that religion possesses over philosophy. (Feuerbach, 'The Necessity of a Reform of Philosophy', in *The Fiery Brook*, p. 148)

171. Louis Althusser, 'Sur Feuerbach', in *Écrits philosophiques et politiques*, vol. 2, Paris, 1995, pp. 241–2 (English translation forthcoming).

172. *Pace* Bensussan, for whom 'revolution and intellectual love are linked, and the subordination of one to the other is always conditional and reversible' (Bensussan, *Moses Hess*, p. 39). Bensussan construes intellectual love as an anticipation of the politics of the post-historical future, for which the revolution sets the stage. However, even before this future is post-historical, it is – for Hess and the thinkers of the 'social' in general – *post-political*.

173. Engels, *Feuerbach and the End of Classical German Philosophy*, MECW 26: 365.

174. GW, p. 333.
175. 'We are forever *purchasing* our *individual existence* with the *loss of our freedom*. And, mark you, not only, as one might think, we *proletarians*, but *we capitalists* too are these miserable creatures who suck each other's blood, *who devour one another and themselves*. None of us can freely develop his life activity; we cannot *create* or act *for one another*.' GW, p. 335.
176. Marx and Engels, 'German or "True" [*Wahre*] Socialism', *Communist Manifesto*, pp. 510–13.
177. As Lukács, for example, affirms, despite his profound understanding of the links between the anti-political socialism of Hess and Lassalle, a fundamental figure in the German labour movement. See Lukács, 'Moses Hess', pp. 183, 188–90, 203.
178. Marx, 'Herr Vogt', *MECW* 17: 79. Marx chooses these dates with an eye to the context (the importance of the religious question). In 1839, Feuerbach published his first texts in the *Hallische Jahrbücher* ('Towards a Critique of Hegel's Philosophy'). In Marx's view, 1846 marked a turning point: late that year, Weitling's dominance over the League came to an end, while his own (and Engels's) interventions in the League began to have greater and greater impact (ibid., pp. 79–81).
179. Although he did not join the League of the Just, Hess befriended two of its leaders, Ewerbeck and Mäurer (Bensussan, *Moses Hess*, p. 75). This was certainly not unrelated to the fact that Ewerbeck and Mäurer gradually came round to the view that the League should break with Étienne Cabet and Wilhelm Weitling and move closer to the *Vorwärts* group (Jacques Grandjonc, *Marx et les communistes allemands à Paris. Vorwärts 1844*, Paris, 1974, p. 62). When Arnold Ruge, one of the leading figures of the German democratic movement, settled in Paris in August 1843, it was Hess who provided him with a map of the various French socialist groups, introducing him to Flore Tristan, Victor Considér-ant, Cabet, Théodore Dézamy, Hugues de Lamennais and Louis Blanc (Espagne, 'Le Saint-Simonisme', p. 30). In 1844, a police informer noted that Hess and Marx were among the 'plotters' who spoke regularly at the Sunday meetings the German workers in Paris held at the *Barrière du Trône*, on the southwestern edge of the city (Bert Andreas, Introduction, *Gründungsdokumente des Bundes der Kommunisten, Juni bis September 1847*, ed. Andreas, Hamburg, 1969, p. 14). In 1847, we find Hess at the head of the Brussels German Workers' Association, which had been created by the Communist League; the Association, in turn, was the moving spirit behind the creation of the Democratic Association for the Unification of All Countries. Among its founding members, besides Hess, were Marx, Engels, Wilhelm Wolff and Georg Weerth, as well as two leaders of the Belgian Revolution, General François Mellinet and Lucien-Léopold Jottrand. (Franz Mehring, *Karl Marx: The Story of His Life*, trans. Edward Fitzgerald, Atlantic City, NJ, 1981, pp. 139 ff.)
180. Cornu, *Moses Hess*, p. 65.
181. The phrase is Cornu's; see ibid., p. 87.
182. See Grandjonc, *Marx*, p. 73.
183. Essentially because most accounts take their dates from Engels's 'On the History of the Communist League' (*MECW* 26: 312-30), a late work that sets out to provide badly needed information about a 'period' that 'today [i.e. in 1885] is almost forgotten' (ibid., p. 312).
184. Thus we can see why Bert Andreas's 1969 publication of the founding documents of the Communist League (see Andreas, *Gründungsdokumente*) was so important: it set the record straight on this point.
185. The first six questions and answers of the draft 'Profession of Faith' provide a rather good illustration of the League's doctrine. Here, by way of example, is the sixth question and answer: '*How do you want to work towards collective property?* Through enlightenment [*Aufklärung*] and by unifying the proletariat.' Engels, 'Entwurf des kommunistischen Glaubensbekenntnisses', in *Marx–Engels Gesamtausgabe (MEGA)*, Berlin, 1972, p. 120.

186. In fact, the draft of the 'Profession of Faith', because it grew out of a compromise and was supposed to serve as a basis for discussion, avoided setting out a clear-cut position on these points. From the seventh question on, Engels's influence becomes more obvious; many of the formulations in the document are clear anticipations of the future 'Principles of Communism'.

187.

Again, it was this 1844 profession of faith, or a very similar text, that Moses Hess persuaded the Paris branches of the League of Communists to adopt in summer 1847, during the discussion of the draft of the 'Communist Profession of Faith' that had been proposed at the founding congress of the new League in June. This led Engels to draft a counter-credo, known as the 'Principles of Communism'; it was the last stage but one in his preparations for writing the *Manifesto*. (Grandjonc, *Marx*, p. 74)

188. See Jean Bruhat, Introduction, *Manifeste du Parti communiste*, Paris, 1983, p. 14.

189. Resorting to a kind of bureaucratic manoeuvre, Engels decided to short-circuit the League's rank-and-file body (the communities) and appeal only to its intermediate level, the district or circle [*Kreis*], because he knew that the balance of forces there was more favourable to him and Marx. His 25–26 October 1847 letter to Marx is eloquent on this subject (*MECW* 38: 135–9).

190. See Engels, 'Principles of Communism', *MECW* 6: 341–5, questions 1 to 10: communism is the theory of, specifically, the emancipation of the proletariat, whose existence (and struggle) coincide with the Industrial Revolution; the proletariat is qualitatively different from all the exploited classes that have gone before it (serfs, slaves, etc.), and even from pre-industrial forms of dependent labour (craft labour or manufacturing).

191. This is the answer to the first question in the 'Principles': 'What is communism?' ('Principles of Communism', p. 341).

192. 'The Communists know only too well that . . . revolutions are not made deliberately and arbitrarily, but that everywhere and all times they have been the necessary *outcome* of circumstances *entirely independent of the will and the leadership of particular parties and entire classes*.' (Principles of Communism, p. 349; emphasis added)

193. See 'Principles of Communism', questions 16–19, 24–25, pp. 349–52, 355–7, which discuss the problem of provisional objectives, alliances, the programme, and the right time and place for the revolution.

194. 'All these circumstances contributed to the quiet revolution that was taking place in the League, and especially among the leaders in London.' ('On the History of the Communist League', p. 320.) This is not an isolated formulation: the whole of Engels's account tends to substantiate the idea that his and Marx's conceptions gained an easy and more or less natural victory over those of their adversaries.

195. Yet this is what Gérard Bensussan says about Hess, echoing, on this point, not only Althusser's essentialist conceptions but also those of Georg Lukács, which are based on diametrically opposed premises.

4   Friedrich Engels Discovers the Proletariat, 1842–1845

1. As Hegel points out in *Elements of the Philosophy of Right*, ed. Allen W. Wood, trans. H. B. Nisbet, Cambridge, 1991, §189, p. 227.

2. Marx, *Economic and Philosophic Manuscripts of 1844* (hereafter *1844 Manuscripts*), *MECW* 3: 333.

3. The Ricardian socialist Thomas Hodgskin published his *Labour Defended Against the Claims of Capital* in 1825, six years before Hegel's death. In his Preface to Book II of *Capital* (1885), Engels mentions the existence of 'an entire literature which in the twenties turned the Ricardian theory of value and surplus value against capitalist

production in the interest of the proletariat'; he cites Hodgskin, William Thompson, Ravenstone and others as its representatives. Engels, Preface to Marx, *Capital*, vol. 2, *MECW* 36: 17f. According to E.P. Thompson, 'the publication of *Labour Defended*, and its reception in the *Trades Newspaper*, represents the first clear point of junction between the "labour economists" or the Owenites and a part of the working-class *movement*' (*The Making of the English Working Class*, Harmondsworth, 1980, p. 857).

4. On the properly theoretical and political dimension of the work of the young (and the not-so-young) Engels, see Lukács's study 'Friedrich Engels als Literaturtheoretiker und Literaturkritiker', in George Lukács, *Karl Marx und Friedrich Engels als Literaturhistoriker*, Berlin, 1947, pp. 63–106.

5. Engels, Letter of 26 July 1842 to Ruge, *MECW* 2: 545.

6. Lukács, *Karl Marx und Friedrich Engels als Literaturhistoriker*, pp. 65–6.

7. Engels, 'Ernst Moritz Arndt', *MECW* 2: 142, 144; translation modified.

8. See the three texts that make up a kind of 'Anti-Schelling' (they are in fact grouped under this general title in the *Marx–Engels Werkausgabe*): 'Schelling on Hegel'; 'Schelling and Revelation'; and 'Schelling, Philosopher in Christ', *MECW* 2: 181–264.

9. Marx, Letter of 3 October 1843 to Feuerbach, *MECW* 3: 350.

10. Many of Engels's first articles (his critique of Ernst Moritz Arndt, the beginnings of his polemic with Schelling, poems, reviews, etc.) were published under the pen name F. Oswald in the newspaper founded by Gutzkow, *Telegraph für Deutschland*.

11. See his letters of 8–11 March 1839 to his brother Hermann and those of 7 January 1839, 21–28 December 1840, 18 February 1841 and 3 March 1841 to his sister Marie, as well as his 18 June 1840 letter to Levin Schücking about his (lost) translations of Shelley's verse.

12. See Moses Hess, Letter of 19 July 1843 to Auerbach: 'last year, as I was about to leave for Paris, Engels, who is now in England, where he is writing a long book on that country, came to Cologne from Berlin. We talked about the questions of the day; Engels, who is a revolutionary of the Year I, left me as a whole-hearted convert to communism. That's how I go about wreaking havoc.' Cited in Cornu, *Moses Hess et la gauche hégélienne*, Paris, 1934, p. 65.

13. And by no means that of Marx, contrary to the myths perpetuated in the canonical account of the formation of Marx's and Engels's thought.

14. Marx, *1844 Manuscripts*, *MECW* 3: 232; original emphasis.

15. Georg Lukács, 'Moses Hess and the Problem of Materialist Dialectics', in *Political Writings*, London, 1972, pp. 183–4.

16. The phrase is Solange Mercier-Josa's (*Théorie allemande et pratique française de la liberté*, Paris, 1993, p. 190; emphasis added).

17. Engels, *Ludwig Feuerbach and the End of Classical German Philosophy*, *MECW* 26: 364.

18. Engels, 'A Fragment of Fourier's on Trade', *MECW* 4: 614; emphasis added.

19. Engels, 'The Internal Crises', *MECW* 2: 371.

20. Ibid., pp. 370–71.

21. On Engels's and Tocqueville's parallel – and contrasting – treatment of the Anglo-Saxon model, see Domenico Losurdo, 'Phénoménologie du pouvoir: Marx, Engels et la tradition libérale', in Georges Labica and Mireille Delbraccio, eds, *Friedrich Engels, savant et révolutionnaire*, Paris, 1997, pp. 51 ff.

22. Engels, 'The Internal Crises', *MECW* 2: 370–71. Carried away by the anti-political dimension of his socialist project, Engels would later (see his August–September 1844 articles in *Vorwärts*) downplay this decisive point. We shall come back to it.

23. See Engels, 'Letters from London', *MECW* 3: 380.

24. The debate about the long-term consequences of Britain's *politico-cultural* backwardness is not about to end, as Tom Nairn's recent work attests (*The Enchanted Glass: Britain and its Monarchy*, London, 1988). It is no longer a question, as the first version of Anderson's and Nairn's theses obliquely suggested, of calling the capitalist development of Great Britain into doubt; nor even, as was suggested by the second version

(Anderson's), of emphasizing the peculiar features of this development, that is, construing its later failures as a consequence of its early supremacy (see Perry Anderson, *English Questions*, London, 1992). According to Nairn's latest work, the fact that Britain did not go through a bourgeois-democratic revolution enabled certain elements of the *ancien régime*, beginning with the monarchy, to construct a very special sort of nationalism around the fetishized image of the royal family, which took the place of the national-popular, democratic-egalitarian dimension typical of the modern nation-state but absent from its British variant. Contrary to what Engels would later affirm about the advanced, 'social' English situation, this nationalism has been a factor in the ongoing de-radicalization of political and intellectual life, and has foreclosed all prospects of revolution.

25. Engels, 'The Internal Crises', *MECW* 2: 370.
26. See the last text Hegel wrote, 'The English "Reform Bill"', in *Hegel's Political Writings*, trans. T.M. Knox, Oxford, 1964, pp. 295–330. Hegel concludes his analysis of the English situation by posing the dilemma 'reform or revolution'.
27. Engels, 'The Internal Crises', *MECW* 2: 373–4.
28. Ibid., p. 374.
29. See especially the first two letters to the *Rheinische Zeitung*, 'The English View of the Internal Crises', *MECW* 2: 368–9; and 'The Internal Crises', *MECW* 2: 370–74. Engels offers a more finely shaded version of the same judgement in *The Condition*. As Eric Hobsbawm points out: 'far from denigrating the bourgeoisie, Engels is manifestly disconcerted by its blindness. He repeats again and again that if it were wise, it would learn to make concessions to the workers' (Preface to *La Situation de la classe laborieuse en Angleterre*, Paris, 1960, p. 22).
30. I take this idea from Costanzo Preve (*La passione durevole*, Milan, 1989, ch. 1, 'Capitalismo senza borghezia').
31. Heinrich Heine, 'Pictures of Travel', *passim*.
32. David Cannadine (see his classic study, 'The Context, Performance and Meaning of Ritual: The British Monarchy and the Invention of Tradition, *c.* 1820–1977', in Eric Hobsbawm and Terence Ranger, eds, *The Invention of Tradition*, Cambridge, 1983, pp. 101–64) and Nairn (*The Enchanted Glass, passim*) have brilliantly shown that this courtly ceremonial is the fruit of a pure *reconstruction*, an imaginary version of the Middle Ages forged by the monarchy in response to the challenge of the French Revolution; in no case was it the sign of an uninterrupted continuity between the medieval past and the present.
33. Engels, 'Letters from London', *MECW* 3: 379–80.
34. Ibid., 380. Towards the end of his life, Engels made a more systematic study of early Christianity, developing a parallel between it and the workers' movement. The idea was, it must be said, rather widespread throughout the nineteenth century. From Leroux to Flora Tristan or Lamennais, Romantic socialism, especially in its French variant, had made it a 'positive' commonplace, before the reactionary criticism of the late nineteenth century, from Taine to Nietzsche, assigned the same parallel a negative value (Christianity as a religion of 'the weak', 'the herd', and so on).
35. Engels, 'Letters from London', *MECW* 3: 387. On the diffusion of Byron and Shelley among the working classes, see ibid., p. 380.
36. Ibid.
37. Ibid.
38. Today, especially after the appearance of E.P. Thompson's monumental work (*The Making, passim*), it is hard to take seriously any study of the history of the English movement that ignores its religious dimension (among other aspects, the role of Methodism and the dissenting Protestant movements, with their marked messianic overtones). It is true, as Thompson also points out (ibid., p. 468), that significant sections of the proletariat, especially in southern England, had effectively abandoned the practice of religion. But the fact remains that 'it is premature, in the 1830s, to

think of the English working people as being wholly open to secular ideology' (ibid., p. 882).

39. See Gareth Stedman Jones's classic study 'Rethinking Chartism', in *Languages of Class: Studies in English Working Class History, 1832–1982*, Cambridge, 1983, pp. 90–180. Stedman Jones has also drawn attention to the selective character of the young Engels's interpretation of the English workers' movement. Marx, he says, adhered to it even more faithfully than its author, whose positions began to shift from 1858 on. See Stedman Jones, 'Karl Marx and the English Labour Movement', in *Marx en perspective*, ed. Bernard Chavance, Paris, 1985, pp. 609–24.

40. See Hodgskin, *Labour Defended*, pp. 104 ff.

41. Engels, 'Letters from London', *MECW* 3: 379.

42. As Engels would later spell out in the article 'Progress of Social Reform on the Continent', to hold fast to principles alone while ignoring 'interests' would be to regress towards 'abstract principle' and 'political nonentity' (*MECW* 3: 407).

43. Engels, 'The Internal Crises', *MECW* 2: 370–71.

44. Ibid., p. 374.

45. Let us recall the dates of a few of the texts by Marx that frame the period preceding his stay in Paris: October–November 1842: 'Debates on the Law on Thefts of Wood', a series of articles that appeared in the *Rheinische Zeitung*; January 1843: 'Justification of the Correspondent from the Mosel', another article published in the *Rheinische Zeitung*; March 1843: correspondence with Ruge and preliminary work on his 'Contribution to the Critique of Hegel's Philosophy of Law'; summer 1843: 'On the Jewish Question'.

46. See Marx's pronouncements on the relations between socialist and communist theories in his September 1843 letter to Ruge (*MECW* 3: 142–3).

47. Marx, Preface to 'A Contribution to the Critique of Political Economy' (1859), *MECW* 29: p. 264.

48. Engels, 'Outlines of a Critique of Political Economy', *MECW* 3: 418.

49. Ibid., pp. 422, 429, 439.

50. On this point, which bears mainly on the relationship between the Smith of the *Theory of Moral Sentiments* and the Smith of *The Wealth of Nations*, see Jean Mathiot, *Adam Smith. Philosophie et économie: De la sympathie à l'échange*, Paris, 1990.

51. Adam Smith, *The Wealth of Nations*, 3 vols., ed. W.B. Todd, Oxford, 1976, vol. 1, p. 24.

52. Smith often takes up this theme – for example, in the chapter on wages. See ibid., pp. 87–90.

53. Ibid., pp. 376–427.

54. Engels, 'Outlines of a Critique of Political Economy', *MECW* 3: 421–2.

55. Ibid., pp. 423–4.

56. Ibid., p. 424.

57. See Gérard Bensussan, *Moses Hess, la philosophie, le socialisme*, Paris, 1985, p. 126.

58. Engels, 'Outlines of a Critique of Political Economy', *MECW* 3: 421. Thus one cannot accept Althusser's interpretation, according to which, in England, Engels discovered 'developed capitalism and a class struggle obeying its own laws and ignoring philosophy and philosophers' (Louis Althusser, *For Marx*, trans. Ben Brewster, London and New York, 1990, p. 81 and note); Labica says much the same thing (Georges Labica, *Le statut marxiste de la philosophie*, Paris, 1976, p. 61). Engels's theoretical 'ultra-leftism', as his writings of 1842–43 as well as *The Condition of the Working-Class in England* (1845) would seem to indicate, speaks – overwhelmingly – German, especially Feuerbach's German. As we shall see, this means that Engels was closer to Hess than to Marx throughout this period.

59. Engels, 'Outlines of a Critique of Political Economy', *MECW* 3: 419.

60. Ibid., p. 424.

61. Ibid., p. 427. Engels goes on to say that 'the struggle of capital against capital, of labour against labour, of land against land, drives production to a fever-pitch at which

production turns all natural and rational relations upside-down [*sie . . . auf den Kopf stellt*]'. Ibid., p. 435.

62. Ibid., p. 419.

63. Ibid., p. 422. In his Paris manuscripts, Marx would utilize this expression in his turn (*1844 Manuscripts, MECW* 3: 290).

64. Engels, 'Outlines of a Critique of Political Economy', *MECW* 3: 420.

65. See especially E.P. Thompson, 'The Moral Economy of the English Crowd in the 18th Century', in *Customs in Common*, London, 1991, pp. 185–258.

66. On Sismondi's vision of things and his place in the comparative genealogy of the term 'industrial revolution' in France and Great Britain, see Gareth Stedman Jones, '*Industrie, Pauperism and the Hanoverian State: The Genesis and the Political Context of the Original Debate about the "Industrial Revolution" in England and France, 1815–1840*', *Papers of the Center for History and Economics*, January 1997. On the Saint-Simonian sources of the term, which Stedman Jones completely neglects, see Jacques Grandjonc, *Communisme/Kommunismus/communism. Origine et développement international de la terminologie communautaire prémarxiste des utopistes aux néo-babouvistes*, 2 vols, Trier, 1989, vol. 1, pp. 128–32.

67. Engels, 'Outlines of a Critique of Political Economy', *MECW* 3: 421.

68. Ibid.

69. Ibid., p. 420.

70. 'The concept of value is violently torn asunder, and . . . each of the separate sides is declared to be the whole'. Ibid., p. 426.

71. 'Thus everything in economics stands on its head. Value, the primary factor, the source of price, is made dependent on price, its own product. As is well known, this inversion [*Umkehrung*] is the essence of abstraction [*Abstraktion*]; on which see Feuerbach'. Ibid., p. 427.

72. Ibid., pp. 441–2.

73. Ibid., p. 434.

74. Ibid., translation modified.

75. In the course of Chapter 3, I briefly described Saint-Simon's seminal role. Let me also mention, among the 'grand narratives' of organization, Louis Blanc's monumental *Organisation du travail* (1839) in G.M. Bravo, *Les socialistes avant Marx*, Paris, 1979, vol. 2, pp. 134–66. The question is whether this organizational schema persists unchanged in Engels's work. He returns to it again at great length in *Anti-Dühring*, in a discussion that was to have major consequences for the workers' movement. See Jean Robelin's admirable review of the question, 'Engels et la rectification du socialisme', in Labica and Delbraccio, eds, *Friedrich Engels*, pp. 41–50.

76. The passing reference to Fourier here is symptomatic. It suggests the idea – which Engels does not develop – of a harmonious society conceived as a vast machine in which the play (emulation) between individual forces will be assigned, once it is stripped of its antagonistic character, its 'proper and rational sphere'. See Engels, 'Outlines of a Critique of Political Economy', *MECW* 3: 435.

77. Ibid., pp. 430–31.

78. Ibid., p. 433.

79. Ibid., p. 434.

80. This is part of the heritage of Babouvism, which was very much alive in the secret societies that flourished under the July monarchy, and constituted a key moment in the autonomous activity of the dominated classes throughout the post-1789 period. Engels knew the Babouvist movement well, as is shown by the account of it that he produced for an English public (Engels, 'Progress of Social Reform on the Continent', *MECW* 3: 393, 396–7).

81. If it is true that 'as long as you continue to produce in the present unconscious, thoughtless manner, at the mercy of chance, for just so long trade crises will remain', it

surely follows that the revolution represents the first instance of a *conscious* process which eliminates crises and the relations that cause them.

82. Engels, 'Progress of Social Reform on the Continent', *MECW* 3: 392.
83. Indeed, the importance of the *national* function of a philosophical transformation has rarely been brought out so well. See ibid., pp. 405–6.
84. Ibid., p. 406; translation modified.
85. Ibid., p. 393.
86. In Fourier's 'social philosophy', Engels discerns, notably, a definition of the human spirit as 'activity' and an identification of labour with enjoyment.
87. Ibid., p. 399.
88. Engels is not unaware that they are 'more favourable to an elective monarchy'. Ibid., p. 397.
89. Engels follows Hess's lead when it is a question of demoting politics in favour of the social, but he remains faithful to the (apparent, at any rate) Anglocentrism of the *Triarchy* at the point where Hess turns back to the classic theme of the confrontation between France and Germany.
90. Engels, 'The Condition of England: The Eighteenth Century', *MECW* 3: 471.
91. This is a commonplace of the historical narrative cast in terms of race and race struggles. I shall have a great deal to say about the uses to which Engels puts this *topos* in *The Condition of the Working-Class in England.*
92. Engels, 'The Condition of England: The Eighteenth Century', *MECW* 3: 469.
93. Ibid., p. 474.
94. 'The abolition of feudal servitude has made "cash-payment the sole relation of human beings" ... the perversion of the human condition is complete.' (Ibid., p. 476.) Hess's critique of money has obviously influenced this passage.
95. 'The democracy towards which England is moving is a *social* democracy.' Engels, 'The Condition of England: The English Constitution', *MECW* 3: 513.
96. Ibid.
97. This at the very moment when, in the polemic with Ruge carried out in the same newspaper, Marx's anti-political attitude is also reaching its zenith.
98. Engels, 'The Condition of England: The English Constitution', *MECW* 3: 489; translation modified.
99. 'The word "king" is the essence of the state, just as the word "God" is the essence of religion, even though neither word has any meaning at all.' (Ibid., p. 493.)
100. After observing that the English workers have already transcended the narrow-mindedness of national particularism, Engels tells us on what *grounds* he, like many others, hails their efforts:

> I found you to be more than mere *English*men, members of a single, isolated nation, I found you to be *Men*, members of the great and universal family of Mankind, who know their interest and that of all the human race to be the same. And as such, as members of this Family of 'One and Indivisible' Mankind, as Human Beings in the most emphatical meaning of the word, as such I, and many others on the Continent, hail your progress in every direction and wish you speedy success. (*Condition, MECW* 4: 298)

101. Such, according to Foucault, is the unprecedented idea underlying 'the analytic of finitude' characteristic of modern humanism: Man takes the place of God (of the Grounds) by virtue of his essential finitude (see Michel Foucault, *The Order of Things: An Archaeology of the Human Sciences*, trans. anon., New York, 1970, pp. 312–13.). Feuerbach's formulations of this idea provide a particularly naive – and therefore transparent – version of it.
102. 'I have continually used the expressions working-men [*Arbeiter*] and proletarians, working-class, propertyless class and proletariat as equivalents.' *Condition, MECW* 4: 304.
103. Engels's *Vorwärts* article goes on to emphasize the social order's capacity for internal

expansion: 'Only in England have individuals as such, without consciously standing for universal principles, furthered national development and brought it near to its conclusion'. Engels, 'The Condition of England: The Eighteenth Century', *MECW* 3: 474.

104. This is how Foucault defines the operating principle governing modern power relations, with their twofold dimension of disciplinary power and bio-power, functionally indissociable from their statification and incorporation into the mechanisms of the capitalist state apparatus (see Michel Foucault, *History of Sexuality*, vol. 1, trans. Robert Hurley, London, 1979, pp. 139 ff.).

105. Engels, *Condition*, *MECW* 4: 401.

106. Ibid., p. 425.

107. Ibid., p. 582.

108. See Robert Owen, 'Essays on the Formation of Character', in *A New View of Society and Other Writings*, ed. G.D.H. Cole, London, 1963 pp. 53 ff. As E.P. Thompson judiciously notes, it is 'the very rigour' of Owen's 'mechanical materialism' which engenders his messianism whenever it is a question of conceiving a change in circumstances, since, for Owen, any notion of transformative or, *a fortiori*, revolutionary practice is ruled out from the start (*The Making*, p. 865).

109. See Miguel Abensour's insightful remarks, 'Robert Owen', in François Châtelet *et al.*, eds, *Dictionnaire des œuvres politiques*, Paris, 1986, pp. 619–32.

110. Thompson, *The Making*, p. 859. Thompson notes that if the ideas of the first Owen had been put into practice, the result would have looked very much like a variant on the workhouse (ibid., p. 861).

111. 'The two great practical philosophers of latest date, Bentham and Godwin, are ... almost exclusively the property of the proletariat.' Engels, *Condition*, *MECW* 4: 528. Well before Engels, Heine ranged the 'Benthamites, the preachers of utility' among the 'revolutionary parties' that were active in England and drew their inspiration from Locke's materialism (Heine, *On the History of Religion and Philosophy in Germany*, in *Selected Prose*, ed. and trans. Ritchie Robertson, Harmondsworth, 1993, pp. 239–40).

112. I have already mentioned Saint-Simon's key role. According to Grandjonc, 'the terms "social science/doctrine social" in French and "social system/ social science" in English effectively fulfil the function of the abstract *socialisme*/socialism, in Fourier's and Saint-Simon's writings as well as in Owen's (and in those of their respective disciples); for its part, the meaning of the term "social" began to shift, from the turn of the century in French and from the 1820s on in English, towards "socialist/socialistic"'. Grandjonc, *Communisme*, p. 105. It was only around the middle of the century that 'social science' and 'socialism', which are still interchangeable in works by Proudhon such as *What is Property?* (1840), came to be clearly distinguished.

113. Consider, for example, the fascination exerted by the themes of 'healthiness' and the 'cure' of the 'pathologies' of society, equated with a 'body' or 'organism', that Durkheim sounds again and again in *The Rules of Sociological Method* (ed. Steven Lukes, trans. W.D. Halls, London, 1982, notably p. 104). The equation of social reorganization with medical care, especially with therapies considered appropriate for the mentally ill, stands out even more clearly in Owen's work. See Robert Owen, *The Revolution in the Mind and Practice of the Human Race*, London, 1849, p. 115. Let us not forget that medicalization constitutes the overriding tendency of the systems of state bio-power. . . .

114. On this point, see Pierre-François Moreau, *Le récit utopique. Droit naturel et roman de l'État*, Paris, 1982.

115. Saint-Simon's 'industrialism', the Fourierist 'societal mechanism' based on a statistical rationalization of the economy of the passions, Owen's complex system of total education, with its scientific pretensions – there was no lack of elaborate projects that aimed 'to bring social technology up to the level of industrial technology' (Abensour, 'Robert Owen', p. 627).

116. Moreau, *Le récit*, p. 142.

117. On neutralization as the basis of the utopian system, see the now classic analysis by Louis Marin, *Utopics: The Semiological Play of Textual Spaces*, trans. Robert A. Vollrath, Atlantic Highlands, NJ, 1984; as well as Fredric Jameson's remarks in 'Of Islands and Trenches: Neutralization and the Production of Utopian Discourse', in *The Ideologies of Theory. Essays, 1971–1986, Vol. 2: The Syntax of History*, Minneapolis, MN, 1988.

118. Engels reserves the term 'social philosophy' for Fourier, whose 'scientific research' and 'cool, unbiased, systematic thought' he contrasts with Saint-Simon's mysticism. See Engels, 'Progress of Social Reform on the Continent', *MECW* 3: 394.

119. Engels, *Anti-Dühring*, *MECW* 25: 249–54. Significantly, what comes in for praise is, without exception, the 'practical' nature of Owenite social engineering, along with the 'technical competence' and the gift for accurate 'calculation' attributed to Owen. In a revelatory passage, Engels goes so far as to say that 'the Owen method of social reform once accepted, there is from the practical point of view little to be said against the actual arrangement of details'.(Engels, *Anti-Dühring*, p. 251). Owen is credited not only for his defence of 'the most clear-cut communism possible', but also for 'the most comprehensive building project of the future communist community, with its ground-plan, front and side and bird's-eye views' (ibid., p. 253).

120. Marc Angenot's iconoclastic book *L'utopie collectiviste. Le grand récit socialiste sous la Deuxième Internationale* (Paris, 1993), offers a gripping archaeological descent into the discursive matrix common to the whole of the workers' movement of the period. Angenot shows that this *grand récit* satisfied an irrepressible need for *representation*, a need inherent in the functioning of socialist doctrine (including the versions of it that claimed to derive from Marx) as a mass ideology adapted to the nascent working-class organizations and their apparatuses.

121. For a fuller treatment of this theme, see Robelin, 'Engels et la rectification du socialisme'; and Jean Robelin, *Marxisme et socialisation*, Paris, 1989, esp. pp. 109–26.

122. As Marc Angenot says, talking about Marx alone. See Angenot, 'Jules Guesde, ou: la fabrication du marxisme orthodoxe', *Actuel Marx*, no. 23, 1998.

123. See Georges Labica's indispensable discussion of it in *Les 'Thèses sur Feuerbach'*, Paris, 1987, pp. 60–65.

124. This association is symptomatic, since Marx's text, as it appears when it is read in the light of others, refers primarily to French materialists such as Helvétius or Holbach (see Marx and Engels, *The Holy Family*, *MECW* 4: 132–3). Their socialist tendencies, viewed in this perspective, are merely extensions of the French materialists' arguments. E.P. Thompson provides one highly significant illustration, among many others, of the reception of the Third Thesis on Feuerbach: he quotes it in Engels's rewritten version, attributing the interpolation about Owen to Marx (*The Making*, p. 865).

125. Here is the *Collected Works* translation of the original text of the Third Thesis (it was, of all the Theses on Feuerbach, the one that Engels revised the most heavily); Engels's addenda and deletions are indicated in brackets:

> The materialist doctrine concerning the changing of circumstances and upbringing [that men are products of circumstances and upbringing, and that, therefore, changed men are products of other circumstances] forgets that circumstances are changed by men and that the educator must himself be educated. This doctrine must, therefore, divide society into two parts, one of which is superior to society [(in Robert Owen, for example)]. The coincidence of the changing of circumstances and of human activity or self-change [Engels struck through the term 'self-change'] can be conceived and rationally understood only as *revolutionary* (*umwälzende*) *practice*. (*MECW* 5: 7)

126. Karl Kautsky, *Le Programme socialiste*, Paris, 1910, p. 127, cited in Angenot, *L'utopie collectiviste*, p. 23.

127. Jules Guesde, Letter of late 1878–early 1879 to Marx, in Marx and Engels, *Le mouvement ouvrier français*, ed. and trans. Roger Dangeville, Paris, 1974, vol. 2, p. 84.

128. Gareth Stedman Jones ('Voir et entendre. Engels, Manchester et l'observation sociale en 1844', *Genèses*, no. 22, 1996, pp. 4–17) rightly emphasizes this pre-eminence of the gaze in *The Condition*. Unfortunately – no doubt because Stedman Jones is carried away by a desire to deny the existence of any 'social determinism' whatsoever – his explanations of this pre-eminence are particularly unconvincing. For the moment, let us content ourselves with noting that the primacy of the gaze, as well as the division between the visible and the invisible that it establishes, are rather hard to reconcile with the Hegelian dialectic of appearance, essence, and the concept, *pace* Stedman Jones. That is because this dialectic presents itself as a radical critique of the primacy of the visual, one of the representative illusions of consciousness that the logic of the concept attempts, precisely, to expose. As for the pure and simple identification of Engels's and Hess's Feuerbachianism with that of Marx, I have already indicated where I stand.

129. Engels, *Condition, MECW* 4: 418.

130. Ibid., p. 419.

131. Ibid., pp. 445–6. The sentence I refer to here reveals a great deal about the nature of the Engelsian gaze. A long list of deformities and of cases of scrofula, tuberculosis, rickets, and other diseases winds its way through the text. As a rule, its is accompanied by extensive quotations of passages taken from the accounts of health inspectors. See, for example, ibid., pp. 394–409, 443–61.

132. Ibid., p. 450. On size and stature, see also ibid., pp. 396, 403, 454, 491.

133. After dwelling at length on the 'immorality' of the Sheffield proletarians (precocious, unbridled sex; teenage prostitution; brutality), Engels puts the finishing touch to his portrait with the remark that 'crimes of a savage and desperate sort are of common occurrence' (ibid., p. 494). On crime, see also ibid., pp. 366, 425.

134. See Foucault, *History of Sexuality*, vol. 1, p. 115 ff.; Michel Foucault, *Discipline and Punish*, trans. Alan Sheridan, London, 1977, pp. 251 ff.

135. That men are 'condemned to domestic occupations' when women find work and men fail to is 'a case', Engels notes, 'that happens very frequently'; he treats it as a 'virtual castration' (ibid., p. 438n.) or even an apocalyptic threat hanging over civilization (ibid., p. 439). The nightmarish vision of this impossible inversion of the roles of the sexes can be construed as an allegory of the radical, traumatic transformation of social conditions attributable to the first 'capitalist revolution'.

136. 'A power that exerts a positive influence on life, that endeavors to administer, optimize, and multiply it, subjecting it to precise controls and comprehensive regulations.' Foucault, *The History of Sexuality*, vol. 1, pp. 137–8.

137. Engels's account suggests that Foucault's periodization needs to be modified; according to Foucault – who, paradoxically, refers to *Capital* on this point – the process of sexualization commenced only in the second half of the nineteenth century. One can, nevertheless, accept his analysis of the process. See Foucault, *History of Sexuality*, vol. 1, pp. 125–6.

138. Étienne Balibar and Immanuel Wallerstein, *Race, Nation, Class*, trans. Chris Turner, London and New York, 1991, p. 282.

139. Throughout *The Condition*, sexual relations are considered from a fourfold point of view which takes into consideration the legal status of the partners, the age at which sexual relations first occur (Engels makes only one allusion to female virginity: pp. 441–2), and, above all, the frequency of sexual relations and their link with drinking, which rounds off the picture of 'immorality' and 'vice'. An especially noteworthy passage links sexuality to crime via the figure of the 'savage and desperate' criminal (p. 494). The terms recurrently associated with proletarian sexual relations are 'unbridled', 'excess' and '[too] early'. See, for example, Engels, *Condition, MECW* 4: 424, 441–2, 482, 483–4, 492, 496, 538–9.

140. For example, in the case of the mines (ibid., p. 538). However, the heat that apparently transforms the mines into proletarian rabbit hutches has the opposite effect in the

factories (ibid., p. 448). The perception of the proletarian body oscillates between the morbid figure of increasing debility and the threatening vision of excessive sexual power.

141. Benjamin discusses the seminal role of Engels's *flâneries* in his essays on Baudelaire ('On Some Motifs in Baudelaire', in *Illuminations*, ed. Hannah Arendt, trans. Harry Zohn, London, 1973, p. 168). Oddly enough, Benjamin says nothing about Heine. See also the chapter on Engels in Henri Lefebvre, *La pensée marxiste et la ville*, Paris, 1972, pp. 9–26. The author of *The Condition* has clearly observed at first hand much of the material he presents, in the course of his indefatigable walks through the fascinating and morbid 'great towns' of London and Manchester. Many descriptions are introduced by phrases such as 'after roaming the streets of the capital for a day or two'; 'I do not remember to have seen'; 'though I thought I knew this region'; 'if one roams the streets a little in the early morning', 'I have seldom traversed Manchester without', etc. See, respectively, Engels, *Condition*, *MECW* 4: 328, 346 and 454, 353, 396, 445.

142. Ibid., p. 349. 'The eye and the nerves of the bourgeoisie': this is a clear example of the 'sensorial triangulation' (sight, hearing and touch, under the dominance of the visual) at the basis of the anatomico-pathological gaze that Michel Foucault discusses in *The Birth of the Clinic: An Archaeology of Medical Perception*, trans. Alan Sheridan, London, 1972, pp. 162 ff. Here Foucault establishes an archaeology of the medical gaze as it was redeployed around new axes, leading to a reorganization of the regimes of the visible (the surfaces and the transparency of language, which are to be traversed; the depth of the body, which is to be penetrated).

143. Without a doubt, the description of London's streets and their crowds, with their simultaneously atomized and massified crowds (Engels, *Condition*, *MECW* 4: 328–9), is a classic example of the genre.

144. See Marin, *Utopics*, p. 212.

145. Heine had earlier described London as a 'stone forest of houses, and amid them the rushing stream of faces of living men'. Heine, *English Fragments*, in *The Sword and the Flame: Selections from Henrich Heine's Prose*, trans. Charles Godfrey Leland, ed. Alfred Werner, London, 1960, pp. 429–30.

146. As one of Engels's contemporaries, Léon Faucher, also observed, 'the town [Manchester] realises in a measure the utopia of Bentham' (cited in Eric Hobsbawm, *The Age of Revolution: Europe 1789–1848*, London, 1992, p. 243). On the reversible relation between utopia and dystopia, see Fredric Jameson's very fine discussion in *The Seeds of Time*, New York, 1994, Part 1, pp. 1–71.

147. Engels, *Condition*, *MECW* 4: 515.

148. See ibid., pp. 345–64.

149. Ibid., p. 350.

150. On city maps as representations of an ideological system, see Marin, *Utopics*, ch. 10, 'The City's Portrait in its Utopics', pp. 201–32. Engels's map of Manchester should be compared with Heine's map of his native Düsseldorf as well as Engels's colourful representation of his native Barmen.

151. This, as we shall see, explains why Marx feels obliged to devote several dozen pages to criticizing a serialized novel (and to the interpretation that someone close to the Young Hegelian movement had made of it): Eugène Sue's *Les Mystères de Paris*.

152. See, for example, an evocative passage in Engels, *Condition*, *MECW* 4: 396–7.

153. Heine, *English Fragments*, pp. 429–30.

154. Engels, *Condition*, *MECW* 4: 297.

155. Walter Benjamin, *Charles Baudelaire: A Lyric Poet in the Era of High Capitalism*, trans. Harry Zohn, London, 1973, p. 37.

156. Foucault, *The Birth of the Clinic*, pp. 162–3.

157. Cited by Benjamin in *Charles Baudelaire*, p. 42; translation modified.

158. See Marx and Engels, *The Holy Family*, ' "Critical criticism" as a Mystery-Monger, or "Critical criticism" as Herr Szeliga', *MECW* 4: 55–77.

159. Engels, 'Continental Movements' (*The New Moral World*, 3 February 1844), *MECW* 3: 415. Lukács, who sees in this 'overestimation of Eugène Sue' a rare 'vestige of idealistic Young-Hegelian views', draws a very apt comparison between the polemic with Sue and the question of 'true socialism' (*Karl Marx und Friedrich Engels als Literaturhistoriker*, pp. 78–9).

160. Engels, *Condition*, *MECW* 4: 364.

161. Ibid., pp. 419–20.

162. On this point, I follow the leads given by Michel Foucault in '*Il faut défendre la société*': *Cours au collège de France (1975–1976)*, Paris, 1997.

163. In a note to the 1892 German edition (ibid., p. 420n.), Engels draws attention to the objective similarity between this passage in *The Condition* and a novel Disraeli wrote around the same time: *Sybil, or the Two Nations*. Disraeli, a converted Jew and Romantic Tory, was an ardent apologist for a racialist, colonialist vision of British policy, but also believed in the 'racial superiority' of the Jews. He provides a perfect illustration of the reversibility of 'pro-Semitism' and anti-Semitism – that is, the oscillation inherent in classifications based on race. Hannah Arendt paints a suggestive portrait of this very Nietzschean personage, 'the potent wizard' of *The Origins of Totalitarianism*, 2nd edn, New York, 1973, pp. 68–75.

164. The *Vorwärts* articles (see above) had already taken up the idea that the English nation is the result of a mixture of 'Germanic and Latin peoples' ('The Condition of England', p. 471; trans. modified).

165. Foucault's 1976 course at the Collège de France examines the formation of this agonistic discourse around the theme of the 'war of the races' and with its subsequent biologizing or class transcription. See '*Il faut défendre*'.

166. Engels, *Condition*, *MECW* 4: 390.

167. Contrary to what Stedman Jones maintains ('Voir sans entendre'), the senses of hearing and smell are not altogether absent from Engels's inquiry. But they occupy a subordinate place within the 'sensorial triangulation' which founds the new bio-political gaze. In any case, the points of convergence between Engels and Carlyle must be sought in this 'racialist' vision of the social, not, as Stedman Jones contends, in the distinction between word and deed and the devaluation of the former in favour of the latter; a distinction of that sort would imply a vision of theory, and of its relation to practice, which is utterly foreign to Engels.

168. Ibid., p. 390.

169. Ibid., p. 391.

170. See his analysis of the way wages fluctuate around an average that is itself historically variable: ibid., pp. 378–81. *Pace* Stedman Jones, then ('Voir sans entendre'), Engels's vision of the Manchester proletariat is in no sense undifferentiated, and he by no means treats its immigrant stratum as 'representative' of the class as a whole. Rather – and this is something else entirely – he makes it a metonymy for the 'proletarianizing' section of the class, extreme but, for that very reason, an integral part of the working-class condition as such.

171. Jacques Bidet has already drawn attention to the non-functional character of the system in his analysis of the relationship between value and the price of labour-power within Marx's schema. The variations in the price of labour-power, which tends to fall below the level of its 'normal' value, depend on a power relationship; this is the sole factor capable of countering the tendency to the undervaluation of labour, which can go so far as to endanger even its physical reproduction. See Jacques Bidet, *Que faire du Capital?*, Paris, 1985, pp. 71–87.

172. Engels, *Condition*, *MECW* 4: 389.

173. Ibid., p. 391.

174. Ibid., p. 354. Engels returns again and again to the theme of the 'indescribable filthiness' of the Irish (ibid., pp. 365, 368, 391–2).

175. On the relationship between Engels and Carlyle, see Michael Levin, *The Condition of*

NOTES TO PAGES 210–212

England Question: Carlyle, Mill, Engels, London, 1998, esp. pp. 140 ff., on their respective visions of the Irish proletariat.

176. 'The pressure of this race has done much to depress wages and lower the working-class.' Engels, *Condition, MECW* 4: 392.

177. Ibid., p. 350.

178. Here I am tempted to evoke both his relationship with the Irish worker Mary Burns, who became his lifelong companion, and, more generally, his 'often *déclassé* love affairs' or his characteristic 'Rabelaisian vitality' (Michelle Perrot, Introduction to *Les filles de Karl Marx, Lettres inédites*, Paris, 1979, p. 20).

179. On the 'savage' and the 'barbarian', see Foucault, *'Il faut défendre'*, p. 173.

180. Benjamin, *Charles Baudelaire*, pp. 87, 83.

181. 'Nineteenth-century medicine was haunted by that absolute eye that cadaverizes life and rediscovers in the corpse the frail, broken nervure of life.' Foucault, *The Birth of the Clinic*, pp. 166 ff.

182. 'Here, then, by means of dialectics, simply becoming clear about the nature of life and death suffices to abolish an ancient superstition. Living means dying.' *Dialectics of Nature*, Notes and Fragments, *MECW* 25: 572. For a partial rehabilitation of the Romantics' *Naturphilosophie*, especially Oken's vitalist intuitions, see *Anti-Dühring*, p. 12; *Dialectics of Nature*, pp. 486, 488. On the connections between vitalism and Engels's conceptions of biology, which were essentially inspired by Haeckel, see Georges Canguilhem, *La connaissance de la vie*, 2nd edn, Paris, 1980, pp. 60 and *passim*, partially translated in *A Vital Rationalist: Selected Writings from Georges Canguilhem*, ed. François Delaporte, trans. Arthur Goldhammer, New York, 1994, pp. 168–73.

183. On the relationship between Claude Bernard and Bichat (Bichat's definition is clearly more agonistic than Bernard's), see Canguilhem, 'Claude Bernard et Bichat', in *Études d'histoire et de philosophie des sciences*, Paris, 1983, pp. 156–62; 'La nouvelle connaissance de la vie', pp. 355 ff.

184. This is yet another constant in Engels's work. In his *Principles of Communism* (1847), he fully endorses Fourier's idea of building 'large palaces' to be scattered over the national territory; they would combine agricultural and industrial activity, and put an end to the division between city and country (*MECW* 6: 351). In *The Housing Question* (1872), he again refers to these ideas of Fourier's and Owen's, envisaging uniform distribution of the population across the country (*MECW* 23: 347, 384–5). He continues in the same vein in *Anti-Dühring* (1878): in order to overcome the city/country split, he says there, it is necessary to go beyond the city, taking Fourier's and Owen's ideas on the subject as one's guide (*Herr Eugen Dühring's Revolution in Science, MECW* 25: 279).

185. On this point, see Hélène Desbrousses and Bernard Peloille, 'Le "Communisme consanguin" dans *L'origine de la famille, de la propriété privée et de l'État'*, *Cahiers pour l'analyse concrète*, no. 30–31, 1993. This aspect of Engels's communitarian nostalgia, fully congruent with the impolitic imagery of the quasi-natural 'extinction' of the state, is reason enough to temper, at least, the re-evaluation of the Romantic vein in Marxism proposed by Michael Löwy (see his *Marxisme et romantisme révolutionnaire*, Paris, 1979).

186. Engels, *The Origin of the Family, Private Property and the State, MECW* 26: 254–6.

187. Ibid., p. 254.

188. The expression 'the war of the poor against the rich', or its equivalents, runs through *The Condition* from beginning to end. See, for example, Engels, *Condition, MECW* 4: 510, 512, 513, 570, 581.

189. Foucault, *'Il faut défendre'*, pp. 57, 69, 71.

190. 'What a sight! This infinitely proceeding division of society into the most manifold races opposed to one another by petty antipathies, uneasy consciences and brutal mediocrity, and which, precisely because of their reciprocal ambiguous and distrustful attitude, are all, without exception although with various formalities, treated by their *rulers* as *licensed existences!*' Marx, 'Contribution to the Critique of Hegel's Philosophy of Law. Introduction', *MECW* 3: 177–8.

191. See Marx, 'Second Address of the General Council of the International Working-Men's Association on the Franco–Prussian War', *MECW* 22: 267.
192. Ibid.
193. For details, see Gilbert Achcar, 'Engels, penseur de la guerre, penseur de la révolution', in Labica and Delbraccio, *Friedrich Engels*, pp. 139–60.
194. In his 11–12 December 1884 letter to August Bebel, Engels, before taking up the military aspect of the proletariat's battle to win power, describes himself 'as [the] representative, so to speak, of the party's General Staff' (*MECW* 47: 234). His interlocutors saw him in the same light. As Wilhelm Liebknecht put it: 'if there had been another revolution in his lifetime, we would have had in Engels our Carnot, the organizer of armies and victories, the military brain' (Wilhelm Liebknecht, 'Reminiscences of Engels', in *Marx and Engels through the Eyes of Their Contemporaries*, trans, anon., Moscow, 1972, p. 97).
195. On the importance, which is systematically underestimated, of this major shift in Engels's thinking, see the indispensable analysis in Jacques Texier, *Révolution et démocratie chez Marx et Engels*, Paris, 1998.
196. Engels, Introduction (1895) to *The Class Struggles in France*, *MECW* 27: 512. Later, Engels compares Social Democracy to a ' "decisive shock force" [*Gewalthaufen:* "shock troops" would be the more accurate translation, as is noted by Achcar, 'Engels', p. 156] of the international proletarian army' (ibid., p. 521). The model of the party-as-army recurs constantly in Engels's last texts. See, for example, his 23 May 1890 article on the English workers' movement ('May 4 in London', *MECW* 48: 66).
197. 'The workman . . . has a clearer eye for facts as they are than the bourgeois, and does not look at everything through the spectacles of personal selfishness. His faulty education saves him from religious prepossessions, he does not understand religious questions, does not trouble himself about them, knows nothing of the fanaticism that holds the bourgeoisie bound. . . .' Engels, *Condition*, *MECW* 4: 421. 'The cultivation of the understanding . . . is wanting in the working-man, whose passions are therefore strong and mighty as those of the foreigner. English nationality is annihilated in the working-man.' Ibid., pp. 501–2.
198. Ibid., pp. 329–30.
199. Marx, 'Contribution to the Critique of Hegel's Philosophy of Law. Introduction', *MECW* 3: 177–8. See also Hegel, *Elements of the Philosophy of Right*, §289, p. 329.
200. Notably, the Marx who comments on this paragraph at length in the Kreuznach manuscript (Marx, 'Contribution to the Critique of Hegel's Philosophy of Law', *MECW* 3: 41–2).
201. Hobbes clearly distinguishes 'the Battell . . . or the act of fighting' from 'the known disposition' or 'the inclination' towards rivalry; this 'inclination', which he considers permanent, is enough to justify speaking of a state of non-peace, and thus of the peculiar sort of sustained conflictuality that he calls 'the warre of every man against every man'. Thomas Hobbes, *Leviathan*, ed. C.B. Macpherson, Harmondsworth, 1981, pp. 185–6. See Foucault's remarks in '*Il faut défendre*', pp. 7 ff.
202. Engels, *Condition*, *MECW* 4: 427; emphasis added.
203. 'Meanwhile, the development of the nation goes its way whether the bourgeoisie has eyes for it or not, and will surprise the property-holding class one day with things not dreamed of in its philosophy.' Ibid.
204. Engels falls back on the notion of *slavery* to designate the dissymmetry constitutive of the relationship of domination based, in his view, on *competition* between proletarians. See Engels, *Condition*, *MECW* 4: 379. Here, obviously, we are in a theoretical space that is very different from the one marked off by the analyses of real subsumption that Marx undertakes in *Capital*.
205. He first used the term late in 1794. See Grandjonc, *Communisme*, vol. 1, p. 71.
206. Babeuf, *Le Tribun*, vol. 2, no. 34, pp. 11–14, cited in Grandjonc, *Communisme*, vol. 1, pp. 64–6.

207. Grandjonc (*Communisme*, vol. 1, p. 70) highlights Saint-Simon's contribution to the development of the idea of 'class struggle'.
208. Victor Considérant, 'Manifeste', *La Démocratie pacifique*, 1 August 1843, p. 2; cited in Grandjonc, *Communisme*, vol. 2, pp. 373–4.
209. Tocqueville seems to waver between a more general theory of 'equal opportunity', where the clock is set back to zero with each new generation – i.e. a state of maximum social mobility (Alexis de Tocqueville, *Democracy in America*, trans. George Lawrence, Garden City, NY, 1969, vol. 1, pp. 50–5) – and a more concrete theory of a neo-Aristotelian kind, hinging on the expansion and stabilization of a fundamentally conservative middle class – i.e. a state of tendential immobility presaging Weber's 'iron cage' (ibid., vol. 2, ch. 21, pp. 634–45; this chapter bears the significant title 'Why Great Revolutions Will Become Rare').
210. Tocqueville, too, is compelled to take a position on the agonistic schemes of the struggle between the classes/races – which he rejects altogether. Ibid., vol. 2, p. 635.
211. Albert Soboul has demonstrated *ad abudantam* that the *extension* of the term 'aristocrats' and the signifiers associated with it 'to the upper strata of what had been the Third Estate', above all *to the bourgeoisie*, was constitutive of the discourse and practice of the *sans-culottes*: 'this helps to underline the separate and distinct character of their contribution to the revolution' (Soboul, *The Parisian Sans-Culottes and the French Revolution, 1793–1794*, trans. Gwynne Lewis, Oxford, 1964, pp. 21–2; emphasis added). Soboul goes on to say that 'extreme sans-culottes no longer used the word "aristocrat" to designate the former nobility, but the bourgeoisie' (ibid., p. 22).
212. Engels, *Condition*, *MECW* 4: 500; the emphasis is in the original, but not in the English translation.
213. Ibid., p. 411.
214. Engels, *Condition*, *MECW* 4: 298.
215. 'Since . . . no single field for the exercise of his manhood is left him, save his opposition to the whole conditions of his life, it is natural that exactly in this opposition he should be most manly, noblest, most worthy of sympathy.' Engels, *Condition*, *MECW* 4: 502. See also ibid., pp. 420f.
216. Ibid., p. 500.
217. Ibid., p. 501.
218. See Chapter 2 above: 'The revolution as the right of (and to) life'.
219. Here I draw on the work of Jean Robelin, who notes the permanence of this line of argument in *Anti-Dühring*. Robelin, 'Engels', in Labica and Delbraccio, *Friedrich Engels*, p. 46.
220. The leaders of the popular movement, under the influence of Rousseau's contractualism, naturally adopted the idea that these were equivalent concepts. See especially the definition of the pact in Jean-Jacques Rousseau, *The Social Contract and Discourses*, trans. G.D.H. Cole *et al.*, London, 1993, Book 1, Chapter 6, pp. 190–93.
221. A speech Babeuf made as he was getting ready to launch his *Manifeste des plébéiens* (November 1795) provides an exemplary illustration of this series of determinations. See *Le Tribun*, vol. 2, no. 34, pp. 11–14, cited in Grandjonc, *Communisme*, pp. 63–6.
222.
Their objects [in forming associations; here, trade unions] were to deal, *en masse*, as a power, with the employers; to regulate the rate of wages according to the profit of the latter, to raise it when opportunity offered, and to keep it uniform in each trade throughout the country. Hence they tried to settle with the capitalists a scale of wages to be universally adhered to, and ordered out on strike the employees of such individuals as refused to accept the scale. (Engels, *Condition*, *MECW* 4: 504)
223.
What gives these Unions . . . their real importance is this, that they are the first attempt of the workers to abolish competition. They imply the recognition of the fact that the supremacy of the bourgeoisie is based wholly upon the competition of

the workers among themselves, i.e., upon their want of cohesion and the setting of individual workers against one another. (Ibid., p. 507 and n.)

224.

The laws determining the rate of wages would, indeed, come into force again in the long run, if the working-men did not go beyond this step of abolishing competition among themselves. But they must go beyond that unless they are prepared to recede again and to allow competition among themselves to reappear. Thus once advanced so far, necessity compels them to go farther; to abolish not only one kind of competition, but competition itself altogether, and that they will do. . . . They will soon learn *how* they have to go about it. (Ibid., pp. 507–8)

225. Ibid., p. 507 and n.
226. Ibid., pp. 526–7.
227. Ibid., p. 524; the emphasis is in the original, but not in the English translation.
228.

In its present form, Socialism can never become the common creed of the working-class. . . . But the true proletarian Socialism having passed through Chartism, purified of its bourgeois elements, assuming the form which it has already reached in the minds of many Socialists and Chartist leaders (who are nearly all Socialists), must, within a short time, play a weighty part in the history of the development of the English people. (Ibid., p. 526)

229. Ibid., p. 309. Engels goes on: 'as in France politics, so in England manufacture and the movement of civil society in general drew into the whirl of history the last classes which had remained sunk in apathetic indifference to the universal interests of mankind'.
230. Engels, *Condition*, *MECW* 4: 320. It is easy to see what the term 'industrial revolution' implied, thanks to Engels's work, and what the English liberal or even radical opposition had sought to escape in avoiding it. See Stedman Jones, '*Industrie*, Pauperisme'.
231. Ibid., p. 512.
232. Ibid.
233. This explains why Engels feels compelled to offer counter-arguments about the legalism of the English, the absence of revolutionary traditions in the English proletariat, etc.
234. See Chapter 2 above: 'Political revolution, social revolution'.
235. See Sylvie Aprile, 'L'Europe en révolution', in *La révolution de 1848 en France et en Europe*, Paris, 1998, p. 187.
236. Nairn, *The Enchanted Glass*, pp. 206–7.
237. See Engels's retrospective essay of June 1885, published in *Neue Zeit* ('England in 1845 and in 1885', *MECW* 26: 295–301); his May 1872 text on the relations between the Irish sections and the British Federal Council ('Relations between the Irish and the British Federal Council', *MECW* 23: 153–6); the articles published in *The Labour Standard* of May–June 1881 on the English workers' movement (*MECW* 24: 376–88); the article of May 1890 published in the *Arbeiter Zeitung* ('May 4 in London', *MECW* 48: 61–6); and various letters, especially those of 17 June 1879 to Edouard Bernstein, *MECW* 45: 360–61; 12 September 1882 to Karl Kautsky, *MECW* 46: 322; 30 August 1883 to August Bebel, *MECW* 47: 54; 11 September 1892 to Laura Lafargue, in Friedrich Engels, *Paul et Laura Lafargue, Correspondance*, Paris, 1959, vol. 3, pp. 205–7).
238. Engels, *Principles of Communism*, p. 352.
239. Ibid., p. 356.
240. Marx and Engels, *Manifesto of the Communist Party*, *MECW* 6: 519. This point is emphasized in Levin, *The Condition of England*, p. 149.
241. See Derrida, *Specters of Marx*, *passim*; Chapter 2 above: 'Exorcizing the spectres'.
242. Engels, *Condition*, *MECW* 4: 322–3.
243. Ibid., pp. 322–3 and nn.
244. Ibid., p. 581.
245. This is why it is quite impossible to maintain, as Stedman Jones does ('Voir et entendre') that Engels makes use of an (antinomical) Carlylean distinction between word and

deed, typical of an irrationalist conception of collective action, which leads Carlyle to contrast 'the chit-chat of [French] philosophers' with the 'the terrifying eruption of the *sans-culottes*' (ibid., p. 17; see Thomas Carlyle, *The French Revolution*, Oxford, 1989, pp. 35–9). Stedman Jones very quickly forgets that Engels 'speaks German', although he highlights the fact earlier in his essay, where his aim is to mock Engels's Feuerbachian humanism and Hegelian teleology.

246. Engels, *Condition*, *MECW* 4: 581–2; the emphasis is in the original, but not in the English translation.

247. Commenting on the sensibility surrounding the French culture of 1848, especially the fact that the bourgeois publishers and the press of the period did not ignore the social, or even semi-socialist, concerns of the day, and noting, as well, the populist tone of literature, the interest the social elites took in popular culture, and so on, Jean-Yves Mollier speaks of 'the ambiance of the day, which inclined the possessing classes to take part in the search for a compromise acceptable to all the social forces endeavouring to transform the country's economic structures'. 'La culture de 48', in *La révolution de 1848*, p. 156.

248. See Gérard Noiriel, *Les ouvriers dans la société française*, Paris, 1986, pp. 30–31.

249. As I pointed out in the introductory section of this chapter, this is clearly the explanation for Engels's many self-critical rectifications.

250. This note is, to be sure, somewhat confused. It is not clear whether Engels thinks that his original formulation should be abandoned for pragmatic reasons, or whether what is involved is, at the conceptual level, a 'bad abstraction'. Engels seems to be suggesting a historicist reading: although the principle he espoused was 'true enough in the abstract' during the French Revolution, it subsequently 'became a mere sentimentalism', and eventually 'disappeared from view altogether in the fire of the revolutionary struggle'. Preface to the second German edition of *The Condition of the Working-Class in England*, *MECW* 27: 314.

251. See Engels's fascinating letters of 22–26 February and 7 and 17 March 1845 to Marx, *MECW* 38: 21–30.

252. Engels, 'Speeches in Elberfeld', 15 February 1845, *MECW* 4: 263.

253. 'A social revolution is the consequence of competition.' Ibid., p. 258.

254. Ibid., p. 262.

255. Ibid., p. 263.

256. Ibid.; original emphasis.

257. Ibid., pp. 263–4.

258. After evoking the atmosphere of 'bigoted' 'piety' reigning under his familial roof, Engels tells Marx about the following incident: '*Pour comble de malheur* I spent yesterday evening with Hess in Elberfeld, where we held forth about communism until two in the morning. Today, of course, long faces over my late return, hints that I might have been in jug. Finally they plucked up enough courage to ask where I had been. – With Hess. – "With Hess! Great heavens!" Pause, intensified Christian dismay in their faces. – "What company you keep!" Sighs, etc.'. Engels, Letter of 17 March 1845 to Marx, *MECW* 38: 29.

5　Karl Marx: From the Public Sphere to Revolutionary Democracy, 1842–1844

1. Engels, Letter of 12 February 1851 to Marx, *MECW* 38: 287.

2. Cited in Sylvie Aprile, 'L'Europe en révolution', in Aprile *et al.*, *La révolution de 1848 en France et en Europe*, Paris, 1998, p. 188.

3. Louis Althusser, *For Marx*, trans. Ben Brewster, London and New York, 1990, p. 54.

4. Marx, Letter of September 1843 to Arnold Ruge, *MECW* 3: 142.
5. 'Whereas you are a *poet*, I am a *critic*, and for me the experiences of 1849 to 1852 are quite enough.' Marx, Letter of 29 February 1860 to Ferdinand Freiligrath, *MECW* 41: 82.
6.

> We see the young Marx at the same time change the *object* of his thought (roughly, he moves from Law to the State, then to Political Economy), change his *philosophical* position (he moves from Hegel to Feuerbach, then to a revolutionary materialism), and change his *political* position (he moves from radical bourgeois liberalism to petty-bourgeois humanism, then to communism). We can say that, in this process, in which the *object* occupies the front of the stage, it is the class (political) position that occupies the determinant place; but it is the philosophical position that occupies the central place, because it guarantees the theoretical relation between the political position and the object of Marx's thought. (Louis Althusser, 'On the Evolution of the Young Marx', in *Essays in Self-Criticism*, trans. Grahame Locke, London, 1976, pp. 158-9)

Let us also note that Althusser refuses to assign politics a 'central' place in order to preserve philosophy's pre-eminence in the field of theoretical mediation.
7. Jacques Rancière emphasizes this point: *La parole ouvrière 1830-1851*, Paris, 1976.
8. At the two extremes of this spectrum, which meet in their common rejection of the Hegelian moment, we find both Althusser, for whom 'the Young Marx was *never strictly speaking a Hegelian*, except in what was virtually the *last* text of his ideological-philosophical period [the *Manuscripts of 1844*]; rather, he was first a Kantian-Fichtean, then a Feuerbachian' (*For Marx*, p. 35; translation modified), and Miguel Abensour (*La démocratie contre l'État*, Paris, 1999, translation forthcoming), who, like many other students of the Young Hegelian movement, puts Marx in the tradition of a philosophy of the subject inspired by Fichte and Bauer.
9. Warren Breckman argues this very cogently: *Marx, the Young Hegelians, and the Origins of Radical Social Theory*, Cambridge, 1999.
10. This is where my reading diverges from Galvano Della Volpe's. Certainly, Della Volpe overemphasizes the break that comes with the texts of 1843 ('Una difficoltà per il compagno Althusser', in *Opere, a cura di Ignazio Ambrogio*, vol. 6, Rome, 1973, pp. 430–31; see also *Rousseau and Marx*, trans. John Fraser, London, 1978, pp. 162 ff.). However, the logical and methodological importance he assigns to it has nothing to do with politics. Moreover, he interprets it as a radical break with Hegel's hypostasized dialectic in favour of 'determinate abstractions'.
11. Marx, 'The Difference Between the Democritan and Epicurean Philosophy of Nature' (hereafter 'Difference'), *MECW* 1: 29.
12. As is already suggested by a poem Marx wrote in his youth, 'Feelings' (1836). It ends with these lines: 'Therefore let us risk our all, / Never resting, never tiring; / Not in silence dismal, dull, / Without action or desiring; / Not in brooding introspection / Bowed beneath a yoke of pain, / So that yearning, dream, and action [*die Tat*]/ Unfulfilled to us remain'. *MECW* 1: 526-7.
13. See Bauer's polemic, written in the period when he was closest to Marx: *The Trumpet of the Last Judgement Against Hegel the Atheist and Antichrist*, trans. Lawrence S. Stepelevich, Lewiston, NY, 1988.
14. Marx, 'Difference', p. 84.
15. Ibid.
16. In their genealogy of the concept of critique in Marx, Paul-Laurent Assoun and Gérard Raulet rightly point out that 'it is not possible to trace a direct line of descent from the philosophical content of the concept of critique in Kant to its content in Marx' (*Marxisme et théorie critique*, Paris, 1978, p. 44).
17. As Emmanuel Renault notes, 'this point was established once and for all in [Marx's] thought'. *Marx et l'idée de critique*, Paris, 1995, p. 34.

18. Marx, 'Difference', p. 87.
19. Marx's *bon mot* is well known: 'Schelling's philosophy is Prussian policy *sub speciæ philosophiæ.*' It occurs in a letter to Feuerbach in which Marx exhorts him to wage an open struggle against Schelling, a suggestion prudently declined by Feuerbach, who had already got his fingers burnt in run-ins with the Prussian authorities (Marx, extract from a letter of 3 October 1843 to Feuerbach, *MECW* 3: 350). Remarks of this sort were standard fare for the left of the day; see, for example, the judgement that Heine made as early as 1835 in *Religion and Philosophy in Germany* (in Heine, *Selected Prose*, ed. and trans. Ritchie Robertson, Harmondsworth, 1993, pp. 85 ff.). Engels, for his part, had already acquired a certain reputation among those vying to outdo one another in attacks on Schelling (see his two broadsides of 1842, 'Schelling and Revelation: Critique of the Latest Attempt of Reaction Against the Free Philosophy'; and 'Schelling, Philosopher in Christ; or, The Transfiguration of Worldly Wisdom into Divine Wisdom', *MECW* 2: 189–264). But Engels was incomparably less influential than Feuerbach.
20. Karl Löwith goes so far as to speak of a 'connection' between Schelling and the Young Hegelians (Löwith, *From Hegel to Nietzsche: The Revolution in Nineteenth-Century Thought*, trans. David E. Green, London, 1965, pp. 115–21). This is an exaggeration, to say the least. Löwith quotes extracts from Schelling's correspondence which indicate that Schelling was persuaded that he had carried the day against Hegel, since he had – at least implicitly – gained the support of Hegel's disciples, who even faithfully attended his lectures. Rosenkranz, although he was among the most loyal of Hegelians, likewise seems, to judge from his diary, to have been briefly carried away by the craze for Schelling (ibid., p. 186).
21. This is the point of departure for Feuerbach's essay 'Towards a Critique of Hegelian Philosophy', which appeared in Ruge's *Hallische Jahrbücher* in 1839, i.e. two years before Marx finished his dissertation. The essay found a large echo in Left Hegelian circles.
22. Whenever Marx talks about '*positive* philosophy', he plainly has Schelling in mind, but his remark about consciousnesses 'engaged merely in the act and immediate energy of development' (Marx, 'Difference', p. 86) seems to apply more directly to positions such as Cieszkowski's.
23. This 'liberalism' must not be confused with the deeply conservative liberalism of a Burke or even a Benjamin Constant, nor, *a fortiori*, with *liberismo*, i.e. economic liberalism (to fall back on a useful terminological distinction that can be made in Italian), even if certain Rhineland liberals (first and foremost David Hansemann) had positions rather similar to those of the 'liberists'. In fact, a number of disparate elements went to make up the foundations of the Rhenish liberalism in question here (a mixture of modern reformism destined for the elites and demands for equality before the law that were quite radical in the German context of the day). These different elements may be situated at the confluence of the ideas of the German Enlightenment and the French Revolution. They find their coherence in the practical functioning of this discursive ensemble, which was an ideological and political current rather than a doctrine in the strict sense. The indispensable work on the subject in French is still Jacques Droz, *Le libéralisme rhénan 1815–1848. Contribution à l'histoire du libéralisme allemand*, Paris, 1940.
24. It is Auguste Cornu's incontestable merit to have grasped the role this reliance on Hegel, especially in Marx's doctoral dissertation, played in setting Marx apart from the rest of the Young Hegelian movement, notably Bauer – this despite Marx's generally negative judgement of Hegel in his dissertation. See Auguste Cornu, *Karl Marx et Friedrich Engels. Leur vie, leur œuvre*, 4 vols, Paris, 1955–70, vol. 1, pp. 202–5, 272–5.
25. Marx, 'Difference', p. 44.
26. Ibid., p. 45.
27. On all these points, see Francine Markovits, *Marx dans le jardin d'Epicure*, Paris, 1974. By an odd circular effect, these features of Epicurean ontology, surging up out of Marxism's limbo, fascinated Althusser in his late quest for an 'aleatory materialism'

centred on singularity and the random encounter. See Louis Althusser, 'Le courant souterrain du matérialisme de la rencontre', in *Écrits philosophiques et politiques*, Paris, 1994, vol. 1, pp. 539–76.

28. Marx, 'Difference', p. 50.
29. Ibid., pp. 50–51.
30. Ibid., p. 52.
31. See Chapter 3 above: 'We Europeans . . .'.
32. See Jonathan Sperber, *Rhineland Radicals: The Democratic Movement and the Revolution of 1848*, Princeton, NJ, 1991, p. 6.
33. Ibid., p. 110.
34. See Lucien Calvié, 'Unité nationale et liberté politique', in Françoise Knopper and Gilbert Merlio, eds, *Naissance et évolution du libéralisme allemand*, Toulouse, 1995, p. 114.
35. Quoted in Pierre Lascoumes and Hans Zander, *Marx: Du 'vol de bois' à la critique du droit. Karl Marx à la Gazette Rhénane, naissance d'une méthede*, Paris, 1984, p. 75.
36. See, for example, Cornu, *Karl Marx*, vol. 2, pp. 142–3; and – for a more detailed, balanced treatment – Jacques Droz, *La formation de l'unité allemande, 1789–1871*, Paris, 1970, pp. 105–27. For Sperber, Rhenish society was 'thoroughly bourgeois', and 'structured around access to the market' (*Rhineland Radicals*, p. 32).
37. Sperber, *Rhineland Radicals*, p. 34.
38. Arno J. Mayer, *The Persistence of the Old Regime*, London, 1981.
39. For instance, Trier boasted 12,000 inhabitants when Marx came into the world there. As for the region's economic capital, Cologne, it had a population of a little over 70,000 when the *Rheinische Zeitung* was founded.
40. As Elisabeth Fehrenbach notes in 'La noblesse en France et en Allemagne' (in Helmut Berding *et al.*, eds, *La Révolution, la France et l'Allemagne. Deux modèles opposés de changement social?*, Paris, 1989, p. 187): 'the Westphalian and Rhenish aristocracies, after their integration into a Prussian state whose bureaucracy and military was not at all to their liking, succeeded in maintaining their internal cohesion and distinctive character thanks to the strength of their regional, aristocratic and family ties, as well as their common allegiance to the Catholic Church'.
41. Pierre Ayçoberry's portrait of the colonial bourgeoisie, supposedly one of the most advanced, is quite revealing (see *Cologne entre Napoléon et Bismarck. La croissance d'une ville rhénane*, Paris, 1981, esp. pp. 119–67). For an overview, see the studies by Hans-Ulrich Wehler and Ute Frevert in Berding *et al.*, eds, *La Révolution, la France et l'Allemagne*.
42. On the question of pauperization, see the data cited by Droz, *La formation*, pp. 111–12, 127–9) as well as Sperber's detailed discussion of the conflicting theses in *Rhineland Radicals*, pp. 34, 36.
43. Ibid., p. 92.
44. This held especially for the Historical School of Law.
45. Marx, 'The Philosophical Manifesto of the Historical School of Law', *MECW* 1: 206.
46. Marx, The Leading Article in No. 179 of the *Kölnische Zeitung* (hereafter 'Leading Article'), *MECW* 1: 201.
47. On this point, see Domenico Losurdo's insightful comments. Losurdo stresses the anti-liberal thrust of this notion in 'La construction du concept universel de l'homme: De la tradition libérale à la Révolution française', in B. Bourgeois and J. d'Hondt, eds, *La philosophie et la Révolution française*, Paris, 1984, pp. 49–58.
48. Hence its need to clothe itself in modern dress, and the use of pairs of contradictory expressions to characterize it. In Marx's view, Romantic discourse is characterized by the divergence between the modernity that serves it as a façade ('all these fragrant modern phrases') and its reactionary content. This explains why he can define the Romantic principle as 'Christian-knightly, modern-feudal' (Marx, 'Proceedings of the Sixth Rhine Province Assembly: First Article. Debates on Freedom of the Press' [hereafter 'Freedom of the Press'], *MECW* 1: 151–2).

49. Ibid., p. 137.
50. Sperber, *Rhineland Radicals*, p. 117.
51. It was, moreover, to Marx that Bruno Bauer addressed the following prophecies:

> The catastrophe will be terrible, and will go from bad to worse; I am even tempted to say that it will be greater and more phenomenal than the one touched off by the birth of Christianity. In view of that, what point is there in engaging in an interminable personal quarrel with blackguards? What is the good of showing dissatisfaction with that breed, when, in one's heart, one is not at all dissatisfied or annoyed or vexed? The future is all too certain for even a moment's hesitation. (Bruno Bauer, Letter of 5 April 1840 to Marx, *MEGA* III, 1, p. 346).

It is easy to see that there already exists, in Bauer, a tendency to dismiss the very down-to-earth constraints of the political struggle in the name of an 'all too certain future', guaranteed by the coming catastrophe.

52. Marx, 'The Supplement to Nos. 335 and 336 of the Augsburg *Allgemeine Zeitung* on the Commissions of the Estates in Prussia' (hereafter 'Supplement'), *MECW* 1: 300.
53. Marx, Leading Article, p. 196.
54. Marx, 'Comments on the Latest Prussian Censorship Instruction' (hereafter 'Censorship'), *MECW* 1: 109–31.
55. Ibid., p. 131.
56. See Marx, [Renard's Letter to Oberpräsident von Schaper, 17 November 1842], *MECW* 1: 283.
57. On all these points, see Chapter 1 above: 'A Foundation for Politics'.
58. Immanuel Kant, 'Perpetual Peace: A Philosophical Sketch', in *Political Writings*, ed. Hans S. Reiss, trans. H.B. Nisbet, 2nd edn, Cambridge, 1991, p. 126.
59. Ibid., p. 122.
60. G.W.F. Hegel, *Elements of the Philosophy of Right*, trans. H.B. Nisbet, ed. Allen Wood, Cambridge, 1991, §258, p. 275.
61. Ibid., §183, p. 221.
62. In a famous passage of *The German Ideology* (*MECW* 5: 93), Marx writes: 'the state of affairs in Germany at the end of the last century is fully reflected in Kant's *Kritik der practischen Vernunft* . . . the impotent German burghers did not get any further than "good will". Kant was satisfied with "good will" alone, even if it remained entirely without result, and he transferred the *realisation* of this good will . . . to the *world beyond*.'
63. 'Civil society is the [stage of] difference which intervenes between the family and the state.' Hegel, *Elements of the Philosophy of Right*, §182, addition, p. 220.
64. Ibid., §187, p. 224.
65. Ibid., §183, p. 221.
66. See Chapter 1 above: 'Superseding the Revolution?'.
67. See Hegel, *Elements of the Philosophy of Right*, §253 and §255, pp. 271–3.
68. For Marx, the Provincial Assemblies are, given the principle they are based on, simply machines for preserving special privileges and producing new ones. See Marx, 'Freedom of the Press', pp. 146–7.
69. 'It is integral to the definition [*Bestimmung*] of the *universal* estate – or more precisely, the estate which devotes itself to the *service of the government* – that the universal is the end of its essential activity'. Hegel, *Elements of the Philosophy of Right*, §303, p. 343.
70. See Marx, 'Justification of the Correspondent from the Mosel', *MECW* 1: 343–6.
71. It was, indeed, the government's inability to relieve the distress of the people, especially the Mosel vine-growers, which gave rise to Marx's reflections. Ibid., p. 346.
72. See Chapter 1 above: 'A Foundation for Politics?'.
73. Marx, 'Censorship', p. 116.
74. Ibid., p. 113.
75. Marx, 'Freedom of the Press', p. 178.
76. Marx, 'Justification of the Correspondent from the Mosel', p. 333. Marx spelled out

what he meant in reply to a speaker in the Assembly who had proposed to outlaw anonymous publications: 'we would point out that in the press it is not the *name* that matters, but that, where a press law is in force, the publisher, and through him the anonymous and pseudonymous writer as well, is liable to prosecution in the courts'. Marx, 'Freedom of the Press', p. 178.

77. Marx, 'Justification of the Correspondent from the Mosel', p. 334.
78. 'Although the mention of names', Marx hastens to add, 'is not permitted in the Diets.' Marx, Letter of May 1843 to Arnold Ruge, *MECW* 3: 140.
79. See Marx, Letter of 5 March 1842 to Arnold Ruge, *MECW* 1: 382.
80. Marx, Letter of September 1843 to Arnold Ruge, *MECW* 3: 145.
81. Heinrich Heine, *On the History of Religion and Philosophy in Germany*, in *Selected Prose*, ed. and trans. Ritchie Robertson, Harmondsworth, 1993, p. 269.
82. This is the title of Book II of Heine's *Ludwig Börne*.
83. Marx, 'Leading Article', p. 195.
84. Ibid., p. 202.
85. Ibid., p. 196.
86. Marx, 'Freedom of the Press', p. 140.
87. Marx, 'Leading Article', p. 201.
88. Ibid.
89. Ibid., p. 192.
90. Marx, 'Justification of the Correspondent from the Mosel', pp. 348–9.
91. Feuerbach develops a doctrine of the head and the heart which, it must be said, is rather confused. He associates the head with the 'French', feminine attributes (sensitivity, dependence, materialism) and the heart with 'German', masculine traits (initiative, independence, idealism). For Feuerbach, 'the true philosopher, the philosopher *identical with life* and *human being*, must be of Franco-German descent'. Feuerbach, 'Provisional Theses for the Reformation of Philosophy', trans. Daniel O. Dahlstrom, in Lawrence S. Stepelevich, ed., *The Young Hegelians: An Anthology*, New York, 1983, p. 164.
92. Marx, 'The Ban on the *Leipziger Allgemeine Zeitung*', *MECW* 1: 313.
93. Marx, 'Freedom of the Press', pp. 164–5.
94. Ibid., pp. 167–8.
95. See Hegel, *Elements of the Philosophy of Right*, §253, pp. 271–2.
96. Marx, 'Justification of the Correspondent from the Mosel', p. 333.
97. 'Truth includes not only the result but also the path to it. The investigation of truth must itself be true; true investigation is developed truth, the dispersed elements of which are brought together in the result. And should not the manner of investigation alter according to the object?' Marx, 'Censorship', p. 113.
98. Marx, 'The Ban on the *Leipziger Allgemeine Zeitung*', pp. 313–14.
99. Marx, 'Freedom of the Press', p. 143. Marx goes on to emphasize the anti-aristocratic, universalistic thrust of his reference to a national/popular principle.
100. See Hegel, *Elements of the Philosophy of Right*, §258 and §270, pp. 275, 292.
101. Marx, Leading Article, p. 193.
102. Thus I disagree with Miguel Abensour, who maintains that 'to call the state "the great organism", to position it beyond all derivation, is to admit in the same breath its primacy and to establish it in the very site of the institution of the social sphere' (Abensour, *La démocratie contre l'état*, p. 25. The translation is Max Blechman's).
103. In the sense defined by Antonio Negri, who turns the conception of the constitutionalist tradition upside down: 'constituent power is tied to the notion of democracy as absolute power. Thus, as a violent and expansive force, constitutive power is a concept connected to the social preconstitution of the democratic totality' (Antonio Negri, *Insurgencies: Constituent Power and the Modern State*, trans. Maurizia Boscagli, Minneapolis, MN, 1999, p. 10).
104. Marx, 'Freedom of the Press', p. 137.
105. Ibid.

106. Ibid., p. 180.
107. See Sperber, *Rhineland Radicals, passim.*
108. Marx, Letter of 25 August 1842 to Dagobert Oppenheim, *MECW* 1: 392.
109. Sperber, *Rhineland Radicals*, p. 92.
110. See, for example, Cornu's 'classic' account of Marx's development in *Karl Marx*, vol. 2, p. 1.
111. Marx, 'Supplement', p. 292.
112. Marx, 'Proceedings of the Sixth Rhine Province Assembly. Third Article. Debates on the Law on Thefts of Wood' (hereafter 'Thefts of Wood)', *MECW* 1: 241.
113. 'It will be found that the customs which are customs of the entire poor class are based with a sure instinct on the *indeterminate* aspect of property; it will be found not only that this class feels an urge to satisfy a natural need, but equally that it feels the need to satisfy a rightful urge.' Ibid., pp. 233–4.
114. Marx, 'Justification of the Correspondent from the Mosel', p. 349.
115. Ibid., p. 351.
116. Marx, 'Thefts of Wood', p. 261.
117. Marx's main argument is encapsulated in his observation that there is a basic asymmetry between the customary rights of the aristocracy, which adopts the forms of modern law only to abolish its content, and the customary rights of the poorer classes, which, even when they are in contradiction with positive law, anticipate the universality of a law based on the freedom and equality of its subjects. Ibid., p. 232.
118. See Florence Gauthier's studies: 'De Mably à Robespierre', in Thompson *et al., La guerre du blé au XVIIème siècle,* Paris, 1988, pp. 11–143; *Triomphe et mort du droit naturel en Révolution,* Paris, 1992.
119. This point, which is generally neglected, is emphasized by Florence Gauthier, 'Critique du concept de "révolution bourgeoise" appliqué aux révolutions des droits of l'homme et du citoyen du XVIIème siècle', *Actuel Marx*, no. 20, 1996, p. 157, and Domenico Losurdo, 'La construction du concept universel d'homme de la tradition libérale à la Révolution française', in Bourgeois and d'Hondt, *La Philosophie et la Révolution française,* pp. 54–5.
120. Marx, 'Supplement', *op. cit.*, p. 305.
121. See Chapter 4 above: 'From the "Social" to "Socialism": The great romance of organization'.
122. See Marx, Letter of September 1843 to Arnold Ruge, p. 143.
123. Marx first took a public stand on the question in reaction to an article in the *Augsburger Allgemeine Zeitung.* See Marx, 'Communism and the Augsburg Allgemeine Zeitung', *MECW* 1: 219.
124. Marx, 'Supplement', p. 306.
125. Louis Antoine de Saint-Just, *Discours et rapports,* ed. Albert Soboul, Paris, 1957, p. 74.
126. Marx, 'Freedom of the Press', p. 143.
127. No doubt the most significant is to be found in the conclusion to the articles on the deliberations of the Sixth Rhine Province Assembly. Here Marx makes use of the classic technique of the art of writing under a regime of censorship that consists in citing the words of an author who is above suspicion – in this instance, the Spartans' reply to the Persian satrap Hydarnes, as reported by Herodotus: ' "You know what it means to be a slave, but you have never yet tried freedom, to know whether it is sweet or not. For if you had tried it, you would have advised us to fight for it, not merely with spears, but also with axes." ' Ibid., p. 181.
128. Ibid., p. 167.
129. Ibid., p. 180.
130. See Feuerbach, 'Provisional Theses for the Reformation of Philosophy', in Stepelevich, ed., *The Young Hegelians*, pp. 164–5.
131. Marx, 'Freedom of the Press', p. 172. Marx, as later texts show, was fascinated by these metaphors: in 'Critique of Hegel's Philosophy of Law. Introduction' (*MECW* 3: 187), he

was to repeat: 'The *head* of this [human] emancipation is *philosophy*, its *heart* is the proletariat.'

132. See Marx, Letter to Dagobert Oppenheim of 25 August 1842, p. 392.
133. Marx, 'Supplement', p. 297.
134. Ibid.
135. Lucien Calvié rightly emphasizes that even the Marx of the *Rheinische Zeitung* was influenced by the reformism of the Young Hegelians 'to the extent that his criticisms of the Prussian state set out from the idea that this state can be reformed, that it is capable of repudiating its reactionary, repressive orientation, returning to its Enlightenment traditions, and, what is more, pursuing the achievements of the Revolutionary and Napoleonic periods in a Rhineland particularly favourable to such developments' (Lucien Calvié, *Le renard et les raisins. La Révolution française et les intellectuels alemands, 1789–1845*, Paris, 1989, p. 133).
136. 'Or does the lady of Augsburg resent our correspondent's expectation that the undeniable collision will be solved "in a *peaceful* way"?' Marx, 'Communism and the Augsburg *Allgemeine Zeitung*', p. 219.
137. Letter of May 1843 to Arnold Ruge, p. 139.
138. Thus Moses Hess, one of the paper's main collaborators, wrote on 6 December 1842 to his friend Auerbach that 'the position of the *Rheinische Zeitung* is now assured, *vis-à-vis* the public as well as the government. It's true that we had a bit of a to-do with the government not long ago, but now everything has been sorted out without our having to make any concessions' (cited in Cornu, *Karl Marx*, vol. 2, p. 91).
139. Lascoumes and Zander, *Du vol de bois, op. cit.*, p. 59.
140. See Cornu, *Karl Marx*, vol. 2, p. 111.
141. Although it had only a few hundred subscribers when it was launched, the *Rheinische Zeitung* boasted 1,820 when Von Schaper wrote to the Minister, according to information he himself cites in his report. The list of subscribers included some 3,400 names shortly before the paper was banned (ibid., p. 99).
142. Marx, Letter of 25 January 1843 to Ruge, *MECW* 1: 397.
143. 'Germany is a state no longer.' Hegel, 'The German Constitution' (manuscript of 1799–1801), in *Hegel's Political Writings*, trans. T.M. Knox, Oxford, 1964, p. 143. Louis Althusser observes that, in this text, 'Hegel adopts the accents of Machiavelli speaking of Italy' (*Machiavelli and Us*, ed. François Matheron, trans. Gregory Elliott, London and New York, 1999, p. 9).
144. On solitude as a condition for taking political initiatives in times of crisis, see the text by Althusser cited above; and Louis Althusser, 'Machiavelli's Solitude', trans. Ben Brewster, in *Machiavelli and Us*, pp. 115–30.
145. Marx, Letter of March 1843 to Arnold Ruge, CW 1: 133; translation modified.
146. See Antonio Negri's suggestive remarks in *The Savage Anomaly: The Power of Spinoza's Metaphysics and Politics*, trans. Michael Hardt, Minneapolis, MN, 1991, ch. 1: 'The Dutch Anomaly', pp. 3–21.
147. Marx, Letter of March 1843 to Arnold Ruge, p. 133.
148. I am in basic agreement with Lucien Calvié's thesis; his work sheds considerable light on this question (see Calvié, *Le renard et les raisins*, p. 135).
149. This is the shortcoming of Harold Mah's interpretation (*The End of Philosophy, The Origin of Ideology: Karl Marx and the Crisis of the Young Hegelians*, Berkeley, CA, 1987), which nevertheless has the merit of taking the critical year 1843 as the focus of the twin crises of the Young Hegelians and the absolutist Prussian regime.
150. Marx, Letter of March 1843 to Arnold Ruge, p. 134.
151. See Michel Foucault, *Madness and Civilization: A History of Insanity in the Age of Reason*, trans. Richard Howard, New York, 1973, p. 11. The *flâneur*, who also finds himself poised on a threshold, might similarly be regarded as a figure descended from this archetype of the wanderer, albeit a somewhat more 'civilized' and 'disciplined' one.
152. Ibid.

153. See Chapter 2 above: 'Waiting for dawn: The German revolution between dream and reality'.
154. To describe this 'new life', Marx borrows a metaphor from Heine's spectrology: 'let the dead bury their dead and mourn them. On the other hand, it is enviable to be the first to enter the new life alive; that is to be our lot'. Marx, Letter of May 1843 to Arnold Ruge, p. 134.
155. Ibid., p. 141.
156. 'You will not say that I have had too high an opinion of the present time; and if, nevertheless, I do not despair of it, that its only because it is precisely the desperate situation that fills me with hope.' Ibid.
157. Marx, Letter of September 1843 to Arnold Ruge, *op. cit.*, p. 142. Ruge, for his part, had already written that 'at any rate, the cause must be grasped by the roots; that is, only philosophy can attain and grasp freedom'. 'A Self-Critique of Liberalism', trans. James A. Massey, in Stepelevich, ed., *The Young Hegelians*, p. 257.
158. In his letter of September 1843 to Ruge (pp. 142–3), Marx again contends that the 'actually existing' communist doctrines are ultimately only 'dogmatic abstraction[s]' that seek to resolve the contradictions of the real world a priori.
159. Ibid., p. 142.
160. Ibid.
161. Marx and Engels, *The German Ideology*, *MECW* 5: 49.
162. Marx, 'Censorship', p. 113.
163. Marx, Letter of September 1843 to Arnold Ruge, p. 144.
164. See Eduard Bernstein, *The Preconditions of Socialism*, trans. Henry Tudor, Cambridge, 1993, p. 190 and *passim*.
165. Moreover, to overcome – if only in regulatory fashion – the dualism that weighs heavily on his system, Bernstein is forced to distinguish the 'higher level of economy and of social life as a whole', towards which everything has to tend, despite all, from the 'more immediate objectives' which nevertheless 'point to' it (ibid., p. 209).
166. Marx, Letter of September 1843 to Arnold Ruge, p. 145.
167. Ibid., p. 144.
168. Significantly, in one of the last articles to appear in his review, Ruge takes aim at Kant, without naming him – or rather, at a certain Kantian spirit typical of this Germanic liberalism: 'whoever is sympathetic', he says, 'watches the battle going on out the window and wishes good luck and blessings on all the heroes of freedom' (Ruge, 'A Self-Critique of Liberalism', p. 242). Thus Marx's critique of Kant in *The German Ideology*, which focuses on the powerlessness of the petty bourgeoisie, has nothing very original about it, at least as far as the language it is couched in is concerned.
169. But let us not forget Engels's surprise when he discovered that the manuscript of *The Holy Family*, Marx's reply to the 'critical criticism' of Bauer and company, had assumed proportions rather reminiscent of the prolixity of the Young Hegelians. See Engels, Letter written *c.* 20 January 1845 to Marx, *MECW* 38: 18.
170. Marx, Letter of May 1843 to Arnold Ruge, p. 141.
171. See Ruge, 'A Self-Critique of Liberalism', pp. 254–5, which excoriates the 'blasé consciousness', overly cultivated and self-satisfied, of the Berlin *Freien*.
172. Marx, 'Contribution to the Crtitique of Hegel's Philosophy of Law. Introduction', p. 181.
173. Ruge, 'A Self-Critique of Liberalism', p. 257.
174. 'In order to secure remission of its sins, mankind has only to declare them for what they actually are.' Marx, Letter of September 1843 to Arnold Ruge, p. 145.
175. Ruge, 'A Self-Critique of Liberalism', p. 259.
176. See. Marx, Letter of May 1843 to Arnold Ruge, pp. 134, 137.
177. Yet this theme makes an appearance in the Kreuznach manuscript, contemporaneous with Marx's correspondence with Ruge. See below: 'The origins of the permanent revolution: "true democracy"'.

178. See Marx, Letter of May 1843 to Arnold Ruge, p. 137.
179. Ibid., p. 139.
180. Ibid., p. 138.
181. 'The critic not only can, but must deal with these political questions (which according to the extreme Socialists are altogether unworthy of attention). In analysing the superiority of the representative system over the social-estate system, the critic in a practical way wins the interest of a large party.' Marx, Letter of September 1843 to Arnold Ruge, p. 144.
182. The anti-political position of 'true socialism', at the heart of the polemic in the *Communist Manifesto*, had a bright future ahead of it in the German workers' movement. Let us recall only the Lassallians' attempts to promote social reform through accommodation with Bismarck's regime, and the now unified Social-Democracy's abandonment, at the Congress of Erfurt (1891), of the call for a 'German republic'. Engels issued a sharp warning against dropping this slogan in his 'Critique of the Erfurt Programme' ('Critique of the Draft Social-Democratic Programme of 1891', *MECW* 27: 217–32; see especially pp. 227–8).
183. At the moment of the autumn 1842 break between the *Freien* and Marx, who had become editor-in-chief of the *Rheinische Zeitung*, Ruge sided with Marx; see Cornu, *Karl Marx*, vol. 2, p. 89. At the same moment, and for similar reasons, the poet Georg Herwegh also broke with the 'Free' in Berlin.
184. This did not escape the attention of the keenest observers, such as Herwegh, who, from the moment the first and only issue of the *Deutsch–Französische Jahrbücher* appeared, detected a 'flagrant contradiction' between Ruge's 'doctrinaire' introduction and Marx's 'incomparably *more striking*' articles. He saw in this contradiction the seeds of a 'new break', a 'new split' between these two tendencies (M. d'Agoult, Letter of 25 February 1844, cited in Solange Mercier-Josa, *Théorie allemande et pratique française de la liberté*, Paris, 1993, pp. 291–2).
185. For Ruge, too, only intellectual differences have the right to an authentic existence. See Ruge, 'A Self-Critique of Liberalism', p. 248.
186. Marx, Letter of May 1843 to Arnold Ruge, p. 141.
187. Ibid.
188. Marx, Letter of September 1843 to Arnold Ruge, p. 143.
189. In his discussion of the political state, Marx in effect retraces the movement of the concept from 'presupposed' to 'posed': '[the political state] everywhere ... assumes that reason has been realized. But precisely because of that it everywhere becomes involved in the contradiction between its ideal function and its real prerequisites. From this conflict of the political state with itself, therefore, it is possible everywhere to develop the social truth.' Ibid.
190. Ibid.
191. Ibid., p. 144.
192. 'By raising the representative system from its political form to the universal form and by bringing out the true significance underlying this system, the critic at the same time compels this party to go beyond its own confines, for its victory is at the same time its defeat' (ibid.). In the process of self-transcendence set in motion when the democratic principle embodied in representative institutions is raised to its 'universal form', we have a first formulation of the theses on 'true democracy' that Marx was elaborating at the same time in his commentary on Hegel's *Elements of the Philosophy of Right* (the above-quoted letter to Ruge was written in Kreuznach).
193. In the Kreuznach manuscript, Marx was to clarify this position even further by talking about the 'annihilation of the political state' in so far as it is a '*merely* political state'. See below: 'Hegel beyond Hegel'.
194. Calvié, *Le renard et les raisins*, p. 136.
195. Marx, Letter of May 1843 to Arnold Ruge, p. 139.
196. Ibid., p. 138; translation modified.

197. 'In political affairs, the French have set the example', says Ruge in 'A Self-Critique of Liberalism', p. 256.
198. From Louis Althusser through Shlomo Avineri and Kostas Papaioannou to Maximilien Rubel, this is a point of convergence among writers whose interpretations of Marx are in other respects poles apart. Among the discordant voices are those of Solange Mercier-Josa, to whose work our reading is deeply indebted, and also André Tosel.
199. To say nothing of the fact that this novelty is illusory in as much as one can well and truly speak of a *Feuerbachian politics* (see below), even if there would appear to be little that is original about Feuerbach's *mélange* of Francophile republicanism and German faith in the omnipotence of ideas and the reformist approach.
200. Thus it is clear that even in Marx's first problematic, that of his 'youth', his object is specifically the *modern* state, the only one to rest on a separation between the social and political spheres. His concern is not a 'general theory of the state' – contrary to what Jean Robelin, for example, affirms in the wake of other Althusserian interpretations of Marx (Robelin, *Marxisme et socialisation*, Paris, 1989, pp. 127–51).
201. See above: 'From civil society to the state'.
202. Marx, Letter of September 1843 to Arnold Ruge, p. 143.
203. Marx, 'Critique of Hegel's Philosophy of Law. Introduction', p. 178.
204. Marx, 'Contribution to the Critique of Hegel's Philosophy of Law', p. 83 (hereafter 'Critique of Hegel's Philosophy of Law').
205. Marx, 'Critique of Hegel's Philosophy of Law. Introduction', p. 178, 181.
206. The 1844 Introduction was to make this point even more clearly.
207. Marx, 'Critique of Hegel's Philosophy of Law. Introduction', p. 175.
208. Ibid.
209. Marx, 'Critique of Hegel's Philosophy of Law', p. 7.
210. The source of Hegel's inversion of the subject/predicate relation is to be sought in this double movement of subjectivization of the Idea and reduction of the actual subjects (i.e. the people, as we shall see) to 'raw material' for the Idea. The accents of Feuerbach's critique reappear here. At the time, Feuerbach maintained that – for Hegel as well as for Spinoza – the Absolute (substance) was 'a mere name', a purely non-determined entity existing outside the categories that would make it possible to conceive it in one respect or another. See, for example, Feuerbach, 'Provisional Theses for the Reformation of Philosophy', p. 157. By turning Hegel's criticisms of Spinoza against Hegel, Feuerbach simply repeats and reinforces Hegel's misunderstandings of the Spinozan system – particularly the one that consists in reducing the attributes to external forms of reflection that have lost all connection with the substance from which they are descended. This is an important point. Marx, for his part, would refuse to treat the modern state as if it were merely unreal; he would insist on its practical dimension as a 'political illusion,' and try to plumb the mystery of the specific mechanisms that spawn it. On Hegel's reading of Spinoza, see Pierre Macherey's illuminating demonstration in *Hegel ou Spinoza*, Paris, 1979, esp. pp. 133–7, 175–80. Galvano Della Volpe had already pointed out the difference between Feuerbach's critique of Hegel, which he considered idealistic/Kantian, and Marx's (Della Volpe, 'Una difficoltà per il compagno Althusser', pp. 430–31).
211. Marx, 'Critique of Hegel's Philosophy of Law', pp. 8–9. As we shall see, it is because of this inversion, which is simply the abstract expression of a political inversion, that Hegel is unable to understand democracy as 'self-determination by the people'.
212. Ibid., p. 10.
213. See ibid., pp. 16–17.
214. Ibid., p. 12.
215. Ibid., p. 18.
216. Ibid., p. 39; translation modified. In his August 1842 essay 'Hegel's "Philosophy of Right" and the Politics of our Times' (in Stepelevich, ed., *The Young Hegelians*,

pp. 211–36), published in the *Deutsche Jahrbücher*, Arnold Ruge had already criticized Hegel's inversion of concept and historical existence, logic and empirical reality.

217. 'The correct method is stood on its head. The simplest thing becomes the most complicated, and the most complicated the simplest. What ought to be the starting point becomes a mystical outcome, and what ought to be the rational outcome becomes a mystical starting point.' Marx, 'Critique of Hegel's Philosophy of Law', p. 40.
218. Ibid., p. 39.
219. Ibid., p. 47.
220. Ibid., pp. 45–6.
221. 'Once the state actually comes to life and civil society frees itself from the corporations by its own radical impulse, the bureaucracy tries to restore them.' Ibid., p. 45.
222. This is the respect in which Marx's analysis of the political illusion goes beyond the Feuerbachian conception of alienation. Thus the Kreuznach manuscript anticipates the 'new concept of alienation' that Emmanuel Renault discerns in the *1844 Manuscripts*, a de-psychologized concept designating, not a non-correspondence internal to human consciousness, but the social reality that engenders this alienated consciousness (Renault, *Marx et l'idée de critique*, p. 59). It follows that Marx did not wait for the break of 1845–48 in order to pose the question of '*the reality* and historical efficacity characteristic of the instance of the state', *pace* Étienne Balibar ('État, parti, idéologie. Esquisse d'un problème', in Balibar *et al.*, *Marx et sa critique de la politique*, Paris, 1979, p. 131). The same criticism could be made of François Furet, who considers the early Marx a 'prisoner to the idea of the subordination of politics to civil society, unable to conceive of the autonomy of politics under any other form than that of illusion' (Furet, *Marx and the French Revolution*, trans. Deborah Kahn Furet, Chicago, 1988, p. 30).
223. Marx, 'Critique of Hegel's Philosophy of Law', p. 46.
224. Ibid., p. 47.
225. Hegel, *The Philosophy of History*, trans. J. Sibree, New York, 1956, p. 43.
226. 'This is the enigma of mysticism. . . . Hegel idealizes the bureaucracy and empiricizes public consciousness.' Marx, 'Critique of Hegel's Philosophy of Law', pp. 60–61.
227. Ibid., p. 127.
228. André Tosel, 'Les critiques de la politique chez Marx', in Balibar *et al.*, *Marx et sa critique de la politique*, p. 20.
229. Marx, 'Critique of Hegel's Philosophy of Law', p. 55.
230. 'The totality of the political state is the *legislature*.' Ibid., p. 118; see also ibid., p. 87.
231. Jacques Guilhaumou, 'Le jeune Marx et le langage jacobin', in Calvié, ed., *Révolutions françaises et pensée allemande 1789–1871*, Grenoble, 1989, p. 109.
232. In a sense not unlike that of 'constitutive power' as defined by Antonio Negri (*Insurgencies, passim*), as long as its absolute character is conceived as that of a process, not as the metaphysical emergence of an already constituted Subject.
233. Marx, 'Critique of Hegel's Philosophy of Law', p. 55; translation modified.
234. Ibid., p. 55.
235. 'According to the law (illusion) the constitution is, but according to reality (the truth) it *develops*. According to its definition the constitution is unalterable, but actually it is altered; only, this alteration is unconscious, it does not have the form of alteration. The *appearance* contradicts the *essence*.' Ibid.
236. Ibid.
237. Ibid., p. 57.
238. Ibid.
239. Abensour rightly emphasizes this (*La démocratie contre l'Etat*, p. 48). Shlomo Avineri makes a similar point; see Avineri, *The Social and Political Thought of Karl Marx*, Cambridge, 1968, pp. 32–3.
240. Marx, 'Die historisch-politische Zeitschrift von L. Ranke', MEGA 4/2: 177–86.
241. 'The constitution is nothing but a compromise between the political and the unpolitical

state. Hence, it is necessarily in itself a treaty between essentially heterogeneous powers.' Marx, 'Critique of Hegel's Philosophy of Law', p. 57.
242. Ibid., p. 119.
243. This is the nub of the argument made by, among many others, François Furet, for whom a 'true' revolution 'destroys the political by absorbing it in the social' (Furet, *Marx and the French Revolution*, p. 25). Furet assumes the relationship between the political and social revolutions to be simply contradictory; the links between the two seem to him to be external and purely instrumental (succession in time, with the political revolution serving as a stepping stone on the way to the social). See ibid., pp. 59–60 and, especially, 88–90.
244. Despite the reservations one may have about the disjunction between the social and the political that underlies Abensour's reading (we shall come back to this), his interpretation has the incontestable merit of clearly distinguishing between the Marxist position on the disappearance of the state as an autonomous, dominant sphere and the disappearance of the political as such (see Abensour, *La démocratie contre l'État*, pp. 76 ff.).
245. This is proved beyond the shadow of a doubt by Marx's annotations, made during the period he spent in Kreuznach, to a recently published German work on the French Revolution, C.F.E. Ludwig's *Geschichte der letzten 50 Jahre* (1834). See Jacques Guilhaumou, 'Note sur Marx, la Révolution française et le manuscrit de Kreuznach', in Étienne Balibar and Gérard Raulet, eds, *Marx démocrate. Le Manuscrit de 1843*, Paris, 2001, pp. 79–88.
246. Marx, 'Critique of Hegel's Philosophy of Law', p. 55.
247. See Chapter 1 above: 'Superseding the Revolution?'
248. Marx, 'Critique of Hegel's Philosophy of Law', p. 80.
249. Ibid., p. 75.
250. Ibid., p. 79; translation modified.
251. Ibid., p. 69.
252. Ibid., p. 79; translation modified. Here Marx uses the term *kommunistisch* ('communistic'; translated as 'communal' in *MECW*) in the Feuerbachian sense in which it designates man's communitarian essence, not in the political sense that the word has in his correspondence with Ruge. (The word does not occur anywhere else in the Kreuznach manuscript.) It is in this sense that Feuerbach called himself a 'communist', notably in his reply to Stirner. See Ludwig Feuerbach, '*The Essence of Christianity* in Relation to *The Ego and Its Own*', trans. Frederick M. Gordon, *The Philosophical Forum* 7, nos 2–4 (1977), p. 91.
253. Marx, 'Critique of Hegel's Philosophy of Law', p. 80.
254. 'It is an historical advance which has transformed the *political estates* into *social* estates, so that, just as the Christians are equal in heaven, but unequal on earth, so the individual members of the nation are *equal* in the heaven of their political world, but unequal in the earthly existence of *society*.' Ibid.
255. Ibid., p. 79.
256. 'It shows Hegel's profundity that he feels the separation of civil from political society as a *contradiction*.' Ibid., p. 75.
257. 'Hegel wants the medieval-estates system, but in the modern sense of the legislature, and he wants the modern legislature, but in the body of the medieval-estates system! This is the worst kind of syncretism.' Ibid., p. 95.
258. See ibid., pp. 84, 89.
259. Ibid., p. 95.
260. Ibid., p. 78.
261. Ibid., p. 79.
262. Ibid., p. 95. In his 1841 dissertation, Marx condemned the use of this term by Hegel's heirs (see *Difference*, p. 84, and above: 'The "party of the concept"'); yet he himself employs it here. Does he slip into making the kind of moral judgement for which he

has only recently criticized others? No doubt he considers himself immune from such criticism because he has done enough in the way of tracing Hegel's 'defect' back to the principle that is responsible for it.

263. Marx, 'Critique of Hegel's Philosophy of Law', pp. 120–21.

264. Della Volpe's Italian school has heavily emphasized this point in its reading of Marx. See Lucio Colletti's analysis of the Kreuznach manuscript in Colletti, *From Rousseau to Lenin: Studies in Ideology and Society*, London, 1972, pp. 256–9.

265. 'Civil society has really raised itself to abstraction from itself, to *political* being as its true, general, essential mode of being only in *elections* unlimited both in respect of the franchise and the right to be elected.' Marx, 'Critique of Hegel's Philosophy of Law', p. 121.

266. 'Political emancipation is, of course, a big step forward. True, it is not the final form of human emancipation in general, but it is the final form of human emancipation within the hitherto existing world order.' Marx, 'On the Jewish Question', *MECW* 3: 155.

267. 'We have seen above all that the first step in the revolution by the working class is to raise the proletariat to the position of ruling class, to win the battle of democracy.' Marx and Engels, *Manifesto of the Communist Party*, *MECW* 6: 504.

268. Marx, *The Civil War in France*, ch. 5, 'The Paris Commune', *MECW* 22: 334.

269. Marx's contemporaries make overabundant use of the word 'true'; doubtless they meant, like him, to call things by their true names at last. Thus Marx's 'true' democracy – a concept of which, to be sure, he made only 'private' use, employing it in the Kreuznach manuscript alone – had its counterpart in Grün's 'true socialism' or Bakunin's 'true communism', both of which (especially the first) enjoyed a genuine public existence. See Cornu, *Karl Marx*, vol. 2, p. 221.

270. Marx, 'Critique of Hegel's Philosophy of Law', pp. 31, 29.

271. Baruch Spinoza, *Tractatus Theologico-Politicus*, trans. Samuel Shirley, Leiden, 1989, p. 243. While he was doing the preliminary research for his 1841 doctoral dissertation, Marx read the *Tractatus* very closely, copying out long passages from it, notably this one from Chapter 16 (see 'Exzerpte aus Benedictus de Spinoza', *MEGA* 4/1: 233–76.)

272. In particular, with respect to the Kreuznach manuscript, Albert Igoin, André Tosel, and, especially, Miguel Abensour.

273. To put matters as succinctly (and schematically) as possible, Spinoza defines the democratic regime as an 'absolute' power towards which every existing regime tends; it creates a perfect equivalence between the regime and the power of the masses. ('For absolute sovereignty, if any such thing exists, is really the sovereignty held by a whole people.' Spinoza, *Tractatus Politicus*, in *The Political Works*, ed. and trans. A.G. Wernham, Oxford, 1958, VIII, §3, p. 371.) However, the idea of a multitude governed solely by the laws of reason is self-contradictory, for it comes down to making human nature an empire within an empire, i.e. to subordinating the order of 'the whole of nature', in which 'man is a tiny part' (ibid., II, §8, p. 273). Spinoza concludes from this that 'those who believe that a people, or men divided over public business, can be induced to live by reason's dictate alone, are dreaming of the poets' golden age or of a fairy-tale' (ibid., I, §5, p. 265).

274. This inversion of Spinoza is already at work in Marx's interpretation of the *Tractatus Theologico-Politicus*. As Alexandre Matheron has brilliantly shown ('Le *Traité théologico-politique* lu par le jeune Marx', *Cahiers Spinoza*, no. 1, 1977, pp. 159–212), the collection of quotations with which Marx fills his notebooks on Spinoza is calculated to reinforce the opposition between two types of state (one theocratic and oppressive, the other democratic), while filtering out everything in Spinoza's argument that tends to establish a continuity between the various forms of power.

275. Spinoza, *Tractatus Politicus*, VIII, §3, pp. 369, 371.

276. Ibid., VII, §31, p. 365.

277. Marx, 'Critique of Hegel's Philosophy of Law', p. 29.

278. Ibid., p. 31.

279. Alexandre Matheron points out that the passages Marx extracts from Chapter 16 of the *Tractatus Theologico-Politicus* allow him to present the democratic state, characteristically, as one which 'rules out the manipulation of the fanaticism of the people by power-seekers', and also ensures 'the gradual disappearance of the religious "furor" of, again, the people, which thereby ceases to be a "populace" and is progressively civilized' ('Le *Traité théologico-politique* lu par le jeune Marx', pp. 202–3).

280. On Spinoza's ambivalent attitude towards the masses, see especially Étienne Balibar, 'Spinoza, l'anti-Orwell. La crainte des masses', in Balibar, *La crainte des masses. Philosophie avant at après Marx*, Paris, 1997, pp. 57–99. Balibar's approach is in large measure a reaction to Antonio Negri's reading (*The Savage Anomaly, passim*), which sets out, precisely, to eliminate all notions of such ambivalence in order to cast Spinoza as a subversive, the theoretician of the power of a multitude endowed with an untamed productive force that is radically irreducible to any mediation.

281. Marx, 'Critique of Hegel's Philosophy of Law', p. 30.

282. Ibid., p. 79.

283. Ibid., p. 58.

284. This is exactly how Abensour views the matter; see *La démocratie contre l'État*, pp. 69–70. According to Abensour, the difference between Marx and Hess comes into play in their differing relations to Spinoza: Marx adopts the Spinozan conception of democracy, whereas Hess takes it in the direction of anarchy and an ethical foundation (ibid., p. 59). In fact, as I have already suggested, what separates the two thinkers is, rather, a radical difference in their approach to the politico-religious realm. In the *Tractatus Theologico-Politicus*, Hess seeks the bases for a reconstruction of the link between the political and religion that would combine an internal reform of religion with democratic reform of the state. This is precisely what Marx finds uninteresting in Spinoza; as the collection of quotes in his notebooks on Spinoza shows, he systematically ignores Spinoza's entire analysis of the anthropological roots of the religious illusion, and all his references to the *credo minimum* and the question of the 'salvation of the ignorant'. The only thing Marx finds of interest in the *Tractatus Theologico-Politicus*, as Alexandre Matheron decisively shows, is the point-by-point opposition of the theocratic state to the secular democratic state (Matheron, 'Le *Traité théologico-politique* lu par le jeune Marx'). Thus it is not possible to range Marx and Hess 'with the political atheists', as Abensour does (*La démocratie*, p. 61). Indeed, Hess explicitly contested this position in his ongoing polemic with the political 'rationalists'.

285. Or rather, as we shall see below, Marx succumbs to this temptation only when he 'flirts' with the anti-political (and social-ist) theme of 'organisation'.

286. Hegel, *Lectures on the Philosophy of World History: Introduction*, trans. H.B. Nisbet, Cambridge, 1975, p. 111: 'the aspects of the people's existence'. The notion of the 'spirit of the people' [*Volksgeist*] makes it possible to conceive of the unity of these different spheres of the life of the people to the extent that they belong to one and the same organism, 'the State . . . the focal point of all the other concrete aspects of the spirit' (ibid., p. 93; trans. modified).

287. Marx, 'Critique of Hegel's Philosophy of Law', p. 112. Abensour manifestly distorts the meaning of the word 'ecstasy' (*La démocratie contre l'État*, pp. 63, 75) by closing his eyes to the fact that, for Marx, it designates, precisely, a dimension of the constitutive illusion of political abstraction, of a politics cut off from its own conditions of possibility – that is, from social relations.

288. See Marx, 'On the Jewish Question', pp. 155–6.

289. Marx, 'Critique of Hegel's Philosophy of Law', p. 75.

290. Ibid., p. 28.

291. Ibid., p. 31.

292. In the Kreuznach manuscript, and, even more obviously, in 'On the Jewish Question', the United States represents a sort of touchstone for radical criticism, since, in order to remain faithful to its own essence, such criticism has to abandon its obsolete forms (the

critique of religion that, *à la* Bruno Bauer, remains within the bounds of religious discourse) in order to become criticism of the political state.

293. Marx, 'Critique of Hegel's Philosophy of Law', p. 31.

294. Ibid., p. 30.

295. Ibid., pp. 30–31.

296. Ibid., p. 30. This imprecise formulation has inspired various hypotheses. It seems to me that what is in question is a rather diffuse theme that is common to all social-ist thought, Saint-Simon's not excluded; one that it would be very hard to assign to a particular author. This no doubt explains Marx's use of the plural: 'the French of the modern epoch . . .'.

297. On this point, Abensour rightly maintains, against Avineri (and, indirectly, Rubel), that the reduction of the political state in the Kreuznach manuscript, which simply reduces the state to its particularity, differs both from its pure and simple disappearance and, no less, from its complete resorption in communist society; hence it also differs from the subsequent problematic of the withering away of the state (*La démocratie contre l'État*, p. 76).

298. The first alternative may be regarded as the canonical interpretation of Marx's 'transition' to communism; the second is defended by Miguel Abensour, in line with his 'ecstatic' conception of the originary political act (*La démocratie contre l'État*, p. 85).

299. This is the constitutive act of Marxian politics, which Étienne Balibar defines in these sharply condensed terms: 'to transgress the limits of the recognized – and artificially separated – political sphere, which are only ever the limits of the established order, politics has to get back to the "non-political" conditions of that institution (conditions which are, ultimately, eminently political). It has, in other words, to get back to the economic contradictions, and gain a purchase on these from the inside.' 'Three Concepts of Politics', in *Politics: The Other Scene*, trans. Chris Turner, London and New York, 2002.

300. Similarly, in 'On the Jewish Question', human emancipation will take the form of a self-critical supersession of political emancipation: with political emancipation, says Marx, 'man frees himself through the *medium of the* state . . . he frees himself *politically* from a limitation when, in contradiction with himself, he raises himself above this limitation in an *abstract*, limited, and *partial* way' (Marx, 'On the Jewish Question', p. 152; emphasis added).

301. See Marx, 'Critique of Hegel's Philosophy of Law', pp. 30–31. Moreover, Marx spells out that this material penetration is completely different from a top–down organization of the various spheres of social life, the characteristic pretension of the abstract state.

302. This point – which is crucial, bearing as it does on the very sources of revolutionary theory and practice – is obscured by interpretations which concede that Marx is a democrat, but argue that he is an anti-Jacobin democrat. See, for example, Shlomo Avineri, according to whom Marx regarded Jacobinism as a form of straightforward political subjectivism culminating in the Terror (Avineri, *The Social and Political Thought*, pp. 185–201); or Michaël Löwy, who, paradoxically, finds himself repeating the ortho-doxy of the vulgate when he makes Jacobinism a simple 'bourgeois' phenomenon (Löwy, *La théorie de la révolution*, p. 26). For a rectification, see Jacques Texier, *Révolution et démocratie chez Marx et Engels*, Paris, 1998, p. 18 and *passim*.

303. Marx, 'Critique of Hegel's Philosophy of Law', p. 80.

304. Hegel, *Elements of the Philosophy of Right*, §195, §243–4, pp. 231, 266. On this point, see also Chapter 1 above: 'The aporias of bourgeois society'.

305. Marx, 'Critique of Hegel's Philosophy of Law', p. 80.

306. Ibid.

307. 'This will be further considered in the section on "civil society".' Ibid., p. 81.

308. 'For all his other qualities in civil society *appear* inessential to the human being, the individual, as external qualities which indeed are necessary for his existence in the whole, i.e., as a link with the whole, but a link that he can just as well throw away again.' Ibid.

309. 'Present-day civil society is the realized principle of *individualism*; the individual exist-ence is the final goal; activity, work, content, etc., are *mere* means.' Ibid.
310. See Chapter 4 above: 'From the "social" to "socialism": the great romance of organization'.
311. Marx reduces the political state to the 'state of the understanding' developing in externality, a term that Hegel, for his part, had used to refer to a moment prior to the state, namely, the sphere of civil society. Marx, 'Critique of Hegel's Philosophy of Law', p. 10.
312. Ibid., p. 119.
313. 'In democracy, the constitution, the law, *the state itself*, insofar as it is a political constitution, is only the self-determination of the people, and a particular content of the people.' Ibid., p. 31; emphasis added.
314. Marx, 'On the Jewish Question', p. 168. In the polemic Marx waged against Ruge in the summer of 1844, when his 'flirt' with Feuerbach and the social-ist problematic was at its most intense, Marx was to pose the question of organization in an explicitly anti-political – or, more precisely, metapolitical – sense: '*socialism* cannot be realized without *revolution*. It needs this *political act* insofar as it needs *destruction* and *dissolution*. But where its *organising activity* begins, where its *proper object*, its *soul*, comes to the fore – there socialism throws off the political cloak.' Marx, 'Critical Marginal Notes on the Article "The King of Prussia and Social Reform". By a Prussian', *MECW* 3: 206.
315. Which are obviously only a secularized version of religious transcendence, transformed into a religion of divinized Man. See Chapter 3 above: 'The "religion of love and humanity"'.
316. 'As far as the *Rheinische Zeitung* is concerned I would not remain *under any conditions*; it is impossible for me to write under Prussian censorship or to live in the Prussian atmosphere.' Marx, Letter of 13 March 1843 to Arnold Ruge, *MECW* 1: 400.
317. The expression is Marx's; see his letter of September 1843 to Ruge, p. 142.
318. 'I have abandoned my plan to settle in Cologne, since life there is too noisy for me, and an abundance of good friends does not lead to better philosophy.' Marx, Letter of 27 April 1842 to Ruge, *MECW* 1: 387.
319. Grandjonc, *Marx et les communistes allemands à Paris. Vorwärts 1844*, Paris, 1974, p. 45.
320. The result was his 'Critical Marginal Notes on the Article "The King of Prussia and Social Reform". By a Prussian', pp. 189–206.
321. We learn from Ruge's correspondence, particularly the letters he wrote to Feuerbach and Marx in the spring and summer of 1843, that among the French collaborators they had in mind were Pierre Leroux, Louis Blanc, Proudhon and Lamartine, as well as the Fourierists of *Démocratie pacifique*, who had been contacted through Victor Considérant. See Maximilien Rubel, 'Notice sur la "Déclaration Ruge–Marx"', in Marx, *Œuvres*, vol. 3, pp. 1348–9.
322. Hereinafter referred to as the '1844 Introduction'.
323. Religion as the 'opium of the people'; 'the arm of critique which cannot replace the critique of arms', etc.
324. See Georges Labica, *Le statut marxiste de la philosophie*, Paris, 1976, p. 83; and Löwy, *La théorie de la révolution*, p. 69.
325. Marx, 'Critique of Hegel's Philosophy of Law. Introduction', p. 175.
326. Ibid.
327. Ibid., p. 176.
328. Ibid.
329. 'For we shared the restorations of the modern nations although we had not shared their revolutions. . . . We – and our shepherds first and foremost – never found ourselves in the company of freedom except once – on the *day of its* burial.' Ibid., pp. 176–7.
330. Hegel, *The Philosophy of History*, p. 23.
331. Marx, 'Critique of Hegel's Philosophy of Law. Introduction', pp. 177–8.
332. Heine left Paris for Germany on 21 October and returned on 18 December. He must

therefore have met Marx after the latter date; he was probably introduced to him by Ruge in December 1843.

333. Marx, 'Critique of Hegel's Philosophy of Law. Introduction', p. 178.

334. 'The modern *ancien régime* is only the *comedian* of a world order whose *true heroes* are dead. . . . The last phase of a world-historical form is its *comedy*.' Ibid., p. 179.

335. See Chapter 2 above: 'From tragedy to comedy: The impossible historical repetition'. Brecht's use of the word 'epic' should likewise be considered against the background of this tradition. According to Fredric Jameson, its origins may be traced to Goethe's and Schiller's exchange on the subject of Greek epic. See Jameson, *Brecht and Method*, London and New York, 1998, p. 52.

336. 'As the ancient peoples went through their pre-history in imagination, in *mythology*, so we Germans have gone through our post-history in thought, in *philosophy*. We are *philosophical* contemporaries of the present without being its *historical* contemporaries.' Marx, 'Critique of Hegel's Philosophy of Law. Introduction', p. 180.

337. Ibid., p. 181.

338. Ibid., pp. 180–81.

339. Ibid., p. 182.

340. Ibid., p. 181.

341. Ibid., p. 182.

342. Ibid.

343. It is only a slight exaggeration to say that Maximilien Rubel makes this formula the touchstone of his 'ethical' interpretation of Marx's thought – an interpretation that is ultimately compatible with Kant's normativism, the superficial references to Spinoza notwithstanding.

344. Marx, 'Critique of Hegel's Philosophy of Law. Introduction', p. 175.

345. 'Germany's *revolutionary* past is theoretical, it is the *Reformation*. As the revolution then began in the brain of the *monk*, so now it begins in the brain of the *philosopher*.' Ibid., p. 182.

346. Ibid., p. 183.

347. See Chapter 2 above: 'A national-popular narrative'.

348. Marx, 'Critique of Hegel's Philosophy of Law. Introduction', p. 183.

349. Ibid., p. 182.

350. On this question, see Étienne Balibar, *The Philosophy of Marx*, trans. Chris Turner, London and New York, 1995, pp. 21–41.

351. At the very same moment, writing in the *Allgemeine Literatur-Zeitung*, the Bauer brothers were drawing a conclusion from the crisis that was the exact opposite of Marx's: 'the true enemy is to be sought in the mass and nowhere else. . . . As we have said, criticism has ceased to have a political character. Only recently, it continued to pit ideas against ideas, systems against systems, opinions against opinions; now it has rejected all ideas, all systems, all opinions' (cited in Cornu, *Karl Marx*, vol. 3, pp. 15–16n.).

352. Marx, 'Critique of Hegel's Philosophy of Law. Introduction', p. 183.

353. See above: 'From civil society to the state'; Chapter 1 above: 'The aporias of bourgeois society'.

354. Marx, 'Critique of Hegel's Philosophy of Law. Introduction', p. 183.

355. My reading is thus diametrically opposed to Agnes Heller's (see *The Theory of Need in Marx*, London, 1976). Heller elaborates a normative conception of need on the basis of an (inverted) Fichtean conception of the objectivization of an 'ought' [*Sollen*] that is transformed into a collective duty-grounded 'Being' (pp. 76–7).

356. Marx, 'Critique of Hegel's Philosophy of Law. Introduction', p. 183.

357. 'How can [Germany] leap, in a single *salto mortale*, not only over its own limitations, but at the same time over the limitations of the modern nations, over limitations which in reality it must feel and strive for as bringing emancipation from its real limitations?' Ibid.; translation modified.

358. Kant, 'On the Common Saying: This May Be True in Theory, But It Does Not Apply in

Practice', in *Political Writings*, ed. Hans Reiss, trans. H.B. Nisbet, 2nd edn, Cambridge, 1991, p. 186.

359. 'On what is a partial, a merely political revolution based? On the fact that *part of civil society* emancipates itself and attains *general* domination; on the fact that a definite class, proceeding from its particular situation, undertakes the general emancipation of society.' Marx, 'Critique of Hegel's Philosophy of Law. Introduction', p. 184.

360. Ibid., p. 185.

361. Ibid., p. 184.

362. Ibid., p. 186.

363. Ibid.

364. Ibid.

365. Ibid., p. 187.

366. This is no doubt the only time that Marx evokes an 'in itself' and 'for itself' and speaks, in those terms, of a 'being' of the proletariat, whose 'aim and historical action', he says, 'is visibly and irrevocably foreshadowed'. Marx and Engels, *The Holy Family*, p. 37.

367. Marx, 'Critique of Hegel's Philosophy of Law', p. 80.

368. Marx, 'Critique of Hegel's Philosophy of Law. Introduction', p. 175.

369. Ibid., p. 186.

370. See Ernesto Laclau and Chantal Mouffe, *Hegemony and Socialist Strategy*, London, 1985.

371. Marx, 'Critique of Hegel's Philosophy of Law. Introduction', p. 187.

372. Hegel, *Elements of the Philosophy of Right*, §279 and addition, pp. 316–21.

373. Labica, *Le statut marxiste de la philosophie*, p. 112. Labica rightly remarks that Marx's refusal to associate himself with socialism and communism in this period proceeds not from his lack of knowledge of them, but from a desire to create a theory of his own, which ruled out 'conversion' to an already existing doctrine.

374. See Löwy, *La théorie de la révolution chez le jeune Marx*, pp. 72–4. Maurice Barbier makes a similar argument in *La pensée politique de Karl Marx*, Paris, 1973, p. 74.

375. See the conclusion of '*Volksgeist* and revolution' above.

376. As Fernando Claudin rightly remarks in *Marx, Engels et la révolution de 1848*, Paris, 1980, p. 59. In his famous 'Address of the Central Authority to the League – March 1850' (*MECW* 10: 277–87), delivered at a moment when he was trying to rekindle the revolutionary process after a series of defeats, Marx defined an internal threshold within it: to 'make the revolution permanent', the proletariat would have to win 'a position of dominance' by affirming the independence of its political practice.

377. Engels, Introduction to Marx, 'The Class Struggles in France, 1848 to 1850' [1895], *MECW* 27: 512.

378. It hardly needs to be said that the Social-Democratic movement considered Engels's version a founding text throughout the period of the Second International. Kautsky's view of history – which gave theoretical expression to a certain common sense prevalent in the workers' movement of the day, quite as much as it helped to shape it – is a logical consequence of this version of things. Even the theoretician whose name and destiny are linked to the concept of permanent revolution, Leon Trotsky, adopted this line of argument, although he developed a more finely tuned version of it. Yet it would be employed *ad nauseam* to refute his own conceptions! (See Trotsky, '1789–1848–1905', in *Results and Prospects*, trans. Brian Pearce, London, 1982, pp. 184–93.

379. Walter Benjamin, 'Theses on the Philosophy of History', in *Illuminations*, ed. Hannah Arendt, trans. Harry Zohn, London, 1973, p. 255.

380. This point is underscored by Georg Lukács in *The Destruction of Reason*, trans. Peter Palmer, London, 1980, pp. 58–9 and *passim*. On the process of effacing 1848 from German history, particularly during the Bismarckian period, see Sperber's remarks in *Rhineland Radicals*, p. 15 and *passim*.

381. It is Rosa Luxemburg who takes this symbolic step in her December 1918 speech before the founding congress of the German Communist Party. See Luxemburg, *Spartacus*,

London, 1971, esp. pp. 9–11; and, in more theoretical terms, Karl Korsch, *Marxism and Philosophy*, trans. Fred Halliday, New York, 1971, pp. 51 ff.

382. This is the question that Lucien Calvié asks after evoking the fable of the fox and the grapes from which he takes the title of his book. See Calvié, *Le renard et les raisins*, p. 11.

383. Marx, 'Critique of Hegel's Philosophy of Law. Introduction', p. 186.

384. Marx, 'Critical Marginal Notes on the Article "The King of Prussia and Social Reform"', p. 202.

385. Marx, 'Critique of Hegel's Philosophy of Law. Introduction', p. 187.

386. Rosa Luxemburg, *Selected Political Writings*, trans. William D. Gram, London, 1972, p. 305.

Conclusion: Self-Criticisms of the Revolution

1. Independently, that is, of any normative analysis or commentary that would accord primacy to the Anglo-American revolutions or 'Atlantic traditions', whether in the register of political philosophy (the revolution for 'freedom' as opposed to the one for happiness, which is always liable to drift in a totalitarian direction, as Hannah Arendt likes to point out) or the history of ideas (J.G.A. Pocock's 'republican moment').

2. Francis Fukuyama, *The End of History and the Last Man*, New York, 1992, p. 46.

3. This is the title of the first part of François Furet's *Interpreting the French Revolution*, trans. Elborg Forster, Cambridge, 1981, pp. 1–79.

4. 'The Revolution ... ushered in a world where mental representations of power governed all actions, and where a network of signs completely dominated political life' (ibid., p. 48). On the Revolution's 'frenzied preoccupation with power', see pp. 48, 54.

5. 'The Revolution was over, since France had returned to its history or, rather, reconciled its two histories.' Ibid., p. 79.

6. *Ibid.*, p. 29; translation modified.

7. *Ibid.*, p. 12.

8. André Tosel, 'Quelle théorie de l'histoire pour le temps de la crise des philosophies de l'histoire?', *La Pensée*, no. 315, 1998, p. 138.

9. Jean-François Lyotard, *The Postmodern Condition*, trans. Geoff Bennington and Brian Massumi, Manchester, 1984, p. 37: 'The grand narrative has lost its credibility, regardless of what mode of unification it uses, regardless of whether it is a speculative narrative or a narrative of emancipation.'

10. Whose grounds are to be found in the *homology* between two tripartite schemes, that of the human soul (desire, the *thymos*, and the *megalothymia*) and that of the social world (the economic, the political and the cultural), of which liberalism represents, as it were, the apperceptive unity: the optimal equilibrium between a market economy driven by the imperatives of competition and productivity (which correspond to the first level of the human soul, the desire for security and the acquisition of goods); parliamentary democracy, which reflects the second level of the soul, *thymos* or the struggle for recognition; and a culture that leaves room for a more aristocratic element, an ethos of the 'strong' counterbalancing, in some way, the democratic passion (which corresponds to the third level of the soul, the *megalothymia*). See Jacques Derrida's withering critique in *Specters of Marx*, trans. Peggy Kamuf, New York, 1994, pp. 55–75.

11. As Perry Anderson believes; see his 'The End of History', in *Zones of Engagement*, London, 1992, p. 283.

12. Furet, *Interpreting the French Revolution*, p. 25; translation modified.

13. On the frequent comparisons that those who participated in the French strikes of November–December 1995 made between themselves and the *sans-culottes*, see Claude Leneveu, 'Un automne brûlant à Nantes', in *Société française*, 4/54, 1996, p. 13; Jacques

Guilhaumou, *La parole des 'sans'. Les mouvements actuels à l'épreuve de la Révolution française*, Fontenay-Saint-Cloud, France, 1998, *passim*. On the rhetoric of the strike movement and the strikers' historical references, see the two studies by Hélène Desbrousses and Bernard Peloille, 'Expérience mémorable et horizon d'attente' (in Claude Leneveu and Michel Vakaloulis, eds, *Faire mouvement*, Paris, 1997, pp. 121–42); ' "Tous ensemble" pour quoi, contre quoi?' (in Sophie Béroud and René Mouriaux, eds, *Le souffle de décembre*, Paris, 1997, pp. 131–69). On the resurgence of the tradition of direct action and the recourse to riots, see Leneveu, 'Nantes: le théâtre des émeutes urbaines', in Leneveu and Vakaloulis, eds, *Faire mouvement*, pp. 143–69. Tellingly, a recent book that calls itself an 'inquiry into the far left' (this is its subtitle) is entitled *Les nouveaux sans-culottes* (by Jean-Christophe Brochier and Hervé Delouche, Paris, 2000).

14. François Furet, 'L'idée française de Révolution' and 'L'énigme française', *Le Débat*, no. 96, 1997.
15. See Guilhaumou, *La parole des 'sans'. Les mouvements actuels à l'épreuve de la Révolution française*.
16. Thus it was a 'bourgeois', 'exclusively political' revolution, according to a certain Marx or a certain Marxism; an essentially 'social' revolution, hostile to the cause of freedom, according to a certain liberalism.
17. Georg Lukács, *Demokratisierung Heute und Morgen*, Budapest, 1985.
18. This history, in which sailors, pirates, conspirators and rebellious slaves played the leading roles, is superbly reconstructed in Peter Linebaugh and Marcus Rediker, *The Many-Headed Hydra: The Hidden History of the Revolutionary Atlantic*, London and New York, 2000.
19. In his study of the *Vormärz* Rhineland, Jonathan Sperber points out that the partisans of 'true socialism' did not usually situate themselves to the left of the spectrum of the opposition, and that when they did, it was rather *despite* than *because of* their social ideals, 'which tended to moderate rather than radicalize their political ideas' (Sperber, *Rhineland Radicals: The Democratic Movement and the Revolution of 1848*, Princeton, NJ, 1991, p. 118). The 'true socialists' did not make a special bid for working-class or popular support, unlike certain fractions of the radical democrats; they were active within the democratic camp in the broad sense of the word, and addressed a cultivated, rather well-off public. An examination of the cases in which the newspaper *Triersche Zeitung*, where the influence of 'true socialism' predominated, came under fire from the censors shows that their object was the paper's political options, whenever they were openly declared, not its 'socialist' references (ibid., pp. 122–6).
20. As Etienne Balibar suggests in 'Quel communisme après le communisme?', in Eustache Kouvélakis, ed., *Marx 2000*, Paris, 2000, esp. pp. 79–81.

Afterword

1. After its long 1960s–70s history of dissident currents, expulsions and waves of members leaving, the UEC was entirely aligned with the French Communist Party and *de facto* worked as a training ground for future party cadres.
2. Pierre Juquin (born 1930) was a long-standing member of the PCF, joining its central committee in 1964 and its politburo in 1979. He played an important role during the Eurocommunist period of the party, collaborating closely with its secretary general, Georges Marchais. He was removed from the politburo in 1984 when he sided with a broader challenge to the leadership from within party ranks. In 1987, Juquin left the party, followed by thousands of party members and cadres, and stood in the 1988 presidential elections, with the support of some other organisations of the extra-parliamentary left (most significantly

the Trotskyist *Ligue communiste révolutionnaire* [LCR] and the left-socialist *Parti socialiste unifié* [PSU]; see notes 6 and 7). Despite a successful militant campaign, his electoral performance was poor (2.1 per cent, versus 6.8 per cent for the PCF candidate André Lajoinie) and led to the fragmentation of the coalition that supported him.

3. Georges Labica (1930–2009) was a Marxist philosopher and author of numerous books. A member of the PCF from 1954 onwards, in 1956 he was appointed as a high school philosophy teacher in Algiers. He quickly joined the ranks of the National Liberation Front (FLN), from 1960 onwards taking part in the editorial team of its main organ, *El Moudjahid*. Labica spent the end of the war in clandestinity in Algiers, having had a price placed on his head by the Secret Army Organisation (OAS), a far-right paramilitary group active among French army officers. After independence, he taught at the University of Algiers, where he played a prominent role in organising philosophy teaching. He remained in Algeria until late 1968 but took part in that May's Paris '*événements*'. Returning to France, he taught at the Paris Nanterre University, and he was again active as a PCF militant. He left the party in 1982, after being one of the driving forces in the internal dissident current around the '*Union dans les luttes*' movement. An active anti-imperialist activist, he was honorary president of the *Comité de vigilance pour une paix réelle au Proche-Orient* (CVPR-PO), president of *Résistance démocratique international* and a member of *L'Appel Franco-Arabe*. For a website devoted to Georges Labica, see labica. lahaine.org.

4. See André Tosel, 'The Development of Marxism: From the End of Marxism-Leninism to a Thousand Marxisms – France-Italy 1975–2005', in Jacques Bidet, Stathis Kouvelakis, eds, *Critical Companion to Contemporary Marxism*, Chicago, Haymarket, 2009, p. 49.

5. François Cusset, *La décennie. Le grand cauchemar des années 1980*, Paris, La Découverte, 2006.

6. *Ligue communiste révolutionnaire*, founded in 1966 (as *Jeunesse communiste révolutionnaire*) by members expelled from the UEC. From 1969, it became the French section of the Trotskyist Fourth International (United Secretariat). It dissolved in 2009, to create the *Nouveau parti anticapitaliste*.

7. *Parti socialiste unifié*, a socialist party founded in 1960 by dissidents of the socialist SFIO (*Section française de l'Internationale Ouvrière*) who opposed the colonialist policy of its leadership under Guy Mollet. Advocating self-management, and close for a long period to the CFDT (*Confédération française démocratique du travail*) trade union, the PSU reached its height in the years following May 1968, when it became a platform able to rally many tendencies of the far left.

8. Louis Althusser, 'Marx in His Limits', in *Philosophy of the Encounter: Later Writings 1978–1987*, London, Verso, 2006, pp. 7–162.

9. These three texts written in 1978 appear in the collection *Solitude de Machiavel et autres textes*, Paris, PUF, 1998, pp. 267–309. The first two are available, together with other important contributions to the debate, in the 'Crisis of Marxism' dossier of translations published 18 December 2017 in *Viewpoint*, viewpointmag.com.

10. See, for example, his interviews with Fernanda Navarro, first published in Mexico in 1988; in *Philosophy of the Encounter*, p. 258; or in his autobiography, *The Future Lasts A Long Time*, London, Chatto & Windus, 1993, p. 148.

11. See note 7.

12. Georges Labica, *Marxism and the Status of Philosophy*, Leiden, Brill, forthcoming (1st edition: Sussex, Harvester Press, 1980).

13. Lucien Goldmann, 'Is There a Marxist Sociology?', *International Socialism* 34, Autumn 1968, pp. 13–21, available at marxists.org.

14. Isabelle Garo, *Foucault, Deleuze, Althusser et Marx. La politique dans la philosophie*, Paris, Demopolis, 2011.

15. In *The Poems of Heine*, London, Bell and Daldy, 1866, p. 401.

16. Stathis Kouvelakis, 'La forme politique de l'émancipation', in Jean-Numa Ducange, Isabelle Garo, eds, *Marx politique*, Paris, La Dispute, pp. 39–90.

17. Étienne Balibar, 'Marxism and the Idea of Revolution: The Messianic Moment in Marx', in Dipesh Chakrabarty et al., eds, *Historical Teleologies in the Modern World*, London, Bloomsbury Academic, 2015, pp. 235–50

18. A still-ongoing project to publish Marx and Engels's collected works, begun in the German Democratic Republic in the 1970s.

19. See Terrell Carver, *Friedrich Engels: His Life and Thought*, London, Palgrave Macmillan, 1991; Georges Labica, *Marxism and the Marxist Status of Philosophy*.

20. Henri Lefebvre, *Marxist Thought and the City*, Minneapolis, University of Minnesota Press, 2016.

21. Jacques Texier, *Révolution et démocratie chez Marx et Engels*, Paris, PUF, 1998.

22. André Tosel, 'Formes de mouvement et dialectique "dans" la nature selon Engels', in *Études sur Marx (et Engels). Vers un communisme de la finitude*, Paris, Kimé, 1996, pp. 105–38.

23. Francis Wheen, *Karl Marx: A Life*, London, Norton, 2001; Jonathan Sperber, *Karl Marx: A Nineteenth-Century Life*, London, Liveright, 2014; Jacques Attali, *Karl Marx ou l'esprit du monde*, Paris, Fayard, 2005.

24. Roberto Finelli, *A Failed Parricide: Hegel and the Young Marx*, Leiden, Brill, 2015; Gareth Stedman Jones, *Karl Marx: Greatness and Illusion*, London, Allen Lane, 2016; Warren Breckman, *Marx, The Young Hegelians, and the Origins of Radical Social Theory: Dethroning the Self*, Cambridge, Cambridge University Press, 2001; Douglas Moggach, ed, *The New Hegelians: Politics and Philosophy in the Hegelian School*, Cambridge, Cambridge University Press, 2011.

25. Franck Fischbach, *Philosophies de Marx*, Paris, Vrin, 2015; Emmanuel Renault, *Marx et la philosophie*, Paris, PUF, 2014.

26. David Leopold, *The Young Karl Marx: German Philosophy, Modern Politics, and Human Flourishing*, Cambridge, Cambridge University Press, 2009.

27. Neil McLaughlin, 'Review of Stathis Kouvelakis, *Philosophy and Revolution: From Kant to Marx*', *Contemporary Sociology* 33:3, 2004, pp. 375–6.

28. In Georg Lukács, *The Process of Democratization*, New York, SUNY Press, 1991.

Index